THE PEOPLE OF INDIA

THE
PEOPLE OF INDIA

BY

SIR HERBERT RISLEY, K.C.I.E., C.S.I.,

DIRECTOR OF ETHNOGRAPHY FOR INDIA, OFFICIER D'ACADEMIE, FRANCE, CORRESPONDING MEMBER OF THE ANTHROPOLOGICAL SOCIETIES OF ROME AND BERLIN, AND OF THE ANTHROPOLOGICAL INSTITUTE OF GREAT BRITAIN AND IRELAND.

SECOND EDITION, EDITED BY
W. CROOKE, B.A.
LATE OF THE INDIAN CIVIL SERVICE

"In good sooth, my masters, this is no door. Yet is it a little window, that looketh upon a great world."

WITH 36 ILLUSTRATIONS AND AN ETHNOLOGICAL MAP OF INDIA

GYAN

Published by

GYAN

Gyan Publishing House
5, Ansari Road
Daryaganj, New Delhi-110002
Phone: 011-47034999, 9811692060
E-mail: books@gyanbooks.com

Distribution Network
gyanbooks.com
India, USA, Canada, UK, Australia, France

ISBN : 978-81-212-2788-9 (HB)
First Published, 1915

2nd Impression 2021

Printed at: Gyan Press, Delhi.

The People of India
Author: Sir Herbert Risley

THE PEOPLE OF INDIA

BY

SIR HERBERT RISLEY, K.C.I.E., C.S.I.
DIRECTOR OF ETHNOGRAPHY FOR INDIA, OFFICIER D'ACADEMIE, FRANCE,
CORRESPONDING MEMBER OF THE ANTHROPOLOGICAL SOCIETIES OF ROME AND BERLIN,
AND OF THE ANTHROPOLOGICAL INSTITUTE OF
GREAT BRITAIN AND IRELAND

SECOND EDITION, EDITED BY

W. CROOKE, B.A.
LATE OF THE INDIAN CIVIL SERVICE

"In good sooth, my masters, this is no door. Yet is it a little window, that looketh upon a great world"

WITH 36 ILLUSTRATIONS AND AN ETHNOLOGICAL MAP OF INDIA

CALCUTTA & SIMLA: THACKER, SPINK & CO.
LONDON: W. THACKER & CO., 2, CREED LANE, E.C.
1915

Lafayette

SIR HERBERT HOPE RISLEY,

K.C.I.E., C.S.I.

TO

SIR WILLIAM TURNER, K.C.B.

CHIEF AMONG ENGLISH CRANIOLOGISTS

THIS SLIGHT SKETCH OF A

LARGE SUBJECT

IS WITH HIS PERMISSION

RESPECTFULLY DEDICATED

PREFACE TO THE FIRST EDITION

In an article on "Magic and Religion" published in the *Quarterly Review* of last July, Mr. Edward Clodd complains that certain observations of mine on the subject of "the impersonal stage of religion" are hidden away under the "prosaic title" of the Report on the Census of India, 1901. The charge is just, and the offence is aggravated by the fact that the Report in question weighs seven pounds and is cumbered with many statistics. Mr. Clodd's grievance may, however, perhaps be thought to justify me in venturing to reprint, in a more handy form, the less dreary portions of my own contributions to the Report, with such revision and expansion as seemed to be called for. Two new chapters have been added. One of these, Caste in Proverbs and Popular Sayings, is an attempt to give a much-described people the chance of describing themselves in their own direct and homely fashion. It is, in fact, a mosaic of proverbs, selected from the ample material which will be found in Appendix I, and fitted together into a connected whole with the minimum of comment and explanation. In the chapter on Caste and Nationality I have endeavoured to analyse the causes and to forecast the prospects of the Indian nationalist movement of recent years. Being anxious above all things to avoid giving offence, I submitted the proofs to Mr. Nagendra Nath Ghose, Fellow of the Calcutta University, and Editor of the *Indian Nation*, a sober thinker, who holds that the people of India "should conceive national unity as their chief aim, and the realisation of it as their chief duty."* Mr. Ghose gives me the comforting assurance—"I have discovered no sentiment with which I am not in agreement."

For the same reason the chapter on Caste and Religion, which contains a certain amount of new matter, was laid before my friend Mr. Justice Mookerjee, Vice-Chancellor of the Calcutta University, one of the most learned, and not the least orthodox, of living Hindus. Dr. Mookerjee has been good enough to write to me: "I have very carefully read over the proof which you so kindly sent me. I have never read

* *Hindustan Review*, Nov. and Dec. 1904.

anything so illuminating on the subject, and I have not come across any statement to which exception may justly be taken." I trust, therefore, that it may be recognised, even by those who dissent from my views, that these delicate subjects have been approached in a spirit which escapes Darmesteter's telling criticism "Mais à ces maîtres honnêtes manque le don suprême, le seul qui fasse pardonner les supériorités écrasantes : la sympathie."

I am indebted to Rai Bahadur Lala Baij Nath, Judge of Ghazipur, for the following criticism of my definition of Hinduism, as it appeared in the Census Report:—"The Census Commissioner's [definition] would have approached nearest to the mark, so far as modern Hindu society is concerned, if he had omitted the word 'two' both from the sets of ideas and the conceptions of the world and of life." * The amendment suggested is gratefully accepted and has been duly carried out.

My thanks are also due to Mr. Justice Sarada Charan Mitra, of the Calcutta High Court, for revising the translation of a notable speech of his quoted in the chapter on Caste and Marriage, and to Mr. B. A. Gupte, F.Z.S., Assistant Director of Ethnography, for much assistance in the collection of material and the revision of proofs.

The illustrations require a word of explanation. With the exception of the frontispiece, which was presented to me some years ago by one of the persons there depicted, all of them are taken from the *Ethnology of Bengal*, by the late Colonel E. T. Dalton, formerly Commissioner of Chutia Nagpur. The book is now a rare one, and I am informed that the entire stock was destroyed by an unfortunate accident some years ago. The lithographs which it contains represent only two out of the seven main types traceable in India, and thus fail to cover the whole of the subject dealt with in the present work. It seemed, however, to my publishers worth while, and to myself as a lover of Chutia Nagpur and its people a pious duty, to preserve from oblivion these fine pictures, one of which, the study of Juāng female attire by my friend the late Mr. Tosco Peppé, is, I believe, absolutely unique. I trust that Sir Benjamin Simpson, the sole survivor of the artists who assisted Colonel Dalton, will recognise the excellence of our intentions and will pardon the shortcomings of the process employed.

H. H. RISLEY.

---

* *Hinduism: Ancient and Modern.* New Edition, 1905, p. 6.

PREFACE TO THE NEW EDITION

Soon after the death of her husband, Lady Risley entrusted to me a large collection of papers connected with Anthropology, which he had brought with him from India. He intended to prepare new editions of the present work and of his *Tribes and Castes of Bengal*, and to write an account of the people of Eastern Bengal. But his health failed soon after his retirement from the Indian Civil Service, and he was unable to do any work in connection with these projects. It was therefore decided to issue a memorial edition of *The People of India*, the preparation of which was entrusted to me. On examining his papers nothing in the shape of notes for this revised edition could be discovered. Under these circumstances it was decided to reprint the text as it stood in the first edition, which was issued in limited numbers and had fallen out of print soon after publication. Accordingly, no attempt has been made to revise the text, except by bringing the statistics up to date, securing uniformity in the transliteration of vernacular terms, and adding, in square brackets, some notes and references mainly collected from the Reports of the Census of India and its Provinces which was carried out in 1911 by Mr. E. A. Gait, C.S.I., C.I.E. The publication of this edition has therefore been postponed until the arrival in England of a full set of the Census Reports.

I have also added an Introduction containing a short memoir of Sir H. Risley, confined to his official life and his work in Anthropology, with some remarks on questions connected with this book which have been raised since its publication, and a bibliography of his Anthropological writings, so far as I have been able to trace them.

The illustrations of the original edition consisted of reproductions from the late Colonel E. T. Dalton's *Descriptive Ethnology of Bengal*. These were confined to the tribes of Bengal and Assam. In order to render the book more interesting and useful to Anthropologists, in the present edition these have been supplemented by a collection of photographs, some of which were procured by the publishers in India, and a few others for which I am indebted to Messrs. E. Thurston, E. H. Mann, Major Nicolas, B. A. Gupte, and Pandit Giraj Kishor Dutt, Rai Bahadur.

In preparing this edition I beg to acknowledge assistance from Messrs. J. Kennedy and V. A. Smith, late of the Indian Civil Service. The memoir of Sir H. Risley is to a great extent based on that contributed to *Man* (vol. xii) by Mr. J. D. Anderson, supplemented by notes from Mr. Keith Jopp, the Warden of New College, and the Headmaster of Winchester College. Mr. B. A. Gupte, who acted as Personal Assistant to Sir H. Risley while he was Director of Ethnography for India, has kindly aided in the preparation of the bibliography of his writings. Miss Ethel E. Risley has contributed the photograph from which the frontispiece is taken, and has read the memoir of her brother in proof.

W. CROOKE.

INTRODUCTION

HERBERT HOPE RISLEY, only son of Rev. John Holford Risley, Rector of Akeley, Bucks, and Fanny Elton, his wife, daughter of John Hope, late of the Bengal Medical Service, was born on 4th January, 1851. He belonged to one of the "Founder's Kin" families of Winchester. Most of his family, including his father, were, during the last two or three centuries, educated at Winchester, which he entered in 1864. He had a distinguished school career, winning the Goddard Scholarship and the Moore Stevens Divinity Prize in 1868, and the King's Gold Medal for the Latin Essay in 1869.

On 15th October, 1869, he entered New College, Oxford; took a Second Class in the School of Law and Modern History, Michaelmas Term, 1872, and received his B.A. degree in January, 1873. He had been selected for an appointment in the Civil Service of India in April, 1871. As the Warden, Rev. W. A. Spooner, D.D., writes: "This early selection to the Indian Civil Service partly explains and partly accounts for his comparative failure in the Schools. His great friends in College were Mr. Keith Jopp, who also entered the Indian Civil Service, and Dr. G. B. Longstaff. All three of them, if my memory does not play me false, were very keen members of the University Volunteer Corps." Mr. Keith Jopp confirms the accuracy of the Warden's recollections, and adds that "even then he had charming manners and great powers of writing."

On reaching India in 1873 Risley had the good fortune to start his service in the district of Midnapur, part of which fringes on the plateau of Chota Nāgpur, a land of hills and forests, situated to the south of the Ganges valley, the home of several interesting tribes whose culture was of a very primitive type. Here he gained his first opportunity for work in Anthropology. His interest in the forest tribes continued during his life, and it was due to his initiative that the late

Rev. P. Dehon, S.J., compiled his valuable monograph on the Oraons.*

In 1869 Sir W. W. Hunter had commenced the Statistical Survey of India, the results of which were embodied in the first edition of the *Imperial Gazetteer* published in 1881. The survey of the Province of Bengal was undertaken by Hunter himself, and the interest displayed by Risley in the anthropology, linguistics, and sociology of India led to his appointment on the staff of the Survey, as Assistant Director of Statistics, early in 1875. The volume on the hill districts of Hazāribāgh and Lohārdaga was compiled by Risley. His wide knowledge of rural life and the lucidity of his literary style displayed in this book marked him out for further promotion. After little more than three years' service he began to act as Assistant Secretary to the Government of Bengal, and in 1879 he officiated as Under Secretary in the Home Department of the Government of India. "It was at this period of his career," writes Mr. Anderson, "that he met and married the accomplished German lady, whose linguistic attainments aided him in his wide reading on anthropology and statistical subjects in foreign languages." In 1880 he once more returned to district work among his old friends the jungle folk of Chota Nāgpur; and after an interval again spent in the Bengal Secretariat, he was placed in charge of an enquiry into the Ghātwāli and other primitive forms of land tenure in the district of Mānbhum.

In 1885 Sir Rivers Thompson, then Lieutenant-Governor of Bengal, decided that it was advisable to collect detailed information on the castes, tribes, and sociology of that Province. Risley was naturally selected as the officer best qualified to undertake the work. At the beginning of this investigation, which extended over some years, he had the good fortune to meet Dr. James Wise, then retired from the Indian Medical Service, who during ten years' occupancy of the post of Civil Surgeon of Dacca, had collected much valuable information on the people of Eastern Bengal. A summary of this was published privately by him in 1883 under the title of *Notes on the Races, Castes, and Trades of Eastern Bengal.* On the sudden death of Dr. Wise in 1886, his widow made over his papers to Risley "on the understanding that after testing the data contained in

---

* "Religion and Customs of the Uraons," *Memoirs Asiatic Society of Bengal*, 1906, p. 121 *et seq.*

them as far as possible in the manner contemplated by Dr. Wise himself, I should incorporate the results in the ethnographic volumes of the present work, and by dedicating these volumes to Dr. Wise, should endeavour to preserve some record, however imperfect, of the admirable work done by him during his service in India." *

To complete this work Risley was placed on special duty. For the description of the jungle tribes of Chota Nāgpur and Assam the materials collected by Colonel E. T. Dalton and published in 1872 under the title of *The Descriptive Ethnology of Bengal* were available. The papers of Dr. Wise were used for the accounts of the people of Eastern Bengal, and for the remaining parts of the Province a large staff of correspondents, including Government officials, missionaries, planters, and native gentlemen, supplied ample information. The results of the Ethnographic Survey of Bengal were published in a preliminary edition in 1891 under the title of *The Tribes and Castes of Bengal,* consisting of two volumes of the "Ethnographical Glossary," and two of "Anthropometric Data," the latter prepared under the advice of Sir W. H. Flower, Director of the Natural History Museum, South Kensington, and Sir W. Turner, the eminent Edinburgh anthropologist. The Introductory Essay prefixed to this work was the first attempt to apply, in a systematic way, the methods of anthropometry to the analysis of the people of an Indian Province. The most important result of the inquiry was that there appears to be, from the physical point of view, no difference between the so-called "Dravidian" and "Kolarian" races occupying the hill country to the south of Bengal. The newer learning has now identified the Austro-Asiatic group of languages, with Mūndā as one of its sub-branches. With this new position Risley was not spared to deal.

Among other anthropological work done during this period was the Introduction to the Gazetteer of Sikkim published in 1894, and a monograph on "Widow and Infant Marriage," which formed the basis of the views expressed on these subjects in the following pages.

About this time financial difficulties, the result of a succession of disastrous famines, impeded the prosecution of the Ethnological Survey of the Indian Empire, and it was not till the Viceroyalty of Lord Curzon that Risley was appointed

* *The Tribes and Castes of Bengal,* vol. i., Introductory Essay, p. xv.

Honorary Director of the Survey, the general principles of which were described in his paper entitled "The Study of Ethnology in India."* "What he thought of the administrative and political value of ethnological enquiries," writes Mr. Anderson, "may be gathered from a charming discourse on 'India and Anthropology' delivered to the boys at Winchester in 1910 [vide *Man*, vol. x., p. 163 *et seq.*], in which he paid a kindly tribute to his friend Dr. Jackson. He quoted, too, the words of another old friend, Sir Bamfylde Fuller, that 'nothing wins the regard of an Indian so easily as a knowledge of facts connected with his religion, his prejudices, or his habits. We do but little to secure that our officers are equipped with these passports to popular regard.' Thus, in one of the last of his public utterances, Sir Herbert Risley stated his deliberate conviction that it is only right 'to teach the anthropology of India to men of the Indian services.'" This question was again raised in 1913 by Sir R. Temple in his Presidential Address delivered before the Anthropological Section at the Birmingham meeting of the British Association, which attracted much attention among all those who are interested in the training of candidates for the Indian Civil Service. An appeal, widely supported by British anthropologists, has recently been submitted to the Government, pleading for the encouragement of anthropological studies in the older Universities, which have already established flourishing Schools, and for the extension of these in the more modern Universities and Colleges.

In 1890 Risley served as member and secretary of a Commission appointed to enquire into the working of the Indian police. After a brief reversion to district duty he resumed work in the Secretariats of Bengal and of the Imperial Governments. The decennial Census of the Empire was fixed to be carried out in 1901, and in 1899 he was appointed Census Commissioner. His administrative ability was proved in the difficult task of organising a competent staff, in consulting with the Provincial Governments, and in formulating an elaborate code of regulations which formed the basis on which the Census of 1901 and that of 1911 were conducted. The results of the Census carried out under his charge were reviewed in an exceptionally interesting report prepared by him with the assistance of his friend, Mr. E. A. Gait, in which he developed his views on the origin and classification of the Indian races

* *Journal Royal Anthropological Institute*, vol. xx., 1891, p. 235 *et seq.*

largely on the basis of anthropometry. Portions of this report, with some additions and revision, were republished in 1908 under the title of *The People of India*.

After the completion of this work he was appointed Home Secretary in Lord Curzon's administration, and in 1909 he became a temporary member of the Council of the Governor-General. When, in the viceroyalty of Lord Minto, the arduous and delicate task of reforming and extending the Provincial Councils, in order to satisfy the aspirations of the more advanced section of the people, was undertaken, the heaviest portion of the work was entrusted to Risley, and the strain of these duties on a constitution which at no time was robust doubtless laid the seeds of the fatal disease which was soon to end his life. In these, the final years of his service in India, besides his official duties, he took his share in various activities. He was Director of the Ethnological Survey, President on three occasions of the Asiatic Society of Bengal, a Trustee of the Indian Museum, Secretary of the Queen Victoria Memorial Committee, and a member of the Committee of Lady Dufferin's Fund for providing medical and surgical aid for native women. His work on Constitutional Reform was so important that his service was extended for two years on the expiry of thirty-five years, the maximum term of office prescribed for members of the Indian Civil Service.

At a farewell dinner given in his honour at Calcutta on 7th February, 1910, by Lord and Lady Minto, the Viceroy remarked that "he did not know what he should have done without his assistance in the Reforms scheme," and he paid the highest tribute to his literary abilities, his foresight and industry, which had all been of invaluable assistance to the Government of India. The country could ill afford to spare so able a servant, and he wished him all success in the future.

In February, 1910, he resigned the service. Soon after his arrival in England he was appointed to succeed Sir C. J. Lyall as Permanent Secretary in the India Office. He was able to do little more than take charge of his new duties when his health finally broke down, and he fell the victim to a fatal and painful disease, borne with unflinching courage and with characteristic and touching consideration for those who strove to alleviate his sufferings. He died at Wimbledon on 30th September, 1911, leaving a widow, a son, now an officer in the Indian army, and a daughter to mourn his loss.

In the course of a long Indian career he worthily maintained the traditions of the service to which he belonged. He proved that the study of the native races may be conducted side by side with the most engrossing public work, and forms one of the best means of relaxation amidst its labours and anxieties. He showed a wide sympathy with all classes of the people, and it was his privilege at the close of his official career to be associated with measures calculated to improve the relations of its subjects with the British Government. Some of the native journals, in their sympathetic comments on his career, did not fail to recall that one of the services to the people with which his name was associated was a scheme for the sale through the agency of the Post Office of cheap packets of quinine among the malaria-stricken people of the Ganges Delta.

His services as an administrator and an anthropologist were recognised by the bestowal of the Order of Companion of the Star of India in 1904 and the Knighthood of the Order of the Indian Empire in 1907. He was elected Officier d'Académie Française and corresponding member of the Anthropological Societies of Berlin and Rome. One of his last literary tasks was to prepare the Annual Address as President of the Royal Anthropological Institute, which illness prevented him from delivering in person.

The value of Risley's work on the ethnology of India has been so widely recognised that it is unnecessary to discuss it in detail. He was a pioneer in the application of scientific methods to the classification of the races of India; and, like all pioneer work, some of his conclusions are open to criticism in the light of later researches. The words of Sir J. G. Frazer in reference to the study of comparative religion may well apply to Indian ethnology: "In this as in other branches of study it is the fate of theories to be washed away like children's castles of sand by the rising tide of knowledge." * The problems of Indian ethnology are still so obscure and in many directions our knowledge is so imperfect, that in the following pages no attempt will be made to express a dogmatic opinion upon them. All that it is proposed to do is to indicate some of the questions treated in this work which have formed the subject of controversy since the first edition was issued.

First, one of the main assumptions underlying his attempt to classify the races of India on the basis of anthropometry is

---

* *The Golden Bough*, 3rd ed., Part vii., vol. i., Preface, p. xi.

that "nowhere else in the world do we find the population of a large continent broken up into an infinite number of mutually exclusive aggregates, the members of which are forbidden by an inexorable social-law to marry outside the group to which they belong. . . . In this respect India presents a remarkable contrast to most other parts of the world, where anthropometry has to confess itself hindered, if not baffled, by the constant intermixture of types obscuring and confusing the data ascertained by measurements." *

In reply to this it has been urged that Risley has exaggerated the isolation of the present grouping of the people; that caste, in its modern, rigid form, is of comparatively recent origin. The older custom, for instance, recognised the possibility of a Kshatriya becoming a Brāhman, or *vice versâ;* and although a man was supposed to take his first wife from his own class, there was no binding rule to this effect, while in any case he was free to take a second wife from a lower class.† Similar laxities of practice prevail at the present time among certain communities in the Himalayan districts of the Panjāb.‡ The long periods of anarchy through which most parts of India have passed, some notorious facts of modern peasant life—the pressure of hypergamy which produces a scarcity of brides in the higher groups and leads to the purchase of low-born girls, the weakness of moral control among certain classes §—produce miscegenation. Caste, again, has been habitually modified by the action of the Rājās, who claimed the right of promoting and degrading members of the various castes. The process of amalgamation of caste and tribal groups is specially observable in the case of the forest tribes when they come in contact with Hinduism. Each of them shows a ragged fringe in which the more primitive type is found intermingled with the more civilised race. In the case of certain areas, like Burma, Kashmīr, Gujarāt, the existing population represents a mixture of various races which have amalgamated within the historical period. ‖

* *Infra*, p. 25 *et seq.*

† E. A. Gait, in Hastings' *Encyclopædia of Religion and Ethics*, vol. iii., 1910, p. 234.

‡ H. A. Rose, *Glossary of the Tribes and Castes of the Punjab and North-West Frontier Province*, vol. ii., 1911, pp. 130, 256 *et seq.*, 460 note: *Census Report, Punjab*, 1911, Vol. i., p. 270.

§ *Census Report, Punjab*, 1911, vol. i., p. 293, *United Provinces*, 1911, vol. i., p. 327 *et seq.*

‖ *General Indefinite Characteristics of the Tribes of Burma*, 1906, p. vi.; *Census Report, Kashmir*, 1911, vol. i., p. 204; Sir G. Grierson, *Linguistic Survey of India*, vol. ix., part ii., 1908, p. 324.

It is impossible here to discuss at length the wide and difficult question of the value of anthropometry as a test of race, on which controversy is still active. "Of late years," says Mr. O'Malley, "anthropometry as a test of race has begun to fall out of favour." * Perhaps it may be safer to say that measurements collected in a haphazard fashion among the larger composite groups, like Brāhmans, Rājputs, Nāyars, or Vellālas, which include all sorts and conditions of men, must remain of doubtful value, unless it is certain that the individuals who have been examined belong to sub-castes or families which have not been contaminated by union with outsiders. Mr. Gait, discussing the variability of caste to which reference has been made, writes: "It is desirable to point out the practical bearing on the point at issue of the facts which have been adduced in the preceding paragraphs regarding caste changes. Those which I have described as discontinuous, whereby a whole community raises its social rank, though disturbing the correlation between caste and status which Risley alleged to exist, have in themselves no effect on the racial composition of the community, unless in time the upstarts succeed in intermarrying with some other social group. But the changes arising from the transfer of individuals or groups from one caste to another would clearly disturb the homogeneity of the castes receiving them. This would be the case, for instance, when the men are in the habit of taking wives from other castes of lower status. Still more would it be the case amongst the functional castes. If it be conceded that such castes have received successive accretions of groups from outside, it follows that the main caste is seldom a homogeneous body, and that measurements taken, as they have almost invariably been, without regard to the sub-caste, cannot be expected to give uniform results. The individual sub-castes are more likely to consist of persons having a common origin, but this also is by no means an invariable rule. The processes of fission and fusion have no doubt been in operation from the earliest times; and the sub-castes of to-day, though more uniform in type than the castes of which they form part, were probably in their time formed out of different groups, which in course of time have become so closely intermingled that all traces of the original distinctions have disappeared." †

---

* *Census Report, Bengal,* 1911, vol. i., p. 517.

† *Census Report, India,* 1911, vol. i., p. 381; cf. *Man,* xiv., 1914, p. 207.

Secondly, it has been urged that Risley devoted too little attention to the influence of environment in modifying bodily structure. The views of Professor Franz Boas, who claims to have proved that the head-forms of immigrants to the United States rapidly become modified in their environment, have not been universally accepted.* But the stress laid on these influences by Professor W. Ridgeway deserve more attention than they have hitherto received in India.† It can hardly, it is urged, be possible that the differences of climate, soil, and food supplies throughout the Indian Peninsula fail to exert their influence on the physical characteristics of the population. The contrast between the deltas of the great rivers and regions like the Panjāb, the Deccan, or the forest and hill tracts, is obvious. Differences in the food supply equally deserve investigation, when we compare the races of Bengal or Madras, who mainly subsist on rice, with the people of the Deccan whose staple food is millet, the Panjābi who eats wheat or barley, the jungle-dwellers who largely use the wild products of the forest.

Thirdly, since this book was written, the problem of the Aryan and the Dravidian has assumed new forms. It has been urged that it is difficult to maintain Risley's theory of a movement of Aryan tribes into the Panjāb who retained their original Indo-Aryan type, in spite of the fact that this province has been the scene of continuous foreign immigration—Iranian, Scythian, Hun, Mongol, Persian. Again, writers of the South Indian school maintain the predominance of the Dravidian element in the present population, and regard the distinction between the Aryan and their Dasyu predecessors as one of cult and not of race.‡

Fourthly, as regards the Dravidian type, the researches of Mr. E. Thurston show that it is far from uniform;§ and Risley's extension of this term to include not only the hill tribes of Central India but much of the menial population of the northern plains, is disputed in view of recent work in linguistics which proves that the Mon-Khmer form of speech stretches right across the centre of continental India, and at one time covered the greater part of Further India and the

---

* *The American Anthropologist*, N.S., vol. xiv., No. 3, July–September, 1912, p. 530 *et seq.*; *Man*, xiv., 1914, p. 206 *et seq.*

† *Report, British Association*, 1905, p. 832 *et seq.*

‡ P. T. Srinivas Iyengar, *Life in Ancient India in the Age of the Mantras*, 1912, p. 9 *et seq.*

§ *The Castes and Tribes of Southern India*, 1909, vol. i., Introduction, p. xxxvi. *et seq.*

present Province of Assam.* This widespread extension of Mon-Khmer speech may be assumed to imply a westward movement of these races. This, and not a Dravidian element, survives in the menial population of the northern plains.

Fifthly, the views expressed in this work on the origin of the Rājputs, Jāts, and Marāthas have met with vigorous criticism. Accepting the fact that the people of Central Asia are of an uniform brachycephalic type, Risley argued that it was impossible to suppose that the long-headed Rājputs and Jāts could be descended from races entering India from that region. It is now believed by many scholars that the term Scythian or Hun does not represent homogeneous ethnical types; that as the Greeks and Romans confounded Gauls with Germans—and to most Greeks a Scythian was any barbarian from the east of Europe,—so it is held to be possible that the Hindus termed any savage enemy who crossed the Himālaya a Saka or a Hūna, migrants from a region which displays many different physical types.† It is now generally admitted that these Hun princes rapidly became Hinduised, and that from one of their clans, the Gurjara, the present Rājputs were largely, if not wholly, derived.‡

As regards the Marāthas, Risley suggested that they originated in bodies of Scythians, driven from the grazing-grounds of the Western Panjāb towards the south, where they intermingled with the Dravidian type. There seems to be, however, no historical, or even traditional, evidence of a Scythian migration into the Deccan. The Marāthas are closely connected with a mixed race of cultivators, extending over a wide area from the Deccan to the valley of the Ganges, and known as Kunbi or Kurmi. The Marātha group has now succeeded in asserting its superiority over its humbler kinsfolk, with whom they practise hypergamy, that is to say, they take brides from the latter, while the higher Marātha families refuse to give their daughters to Kunbi husbands.§ In some places these higher-class Marāthas have succeeded in acquiring the right of connubium with certain Rājput septs; but the fact that their

* *Census Report, India*, 1901, vol. i., p. 257 *et seq.*; 1911, vol. i., p. 322 *et seq.*

† E. H. Minns, *Scythians and Greeks*, 1913, p. 35; T. A. Joyce, *Journal Royal Anthropological Institute*, vol. xlii, 1912, p. 450 *et seq.*

‡ V. A. Smith, *Early History of India*, 3rd edit., 1914, pp. 322, 407 *et seq.*; *Journal Royal Asiatic Society*, January–April, 1909; D. R. Bhandarkar, *Journal Asiatic Society, Bengal*, 1909, p. 167 *et seq.*

§ *Census Report, Central Provinces*, 1911, vol. i., p. 135; *Ethnographic Survey, Central Provinces*, vol. ix., 1911, p. 123 *et seq.*

tribal organisation retains the totemistic form connects them with the pre-Aryan people. The brachycephalic form of skull which is said to prevail in parts of the Deccan was the basis of Risley's theory. But this is probably not the result of Scythian migration, but of some early tribal movement, perhaps by sea or along the coast route.*

Had Risley lived to revise this work he would certainly have considered these and other criticisms. It cannot be too clearly stated that on many or most of these problems no complete certainty has yet been attained. Much further investigation, more extended and more careful collection of anthropometric data, will be needed before the study of the ethnology of India can be placed on a scientific basis. The great value of Risley's work lies in the fact that he opened out fresh fields of enquiry, and gave a new impulse to the study of man in India.

---

* W. Crooke, "Rajputs and Mahrattas," *Journal Royal Anthropological Institute*, vol. xi., 1910, p. 46 *et seq.*

CONTENTS

CHAPTER I

THE PHYSICAL TYPES

CHAPTER II

SOCIAL TYPES

CHAPTER III

CASTE IN PROVERBS AND POPULAR SAYINGS

CHAPTER IV

CASTE AND MARRIAGE

CHAPTER V

CASTE AND RELIGION

CHAPTER VI

THE ORIGIN OF CASTE

CHAPTER VII

CASTE AND NATIONALITY

APPENDIXES

LIST OF ILLUSTRATIONS

BIBLIOGRAPHY OF THE ANTHROPOLOGICAL WRITINGS OF SIR H. H. RISLEY

1.—*The Statistical Account of Bengal*, edited by W. W. Hunter, vol. xvi.: Districts of Hazāribāgh and Lohārdaga. London, 1877.

2.—*Sikkim and Tibet*, "Blackwood's Edinburgh Magazine," May, 1890.

3.—*The Race Basis of Indian Political Movements*, "Contemporary Review," May, 1890.

4.—*Hindu Infant Marriage*, "Blackwood's Edinburgh Magazine," December, 1890.

5.—*The Study of Ethnology in India*, "Journal Anthropological Institute," vol. xx., pp. 235 *et seq.* London, 1890.

6.—*The Tribes and Castes of Bengal*, 4 vols.: vol. i., ii., "Ethnographic Glossary"; iii., iv., "Anthropometric Data." Calcutta, 1891.

7.—*Anthropometric Instructions*, "Journal Asiatic Society of Bengal," vol. lxii., pt. iii., pp. 95 *et seq.* Calcutta, 1893.

8.—*Measurements of Cingalese Moormen and Tamils taken in Ceylon, in November*, 1892, ibid., vol. lxii., pt. iii., pp. 33 *et seq.* Calcutta, 1893.

9.—*The Gazetteer of Sikkim*, Introduction. Calcutta, 1894.

10.—*Widow and Infant Marriage.* Calcutta, 1894.

11.—*Notes on Nepaul*, Introduction. Calcutta, 1896.

12.—*Presidential Anniversary Address*, "Asiatic Society of Bengal, Proceedings," pp. 18 *et seq.* Calcutta, 1899.

13.—*Presidential Anniversary Address*, "Asiatic Society of Bengal, Proceedings," pp. 21 *et seq.* Calcutta, 1900.

14.—*Note on some Indian Tatu-Marks*, *Man*, Article No. 74, pp. 97 *et seq.*, Anthropological Institute. London, 1902.

15.—*Extracts from Correspondence relating to the Origin of the Gipsies*, *ibid.*, Article No. 126, pp. 180 *et seq.*, Anthropological Institute. London, 1902.

16.—*Manual of Ethnography for India.* Calcutta, 1903.

17.—*Report Census of India*, 1901, vol. i. in collaboration with E. A. Gait; vol. ii., Ethnographic Appendixes. Calcutta, 1903.

18.—*Presidential Annual Address*, "Asiatic Society of Bengal, Proceedings," pp. 22 *et seq.* Calcutta, 1904.

19.—F. B. Bradley-Birt, *The Story of an Indian Upland*, Introduction. London, 1905.

20.—*Anthropometric Data from Bombay, Burma, Baluchistan, North-West Borderland.* Calcutta, 1906–09.

21.—*The People of India.* Calcutta, 1908.

22.—*The Indian Councils at Work*, "Blackwood's Edinburgh Magazine," November, 1900.

23.—*Manual of Anthropometry.* Calcutta, 1909.

24.—*Presidential Address*, "The Methods of Ethnography," "Journal Royal Anthropological Institute," vol. xli., pp. 8 *et seq.* London, 1911.

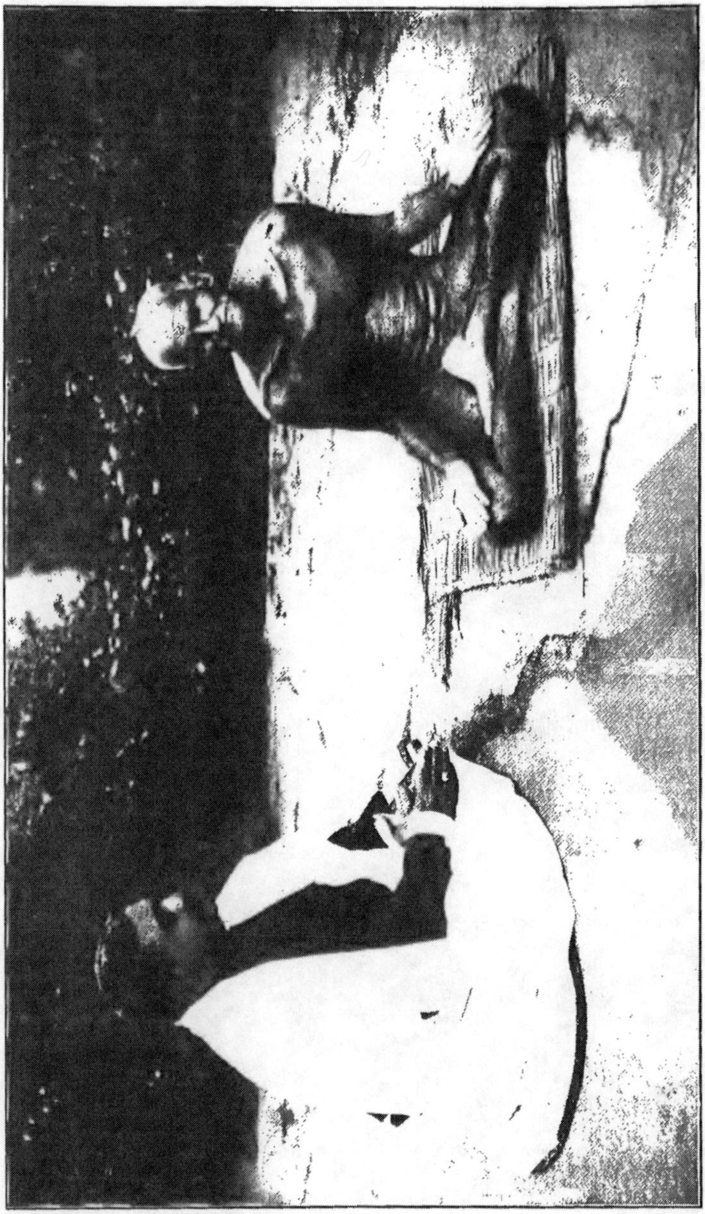

PEOPLE OF INDIA

CHAPTER I

THE PHYSICAL TYPES

ἐπεὶ ἦ μάλα πολλὰ μεταξύ,
οὔρεά τε σκιόεντα θάλασσά τε ἠχήεσσα
Il. I. 156–7.

Ethnic isolation of India.

In respect of those decisive physical features which determine the course of the national movements of mankind, India may be described as an irregularly triangular or pear-shaped fortress, protected on two sides by the sea and guarded on the third by the great bulwark of mountain ranges of which the Himalaya forms the central and most impregnable portion.* As these ranges curve westward and southward towards the Arabian Sea, they are pierced by a number of passes, practicable enough for the march of unopposed armies, but offering small encouragement to the halting advance of family or tribal migration. On the east, though the conformation of the barrier is different, its secluding influence is equally strong. The ridges which take off from the eastern end of the Himalaya run for the most part north and south, and tend to direct the main stream of Mongolian colonization towards the river

* Professor Huxley's comparison of the shape of India to "the diamond on a pack of cards, having a north angle at Ladakh, a south angle at Cape Comorin, a west angle near the mouth of the Indus, and an east angle near that of the Ganges," is possibly more accurate than that adopted in the text. It brings out the great projections of the Punjab and Kashmir towards the north and the long straight line of frontier which forms the north-western side of the diamond. On the whole, however, the triangular aspect seems to catch the eye more as one looks at a map and is thus better suited for descriptive purposes. Huxley's description is to be found in the first volume of the Journal of the Ethnological Society of London. His simile is curiously analogous to the "rhomboid" of Eratosthenes and other Greek geographers.

basins of Indo-China rather than towards India itself. On either frontier, where the mountains become less formidable, other obstacles intervene to bar the way. On the western or Iranian march the gap between the Suleiman range and the Arabian Sea is closed by the arid plateaux and thirsty deserts of Makran; to the east, the hills of the Turanian border rise in a succession of waves from a sea of trackless forest. On either side, again, at any rate within historic times, the belt of debatable land which veiled a dubious and shifting frontier has been occupied by races of masterless men knowing, in the west, no law save that of plunder and vendetta, and in the east, owning no obligation but the primitive rule that a man must prove his manhood by taking the stranger's head. Along the coast line conditions of a different character tended equally to preclude immigration on a large scale. The succession of militant traders who landed on the narrow strip of fertile but malarious country which fringes Western India, found themselves cut off from the interior by the forest-clad barrier of the Western Ghāts; while on the eastern side of the peninsula, the low coast, harbourless from Cape Comorin to Balasore, is guarded by dangerous shallows backed by a line of pitiless surf.*

The country thus isolated by physical and historical causes comprises three main regions, the Himalaya or abode of snow; the Middle Land, or Madhyadesa, as the river plains of Northern India are called in popular speech; and the southern table-land of the Deccan with its irregular hill ranges rising out of undulating plains. Each region possesses an ethnic character of its own, and has contributed a distinct element to the making of the Indian people. The Deccan, itself one of the most ancient geological formations in the world, has, since the dawn of history, been the home of the Dravidians, the oldest of the Indian races. The most recent of the three regions, the alluvial plains of the north, formed in pre-historic times the highway of the Aryan advance into India, and a large section of its inhabitants still cherishes the tradition of remote Aryan descent. The influence of the

[* The geographical isolation of India has probably been overestimated (V. A. Smith, *History of Fine Art in India and Ceylon*, 1911, p. 377). Commercial intercourse with the Tigris-Euphrates valley was active during the period 700–300 B.C. (J. Kennedy, "The Early Commerce of Babylon with India," *Journal Royal Asiatic Society*, 1908, pp. 241–88). At the close of the 1st century A.D., white slaves were imported into Western India, and the trade in Abyssinian slaves has left evidence of negro blood among some castes in the same region (*Periplus Maris Erythraei*, ch. 49; *Bombay Gazetteer*, xi., 1883, p. 433 n.).]

Himalaya has been mainly negative. It has served as a barrier against incursions from the north, but all along the line of the hills, even among people whose speech is of Rajput origin, distinct traces may be observed of an intermixture of Mongolian blood.

The Empire of to-day has outgrown its ancient limits, and now embraces the Indo-Iranian region of Baluchistan and the Indo-Chinese region of Burma. If we speak of India as a fortress, these are the outworks which guard its flanks. Nor is it pressing metaphor too far to describe Baluchistan as a great natural glacis stretching westward from the crest of the ramparts of India till it loses itself in the plains of Kandahar. Its surface is a medley of rocky peaks, narrow passes, intricate ravines and broken ranges of barren hills, which bristle at every point with defensive positions. The people show no trace of Indian culture, and are as rugged as the land in which they dwell. Arab or Afghan by tradition, Scythian or Turki by type, but probably a blend of several stocks, they are fitting guardians of the inhospitable wastes which separate India from Iran.

The Eastern outpost, Burma, presents the sharpest of contrasts to Baluchistan. Broad stretches of alluvial rice-land fringe the coast strip and run up into the interior, gradually thinning out as they approach the highlands of earlier formation through which the great rivers have forced their way. Cut off from India by a series of forest-clad ranges, which restricted the interchange of population by land, Burma lay open on the north, east and south to the inroads of a succession of Mongolian races who bore rule in turn and combined to form the type which we know as Burmese. In the hands of a maritime power Burma commands the eastern gate of the Empire, and the growing Indian element in the population owes its existence to the English control of the sea.

External Factors.

These are the external factors of the problem of Indian ethnology. The main results of their influence are obvious enough. An unbroken chain of snow-clad peaks and of passes only practicable at certain seasons opposes an effectual obstacle to the fusion of contrasting types. Ranges of lower elevation, intersected by frequent valleys, form no bar to hostile incursions and yield but scanty protection to a weaker race. Long stretches of fertile plains, traversed by navigable rivers and lying open to the march of armies, lend themselves to that crushing out of racial distinctions which conquest brings in its train. Isolated hill ranges and lofty plateaux, guarded by fever-haunted forests and offering no prospect of profit or plunder, furnish an abiding refuge for tribes which are compact enough to emigrate *en masse*. Lastly, a coast line almost devoid of sheltering harbours, while it may invite a daring invader, fails to foster the maritime skill and enterprise which alone can repulse his landing.

Internal Factors.

For the internal factors—the races which lived and struggled within the environment roughly sketched above—we must depend to a great extent upon speculative data. Living organisms are more complex and less stable than their material surroundings. The hills may not be everlasting, as poets have imagined, but they outlive countless generations of men, and the changes that time works in their structure do impress on them some record, however imperfect, of processes which it has taken ages to complete. Man alone passes and leaves nothing behind. India in particular is conspicuous for the absence of the pre-historic evidence of which ethnologists in Europe have made such admirable use. There are no cave deposits, no sepulchral mounds or barrows, no kitchen middens, no lake dwellings, no ancient fortified towns such as modern research is now unearthing in Greece,* and no sculptured bones or weapons portraying the vicissitudes of the life of primitive man. The climate and the insects have obliterated all perishable vestiges of the past, and what nature may have spared a people devoid of the historic sense has made no effort to preserve. To fill the blank we are thrown back mainly on conjecture. Yet in India conjecture starts from a more solid basis than in the progressive countries of the Western world. For here we have before our eyes a society in many respects still primitive, which preserves, like a palimpsest manuscript, survivals of immemorial antiquity. In a land where all things always are the same we are justified in concluding that what is happening now must have happened, very much in the same way, throughout the earlier stages of human society in India. Observation of the present is our best guide to the reconstruction of the past.

---

* In an instructive paper recently published Professor Kabbadias, Director of Antiquities in Greece, shows that in pre-historic times fortified towns occupied the place taken in other countries by pile-dwellings, *Man*, Decr., 1904, No. 112.

On a stone panel forming part of one of the grandest Buddhist monuments in India, the great tope at Sānchi, a carving in low relief depicts a strange religious ceremony.* Under trees with conventional foliage and fruits, three women, attired in tight clothing without skirts, kneel in prayer before a small shrine or altar. In the foreground, the leader of a procession of monkeys bears in both hands a bowl of liquid and stoops to offer it at the shrine. His solemn countenance and the grotesquely adoring gestures of his comrades seem intended to express reverence, devotion, and humility. In the background four stately figures, two men and two women of tall stature and regular features, clothed in flowing robes and wearing elaborate turbans, look on with folded hands in apparent approval of this remarkable act of worship. Antiquarian speculation has for the most part passed the panel by unnoticed, or has sought to associate it with some pious legend of the life of Buddha. A larger interest, however, attaches to the scene, if it is regarded as the sculptured expression of the race sentiment of the Aryans towards the Dravidians, which runs through the whole course of Indian tradition and survives in scarcely abated strength to the present day. In this view the carving would belong to the same order of ideas as the story in the Rāmāyaṇa of the army of apes who assisted Rāma in the invasion of Ceylon. It shows us the higher race on friendly terms with the lower, but keenly conscious of the essential difference of type and taking no active part in the ceremony at which they appear as sympathetic but patronizing spectators. An attempt is made in the following pages to show that the race sentiment which inspired this curious sculpture, rests upon a foundation of facts which can be verified by scientific methods; that it supplied the motive principle of caste; that it continues, in the form of fiction or tradition, to shape the most modern developments of the system; and, finally, that its influence has tended to preserve in comparative purity the types which it favours.

The race basis of Indian society.

It is a familiar experience that the ordinary untravelled European, on first arriving in India, finds much difficulty in distinguishing one native of the country from another. To his untrained eye all Indians are black; all have the same

[* For an illustration of this relief see F. C. Maisey, *Sanchi and its Remains*, 1892, Plate ix, Fig. 1. The value of this relief, from the point of view of anthropology, has been disputed (*Census Report, Punjab*, 1911, vol. i., p. 400).]

cast of countenance; and all, except the "decently naked" labouring classes, wear loose garments which revive dim memories of the attire of the Greeks and Romans. An observant man soon shakes off these illusions and realizes the extraordinary diversity of the types which are met with everywhere in India. The first step in his education is to learn to tell a Hindu from a Muhammadan. A further stage is reached when it dawns upon him that the upper classes of Hindus are much fairer than the lower and that their features are moulded on finer lines. Later on, if opportunity favours him, he comes to recognize at a glance the essential differences between the Punjabi and the Bengali, the Pathān and the Gurkha, the Rajput and the "Jungly" tea coolie: he will no longer take a Marāthā Brāhman for a Madrasi, or an Oriya for a native of Kashmir. He learns, in short, to distinguish what may be called the provincial types of the people of India, the local, racial, or linguistic aggregates which at first sight seem to correspond to the nations of Europe. But the general impressions thus formed, though accurate enough so far as they go, are wanting in scientific precision. They cannot be recorded or analyzed; no description can convey their effect; they melt away in the attempt to fix them, and leave nothing behind.

The Data of Ethnology.

The modern science of ethnology endeavours to define and to classify the various physical types, with reference to their distinctive characteristics, in the hope that when sufficient data have been accumulated it may be possible in some measure to account for the types themselves, to determine the elements of which they are composed, and thus to establish their connexion with one or other of the great families of mankind. In India, where historical evidence can hardly be said to exist, the data ordinarily available are of three kinds—physical characters, linguistic characters, and religious and social usages. Of these the first are by far the most trustworthy. Most anthropologists, indeed, are now inclined to adopt without much question the opinion of the late Sir William Flower, who wrote to me some years ago that "physical characters are the best, in fact the only true tests of race, that is, of real affinity; language, customs, etc., may help or give indications, but they are often misleading."

The claims of language to share in the settlement of questions of race cannot, however, be dismissed in a single sentence.

Nearly twenty years ago, when the ethnographic survey of Bengal was in progress, the late Professor Max Müller sent me a long letter, since published in his collected works, in which he protested against "the unholy alliance" of the two sciences of ethnology and comparative philology. At first sight it is hard to understand why two lines of research, dealing with different subjects and working towards different ends, should be charged with nefarious collusion for the purpose of perverting the truth. A clue to the grounds of the accusation is, however, furnished by Sir Henry Maine's remark that the study of the sacred languages of India has given to the world "the modern science of Philology and the modern theory of Race." The study of Sanskrit received its first impetus from the publication by Sir William Jones of translations of Kālidāsa's Sakuntala in 1789 and of the Institutes of Manu in 1794.* The discovery was announced and its importance emphasised in Friedrich von Schlegel's treatise on the Language and Wisdom of the Hindus; but even with this assistance the fresh ideas took more than a generation to spread beyond the narrow circle of Orientalists and to impress themselves upon the main current of European thought. The birth of a new science, based upon an ancient language of which most people then heard for the first time, was inaugurated by Friedrich Bopp's Comparative Grammar of the Indo-European languages. The editions of this work extend over the period 1833—1852, so that the beginnings of Comparative Philology coincide in point of time with the popular upheaval which found expression in the revolutionary movements of 1848. The belief that linguistic affinities prove community of descent was one which commended itself alike to populations struggling for freedom and to rulers in search of excuses for removing a neighbour's landmark. The old idea of tribal sovereignty seemed almost to have revived when Napoleon III. assumed the title of Emperor of the French and justified his annexation of Savoy by the plea that territory where French was spoken ought to belong to France. As the principle gained strength and was invoked on a larger

Language and Race.

[* Professor A. A. Macdonell points out that "the first impulse to the study of Sanskrit was given by the practical administrative needs of our Indian possessions. Warren Hastings, at that time Governor-General, clearly seeing the advantage of ruling the Hindus as far as possible according to their own laws and customs, caused a number of Brahmans to prepare a digest based on the best ancient legal authorities. An English version of this Sanskrit compilation, made through the medium of a Persian translation, was published in 1776." (*A History of Sanskrit Literature*, 1900, p. 2.)]

scale it gave rise to the political aspirations implied in the terms Pan-Teutonism, Pan-Hellenism, Pan-Slavism; it helped the cause of German unity; it was appealed to in the name of united Italy; and, if carried to its logical conclusion, it may some day contribute to the disruption of the Austrian Empire.

Thus we find Comparative Philology, in the hands of ardent patriots and astute diplomatists, trespassing on the domain of ethnology and confusing for political purposes the two distinct conceptions of race and nationality. But the ethnologists themselves were not free from blame. So far from resisting the encroachment on their territory they lent their authority to the prevailing tendency and based their classification of races mainly upon linguistic characters. For this they may well be held to have had some substantial excuses. In the first place linguistic data are far easier to collect on a large scale, and far easier to examine when collected, than the physical observations which form the main basis of ethnological conclusions. The vast array of languages and dialects which fill the sixteen volumes of Dr. Grierson's Linguistic Survey of India was brought together from the most distant corners of the Empire by the simple device of circulating for translation the parable of the Prodigal Son (the fatted calf, in deference to Hindu sentiment, being discreetly transformed into a goat), together with a small number of common words and phrases. But to have recorded the physical characters of the people on a similar scale would have cost an immense sum; the operations would have extended over many years; and the results would probably have been vitiated by the personal divergencies of the numerous observers whom it would have been necessary to employ.

Secondly, languages lend themselves far more readily to precise classification than the minute variations of form and feature which go to make up an ethnic type. Thirdly,—and this is perhaps the most important point of all—while there are practically no mixed languages, there are hardly any pure races. Judged by the only sound test, that of grammatical structure as distinguished from mere vocabulary, all languages may be regarded as true genera and species from which no hybrid progeny can arise. Words may be borrowed on a larger or smaller scale, but the essential structure of the language remains unchanged, the foreign elements being forced into an indigenous mould. Thus French people who have taken to afternoon tea have evolved the verb "*five o'cloquer*"; a Bengali clerk who is late for office will say *āmi miss-train kariyāchhi*, converting a mangled English phrase into a characteristic verbal noun; and a Berlin tram-conductor, who was explaining to me how his working hours had come to be reduced, summed up the position with the words "*wir haben nämlich streikirt.*" In each case a foreign phrase has been taken to express an imported idea; but this phrase has been absorbed and dealt with in accordance with the genius of the language, and there is no approach to structural hybridism. Races, on the other hand, mix freely; they produce endless varieties; and it can hardly be said even now that any satisfactory agreement has been arrived at as to the system on which such varieties should be classified.

These considerations go some way towards accounting for the "unholy alliance" which politics and the spirit of classification have combined to bring about between two distinct sciences. They fail, however, to give us much assistance in the solution of the main question—what are the true relations between Ethnology and Philology? Within what limits can we argue from correspondences of language to community of race or from differences of language to diversity of race? Are we to hold with Schwiker and Hale that language is the only true test of racial affinities; or should we follow Sayce's opinion that "identity or relationship of language can prove nothing more than social contact"? The mere fact that speech is a physiological function, depending in the last resort on the structure of the larynx, suggests that the latter view may be too absolutely expressed. That some races produce sounds which other races can only imitate imperfectly is a matter of common observation, and may reasonably be ascribed to differences of vocal machinery. The clicks of the Bushman and Hottentot, the gutturals of Arabic and the dental and cerebral consonants of the Indian vernaculars present varying degrees of difficulty to the average European. Similar differences of phonetic capacity may be observed among the Indian races. Bengalis, as Dr. Grierson has pointed out, "cannot pronounce a clear *s* but make it *sh*"; the natives of Western India tend to turn *v* into *w*; and nearly all Orientals find a difficulty in starting a word like Smith without prefixing a vowel and turning it into "I-Smith." Even within the range of a single language, dialectic variations occur which may be due to physical causes. The gobbling speech of the people of

Chittagong and Eastern Bengal, and their inability to negotiate certain consonants, seem to suggest that their original tongue belonged to the Tibeto-Burman family, and that their vocal apparatus must differ materially from that of their Western neighbours.* Whether it will ever be possible to define these variations, and to correlate them with racial characteristics, is a question for students of the physiological side of the modern science of phonetics.

The truth as to the relation between race and language probably lies somewhere between the extreme views noticed above, but it can only be reached by an examination of the facts. There are four possible cases:—

(1) where both language and physical type have been changed by contact with other races or communities, as have happened with the Bengali-speaking Kochh, who have lost their tribal language while their original Mongoloid type, still clearly discernible among their congeners in Assam, has been modified by intermixture with a Dravidian element;

(2) where the language has changed but the racial type has remained the same, as with the Gauls, Normans, and Lombards in Europe, the Negroes in America, and the Ahoms, Bhumij and many others in India;

(3) where the original language has been retained but the racial type has changed, as with the Basques and Magyars in Europe, the Khas in Nepal, and a large proportion of the Rajputs all over India;

(4) where both language and physical type are unchanged, as with the Andamanese, the Santals, the Mundas, the Manipuris and many others.

In the first two cases an appeal to language would clearly be ineffectual unless historical evidence were forthcoming to show what the original language had been. In India the *genius loci* has not turned to history, and almost the only instance in which ancient records throw light upon the origin of a tribe is that of the Ahoms, a Shan people who entered Assam early in the thirteenth century and within the next three hundred years conquered and gave their name to the country. Towards the end of the seventeenth century they

[* "So full of consonants are Tibetan words that most of them could be articulated with almost semi-closed mouth, evidently from the enforced necessity to keep the lips closed as far as possible against the cutting cold when speaking" (L. A. Waddell, *Lhasa and its Mysteries*, 3rd ed., 1906, p. 144).]

embraced Hinduism, lost their original language, and "became, like Brāhmans, powerful in talk alone." Their chronicles (*buranji* or "store of instructions for the ignorant") were kept up by their priests in Ahom, "an old form of the language which ultimately became Shan," and are the chief authority for the early history of Assam.

To the remaining two cases we may apply a canon which I suggested to Dr. Grierson some two years ago, and which he has embodied in his chapter on Language in the Census Report of 1901. I would now state it somewhat more fully thus:—

(1) In areas where several languages are spoken, one or more of them will usually be found to be gaining ground, while others are stationary or declining: the condition of stable equilibrium is comparatively rare. The former may be described in relation to any given area as *dominant*, the latter as *decadent* or *subordinate* languages. What languages belong to either class is, in each case, a matter of observation.

(2) The fact that a particular tribe or people uses a *dominant* language does not of itself suggest any inference as to their origin.

(3) The fact that such a group speaks a *decadent* language may supply evidence of their origin, the value of which will vary with circumstances.

It must be admitted, however, that these propositions do not carry us very far, and that in their application to particular cases they tend to break down just at the point where the enquiry begins to be interesting. Of course it is obvious enough that the fact that the Rājbansi-Kochh and the Bhumij both speak Bengali does not prove them to be of Indo-Aryan descent. On this point their physical type would be conclusive, even if we had not independent evidence that a few generations ago they spoke tribal languages of their own. Similarly, when one finds two small and isolated communities in Bengal, the Siyālgirs of Midnapur and the Kichaks of Dacca, speaking Bhīl dialects of Gujarāti, one is naturally disposed to infer that these people must have come from Gujarāt, and are probably related in some way to the Bhīls. But here again there is room for doubt. Although both Kichaks and Siyālgirs are now of settled habits, the traditions of the former, and the usages and occupations of both, suggest that at no very distant date they formed part of that miscellaneous multitude of gipsy folk whose origin is no less of a mystery in India than in other parts of the world. To people of their habits—the Kichaks say that their ancestors were dacoits, and the Siyālgirs are credited with thievish proclivities—the possession of a special *argot* would be an obvious convenience, and it seems simpler to suppose that this circumstance led to the wide diffusion of the dialect than to argue that the small groups which make use of it in Bengal must be fragments of a distant and compact tribe like the Bhīls. Thieves' patters have a family likeness all the world over, but no one has yet attempted to trace the speakers to a common ancestor.

Other minor instances deserve passing mention. The Vaidu herbalists of Poona, who speak Marāthi to their neighbours, explain the fact that they use Kanarese among themselves by the tradition that they were brought from the Kanara country by one of the Peshwas and settled in Kirki. The Kāsār coppersmiths of Nasik speak Gujarāti at home and Marāthi out of doors. The men dress like Marāthas, but the women still wear the characteristic petticoat (*ghāgra*) of Gujarāt instead of the Marātha *sāri*. In both these cases linguistic evidence points to a migration; but the value of the deduction is small. For we know historically that the migration must have been a recent one and it could probably be established on independent grounds. Nor do linguistic considerations throw any light upon the curious question how it is that the Mundas and Oraons, two distinct tribes of identical physical type, speak languages which differ widely in respect of structure and vocabulary.

But perhaps the most notable illustration of the weakness of the argument from affinity of language to affinity of race is afforded by Brāhūi. One of the maps in Dr. Grierson's chapter on language in the Census Report for India in 1901, shows the distribution of the Dravidian languages. Most of the Dravidian-speaking areas are massed in the south of India, while a few outlying patches represent Gond in the Central Provinces and Kandh, Kurnkh, and Malto in Bengal. Otherwise the map is blank save for Brāhūi, a tiny island of Dravidian speech far away in Baluchistan where it is surrounded on all sides by Indo-Aryan languages. As to the Dravidian affinities of the Brāhūi language, I understand that there is practical agreement among linguistic authorities. Concerning the conclusions to be drawn from this fact opinions differ widely. One school founds upon it the hypothesis that the Dravidians entered India from beyond the north-west frontier, while another regards the Brāhūi as an outpost of the main body of Dravidians in Southern India. Both assume identity of race, and both ignore the essential fact that, as is shown at length below, few types of humanity can present more marked physical differences than the Brāhūi and the Dravidian. How then can we explain the resemblances of language? Surely only by assuming that at some remote period the two races must have been in contact and that the speech of one influenced that of the other. Thus what seems at first sight to be a crucial instance serves merely to bring out the uncertainty that besets any attempt to argue from language to race. Here, if anywhere, is a decadent and isolated language; here, if anywhere, it ought to tell a plain tale; and here, when confronted with other evidence, it conspicuously fails us. Thus we end very much where we began, with the rather impotent conclusion that in questions of racial affinity, while the testimony of language should certainly be considered, the chances are against its telling us anything that we did not know already from other and less dubious sources.

Indefinite physical characters.

For ethnological purposes physical characters may be said to be of two kinds—*indefinite* characters which can only be described in more or less appropriate language, and *definite* characters which admit of being measured and reduced to numerical expression. The former class, usually called descriptive or secondary characters, includes such points as the colour and texture of the skin; the colour, form, and position of the eyes; the colour and character of the hair; and the form of the face and features. Conspicuous as these traits are, the difficulty of observing, defining, and recording them is extreme. Colour, the most striking of them all, is perhaps the most evasive, and deserves fuller discussion as presenting a typical instance of the shortcomings of the descriptive method. Some forty years ago the French anthropologist Broca devised a chromatic scale consisting of twenty shades, regularly graduated and numbered, for registering the colour of the eyes, and thirty-four for the skin. The idea was that the observer would consult the scale and note the numbers of the shades which he found to correspond most closely with the colouring of his subjects. Experience, however, has shown that with a scale so elaborate as Broca's the process of matching colours is not so easy as it looks; that different people are apt to arrive at widely different conclusions; and that even when the numbers have been correctly registered no one can translate the result of the observations into intelligible language. For these reasons Broca's successor Topinard reverted to the method of simple description, unaided by any scale of pattern colours. He describes, for example, the mud-coloured hair so common among the peasants of Central Europe as having the colour of a dusty chestnut. In the latest edition of the Anthropological Notes and Queries published under the auspices of the British Association, an attempt is made to combine the two systems. A greatly simplified colour scale is given, and each colour is also briefly described. I doubt, however, whether it is possible to do more than to indicate in very general terms the impression which a particular colour makes upon the observer. In point of fact the colour of the skin is rather what may be called an artistic expression, dependent partly upon the action of light, partly on the texture and transparency of the skin itself, and partly again on the great variety of shades which occur in every part of its surface. It is hopeless to expect that this complex of characters can be adequately represented by a patch of opaque paint which is necessarily uniform throughout and devoid of any suggestion of light and shade.

The difficulty which besets all attempts to classify colour is enhanced in India by the fact that, for the bulk of the population, the range of variation, especially in the case of the eyes and hair, is exceedingly small. The skin, no doubt, exhibits extreme divergencies of colouring which any one can detect at a glance. At one end of the scale we have the dead black of the Andamanese, the colour of a blackleaded stove before it has been polished, and the somewhat brighter black of the Dravidians of Southern India, which has been aptly compared to the colour of strong coffee unmixed with milk. Of the Irulas of the Nilgiri jungles, some South Indian humourist is reported to have said that charcoal leaves a white mark upon them. At the other end one may place the flushed ivory skin of the typical Kashmiri beauty and the very light transparent brown—"wheat-coloured" is the common vernacular description—of the higher castes of Upper India, which Emil Schmidt compares to milk just tinged with coffee and describes as hardly darker than is found in members of the swarthier races of Southern Europe. Between these extremes we find countless shades of brown, darker or lighter, transparent or opaque, frequently tending towards yellow, more rarely approaching a reddish tint, and occasionally degenerating into a sort of greyish black which seems to depend on the character of the surface of the skin. It would be a hopeless task to attempt to register and to classify these variations. Nor, if it were done, should we be in a position to evolve order out of the chaos of tints. For even in the individual minute gradations of colour are comparatively unstable, and are liable to be affected not only by exposure to sun and wind, but also by differences of temperature and humidity. Natives of Bengal have assured me that people of their race, one of the darkest in India, become appreciably fairer when domiciled in Hindustan or the Punjab; and the converse process may be observed not only in natives of Upper India living in the damp heat of the Ganges delta, but in Indians returning from a prolonged stay in Europe, who undergo a perceptible change of colour during the voyage to the East. The fair complexion of the women of the shell-cutting Saṇkāri caste in Dacca is mainly due to their seclusion in dark rooms, and the Lingāyats of Southern India who wear a box containing a tiny phallus tied in a silk cloth round the upper arm, show, when they take it off, a pale band of skin contrasting sharply with the colour of the rest of the body.

Still less variety is traceable in the character of the eyes and hair. From one end of India to the other, the hair of the great mass of the population is black or dark brown, while among the higher castes the latter colour is occasionally shot through by something approaching a tawny shade. Straight hair seems, on the whole, to predominate, but hair of a wavy or curly character appears in much the same proportion as among the races of Europe. The Andamanese have woolly or frizzy hair, oval in section and curling on itself so tightly that it seems to grow in separate spiral tufts, while in fact it is quite evenly distributed over the scalp. Although the terms woolly and frizzy have been loosely applied to the wavy hair not uncommon among the Dravidians, no good observer has as yet found among any of the Indian races a head of hair that could be correctly described as woolly. Throughout India the eyes are almost invariably dark brown. Occasional instances of grey eyes are found among the Konkanasth Brāhmans of Bombay, and the combination of blue eyes, auburn hair, and reddish blonde complexion is met with on the north-western frontier. On the Malabar coast in the south, Mr. Thurston had noticed several instances of pale blue and grey eyes combined with a dark complexion and has even seen a Syrian Christian baby of undoubted native parentage with bright carroty hair. The Syrian Christians of South Travancore say, indeed, that they differ from Northerners in having a red tinge to the moustache.

Definite physical characters.

When we turn to the definite or anthropometric characters we find ourselves upon firmer ground. The idea of applying instruments of precision to the measurement of the human body was familiar to the Egyptians and the Greeks, both of whom appear to have made extensive experiments with the object of arriving at a "canon" or ideal type, showing the proportions which various parts of the body should bear to the entire figure and to each other. Such canons were usually expressed either in terms of a particular member of which the rest were supposed to be multiples, or in fractional parts of the entire stature. Thus, according to Lepsius, the Egyptian canon is based on the length of the middle finger and this measure is supposed to be contained nineteen times in the full stature, three times in the head and neck, eight times in the arm, and so forth. The Greek canon, on the other hand, as restored by Quetelet, expresses the limbs and other dimensions in thousandth parts of the entire stature. Concerning this canon a curious story is told by Topinard, not without interest in its bearings upon the relations of Egyptian and Greek art. In 1866, the eminent French anthropologist Broca was asked on behalf of an artist who was engaged in the attempt to reconstruct the Greek standard, to provide a skeleton corresponding in its proportions to certain measurements derived from an examination of the Belvedere Apollo. After some search Broca found in the Museum of the Anthropological Society at Paris a skeleton of the type required. It was that of a Soudanese negro named Abdullah, and from this Broca concluded that the famous statue of Apollo had been modelled on the Egyptian canon, which in his opinion had been derived by Egyptian sculptors from the study of the Nubian negroes whom they employed as models.

The Roman canon handed down in the treatise *De Architectura* of Vitruvius was taken up and developed in the early days of the Renaissance by Leo Battista Alberti, himself, like Vitruvius, an architect, and a curious enquirer into the secret ways of nature and of the human frame. Forty years later Leonardo da Vinci, in his *Trattato della pittura*, expressed the general opinion that the proportions of the body should be studied in children and adults of both sexes, and refuted the opinion of Vitruvius that the navel should be deemed the centre of the body. Following Leonardo's suggestions, Albrecht Dürer addressed himself to the task of working out the proportions of the body for different ages and sexes, for persons of different heights, and for different types of figure. In his "*Four books on the proportions of the human figure*," published at Nürnberg in 1528, the year of his death, Dürer discussed the difficult question of the so-called "orientation" or adjustment of the head in an upright position, and he is believed by the authors of the *Crania ethnica* to have also anticipated Camper's invention of the facial angle. Jean Cousin, a French contemporary of Dürer's, took the nose as his unit of length and represented the ideal head as measuring four noses, and the ideal stature as equivalent to eight heads or thirty-two noses. Cousin's system, slightly modified by Charles Blanc, holds its own at the present day as the *canon des ateliers* of French artists, preference, however, being given in ordinary parlance to the head rather than the nose as the unit of length.

All these canons, it will be observed, approach the subject purely from the artistic point of view; and so far from taking account of the distinctive characters of particular races, incline to sink these in the attempt to frame a general canon of the proportions of the body which should hold good for the whole of mankind. Such an endeavour would be foreign to the purpose of anthropology, which fixes its attention on points of difference rather than of resemblance, and seeks by examination and analysis of such differences to form hypotheses concerning the genesis of the distinct race stocks now in existence. It would perhaps be fanciful to trace the germs of anthropometric research in the statement of Herodotus that the skulls of the Persian soldiers slain at the battle of Platæa were thin, and those of the Egyptians were thick, or to cite his explanation, that the former lived an indoor life and always wore hats, while the latter shave their heads from infancy and exposed them to sun without covering, as the earliest instance of the modern scientific doctrine of the influence of external conditions. But when Ctesias speaks of the small stature, black complexion, and snub noses of the inhabitants of India, we feel that the description is precise enough to enable us to identify them with the *Dasyus* and *Nishādas* of early Sanskrit

The data now available.

literature, and we are almost tempted to wonder whether the Greek physician, who was doubtless acquainted with the canon of Polycletus, may not have devised some accurate method of recording the racial characteristics of which he was so close an observer. Curiously enough the famous potter, Bernard de Palissy, was the first to throw out, in a humorous dialogue published in 1563, the idea of measuring the skull for purposes other than artistic. The passage quoted by Topinard is too quaint to be omitted here:—"Quoy voyant il me print envie de mesurer la teste d'un homme pour sçavoir directement ses mesures, et me semble que la sauterelle, la régle, et le compas me seroient fort propres pour cest affaire, mais, quoy qu'il en soit, je n'y sceu jamais trouver une mesure osseuse, parce que les folies qui estaient en ladite teste luy faisaient changer ses mesures."

Method of treatment adopted.

Palissy, however, cannot be seriously put forward as the founder of scientific craniometry, and that title perhaps most properly belongs to the Swedish naturalist, Anders Retzius, who in 1842 hit upon the device of expressing one of the chief characters of the skull by the relation of its maximum breadth to its maximum length, the latter being taken to be one thousand. In this way he distinguished two forms of skull—the *dolicho-cephalic*, or long-headed type, in which the length exceeds the breadth by about one-fourth, and the *brachy-cephalic*, or short-headed type, in which the length exceeds the breadth by a proportion varying from one-fifth to one-eighth. Thus according to Retzius the Swedes are long-headed in the proportion 773 : 1000, and the Lapps short-headed in the proportion 865 : 1000. He also distinguished two types of face—the orthognathic, in which the jaws and teeth project either not at all, or very little beyond a line drawn from the forehead, and the prognathic, in which this projection is very marked. His classification of races was based upon these characteristics. In 1861 Broca improved Retzius' system by expressing it in hundredths instead of thousandths, by introducing an intermediate group, called *mesati-cephalic* or medium-headed and ranging from 77·7 to 80 per cent., and by giving the name of cephalic index to the relation between the two diameters. Numerous other measurements, which are described in the literature of the subject, have since been introduced.

In the earlier days of anthropology, it was natural that the attention of students should have been directed mainly to the examination of skulls. Craniometry seemed to offer a solution of the problems regarding the origin and antiquity of the human race which then divided the scientific world. Its precise method promised to clear up the mystery of the prehistoric skulls discovered in the quaternary strata of Europe, and to connect them on the one side with a possible Simian ancestor of mankind and on the other with the races of the present day. The latter line of research led on to the measurements of living subjects, which have since been undertaken by a number of enquirers on a very large scale. Anthropometry which deals with living people, while craniometry is concerned exclusively with skulls, possesses certain advantages over the elder science. For reasons too technical to enter upon here, its procedure is in some respects less precise and its results less minute and exhaustive than those of craniometry. These minor shortcomings are, however, amply made up for by its incomparably wider range. The number of subjects available is practically unlimited; measurements can be undertaken on a scale large enough to eliminate, not merely the personal equation of the measurer, but also the occasional variations of type arising from intermixture of blood; and the investigation is not restricted to the characters of the head, but extends to the stature and the proportions of the limbs. A further advantage arises from the fact that no doubts can be cast upon the identity of the individuals measured. In working with skulls, whether prehistoric or modern, this last point has to be reckoned with. The same place of sepulture may have been used in succession by two different races, and the skulls of conquering chiefs may be mixed with those of alien slaves or of prisoners slain to escort their captors to the world of the dead. The savage practice of head-hunting may equally bring about a deplorable confusion of cranial types; famine skulls may belong to people who have wandered from no one knows where; and even hospital specimens may lose their identity in the process of cleaning. In the second of his elaborate monographs on the craniology of the people of India Sir William Turner observes * that among the Oriya skulls belonging to the Indian Museum, which were lent to him for examination, some crania partake "of Dravidian, others of Aryan characters," while in others again there is "a trace of

Craniometry and Anthropometry.

* *Transactions of the Royal Society of Edinburgh*, Vol. XL. Pars 1. (No. 6).

Mongolian or other brachy-cephalic intermixture." He surmises, therefore, that "no proper history of the dead had been obtained, and that in consequence the skulls had not been accurately identified." As a matter of fact most of these skulls were acquired during the Orissa famine of 1866, and the only description they bear is "Oriya" or "Orissa," the word "Hindu" being occasionally added. To any one who is acquainted with the conditions which prevailed in Orissa at that time it is obvious that a given skull may have belonged to a broad-nosed Dravidian from the hill tracts, to a high caste Hindu of the coast strip, or to a Mongoloid pilgrim from Nepal who died of starvation or cholera while seeking salvation at Jagannath. The characters of the skulls themselves render it probable that all of these indefinite groups are represented in the collection.

Anthropometry in India.

Scientific anthropometry was introduced into India on a large scale twenty years ago in connexion with the ethnographic survey of Bengal then in progress. The survey itself was a first attempt to apply to Indian ethnography the methods of systematic research sanctioned by the authority of European anthropologists. Among these the measurement of physical characters occupies a prominent place, and it seemed that the restrictions on intermarriage, which are peculiar to the Indian social system, would favour this method of observation, and would enable it to yield peculiarly clear and instructive results. A further reason for resorting to anthropometry was the fact that the wholesale borrowing of customs and ceremonies which goes on among the various social groups in India makes it practically impossible to arrive at any certain conclusions by examining these practices. Finally, the necessity of employing more precise methods was accentuated by Mr. Nesfield's * uncompromising denial of the truth of "the modern doctrine which divides the population of India into Aryan and aboriginal," and his assertion of the essential unity of the Indian race, enforced as it was by the specific statements that "the great majority of Brahmans are not of lighter complexion or of finer and better bred features than any other caste," and that a stranger walking through the class rooms of the Sanskrit College at Benares "would never dream of supposing" that the high caste students of that exclusive institution "were

* Nesfield's *Brief View of the Caste System of the North-West Provinces and Oudh.*

distinct in race and blood from the scavengers who swept the roads." A theory which departed so widely from literary tradition, from the current beliefs of the people, and from the opinions of most independent observers called for the searching test which anthropometry promised to furnish, and the case was crucial enough to put the method itself on its trial. The experiment has been justified by its results.

In 1890 I published in the Journal of the Anthropological Institute,* under the title "The Study of Ethnology in India," a summary of the measurements of eighty-nine characteristic tribes and castes of Bengal, the United Provinces of Agra and Oudh, and the Punjab. These measurements were taken in accordance with a scheme approved by the late Sir William Flower of the British Museum and Professor Topinard of Paris. Topinard's instruments were used, and his instructions were closely followed throughout. Analysis of the data rendered it possible to distinguish in the area covered by the experiment three main types, which were named provisionally Aryan, Dravidian, and Mongoloid. The characteristics of these types will be discussed fully below. Here it is sufficient to remark that the classification was accepted at the time by Flower, Beddoe, and Haddon in England, by Topinard in France, and by Virchow, Schmidt, and Kollmann in Germany. It has recently been confirmed by the high authority of Sir William Turner, who has been led by the examination of a large number of skulls to the same conclusions that were suggested to me by measurements taken on living subjects, and has been good enough to quote and adopt my descriptions of the leading types in his monographs † on the subject. Similar confirmation is furnished in the case of the Punjab by the craniometric researches of Lieutenant-Colonel Sir Havelock Charles.‡ Great additions have since been made to the number of measurements on living subjects by the exertions of Mr. Edgar Thurston, Superintendent of Ethnography for Southern India, under the comprehensive scheme of research sanctioned by Lord Curzon; by Sir T. H. Holland, Director of the Geological Survey of India, who has contributed important data for the Coorgs and Yeruvas of

* J. A. I., XX, 235.

† "Contributions to the Craniology of the People of the Empire of India." *Transactions of the Royal Society of Edinburgh*, Vol. XXXIX., Part III. (No. 28); Vol. XL., Part I. (No. 6).

‡ *Journal of Anatomy and Physiology*, Vol. XXVII., p. 20.

Southern India and the Kanets of Kulu and Lahoul;* by my anthropometric assistants, Rai Sahib Kumud Behāri Sāmanta and Mr. B. A. Gupte, who have carried out under my instructions an extensive series of measurements in Baluchistan, Rajputana, Bombay, Orissa, and Burma; and by Lieutenant-Colonel Waddell, C.B., C.I.E., of the Indian Medical Service, who has published some valuable data for Assam, and parts of Bengal in the Journal of the Asiatic Society of Bengal.†

It is clearly impossible, within the compass of this sketch, to enter upon a full analysis of all the measurements which have been collected. I have therefore selected three characters, the proportions of the head, the proportions of the nose, and the stature, and have included them in the tables appended to this volume. For two groups I have also taken the orbito-nasal index, which affords a very precise test of the comparative flatness of face, determined mainly by the prominence or depression of the root of the nose in relation to the bones of the orbit and cheek, which is a distinctive characteristic of the Mongolian races. The measurements are arranged under the seven types, into which I now propose to divide the population; in every case the average and the maximum and minimum indices or dimensions are shown; and for each type diagrams are given, showing the seriation of the data for the tribes or castes selected as characteristic of the type. It need hardly be added that the conclusions which I have ventured to put forward are necessarily provisional, and will be of use mainly as a guide to research, and as an indication of the progress made up to date in this line of enquiry. During the next few years the data will be greatly added to by the ethnographic survey, and we may then hope to be in a position to make some approach to a final classification of the people of India on the basis of their physical characters.

General classification of mankind: the three primary types.

Meanwhile, it may be of service to point out that no natural classification of the varieties of the human species has as yet been arrived at. Certain extreme types can, of course, be readily distinguished. No one can fail to recognize the enormous structural differences between an Andamanese and a Chinaman, an Englishman, and a Negro, or a Patagonian and a Hottentot.

[* *Journal Asiatic Society, Bengal*, Vol. LXV., Part III., 1901, p. 59 *et seq.* *Journal Anthropological Institute*, Vol. XXXII., 1902, p. 96 *et seq.*]

† J. A. S. B., Vol. LXIX., Part III., 1900.

But owing to the tendency of individuals to vary, and to the intermixture of races, which has gone on more or less at all times, and is continually increasing with modern improvements in communications, the apparently impassable gulf between the extreme types is bridged over by a number of intermediate or transitional forms, which shade into each other by almost imperceptible degrees. It is therefore practically impossible to divide mankind into a number of definite groups in one or other of which every individual will find a place. Even as regards the primary groups there has been great diversity of opinion, and the number suggested by different writers ranges from two to more than sixty. In the main, however, as Flower has pointed out, there has always been a tendency to revert to the four primitive types sketched out by Linnæus—the European, Asiatic, African, and American, reduced by Cuvier to three by the omission of the American type. Flower himself is of opinion "that the primitive man, whatever he may have been, has, in the course of ages, divaricated into three extreme types, represented by the Caucasian of Europe, the Mongolian of Asia, and the Ethiopian of Africa," and "that all existing individuals of the species can be ranged around these types, or somewhere or other between them." He therefore adopts as the basis of his classification the following three types :—

I. The Ethiopian, Negroid, or black type with dark or nearly black complexion; frizzly black hair, a head almost invariably long (dolicho-cephalic); a very broad and flat nose; moderate or scanty development of beard; thick, everted lips; large teeth; and a long forearm.

The Negroid type is again sub-divided into four groups, with only one of which we are concerned here. This is the Negrito, represented within the Indian Empire by the Andamanese enumerated for the first time in the Census of 1901 and possibly by the Semangs of the jungles of Malacca, some of whom may have wandered up into the Mergui district of Burma.* In respect of colour and hair, the Andamanese closely resemble the Negro, but they have broad heads, their facial characters are different, and they form a very distinct group which has not been affected by intermixture with other races.

II. The Mongolian, Xanthous, or yellow type, with yellow

[* For the physical characteristics of the Semang, see W. W. Skeat, C. O. Blagden, *The Pagan Races of the Malay Peninsula*, 1906, Vol. I., p. 19 *et seq.*]

or brownish complexion. These races have coarse straight hair without any tendency to curl; they are usually beardless or nearly so; they are mostly broad-headed; the face is broad and flat with projecting cheek-bones; the nose small, and conspicuously depressed at the root; the eyes sunken and the eyelids peculiarly formed so as to give the eye itself the appearance of slanting downwards; the teeth of moderate size.

The Northern or Mongolo-Altaic group of Mongolians includes the nomadic races of Central Asia whose influence on the population of India will be discussed later on. The Tibetans and Burmese are members of the Southern Mongolian group.

III. The Caucasian, or white type, has usually a fair skin; hair fair or dark, soft, straight or wavy; beard fully developed; the head-form is long or medium; the face narrow; the nose narrow and prominent; the teeth small and the forearm short.

Following Huxley, Flower divides the Caucasians into two groups:—

(*a*) The Xanthochroi or blonde type, with fair hair, light eyes and fair complexion. They "chiefly inhabit Northern Europe, but, much mixed with the next type, they extend as far as Northern Africa and Afghanistan."

(*b*) Melanochroi, "with black hair and eyes, and skin of almost all shades from white to black." Flower includes in this group not only the great majority of the inhabitants of Southern Europe, Northern Africa, and South-West Asia, consisting mainly of the Aryan, Semitic, and Hamitic families, but also the Dravidians of India, and the Veddahs of Ceylon.

Here we are confronted at once with the drawbacks which attend all attempts at systematic arrangement. It is difficult not to distrust a classification which brings together in the same category people of such widely different appearance, history, and traditions as the modern Greeks and Italians, and the black, broad-nosed Dravidians of Central and Southern India. Peschel's arrangement seems to be in closer accordance with the facts established by recent observations. He divides the Caucasian type into (*a*) Indo-Germans, (*b*) Semites, (*c*) Hamites or Berbers, and includes the "Hindus" (non-

Dravidian Indians) in the first of these groups. The Dravidians are classed with Sinhalese and Veddahs as people of uncertain origin. Huxley treats them as Australoid.

Their application to India.

In respect of classification the general position in India is closely parallel to that described above. It is easy enough to distinguish certain well-marked types. Our difficulties begin when we attempt to carry the process of classification further and to differentiate the minor types or subtypes which have been formed by varying degrees of intermixture between the main types. The extremes of the series are sharply defined, but the intermediate types melt into each other, and it is hard to say where the dividing line should be drawn. Here measurements are of great assistance, especially if they are arranged in a series so as to bring out the relative preponderance of certain characters in a large number of the members of particular groups. This is well illustrated by the diagrams in Appendix III., and will be more fully dwelt upon below. We are further assisted by the remarkable correspondence that may be observed at the present day in all parts of India, except the Punjab, between variations of physical type and differences of grouping and social position. This, of course, is due to the operation of the caste system, which in its most highly developed form, the only form which admits of precise definition, is, I believe, entirely confined to India. Nowhere else in the world do we find the population of a large continent broken up into an infinite number of mutually exclusive aggregates, the members of which are forbidden by an inexorable social law to marry outside of the group to which they themselves belong. Whatever may have been the origin and the earlier developments of caste, this absolute prohibition of mixed marriages stands forth now as its essential and most prominent characteristic, and the feeling against such unions is so deeply engrained in the people that even the theistic and reforming sect of the Brahmo Samāj has found a difficulty in freeing itself from the ancient prejudices, while the Lingāyats of Western and Southern India have transformed themselves from a sect into a caste within recent times. In a society thus organized, a society putting an extravagant value on pride of blood and the idea of ceremonial purity, differences of physical type, however produced in the first instance, may be expected to manifest a high degree of persistence, while methods which seek to

Conditions favourable to anthropometry.

trace and express such differences find a peculiarly favourable field for their operations. In this respect India presents a remarkable contrast to most other parts of the world, where anthropometry has to confess itself hindered, if not baffled, by the constant intermixture of types obscuring and confusing the data ascertained by measurements. Thus in Europe, as Topinard observes, there is nothing to prevent the union "of the blonde Kymri with the dark-haired dweller on the Mediterranean, of the broad-headed Celt with the long-headed Scandinavian, of the tiny Laplander with the tall Swede." In fact, all the recognized nations of Europe are the result of a process of unrestricted crossing which has fused a number of distinct tribal types into a more or less definable national type. In India the process of fusion has long ago been arrested, and the degree of progress which it had made up to the point at which it ceased to operate is expressed in the physical characteristics of the groups which have been formed. There is consequently no national type and no nation or even nationality in the ordinary sense of these words.

Shape of the head.

The measurements themselves require a few words of explanation, which will be given in as popular language as the nature of the subject permits. The form of the head is ascertained by measuring in a horizontal plane the greatest length from a definite point on the forehead (the glabella) to the back of the head, and the greatest breadth a little above the ears. The proportion of the breadth to the length is then expressed as a percentage, called the cephalic index, the length being taken as 100. Heads with a breadth of 80 per cent. and over are classed as broad or brachy-cephalic; those with an index under 80, but not under 75, are called medium heads (meso- or mesati-cephalic); long or dolicho-cephalic heads are those in which the ratio of breadth to length is below 75 per cent.

Its value as a test of race.

It is not contended that these groupings correspond to the primary divisions of mankind. Long, broad and medium heads are met with in varying degrees of preponderance among the white, black, and yellow races. But within these primary divisions the proportions of the head serve to mark off important groups. Topinard shows how the form expressed by the index separates the long-headed Scandinavian people from the broad-headed Celts and Slavs; while the Esquimaux are distinguished on similar grounds from the Asiatic Mongols, and the Australians from the Negritos. All authorities agree in regarding the form of the head as an extremely constant and persistent character, which resists the influence of climate and physical surroundings, and (having nothing to do with the personal appearance of the individual) is not liable to be modified by the action of artificial selection. Men choose their wives mainly for their faces and figures, and a long-headed woman offers no greater attractions of external form and colouring than her short-headed sister. The intermixture of races with different head-forms will, of course, affect the index, but even here there is a tendency to revert to the original type when the influence of crossing is withdrawn. On the whole, therefore, the form of the head, especially when combined with other characters, is a good test of racial affinity. It may be added that neither the shape nor the size of the head seems to bear any direct relation to intellectual capacity. People with long heads cannot be said to be cleverer or more advanced in culture than people with short heads.

Shape of the head in India.

In relation to the rest of Asia, India may be described as an area of mainly long-headed people separated by the Himalaya and its offshoots from the Mongolian country, where the broad-headed types are more numerous and more pronounced than anywhere else in the world. At either end of the mountain barrier, broad heads are strongly represented in Assam and Burma on the east, and in Baluchistan on the west, and the same character occurs in varying degrees in the Lower Himalayas and in a belt of country on the west of India extending from Gujarāt through the Deccan to Coorg, the limits of which cannot at present be defined precisely. In the Punjab, Rajputana, and the United Provinces, long heads predominate, but the type gradually changes as we travel eastwards. In Bihar medium heads prevail on the whole, while in certain of the Bengal groups a distinct tendency towards brachy-cephaly may be observed, which shows itself in the Muhammadans and Chandāls of Eastern Bengal, is more distinctly marked in the Kāyasths, and reaches its maximum development among the Bengal Brāhmans. In Peninsular India south of the Vindhya ranges, the prevalent type seems to be mainly long-headed or medium-headed, short heads appearing only in the western zone of country referred to above. But the population of the coast has been much affected by foreign influence, Malayan or Indo-Chinese on the east, Arab,

Persian, African, European and Jewish on the west, and the mixed types thus produced cannot be brought under any general formula.

Shape of the nose: the nasal index.

The proportions of the nose are determined on the same principle as those of the skull. The length and breadth are measured from certain specified points, and the latter dimension is expressed as a percentage of the former. The nasal index, therefore, is simply the relation of the breadth of the nose to its length. If a man's nose is as broad as it is long—no infrequent case among the Dravidians—his index is 100. The results thus obtained are grouped in three classes—narrow or fine noses (leptorrhine) in which the width is less than 70 per cent. of the length; broad noses (platyrrhine) in which the proportion rises to 85 per cent. and over, and medium noses (mesorrhine) with an index of from 70 to 85. The index, as Topinard points out, expresses with great accuracy the extent to which the nostrils have been expanded and flattened out or contracted and refined, the height in the two cases varying inversely. It thus represents very distinctly the personal impressions which a particular type conveys to the observer. The broad nose of the Negro or of the typical Dravidian is his most striking feature, and the index records its proportions with unimpeachable accuracy. Where races with different nasal proportions have intermixed, the index marks the degree of crossing that has taken place; it records a large range of variations; and it enables us to group types in a serial order corresponding to that suggested by other characters. For these reasons the nasal index is accepted by all anthropologists as one of the best tests of racial affinity.

Correspondence with social groupings.

Speaking generally, it may be said that the broad type of nose is most common in Madras, the Central Provinces and Chutia Nāgpur; that fine noses in the strict sense of the term are confined to the Punjab and Baluchistan, and that the population of the rest of India tends to fall within the medium class. But the range of the index is very great. It varies in individual cases from 122 to 53, and the mean indices of different groups differ considerably in the same part of the country. The average nasal proportions of the Māl Pahāria tribe of Bengal are expressed by the figure 94·5, while the pastoral Gūjars of the Punjab have an index of 66·9, the Sikhs of 68·8 and the Bengal Brāhmans and Kāyasths of 70·4. In other words, the typical Dravidian, as represented by the Māl Pahāria, has a nose as broad in proportion to its length as the Negro, while this feature in the Indo-Aryan group can fairly bear comparison with the noses of sixty-eight Parisians, measured by Topinard, which gave an average of 69·4. Even more striking is the curiously close correspondence between the gradations of racial type indicated by the nasal index and certain of the social data ascertained by independent enquiry. If we take a series of castes in Bengal, Bihar, the United Provinces of Agra and Oudh, or Madras, and arrange them in the order of the average nasal index, so that the caste with the finest nose shall be at the top, and that with the coarsest at the bottom of the list, it will be found that this order substantially corresponds with the accepted order of social precedence. Thus in Bihar or the United Provinces the casteless tribes, Kols, Korwas, Mundās and the like, who have not yet entered the Brahmanical system, occupy the lowest place in both series. Then come the vermin-eating Musahars and the leather-dressing Chamārs. The fisher castes, Bauri, Bind, and Kewat, are a trifle higher in the scale; the pastoral Goālā, the cultivating Kurmi, and a group of cognate castes from whose hands a Brāhman may take water, follow in due order, and from them we pass to the trading Khatris, the landholding Bābhans and the upper crust of Hindu society. Thus, for those parts of India where there is an appreciable strain of Dravidian blood it is scarcely a paradox to lay down, as a law of the caste organization, that the social status of the members of a particular group varies in inverse ratio to the mean relative width of their noses. Nor is this the only point in which the two sets of observations—the social and the physical—bear out and illustrate each other. The character of the curious matrimonial groupings for which the late Mr. J. F. McLennan devised the useful term exogamous, also varies in a definite relation to the gradations of physical type. Within a certain range of nasal proportions, these sub-divisions are based almost exclusively on the totem. Along with a somewhat finer form of nose, groups called after villages and larger territorial areas, or bearing the name of certain tribal or communal officials, begin to appear, and above these again we reach the eponymous saints and heroes who in India, as in Greece and Rome, are associated with a certain stage of Aryan progress.

The comparative flatness of the Mongolian face is a peculiarity which cannot fail to strike the most casual observer. On closer examination this characteristic will be seen to be intimately connected with the formation of the cheek-bones, the margins of the bony sockets of the eyes, and the root of the nose. No precise measurements can be made of the cheek-bones on the living subject, for it is impossible to fix any definite points from which the dimensions can be taken. Some years ago, however, Mr. Oldfield Thomas devised a method of measuring the relative projection of the root of the nose above the level of the eye-sockets, which expresses very accurately the degree of flatness of face met with in different types. It was used by him for skulls, but it has the great advantage of being equally applicable to living persons, and at Sir William Flower's suggestion it has been extensively used in India, especially among hill tribes and wherever there was reason to suspect an intermixture of Mongolian blood. The principle on which it proceeds can be described without resorting to technical language. Any one who looks at a Gurkha in profile will readily observe that the root of the nose rises much less above the level of the eye-sockets than is the case with Europeans or natives of Upper India. The object is to determine the comparative elevation of the lowest point on the root of the nose above the plane of the eye-sockets. This is done by marking a point on the front surface of the outer edge of each orbit and a third point on the centre of the root of the nose where it is lowest. The distance between the two orbital dots is then measured in a direct line and also the distance from each of these to the dot on the bridge of the nose. The former dimension represents the base of a triangle, and the latter its two sides. The index is formed by calculating the percentage of the latter dimension on the former. If, as is sometimes the case, the bridge of the nose is let down so low that it does not project at all beyond the level of the orbits, the two dimensions will obviously be of equal length and the index will be 100. If, on the other hand, the elevation of the bridge of the nose is marked, the index may be as high as 127 or 130. In the paper already referred to, which dealt only with skulls, Mr. Thomas proposed the division of the index into three classes :—

Shape of face: orbitonasal index.

Platyopic	below 107·5.
Mesopic	107·5 to 110·0.
Pro-opic	above 110·0

The experience gained in India, which extends to a large

number of castes and tribes in all parts of the country, has led me to adopt the following grouping for the living subject:—

Platyopic	below 110.
Mesopic	110 to 112·9.
Pro-opic	113 and over.

This brings the Mongoloid people of Assam and the Eastern Himalayas within the platyopic group, and effectually differentiates them from the broad-headed races of Baluchistan, Bombay and Coorg. It also separates the Indo-Aryans from the Aryo-Dravidians.

Stature in Europe and India.

Topinard's classification of stature, which is generally accepted, comprises four groups:—

Tall statures,	170 c.m.	(5′ 7″) and over
Above the average,	165 c.m.	(5′ 5″) and under 170 c.m. (5′ 7″)
Below the average,	160 c.m.	(5′ 3″) and under 165 c m. (5′ 5″)
Small statures,	under 160 c.m. (5′ 3″)	

Much has been written on the subject of the causes which affect the stature. The general conclusion seems to be that in Europe the question is a very complicated one, and that the influence of race is to a great extent obscured by other factors, such as climate, soil, elevation, food supply, habits of life, occupation, and natural or artificial selection. Most of these causes also come into play in India, but not necessarily to the same extent as in Europe. The influence of city life, which in civilized countries as a rule tends to reduce the stature and to produce physical degeneracy, is comparatively small in India, where from fifty to eighty-four per cent. of the population are engaged in agriculture and live an outdoor life. Nor are the conditions of factory industries in India so trying or so likely to affect growth as in Europe. The operatives do not attend so regularly nor do they work so hard, and many of them live in the country for a great part of the year, coming into the mills only when there is nothing to be done in the fields. Some of the indigenous hand-loom weavers, however, show the lowest mean stature yet recorded—a fact which is probably due to the unwholesome surroundings in which they live. In India, as in Europe, the dwellers in the hills are generally shorter than the people of the plains, and within the hill region it may in either case be observed that the stature is often greater at high than at moderate altitudes—a fact which has been ascribed to the influence of a rigorous climate in killing off all but vigorous individuals. In India the prevalence of malaria in the lower levels and the less healthy conditions of life would probably tend to bring about the same result. On the whole, however, the distribution of stature in India seems to suggest that race differences play a larger part here than they do in Europe. The tallest statures are massed in Baluchistan, the Punjab, and Rajputana; and a progressive decline may be traced down the valley of the Ganges until the lowest limits are reached among the Mongoloid people of the hills bordering on Assam. In the south of India the stature is generally lower than in the plains of the north. The minimum is found among the Negritos of the Andaman Islands, whose mean stature is given by Deniker as 1485 mm. or 4 feet 10½ inches.

The seven physical types.

These physical data enable us to divide the people of the Indian Empire into seven main physical types, the distribution of which is shown in the coloured map at the end of this volume. If we include the Andamanese, the number of types is eight, but for our present purpose this tiny group of Negritos may be disregarded. Curious and interesting as they are from the point of view of general anthropology, the Andamanese have had no share in the making of the Indian people. They survive—a primitive outlier—on the extreme confines of the Empire to which they belong merely by virtue of the accident that their habitat has been selected as a convenient location for a penal settlement. I have, however, thought it worth while to take this opportunity of publishing the measurements of 200 Andamanese, 100 males and 100 females, which were taken some years ago by Major Molesworth, I.M.S., then Surgeon at Port Blair, in the hope that they may be of service to any one who has the leisure to undertake a monograph on the subject. The conclusions suggested by Major Molesworth's measurements of living subjects seem to coincide with those arrived at by the late Sir William Flower from an examination of a series of forty-eight skulls, and confirmed by Sir William Turner in the monograph referred to above. These observers agree in describing the Andamanese as short-headed, and broad-nosed, with a low cranial capacity. Their heads differ in essential particulars from those of the Dravidians, and Sir William Turner considers that no direct evidence of either a past or a present Negrito population in India has yet been obtained.

Counting from the western frontier of India, we may determine the following distinctive types :—

I. The *Turko-Iranian* type, represented by the Baloch, Brāhūi, and Afghāns of the Baluchistan Agency and the North-West Frontier Province; probably formed by a fusion of Turki and Persian elements in which the former predominate. Stature above mean; complexion fair; eyes mostly dark, but occasionally grey; hair on face plentiful; head broad; nose moderately narrow, prominent, and very long.

II. The *Indo-Aryan* type, occupying the Punjab, Rajputana, and Kashmir, and having as its characteristic members the Rajputs, Khatris, and Jāts. This type approaches most closely to that ascribed to the traditional Aryan colonists of India. The stature is mostly tall; complexion fair; eyes dark; hair on face plentiful; head long; nose narrow and prominent, but not specially long.

III. The *Scytho-Dravidian* type of Western India, comprising the Marātha Brāhmans, the Kunbis, and the Coorgs; probably formed by a mixture of Scythian and Dravidian elements, the former predominating in the higher groups, the latter in the lower. The head is broad; complexion fair; hair on face rather scanty; stature medium; nose moderately fine and not conspicuously long.

IV. The *Aryo-Dravidian* type found in the United Provinces of Agra and Oudh, in parts of Rajputana, in Bihar and Ceylon, and represented in its upper strata by the Hindustāni Brāhman and in its lower by the Chamār. Probably the result of the intermixture, in varying proportions, of the Indo-Aryan and Dravidian types, the former element predominating in the lower groups and the latter in the higher. The head-form is long with a tendency to medium; the complexion varies from lightish brown to black; the nose ranges from medium to broad, being always broader than among the Indo-Aryans; the stature is lower than in the latter group, and is usually below the average by the scale given above.

V. The *Mongolo-Dravidian* type of Lower Bengal and Orissa, comprising the Bengal Brāhmans and Kāyasths the Muhammadans of Eastern Bengal, and other groups peculiar to this part of India. Probably a blend of Dravidian and Mongoloid elements with a strain of Indo-Aryan blood in the higher groups. The head is broad; complexion dark; hair on face usually plentiful; stature medium; nose medium with a tendency to broad.

VI. The *Mongoloid* type of the Himalayas, Nepal, Assam,

and Burma, represented by the Kanets of Lahoul and Kulu, the Lepchās of Darjeeling, the Limbus, Murmis and Gurungs of Nepal, the Bodo of Assam, and the Burmese. The head is broad; complexion dark with a yellowish tinge; hair on face scanty; stature small or below average; nose fine to broad; face characteristically flat; eyelids often oblique.

VII. The *Dravidian* type extending from Ceylon to the valley of the Ganges and pervading the whole of Madras, Hyderabad, the Central Provinces, most of Central India, and Chutia Nāgpur. Its most characteristic representatives are the Paniyans of the South Indian hills and the Santāls of Chutia Nāgpur. Probably the original type of the population of India, now modified to a varying extent by the admixture of Aryan, Scythian, and Mongoloid elements. In typical specimens the stature is short or below mean; the complexion very dark, approaching black; hair plentiful with an occasional tendency to curl; eyes dark; head long; nose very broad, sometimes depressed at the root, but not so as to make the face appear flat.

Before proceeding to describe the types in further detail, a few words of preliminary explanation are essential. In the first place, it must be clearly understood that the areas occupied by the various types do not admit of being defined as sharply as they are shown on the map. They melt into each other insensibly, and although at the close of a day's journey from one ethnic tract to another, an observer whose attention had been directed to the subject would realise clearly enough that the physical characteristics of the people had undergone an appreciable change, he would certainly be unable to say at what particular stage in his progress the transformation had taken place. Allowance, therefore, must be made for the necessary conditions of map-making, and it must not be supposed that a given type comes to an end as abruptly as the patch of colour which indicates the area of its maximum prevalence. Secondly, let no one imagine that any type is alleged to be in exclusive possession of the locality to which it is assigned. When, for example, Madras is described as a Dravidian and Bengal as a Mongolo-Dravidian tract, that does not mean that all the people of Madras and Bengal must of necessity belong to the predominant type. From time immemorial in India a stream of movement has been setting from west to east and from north to south—a tendency impelling the higher types towards the territories occupied by the lower. In the

Limitations of the scheme.

course of this movement representatives of the Indo-Aryan type have spread themselves all over India as conquerors, traders, landowners, or priests, preserving the original characteristics in varying degrees, and receiving a measure of social recognition dependent in the main on the supposed purity of their descent from the original immigrants.* Family and caste traditions record countless instances of such incursions, and in many cases the tradition is confirmed by the concurrent testimony of historical documents and physical characteristics. Even in the provinces farthest removed from the Indo-Aryan settlements in North-Western India, members of the upper castes are still readily distinguishable by their features and complexion from the mass of the population, and their claims to represent a different race are thrown into relief by the definition now for the first time attempted of the types which predominate in different parts of India. Until the existence of a lower type has been established, no special distinction is involved in belonging to a higher one. Thirdly, it may be said that the names assigned to the types beg the highly speculative question of the elements which have contributed to their formation. The criticism is unanswerable. One can but admit its truth, and plead by way of justification that we must have some distinctive names for our types, that names based solely on physical characters are no better than bundles of formulæ, and that if hypotheses of origin are worth constructing at all, one should not shrink from expressing them in their most telling form.

Turko-Iranian type.

The *Turko-Iranian* type is in practically exclusive possession of Baluchistān and the North-West Frontier Province. Its leading characteristics are the following:—

(i) The head is broad, the mean indices ranging from 80 in the Baloch of the Western Punjab to 85 in the Hazāra of Afghanistan. I put aside as doubtful cases the Hunzas, Nagars, and Kāfirs and the Pathāns of the North-Western Punjab. For the first three the data are scanty, and it is possible that further enquiry might lead to their inclusion in the Indo-Aryan type. In the case of the last the individual indices vary from 69 to 87, and although broad heads

* An effective parallel might be drawn between the predatory invasions of the Rajputs and the settlements effected by the Normans in Sicily, Southern Italy and Greece. Both sets of movements arose from similar impulses, both have left unmistakable traces behind, and both ended in the comparative absorption of the conquering race.

preponderate on the whole, there is a sufficient proportion of long heads to warrant the suspicion of some mixture of blood.

(ii) The proportions of the nose (nasal index) are fine or medium, the average indices running from 67·8 in the Tarin to 80·5 in the Hazāra. Some of the individual indices are high and one Hazāra attains the remarkable figure of 111. These abnormalities may probably be accounted for by the importation of Abyssinian slaves. The proportions of the nose, however, are less distinctive of the type than its great absolute length, which varies in individual cases from 56 mm. among the Hazāras to 65 among the Brāhūi. The one feature indeed that strikes one in these people is the portentous length of their noses, and it is probably this peculiarity that has given rise to the tradition of the Jewish origin of the Afghāns. Some of the Scythian coins exhibit it in a marked degree. As M. Ujfalvy * has pointed out, the lineaments of Kadphises II survive in the Dards of to-day, and the remark holds good of most of the people whom I have ventured to include in the Turko-Iranian type.

(iii) The mean orbito-nasal index, which measures the relative flatness of the face, ranges with the Turko-Iranians from 111 in the Hazāra to 118 in the Baloch, Brāhūi, and Dehwār. The highest individual index (131) occurs among the Pathāns of the North-Western Punjab and the lowest (118) among the Kāfirs. The type as a whole is conspicuously proopic, and there are no signs of that depression of the root of the nose and corresponding flatness of the cheek bones to which the appearance popularly described as Chinese or Mongolian is due. In respect of this character the Hazāras seem to be an exception. In them the individual indices form a continuous curve of striking regularity from 103 to 120, and it is a question whether the tribe ought not to be included in the Mongoloid type. I prefer, however, to show them as Turko-Iranian, for it seems possible that they partake of the elements of both types and represent the points of contact between the two.

(iv) The average stature varies from 162 in the Baloch of Makrān to 172 to the Achakzai Pathān of Northern Baluchistān. The figure for the Hazāra is 168, which makes for their inclusion in the Turko-Iranian rather than in the Mongoloid group; but the subjects measured belonged to one of the

* L'Anthropologie, IX., 407. *Mémoire sur les Huns blancs.*

regiments at Quetta and were probably rather above the average stature of the tribe.

Indo-Aryan type.

The *Indo-Aryan* type predominates in Rajputana, the Punjab, and the Kashmir valley, though in parts of these areas it is associated to a varying extent with other elements. It is readily distinguishable from the Turko-Iranian. Its most marked characteristics may be summarised as follows:—

(i) The head-form is invariably long, the average index ranging from 72·4 in the Rajput to 74·4 in the Awān. The highest individual index (86) is found among the Khatris and the lowest (64) among the Rajputs. The seriations bring out very clearly the enormous preponderance of the long-headed type and present the sharpest contrast with those given for the Turko-Iranians.

(ii) In respect of the proportions of the nose there is very little difference between the two types. The Indo-Aryan index ranges from 66·9 in the Gūjar to 75·2 in the Chuhrā, and there are fewer high individual indices; but between the seriations there is not much to choose. On the other hand the Indo-Aryans, notwithstanding their greater stature, have noticeably shorter noses than the Turko-Iranians.

(iii) Concerning the orbito-nasal index there is little to be said. All the members of the Indo-Aryan type are placed by their average indices within the pro-opic group; their faces are free from any suggestion of flatness, and the figures expressing this character run in a very regular series. The highest index (117·9) occurs among the Rajputs and the lowest (113·1) amongst the Khatris.

(iv) The Indo-Aryans have the highest stature recorded in India, ranging from 174·8 in the Rajput to 165·8 in the Arora. Individual measurements of Rajputs rise to 192·4 and of Jāts (Sikhs) to 190·5. Stature alone, therefore, were other indications wanting, would serve to differentiate the Indo-Aryan from the Aryo-Dravidian type of the United Provinces and Bihar.

The most important points to observe in the Indo-Aryan series of measurements are the great uniformity of type and the very slight differences between the higher and the lower groups. Socially, no gulf can be wider than that which divides the Rajputs of Udaipur and Mārwār from the scavenging Chuhrā of the Punjab. Physically, the one is cast in much the same mould as the other; and the difference in mean height which the seriations disclose is no greater than might easily be accounted for by the fact that in respect of food, occupation, and habits of life, the Rajput has for many generations enjoyed advantages, telling directly on the development of stature, which circumstances have denied to the Chuhrā. Stature we know to be peculiarly sensitive to external influences of this kind. Other and more subtle influences re-act upon environment and tend to modify the type. Sikhism has transformed the despised Chuhrā into the soldierly Mazhabi. Who shall say that military service might not have the same effect on groups belonging to the lower social strata of the Punjab, whose physical endowment is hardly inferior to that observed at the top of the scale?

Scytho-Dravidian type.

The *Scytho-Dravidian* type occurs in a belt of country on the west of India extending from Gujarat to Coorg. It is represented at one extreme of this belt by the Nāgar Brāhmans of Gujarat and at the other by the remarkable people who have given their name to the little province of Coorg. Excluding the Kātkaris, who really belong to the Dravidian type, the leading characteristics of the Scytho-Dravidians are the following:—

(i) The head-form ranges from 76·9 in the Deshasth Brāhmans to 79·7 in the Nāgar Brāhmans and 79·9 in the Prabhus and the Coorgs, while the maximum individual indices rise as high as 92 with the Marātha Kunbis and the Shenvi Brāhmans. In the case of the three type specimens—the Nāgar Brāhmans, the Prabhus, and the Coorgs—the mean index is virtually 80, and the predominance of the broad-headed type is unmistakable. The seriations show that the gradation of the type is fairly regular, and a comparison with the diagrams of the Indo-Aryans brings out marked differences of head-form, where the features and complexion taken by themselves would appear to point to an identical origin. Both indices and maxima are noticeably lower than among the Turko-Iranians.

(ii) In the proportions of the nose there is nothing much to remark. The mean indices vary from 72·0 in the Coorg to 81·9 in the Mahār, the Nāgar Brāhman giving 73·1 and the Prabhu 75·8. The length of the nose, whether we look to the averages or the maxima, is distinctly less than among the Turko-Iranians, the type most closely allied to the Scytho-Dravidian.

(iii) The mean orbito-nasal index varies from 113·1 in the Son-Koli to the very high figure of 120 in the Coorg. It deserves notice, however, that the minimum indices run very low, and that the range between the highest maximum (132) and the lowest minimum (103) is considerable and points to some mixture of blood.

(iv) The mean stature varies from 160 in the case of the Kunbis in 168·7 in the Coorgs, and an examination of the figures will show that it is, on the whole, lower than among the Turko-Iranians.

The type is clearly distinguished from the Turko-Iranian by a lower stature, a greater length of head, a higher nasal index, a shorter nose and a lower orbito-nasal index. All of these characters, except perhaps the last, may be due to a varying degree of intermixture with the Dravidians. In the higher types the amount of crossing seems to have been slight; in the lower the Dravidian elements are more pronounced, while in the Kātkari the long head and wide nose are conspicuous.

Aryo-Dravidian type.

The *Aryo-Dravidian* or *Hindustāni* type extends from the eastern frontier of the Punjab to the southern extremity of Bihar, from which point onwards it melts into the Mongolo-Dravidian type of Bengal Proper. It occupies the valleys of the Ganges and Jumna, and runs up into the lower levels of the Himalayas on the north and the slopes of the Central Indian plateau on the south. Its higher representatives approach the Indo-Aryan type, while the lower members of the group are in many respects not very far removed from the Dravidians. The type is essentially a mixed one, yet its characteristics are readily definable, and no one would take even an upper class Hindustāni for a pure Indo-Aryan, or a Chamār for a genuine Dravidian. Turning now to details, we find the following results :—

(i) The head-form is long, with a tendency towards medium. The average index varies from 72·1 in the Kāchhi and Koiri of Hindustan to 76·8 in the Dosādh of Bihar and 76·7 in the Bābhan. The highest individual index (90) occurs among the Bābhans of Bihar, and the lowest (62) among the Bhars of Hindustan. But the head-form throws little light upon the origin and affinities of the type, and would of itself barely serve to distinguish the Aryo-Dravidian from the Indo-Aryan. Nor, indeed, would one expect it to do so, for the pure Dravidians are themselves a long-headed race, and the Hindustāni people might well have derived this character from the Dravidian element in their parentage.

(ii) The distinctive feature of the type, the character which gives the real clue to its origin, and stamps the Aryo-Dravidian as racially different from the Indo-Aryan, is to be found in the proportions of the nose. The average index runs in an unbroken series from 73·0 in the Bhuinhār or Bābhan of Hindustan and 73·2 in the Brāhman of Bihar to 86 in the Hindustāni Chamār and 88·7 in the Musahar of Bihar. The order thus established corresponds substantially with the scale of social precedence independently ascertained. At the top of the list are the Bhuinhārs, who rank high among the territorial aristocracy of Hindustan and Bihar; then come the Brāhmans, followed at a slight but yet appreciable interval by the clerkly Kāyasths with an index of 74·8; while down at the bottom the lower strata of Hindu society are represented by the Chamār, who tans hides and is credibly charged with poisoning cattle, and the foul-feeding Musahar who eats pigs, snakes, and jackals, and whose name is popularly derived from his penchant for field-rats. The seriations tell the same tale as the averages, and mark the essential distinction between the Aryo-Dravidian and Indo-Aryan types. The Hindustāni Brāhmans, with a slightly lower mean index than the Chuhrās of the Punjab, have a far larger proportion of the broad noses, which point to an admixture of Dravidian blood.

(iii) The statistics of height lead to a similar conclusion. The mean stature of the Aryo-Dravidians ranges from 166 centimetres in the Brāhmans and Bhuinhārs to 159 in the Musahar, the corresponding figures in the Indo-Aryan being 174·8 and 165·8. The one begins where the other leaves off.

Mongolo-Dravidian type.

The *Mongolo-Dravidian* or *Bengali* type occupies the delta of the Ganges and its tributaries from the confines of Bihar to the Bay of Bengal. It is one of the most distinctive types in India, and its members may be recognized at a glance throughout the wide area where their remarkable aptitude for clerical pursuits and their keen sense of family obligations have procured them employment. Within its own habitat the type extends to the Himalayas on the north and Assam on the east, and probably includes the bulk of the population of Orissa. The western limit coincides approximately with the hilly country of Chutia Nāgpur and Western Bengal.

(i) The broad head of the Bengali, of which the mean index varies from 79·0 in the Brāhman to 83·0 in the Rājbansi Magh, effectually differentiates the type from the Indo-Aryans or

Aryo-Dravidians. The seriation of the cephalic index for the Brāhmans of East Bengal is very regular in its gradations, and presents a striking contrast with the corresponding diagrams for the Hindustāni Brāhmans and the Rajput. Here, as elsewhere, the inferences as to racial affinity suggested by the measurements are in entire accord with the evidence afforded by features and general appearance. For example, it is a matter of common knowledge that the Rājbansi Magh of Chittagong, who is in great demand as a cook in European households in India and usually prospers exceedingly, resembles the upper class Bengali of Eastern Bengal so closely that it takes an acute observer to tell the difference between the two.

(ii) The mean proportions of the nose range from 70·3 in the Brāhmans and Kāyasths to 84·7 in the Mals of Western Bengal and 80 in the Kochh. The number of high individual indices brings out the contrast with the Indo-Aryans, and points to the infusion of Dravidian blood. In the Brāhman seriation the finer forms predominate, and it is open to any one to argue that, notwithstanding the uncompromising breadth of the head, the nose-form may, in their case, be due to the remote strain of Indo-Aryan ancestry to which their traditions bear witness.

(iii) The stature varies from 167 in the Brāhmans of Western Bengal to 159 in the Kochh of the Sub-Himalayan region.

The seriations of the Kochh deserve special notice for the indications which they give of the two elements that have combined to form the Mongolo-Dravidian type. In writing about them fifteen years ago I ventured, on the evidence then available, to describe them as a people of Dravidian stock who, being driven by pressure from the west into the swamps and forests of Northern and North-Eastern Bengal, were there brought into contact with the Mongoloid races of the Lower Himalayas and the Assam border, with the result that their type was affected in a varying degree by intermixture with these races. On the whole, however, I thought that Dravidian characteristics predominated among them over Mongolian. My conclusions, which coincided in the main with those of Colonel Dalton and other observers, have been questioned by Lieutenant-Colonel Waddell, C.B., C.I.E., in a paper on the *Tribes of the Brahmaputra Valley.** Colonel Waddell, who has observed

* J. A. S. B., Vol. LXIX., Part III., 190. [Major A. Playfair, *The Garos*, 1909, pp. 18 *et seq.*]

and measured the Kochh both in North-Eastern Bengal and in Assam, denies their Dravidian origin, and describes them as "distinctly Mongoloid though somewhat heterogeneous." For purposes of comparison I have included both his measurements and my own in the same diagram. As regards the head-form and the stature, the two sets of observations are practically identical. In the case of the nose, Colonel Waddell's data show a far higher proportion of broad noses than mine, and clearly point to a strong Dravidian element. On the other hand, the orbito-nasal index exhibits, though in a less degree, some distinctive Mongoloid characteristics. One can ask for no better illustration of the efficacy of the method of anthropometry in its application to a mixed or transitional type than the fact that, while two independent observers have formed different opinions as to the relative preponderance of its component elements, the data obtained by them from two distinct series of individuals correspond to the remarkable extent indicated by the Kochh diagram. There is, of course, no real conflict of opinion between Colonel Waddell and myself. The whole question turns upon the point of view of the observer. Take the Kochh in Dinajpur and Rangpur, and they strike you as in the main Dravidian; travel further east, and include in your survey the cognate Kachāri of Assam, and there is no mistaking the fact that Mongoloid characteristics predominate. The same may be said of the Bengali type as a whole. In Western Bengal the Dravidian element is prominent; in Dacca and Mymensingh the type has undergone a change, which scientific methods enable us to assign to the effect of intercourse with a Mongolian race.

Mongoloid type.

On its northern and eastern frontier India marches with the great Mongolian region of the earth. The effect of this contact with an almost exclusively broad-headed population is indicated in yellow on the map, and a glance will show how the area within which this particular foreign influence has impressed itself upon India widens gradually from west to east. The Punjab and Hindustan are left virtually untouched; the Bengalis exhibit a type sensibly modified in the direction of Mongolian characters; the Assamese are unmistakably Mongoloid, and in Burma the only non-Mongolian elements are the result of recent immigration from India. This condition of things is of course mainly due to the intervention of the great physical barrier of the Himalayas, "the human equator of the earth," as an American anthropologist* has called it, which throughout its length offers an impassable obstacle to the southward extension of the Mongolian races. But other causes also enter in. No one who is acquainted with the population of the Lower Himalayas can have failed to observe that in the west there has been a substantial intermixture of Indo-Aryan elements, while in the east the prevailing type down to the verge of the plains is exclusively Mongoloid. The reason seems to be that the war-like races of the Punjab and Hindustan invaded the pleasant places of the hills and conquered for themselves the little kingdoms which once extended from the Kashmir valley to the eastern border of Nepal. The Dogrās or Hill Rajputs of Kāngra, and the Khas of Nepal form the living record of these forgotten enterprises. Further east the conditions were reversed, neither Bengalis nor Assamese have any stomach for fighting; they submitted tamely to the periodical raids of the hill people, and the only check upon the incursions of the latter was their inability to stand the heat of the plains. They occupied, however, the whole of the lower ranges and held the Duārs or "gates" of Bhutan until dispossessed by us. Thus in the Eastern Himalayas none of the plains people made good a footing within the hills, which remain to this day in the exclusive possession of races of the Mongoloid type.

The summaries of measurements given in the appendix relate to a fairly large number of subjects and the type is distinct.

(i) The prevalent head-form is broad, but the mean indices show some remarkable departures from this type. The Jaintia index is 72·9, thus falling within the long-headed category, and several tribes have indices between 75 and 80. These low indices are, however, based upon a comparatively small number of subjects, and it seems not unlikely that a larger series of measurements may sensibly modify the average. In any case a great deal of work will have to be done before we are in a position to determine the probable affinities of the numerous Mongoloid tribes who inhabit the hilly region between India and China.

(ii) The nose-form appears at first sight to show a great range of variations, but on closer examination it will be seen that the higher indices are for the most part confined to tribes for which the data are scanty. In the larger groups the mean index ranges from 67·2 for the Lepchās to 84·5 for the Chakmās

---

* Ripley. *The Races of Europe*, p. 45.

and 86·3 for the Khasiās; the Tibetans (73·9) and the Murmis (75·2) falling between these extremes. The highest mean index (95·1) occurs among the Mānde or Gāro, in one of whom, according to Lieutenant-Colonel Waddell, the width of the nose exceeds its height to an extent indicated by the surprising ratio of 117. But only 34 Gāros have been measured, and looking to the possibilities of crossing one can scarcely regard the figures as conclusive. On the measurements given in the table there may be some question whether the Mānde should not be classed as Mongolo-Dravidian, and this view may be thought to derive some support from Buchanan's description of them as a wild section of the Kochh.*

(iii) Under the head of stature there is nothing much to remark. The Gurungs (169·8) are the tallest and the Miris (156·4) the shortest of the tribes included in the table. The 106 Tibetans show an average of 163·3, which may be regarded as fairly typical. The tallest individuals (176) are found among the Tibetans and Murmis; the shortest (141) are the Khambus and the Khasiās.

(iv) The characteristic orbito-nasal index, which measures the relative flatness or prominence of the root of the nose and the adjacent features, yields singularly uniform results. The average varies in the large groups, which alone are worth considering, from 106·4 in the Chakmā to 109·1 in the Tibetan. For the Lepchās Lieutenant-Colonel Waddell's observations yield a mean index of 105·8, with a maximum of 119 and a minimum of 92, against my average of 101·8 ranging from 133 to 103. As my figures relate to a larger number of subjects (57 against 36), I have selected them in preference to his for inclusion in the diagram showing seriation. A glance at the diagrams given for the Lepchās of Darjeeling and the Chakmās of the Hill Tracts of Chittagong will show how regularly the gradations of the indices are distributed, and will bring out better than any description the correspondences and divergences of type.

Dravidian type.

The *Dravidian* race, the most primitive of the Indian peoples, occupies the oldest geological formation in India, the medley of forest-clad ranges, terraced plateaux, and undulating plains which stretches, roughly speaking, from the Vindhyas to Cape Comorin. On the east and west of the peninsular area the domain of the Dravidian is conterminous with the Ghāts; while farther north

[* In M. Martin, *Eastern India*, iii., 1838, p. 538, *et seq.*]

it reaches on one side to the Aravallis and on the other to the Rajmahal hills. Where the original characteristics have been unchanged by contact with Indo-Aryan or Mongoloid people the type is remarkably uniform and distinctive. Labour is the birthright of the pure Dravidian, and as a coolie he is in great demand wherever one meets him. Whether hoeing tea in Assam, the Duārs and Ceylon, planting sugar-cane in far Fiji, cutting rice in the swamps of Eastern Bengal, or doing scavenger's work in the streets of Calcutta, Rangoon, and Singapore, he is recognizable at a glance by his black skin, his squat figure and the negro-like proportions of his nose. In the upper strata of the vast social deposit which is here treated as Dravidian these typical characteristics tend to thin out and disappear, but even among them traces of the original stock survive in varying degrees. We must look to the researches of Mr. Thurston,* who is conducting the ethnographic survey of Southern India, to define and classify the numerous sub-types thus established and to determine the causes which have given rise to them.

Turning now to the actual measurements we find the following specific characters:—

(i) The head-form is usually medium with a tendency in the direction of length. The mean indices range in Southern India from 71·7 in the Badaga of the Nilgiris and 72·9 in the Kādir of the Anamalai Hills to 76·6 in the Shānāṇs of Tinnevelly. The Tiyans (73), Nāyars (73·2), Cheruman (73·4), Palli (73), Parāyan or Pariah (73·6), Irula (73·1) and several others also fall well within the long-headed group. In Chutia Nāgpur, on the other hand, the type is uniformly medium. Among the large groups the Chik (73·8), the Muṇda (74·5), the Māle (74·8), the Kharia (74·5), and the Korwa (74·4) are just included in the long-headed division; while for all the others the mean index ranges about 75 and 76. In this part of India the physical conformation of the country, the vast stretches of fever-haunted jungle, the absence of roads, and the compact tribal organization and independent spirit of the Dravidian races have tended to preserve them singularly free from the intrusion of foreign influence, and for these reasons I believe that their measurements may be taken as fairly typical. The seriation given for the Santāls shows how regularly the individual indices are graduated.

(ii) In Southern India the mean proportions of the nose

[* *Castes and Tribes of Southern India*, 1909, vol. i., Intro., p. xxxvii, *et seq.*]

vary from 69·1 in the Lambādis of Mysore, and 73·1 in the Vellālas of Madras to 95·1 in the Paniyans of Malabar. In Chutia Nāgpur and Western Bengal the range of variation is less marked, and the mean indices run from 82·6 in the Kurmi of Mānbhum in a gradually ascending series to 94·5 in the Māle of the Santāl Parganas. The Asur figure of 95·9 may be left out of account as it relates only to two subjects. In both regions the mean proportions of the nose correspond in the main to the gradations of social precedence, and such divergencies as occur admit of being plausibly accounted for. At the head of the physical series in Southern India stand the Lambādi with a mean index of 69·1. They do not employ the local Brāhmans as priests, and their touch is held to convey ceremonial pollution. But there is reason to believe that they are a nomadic people from Upper India, and that their social rank is low merely because they have not been absorbed in the social system of the South. Next come the Vellālas, the great cultivating caste of the Tamil country, with a mean index of 73·1. They are classed as *Sat* or pure Sudras; the Brāhmans who serve them as priests will take curds and butter from their hands and will cook in any part of their houses. The Tamil Brāhmans themselves belong, indeed, to a lower physical type; but their mean index of 76·7 has probably been affected by the inclusion in the group of some tribal priests, who obtained recognition as Brāhmans when their votaries insensibly became Hindus. Then follow the Palli (77·9), a large group mainly employed in agriculture, who claim twice-born rank and frequently describe themselves as *Agnikula* or fire-born Kshatriyas. Low down in the social as in the physical scale are the Parāiyan or Pariah, with an index of 80, whose mere vicinity pollutes, but whose traditions point to the probability that their status was not always so degraded as we find it at the present day. This conjecture derives some support from the fact that the Kādir, Mukkuvan and Paniyan with substantially broader noses yet take higher social rank.

(iii) Among the Dravidians of Southern India the mean stature ranges from 170 in the Shānān of Tinnevelly to 153 in the Pulaiyan of Travancore; and individual measurements vary from 182·8 in the former group to 143·4 in the latter. Mr. Thurston has drawn my attention to the well-marked correlation between stature and the proportions of the nose which is brought out by the following statement:—

		Mean stature.	Mean nasal index.
Agamudaiyan	...	165·8	74·2
Badaga	...	164·1	75·6
Tiyan	...	163·7	75
Tamil Brāhman	...	162·5	76·7
Palli	...	162·5	77·3
Tamil Parāyan	...	162·1	80
Irula	...	159·9	80·4
Kādir	...	157·7	89·8
Paniyan	...	157	95·1

In Chutia Nāgpur and Western Bengal the stature is more uniform, varying from 162·7 in the Orāon of Ranchi to 157·7 in the Māl Pahāria and Māle of the Santāl Parganas, and the correlation with the proportions of the nose, though traceable, is less distinct.

Origins of types.

The origins of these types are hidden in the mist which veils the remote era of the Aryan advance into India. Within that dim region evidence is sought for in vain. Our only guides are tradition and conjecture, aided by the assumption, which the history of the East warrants us in making, that in those distant ages types were formed by much the same processes as those that we find in operation to-day. Such are our materials for a study of the evolution of the Indian people. At the best the picture can present but shadowy outlines. All that can be demanded of it is that it should accord in the main with the scanty data furnished by what passes for history in India, and at the same time should offer a consistent and plausible explanation of the ethnic conditions which prevail at the present time.

The oldest of the seven types is probably the Dravidian. Their low stature, black skin, long heads, broad noses, and relatively long fore-arm distinguish them from the rest of the population, and appear at first sight to confirm Huxley's surmise that they may be related to the aborigines of Australia. Linguistic affinities, especially the resemblance between the numerals in Mundāri and in certain Australian dialects, and the survival of some abortive forms of the boomerang in Southern India, have been cited in support of this view, and an appeal has also been made to Sclater's hypothesis of a submerged continent of Lemuria, extending from Madagascar to the Malay Archipelago, and linking India with Africa on the one side and Australia on the other. But Sir William Turner's comparative study of the characters of Australian and Dravidian crania has not led him to the conclusion that these data can be adduced in support of the theory of the unity of the two peoples.

The facts which cast doubt on the Australian affinities of the Dravidians finally refute the hasty opinion which seeks to associate them with the tiny, broad-headed, and woolly-haired Negritos of the Andamans and the Philippines. This is the last word of scientific authority, and here we might leave the subject, were it not that another theory of the origin of the Dravidians was adopted by Sir William Hunter in the account of the non-Aryan races of India given by him in *The Indian Empire*. According to this view there are two branches of the Dravidians—the Kolarians speaking dialects allied to Mundāri, and the Dravidians proper whose languages belong to the Tamil family. The former entered India from the north-east and occupied the northern portion of the Vindhya table-land. There they were conquered and split into fragments by the main body of Dravidians, who found their way into the Punjab through the north-western passes and pressed forward towards the south of India. The basis of this theory is obscure. Its account of the Dravidians seems to rest upon a supposed affinity between the Brāhūi dialect of Baluchistan and the languages of Southern India; while the hypothesis of the north-eastern origin of the Kolarians depends on the fancied recognition of Mongolian characteristics among the people of Chutia Nāgpur. But in the first place the distinction between Kolarians and Dravidians is purely linguistic and does not correspond to any differences of physical type. Secondly, it is extremely improbable that a large body of very black and conspicuously long-headed types should have come from the one region of the earth which is peopled exclusively by races with broad heads and yellow complexions. With this we may dismiss the theory which assigns a trans-Himalayan origin to the Dravidians. Taking them as we find them now it may safely be said that their present geographical distribution, the marked uniformity of physical characters among the more primitive members of the group, their animistic religion, their distinctive languages, their stone monuments and their retention of a primitive system of totemism justify us in regarding them as the earliest inhabitants of India of whom we have any knowledge.

Dravidian.

The Indo-Aryan type. Its non-Indian origin.

Upon the interminable discussions known as the Aryan controversy there is no need to enter here. Whether anything that can properly be described as an Aryan race ever existed; whether the heads of its members were long, according to

Penka, or short according to Sergi; whether its original habitat was Scandinavia, the Lithuanian steppe, South-Eastern Russia, Central Asia, or India itself, as various authorities have held; or again whether the term Aryan is anything more than a philological expression denoting the heterogeneous group of peoples whose languages belong to the Aryan family of speech —these are questions which may for our present purpose be left unanswered. We are concerned merely with the fact that there exists in the Punjab and Rajputana at the present day, a definite physical type, represented by the Jāts and Rajputs, which is marked by a relatively long (dolicho-cephalic) head; a straight, finely cut (leptorrhine) nose; a long, symmetrically narrow face; a well-developed forehead, regular features, and a high facial angle. The stature is high and the general build of the figure is well proportioned, being relatively massive in the Jāts and relatively slender in the Rajputs. Throughout the group the predominant colour of the skin is a very light transparent brown, with a tendency towards darker shades in the lower social strata. Except among the Meos and Mīnas of Rajputana, where a strain of Bhīl blood may perhaps be discerned, the type shows no signs of having been modified by contact with the Dravidians; its physical characteristics are remarkably uniform; and the geographical conditions of its habitat tend to exclude the possibility of intermixture with the black races of the south. In respect of their social characters the Indo-Aryans, as I have ventured to call them, are equally distinct from the bulk of the Indian people. They have not wholly escaped the contagion of caste; but its bonds are less rigid among them than with the other Indian races; and the social system retains features which recall the more fluid organization of the tribe. Marriage in particular is not restricted by the hard and fast limits which caste tends to impose, but is regulated within large groups by the principle of hypergamy or 'marrying up' which was supposed to govern the connubial relations of the four original classes (*varna*) in the system described by Manu. Even now Rajputs and Jāts occasionally intermarry, the Rajputs taking wives from the Jāts, but refusing to give their own maidens in return. What is the exception to-day is said to have been the rule in earlier times. In short, both social and physical characters are those of a comparatively homogeneous community which has been but little affected by crossing with alien races.

The uniformity of the Indo-Aryan type can be accounted

for only by one of two hypotheses, (1) that its members were indigenous to the Punjab, (2) that they entered India in a compact body or in a continuous stream of families from beyond the north-west frontier. It is clear that they could not have come by sea, and equally clear that they could not have found their way into India round the Eastern end of the Himalayas. The theory that the Punjab was the cradle of the Aryan race was propounded by a writer in the *Journal of the Royal Asiatic Society** about fifty years ago, on the basis of some rather crude linguistic speculations; but it met with no acceptance, and the opinion of European scholars from Von Schlegel down to the present time is unanimous in favour of the foreign origin of the Indo-Aryans. The arguments appealed to are mainly philological. Vedic literature, indeed, as Zimmer † admits, throws but scanty light upon the subject, for no great weight can be laid upon the identification of the River Rasā with the Araxes, the name by which the Jaxartes was known to Herodotus. Following authority, however, we may assume for our present purpose that the ancestors of the Indo-Aryans came into India from the north-west, and that at the time of their arrival the peninsula, as far as the valley of the Ganges and Jumna, was in the possession of the Dravidians. The only indication of the latter people having extended further to the west, is to be found (as has been mentioned already) in the survival of Brāhūi, an island of supposed Dravidian speech, among the Iranian languages of Baluchistan. But the present speakers of Brāhūi are certainly not Dravidians by race; and we find no traces of Dravidian blood among the Indo-Aryans of to-day. It seems probable, therefore, that when the Indo-Aryans entered the Punjab they brought their own women with them, and were not reduced to the necessity of capturing Dravidian brides. On no other supposition can we explain the comparative purity of their type.

The mode of its entry into India.

Now, if the physical and social conditions of the Indian Borderland had been the same in those remote ages as we find them at the present day, it is difficult to see how the slow advance of family or tribal migration could have proceeded on a scale large enough to result in an effective occupation of the Punjab. The frontier strip itself, a mere tangle of barren hills and narrow valleys, is ill-adapted to serve as an *officina gentium*;

* *J. R. A. S.*, XVI., 172-200.

† Zimmer, *Altindisches Leben*, pp. 15 and 101.

while a pastoral people, moving by clans or families from more favoured regions further west, would have found their way barred by obstacles which only the strongest members of the community could have surmounted. The women and children must have been left behind or they would have perished by the way. Again, given the present rainfall and climate of the countries adjacent to India, where should we find to-day, within a measurable distance of the frontier, the favoured region that would give off the swarm of emigrants required to people the Punjab? Surely not in south-eastern Persia, with its inhospitable deserts of shifting sand; nor on the dreary Central Asian steppes where only a scanty nomadic population finds a meagre subsistence. But is it certain that during the three or four thousand years that may have elapsed since the Aryans began to press forward into India the climate of the countries through which they passed may not have undergone a material change? There is an appreciable amount of evidence, the value of which I am anxious not to overrate, in favour of this supposition. The late Mr. W. T. Blanford, writing in 1873,* thought it probable that the rainfall both in Central Asia and Persia had fallen off greatly in modern times, and that owing mainly to this cause, and in a less degree to the destruction of trees and bushes, the climate had become perceptibly drier, cultivation had fallen off and the population had greatly declined in numbers. Nearly thirty years later, we find Mr. Blanford's views confirmed and developed by Mr. E. Vredenburg in his geological sketch of the Baluchistan Desert and part of Eastern Persia.† Mr. Vredenburg applies to the problem the known principles of physical geography and shows how, given a dwindling rainfall in a tract situated like Eastern Persia and Baluchistan, evaporation is bound to produce the present condition of perennial drought. As the rainfall declines fertile plains relapse into deserts; lakes are transformed into hideous salt marshes; the springs in the hills dry up and an era of desolation sets in. No human agency, however corrupt, no mere misgovernment, however colossal, could bring about such widespread disaster. The village communities, give them but earth and water, would outlast the conqueror and the marauder, as they have done in India. The forces of nature alone could defeat their patient industry. It is the great merit of Mr. Vredenburg's paper that it indicates the

* *Quart. Jour. Geol. Soc.*, XXIX. (1873).

† *Mem. Geol. Survey of India*, XXXI., Pt. 2.

true cause of the facts observed and exposes the fallacy of the belief, countenanced by a long series of travellers, that oriental inertia and corruption are solely or chiefly answerable for the present condition of Baluchistan. In illustration of the state of things which must have existed in some former age, he tells us how in the desolate valleys of the State of Khārān there exist hundreds of stone walls, known locally as *gorbands* or "dams of the infidels," which mark the edges of ancient terraced fields, and retain even now remnants of soil which once was cultivated. A legend still survives that the builders of these walls carried the earth in bags on their backs from the alluvial desert on the south, a form of labour which the indolent Baloch would regard as degrading to the dignity of a man. Toil of this sort, whether the soil was transported by beasts of burden or by men, can only have been undertaken in the certain hope of a substantial return. No one would construct fields in a rainless wilderness of ravines, or build walls which have lasted for centuries to retain water where water there was none. Nor is it likely that the cultivation was confined to the hills. Arguing from what one sees in India, it seems far more likely that these terraced fields represent the overflow of a flourishing agricultural community driven up into the hills by the pressure of population in the plains. Gradually as the climate changed, the level alluvial tracts, deprived of rainfall, lapsed into desert; the bulk of the population drifted on into the Punjab, while those who remained behind turned their ploughshares into swords and eked out by pillage the meagre livelihood to be won from patches of soil in the hills. Last of all, the springs on which this scanty cultivation depended shrank and disappeared, till nothing was left but the stone walls to recall the labours of the forgotten people who built them.

The picture which these observations enable us to construct of a country of great lakes and fertile plains extending from the centre of Persia to the western confines of India, or let us say from the Dasht-i-Kavīr in western Khorāsān to the deserts of Registān and Khārān, may help to throw light upon the problem of the Indo-Aryan advance into the Punjab. The population of such a tract, as they began to press on their own means of subsistence or were pushed forward by incursions from the west, would naturally have moved on by tribes and families, without any disturbance of their social order, and would have occupied the valley of the Indus. Arriving there as an organized society, like the children of Israel when they entered Palestine, they would have had no need and no temptation to take to themselves any Dravidian daughters of Heth, and they would have preserved their type as distinct as we find it in the Punjab to-day. The movement must, of course, have been gradual and must have extended over many centuries, during which time the climate continued to dry up and the possibilities of agriculture to decline. When the new conditions had become fully established the north-western frontier of India was closed to the slow advance of family or tribal migration and remained open only to bands of fighting men or adventurous nomads, who could force their way through long zones of waterless deserts ending in a maze of robber-haunted hills. Armed invasion took the place of peaceful colonization. But the invaders, however great their strength, could in any case bring relatively few women in their train. This indeed is the determining factor both of the ethnology and of the history of India. As each wave of conquerors, Greek, Scythian, Arab, Moghal, that entered the country by land became more or less absorbed in the indigenous population, their physique degenerated, their individuality vanished, their energy was sapped, and dominion passed from their hands into those of more vigorous successors. *Ex Occidente Imperium;* the genius of Empire in India has come to her from the West; and can be maintained only by constant infusions of fresh blood from the same source.

The scanty glimpses that are obtained of the history of this region in the distant past bear out the conclusions of the scientific observer. Three hundred years before the Christian era, Alexander's lieutenant Krateros conducted half of the army which had invaded India, consisting of some fifty thousand men encumbered with elephants, invalids and heavy baggage, from Quetta to Kandahar and thence by the Helmund Valley to Narmashir in Seistān. The route which he followed crossed the southern end of the Dasht-i-Lūt or Desert of Desolation, and traversed nearly two hundred miles of what is now an absolute waste "either waterless or supplied with the most brackish wells." * Arrian's account of the march makes no mention of disaster, and Krateros appears to have joined Alexander without any material loss either of elephants or invalids. Strabo again, who described Kirmān about 20 B.C. in

* *Explorations in Turkestan, with an Account of the Basin of Eastern Persia and Seistan.* Expedition of 1903, under the direction of Raphael Pumpelly; Washington, 1905.

a treatise on geography for the use of Roman administrators, speaks of it as a fertile and well-wooded country watered by rivers and producing everything.

Yet when Major Sykes passed through a part of the same tract in 1893–94 he found it covered with ancient ruins and had difficulty in procuring forage for the camels of his small party numbering only about twenty men. Clearly the whole face of the country must have been transformed in the interval. Was this the work of nature or of man? Has the disappearance of the population been brought about by physical causes, such as diminished rainfall, the shifting of river courses, the inroads of wind-driven sand, and the shrinking of the crust of the earth? Or need we look no further than the familiar incidents of Oriental misgovernment—incessant wars, general lawlessness, official corruption and neglect of natural resources? To these questions an answer is supplied by Mr. Ellsworth Huntington's paper on the Basin of Eastern Seistan and Persia, which forms part of the report of the explorations conducted in Turkestan and Persia in 1903 with the support of the Carnegie Institution of Washington.* Here it is shown that the main cause of the desolation now prevailing is the aridity of the climate due to the high mountains which "on every side shut out the moisture of the sea and shut in the people." Ever since the end of the Tertiary era the geological history of the country has been marked by a series of epochs of "prolonged rivers and expanded lakes," alternating with epochs when the rivers were curtailed and the lakes contracted; while throughout the period earth-movements have taken place tending to elevate the barren hills and extend their area and to reduce both the size and the productive capabilities of the habitable basins which they enclose. By the side of these overwhelming physical forces the influence of mere human agencies, such as foreign invasions and native misgovernment, sinks into insignificance. The argument is

[* See his "The Pulse of Asia," 1907, chap. xvi., p. 315, *et seq.* In a lecture delivered by Professor J. W. Gregory to the Royal Geographical Society on December 8, 1913 (*The Times*, December 9, 1913), after a survey of the conditions in Africa, Asia, and America, he observed that, owing to the varied nature of the evidence to be considered, the extensive and scattered literature whence much of that evidence had to be gleaned, and the contradictory opinions expressed by high authorities, the problem whether the earth was drying up was hedged about with difficulties. Archæological and historical evidence showed that Central Asia and even the coasts of Persia and Baluchistan had a very arid climate in the earliest times of which we had human record. Though it must be admitted that, while there was a strong balance of opinion in favour of the view that aridity was being still increased, there were weighty authorities on the other side.]

clinched by the effective comparison which Mr. Huntington draws between the four provinces of Khorāsān, Azerbaijān, Kirmān and Seistān, all of which are equally badly governed. The two former have been devastated by repeated invasions of the most savage character, but they enjoy a relatively abundant rainfall; the two latter have suffered less severely from war, but are afflicted by more or less permanent drought. Khorāsān and Azerbaijān are the most populous and flourishing provinces of Persia; Seistān and Kirmān have been depopulated almost beyond hope of recovery. In Persia, as in India, nature is stronger than man.

The Aryo-Dravidians: Dr. Hoernle's theory.

For the origin of the Aryo-Dravidian type we need not travel beyond the ingenious hypothesis put forward by Dr. Hoernle twenty-six years ago and confirmed by the recent researches of Dr. Grierson's Linguistic Survey. This theory supposes that after the first swarm of Indo-Aryans had occupied the Punjab, a second wave of Aryan-speaking people, the remote ancestors of the Aryo-Dravidians of to-day, impelled by some ethnic upheaval, or driven forward by the change of climate in Central Asia to which we have referred above, made their way into India through Gilgit and Chitrāl and established themselves in the plains of the Ganges and Jumna, the sacred Middle-land (*Madhyadesa*) of Vedic tradition. Here they came in contact with the Dravidians; here by the stress of that contact, caste was evolved; here the Vedas were composed, and the whole fantastic structure of orthodox ritual and usage was built up. For the linguistic evidence in favour of this view I must refer the reader to Dr. Grierson's chapter on language in the Report on the Census of India, 1901. For my present purpose it is sufficient to note that the record of physical characters bears out the conclusions suggested by philology. The type of the people now dwelling in the Middle-land is precisely what might have been expected to result from the incursion of a fair long-headed race, travelling by a route which prevented women from accompanying them, into a land inhabited by dark-skinned Dravidians. The men of the stronger race took to themselves the women of the weaker, and from these unions was evolved the mixed type which we find in Hindustan and Bihar. The degree of intermixture varied to the extent indicated in the tables of measurements; at one end of the scale the type approaches the Indo-Aryan, at the other it almost merges in the Dravidian.

It may be said that the theory of a second wave of Aryans, resting as it does on the somewhat uncertain data of philology, is not really required for the purpose of explaining the facts. Why should we not content ourselves by assuming that the original Indo-Aryans outgrew their settlements on the Indus and threw off swarms of emigrants who passed down the Ganges valley, modifying their type as they went by alliances with the Dravidian inhabitants? But on this view of the problem it is difficult to account for the marked divergence of type that distinguishes the people of the Eastern Punjab from the people of Western Hindustan. If there had been no second and distinct incursion coming in like a wedge behind the original colonists, no such sharp contrast would now be discernible. One type would melt into the other by imperceptible gradations, and scientific observation and popular impressions would not concur, as they do, in affirming that a marked change takes place somewhere about the longitude of Sirhind—a name which itself preserves the tradition of an ethnic frontier. Nor is this the only point in favour of Dr. Hoernle's hypothesis. That theory further explains how it is that the Vedic hymns contain no reference to the route by which the Aryans entered India or to their earlier settlements on the Indus; and it accounts for the antagonism between the eastern and western sections and for the fact that the latter were regarded as comparative barbarians by the more cultured inhabitants of the Middle-land.

The Mongolo-Dravidians.

When we leave Bihar and pass on eastward into the steamy rice-fields of Bengal, the Indo-Aryan element thins out rapidly and appears only in a sporadic form. The bulk of the population is Dravidian, modified by a strain of Mongoloid blood which is relatively strong in the east and appreciably weaker in the west. Even in Bengal, however, where the Indo-Aryan factor is so small as to be hardly traceable, certain exceptions may be noticed. The tradition cherished by the Brāhmans and Kāyasths of Bengal that their ancestors came from Kanauj at the invitation of King Adisur to introduce Vedic ritual into an unhallowed region is borne out to a substantial degree by the measurements of these castes, though even among them indications are not wanting of occasional intermixture with Dravidians.* If, however, the type is regarded as a whole the racial

* Mr. Romesh Chandra Dutt, C.I.E., pointed out long ago that "aboriginal blood enters largely in [*sic*] the existing Brahman community of Bengal." *Calcutta Review*, LXXV., p. 238.

features are seen to be comparatively distinct. The physical degeneration which has taken place may be due to the influence of a relaxing climate and an enfeebling diet, and still more perhaps to the practice of marrying immature children, the great blot on the social system of the upper classes of Bengal.

The Scytho-Dravidian type: its history.

Of the foreign elements that have contributed to the making of the Indian people two have now been passed in review. We have seen the Indo-Aryan type maintaining a high degree of purity in the Punjab and Rajputana, transformed by an increasing admixture of Dravidian blood in Hindustan and Bihar, and vanishing beyond recognition in the swamps of Lower Bengal. We have found the Mongoloid races predominant on the eastern and northern frontiers, confined to the hills where the people of the plains were strong, but further east, where they came in contact with feebler folk, mixing with the Dravidian element to form the type characteristic of the mass of the population of Bengal and Assam. A third foreign element still remains to be accounted for. It has long been known, mainly from Chinese sources supplemented by the evidence of coins and the uncertain testimony of Indian tradition, that long after the settlement of the Indo-Aryans in the Punjab successive swarms of nomadic people, vaguely designated Sakas or Scythians, forced a way into India from the west, and established their dominion over portions of the Punjab, Sind, Gujarat, Rajputana, and Central India. The impulse which started them on their wanderings may be traced in some instances to tribal upheavals in far distant China, while in other cases hordes already on the move were pushed forward from Central Asia. All these people came from regions which, so far as we know, have from time immemorial been occupied by broadheaded races.

In the time of the Achæmenian kings of Persia the Scythians, who were known to the Chinese as Ssĕ, occupied the regions lying between the lower course of the Sillis or Jaxartes and Lake Balkash. We learn from Herodotus that according to the opinion of classical antiquity these Scythians were riding people who wore breeches and used bows of a fashion of their own. It may be gathered from other sources that their empire extended up to the plains of Eastern Turkestan. In the sixth century B.C. the Scythians, who were then renowned for their valour and their riches, came within the scope of the ambitious policy of Cyrus. Their king Amorges was made prisoner, but Sparethra, his wife, rallied the remains of the army, repulsed the Persians, and compelled them to surrender her husband in exchange for the prisoners she had taken. Notwithstanding this temporary success, the Scythians were nevertheless recognised as tributaries of the Persians, and the portion of Turkestan which they occupied formed the twentieth Satrapy of the Persian Empire. Later on they seem to have regained their independence, for at the battle of Arbela we find them fighting on the Persian side no longer as subjects but allies. The fragments of early Scythian history which may be collected from classical writers are supplemented by the Chinese annals, which tell us how the Ssē, originally

Its possible origin.

located in Southern China, occupied Sogdiana and Transoxiana at the time of the establishment of the Græco-Bactrian monarchy about the year 165 B.C. Dislodged from these regions by the Yuechi, who had themselves been put to flight by the Huns, the Ssē invaded Bactriana, an enterprise in which they were frequently allied with the Parthians. To this circumstance, says Ujfalvy, may be due the resemblance which exists between the Scythian coins of India and those of the Parthian kings. At a later period the Yuechi made a further advance and drove the Scythians or Sakas out of Bactriana, whereupon the latter crossed the Paropanisus and took possession of the country called after them Sakastān, comprising Segistān, Arachosia, and Drangiana. But they were left in possession only for a hundred years, for in the year 25 B.C. the Yuechi disturbed them afresh. A body of Scythians then emigrated eastward and founded a kingdom in the western portion of the Punjab. The route they followed in their advance upon India is uncertain, but to a people of their habits who were already located in Sakastān it would seem that the march through Baluchistan and Kachhi would have presented no serious difficulty. Among the sculptured figures on the rock of Behistun there is one which bears the name of Sakuka, the Scythian. Khanikoff, writing in 1866, professed to recognise in this figure the features of a Kirghiz of the present day. Ujfalvy, however, regards the statement as doubtful. He says that he has never seen a Kirghiz with such a luxuriant beard, and the physiognomy of the figure in question appears to him to be Turko-Tartar presenting a mixture of Mongolian and Aryan lineaments.

The Indo-Scythian Yuechi, afterwards known as the

Tokhari, while settled in Eastern Turkestan to the south of the Tian Shan range were defeated by the Hiung-nu or Huns in 201–265 B.C. They fled towards the west, crossed the mountains and took possession of the part of Bactriana inhabited by the Tajiks. A portion of them remained in Eastern Turkestan in the mountainous country to the south-west of Khotan. The Chinese called these people the Siao or Little Yuechi, in order to distinguish them from the others, whom they designated the Ta or Great Yuechi. The Yuechi occupied Central Asia and the north-west of India for more than five centuries from 136 B.C. to 425 A.D. The Hindus called them Sakas and Turushkas, but their kings seem to have known of no other dynastic title than that of Kushan. The Chinese annals tell us how Kitolo, Chief of the Great Kushans, whose name is identified with the Kidara of the coins, giving way before the incursions of the Ephthalites, crossed the Paropanisus and founded in the year 425 of our era the kingdom of Gandhāra, of which in the time of his son Peshawar became the capital. Fifty years later the Ephthalites took possession of Gandhāra and forced the Kushans to retreat into Chitrāl, Gilgit, and Kashmir.

Just at the time when the Kushans were establishing themselves in Gandhāra, the Ephthalites or Hoa of the Chinese annals, who were then settled on the north of the Great Wall of China, being driven out of their territory by the Juan-Juan, started westward and overran in succession Sogdiana, Khwarizm, Bactriana, and finally the north-west portion of India. Their invading movements reached India in the reign of Skanda Gupta, 452—480, and brought about the disruption of the Gupta Empire. The Ephthalites were known in India as Huns. The leader of the invasion of India, who succeeded in snatching Gandhāra from the Kushans, and established his capital at Sakala, is called by the Chinese Laelih, and the inscriptions enable us to identify him with the original Lakhan Udayaditya of the coins. His son Toramana (490—510) took possession of Gujarat, Rajputana and a portion of the Ganges valley, and in this way the Huns came into possession of the ancient Gupta Kingdom. Toramana's successor Mihirakula (510—540) added at the beginning of his reign Kashmir to his kingdom, but eventually succumbed to the combined attack of a confederation of the Hindu princes of Malwa and Magadha.*

[* The account in the text of the Scythians and Huns needs to be corrected. The facts have been carefully collected by V. A. Smith, *Early History of India*, 3rd ed., 1914,

These are the historical data. Scanty as they are, they serve to establish the fact that during a long period of time swarms of nomadic people, whose outlandish names are conveniently summed up in the generic term Scythian, poured into India, conquered and governed. Their coins are now the sole memorial of their rule, but their inroads probably began many centuries before coins were struck or annals compiled. Of the people themselves all traces seem to have vanished, and the student who enquires what has become of them finds nothing more tangible than the modern conjecture that they are represented by the Jāts and Rajputs. But the grounds for this opinion are of the flimsiest description and consist mainly of the questionable assumption that the people who are called Jāts at the present day must have something to do with the people who were known to Herodotus as Getae. Now apart from the fact that resemblances of names are mostly misleading—witness the Roman identification of these very Getae with the Goths—we have good historical reasons for believing that the Scythian invaders of India came from a region occupied exclusively by broad-headed races and must themselves have belonged to that type. They were, by all accounts, nations or hordes of horsemen, with broad faces and high cheek-bones, short and sturdy of stature, and skilled in the use of the bow. In their original homes on the Central Asian steppes their manner of life was that of pastoral nomads; and their instincts were of the predatory order. It seems therefore *primâ facie* unlikely that their descendants are to be looked for among tribes who are essentially of the long-headed type, tall, heavy men without any natural aptitude for horsemanship, settled agriculturists with no traditions of a nomadic and marauding past. Still less probable is it that waves of foreign conquerors,

p. 248 *et seq.*; and for the Scythians, by E. W. Minns, *Scythians and Greeks*, 1913, *Encyclopædia Britannica*, 11th ed., 1911, vol. xxiv. p. 526 *et seq.* For the Huns, see Sir C. Eliot, *Ency. Brit.*, vol. xiii. p. 932 *et seq.* Mr. V. A. Smith, who has kindly read the account in the text, remarks that there is no evidence that the Sakas came from regions exclusively occupied by broad-headed races; that the Chinese did not designate *all* Scythians as Ssē, this title being apparently confined to the tribes on the Jaxartes; that Sillis, unless it represents a form of Syr-darya, has not been traced as a name for the Jaxartes; that the account by Herodotus cannot be extended to the Saka; that the Indians, not the Saka, were included in the twentieth Satrapy of the Persian Empire; that there is no authority for including Arachosia and Drangiana in Sakastān; the date and course of the invasion of the Panjab are uncertain; the evidence of the Behistun figures does not settle the ethnological problem; Kushān was not a dynastic title; Kitolo was chief of the Little, not the Great Kushāns; Peshawar was the capital of Gandhāra ages before the Saka invasion; there is no evidence that the Kushāns retreated before the Ephthalites into Chitrāl or Gilgit; the reign of Skanda Gupta extended from about 455 to 480 A.D.; there is no ground for identifying Laelih with Lakhan Udayaditya, nor was Toramāna son of the latter.]

entering India at a date when the Indo-Aryans had long been an organized community, should have been absorbed by them so completely as to take rank among their most typical representatives, while the form of their heads, the most persistent of racial distinctions, was transformed from the extreme of one type to the extreme of another without leaving any trace of the transitional forms involved in the process. Such are the contradictions which beset the attempt to identify the Scythians with the Jāts and Rajputs. The only escape from them seems to lie in an alternative hypothesis which is suggested by the measurements summarised in the Scytho-Dravidian table. These data show that a zone of broad-headed people may still be traced southwards from the region of the Western Punjab, in which we lose sight of the Scythians, right through the Deccan till it attains its furthest extension among the Coorgs. Is it not conceivable that this may mark the track of the Scythians who first occupied the great grazing country of the Western Punjab and then, pressed upon by later invaders and finding their progress eastward blocked by the Indo-Aryans, turned towards the south, mingled with the Dravidian population and became the ancestors of the Marāthas? The physical type of the people of the Deccan accords fairly well with this theory, while the arguments derived from language and religion do not seem to conflict with it. For, after entering India the Scythians readily adopted an Aryan language written in the Kharosthi character and accepted Buddhism as their religion. These they would have carried with them to the south. Their Prākrit speech would have developed into Marāthi, while their Buddhistic doctrines would have been absorbed in that fusion of magic and metaphysics which has resulted in popular Hinduism. Nor is it wholly fanciful to discover some aspects of Marātha history which lend it incidental support. On this view the wide-ranging forays of the Marāthas; their guerrilla methods of warfare; their unscrupulous dealings with friend and foe; their genius for intrigue, and their consequent failure to build up an enduring dominion; and finally the individuality of character and tenacity of purpose which distinguish them at the present day—all these may be regarded as part of the inheritance which has come to them from their Scythian ancestors.

CHAPTER II

SOCIAL TYPES

κρῖν' ἄνδρας κατὰ φῦλα, κατὰ φρήτρας, Ἀγάμεμνον,
ὡς φρήτρη φρήτρηφιν ἀρήγῃ, φῦλα δὲ φύλοις.

Il. II. 362-3.

Social divisions: the tribe.

UP to this point I have been dealing with the racial divisions of the people of India, with ethnology properly so called. I turn now to their social divisions, to the ethnographic data as distinguished from the ethnological. These divisions are either tribes or castes, which in their turn are further subdivided with reference usually to matrimonial considerations. A tribe as we find it in India is a collection of families or groups of families bearing a common name which as a rule does not denote any specific occupation; generally claiming common descent from a mythical or historical ancestor, and occasionally from an animal, but in some parts of the country held together rather by the obligations of blood feud than by the tradition of kinship; usually speaking the same language and occupying, professing, or claiming to occupy a definite tract of country. A tribe is not necessarily endogamous; that is to say, it is not an invariable rule that a man of a particular tribe must marry a woman of that tribe and cannot marry a woman of a different tribe.

Types of tribes.

We may distinguish several kinds of tribes in various parts of India, and although it cannot be said that each of the seven racial types has its own distinctive form of tribe, nevertheless the correspondence between the two sets of groupings is sufficiently close to warrant the conjecture, that each type was originally organized on a characteristic tribal basis and that, where tribes have disappeared, their disappearance has been effected by caste insensibly absorbing and transforming the tribal divisions which it found in possession of particular localities. In describing the varieties of tribes I shall therefore follow the ethnic types already determined by physical characters.

The Dravidian tribe.

The *Dravidian* tribe exists in its most compact and vigorous form among the people of Chutia Nāgpur. Descriptions of two typical instances are given in the Appendix under the heads of Munda and Santāl. Such a tribe is generally divided into a number of exogamous groups, each of which bears the name of an animal or plant common in the locality. Usually also there is a distinct village organization comprising in its most developed forms a headman with his assistant and a priest with various acolytes whose business it is to propitiate the various undefined powers from whom physical ills are to be apprehended. Another remarkable instance of the tribal organization of the Dravidians is to be found among the Kandhs or Kondhs of the Orissa Kandh Māls, once infamous for the human sacrifices which they offered to the earth goddess with the object of ensuring good crops and immunity from disease and accidents. A grim memorial of these forgotton horrors is to be seen in the Madras Museum in the form of a rude representation in wood of the head and trunk of an elephant pivoted on a stout post. To this the victim was bound head downwards and the machine was slowly turned round in the centre of a crowd of worshippers who hacked and tore away scraps of flesh to bury in their fields, chanting the while a ghastly hymn, an extract from which illustrates very clearly the theory of sympathetic magic underlying the ritual—

As the tears stream from thine eyes,
So may the rain pour down in August;
As the mucus trickles from thy nostrils,
So may it drizzle at intervals;
As thy blood gushes forth,
So may the vegetation sprout;
As thy gore falls in drops,
So may the grains of rice form.

A number of these wooden elephants, which had been used at sacrifices, were found and burnt by the British officers who put down human sacrifice in the Kandh country. The worm-eaten specimen at Madras is probably unique.* The Kandhs are divided into 50 *gochis* or exogamous sects, each of which bears the name of a *muta* or village, believes all its members to be descended from a common ancestor, and as a rule dwells as

[* For a photograph of the Meriah sacrifice post in the Madras Museum, see E. Thurston, *Tribes and Castes of Southern India*, 1909, vol. iii. p. 377: for details of this rite, Sir J. G. Fraser, *The Golden Bough*, 3rd ed. pt. v., 1912, p. 245 *et seq.*]

a body of blood-relations in the commune or group of villages after which it is called. The Kandh *gochi* appears, therefore, to represent the nearest approach that has yet been discovered to the local exogamous tribe believed by Mr. McLennan to be the primitive unit of human society.

The Mongoloid tribe.

The *Mongoloid* type of tribe as found in the Naga Hills is divided somewhat on the same pattern as the Kandhs into a number of *khels*, each of which is in theory an exogamous group of blood relations dwelling apart in its own territory and more or less at war with the rest of the world. Each *khel* fortifies the locality which it inhabits with a stockade, a deep ditch full of bamboo caltrops, and a craftily devised ladder, and raids are constantly made by one upon the other for the purpose of capturing wives. So far as our present researches have gone no very clear traces have been found of totemism among the Mongoloid races of India,* but the Mongoloid people of the Eastern Himalayas and the Chittagong Hills have a singular system of exogamous groups based upon their real or mythical ancestors. Instances of this grotesque variant of eponymy are the Chakma clans *Ichāpochā*, "the man who ate rotten shrimps," *Pirā bhāngā*, "the fat man who broke the stool," *Aruyā*, "the skeleton," and so forth.†

The Turko-Iranian tribes: the Afghan type.

Among the *Turko-Iranians* there seem to be two distinct types of tribe:—

The Baloch and Brahui type.

(*a*) Tribes based upon kinship like the Afghān group of tribes, otherwise known as Pathāns or speakers of the Pashtu language, who trace their lineage to one Qais Abdul Rashīd who lived in the country immediately to the west of the Takht-i-Sulaimān and was thirty-seventh in descent from Malik Tālūt (King Saul). In theory, says Mr. Hughes-Buller in his admirable account of the tribal system of Baluchistan,‡ "an Afghan tribe is constituted from the number of kindred groups of agnates; that is to say, descent is through the father, and the son inherits the blood of his father. Affiliated with a good many tribes, however, are to be found a certain number of alien groups known as *Mindūn* or *Hamsayah*. The latter

[* Instances of totemism among the tribes of Assam are recorded by Major A. Playfair, *The Garos*, 1909, p. 64 *et seq.*, and by S. Endle, *The Kachāris*, 1911. p. 24 *et seq.* Among the Khāsis the evidence is doubtful, Major P. R. Gurdon, *The Khasis*, 1907, p. 66. Also in Sir J. G. Frazer, *Totemism and Exogamy*, 1910, vol. ii. p. 318 *et seq.*; iv. p. 295 *et seq.*]

[† Risley, *Tribes and Castes of Bengal*, vol. ii. App. i. p. 31 *et seq.*]

[‡ *Census Report, Baluchistan*, 1901, vol. i. p. 119 *et seq.*]

term means 'living in the same shade.' These groups are admittedly not united to the tribe by kinship." They do not, indeed, even claim descent from the common ancestor, and the nature of the tie that binds them to the tribe is best expressed in the picturesque phrase which describes them as *Neki aur badi men sharik,* "partners for better or worse"; in other words, active participators in any blood-feud that the tribe may have on their hands. Yet such is the influence of the idea of kinship upon which the tribe is based that the alien origin of the *Hamsayah* is admitted with reluctance, and although for matrimonial purposes they are looked upon as inferior, the tendency is continually to merge the fact of common vendetta in the fiction of common blood. These are the two leading principles which go to the making of an Afghān tribe. There are also —Mr. Hughes-Buller explains—"two other ties which unite the smaller groups: common pasture, or, more important still, common land and water, and common inheritance. The area occupied by each section can be pretty easily localized, and a group which separates itself permanently from the parent stock and makes its way to a remote locality, where it either sets up for itself or joins some other tribe, ceases to have any part or portion with the parent stock. Here the test question is: 'Has the individual or group on separating from the parent stock, departed only temporarily or permanently?' For, among a population largely composed of graziers, there must be constant fission, groups leaving the locality of the majority for other places as pasture or water are required for the flocks. Where the change is only temporary, groups retain as a matter of course their union with the group to which they belong. There are others, however, who wish to sever their connection with the parent group permanently, and, once this has been done, the idea of participation in the common good and ill of the parent stock disappears. Common inheritance can, in the nature of things, only be shared by the more minute groups, and this, in the absence of blood-feud, is the bond of unity in the family or *Kahol.* And this leads me to explain that all the four principles which I have mentioned do not affect every group equally. Thus, the smaller groups or *Kahols,* which in most cases correspond with the family, are united by kinship and common inheritance, but within the family group there can be no blood-feud. For blood-feud can only be carried on when help is given from outside, and no one will help the murderer within the family. Leaving the lowest group, we find that common good and ill, merging in the fiction of kinship, is the influence affecting all the groups, even the largest unit, of the tribe. Common land and water are only shared by comparatively minute groups, *i.e.*, by the *Khel* or *Zāī*, but the groups united by common locality, and possibly by common grazing, are both numerous and large."

(*b*) The second type of Turko-Iranian tribe is based, primarily, not upon agnatic kinship, but upon common good and ill; in other words, it is cemented together by the obligations arising from the blood-feud. There is no eponymous ancestor, and the tribe itself does not profess to be composed of homogeneous elements. In the case of the Marri tribe of Baloch Mr. Hughes-Buller has shown that "Brāhūis, Baloch from the Punjab, Baloch from other parts of Afghanistan, Khetrāns, Afghāns, Jāts, all gained easy admission to the tribe. As soon as a man joined the tribe permanently he became a participator in good and ill. Then, having shown his worth, he was given a vested interest in the tribal welfare by acquiring a portion of the tribal lands at the decennial division, and his admission was sealed with blood by women from the tribe being given to him or his sons in marriage. Starting, therefore, with the principle of participation in common good and common ill, participation in the tribal land came to be the essence of tribesmanship among the Marris. The process is easy to follow: Admission to participation in common blood-feud; then admission to participation in tribal land; and lastly admission to kinship with the tribe. It was not until after a man or group had been given a share of tribal land at the decennial distribution that women were given to him or them in marriage." The same principles hold good in the case of the Brāhūi, who, like the Baloch, appear both by their history and by their physique to be of Central Asian or Scythian origin, though their numbers have been recruited from among Afghāns, Kurds, Jāgdals, Baloch, and other elements, all probably belonging to the same ethnic stock.

Both Baloch and Brāhūi possess an elaborate organization for offensive and defensive purposes, based in each case on the principle that the clan or section must provide for the service of the tribe a number of armed men proportioned to the share of the tribal land which it holds. The Brāhūi system, introduced by Nasir Khān about the end of the seventeenth century, is somewhat the more complete of the two, and binds together all the Brāhūi tribes in a regular confederacy which is now, according to Mr. Hughes-Buller, beginning to regard the British Government as its effective suzerain. A full account of the Brāhūi taken from Mr. Hughes-Buller's report on the first census of Baluchistan will be found in the ethnographic volume of the Imperial Census Report for 1901.

Marriage in Baluchistan.

None of the numerous tribes comprised in the names Afghān, Brāhūi, Baloch are strictly endogamous, and stalwart aliens, whose services are considered worth having, are admitted into the tribe by the gift of a wife, or perhaps one should rather say the loan, for, in the absence of stipulations to the contrary, a woman so given goes back to her own family on the death of her husband. Among the Baloch and Brāhūi, however, a distinct tendency towards endogamy results from the practice of marrying a woman of the same group, a near kinswoman, or, if possible, a first cousin. This seems to be due partly to the feeling that a woman's marriage to an outsider deprives the tribe of the accession of strength that may accrue to it from her offspring; and partly also to the belief that "while among animals heredity follows the father, among human beings it follows the mother. It is argued, therefore, that there is more hope of the stock remaining pure if a man marries a woman who is nearly related to him." In marked contrast to the Baloch and Brāhūi, the business instincts of the Afghān lead him to regard women as a marketable commodity, and under the system of *walwar* or payment for wives "girls are sold to the highest bidder, no matter what his social status." It is possible, however, that in a tribe of comparatively homogeneous descent the sentiment in favour of purity of blood may operate less strongly than in a tribe of admittedly composite structure.

The word "caste."

We shall see in a later chapter how the word *fetish*, which has had a great vogue in the history of religion, owes its origin to the Portuguese navigators who were brought into contact with the strange religious observances of the natives of West Africa. In the same way *caste*, which has obtained an equally wide currency in the literature of sociology, comes from the Portuguese adventurers who followed Vasco de Gama to the west coast of India. The word itself is derived from the Latin *castus* and implies purity of breed. In his article on caste in "Hobson-Jobson," Sir Henry Yule quotes a decree of the sacred council of Goa dated 1567, which recites how in some parts of that province "the Gentoos divide themselves into distinct races or castes (*castas*) of greater or less dignity, holding the Christians as of lower degree, and keep these so superstitiously that no one of a higher caste can eat or drink with those of a lower." From that time to this it has been assumed without much critical examination that the essential principle of caste is mainly concerned with matters of eating and drinking. It need not surprise us to find foreign observers laying stress upon the superficial aspects of a social system which they understood but imperfectly, and overlooking the material fact that the regulations affecting food and drink are comparatively fluid and transitory, while those relating to marriage are remarkably stable and absolute.

Definition of caste.

A caste may be defined as a collection of families or groups of families bearing a common name; claiming common descent from a mythical ancestor, human or divine; professing to follow the same hereditary calling; and regarded by those who are competent to give an opinion as forming a single homogeneous community. The name generally denotes or is associated with a specific occupation. A caste is almost invariably endogamous in the sense that a member of the large circle denoted by the common name may not marry outside that circle, but within the circle there are usually a number of smaller circles each of which is also endogamous. Thus it is not enough to say that a Brāhman at the present day cannot marry any woman who is not a Brāhman; his wife must not only be a Brāhman, she must also belong to the same endogamous division of the Brāhman caste.

M. Senart's description.

By the side of this rigid definition I may place the general description of caste which is given by M. Emile Senart in his fascinating study of the caste system of India. After reminding his readers that no statement that can be made on the subject of caste can be considered as absolutely true, that the apparent relations of the facts admit of numerous shades of distinction, and that only the most general characteristics cover the whole of the subject, M. Senart goes on to describe a caste as a close corporation, in theory at any rate rigorously hereditary; equipped with a certain traditional and independent organization, including a chief and a council; meeting on occasion in assemblies of more or less plenary authority, and joining in the celebration of certain festivals; bound together by a common occupation; observing certain common usages which relate more particularly to marriage, to food and to questions of ceremonial pollution; and ruling its members by the exercise of a jurisdiction the extent of which varies, but which succeeds, by the sanction of certain penalties and above all by the power of final or revocable exclusion from the group, in making the authority of the community effectively felt.

An English parallel.

These, in the view of one of the most distinguished of French scholars, are the leading features of Indian caste. For my own part I have always been much impressed by the difficulty of conveying to European readers who have no experience of India even an approximate idea of the extraordinary complexity of the social system which is involved in the word "caste." At the risk of being charged with frivolity I shall, therefore, venture on an illustration, based on one which I published in *Blackwood's Magazine* a good many years ago, of a caste expressed in terms of an English social group. Let us take an instance, and, in order to avoid the fumes of bewilderment that are thrown off by uncouth names, let us frame it on English lines. Let us imagine the great tribe of Smith, the "noun of multitude," as a famous headmaster used to call it, to be transformed by art magic into a caste organized on the Indian model, in which all the subtle *nuances* of social merit and demerit which *Punch* and the society papers love to chronicle should have been set and hardened into positive regulations affecting the intermarriage of families. The caste thus formed would trace its origin back to a mythical eponymous ancestor, the first Smith who converted the rough stone hatchet into the bronze battleaxe and took his name from the "smooth" * weapons that he wrought for his tribe. Bound together by this tie of common descent, they would recognize as the cardinal doctrine of their community the rule that a Smith must always marry a Smith, and could by no possibility marry a Brown, a Jones, or a Robinson. But over and above this general canon three other modes or principles of grouping within the caste would be conspicuous. First of all, the entire caste of Smith would be split up into an indefinite number of "in-marrying" clans based upon all sorts of trivial distinctions. Brewing Smiths and baking Smiths, hunting Smiths and shooting Smiths, temperance Smiths and

* Skeat, *Etymological Dictionary*, *s.v.* "Smith." ["The relations of the stem are doubtful. The original stem was *app.* craftsman, skilled worker, in metal, wood, or other material, and this general sense remains in Icelandic," *New English Dictionary*, *s.v.*]

licensed-victualler Smiths, Smiths with double-barrelled names and hyphens, Smiths with double-barrelled names without hyphens, Conservative Smiths, Radical Smiths, tinker Smiths, tailor Smiths, Smiths of Mercia, Smiths of Wessex—all these and all other imaginable varieties of the tribe Smith would be as it were crystallized by an inexorable law forbidding the members of any of these groups to marry beyond the circle marked out by the clan-name. Thus the Unionist Mr. Smith could only marry a Unionist Miss Smith, and might not think of a Home Rule damsel; the free-trade Smiths would have nothing to say to the tariff reformers; a hyphen-Smith could only marry a hyphen-Smith, and so on. Secondly, within each class enquiry would disclose a number of "out-marrying" groups, bearing distinctive names, and governed by the rule that a man of one group could in no circumstances marry a girl of the same group. In theory each group would be regarded as a circle of blood-kindred and would trace its descent from a mythical or historical ancestor like the Wayland-Smith of the Berkshire hills, the Captain Smith who married Pocahontas, or the Mr. W. H. Smith of the railway bookstalls. The name of each would usually suggest its origin, and marriages within the limits defined by the group-name would be deemed incestuous, however remote the actual relationship between the parties concerned. A Wayland could not marry a Wayland, though the two might come from opposite ends of the kingdom and be in no way related, but must seek his bride in the Pocahontas or bookstall circle, and so on. Thus the system, the converse of that just described, would effect in a cumbrous and imperfect fashion what is done for ourselves by the table of prohibited degrees at the end of the Prayer-book—cumbrous because it would forbid marriage between people who are in no sense relations, and imperfect because the group-name would descend in the male line and would of itself present no obstacle to a man marrying his grandmother. Thirdly, running through the entire series of clans we should find yet another principle at work breaking up each in-marrying clan into three or four smaller groups which would form a sort of ascending scale of social distinction. Thus the clan of hyphen-Smiths, which we take to be the cream of the caste—the Smiths who have attained to the crowning glory of double names securely welded together by hyphens—would be again divided into, let us say, Anglican, Dissenting, and Salvationist hyphen-Smiths, taking regular rank in that order. Now the rule of this series of groups would be that a man of the highest or Anglican group might marry a girl of his own group or of the two lower groups, that a man of the second or Dissenting group might take a Dissenting or Salvationist wife, while a Salvationist man would be restricted to his own group. A woman, it will be observed, could under no circumstances marry down into a group below her, and it would be thought eminently desirable for her to marry into a higher group. Other things being equal, it is clear that two-thirds of the Anglican girls would get no husbands, and two-thirds of the Salvationist men no wives. These are some of the restrictions which would control the process of match-making among the Smiths if they were organized in a caste of the Indian type. There would also be restrictions as to food. The different in-marrying clans would be precluded from dining together, and their possibilities of reciprocal entertainment would be limited to those products of the confectioner's shop into the composition of which water, the most fatal and effective vehicle of ceremonial impurity, had not entered. Water pollutes wholesale, but its power as a conductor of malign influence admits of being neutralized by a sufficient admixture of milk, curds, whey, or clarified butter—in fact, of anything that comes from the sacred cow. It would follow from this that the members of our imaginary caste could eat chocolates and other forms of sweetmeats together, but could not drink tea or coffee, and could only partake of ices if they were made with cream and were served on metal, not porcelain, plates. I am sensible of having trenched on the limits of literary and scientific propriety in attempting to describe an ancient and famous institution in unduly vivacious language, but the parallel is as accurate as any parallel drawn from the other end of the world can well be, and it has the advantage of being presented in terms familiar to European readers. The illustration, indeed, may be carried a step further. If we suppose the various aggregates of persons bearing the two or three thousand commonest English surnames to be formed into separate castes and organized on the lines described above, so that no one could marry outside the caste-name and could only marry within that limit subject to the restrictions imposed by differences of residence, occupation, religion, custom, social status, and the like—the mental picture thus formed will give a fairly adequate idea of the bewildering complexity of the Indian caste system.

Conversion of tribes into castes.

All over India at the present moment tribes are gradually and insensibly being transformed into castes. The stages of this operation are in themselves difficult to trace. The main agency at work is fiction, which in this instance takes the form of the pretence that whatever usage prevails to-day did not come into existence yesterday, but has been so from the beginning of time. It may be hoped that the Ethnographic Survey now in progress will throw some light upon the singular course of evolution by which large masses of people surrender a condition of comparative freedom and take in exchange a condition which becomes more burdensome in proportion as its status is higher. So far as my own observation goes, several distinct processes are involved in the movement, and these proceed independently in different places and at different times.

(1) The leading men of an aboriginal tribe, having somehow got on in the world and become independent landed proprietors, manage to enrol themselves in one of the more distinguished castes. They usually set up as Rajputs, their first step being to start a Brāhman priest, who invents for them a mythical ancestor, supplies them with a family miracle connected with the locality where the tribe is settled, and discovers that they belong to some hitherto unheard-of clan of the great Rajput community. In the earlier stages of their advancement they generally find great difficulty in getting their daughters married, as they will not take husbands from their original tribe and Rajputs of their adopted caste will, of course, not condescend to alliances with them. But after a generation or two their persistency obtains its reward and they intermarry, if not with pure Rajputs, at least with a superior order of manufactured Rajputs whose promotion into Brahmanical society dates far enough back for the steps by which it was gained to have been forgotten. Thus a real change of blood may take place, as indeed one is on occasion in a position to observe, while in any case the tribal name is completely lost and with it all possibility of correctly separating this class of people from the Hindus of purer blood and of tracing them to any particular Dravidian or Mongoloid tribe. They have been absorbed in the fullest sense of the word, and henceforth pass and are locally accepted as high-class Hindus. All stages of the process, family miracle and all, can be illustrated by actual instances taken from the leading families in various parts of India. The most picturesque instance of the class of legend to

which I refer is that associated with the family of the Maharajas of Chutia Nāgpur, who call themselves Nāgbansi Rajputs, and on the strength of their mythical pedigree have probably succeeded in occasionally procuring wives of reputed Rajput blood. The story itself is a variant of the well-known Lohengrin legend. It tells how a king of the Nāgas or snakes, the strange prehistoric race which figures so largely in Indian mythology, took upon himself human form and married a beautiful Brāhman girl of Benares. His incarnation, however, was in two respects incomplete, for he could not get rid of his forked tongue and his evil-smelling breath. Consequently, as the story goes, in order to conceal these disagreeable peculiarities he always slept with his back to his wife. His precautions, however, were unsuccessful, for she discovered what he sought to conceal, and her curiosity was greatly inflamed. But the snake king, being bound by the same condition as his Teutonic prototype, could only disclose his origin at the cost of separation from his wife. Accordingly, by a device familiar to Indian husbands, he diverted her attention by proposing to take her on a pilgrimage to the shrine of Jagannāth at Puri in Orissa. The couple started by the direct route through the hills and forests of Chutia Nāgpur, and when they reached the neighbourhood of the present station of Rānchi the wife was seized by the pains of childbirth. Her curiosity revived, and she began to ask questions. By folklore etiquette questions asked on such an occasion must be answered, and her husband was compelled to explain that he was really the Takshak Raja, the king of the snakes. Having divulged this fatal secret he did not, like Lohengrin, make a dignified exit to the strains of slow music. He straightway turned into a gigantic cobra, whereupon his wife was delivered of a male child and died. The poor snake made the best of the trying position in which he found himself; he spread his hood and sheltered the infant from the rays of the midday sun. While he was thus occupied, some wood-cutters of the Mūndā tribe appeared upon the scene, and decided that a child discovered in such remarkable circumstances must be destined to a great future and should at once be adopted as their chief. That is the family legend of the Nāgbansi Rajas of Chutia Nāgpur.* It was received with derisive merriment by a number of genuine Rajputs who attended a conference which I held at Mount Abu in 1900 for the purpose of organizing the census of Rajputana. They

* [E. T. Dalton, *Descriptive Ethnology of Bengal*, 1872, p. 165 *et seq.*]

had never heard of such a thing as a Nāgbansi Rajput, but they entirely appreciated the point of the story. Similar tales, associated sometimes with a peacock, sometimes with a cow, sometimes with other animals or trees, are told of various land-owning families which have attained brevet rank as local Rajputs. Any one who has the curiosity to inquire into the distribution of tenures on the estates of these manufactured Rajputs will usually find that a number of the best villages lying round the residence of the Chief are held on peppercorn rents by the descendants of the Brāhmans who helped him to his miraculous pedigree.

(2) A number of aborigines, as we may conveniently call them, though the term begs an insoluble question, embrace the tenets of a Hindu religious sect, losing thereby their tribal name and becoming Vaishnavas, Lingāyats, Rāmāyats, or the like. Whether there is any mixture of blood or not will depend upon local circumstances and the rules of the sect regarding intermarriage. Anyhow, the identity of the converts as aborigines is usually, though not invariably, lost, and this also may, therefore, be regarded as a case of true absorption.

(3) A whole tribe of aborigines, or a large section of a tribe, enrol themselves in the ranks of Hinduism under the style of a new caste, which, though claiming an origin of remote antiquity, is readily distinguishable by its name from any of the standard and recognized castes. Thus the great majority of the Kochh inhabitants of Jalpaiguri, Rangpur, and part of Dinājpur now invariably describe themselves as Rājbansis or Bhanga Kshatriyas—a designation which enables them to represent themselves as an outlying branch of the Kshatriyas of Hindu tradition who fled to north-eastern Bengal in order to escape from the wrath of Parasu-Rāma. They claim descent from Raja Dasaratha, the father of Rāma, they keep Brāhmans, imitate the orthodox ritual in their marriage ceremony, and have begun to adopt the Brahmanical system of *gotras*. In respect of this last point they are now in a curious state of transition, as they have all hit upon the same *gotra* (Kāsyapa) and thus habitually transgress the primary rule of the Brahmanical system, which absolutely prohibits marriage within the *gotra*. But for this defect in their connubial arrangements—a defect which will probably be corrected in course of time as they and their priests rise in intelligence—there would be nothing in their customs to distinguish them from Indo-Aryan Hindus; although there has been no mixture

of blood and they remain thoroughly Kochh under the name of Rājbansi. It is right to add that, however baseless the tradition must be in the case of the tribe as a whole, it does not follow that it may not enshrine a grain of fact as applied to their Chief. The Rajputs in India, like the Normans in Europe, travelled far afield in their conquering excursions. In a country where history masquerades in the garb of legend there is nothing *prima facie* improbable in the conjecture that the story of the Bhanga-Kshatriyas may be really a mythological version of the true origin of the reigning family of Cooch Bihār. A Chief of the higher race ruling a people of the lower is a phenomenon too common to require explanation.

(4) A whole tribe of aborigines, or a section of a tribe, become gradually converted to Hinduism without, like the Rājbansis, abandoning their tribal designation. This is what has happened among the Bhūmij of Western Bengal. Here a pure Dravidian race have lost their original language and now speak only Bengali; they worship Hindu gods in addition to their own (the tendency being to relegate the tribal gods to the women) and the more advanced among them employ Brāhmans as family priests. They still retain a set of totemistic exogamous sub-divisions closely resembling those of the Mundas and the Santāls. But they are beginning to forget the totems which the names of the sub-divisions denote, and the names themselves will probably soon be abandoned in favour of more aristocratic designations. The tribe will then have become a caste in the full sense of the word, and will go on stripping itself of all customs likely to betray its true descent. The physical characteristics of its members will alone survive. With their transformation into a caste the Bhūmij will be more strictly endogamous than they were as a tribe, and even less likely to modify their physical type by intermarriage with other races.

Types of Caste.

By such processes as these, and by a variety of complex social influences whose working cannot be precisely traced, a number of types or varieties of caste have been formed which admit of being grouped as follows:—

(i) Tribal castes.

(*i*) *The tribal type*, where a tribe like the Bhūmij referred to above has insensibly been converted into a caste, preserving its original name and many of its characteristic customs, but modifying its animistic practices more and more in the direction of orthodox Hinduism and ordering its manner of life in accordance with the same model. Numerous instances of this process are to be found all over India; it has been at work for centuries and it has even been supposed that the Sudras of Indo-Aryan tradition were originally a Dravidian tribe which was thus incorporated into the social system of the conquering race. Considerations of space preclude me from attempting an exhaustive enumeration of the castes which may plausibly be described as tribes absorbed into Hinduism, but I may mention as illustrations of the transformation that has taken place, the Ahīr, Dom, and Dosādh of the United Provinces and Bihar; the Gūjar, Jāt, Meo, and Rajput of Rajputana and the Punjab; the Koli, Mahār, and Marātha of Bombay; the Bagdi, Bāuri, Chandāl (Nāmasudra), Kaibartta, Pod, and Rājbansi-Kochh of Bengal; and in Madras the Māl, Nāyar, Vellāla, and Paraiyan or Pariah, of whom the last retain traditions of a time when they possessed an independent organization of their own and had not been relegated to a low place in the Hindu social system.

(ii) Functional castes.

(*ii*) *The functional or occupational type* of caste is so numerous and so widely diffused and its characteristics are so prominent that community of function is ordinarily regarded as the chief factor in the evolution of caste. Whatever the original impulse may have been, it is a matter of observation at the present day not only that almost every caste professes to have a traditional occupation, though many of its members have abandoned it, but that the adoption of new occupations or of changes in the original occupation may give rise to sub-divisions of the caste which ultimately develop into entirely distinct castes. Thus among the large castes shown in the maps at the end of this volume the Ahīrs are by tradition herdsmen; the Brāhmans priests; the Chamārs and Mochis workers in leather; the Chuhras, Bhangis, and Doms scavengers; the Dosādhs village watchmen and messengers; the Goālas milkmen; the Kaibarttas and Kewats fishermen and cultivators; the Kāyasths writers; the Koiri and Kāchhi market gardeners; the Kumhārs potters; the Pods fishermen; and the Teli and Tili oil-pressers and traders. But the proportion of a caste that actually follows the traditional occupation may vary greatly. It is shown in the Bengal Census Report * that 80 per cent. of the Ahīrs in Bihar are engaged in agriculture; that of the Bengal Brāhmans only 17 per cent. and

* [*Census Report, Bengal*, 1901, vol i. p. 486.]

of the Bihar Brāhmans only 8 per cent. are engaged in religious functions; that not more than 8 per cent. of the Chamārs in Bihar live by working in leather, the remainder being cultivators or general labourers; that two-thirds of the Kāyasths in Bengal are agriculturists, and that only thirty-five per cent. of the Telis follow their traditional profession. A remarkable instance of the formation of a caste on the basis of distinctive occupation is supplied by the Garpagāri or hail-averter in the Marātha districts of the Central Provinces, a village servant whose duty it is to control the elements and protect the crops from the destructive hail-storms which are frequent in that part of India. For this, says Mr. Russell, "he receives a contribution from the cultivators; but in recent years an unavoidable scepticism as to his efficiency has tended to reduce his earnings. Mr. Fuller told me that on one occasion when he was hastening through the Chanda District on tour and pressed for time, the weather at one of his halting places looked threatening, and he feared that it would rain and delay the march. Among the villagers who came to see him was the local Garpagāri, and not wishing to neglect any chance he ordered him to take up his position outside the camp and keep off the rain. This the Garpagāri did, and watched through the night. In the event the rain held off, the camp moved, and that Garpagāri's reputation was established for life." * Changes of occupation in their turn, more especially among the lower castes, tend to bring about the formation of separate castes. The Sadgops of Bengal have within recent times taken to agriculture and broken away from the pastoral caste to which they originally belonged; the educated Kaibarttas and Pods are in course of separating themselves from their brethren who have not learnt English; the Madhunāpit are barbers who became confectioners; the Chāsadhobas washermen who took to agriculture. But perhaps the best illustration of the contagious influence of the fiction that differences of occupation imply a difference of blood is to be found in the list of Musalman castes enumerated by Mr. Gait in the Bengal Census Report of 1901.† This motley company includes the Abdāl of Northern and Eastern Bengal, who circumcise Muhammadan boys and castrate animals, while their women act as mid-wives; the Bhatiyāra or inn-keepers of Bihar; the butchers (Chik and Kasāi); the drummers (Nagārchi and Dafāli), of whom the latter exorcise evil spirits and avert

* *Census Report of the Central Provinces*, 1901, vol. i. p. 178.
† [Vol. i. p. 443 *et seq.*]

the evil eye by beating a drum (*daf*) and also officiates as priests at the marriages and funerals of people who are too poor to pay the regular Qāzi; the cotton-carders (Dhunia or Nadāf) numbering 200,000 in Bengal; the barbers (Hajjām or Turk-Nāia); the Jolāha weavers, cultivators, bookbinders, tailors, and dyers numbering nearly a quarter of a million in Bengal and nearly three millions in India; the oil-pressers (Kalu); the greengrocers (Kunjra); the embroiderers (Patwa), and a number of minor groups. All of these bodies are castes of the standard Hindu type with governing committees (*panchāyats* or *mātbars*) of their own who organize strikes and see that no member of the caste engages in a degrading occupation, works for lower wages than his brethren, eats forbidden food, or marries a woman of another caste. Breaches of these and various other unwritten ordinances are visited in the last resort by the extreme penalty of excommunication. This means that no one will eat or smoke with the offender, visit at his house, or marry his daughter, while in extreme cases he is deprived of the services of the barber and the washerman.

(iii) Sectarian castes.

(*iii*) *The sectarian type* comprises a small number of castes which commenced life as religious sects founded by philanthropic enthusiasts who, having evolved some metaphysical formula offering a speedier release from the *tædium vitæ* which oppresses the East, had further persuaded themselves that all men were equal, or at any rate that all believers in their teaching ought to be equal. As time went on the practical difficulties of realizing this ideal forced themselves upon the members of the sect; they found their company becoming unduly mixed; and they proceeded to reorganize themselves on the lines of an ordinary caste. A notable instance of this tendency to revert to the normal type of Hindu society is to be found in the present condition of the Lingāyat or Virshaiv caste of Bombay and Southern India, which numbers 2,900,000 adherents. Founded as a sect in the twelfth century by a reformer who proclaimed the doctrine of the equality of all who received the eightfold sacrament ordained by him and wore on their persons the mystic *phallus* emblematic of the god Siva, the Lingāyat community had begun by the close of the seventeenth century to develop endogamous sub-castes based upon the social distinctions which their founder had expressly abjured. At the recent Census the process of transforming the sect into a caste had advanced still further. In a petition presented to the Government of India the members of the Lingāyat community protested against the "most offensive and mischievous order" that all of them should be entered in the Census papers as belonging to the same caste, and asked that they might be recorded as Virshaiv Brāhmans, Kshatriyas, Vaisyas, or Sudras, as the case might be. It would be difficult to find a better illustration of the essentially particularist instinct of the Indian people, of the aversion with which they regard the doctrine that all men are equal, and of the growing attraction exercised by the aristocratic scheme of society which their ancient traditions enshrine. The legend of the four original castes may have no historical foundation, but there can be no question as to the spread of its influence or the strength of the sentiment which it inspires.

A somewhat similar case is that of the Sarāks of western Bengal, Chutia Nāgpur, and Orissa, who seem to be a Hinduized remnant of the early Jain people to whom local legends ascribe the ruined temples, the defaced images, and even the abandoned copper mines of that part of Bengal. Their name is a variant of Srāvaka (Sanskrit "hearer"), the designation of the Jain laity; they are strict vegetarians, never eating flesh, and on no account taking life, and if in preparing their food any mention is made of the word "cutting," the omen is deemed so disastrous that everything must be thrown away. In Orissa they call themselves Buddhists and assemble once a year at the famous cave temples of Khandagiri near Cuttack to make offerings to the Buddhist images there and to confer on religious matters. But these survivals of their ancient faith have not saved them from the all-pervading influence of caste. They have split up into endogamous groups based partly on locality and partly on the fact that some of them have taken to the degraded occupation of weaving, and they now form a Hindu caste of the ordinary type. The same fate has befallen the Gharbāri Atīths, the Sānnyāsi, the Jugis, the Jāti-Baishtams of Bengal, the Bānhra of Nepal—Newārs, who were originally Buddhist priests but abandoned celibacy and crystallized into a caste—and the Bishnois and Sādhs of the United Provinces. The Bishnois of Rohilkhand, says Mr. Burn,* are divided into nine endogamous groups of sub-castes "called after the castes from which they were recruited. New converts take their place in the appropriate sub-castes." In the case of the Sādhs "recruits are no longer admitted, and it is peculiar that no endogamous or exogamous divisions exist, the only restriction on marriage

* *Census Report of the United Provinces*, 1901, vol. i. p. 214.

being that intermarriage is forbidden between two families as long as the recollection of a former marriage connexion between them remains. The instance is of special interest as the quality maintained by the tenets of the sect; which has developed into a caste, has not yet been destroyed, as is usual in such cases." A still more remarkable, because a more modern, case is mentioned by Sir Henry Cotton, who states that "the more self-assertive portion of the Brahmo community" appears to be "in the course of forming" a new caste. All these curious developments serve to illustrate the comparatively insignificant part that religion has played in the shaping of the caste system, and the strength of the tendency to *morcellement*, to splitting up into fractional groups, that is characteristic of Hindu society. So long as the sectarian instinct confines itself to expressing a mere predilection for one god rather than another, or simply develops a new cult, however fantastic, which permits men to indulge in the luxury of religious eccentricity without quitting the narrow circle of their social environment, its operations are undisturbed and the sects which it forms may flourish and endure. But directly it invades the social sphere and seeks to unify and amalgamate groups of theoretically different origin it comes in contact with a force too strong for it and has to give way. Race dominates religion; sect is weaker than caste.

Even Christianity has not altogether escaped the subtle contagion of caste. Almost everywhere in India a tendency has been observed on the part of converts from Hinduism to group themselves according to the castes to which they originally belonged. This sometimes assumes the form of a division into two groups, the higher restricted to those who were members of the 'clean' castes from whom Brāhmans can take water, while the lower comprises all those of inferior rank. On the west coast the retention of caste distinctions was deliberately recognized by the Portuguese missionaries, and the results of this policy have survived down to the present day. The Indian Roman Catholic Christians of the Konkan, the low-lying strip of coast between the Western Ghāts and the sea, are divided into Bambans or Bammans (Brāhmans), Charodas or Chardos (Kshatriyas or Chhatris), Sudirs (Sudras), Renders (drawers of palm-juice), Gavids or Gavdas (salt-makers), Modvals (washermen), Kumbārs (potters), and Kāphris or Sidis (labourers), whose thick lips, slanting foreheads and curly beards suggest an infusion of Somali blood. Intermarriages among these groups, while not absolutely forbidden, are said to be rare, though in South Kanara such unions "are gradually becoming more frequent in cases in which members of castes other than the Bammans have succeeded in obtaining a good position in the official, legal, or commercial community." * Infant marriage is forbidden among the Konkani Christians, but girls are married as soon as they are twelve years old, and sometimes even before that age under a special dispensation from the Bishop. Widow marriage, though not forbidden, "is as much condemned as among the pagans." Many of them, especially the women, cannot bear the idea of eating beef, and they observe the characteristic Hindu prohibition against a wife addressing or speaking of her husband by his name. The marriage ceremony is performed in Church according to Christian rites, but it is preceded and followed by observances which are palpable survivals from the Hindu customs of betrothal and marriage. These include the formal bathing of the betrothed couple, the giving of a dinner to the poor for the benefit of the deceased ancestors of the family, the tying of a *tāli* or lucky necklace (which sometimes has a cross or a figure of the infant Jesus as a pendant) round the bride's neck, the exchange of presents, and the formal transfer of the bride to her husband's family.

Further south in the little State of Cochin on the Malabar coast, where Christianity has been established for many centuries and is believed by some authorities to date from apostolic times, a different principle has asserted itself. In the course of ages, disputes as to theological doctrine, ecclesiastical ritual, or spiritual supremacy have led to the formation among the non-Protestant Christians in Cochin of a number of sects—the Roman Catholics of the Latin rite, who use the Liturgy of the Romish Church in Latin, and are further subdivided into the Three Hundred, the Five Hundred, and the Seven Hundred, obscure schisms possibly derived merely from the number of families that were converted by the Portuguese missionaries on successive occasions; the Roman Catholics of the Syrian rite, who used the Romish Liturgy in ancient Syriac; the Chaldean Syrians, who are under the Patriarch

---

* *Manual of South Kanara.* J. Sturrock, I.C.S., 1894. *Vide* also *Bombay Gazetteer*, vol. xv., part i., 1883, p. 382; and *Indian Caste*, by Mr. J. A. Saldanha, 1904. [" Broadly speaking, it may be said that the Catholic Church tolerates, the Protestant Church condemns, this idea of caste. The practical outcome of the matter is that among high caste people the Roman Catholic Church alone has made appreciable progress." Some missionaries of that Church, however, dispute these conclusions, *Madras Census Report*, 1911, vol. i. p. 60 *et seq.*]

of Babylon, and differ in several minute points of ritual from the Romo-Syrians; the Jacobite Syrians, who are under the Patriarch of Antioch; and the Reformed or St. Thomas Syrians, an offshoot of the Jacobites who recognize the supremacy neither of the Pope nor of the Patriarch of Antioch and obey a Bishop of their own. These last have come to some extent under Protestant influence, and they insist upon the title of St. Thomas Syrians as marking their close adherence to the teaching and ritual of the apostolic age. They deny that the Bible should be interpreted by the traditions of the Church; they reject confession, absolution, fasting, the invocation of Saints, and the veneration of relics; they object to masses for the dead and dispute the doctrine of baptismal regeneration. Of these seven sects the first five appear to have crystallized into regular castes between the members of which no intermarriage is possible. The two branches of the Jacobite Syrians still intermarry, subject to a further distinction between residents of the northern and southern divisions of the State, the former of whom claim to be superior to the latter on the ground of their descent from the first colonists from Syria.*

(iv) Castes formed by crossing.

(*iv*) *Castes formed by crossing.*—Modern criticism has been especially active in its attacks on that portion of the traditional theory which derives the multitude of mixed or inferior castes from an intricate series of crosses between members of the original four. No one can examine the long lists which purport to illustrate the working of this process without being struck by much that is absurd and inconsistent. But in India it does not necessarily follow that, because the individual applications of a principle are ridiculous, the principle itself can have no foundation in fact. The last thing that would occur to the literary theorists of those times, or to their successors the *pandits* of to-day, would be to go back upon actual facts, and to seek by analysis and comparison to work out the true stages of evolution. They found, as I infer from plentiful experience of my own, the *a priori* method simpler and more congenial. That at least did not compel them to pollute their souls by the study of plebeian usage. Having once got hold of a formula, they insisted, like Thales and his contemporaries, on making it account for the entire order of things. Thus, castes which were compact tribes, castes which had been developed out of corporations like the mediæval trade guilds, and castes which expressed

* [C. Achyuta Menon, *The Cochin State Manual*, 1911, p. 217 *et seq.*]

the distinction between fishing and hunting, agriculture and handicrafts, were all supposed to have been evolved by interbreeding.

But the initial principle, though it could not be stretched to explain everything, nevertheless rests upon a residuum of historical fact. It happens that we can still observe its workings among a number of Dravidian tribes, which, though not yet drawn into the vortex of Brahmanism, have been in some degree affected by the example of Hindu organization. As regards inter-tribal marriages, they seem to be in a stage of development through which the Hindus themselves may have passed. A man may marry a woman of another tribe, but the offspring of such unions do not become members of either the paternal or maternal groups, but belong to a distinct endogamous aggregate, the name of which often denotes the precise cross by which it was started. Among the large tribe of Mūndās we find, for instance, nine such groups—Khāngār-Mūndā, Kharia-Mūndā, Konkpat-Mūndā, Karanga-Mūndā, Mahili-Mūndā, Nāgbansi-Mūndā, Orāon-Mūndā, Sad-Mūndā, Savar-Mūndā—descended from intermarriages between Mūndā men and women of other tribes.* The Mahilis again have five sub-tribes of this kind, and themselves trace their descent to the union of a Mūndā with a Santāl woman. Illustrations of this sort might be multiplied almost indefinitely. The point to be observed is that the sub-tribes formed by inter-tribal crossing are from an early stage complete endogamous units, and that they tend continually to sever their slender connexion with the parent group, and stand forth as independent tribes. As soon as this comes to pass, and a functional or territorial name disguises their mixed descent, the process by which they have been formed is seen to resemble closely that by which the standard Indian tradition seeks to explain the appearance of other castes alongside of the classical four.

Within the limits of the regular caste system Mr. Gait mentions the Shāgirdpeshās of Bengal as the only true caste in this Province "which takes its origin from miscegenation, and which is still adding to its numbers in the same way. Amongst the members of the higher castes of Orissa who do not allow widow remarriage, and also amongst the Kāyasth immigrants from Bengal, it is a common practice to take as maid-servants and concubines women belonging to the lower clean castes such as Chāsa and Bhandāri. The offspring of these

* [See Sarat Chandra Roy, *The Mundas and their Country*, 1912, p. 400 *et seq.*]

maid-servants are known as Shāgirdpeshā. They form a regular caste of the usual type and are divided into endogamous groups with reference to the caste of the male parent. Kāyasth Shāgirdpeshās will not intermarry with Karan Shāgirdpeshās, nor Rajput Shāgirdpeshās (their number is very small) with those of Kāyasth origin, but intermarriage between the Shāgirdpeshās of Karan and of Khandāit descent sometimes takes place, just as such marriages sometimes occur between persons belonging to the castes to which they owe their origin. The caste of the mother makes no difference in the rank of the children, but those who can count several generations from their original progenitor rank higher than those in whose case the stigma of illegitimacy is more recent.

"The word Shāgirdpeshā, which is commonly pronounced Sāgarpeshā, means servant, and is applied with reference to the traditional occupation, which is domestic service. It is said that the word should properly be confined to the offspring of Bengali Kāyasths, and that the illegitimate children of Karans and other castes of Orissa should be called Krishnapakshi, or Antarpuā, or, again, Antarkaran, Antarkhandāit, etc. This distinction, however, is not observed in practice. The relationship between the legitimate children of a man of good caste and their bastard brothers and sisters is recognized, but the latter cannot eat with the former, hence they are called *bhātāntar*, or separated by rice. They are entitled to maintenance, but cannot inherit their father's property so long as there are any legitimate heirs. They usually serve in their father's house until they grow up and marry; male children are then usually given a house and a few *bighas* of land for their support. The Shāgirdpeshās are also sometimes known as *Golām* (slave)—a term which is also applied to the Sudras of Eastern Bengal, who appear in several respects to be an analogous caste. Another appellation is *Kothā po* (own son), as distinguished from *Prajā po* (tenant son), which formerly denoted a purchased slave. Their family name is usually Singh or Dās. Some of them have taken to cultivation, but they will not themselves handle the plough. They usually live in great poverty. It is said to be impossible for a Shāgirdpeshā under any circumstances to obtain admission to his father's caste. If a man of that caste were to marry a Shāgirdpeshā woman he would be outcasted and his children would become Shāgirdpeshā. Persons of higher rank (usually outcasts) are admitted to the caste. A feast is given by the applicant for admission, and he is then formally acknowledged as a caste-fellow.

"In their social observances the Shāgirdpeshās follow the practices of the higher castes. They forbid the remarriage of widows and do not allow divorce. Polygamy is only permitted when good cause is shown, *e.g.*, if the first wife is barren or diseased. They belong to the Vaishnava sect, worship the ordinary Hindu gods, and employ good Brāhmans. The binding portion of the marriage ceremony is the joining of the hands of bride and bridegroom by the officiating priest. Shāgirdpeshās of the first generation, being illegitimate, cannot perform their father's *srādh*. They usually cremate their dead. In spite of their number (about 47,000) the caste is said to be of quite recent origin, and it is asserted that it did not exist a century and-a-half ago." *

An older and more instructive illustration, dating possibly from before the Christian era, of the formation of a caste by crossing, is furnished by the Khas of Nepal, who are the offspring of mixed marriages between Rajputs or Brāhman immigrants and the Mongolian women of the country. "The females," † says Hodgson, "would indeed welcome the polished Brāhmans to their embraces, but their offspring must not be stigmatized as the infamous progeny of a Brāhman and a Mlechha—must, on the contrary, be raised to eminence in the new order of things proposed to be introduced by their fathers. To this progeny also, then, the Brāhmans, in still greater defiance of their creed, communicated the rank of the second order of Hinduism; and from these two roots, mainly, sprung the now numerous, predominant, and extensively ramified tribe of the Khas, originally the name of a small clan of creedless barbarians, now the proud title of the Kshatriyas, or military order of the kingdom of Nepal. The offspring of original Khas females and of Brāhmans, with the honours and rank of the second order of Hinduism, got the patronymic titles of the first order, and hence the key to the anomalous nomenclature of so many *stirpes* of the military tribes of Nepal is to be sought in the nomenclature of the sacred order. It may be added, as remarkably illustrative of the lofty spirit of the *Parbattias*, that in spite of the yearly increasing sway of Hinduism in Nepal, and of the various attempts of the Brāhmans in high office to

* *Census Report, Bengal*, 1901, vol. i., p. 433, *et seq.*

† Essay on the Origin and Classification of the Military Tribes of Nepal, J. A. S. B., 1833, p. 217.

procure the abolition of a custom so radically opposed to the creed both parties now profess, the Khas still insist that the fruit of commerce (marriage is out of the question) between their females and males of the sacred order shall be ranked as Kshatriyas, wear the thread, and assume the patronymic title." The Khas now call themselves Chhattris or Kshatriyas—a practice which, according to Colonel Vansittart,* dates from Sir Jang Bahadur's visit to England in 1850. Allied to the Khas are the Ektharia and the Thākurs, both of Rajput parentage on the male side, the Thākur ranking higher because their ancestors are supposed to have been rulers of various petty States in Nepal. The Matwāla Khas, again, are the progeny of Khas men and Magar women, and the Uchai Thākurs are of the same lineage on the female side.

The Sūdra caste of Eastern Bengal, the Rājbansi Baruas of Chittagong, believed to be the offspring of Burmese fathers and Bengali mothers, the Vidurs of the Central Provinces, who claim Brāhman parentage on the male side and, though now marrying among themselves, still receive into their community the children of mixed unions between Brāhmans and women of other castes, are minor instances of the same process. The Boria caste of Assam is said by Mr. Allen † to comprise the offspring of Brāhman and Ganak widows and their descendants, and the children of Brāhmans who attained puberty before marriage, and so had to be married to men of lower caste. The name Boria is popularly derived from *bari*, a widow, but the members of the caste prefer to call themselves *Sut* or *Suta*, the Shastric designation of the children of a Brāhman woman by a Kshatriya, or Vaisya father. Borias are more numerous in Nowgong than in any other district of Assam, though the number of Brāhmans there is comparatively small. On pointing this out to an educated Brāhman of Nowgong, Mr. Allen received the singular explanation that "the Gosāins and Mohants of that district had put pressure upon householders to give away young Brāhman widows in marriage to men of lower castes to prevent the society from becoming demoralized."

(v) National castes.

(*v*) *Castes of the national type.*—Where there is neither nation nor national sentiment, it may seem paradoxical to talk about a national type of caste. There exist, however, certain groups, usually regarded as castes at the present day, which cherish traditions of bygone

* *Notes on Nepal*, 1896, p. 89.

† *Census Report of Assam*, 1901, vol. i., p. 124, *et seq.*

sovereignty and seem to preserve traces of an organization considerably more elaborate than that of an ordinary tribe. The Newārs, a mixed people of Mongoloid origin, who were the predominant race in Nepal proper until the country was conquered and annexed by the Gurkha Prithi Nārāyan in 1768, may be taken as an illustration of such a survival. The group comprises both Hindus and Buddhists. The latter are at present slightly more numerous, but the former are said to be gaining ground by more frequent conversions. The two communities are quite distinct, and each is divided into an elaborate series of castes. Thus, among the Hindu Newārs, we find at the top of the social scale the Devabhaja, who are Brāhmans and spiritual teachers; the Surjyabansi Mal, members of the old royal family; the Sreshta, consisting of ministers and other officials; and the Japu, who are cultivators. Then comes an intermediate group including, among others, the Awā, masons; the Kawmi, carpenters and sweetmeat-makers, an odd combination of trades; the Chhīpi, dyers of cloth; the Kāu, blacksmiths; and the Nāu, barbers. Lowest of all are the Pāsi, washermen; the Jugi, tailors and musicians; the Po, sweepers, burners of dead bodies, and executioners; and the Kulu, drummakers and curriers.

If the Marāthas can be described as a caste, their history and traditions certainly stamp them as a caste of the national type. They number five millions at the present census, 3,279,000 in Bombay, 1,538,000 in Hyderabad, 79,000 in Madras, 45,000 in Mysore, 93,000 in the Central Provinces and Berar, 28,000 in Central India. According to Mr. Enthoven,* the Bombay Marāthas "may be classified as a tribe with two divisions, Marātha and Marātha Kunbi, of which the former are hypergamous to the latter, but were not originally distinct. It remains to be explained that the Kunbis also consist of two divisions, Desh Kunbis numbering 1,900,000, and Konkani Kunbis, of which there are 350,000 recorded. Intermarriage between these divisions is not usual. The barrier, however, seems to be purely geographical. It may not withstand the altered conditions due to improvements in communications, and it is not apparently based on any religious prohibition of intermarriages. The fact that the Kunbis consist of two branches must, however, be borne in mind in attempting to arrive at a correct description of the tribal configuration." The highest class of Marāthas is supposed to consist of

* *Census Report of Bombay*, 1901, vol. i., p. 183, *et seq.*

ninety-six families, who profess to be of Rajput descent and to represent the Kshatriyas of the traditional system. They wear the sacred thread, marry their daughters before puberty, and forbid widows to marry again. But their claim to kinship with the Rajput is effectually refuted by the anthropometric data now published, and by the survival among them of *kuldevaks* or totems, such as the sun-flower, the *kadamba* tree (*Nauclea Kadamba*), the mango, the conch-shell, the peacock's feather, and turmeric, which are worshipped at marriages and at the ceremony of dedicating a new house, while their close connexion with the Kunbis is attested by the fact that they take Kunbi girls as wives, though they do not give their own daughters to Kunbi men. A wealthy Kunbi, however, occasionally gains promotion to and marries into the higher grade and claims brevet rank as a Kshatriya. The fact seems to be that the ninety-six superior families represent Kunbis who came to the front during the decline of the Moghal Empire, won for themselves princedoms or estates, claimed the rank of landed gentry, and asserted their dignity by refusing their daughters to their less distinguished brethren.

(vi) Castes formed by migration.

(*vi*) *Castes formed by migration.*—If members of a caste leave their original habitat and settle permanently in another part of India, the tendency is for them to be separated from the parent group and to develop into a distinct caste. The stages of the process are readily traced. In the first instance it is assumed that people who go and live in foreign parts must of necessity eat forbidden food, worship alien gods, and enter into relations with strange women. Consequently, when they wish to take wives from among their own people, they find that their social status has been lowered, and that they have to pay for the privilege of marrying within the parent group. This luxury grows more and more expensive, and in course of time the emigrants marry only among themselves and thus become a sub-caste usually distinguished by a territorial name, such as Jaunpuria, Tirhutia, Bārendra, and the like. Mr. Gait has pointed out that "the prolonged residence of persons of Bihar castes in Bengal generally results in their being placed under a ban as regards marriage," * and I had observed some years earlier that up-country barbers who settle in Bengal are called *khotta* and practically form a separate subcaste, as Bengali barbers will not intermarry with them, while they are regarded as impure by the barbers of Upper India and

* [*Census Report*, *Bengal*, 1901, vol. i., p. 355 *note*.]

Bihar by reason of their having taken up their residence in Bengal. If the process of differentiation is carried a step further (as indeed usually happened before the potent influence of railways had made itself felt), and the settlers assume a distinctive caste-name, all traces of their original affinities disappear and there remains only a dim tradition of their migration "from the West," the quarter whence, in Bengal at any rate, promotion is believed to come. Owing to this loss of identity the number of instances in which we can point with certainty to the formation of castes by migration is comparatively small. Mr. Russell, writing of the Central Provinces, tells us how a native gentleman said to him, in speaking of his people, that "when a few families of Khedāwal Brāhmans from Gujarat first settled in Damoh, they had the greatest difficulty in arranging their marriages. They could not marry with their caste-fellows in Gujarat, because their sons and daughters could not 'establish themselves,' that is, could not prove their identity as Khedāwāl Brāhmans; but since the railway has been opened, intermarriages take place freely with other Khedāwāls in Gujarat and Benares." * So the geographical isolation of Chhattisgarh, the country of the "thirty-six forts" of the Haihaibansi dynasty of Ratanpur, has led to the social isolation of the inhabitants. "The Chhattisgarhi Brāhmans," says Mr. Russell, "form a class apart, and up-country Brāhmans will have nothing to do with them." The contempt in which the people of this tract are held by their neighbours, finds expression in the following depreciatory verses:

Wah hai Chhattisgarhi desh,
Jahān Gond hai naresh,
Niche bursi upar khāt,
Lagā hai chongi kā thāt,
Pahile jutā pichhe bāt,
Tab āwe Chhattisgarhi hāt.

Which may be rendered thus :—

"This is Chhattisgarh, where the Gond is king of the jungle,
Under his bed is a fire, for he cannot pay for a blanket;
Nor for a hookah indeed,—a leaf-pipe holds his tobacco.
Kick him soundly first and then he will do what you tell him." †

The verses reflect the intolérant and domineering attitude of the Indo-Aryan towards the Dravidian, of the high-caste man towards the low, that has been characteristic of Indian society from the earliest times down to the present day.

* [*Census Report*, *Central Provinces*, 1901, vol. i., p. 156.]
† [*Ibid.*, p. 147.]

A good illustration of the formation of a caste by migration is to be found in the traditions of the Nambudri or Namputiri Brāhmans of Malabar. These Brāhmans claim to have come to the west coast from various sacred localities in Kathiawar and the northern Deccan; Mr. Fawcett describes them as "the truest Aryans in Southern India;" * and their complexion and features seem to lend some support to the tradition which assigns to them a foreign origin. Whatever their original stock may have been, they are now an entirely separate caste differing from the Brāhmans of other parts of India by their systematic practice of polygamy; by their rejection of infant marriage; by their restriction of marriage to the eldest son, the other brothers entering into polyandrous relations with Nāyar women; and by the curious custom of ceremonial fishing which forms part of their marriage ritual. Another instance of the same process is furnished by the Rārhi Brāhmans of Bengal. The current legend is that early in the eleventh century A.D., Adisura or Adisvara, Raja of Bengal, finding the Brāhmans then settled in his dominions too ignorant to perform for him certain Vedic ceremonies, applied to the Raja of Kanauj for priests conversant with the sacred ritual of the Aryans. In answer to his request there were sent to him five Brāhmans of Kanauj, one of them a son of the Raja, who brought with them their wives, their sacred fire, and their sacrificial implements. It is said that Adisura was at first disposed to treat them with scanty respect, but he was soon compelled to acknowledge his mistake and to make terms with people who had a monopoly o the magical powers associated with the correct performance of ancient ritual. He then made over to them five populous villages, the number of which was subsequently increased to fifty-six. The tradition seems to chronicle an early *brahmottar* grant, the first perhaps of the long series of similar transactions that has played so important a part in the history of land tenures, in the development of caste influence and custom, and in promoting the spread of orthodox Hinduism throughout Bengal. Adisura did what the Rajas of outlying and unorthodox tracts of country (such as Bengal was in the eleventh century) have constantly done since and are doing still. A local chief, far removed from the great centres of Brahmanical lore, somehow becomes aware of his ceremonial shortcomings. In many cases, as indeed is narrated of Adisura himself, a wandering priest brings home to him that his outlandish ritual

* [*Bulletin Madras Government Museum*, vol. iii. part i., p. 33.]

is not up to the orthodox standard. He sends for Brāhmans, gives them grants of land near his own residence, and proceeds at their dictation to reform his ways on the model of the devout kings whom Brahmanical literature holds up as the ideal for a Raja to follow. The Brāhmans find for him a pedigree of respectable antiquity and provide him with a family legend, and in course of time, by dint of money and diplomacy, he succeeds in getting himself recognized as a member of the local Rajput community. But that does not mean that the real Rajputs will acknowledge his pretensions; nor will Brāhmans who have attached themselves to his fortunes retain their status among the community from which they have broken off. It will be said of them, as is said of the Brāhman immigrants into Bengal, that they have married local women, eaten forbidden food, adopted strange customs, and forgotten the endless details of the elaborate ritual which they set forth to teach. As priests *in partibus infidelium* they will be regarded with suspicion by the Brāhmans of their original stock; they will have to pay high for brides from among their own people, and eventually will be cut off altogether from the *jus connubii.* When that stage has been reached they will have become to all intents and purposes a separate caste retaining the generic name of Brāhman, but forming a new species and presenting a distinctive type. And this great change will have been brought about by the simple fact of their abandoning the habitat of their original community.

Occasionally it may happen that social promotion, rather than degradation, results from a change of residence. In Chanda, a remote district of the Central Provinces, a number of persons returned themselves as Barwaiks and the designation, being unknown in the Census office, was referred to the district officer for explanation. It was stated in reply that the Barwaiks were a clan of Rajputs from Orissa who had come to Nāgpur in the train of the Bhonsla Rajas and had taken military service under them. Now in Chutia Nāgpur the Baraiks or Chik-Baraiks are a sub-caste of the Pans—the helot weavers and basketmakers who perform a variety of servile functions for the organized Dravidian tribes and used to live in a kind of Ghetto in the villages of the Kandhs (Khonds) for whom they purveyed children destined for human sacrifice and, when they had failed to steal other people's children, sold their own for this ghastly purpose. Mr. Russell observes that "though it is possible that the coincidence may be accidental, still there seems good reason to fear that it is from these humble beginnings that the Barwaik sept of Rajputs in Chanda must trace its extraction. And it is clear that before the days of railways and the half-anna post an imposture of this sort must have been practically impossible of detection." * The conjecture seems a plausible one, and the fact that Baraik is a title actually in use among the Jadubansi Rajputs may have helped the Pans to establish their fictitious rank.

(vii) Castes formed by changes of customs.

(*vii*) *Castes formed by changes of custom.*—The formation of new castes as a consequence of the neglect of established usage or the adoption of new ceremonial practices or secular occupations has been a familiar incident of the caste system from the earliest times. We are told in Manu † how men of the three twice-born castes, who have not received the sacrament of initiation at the proper time, or who follow forbidden occupations, become Vrātyas or outcasts, intercourse with whom is punished with a double fine, and whose descendants are graded as distinct castes. Living as a Vrātya is a condition involving of itself exclusion from the original caste, and a Brāhman who performs sacrifices for such persons has to do penance. The idea of such changes of status is inherent in the system, and illustrations of its application are plentiful. Sometimes it figures in the traditions of a caste under the form of a claim to a more distinguished origin than is admitted by current opinion. The Skanda Purana, for example, recounts an episode in Parasu Rāma's raid upon the Kshatriyas, the object of which is to show that the Kāyasths are by birth Kshatriyas of full blood, who by reason of their observing the ceremonies of the Sudras are called Vrātya or incomplete Kshatriyas. The Bābhans or Bhuinhārs of the United Provinces and Bihar are supposed, according to some legends, to be Brāhmans who lost status by taking to agriculture, and the Mongoloid Kochh of Northern Bengal describe themselves as Rājbansis, or as Vrātya or Bhanga (broken) Kshatriyas—a designation which enables them to pose as an outlying branch of that exalted community who fled to these remote districts before the wrath of Parasu Rāma, and there allowed their characteristic observances to fall into disuse. At the present day the most potent influence in bringing about elevations or depressions of social status which may result ultimately in the formation of new castes is the practice of

* [*Census Report, Central Provinces*, 1901, vol. i., p. 157.]

† [*Laws*, ii. 39, x. 20, xi. 63.]

widow marriage. With the advance of orthodox ideas that may plausibly be ascribed to the extension of railways and the diffusion of primary education it dawns upon some members of a particular caste that the custom of marrying widows is highly reprehensible, and with the assistance of their Brāhmans they set to work to discourage it. The first step is to abstain from intermarriage with people who practise the forbidden thing, and thus to form a sub-caste which adopts a high-sounding name derived from some famous locality like Ajodhya or Kanauj, or describes itself as *Biyāhut* or *Behutā*, "the married ones," by way of emphasizing the orthodox character of their matrimonial arrangements. Thus the Awadhia or Ayodhya Kurmis of Bihar and the Kanaujia Kurmis of the United Provinces pride themselves on prohibiting the remarriage of widows and are endeavouring to establish a shadowy title to be recognized as some variety of Kshatriya, in pursuance of which, with singular ignorance of the humble origin of the great Marātha houses, they claim kinship with Sivaji, Sindhia and the Bhonsla family of Nāgpur. In Bihar they have succeeded in attaining a higher rank than ordinary Kurmis. Brāhmans take water from their hands; the funeral ceremony is performed on the twelfth day after death, according to the custom of the higher castes; and *kachchi* food prepared by them is eaten by Kahārs, Bhāts, and other castes who would refuse to accept food of this kind from Sudras. They have abandoned domestic service, and the wealthier members of the group exchange presents with the higher castes and are invited by them to ceremonial functions. But although the Awadhias have achieved complete practical separation from the main body of Kurmis no one accepts them as Kshatriyas or Rajputs, nor are they recognized by Hindu public opinion as forming a distinct caste. In the Punjab Sir Denzil Ibbetson* wrote in 1881 that the Gaurwa Rajputs of Gurgaon and Delhi, though retaining the title of Rajput in deference to the strength of caste-feeling and because the change in their customs was then too recent for the name to have fallen into disuse, yet had, for all purposes of equality, communion, or intermarriage, ceased to be Rajputs since they took to *karewa* or widow marriage. And the distinction between the Jāts and Rajputs, both sprung from a common Indo-Aryan stock, is marked by the fact that the former practise and the latter abstain from a usage which more than any other is regarded as a crucial test of relative social position.

* [*Census Report*, 1881, para. 446.]

In allusion to this fact one of the rhyming proverbs of the Punjab makes a Jāt father say—"Come, my daughter, and be married; if this husband dies there are plenty more." The same test applies in the Kāngra Hills, the most exclusive Hindu portion of the Punjab, where Musalman domination was never fully established, and the Brāhman and Kshatriya occupy positions most nearly resembling those assigned to them by Manu. Here the line between the Thakkar and Rāthi castes, both belonging to the lower classes of Hill Rajputs, is said to consist in the fact that Rāthis do and Thakkars do not ordinarily practise widow marriage.

In Southern India movements of the same sort may be observed. Among the begging castes which form nearly one per cent. of the population of the Tamil country in Madras, the Pandārams rank highest in virtue of their abstention from meat and alcohol and more especially of their prohibition of widow marriage. The Pancharamkatti division of the Idaiyan shepherd caste allow widow marriage but connect it with the peculiar neck ornament which their women wear, and say that "Krishna used to place a similar ornament round the necks of the Idaiyan widows of whom he was enamoured, to transform them from widows into married women to whom pleasure was not forbidden." * The story seems to be an *ex post facto* apology for the practice. The Jātāpu again, a branch of the Kandh (Kondh) tribe which has developed into a separate caste, are beginning to discourage widow marriage by way of emphasizing the distinction between themselves and their less civilized brethren.† In Baroda, according to Mr. Dalāl,‡ widow marriage is allowed by some degraded sub-castes of Brāhmans, Tapodhan, Vyās Sārasvat, Rajgor, Bhojak, Tragala and Koligor, which are virtually distinct castes, and also by the Kāthis, Marāthas, Rajputs, Tāghers, and Vadhels. "The higher families, among castes allowing remarriage of widows, do not, as a rule, have recourse to it, as such a marriage is considered undignified for grown-up women. It is this sense of honour and a desire to pass for superior people which has put a stop to widow remarriage among an influential section of the Lewa Kunbis and Sonis."

An account is given in the chapter on marriage and caste of what may be called the internal structure of tribes and caste

---

* [*Census Report, Madras*, 1901, vol. i., p. 155.]
† [*Ibid.*, vol. i., p. 157.]
‡ [*Census Report, Baroda*, 1901, vol. i., p. 491.]

in India—the various endogamous, exogamous, and hypergamous divisions which restrict and regulate matrimony and form the minor wheels of the vast and intricate machinery by which Hindu society is controlled. From the point of view of general ethnology considerable interest attaches to one particular kind of division, to those exogamous groups which are based upon totems. The existence of totemism in India on a large scale has been brought to notice only in recent years: the enquiries instituted in connexion with the census have added materially to our knowledge of the subject; and special attention is being given to it in the ethnographic survey now being conducted in all British provinces and the more important Native States. No apology therefore is needed for mentioning it at length here, since it throws an important sidelight on the development of castes from tribes. At the bottom of the social system, as understood by the average Hindu, we find in the Dravidian region of India a large body of tribes and castes each of which is broken up into a number of totemistic septs. Each sept bears the name of an animal, a tree, a plant, or of some material object, natural or artificial, which the members of that sept are prohibited from killing, eating, cutting, burning, carrying, using, etc. Well-defined groups of this type are found among the Dravidian Santāls and Orāons, both of whom still retain their original language, worship non-Aryan gods, and have a fairly compact tribal organization. The following are specimens selected from among the seventy-three Orāon and the ninety-one Santāl septs:—

Totemism.

Orāon.		Santāl.	
Name of sept.	*Totem.*	*Name of sept.*	*Totem.*
Tirki.	Young mice.	Ergo.	Rat.
Ekka.	Tortoise.	Murmu.	Nilgāi.
Kispotta.	Pig's entrails.	Hānsdā.	Wild goose.
Lakra.	Hyena.	Mārudi.	A kind of grass.
Bāgh.	Tiger.	Besrā.	Hawk.
Kujrar.	Oil from *Kujrar* tree.	Hemron.	Betel palm.
		Saren	The constellation Pleiades.
Gede.	Duck.		
Khoepa.	Wild dog.	Sankh.	Conch-shell.
Minji.	Eel.	Guā.	Areca nut.
Chirra.	Squirrel.	Kārā.	Buffalo.

The Hos of Singhbhum and the Mūndās of the Chutia Nāgpur plateau have also exogamous septs of the same type as the Orāons and Santāls, with similar rules as to the totem being taboo to the members of the group. The lists given in

The Tribes and Castes of Bengal contain the names of 323 Mūndā septs and 46 Ho septs. Six of the latter are found also among the Santāls. The other Ho septs appear to be mostly of the local or communal type, such as are in use among the Kandhs,* but this is not quite certain, and the point needs looking into by some one well acquainted with the Ho dialect, who would probably find little difficulty in identifying the names, as the tribe is known to be in the habit of giving to places descriptive names having reference to their natural characteristics. Nearly all the Mūndā sept names are of the totem type, and the characteristic taboos appear to be recognized. The Tarwār or Talwār sept, for example, may not touch a sword, the Udbāru may not use the oil of a particular tree, the Sindur may not use vermilion, the Baghela may not kill or eat a quail, and, strangest of all, rice is taboo to the Dhān sept, the members of which, though rice is grown all round them, must supply its place with *gondli* or millet. It is difficult not to be sceptical as to the rigid observance of this last prohibition.

In Chutia Nāgpur.

A step higher in the social scale, according to Hindu estimation, the Bhūmij of Mānbhum mark an early stage in the course of development by which a non-Aryan tribe transforms itself into a full-blown caste, claiming a definite rank in the Brahmanical system. With the exception of a few residents of outlying villages bordering on the Mūndā country of the Chutia Nāgpur plateau, the Bhūmij have lost their original language (Mūndāri), and now speak only Bengali. They worship Hindu gods in addition to the fetishistic deities more or less common to them and other Dravidians, but the tendency is to keep the latter rather in the background and to relegate the less formidable among them to the women and children to be worshipped in a hole-and-corner kind of way, with the assistance of a tribal hedge-priest (*Lāyā*), who is supposed to be specially acquainted with their ways. Some of the leading men of the tribe, who call themselves Bhuinhārs, and hold large landed tenures on terms of police service, have set up as Rajputs, and keep a low class of Brāhmans as their family priests. They have, as a rule, borrowed the Rajput class titles, but cannot conform with the Rajput rules of intermarriage, and marry within a narrow circle of pseudo-Rajputs like themselves. The rest of the tribe, numbering at the census of 1901, 370,239, are

* [For Kandh totemism, see J. E. Friend-Pareira, *Totemism among the Khonds*, *Journal Asiatic Society, Bengal*, vol. lxxiii., part iii., 1905, p. 40 *et seq.*]

divided into a number of exogamous groups, of which the following are examples. It is curious to observe in a tribe still in a state of transition, that one of the Brahmanical *gotras*, Sāndilya, has been borrowed from the higher castes, and in the process of borrowing has been transformed from a Vedic saint into a bird:—

BHŪMIJ.

Name of sept.	*Totem.*
Sālrisi.	*Sāl* fish.
Hānsda.	Wild goose.
Leng.	Mushroom.
Sāndilya.	A bird.
Hemron.	Betel palm.
Tumarung.	Pumpkin.
Nāg.	Snake.

At a further stage in the same process of evolution, and on a slightly superior social level, we find the Mahilis, Korās, and Kurmis, all of whom claim to be members of the Hindu community. They have totemistic exogamous sections, of which the following are fairly representative:—

MAHILI.		KORĀ.	
Name of section.	*Totem.*	*Name of section.*	*Totem.*
Dungri.	*Dumur* fig.	Kasyab.	Tortoise.
Turu.	*Turu* grass.	Saulā.	*Sāl* fish.
Kānti.	Ear of any animal.	Kāsibak.	Heron.
		Hānsda.	Wild goose.
Hānsda.	Wild goose.	Butku.	Pig.
Murmu.	Nīlgāi.	Sāmpu.	Bull.

KURMI.

Name of section.	*Totem.*
Kesariā.	*Kesar* grass.
Tarār.	Buffalo.
Dumuriā.	*Dumur* fig.
Chonchmukruār.	Spider.
Hastowār.	Tortoise.
Jālbanuār.	Net.
Sankhowār.	Shell ornaments.
Bāghbanuār.	Tiger.
Katiār.	Silk cloth.

Of these three castes the Mahilis appear to have broken off most recently from the tribe. They still worship some of the Santāl gods in addition to the standard Hindu deities; they will eat food cooked by a Santāl; their caste organization is supervised, like that of the Santāls, by an official bearing the title of Parganāit; they permit the marriage of adults and tolerate sexual intercourse before marriage within the limits of the caste; and they have not yet attained to the dignity of employing Brāhmans for ceremonial purposes. If I may hazard a conjecture on so obscure a question, I should be inclined to class them as Santāls who took to the degraded occupation of basket-making, and thus lost the *jus connubii* within the tribe. In the case of the Korās there is no clue to warrant their affiliation to any particular tribe, but their traditions say that they came from the Chutia Nāgpur plateau, while their name suggests a Dravidian origin, and it seems possible that they may be an offshoot of the Mūndās, who somehow sank from the status of independent cultivators to their present position of earth-cutting and tank-digging labourers. They allow adult marriage, their standard of feminine chastity is low, and they have not yet fitted themselves out with Brāhmans. In the customary rules of inheritance which their *panchāyat* or caste council administers, it is curious to find the usage known in the Punjab as *chundavand*, by which the sons, however few, of one wife take a share equal to that of the sons, however many, of another. The Kurmis may perhaps be a Hinduized branch of the Santāls. The latter, who are more particular about food, or rather about whom they eat with, than is commonly supposed, will eat cooked rice with the Kurmis, and according to one tradition regard them as elder brothers of their own. However this may be, the totemism of the Kurmis of Western Bengal stamps them as of Dravidian descent, and clearly distinguishes them from the Kurmis of Bihar and the United Provinces. They show signs of a leaning towards orthodox Hinduism, and employ Brāhmans for the worship of Hindu gods, but not in the propitiation of rural and family deities or in their marriage ceremonies.

In Orissa.

One more instance of totemism in Bengal deserves special notice here, as it shows the usage maintaining its ground among people of far higher social standing than any of the castes already mentioned. The Kumhārs of Orissa take rank immediately below the Karan or writer caste, and thus have only two or three large castes above them. They are divided into two endogamous sub-castes—Jagannāthi or Oriya Kumhārs, who work standing and make large earthen pots, and Khattya Kumhārs, who turn the wheel sitting and make small earthen pots, cups, toys, etc. The latter are immigrants from Upper India, whose number is comparatively insignificant. For matrimonial purposes the

Jagannāthi Kumhārs are subdivided into the following exogamous sections:—

JAGANNĀTHI KUMHĀR.

Name of section.	*Totem.*
Kaundinya.	Tiger.
Sarpa.	Snake.
Neul.	Weasel.
Goru.	Cow.
Mudir.	Frog.
Bhadbhadria,	Sparrow.
Kurmā.	Tortoise.

The members of each section express their respect for the animal whose name the section bears by refraining from killing or injuring it, and by bowing when they meet it. The entire caste also abstain from eating, and even go so far as to worship the *sāl* fish, because the rings on its scales resemble the wheel which is the symbol of the potter's art. The Khattya Kumhārs have only one section (Kasyapa), and thus, like the Rājbansis of Rangpur, are really endogamous in spite of themselves. The reason, no doubt, is that there are too few of them in Orissa to fit up a proper exogamous system, and they content themselves with the pretence of one. Both sub-castes appear to be conscious that the names of their sections are open to misconception, and explain that they are really the names of certain saints who, being present at Daksha's horse sacrifice, transformed themselves into animals to escape the wrath of Siva, whom Daksha, like Peleus in the Greek myth, had neglected to invite.* It may well be that we owe the preservation of these interesting totemistic groups to the ingenuity of the person who devised this respectable means of accounting for a series of names so likely to compromise the reputation of the caste. In the case of the Khattya Kumhārs, the fact that their single section bears the name of Kasyapa, while they venerate the tortoise (*kachhap*), and tell an odd story by way of apology for the practice, may perhaps lend weight to the conjecture, in itself a fairly plausible one, that many of the lower castes in Bengal who are beginning to set up as pure Hindus have taken advantage of the resemblance in sound between *Kachhap* and *Kasyap* (*chh* and *s* both become *sh* in colloquial Bengali) to convert a totemistic title into an eponymous one, and have gone on to borrow such other Brahmanical *gotras* as seemed to them desirable. If, for example, we analyze the matrimonial arrangements of the

* Muir, *Original Sanskrit Texts*, IV. p. 872.

Bhars of Mānbhum, many of whom are the hereditary personal servants of the pseudo-Rajput Raja of Pachete, we find the foregoing conjecture borne out by the fact that two out of the seven sections which they recognize are called after the peacock and the *bel* fruit, while the rest are eponymous. But this is an exceptionally clear case of survival, and I fear it is hardly possible to simplify the diagnosis of non-Aryan castes by laying down a general rule, that all castes with a section bearing the name Kasyapa who have not demonstrably borrowed that appellation from the Brāhmans, are probably offshoots from some non-Aryan tribe.

In the Bombay Presidency the Kātkaris of the Konkan will not kill a red-faced monkey,* the Vaidus, or herbalists of Poona will not kill a rabbit, and the Vadars whose name is derived from the *Vad* (*Ficus Indica*), will not fell the Indian fig tree. The totemistic character of the septs which regulate marriage is, however, most pronounced in the Kanara district which borders on the Dravidian tract of the South. The rice-growing caste of Hālvakki Vakkal † in Kanara have a number of exogamous septs or *bali* (lit. a creeper) which include the tortoise, the sāmbhar, the monkey, the hog-deer, two sorts of fish, saffron, the acacia and several other trees, and the axe used for felling them. As we find them now, these groups are plainly totemistic. Thus the members of the screw-pine *bali* will neither cut the tree nor pluck its flowers, and those of the *Bargal bali* will not kill or eat the *barga* or mouse-deer. The followers of the *Shirin bali*, named after the *shirkal* tree (*Acacia speciosa*), will not sit in the shade of the tree, and refrain from injuring it in any way. But in Kanara, as in Orissa, there is a tendency to disguise or get rid of these compromising designations as the people who own them rise in the social scale. The Halepāik,‡ once free-booters and now peaceful tappers of toddy trees, are divided into two endogamous groups, one dwelling on the coast and taking its name (*Tengina*) from the cocoanut tree, and the other living in the hills and calling itself *Bainu* after the sago-palm. Each of these again contains a number of exogamous *balis*. The *Tengina* have the wolf, the pig, the porcupine, the root of the pepper plant, turmeric, and the river; to which the *Bainu*

In Bombay.

[* *Ethnographic Survey, Bombay*, No. 134, 1909, pp. 1, 12; *Census Report, Bombay*, 1911, vol. i, p. 269.]

[† *Bombay Census Report*, 1911, vol. i., p. 263.]

[‡ *Ethnographic Survey, Bombay*, No. 12, 1904, p. 2 *et seq.*]

add the snake, the sāmbhar deer, and gold. The members of the *Nāgchampa* group will not wear the flower of that name in their hair, nor will the *Kadave bali* kill a sāmbhar. Two of the *balis* are called after the low castes Mahār and Hole, and it is curious to find that the other groups, though they will take girls from these *balis*, will not give them their own daughters to wife. Among the Halepāiks, unlike most of the Kanara castes, the *bali* descends through the female line, that is to say, the children belong to the *bali* of the mother, not of the father. Similar groups are found among the Suppalig (musicians), the Āger (salt workers and makers of palm-leaf umbrellas), the Ahīr (cowherds), and the Mukur (labourers and makers of shell-lime). Several of these have the elephant for a totem and may not wear ornaments of ivory.

Among the Bhīls of the Sātpura hills, who may be taken to represent the furthest extension westward of the Dravidian type, Major Luard * has discovered forty-one septs, all of which are exogamous. Where two distinct septs have the same totem intermarriage is prohibited. All the septs revere and refrain from injuring or using their totems, and make a formal obeisance when meeting or passing them, while the women veil their faces. Among the totems are moths (*ava*), snakes, tigers, bamboos, *pīpal* and other trees, and a kind of creeper called *gaola* on which the members may not tread, and if they do so accidentally must apologize by making a *salaam*. The *Maoli* sept have as their totem a sort of basket (*kiliya*) for carrying grain which they are forbidden to use. The basket resembles in shape the shrine of the goddess of a certain hill where women may not worship. The *Mori* or peacock sept may not knowingly tread on the tracks of a peacock, and if a woman sees a peacock she must veil her face or look away. The cult of the totem consists in seeking for the footprint of a peacock in the jungle and making a *salaam* to it. The ground is then made smooth round the footprint, a *svāstika* is inscribed in the dust, and offerings of grain are deposited on a piece of red cloth. The *Sanyar* sept worship the cat, but consider it unlucky for their totem to enter their houses and usually keep a dog tied up at the door to frighten it away. The Khangār caste of Bundelkhand, which is cited by Major Luard as an illustration of the conversion of a tribe into a caste, have among their totems horses, iguanas, snakes, cows, elephants, alligators, rice,

In Central India.

[* *Census Report*, *Central India*, 1901, p. 198 *et seq.*]

turmeric, various trees and shrubs, and bricks. The members of the *Īnt* or brick sept may not use bricks in their houses and their domestic architecture is restricted to wattle and mud. The report on the census of Central India also contains a curious instance of the apparent degradation of a caste into a tribe accompanied by the adoption of totems. The Sondhiās or Sundhiās of Malwa are said to be descended from the survivors of a Rajput army who were defeated by Shah Jahan and were ashamed to return to their homes. They therefore stayed in Malwa, married Sondhiā women, borrowed some of the Sondhiā totems and the Sondhiā gods, and in course of time allowed widows to marry again. Ten of the twenty-four septs into which the tribe is divided still cherish traditions of their Rajput origin and, while taking wives from the other septs, refuse to give their daughters in return.

In the Central Provinces.

For the Central Provinces Mr. Russell * gives a long list of totems found among sixteen castes and tribes, including not only the primitive Gonds, Korkus, and Orāons, and the leather-working Chamārs, but also the pastoral Ahīrs, the respectable carpenter caste (Barhai) and the Dhīmars, from all of whom Brāhmans can take water, while the last named are commonly employed by them as personal servants. The list comprises elephants, lions, tigers, bears, wolves, jackals, buffaloes, goats, monkeys, peacocks, parrots, crocodiles, lizards, tortoises, porcupines, scorpions, snakes, also salt, rice, Indian corn, pumpkins, mangoes, cucumbers, lotus leaves, vermilion and a variety of trees. All of these are regarded with reverence, and members of the sept abstain from killing, using or naming them.

In Madras.

In Madras the Boya *shikāri* tribe of the Deccan is divided into 101 totemistic septs, among them *chimalu*, ants; *eddulu*, bulls; *jenneru*, sweet-scented oleander; *jerrabutula*, centipedes; *yenumalu*, buffaloes; and *kusa*, grass. The Jātapu, the civilized division of the Kandhs or Khonds, have among their totems *koaloka*, arrows; *kondacorri*, hill sheep; *kutraki*, wild goats; and *vinka*, white ants. The large agricultural caste of Kapu, numbering nearly three millions, have among their exogamous sections the cock (*kodi*), the sheep (*mekala*), and a shrub known as *tangedu* (*Cassia auriculata*). Of the 102 sections of the trading Komatis six are totemistic, the totems including the tamarind, the *tulsi*

[* *Census Report, Central Provinces*, 1901, vol. i. p. 189 *et seq.*]

(*Ocymum Sanctum*), and the betel vine. The weaving Kurnis count among their totems saffron, gold, cummin, gram, pepper, buffaloes, and certain trees.*

In Assam the Gāros have monkeys, horses, bears, mice, lizards, frogs, crows, pumpkins, and a number of trees among their totems; the Kachāris recognize as totems the tree snail, the *muga* insect, the sesamum plant, the *kumra* or giant gourd, and the tiger. Members of the tiger sept have to throw away their earthenware utensils by way of atonement when a tiger is killed. The louse and the buffalo are the only animal totems on record among the Khāsi; the Kuki have the dog; the Lalung eggs, fish, and pumpkins; the Mikir totems appear to be mainly vegetable. Our information, however, on totemism in Assam is extremely scanty, and the subject requires further investigation.†

In Assam.

For Burma the facts, so far as they go, are thus stated by Mr. Lowis:—

"The question of endogamy naturally leads to that of totemism. Sir George Scott says in the *Upper Burma Gazetteer*: 'All the Indo-Chinese races have a predilection for totemistic birth stories. Some claim to have sprung from eggs, some from dogs, some from reptiles.' The Wās, like a tribe in North-West America cited by Mr. Andrew Lang in his *Custom and Myth*, state that their primæval ancestors were tadpoles. The Palaungs trace their beginnings back to a Nāga princess who laid three eggs, out of the first of which their early ancestor was hatched. An egg-laying Nāga princess figures in the early legendary history of the Mons or Talaings and points to an affinity between the Palaungs and the Talaings which the most recent linguistic research has done much to strengthen. Up to the present

In Burma.

* [Much further information on totemism in Madras will be found in E. Thurston's, *Castes and Tribes of Southern India*, 1909, *passim*: L. K. Anantha Krishna Iyer, *Cochin Tribes and Castes*, vols. i., ii. 1909–12.]

† [See note p. 64 *supra*. Mr. J. McSwiney has not been able to discover any trace of totemistic exogamous clans, in the proper sense, in Assam; *i.e.*, though such sections may have the names of animate or material objects, there does not seem to be any reverence felt for the supposed ancestor. A possible exception is the Jyrwa Nongsiet clan in the west of the Khasi Hills, which believes that its ancestors sprang from a bamboo plant, and in deference to this belief, the members refuse to eat the small green shoots of the bamboo which are the common food of the neighbouring clans (*Census Report*, *Assam*, 1911, vol. i. p. 72). Elsewhere the evidence for the existence of totemism seems to be lacking or doubtful, E. Stack, *The Mikirs*, 1908, p. 15 *et seq.*: T. C. Hodson, *The Meitheis*, 1908, p. 55 *et seq.*, 118: Id. *The Nāga Tribes of Manipur*, 1911, p. 71 *et seq.*: Lieut.-Col. J. Shakespear, *The Lushei Kuki Clans*, 1912, p. 42).]

time all attempts to ascertain the original of the Kachin family names have failed. The totem of the Kachins should, if anything, be a pumpkin, for legend has it that the whole race is descended from a being who was made out of a pumpkin. So far as I can discover, however, their belief in this singular genesis does not deter Kachins from eating the vegetable to which they owe their origin. They do not even appear to be precluded from gathering it under certain circumstances or at a particular period of the year, as is the case with some of the Western Australian tribes." The Southern Chins, on the other hand, are forbidden to kill or eat the King-Crow which hatched "the orginal Chin egg." The bird is regarded in the light of a parent, but, as it is not used as a crest by the Chins, Mr. Houghton is of opinion that it cannot be looked upon as, properly speaking, a totem. The rising sun of the Red Karens is something of the nature of a totemistic badge. Mr. Smeaton refers to it as follows in his *Loyal Karens of Burma* :—

> "Every Red Karen has a rising sun—the crest of his nobility—tattooed on his back. In challenging to combat he does not slap his left folded arm with his right palm, as the rest of the Karens and the Burmans do, but, coiling his right arm round his left side, strikes the tattoo on his back. This action is supposed by him to rouse the magic power of the symbol."

Sir George Scott, however, seems to detect no totemistic inwardness in this tattoo mark, for he sums up the matter under consideration in the following words :—

> "Totemism also shows itself in the prescribed form of names for Shān and Kachin children and in the changing or concealing of personal names, but, so far as is yet known, there is no tribe which habitually takes its family name or has crests and badges taken from some natural object, plant, or animal, though the limiting of marriages between the inhabitants of certain villages only practised both by tribes of Karens and Kachins is no doubt the outgrowth of this totem idea."

Enough has been said to show that totemistic exogamy prevails in India on a fairly large scale, that it is still in active operation, and that it presents features which deserve further investigation in their bearing on the problems of general ethnology. On these grounds I venture to add a few comments on the striking explanation of the origin of totemism which was put forward by Sir J. G. Frazer in the *Fortnightly Review* in 1899.* The subject is one of special interest in India because the Indian evidence seems not only to point to conclusions different from those arrived at by Sir J. G. Frazer on the basis of the Australian data published by Messrs. Spencer and

* *Fortnightly Review*, N. S., LXV, pp. 647-665, 835-852 ; [*Totemism and Exogamy*, 1910, vol. i, p. 91 *et seq.*].

Gillen,* but to suggest a new canon for determining the historical value of ethnographic evidence in general.

Sir J. G. Frazer's theory of totemism.

"A totem," says Sir J. G. Frazer, "is a class of natural phenomena or material object—most commonly a species of animals or plants—between which and himself the savage believes that a certain intimate relation exists. The exact nature of the relation is not easy to ascertain; various explanations of it have been suggested, but none has as yet won general acceptance. Whatever it may be, it generally leads the savage to abstain from killing or eating his totem, if his totem happens to be a species of animals or plants. Further, the group of persons who are knit to any particular totem by this mysterious tie commonly bear the name of the totem, believe themselves to be of one blood, and strictly refuse to sanction the marriage or cohabitation of members of the group with each other. This prohibition to marry within the group is now generally called by the name of exogamy. Thus totemism has commonly been treated as a primitive system both of religion and of society. As a system of religion it embraces the mystic union of the savage with his totem; as a system of society it comprises the relations in which men and women of the same totem stand to each other and to the members of other totemic groups. And corresponding to these two sides of the system are two rough and ready tests or canons of totemism: first, the rule that a man may not kill or eat his totem animal or plant; and second, the rule that he may not marry or cohabit with a woman of the same totem. Whether the two sides—the religious and social—have always co-existed or are essentially independent, is a question which has been variously answered. Some writers—for example, Sir John Lubbock and Mr. Herbert Spencer—have held that totemism began as a system of society only, and that the superstitious regard for the totem developed later, through a simple process of misunderstanding. Others, including J. F. McLennan and Robertson Smith, were of opinion that the religious reverence for the totem is original, and must, at least, have preceded the introduction of exogamy."

The system of totems prevailing in Central Australia is so far parallel to that known in India that it includes, not only animals and plants, but also a number of objects, animate and inanimate. Thus while the Australians have "totems of the wind, the sun, the evening star, fire, water, cloud, and so on,"

* Spencer and Gillen, *Native Tribes of Central Australia*, 1899.

we find among our Dravidians in India the month of June, Wednesday in every week, the moon, the rainbow, and the constellation Pleiades figuring as totems among a number of names which include pretty well the entire flora and fauna of the country where the tribe is settled. But while among the Australians the religious aspect of the totem is relatively more prominent than the social, in India the position is reversed; the social side of the system is very much alive while the religious side has fallen into disuse. It is the religious side on which Sir J. G. Frazer lays stress, and he explains totemism as "primarily an organized and co-operative system of magic designed to secure for the members of the community, on the one hand, a plentiful supply of all the commodities of which they stand in need, and, on the other hand, immunity from all the perils and dangers to which man is exposed in his struggle with nature." In other words, totemism is a primitive Commissariat and General Providence Department which at a later stage took over the business of regulating marriage. The evidence for this proposition is derived from the magical ceremonies called *intichiuma* in which the members of each totem solemnly mimic the animals and plants after which they are called, and eat a small portion of them with the object of ensuring a plentiful supply of the species. Thus the men of the totem called after the Witchetty grub, a succulent caterpillar of some kind which is esteemed a great luxury, paint their bodies in imitation of the grub, crawl through a structure of boughs supposed to represent its chrysalis, chant a song inviting the insect to go and lay eggs, and butt each other in the stomach with the remark "You have eaten much food." The Emu men dress themselves up to resemble Emus and imitate the movements and aimless gazing about of the birds; the Kangaroo men and the men of the Nakea flower totem go through similar mummeries. An admirable collection of the totemistic symbols of the Arunta, together with photographs of the ritual observed in the invocation of the totems themselves, may be seen in the Ethnological department of the Museum at Melbourne.

Now in the first place the doubt occurs to one whether small and moribund tribes, such as the Australians, can fairly be taken to be typical of primitive man. If they could, then man would be primitive still, and we should none of us have got to the point of vexing our souls about the origin of anything. The one distinctive feature of the Australian natives is their incapacity for any sort of progressive evolution.

Surely an atrophied or, it may be, degenerative man of that type is not the sort of ancestor we want to discover; for it is difficult to see what we can learn from him. In Europe, on the other hand, primitive man, so far as we can judge from the traces he has left behind, seems to have been an animal of an entirely different type. He had, indeed, his weaknesses—does not his *vates sacer*, Mr. Andrew Lang, impute to him a diet of oysters and foes—but he fought a good fight with his environment and, as events show, he came out a winner. It seems then that the quest of primitive man ready made and only waiting to be observed and analyzed may be nothing better than a tempting short cut leading to delusion, and that what we must look to is not so much primitive man as primitive usage regarded in its bearing on evolution.

It is from this point of view that I wish to put in a plea for the consideration of the Indian data. Primitive usages may, I would suggest, be divided, as Mr. Bagehot divided political institutions, into the effective and the ineffective, in other words, into those which affect evolution and those which do not. In the case of totemism we can distinguish these two pretty clearly. The magical ritual of the Arunta tribe obviously belongs to the ineffective class. No one outside the Arunta —and even among them one would think there must be augurs—supposes that by performing the most elaborate parody of the demeanour of certain animals a man can really cause them to increase and multiply. In India, on the other hand, our totemistic people have got rid of all such antics, if, indeed, they ever practised them, and retain only the unquestionably effective factor in the system, the rule that a man may not marry a woman of his own totem. They have, it is true, also the rule that people may not eat, injure or make use of their totems, but this prohibition is relatively weak, and in some cases the totems are articles such as rice and salt, which the members of the totem-kin could hardly do without.

Totemism and Exogamy.

Given then a state of things such as this, that tribes which are in no way moribund or degenerate, but on the contrary extremely full of life, retain the effective part of an archaic usage along with the traces of its ineffective parts, may we not reasonably conclude that this effective part, which has stood the wear and tear of ages and contributed to the evolution of the tribe, furnishes the clue to the real origin of the usage itself? Assume this to be so and totemism at once wheels into line and takes the place, which it appears clearly to occupy in India, of a form of exogamy. The particular form presents no great difficulty. Primitive men are like children: they are constantly saying to themselves "Let's pretend," and a favourite and wide-spread form of the game is to pretend to be animals. Only they play it in earnest, and very grim earnest it sometimes is, as any one will discover who has to administer a district where people believe that men can transform themselves into animals at will, or can be so transformed by the agency of witchcraft.

It will be asked, what then is the origin of exogamy? Here again I think the Indian evidence suggests an answer. Just as the special phenomenon of totemism may be explained by reference to the general law of exogamy, so exogamy itself may be traced to the still more general law of natural selection. Nor need we strain the law. We know that there is a tendency in individuals or groups of individuals to vary their habits; and that useful variations tend to be preserved and ultimately transmitted. Now suppose that in a primitive community, such as the Nāga *khel* or the Kandh *gochi*, the men happened to vary in the direction of taking their wives from some other community and that this infusion of fresh blood proved advantageous to the group. The original instinct would then be stimulated by heredity, and the element of sexual selection would, in course of time, come into play. For an exogamous group would have a larger choice of women than an endogamous one, and would thus get finer women, who again, in the course of the primitive struggle for wives, would be appropriated by the strongest and most warlike men. The exogamous groups so strengthened would tend, as time went on, to "eat up," in the expressive Zulu phrase, their endogamous neighbours, or at any rate to deprive them of the pick of their marriageable girls; and the custom of exogamy would spread, partly by imitation, and partly by the extinction of the groups which did not practise it.

The fact that we cannot say how people came to vary in this particular fashion is not necessarily fatal to the hypothesis put forward. In the case of animals other than man we do not call in question the doctrine of natural selection because we cannot trace the precise cause which gave rise to some beneficial variation. It is enough that variations do occur, and that the beneficial ones tend to be transmitted. If, however, an attempt must be made to pierce the veil which shuts off from our view the ages of pre-historic evolution, it does not seem unreasonable to suppose that here and there some half-accidental circumstance, such as the transmission of a physical defect or an hereditary disease, may have given primitive man a sort of warning, and thus have induced the particular kind of variation which his circumstances required. Conquest again may have produced the same effect by bringing about a beneficial mixture of stocks, though it is a little difficult to see, as Mr. Lang pointed out long ago, why the possession of foreign women should have disinclined people to marry the women of their own group. At the same time it is conceivable that the impulse may have been set going by some tribe from which all its marriageable women had been raided and which was thus driven by necessity to start raiding on its own account. I have elsewhere given instances, drawn from the Kandhs and Nāgas, which lend themselves to this view; but I am not sure that we need travel beyond the tendency to accidental variation which appears in all living organisms and may be assumed to have shaped the development of primitive man.

In a country where the accident of birth determines irrevocably the whole course of a man's social and domestic relations, and he must throughout life eat, drink, dress, marry, and give in marriage in accordance with the usages of the community into which he was born, one is tempted at first sight to assume that the one thing that he may be expected to know with certainty, and to disclose without much reluctance, is the name of the caste, tribe, or race to which he belongs. As a matter of fact no column in the Census schedule displays a more bewildering variety of entries, or gives so much trouble to the enumerating and testing staff and to the central offices which compile the results. If the person enumerated gives the name of a well-known tribe, such as Bhīl or Santāl, or of a standard caste like Brāhman or Kāyasth, all is well. But he may belong to an obscure caste from the other end of India; he may give the name of a religious sect, of a sub-caste, of an exogamous sept or section, of a hypergamous group; he may mention some titular designation which sounds finer than the name of his caste; he may describe himself by his occupation or by the province or tract of country from which he comes. These various alternatives, which are far from exhausting the possibilities of the situation, undergo a series of transformations at the hands of the more or less illiterate enumerator

Classification of castes.

who writes them down in his own vernacular, and of the abstractor in the central office who transliterates them into English. Then begins a laborious and most difficult process of sorting, referencing, cross-referencing, and corresponding with local authorities, which ultimately results in the compilation of a table showing the distribution of the inhabitants of India by Caste, Tribe, Race, or Nationality. The arrangement of this table is alphabetical and it consists of two parts. The first is a general list of all the groups returned, with their distribution by religion; while the second shows the distribution by provinces and states of all groups with an aggregate strength of 10,000. An analysis of the table shows that it includes 2,378 main castes and tribes and 43 races or nationalities. With the latter we are not concerned here; as to the former, the question at once arises—on what principle should they be arranged? An alphabetical system is useful for reference, and essential for the purely statistical purposes of a census table. But it does not help us in the least towards presenting an intelligible picture of the social grouping of that large proportion of the people of India which is organized, admittedly or tacitly, on the basis of caste. In this matter a new departure was taken at the Census of 1901. The classification followed in 1891 was then described as "based on considerations partly ethnological, partly historical, and partly, again, functional. The second predominate, for instance, in the first caste group, and the last throughout the middle of the return; but wherever practicable, as it is in the latter portion of the scheme, ethnological distinctions have been maintained. Then, again, it must be mentioned that the functional grouping is based less on the occupation that prevails in each case in the present day than on that which is traditional with it, or which gave rise to its differentiation from the rest of the community." The main heads of the scheme embodying the application of these principles are given at page 188 of the Report on the Census of India for 1891, and its detailed application is shown in Imperial Table XVII.

Judged by its results this scheme is open to criticism in several respects. It accords neither with native tradition and practice, nor with any theory of caste that has ever been propounded by students of the subject. In different parts it proceeds on different principles, with the result that on the one hand it separates groups which are really allied, and on the other includes in the same category groups of widely different origin and status. It is in fact a patch-work classification in which occupation predominates, varied here and there by considerations of caste, history, tradition, ethnical affinity, and geographical position. Illustrations of these defects might be multiplied almost indefinitely, but it is sufficient to mention that the Dravidian Khandāits of Orissa are classed with Rajputs and Bābhans, Jāts, Marāthas, and Nāyars; that Brāhman priests, Mirāsi musicians, and Bahurupia buffoons fall within the same general category; that the Mongoloid Koch, Kachāri, Thāru, and Mech are widely separated; and that more than half of the Musalmans, including the converted aborigines of Eastern Bengal and Assam, are shown as "Musalman Foreign Races," the rest being merged among a number of occupational groups purporting to be endogamous.

Method adopted in Census of 1901.

In organizing the Census of 1901 I suggested to my colleagues that an attempt should be made to arrange the various groups that had to be dealt with on some system which would command general acceptance, at any rate, within the limits of the province to which it was applied. I did not expect that the same system would suit all provinces or even all divisions of the same province; and I was quite prepared to find the preparation of a combined table for the whole of India a task of insuperable difficulty. But I was confident that the provincial results would throw light upon a variety of social movements which at present escape notice; that they would add greatly to the interest of the reports; and that they would provide a sound statistical ground-work for the ethnographic survey of India which is now in progress.

The principle suggested as a basis was that of classification by social precedence as recognized by native public opinion at the present day, and manifesting itself in the facts that particular castes are supposed to be the modern representatives of one or other of the castes of the theoretical Hindu system; that Brāhmans will take water from certain castes; that Brāhmans of high standing will serve particular castes; that certain castes though not served by the best Brāhmans, have nevertheless got Brāhmans of their own, whose rank varies according to circumstances; that certain castes are not served by Brāhmans at all, but have priests of their own; that the status of certain castes has been raised by their taking to infant-marriage or abandoning the remarriage of widows; that the status of some castes has been lowered by their living in a particular locality; that the status of others has been modified by their pursuing some occupation in a special or peculiar way; that some can claim the services of the village barber, the village palanquin-bearer, the village midwife, etc., while others cannot; that some castes may not enter the courtyards of certain temples; that some castes are subject to special taboos, such as that they must not use the village well, or may draw water only with their own vessels, that they must live outside the village or in a separate quarter, that they must leave the road on the approach of a high-caste man, or must call out to give warning of their approach. In the case of the Animistic tribes it was mentioned that the prevalence of totemism and the degree of adoption of Hindu usage would serve as ready tests. All Superintendents, except three who were either defeated by the complexity of the facts or were afraid of hurting people's feelings, readily grasped the main idea of the scheme, and their patient industry, supplemented by the intelligent assistance readily given by the highest native authorities, has added very greatly to our knowledge of an obscure and intricate subject.

The best evidence of the general success of the experiment, and incidentally of the remarkable vitality of caste at the present day, is to be found in the great number of petitions and memorials to which it gave rise, the bulk of which were submitted in English and emanated from the educated classes who are sometimes alleged to be anxious to free themselves from the trammels of the caste system. If the principle on which the classification was based had not appealed to the usages and traditions of the great mass of Hindus, it is inconceivable that so many people should have taken much trouble and incurred substantial expenditure with the object of securing its application in a particular way. Of these memorials the most elaborate was that received from the Khatris of the Punjab and the United Provinces who felt themselves aggrieved by the Superintendent of Census in the latter Province having provisionally classified them as Vaisyas, whereas in the specimen table circulated by me they had been placed in the same group as the Rajputs. A meeting of protest was held at Bareilly, and a great array of authorities was marshalled to prove that the Khatris are lineally descended from the Kshatriyas of Hindu mythology, much as if the modern Greeks were to claim direct descent from Achilles and were to cite the Catalogue of the Ships in the second book of the Iliad in support of their pretensions. In passing orders on their memorial I pointed out that they were mistaken in supposing that this was the first census in which any attempt had been made to classify castes on a definite principle, or that the selection of social precedence as a basis was an entirely new departure. As a matter of fact the scheme of classification adopted in 1891 purported to arrange the groups more or less in accordance with the position generally assigned to each in the social scale, as has been suggested by Sir Denzil Ibbetson in his Report on the Punjab Census of 1881. The result, in the case of the Khatris, was to include them as number 13 in "Group XV—Traders" immediately after the Aroras of the Punjab, ten places lower than the Agarwāls, and several places below the Kāndus and Kasarwānis of the United Provinces and the Subarnabaniks of Bengal. The Rajputs, on the other hand, ranked first in the entire scheme as number I of "Group I—Military and Dominant." In the Bengal Census Report of 1891 the Rajputs were placed among "the patrician class," while the Khatris were grouped with the Baniyas between the Baidyas and Kāyasthas in a group described as "the Vaisyas Proper or Plebeian Middle Class." It was obviously improbable that the Khatris desired this classification to be maintained, and the evidence laid before me not only brought out the conspicuous part played by them in the authentic history of the Punjab in modern times, but seemed to make it clear that in British India at any rate they are generally believed to be the modern representatives of the Kshatriyas of Hindu tradition. For census purposes the fact that most people do hold this belief was sufficient in itself, and it would have been irrelevant to enquire into the grounds upon which the opinion was based. Superintendents of census were accordingly instructed to include the Khatris under the heading Kshatriya in their classification of castes. The decision gave general satisfaction and served to illustrate the practical working of the principle that the sole test of social precedence prescribed was Indian public opinion, and that this test was to be applied with due consideration for the susceptibilities of the persons concerned. The other memorials were disposed of by the Provincial Superintendents on similar lines.

Its practical working.

As no stereotyped scheme of classification was drawn up, but every Province was left to adopt its own system in consultation with its own experts and representative men, it was clearly impossible to draw up any general scheme for the whole of India. One might as well have tried to construct a table of social precedence for Europe, which should bring together on the same list Spanish grandees, Swiss hotel-keepers, Turkish Pashas, and Stock Exchange millionaires, and should indicate the precise degree of relative distinction attaching to each. The problem, in fact, is essentially a local one. Every man has honour in his own country, and India is no more one country than Europe—indeed very much less. The Provincial schemes of classification are summarized in the Census Report of India, 1901, vol. 1, p. 560 *et seq.** Although they cannot be reduced to common terms, they exhibit points of resemblance and difference which deserve some further examination. The first thing to observe is the predominance throughout India of the influence of the traditional system of four original castes. In every scheme of grouping the Brāhman heads the list. Then come the castes whom popular opinion accepts as the modern representatives of the Kshatriyas, and these are followed by the mercantile groups, supposed to be akin to the Vaisyas. When we leave the higher circles of the twice-born, the difficulty of finding a uniform basis of classification becomes apparent. The ancient designation Sūdra finds no great favour in modern times, and we can point to no group that is generally recognized as representing it. The term is used in Bombay, Madras, and Bengal, to denote a considerable number of castes of moderate respectability, the higher of whom are considered "clean" Sūdras, while the precise status of the lower is a question which lends itself to endless controversy. At this stage of the grouping a sharp distinction may be noticed between Upper India and Bombay and Madras. In Rajputana, the Punjab, the United Provinces, the Central Provinces, Bengal, and Assam the grade next below twice-born rank is occupied by a number of castes from whose hands Brāhmans and members of the higher castes will take water and certain kinds of sweetmeats. Below these again is a rather indeterminate group from whom water is taken by some of the higher castes but not by others. Further down, where the test

Its general results.

* [The details of this grouping, which appeared in the first edition of this book, have not been reproduced. Particularly in Bengal, the publication of this so-called "warrant of precedence" led to much agitation and produced a legacy of trouble. It was the signal for an attempt by certain ambitious castes to assert a claim to a rank higher than they deserved, and these claims were supported by various novel expedients. Hence, at the last census the project was abandoned (*Census Reports*, Bengal, 1911, vol. i., p. 440, *et seq.*: Cochin, 1911, vol. i., p. 67: Travancore, 1911, vol. i., p. 233: Assam, 1911, vol. i., p. 116).]

of water no longer applies, the status of a caste depends on the nature of its occupation and its habits in respect of diet. There are castes whose touch defiles the twice-born, but who refrain from the crowning enormity of eating beef; while below these again, in the social system of Upper India, are people like Chamārs and Doms who eat beef and various sorts of miscellaneous vermin. In Western and Southern India the idea that the social status of a caste depends on whether Brāhmans will take water and sweetmeats from its members is unknown, for the higher castes will, as a rule, take water only from persons of their own caste and sub-caste. In Madras especially the idea of ceremonial pollution by the proximity of a member of an unclean caste has been developed with much elaboration. Thus the table of social precedence attached to the Cochin report * shows that while a Nāyar can pollute a man of a higher caste only by touching him, people of the Kammālan group, including masons, blacksmiths, carpenters, and workers in leather, pollute at a distance of twenty-four feet, toddy-drawers (Iluvan or Tiyan) at thirty-six feet, Pulāyan or Cheruman cultivators at forty-eight feet, while in the case of the Paraiyan (Pariahs) who eat beef, the range of pollution is stated to be no less than sixty-four feet. Where these fantastic notions prevail and the authority of the Brāhman is unquestioned, it follows as a necessary consequence that the unhappy people who diffuse an atmosphere of impurity wherever they go are forbidden to enter the high caste quarter of the village, and are compelled either to leave the road when they see a Brāhman coming or to announce their own approach by a special cry like the lepers of Europe in the Middle Ages. Such is the logic of intolerance in parts of Southern India.

The subject of classification is examined fully in some of the Provincial Census Reports, to which the reader is referred for further particulars. No attempt was made to grade every caste. Large classes were formed, and the various groups included in these were arranged in alphabetical order, so as to escape the necessity of settling the more delicate questions of precedence. As an illustration of the method of procedure I may refer to the table of precedence for Bengal Proper, which was compiled by me some years ago and has been adopted by Mr. Gait for the purpose of the Bengal Census Report † after

---

* [*Census Report, Cochin*, 1901, vol. i., p. 181, *et seq.*]

† [1901, vol. i., p. 369, *et seq.*]

careful examination by local committees of Indian gentlemen appointed for the purpose.

The entire Hindu population of this tract, numbering twenty millions, has been divided into seven classes. The first class is reserved for the Brāhmans, of whom there are more than a million, forming six per cent. of the Hindus of Bengal. As every one knows, there are Brāhmans and Brāhmans, of status varying from the Rārhi, who claim to have been imported by Adisura from Kanauj, to the Barna Brāhmans who serve the lower castes and from whose hands pure Brāhmans will not take water. No attempt has been made to deal with these multifarious distinctions in the table. It would be a thankless task to try to determine the precise degree of social merit or demerit that attaches to the Pīrāli Brāhmans, who are supposed to have been forced, some four centuries ago, to smell or, as some say, to eat the beefsteaks that had been cooked for the renegade Brāhman Pīr Ali, the dewān of the Muhammadan ruler of Jessore; to the Vyasokta Brāhmans who serve the Chāsi Kaibartta caste and rank so low that even their own clients will not touch food in their houses; to the Agradāni who preside at funeral ceremonies and take the offerings of the dead; to the Achārji fortune-teller, palmist, and maker of horoscopes; and to the Bhāt Brāhman, a tawdry parody of the bard and genealogist of heroic times, whose rapacity and shamelessness are proverbial.

Social precedence of Hindus in Bengal.

Next in order, at the top of the second class, come the Rajputs, who disown any connexion with Bengal, and base their claims to precedence on their supposed descent from the pure Rajputs of the distant Indo-Aryan tract. Their number (113,405) must include a large number of families belonging to local castes who acquired land and assumed the title of Rajput on the strength of their territorial position. Then follow the Baidyas, by tradition physicians, and the writer caste of Kāyasth. The former pose as the modern representatives of the *Ambastha* of Manu and assert their superiority to the Kāyasthas on the ground that the latter have been pronounced by the High Court of Calcutta to be Sūdras, a Kāyasth judge concurring, and that their funeral usages confirm this finding; that the Sanskrit College, when first opened, admitted only Brāhmans and Baidyas as students; that the Kāyasths were originally the domestic servants of the two higher castes, and when poor take service still; and that native social usage concedes higher rank to the Baidyas at certain ceremonies to which members of the respectable castes are invited. The Kāyasths, on the other hand, claim to be Kshatriyas, who took to clerical work; deny the identity of the Baidyas with the Ambasthas; and describe them as a local caste, unknown in the great centres of Hinduism, who were Sūdras till about a century ago, when they took to wearing the sacred thread, and bribed the Brāhmans to acquiesce in their pretensions. The alphabetical arrangement observed in the table leaves the question an open one.

The third class, numbering three millions, comprises the functional castes originally known as Navasākha, the nine "branches" or "arrows," and other clean Sūdras, from whose hands the higher castes take water, and who are served by high-class Brāhmans. Confectioners, perfume vendors, betel growers, pressers and sellers of oil, gardeners, potters, and barbers figure in this group, the constitution of which appears to have been largely determined by consideration of practical convenience. The preparation of a Hindu meal is a very elaborate performance, involving lengthy ablutions and a variety of ritualistic observances which cannot be performed on a journey, and it is essential to the comfort of the orthodox traveller that he should be able to procure sweetmeats of various kinds without being troubled by misgivings as to the ceremonial cleanliness of the people from whom he buys them. In matters of food and drink caste rules are wisely elastic. It has, I believe, been held that neither ice nor soda-water count as water for the purpose of conveying pollution; there are special exemptions in favour of biscuits and patent medicines, for the last of which the Bengali has an insatiable appetite; and in an outlying district where the only palanquin-bearers available were Dravidian Bhuīyas, I have known them to be given brevet rank as a water-giving (*jalācharaniya*) caste in order that the twice-born traveller might be able to get a drink without quitting his palanquin.

The fourth class includes only two castes—the Chāsi Kaibartta and the Goāla—from whom water is taken by the high castes, but whose Brāhmans are held to be degraded. About the former group I wrote in 1891: "It seems likely, as time goes on, that this sub-caste will rise in social estimation, and will altogether sink the Kaibartta, so that eventually it is possible that they may succeed in securing a place with the Navasākha." The forecast has to this extent been fulfilled that at the recent Census the Chāsi Kaibartta called themselves Māhishya, the name of the offspring of a legendary cross between Kshatriyas and Vaisya, and posed as a separate caste. In Nadia, according to Mr. Gait, "the new idea gained such ground that many Chāsi Kaibarttas in domestic service under other castes threw up their work, saying it was beneath their dignity. Finding, however, that no other means of livelihood were available they were soon fain to return and beg their employers' forgiveness." * The higher castes, moreover, expressed their disapproval of a movement which upset their domestic arrangements by a concerted refusal to take water from the hands of a Chāsi. Notwithstanding these discouragements I have little doubt that by the next Census the Māhishya will have succeeded in establishing their claim.† Their case is of interest for the light that it throws on the evolution of a caste.

The fifth class contains a rather miscellaneous assortment of castes, including the Baishtam, the Sunri, and the Sunbarnabanik, from whom the higher castes do not usually take water. Their precedence is also defined by the fact that although the village barber will shave them he will not cut their toe-nails nor will he take part in their marriage ceremonies. Here again quaint problems of status arise. The Baishtams are a group formed by the conversion to Vaishnavism of members of many different castes, who have embraced the tenets of different Vaishnava sects. In theory inter-marriage between these sects is prohibited, but if a man of one sect wishes to marry a woman of another, he has only to convert her by a simple ritual to his own sect and the obstacles to their union are removed. The social standing of the caste is necessarily low, as it is recruited from among all classes of society, and large numbers of prostitutes and people who have got into trouble in consequence of sexual irregularities are found among its ranks.

---

* [*Census Report, Bengal*, 1901, vol. i., p. 380 *note*.]

† ["The case of these castes who discard the name borne by their ancestors and arrogate a new designation is different. In their case the new name is recognised by the census authorities, if it is generally applied to them by the Hindu community at large and is not used by any other castes. In this way the Chandals have been allowed to be returned as Nama-Sūdras, that term being recognised by the Hindus generally and applying exclusively to them. Similarly, the Chasi Kaibarttas are allowed to return themselves as Mahishya, but though that name has been adopted by the Chasi Kaibarttas in recent times, it has won general recognition and is exclusively applied to the Chasi Kaibarttas. Ten years ago this innovation was resented by conservative Hindus in some places—in Nadia the higher castes went so far as to refuse to take water from the Chasi Kaibarttas—but it is now generally tolerated." *Census Report, Bengol*, 1911, vol. i., p. 443, *et seq.*]

Within the caste, however, many of them retain their old social distinctions, and a Baishtam of Kāyasth origin would not ordinarily take water from the hands of one whose ancestors were Chandāls. Outsiders also recognize these differences and take water from Baishtams who are known to have belonged to one of the clean castes. Where the origin of a Baishtam is unknown, water which he has touched can only be used for washing.

The Subarnabaniks are a mercantile caste peculiar to Bengal Proper, who claim to be the modern representatives of the ancient Vaisya. In spite of their wealth and influence, their high-bred appearance, and the notorious beauty of the women of the caste, their claim to this distinguished ancestry has failed to obtain general recognition. They are excluded from the ranks of the Navasākha, or nine clean Sūdra castes, and none but Vaidik Brāhmans will take water from their hands. To account for the comparatively low status assigned to them, the Subarnabaniks cite a variety of traditions, some of which, however unsupported by historical evidence, deserve to be briefly mentioned here as illustrations of the kind of stories which tend to grow up wherever the business talents and practical ability of a particular community have advanced it in the eyes of the world conspicuously beyond its rank in the theoretical order of castes. These people, for example, say that their ancestors came to Bengal from Oudh during the reign of Adisura, who was struck by their financial ability and conferred on them the title of Subarnabanik, or trader in gold, as a mark of his favour. They then wore the Brahmanical thread, studied the Vedas and were generally recognized as Vaisyas of high rank. The stories of their degradation all centre round the name of Ballāl Sen, who was Raja of Eastern Bengal in 1070 A.D. His intrigue with a beautiful Pātni girl is said to have been ridiculed on the stage by some young Subarnabaniks, while the entire body refused to be present at the penance whereby the king affected to purify himself from the sin of intercourse with a maiden of low caste. Another cause of offence is said to have been the refusal of a leading Subarnabanik to lend Ballāl large sums of money to carry on war with Manipur. Authorities differ concerning the method by which the Raja obtained his revenge. Some say that in the course of the penance already referred to, a number of small golden calves had been distributed to the attendant Brāhmans. One of these Brāhmans was suborned by Ballāl

Sen to fill the hollow inside of a calf with lac-dye, and to take the figure to a Subarnabanik for sale. In testing the gold the Subarnabanik let out the lac-dye, which was at once pronounced to be blood. Having thus fastened upon the caste the inexpiable guilt of killing a cow, Ballāl Sen publicly declared them and their Brāhmans to be degraded, deprived them of the right to wear the sacred thread, and threatened with similar degradation any one who should eat or associate with them.

In default of independent testimony to the accuracy of this tradition we can hardly accept it as a narrative of historical events. It is no doubt conceivable that a despotic monarch might order the social degradation of a particular class of his subjects provided that it were not too numerous or too influential; and it is generally believed that Ballāl Sen did effect some changes of this kind in the relative status of certain families of Brāhmans. Notwithstanding this, the story of the depression of an entire caste from a very high to a comparatively low rank in the social system makes a large demand on our belief, and inclines one to suspect that it may have been evolved in recent times to account for the position actually occupied by the caste being lower than that to which their riches and ability would entitle them to lay claim. From this point of view, the conjecture that the Subarnabaniks are Hindustani Baniyas, who lost status by residing in Bengal and marrying Bengali women, seems to deserve some consideration.

The sixth class includes a long list of castes, numbering nearly eight millions, who abstain from eating beef, pork, and fowls, but from whom the higher castes will not take water. They are served by degraded Brāhmans; the regular barbers refuse to shave them; and some of them have special barbers of their own. Most of them, however, can get their clothes washed by the village washerman. The typical members of the group, according to the census of 1911, are the Bāgdi, (1,041,892), Dravidian cultivators and labourers, the Jaliya or fishing Kaibartta (375,936), the Namasudra or Chandāl (2,087,162), the Pod (536,591), fishermen and cultivators, and the Rājbansi-Koch (2,049,454), nearly all of whom are small cultivators.

The seventh class represents the lowest grade of the Bengal system, castes who eat all manner of unclean food, whose touch pollutes, whom no Brāhman, however degraded, will serve, and for whom neither barber nor washerman will work. It comprises the scavenging Doms and Hāris, the leather-working Chamārs and Mochis, and the Bauris who eat rats and revere the dog as their totem because, as they told Colonel Dalton, it is the right thing to have a sacred animal of some kind, and dogs are useful while alive and not very nice to eat when dead.*

Social precedence among Muhammadans.

Islam, whether regarded as a religious system or as a theory of things, is in every respect the antithesis of Hinduism. Its ideal is strenuous action rather than hypnotic contemplation; it allots to man a single life and bids him live it and make the best of it; its practical spirit knows nothing of a series of lives, of transmigration, of *karma*, of the weariness of existence which weighs upon the Indian mind. For the dream of absorption into an impersonal *Weltgeist* it substitutes a very personal Paradise made up of joys such as all Orientals understand. On its social side the religion of Muhammad is equally opposed to the Hindu scheme of a hierarchy of castes, an elaborate stratification of society based upon subtle distinctions of food, drink, dress, marriage, and ceremonial usage. In the sight of God and of His Prophet all followers of Islam are equal. In India, however, caste is in the air; its contagion has spread even to the Muhammadans; and we find its evolution proceeding on characteristically Hindu lines. In both communities foreign descent forms the highest claim to social distinction; in both, promotion cometh from the West. As the twice-born Aryan is to the mass of Hindus, so is the Muhammadan of alleged Arab, Persian, Afghān or Moghal origin to the rank and file of his co-religionists. And just as in the traditional Hindu system men of the higher groups could marry women of the lower while the converse process was vigorously condemned, so within the higher ranks of the Muhammadans a Saiyad will marry a Shekh's daughter but will not give his daughter in return, and inter-marriage between the upper circle of *soi-disant* foreigners and the main body of Indian Muhammadans is generally reprobated, except in parts of the country where the aristocratic element is small and must arrange its marriages as best it can. Even there, however, it is only under the stress of great poverty that a member of the *Ashrāf* or "noble" class will give his daughter to one of the *Ajlāf* or "low people," as converts of indigenous origin are called in Bengal. Of course, the limits of the various groups are not defined as sharply as they are with the Hindus. The well-known proverb, which occurs in various

* [*Descriptive Ethnology of Bengal*, 1872, p. 327.]

forms in different parts of Northern India—"Last year I was a Jolāha; now I am a Shekh; next year if prices rise, I shall become a Saiyad"—marks the difference, though analogous changes of status are not unknown among Hindus, and, as Mr. Gait observes, "promotion is not so rapid in reality as it is in the proverb." But speaking generally, it may be said that the social cadre of the higher ranks of Muhammadans is based on hypergamy with a tendency in the direction of endogamy, while the lower functional groups are strictly endogamous, and are organized on the model of regular castes with councils and officers who enforce the observance of caste rules by the time-honoured sanction of boycotting.

According to Mr. Gait the Bengal Muhammadans "recognize two main social divisions: (1) Ashrāf or Sharīf and (2) Ajlāf, which in Bengali has been corrupted to Atrāp. The first, which means 'noble' or 'persons of high extraction,' includes all undoubted descendants of foreigners and converts from the higher castes of Hindus.* All other Muhammadans, including the functional groups to be presently mentioned, and all converts of lower rank are collectively known by the contemptuous term Ajlāf, 'wretches' or 'mean people'; they are also called Kamīna or Itar, 'base' or 'Razīl,' a corruption of Rizāl, 'worthless.' This category includes the various classes of converts who are known as Nāo Muslim in Bihar and Nasya in North Bengal, but who in East Bengal, where their numbers are greatest, have usually succeeded in establishing their claim to be called Shekh. It also includes various functional groups such as that of the Jolāha or weaver, Dhunia or cotton-carder, Kulu or oil-presser, Kunjra or vegetable-seller, Hajjām or barber, Darzi or tailor, and the like. Of these divisions, the Ashrāf takes no count. To him all alike are Ajlāf. This distinction, which is primarily one between the Muhammadans of foreign birth and those of local origin, corresponds very closely to the Hindu division of the community into Dwijas or castes of twice-born rank, comprising the various classes of the Aryan invaders, and the Sūdras or aborigines whom they subdued. Like the higher Hindu castes, the Ashrāf consider it degrading to accept menial service or to handle the plough. The traditional occupation of the Saiyads is the priesthood, while the Moghals and Pathāns correspond to the Kshatriyas of the Hindu regime.

* In some places many of the Moghals and Pathāns are regarded as Ajlāf.

"In some places a third class, called Arzāl or 'lowest of all,' is added. It consists of the very lowest castes, such as the Halālkhor, Lālbegi, Abdāl, and Bediya, with whom no other Muhammadan would associate, and who are forbidden to enter the mosque or to use the public burial ground." *

I have described the Bengal scheme of social precedence at some length, because of the curious beliefs and traditions which it embodies and by reason of the testimony which it bears to the remarkable stability of the caste instinct in spite of the many modern influences which seem at first sight to be sapping its foundations. The scheme deals, moreover, with conditions with which I am to some extent familiar, and it represents an advanced stage of a process which appears to me to be going on with varying degrees of rapidity in all parts of India where Hindu sentiment and tradition are the dominant factors of social development. The extension of railways which indirectly diffuses Brahmanical influence and at the same time weakens trivial caste restrictions; the tendency to revive the authority of the Hindu scriptures and to find in them the solution of modern problems; the advance of vernacular education which increases the demands for popular versions of, and extracts from, these writings, and the spread of English education which encourages sceptical tendencies;—these are among the causes which, in my opinion, are tending on the one hand to bring about among the population regarded as a whole a more rigid observance of the essential incidents of caste, especially of those connected with marriage, and on the other to introduce greater laxity in respect of the minor injunctions which are concerned with food and drink.

Case of Baluchistan.

On the outskirts of the Empire there are two regions where Hindu standards of social precedence and Hindu notions of caste are neither recognized nor known. In Baluchistan, until less than a generation ago, Hindus were tolerated only as a useful class of menials who carried on the petty trade which the fighting races deemed below their dignity. They adopted the device, not unknown in mediæval Europe, of putting themselves under the protection of their more powerful neighbours, and Mr. Hughes-Buller tells us that even now a Hindu when asked to what caste he belongs "will often describe himself by the name of the tribal group to whom he holds himself attached.

* [*Census Report, Bengal*, 1901, vol. i., p. 439.]

Their position generally was extremely degraded, and may best be gauged by the fact that among Baloch, Brāhūi, and Afghāns there was an unwritten rule that in the course of raids and counter raids women, children and Hindus were to be spared." * Among the non-Hindu people of Baluchistan the question of social precedence is intricate and obscure and its details must be studied in Mr. Hughes-Buller's excellent report. Of the three chief races the Afghāns rank highest in virtue of their former sovereignty; then comes the Baloch who also once bore rule, and last the Brāhūi who were in power at the time of the British occupation. The relative position of the two latter tribes is indicated by various proverbs, by the attempts of the Brāhūi to trace their descent to the Baloch, and by the fact that "no self-respecting Baloch will give his daughter to a Brāhūi." The test of marriage, however, appears not to apply to the Afghān, who regards the question as a matter of business and will sell his daughter to any man who can pay her price. Below these races come the Jāts, a term which seems to be loosely used to denote all sorts of menial classes, including professional musicians (Langahs), blacksmiths (Loris), and leather-workers (Mochis). But even here there is no hard and fast prohibition of intermarriage, and both Baloch and Brāhūi will take wives from among the Jāts. Within the circle of each tribe a condition of theoretical equality appears to prevail, tempered by personal considerations arising from capacity to lead, religious sanctity, age and kinship with a ruling family.

In Burma caste is so little known that the Burmese language possesses no word for it, while one of the difficulties of conducting the Census of the numerous Indian immigrants is the impossibility of making the average Burman enumerator understand the meaning of the Indian term *zāt* or *jāt.* Differences of religion he can grasp in a vague sort of way, he has a notion of what is meant by race, but caste remains to him an insoluble mystery—a thing with which his democratic spirit, regardless of social distinctions, has no sympathy whatever. Mr. Lowis assures us that there are not and never have been any true castes in Burma, though a class of landed proprietors in Minbu known as the Thugaungs appear to be endogamous, and thirty-six professional groups with hereditary occupations are said to have existed among the Chins.†

* [*Census Report*, 1901. Part I, p. 134.]

† [*Census Report*, 1901, vol. i., p. 109; cf. *Report*, 1911, vol. i., p. 240.]

No attempt can be made here to analyse and explain the distribution of the 2,300 castes and tribes which have been enumerated in the Census. The mere bulk of the undertaking would in any case ensure its failure; the mass of detail would be tedious and bewildering; while the causes which have determined the settlement and diffusion of particular groups belong more properly to local history and are, in any case, largely a matter of conjecture. In order, however, to give some idea of the facts and to provide a statistical basis for further researches, I have selected thirty-six of the principal tribes and castes and have shown their distribution by Provinces and States in the series of small maps annexed to this volume. The maps are constructed on the principle of graphic representation recommended by M. Bertillon. The strength of the caste to which a map relates is depicted in each province by a rectangle, of which the base indicates the total population of the province, while the height denotes the proportion which the numbers of the caste bear to the total population; thus the area of the rectangle gives the actual strength of the caste. Most of the names have also been entered in the large map showing the physical types.

Distribution of Social groups.

A glance at the maps will show that some castes are diffused over the whole of India, while others are localized in particular provinces or tracts of country. The typical instance of a widely diffused caste is furnished by the Brāhmans, who number nearly fifteen millions, and represent a proportion of the total population ranging from ten per cent. in the United Provinces, Central India, and Rajputana to three per cent. in Madras, the Central Provinces and Bengal, and two per cent. in Assam and Chutia Nagpur. The distribution accords fairly well with the history and traditions of the caste. They are strongest in their original centre, numbering nearly five millions in the United Provinces, and weakest in the outlying tracts, peopled mainly by non-Aryan races, which their influence has even now only imperfectly reached. There can, however, be little doubt that many of the Brāhmans of the more remote tracts have been manufactured on the spot by the simple process of conferring the title of Brāhman on the tribal priests of the local deities. The so-called Barna Brāhmans who serve the lower castes of Bengal probably obtained sacerdotal rank in this fashion. That the priestly caste is not of altogether unmixed descent is

Diffused groups.

attested by the numerous legends of Rajas, who, having sworn a rash oath to feed a stated number of Brāhmans, usually a lakh and a quarter, found the supply run out and were obliged to make them up for the occasion out of any materials that were at hand. A similar conclusion may perhaps be drawn from the well-known distich—

Kariā Brāhman, gorā Chamār,
Inke sāth na utariye pār.
If the Brāhman be black,
Or the Chamār be fair ;
At the ford of the river
Let the wise man beware !

As with the Brāhmans so in the chief functional groups the tendency is towards wide diffusion, and their racial composition probably varies materially in different provinces. Owing to differences of language the maps fail to bring out the complete facts in relation to the whole of India. Thus the leather workers (Chamār and Muchi) of Upper India, numbering over eleven millions and forming twelve per cent. of the population of the United Provinces, correspond with the Chakkiliyan (486,884) and Madiga (755,316) of Madras, but the map does not include these. The large pastoral group (Ahīr and Goāla) numbering nearly ten millions in Upper India and forming eight per cent. of the population of the United Provinces appears in the South of India under the names Gola (855,221) and Idaiyan (694,829), neither of which are taken account of in the map. The same may be said of the potters (Kumhār) and the oilmen (Teli, and Tili) both widely diffused functional groups whose distribution is imperfectly exhibited in the maps. In each province such groups form, of course, distinct castes which have probably been evolved independently.

Of the localized groups a large number are admittedly tribes.

Localized groups.

The Bhīl, Gond, Koli, and Santāl come within this category and are still outside the Hindu social system. The Doms, Dosādhs, Gūjars, Jāts, Kaibarttas, Nāmasūdras (Chandāls) Pods, Nāyars, Pallis, Paraiyans (Pariahs), and Rājbansi-Koch represent tribes which have been transformed into castes at a comparatively recent date and retain some traces of the tribal stage of development.

The three Muhammadan maps—Jolāha, Pathān and Saiyad—

Muhammadan groups.

are of interest for the light that they throw upon the spread of Islam. The Jolāha weavers number nearly three millions in all, and the solid blocks which they form in the Punjab (695,216), in the United Provinces (923,042), and in Bengal (1,242,049), seem to mark the area in which the lower classes of the community were converted *en masse* to a faith which seemed to hold out to them the prospect of a social status unattainable under the rigid system of caste. The Pathān map denotes a different order of phenomena, and may be taken to indicate roughly the degree of diffusion of the main body of the foreign Musalmān element and their descendants. It shows us the sturdy, pugnacious, enterprising Pathān pushing forward from the frontier and establishing himself among the feebler folk of India wherever there was fighting to be done or money to be made. The Saiyad map on the other hand seems to give some clue to the distribution of the upper classes of the immigrant Musalmāns.

CHAPTER III

CASTE IN PROVERBS AND POPULAR SAYINGS

Volito vivu' per ora virum.
Ennius.

Proverbs in general: various definitions.

In all ages and countries the study of proverbs and popular sayings has appealed by its human interest to many sorts of minds. Plato, Aristotle and Theophrastus are believed to have collected the proverbs of their day, and many of Lucian's wittiest sayings are pointed from the same armoury. In the later middle age both Erasmus * and Scaliger made collections of proverbs, unfortunately only of classical proverbs, and the former defined a proverb as "*Celebre dictum scita quadam novitate insigne.*" This earliest definition seems to overlook some of the essential features of the best proverbs—their brevity, their bearing on the practical conduct of every-day life, and their origin in the speech of the people. What makes a proverb, as M. Dejardin † excellently puts it, "*c'est sa vogue populaire.*" Erasmus fails to bring out this point and thus does not distinguish the proverb from the apophthegm, the brilliant expression of the concentrated thought of the learned, and from the aphorism which aims at scientific precision and corresponds, in the domain of ethics, to the axiom of mathematical reasoning. Voltaire illustrates the distinction admirably when he says of Boileau's poetry that one finds in it some expressions which have passed into proverbs and others which deserve to rank as maxims. "Maxims," he goes on to say, "are elevated, wise and useful; they are made for the witty and appeal to cultivated taste. Proverbs on the other hand are for the vulgar, for the common man, whom," he observes characteristically, "one meets in all ranks of society."

---

* *Desiderii Erasmi Roterodami Proverbiorum Epitome retractata ab M. Io. Christ, Messerschmid*, Lipsiæ, 1758.

† *Dictionnaire des Spots ou Proverbes Wallons*, Liège, 1863.

Other writers have dwelt upon other points of the genuine proverb. The grammarian Donatus insists that it must be *accommodatum rebus temporibus,* must fit the facts and the period: the philologist Festus, looking to the etymology of the word, lays stress on its quality as *ad agendum apta,* a guide in the business of life. A modern writer who is impressed both by the brevity and by the selfish and heartless tone of many proverbs describes them as "the algebra of materialism." The epigram is ingenious and hits off the tendency of the proverb to get condensed into a paradoxical formula such as *Festina lente,* but the reference to materialism seems hardly appropriate. To describe proverbs as the algebra of *popular pessimism* would in some respects be nearer to the truth.

As might be expected, the most exhaustive and careful definition, albeit a trifle ponderous, has been made in Germany. According to Borchart * a proverb is a saying current among the people which sets forth in thoroughly popular language, and with studied brevity, a truth acknowledged by all. By the side of this we may place Rivarol's opinion that proverbs represent the fruits of popular experience and, as it were, the common-sense of all ages compressed into a formula. And we may conclude the series with the admirable phrase commonly attributed to Lord John Russell, but probably suggested to him by a variety of sayings of the same type which are current in many countries, "The wisdom of many and the wit of one." Of this it may fairly be said that to define a proverb by a proverb is a triumph of definition.

Classified as general and particular.

There are, however, proverbs and proverbs. Some contain a truth of general application which holds good for all time and stands its ground in the face of social change and political or economic revolution. Such proverbs are based on universal experience and embody the common-sense of mankind. Their form, indeed, may differ widely, but the underlying idea is everywhere the same and everywhere has given rise spontaneously to some telling phrase. Our own proverb "Coals to Newcastle" figures in the delicate irony of the Greeks as "Owls to Athens." Other proverbs again have a more limited range. They express a truth rooted in experience, but the experience is that of a particular people or of a particular country, and the sayings in which it is summed up are coloured by the spirit

* *Die Sprichwörtlichen Redensarten im Deutschen Volksmund nach Sinn und Ursprung erläutert;* Leipzig, 1888.

of the time when they were coined and of the nation which produced them. They hold good for their birth-place, but not for all the world.

Indian proverbs of caste.

It need hardly be said that the proverbs and sayings relating to caste which are brought together in Appendix I and are commented on in this chapter belong for the most part to the second of the two classes noticed above. In respect both of their subject-matter and of their form they are local and particular rather than universal and general. Yet now and then one finds a truth of universal experience rendered in terms of caste relations, and the fact is instructive in so far as it bears witness to the supremacy of the caste sentiment in India and to the prominent place that it occupies in the daily life of the people.

A village portrait gallery.

No one indeed can fail to be struck by the intensely popular character of Indian proverbial philosophy and by its freedom from the note of pedantry which is so conspicuous in Indian literature. These quaint sayings have dropped fresh from the lips of the Indian rustic; they convey a vivid impression of the anxieties, the troubles, the annoyances, and the humours of his daily life; and any sympathetic observer who has felt the fascination of an oriental village would have little difficulty in constructing from these materials a fairly accurate picture of rural society in India. The *mise en scène* is not altogether a cheerful one. It shows us the average peasant dependent upon the vicissitudes of the season and the vagaries of the monsoon, and watching from day to day to see what the year may bring forth. Should rain fall at the critical moment his wife will get golden earrings, but one short fortnight of drought may spell calamity when "God takes all at once." Then the forestalling Baniya flourishes by selling rotten grain, and the Jāt cultivator is ruined. First die the improvident Musalmān weavers (Jolāhā), then the oil-pressers for whose wares there is no demand; the carts lie idle, for the bullocks are dead, and the bride goes to her husband without the accustomed rites. But be the season good or bad, the pious Hindu's life is ever overshadowed by the exactions of the Brāhman—"a thing with a string round its neck" (a profane hit at the sacred thread), a priest by appearance, a butcher at heart, the chief of a trio of tormentors gibbeted in the rhyming proverb:—

The Brāhman.

Is dunyā men tīn kasāī,
Pisu, khatmal, Brāhman bhāī.

Which may be rendered—

"Blood-suckers three on earth there be,
The bug, the Brāhman and the flea."

Before the Brāhman starves the King's larder will be empty; cakes must be given to him while the children of the house may lick the grindstone for a meal; his stomach is a bottomless pit; he eats so immoderately that he dies from wind. He will beg with a lakh of rupees in his pocket, and a silver begging-bowl in his hand. In his greed for funeral fees he spies out corpses like a vulture, and rejoices in the misfortune of his clients. A village with a Brāhman in it is like a tank full of crabs; to have him as a neighbour is worse than leprosy: if a snake has to be killed the Brāhman should be set to do it, for no one will miss him. If circumstances compel you to perjure yourself, why swear on the head of your son, when there is a Brāhman handy? Should he die (as is the popular belief) the world will be none the poorer. Like the devil in English proverbial philosophy, the Brāhman can cite scripture for his purpose; he demands worship himself but does not scruple to kick his low-caste brethren; he washes his sacred thread but does not cleanse his inner man; and so great is his avarice that a man of another caste is supposed to pray "O God, let me not be reborn as a Brāhman priest, who is always begging and is never satisfied." He defrauds even the gods; Vishnu gets the barren prayers while the Brāhman devours the offerings. So Pan complains in one of Lucian's dialogues that he is done out of the good things which men offer at his shrine.

The Baniya.

The next most prominent figure in our gallery of popular portraits is that of the Baṇiya, money-lender, grain-dealer and monopolist, who dominates the material world as the Brāhman does the spiritual. His heart, we are told, is no bigger than a coriander seed; he has the jaws of an alligator and a stomach of wax; he is less to be trusted than a tiger, a scorpion, or a snake; he goes in like a needle and comes out like a sword; as a neighbour he is as bad as a boil in the armpit. If a Baniya is on the other side of a river you should leave your bundle on this side, for fear he should steal it. When four Baniyas meet they rob the whole world. If a Baniya is drowning you should not give him a hand: he is sure to have some base motive for drifting down stream. He uses light weights and swears that the scales tip themselves; he keeps his accounts in a character that no one but God can read; if you borrow from him, your debt mounts up like a refuse heap or gallops like a horse; if he talks to a customer he "draws a line" and debits the conversation; when his own credit is shaky he writes up his transactions on the wall so that they can easily be rubbed out. He is so stingy that the dogs starve at his feast, and he scolds his wife if she spends a farthing on betel-nut. A Jain Baniya drinks dirty water and shrinks from killing ants and flies, but will not stick at murder in pursuit of gain. As a druggist the Baniya is in league with the doctor; he buys weeds at a nominal price and sells them very dear. Finally, he is always a shocking coward: eighty-four Khatris will run away from four thieves.

The Kāyasth.

Nor does the clerical caste fare better at the hands of the popular epigrammatist. Where three Kāyasths are gathered together a thunderbolt is sure to fall; when honest men fall out the Kāyasth gets his chance. When a Kāyasth takes to money-lending he is a merciless creditor. He is a man of figures; he lives by the point of his pen; in his house even the cat learns two letters and a half. He is a versatile creature, and where there are no tigers he will become a shikāri; but he is no more to be trusted than a crow or a snake without a tail. One of the failings sometimes imputed to the educated Indian is attacked in the saying, "Drinking comes to a Kāyasth with his mother's milk."

The Jāt.

Considering the enormous strength of the agricultural population of India, one would have expected to find more proverbs directed against the great cultivating castes. Possibly the reason may be that they made most of the proverbs, and people can hardly be expected to sharpen their wit on their own shortcomings. In two Provinces, however, the rural Pasquin has let out very freely at the morals and manners of the Jāt, the typical peasant of the Eastern Punjab and the western districts of the United Provinces. You may as well, we are told, look for good in a Jāt as for weevils in a stone. He is your friend only so long as you have a stick in your hand. If he cannot harm you he will leave a bad smell as he goes by. To be civil to him is like giving treacle to a donkey. If he runs amuck it takes God to hold him. A Jāt's laugh would break an ordinary man's ribs. When he learns manners, he blows his nose with a mat, and there is a great run on the garlic. His baby has a plough-tail for a plaything. The Jāt stood on his own corn-heap and called out to the King's elephant-drivers, "Hi there, what will you take for those little donkeys?" He is credited with practising fraternal polyandry, like the Venetian nobility of the early eighteenth century, as a measure of domestic economy, and a whole family are said to have one wife between them.

The Kunbi or Kurmi.

The Kunbi is not so roughly handled as the Jāt, but some unpleasant things are said about him. You will as soon grow a creeper on a rock as make him into a true friend. He is as crooked as a sickle, but you can beat him straight. If he gets a stye on his eyelid he is as savage as a bull. He is so obstinate that he plants thorns across the path. If it rains in the Hathiya asterism (end of September), and there is a bumper crop, he gives his wife gold ear-rings. You may know her by the basket on her head and the baby on either hip.

The Barber.

In the peculiar ways of the artisans and of the castes who are engaged in personal service the makers of proverbs have found abundant material for vituperative sarcasm. Of the village barber, who is also a marriage broker, a surgeon, a chiropodist, and a quack, it is said, "Among men most deceitful is the barber, among birds the crow, among things of the water the tortoise"—a sentiment reminding one how on a celebrated occasion Br'er Tarrypin outwitted Br'er Rabbit. Barbers, doctors, pleaders, prostitutes —all must have cash down. A barber learns by shaving fools, for which reason you should stick to your barber but change your washerman, since a new Dhobi washes clean. You may hammer a barber on the head with a shoe, but you will not make him hold his tongue. A barber found a purse, and all the world knew it. Of the inquisitive barber the wise say, "Throw a dog a morsel to stop his mouth," which, if applied to the modern representative of pertinacious curiosity, might read, "Choke off a reporter with a scrap of stale news." A barber out of work bleeds the wall or shaves a cat to keep his hand in. A barber's penny, all profit and no risk. A burglary at a barber's: stolen, three pots of combings! If you go back four generations you will find that your uncle was a barber, the suggestion being that the barber is sometimes unduly intimate with the inmates of the zenana.

The Goldsmith.

Trust not the goldsmith; he is no man's friend, and his word is worthless. If you have never seen a tiger, look at a cat; if you have never seen a thief, look at a Sonār. The goldsmith, the tailor and the weaver are too sharp for the angel of death; God alone knows where to have them. A Sonār will rob his mother and sister; he will filch gold even from his wife's nose-ring; if he cannot steal his belly will burst with longing. He will ruin your ornament by substituting base metal for the gold you gave him, and will clamour for wages into the bargain. A pair of rogues: the goldsmith and the man who sifts his ashes for scraps.

The Potter.

The potter gets off cheaper than the rest; his honesty is not impeached, though his intelligence is held up to ridicule, and there is a vein of philosophy in some of the sayings about him. He is always thinking of his pots, and if he falls out with his wife he finds a solace in pulling his donkey's ears. But when the clay is on the wheel the potter may shape it as he will, though the clay rejoins, "Now you trample on me, one day I shall trample on you." Turned on the wheel yet no better for it; praise not the pot till it has been fired; are general proverbs of life to which there are numerous parallels. If you are civil to a potter he will neither respect you nor will he sell you his pots. The frequency of petty thefts in India is illustrated by the saying, "The potter can sleep sound; no one will steal his clay." He lives penuriously, and his own domestic crockery consists of broken pots. He is a stupid fellow—in a deserted village even a potter is a scribe—and his wife is a meddlesome fool, who is depicted as burning herself, like a Hindu wife, on the carcase of the Dhobi's donkey (*Dhobī ke gadhe par Kumhārin satī huī*).

The Blacksmith.

A blacksmith's single stroke is worth a goldsmith's hundred; but a Lohār is a bad friend; he will either burn you with fire or stifle you with smoke. His shop is always in an untidy mess; it is like the place where donkeys roll. Sparks are the lot of the blacksmith's legs. Such is his good nature that a monkey begged of him a pair of anklets. But you should not buy his pet *maina*, even if you can get it for a farthing, for the bird will drive you mad by mimicking the noise of the hammer. "To sell a needle in the Lohārs' quarter," is one of the Indian analogues of our "'Coals to Newcastle.'" "Before the smith can make a screw he must learn to make a nail" is a proverbial truism apparently of comparatively modern origin.

The Carpenter.

The carpenter thinks of nothing but wood, and his wife walks and talks in time to the noise of the plane. When out of work he keeps his hand in by planing his friends' buttocks. "The carpenter's face" is cited as a type of unpunctuality, since it is never to be seen at the time when he promised to come. "A whore's oath and a Sutār's chip" are examples of worthlessness. A fool of a Barhāi has neither chisel nor adze and wants to be the village carpenter!

The oil-presser and dealer in oil.

The oil-presser is no man's friend; he earns a rupee and calls it eight annas. He sits at ease while his mill goes round, and beguiles his hours of leisure by inventing improper stories, so that when two Telis meet their talk is unfit for publication. His unfortunate bullock is always blindfold, and walks miles and miles without getting any further. Once upon a time the bullock was lost, and the Teli is still looking for the peg to which it was tied. On another occasion his bullock took to fighting and the owner was sued before the Kāzi for damages. The Kāzi's finding ran thus: "What made the beast fight? The oil-cake you fed it on; so give me the ox and pay damages into the bargain." His wife saves a little oil by giving short measure to her customers, but "God takes all at once" when the jar breaks and the thick dust sucks up its contents. His daughter, on the other hand, is represented as giving herself airs and wondering what oil-cake can be.

The Tailor.

The tailor, the goldsmith and the weaver, these three are too sharp for the angel of death; God alone knows where to have them. The tailor's "this evening" and the shoemaker's "next morning" never come. However sharp his sight, a Darzi sees nothing, because he cannot take his eyes off his work. The influence of Hindu caste on Muhammadans is illustrated by the saying, "A Darzi's son is a Darzi and must sew as long as he lives." A Darzi steals your cloth and makes you pay for sewing it. When a tailor is out of work he sews up his son's mouth. The estimation in which he is held by his neighbours may be gauged by the saying, "A snake in a tailor's house: who wants to kill it?"

The Washerman.

All the world have their clothes washed, but the Dhobi is always unclean (ceremonially), and to see him the first thing in the morning is sure to bring bad luck. His finery is never his own, but no one has so many changes of linen as a Dhobi. He will not hesitate to use the king's scarf as a loin cloth; at his wedding the clothes of his customers are spread as carpets for the guests; and his son is the dandy of the village on a whistle and a bang, that is to say, by wearing other people's clothes which his father washes by giving them a bang on a stone and whistling. As for soap, none is used unless there are enough Dhobis to set up competition. When there is a robbery in the Dhobi's house the neighbours lose their clothes. He tears people's clothes and says it was the wind, but he is careful not to damage his father's things. You should change your Dhobi as you change your linen, for a new Dhobi washes clean. In a Koiri village the Dhobi is the accountant, for he is the only man who can add two and two together. He knows when the village is poor just as the orderly knows when his master has been degraded. The Dhobi's donkey is habitually overworked, and must carry huge bundles of linen while "its life oozes out of its eyes."

The Fisherman.

The occupation of fishing ranks rather low as it involves the taking of life, but most Indians are great fish-eaters and one would have expected to find more proverbs dealing with the subject. The few that I have collected seem to suggest that the manners of fishing folk are much the same everywhere. "A fisherman's tongue" corresponds to our "Billingsgate"; a Māchhi woman will scold even when she is dead; three clouts from an oilwoman are better than three kisses from a fishwife. There is a touch of local colour in the Sind saying, "Sometimes the float is uppermost, sometimes the fisherman," a reference to the practice of fishing balanced face downwards on an earthen pot which is liable to break or capsize.

The Weaver.

In all parts of India the stupidity of the weaver, especially of the Muhammadan weaver (Jolāhā), is the staple subject of proverbial philosophy. His loom being sunk in the ground, he is said to dig a pit and fall into it himself. If he has a pot of grain he thinks himself a Rājā. He goes out to cut grass when even the crows are flying home to roost. He finds the hind peg of a plough, and proposes to start farming on the strength of it. If there are eight Jolāhās and nine *huqqas*, they fight for the odd one. The Jolāhā goes to see a ram fight and gets butted himself. Being one of a company of twelve who had safely forded a river, he can only find eleven, as he forgets to count himself, and straightway goes off to bury himself in the belief that, as he is missing, he must be dead. Some Jolāhās walking across country come to a field of linseed looking blue in the moonlight; they wonder how deep the water is and hope that all of them can swim. A Jolāhā gets into his boat and forgets to weigh the anchor; after rowing all night he finds himself at home and rejoices in the thought that the village has followed him out of pure affection. A crow snatches a piece of bread from a Jolāhā's child and flies with it to the roof; the prudent father takes away the ladder before he gives the child any more. A Jolāhā hears the Korān being read and bursts into tears; on being asked what passage moves him so, he explains that the wagging beard of the Mullā reminded him of a favourite goat that he had lost. When his dogs bark at a tiger he proceeds to whip his child. He has no sense of propriety; he will crack indecent jokes with his mother and sister, and his wife will pull her father's beard. As a workman he is dilatory and untrustworthy. He will steal a reel of thread when he gets the chance; he has his own standard of time; he lies like a Chamār; and even if you see him brushing the newly woven cloth, you must not believe him when he says that it is ready.

The Tanner and Shoemaker.

Below these more or less respectable members of rural society, we find a number of outcast groups, village menials, or broken tribes some of whom pollute the high-caste man even at a distance, while others are guilty of the crowning enormity of eating beef. Among these the Chamār, tanner, shoemaker, cobbler, and cattle-poisoner, is the subject of a number of injurious reflexions. Though he is as wily as a jackal, he is also so stupid that he sits on his awl and beats himself for stealing it. He laments that he cannot tan his own skin. He knows nothing beyond his last, and the shortest way to deal with him is to beat him with a shoe of his own making, a practical axiom which is expressed in the saying that "old shoes should be offered to the shoemaker's god." "Stitch, stitch" is the note of the cobblers' quarter; "stink, stink" of the street where the tanners live. The Chamār's wife goes barefoot, but his daughter, when she has just attained puberty, is as graceful as an ear of millet. The functions of the Chamārin as the Mrs. Gamp of the village are rather inelegantly referred to in the saying, "There is no hiding the belly from the midwife." The hides and bones of dead cattle are the perquisite of the Chamār, and in some of the great grazing districts he is credibly suspected of assisting nature by means of a bolus of arsenic, craftily wrapped in a leaf or a petal of the *mahua* flower, and dropped where the cattle are feeding. A humorous allusion to this practice, which is exceedingly difficult to detect, may be traced in the proverb which represents the Chamār as enquiring after the health of the village headman's buffalo. In these latter days Chamārs are no longer forbidden to drink Ganges water, and this perversion of the old order of things is said to have caused "the righteous to die while the wicked live."

The Dom.

The Doms, among whom we find scavengers, vermin-eaters, executioners, basket-makers, musicians, and professional burglars, probably represent the remnants of a Dravidian tribe crushed out of recognition by the invading Aryans and condemned to menial and degrading occupations. Sir G. Grierson has thrown out the picturesque suggestion that they are the ancestors of the European gipsies, and that Rom or Romany is nothing more than a variant of Dom. In the ironical language of the proverbs the Dom figures as "the lord of death" because he provides the wood for the Hindu funeral pyre. He is ranked with Brāhmans and goats as a creature useless in time of need. A common and peculiarly offensive form of abuse is to tell a man that he has eaten a Dom's leavings. A series of proverbs represents him as making friends with members of various castes and faring ill or well in the process. Thus the Kanjar steals his dog, and the Gūjar loots his house; on the other hand the barber shaves him for nothing, and the silly Jolāhā makes him a suit of clothes. His traditions associate him with donkeys, and it is said that if these animals could excrete sugar Doms would no longer be beggars. "A Dom in a palanquin and a Brāhman on foot" is a type of society turned upside down. Nevertheless, outcast as he is, the Dom occupies a place of his own in the fabric of Indian society. At funerals he provides the wood and gets the corpse-clothes as his perquisite; he makes the discordant music that accompanies a marriage procession; and baskets, winnowing-fans, and wicker articles in general are the work of his hands.

In the west of India Mahārs and Dheds hold much the same place as the Dom. In the walled villages of the Marāthā country the Mahār is the scavenger, watchman and gate-keeper. His presence pollutes; he is not allowed to live in the village;

and his miserable shanty is huddled up against the wall outside. But he challenges the stranger who comes to the gate, and for this and other services he is allowed various perquisites, among them that of begging for broken victuals from house to house. He offers old blankets to his god, and his child's playthings are bones. The Dhed's status is equally low. If he looks at a water jar he pollutes its contents; if you run up against him by accident, you must go off and bathe. If you annoy a Dhed he sweeps up the dust in your face. When he dies, the world is so much the cleaner. If you go to the Dheds' quarter you find there nothing but a heap of bones.

The Mahār and Dhed.

This relegation of the low castes to a sort of Ghetto is carried to great lengths in the south of India where the intolerance of the Brāhman is very conspicuous. In the typical Madras village the Pāriahs—"dwellers in the quarter" (*pārā*) as this broken tribe is now called *—live in an irregular cluster of conical hovels of palm leaves known as the *pārchery*, the squalor and untidiness of which present the sharpest contrast to the trim street of tiled masonry houses where the Brāhmans congregate. "Every village," says the proverb, "has its Pāriah hamlet"—a place of pollution the census of which is even now taken with difficulty owing to the reluctance of the high-caste enumerator to enter its unclean precincts. "A palm-tree," says another, "casts no shade; a Pāriah has no caste and rules." The popular estimate of the morals of the Pāriah comes out in the saying, "He that breaks his word is a Pāriah at heart"; while the note of irony predominates in the pious question, "If a Pāriah offers boiled rice will not the god take it?" the implication being that the Brāhman priests who take the offerings to idols are too greedy to inquire by whom they are presented.

The Pāriah.

The organized animistic tribes, who are wholly outside the bounds of Hinduism, seem for the most part to have escaped the attention of the makers of proverbs, probably because they have no specific place in the communal life of the village. The Bhīl alone, hunter, blackmailer, and highway robber, has impressed his curious personality upon the people of the jungle country of Western India and Rajputana. He is, we are told, the king of the jungle; his

The Bhīl.

* [Bishop Caldwell (*Dravidian Grammar*, 2nd edit., 1875, p. 549) derives it from Tamil *parei*, "a drum"; but this has been questioned. E. Thurston, *Castes and Tribes of Southern India*, 1909, vol. vi., p. 77 *et seq.*]

arrow flies straight. He is always ready for a fight, but he is also a man of his word, and with a Bhīl for escort your life is safe. If you manage to please him he is a Bhīl; if you rub him the wrong way up he is the son of a dog. He has a large number of children, and in his household there is no dawdling as the family is always on the move.

From the wilds of Assam comes the quaint saying, "The Nāga's wife gets a baby; the Nāga himself takes the medicine." This sounds rather like a reminiscence of the *couvade*, but it may be nothing more than a reflexion on the intelligence of the Nāgas.

Comparative Proverbs.

Of the proverbs discussed in the foregoing paragraphs each has for its subject a particular caste and contains no reference to any other. I now turn to a class of proverbs which it will be convenient to group separately, since each of them deals with several castes and seizes upon their points of difference or resemblance. These comparative proverbs are curious in themselves, and throw a good deal of light on the relative estimation accorded to different castes by popular opinion. Here again the Brāhman bulks large and figures in queer company. A black Brāhman, a fair Sūdra, an under-sized Musalmān, a *ghar-jamai* (a son-in-law who lives with and on his father-in-law), an adopted son are all birds of a feather. Trust not a black Brāhman or a fair Pāriah. A dark Brāhman, a fair Chuhra, a woman with a beard—these three are contrary to nature. The Kunbi died from seeing a ghost; the Brāhman from wind in the stomach; the goldsmith from bile. The first is superstitious; the second over-eats himself; the third sits too long over his fire. A Brāhman met a barber; "God be with you" said the one, but the other held up his looking-glass, thus countering the Brāhman's demand for a fee for his professional blessing by asserting his own claim to be paid for shaving people. Brāhmans are made to eat, Bhavaiyas to play and sing, Kolis to commit robbery, and widows to mourn. The Mulla, the Bhāt, the Brāhman, and the Dom, these four were not born on giving day. A Brāhman for a minister, a Bhāt for favourite, and the Rājā's fate is sealed. A Dom, a Brāhman, and a goat are of no use in time of need. If you cannot ruin yourself by keeping a Brāhman servant, taking money from a Kasāi, or begetting too many daughters, you will do it by going to law with bigger men. The Brāhman is lord of the water; the Rajput lord of the land; the Kāyasth lord of the pen; and the Khatri lord of the back, *i.e.*, a coward. A Khatri woman brings forth sons always; a Brāhman woman only now and then—a rather cryptic utterance which may perhaps be a hit at the practice of female infanticide imputed to the Khatris.

Kāyasths, Khatris, and cocks support their kin; Brāhmans, Doms and Nāis destroy theirs. Bribe a Kāyasth; feed a Brāhman; water paddy and betel; but kick a low-caste man. A Turk wants toddy; a bullock wants grain; a Brāhman wants mangoes; and a Kāyasth wants an appointment. A Dhobi is better than a Kāyasth; a Sonār is better than a cheat; a dog is better than a deity; and a jackal better than a Pandit. Kāzis, Kasbīs, Kasāis, and Kāyasths—the four bad K's. There be three that dance in other people's houses and profit by their misfortunes—the Kāyasth, the Baidya, and the Dalāl or tout who promotes litigation. You may know a good Kāyasṭh by his pen; a good Rajput by his moustache; and a good Baidya by his searching medicine. From the last sentiment it would appear that the *messorum dura ilia* are much the same all over the world and that the Indian cultivator, like the English villager, wants his physic nasty and wants it strong.

When the tax collector is a Jāt, the money-lender a Brāhman, and the ruler of the land a Baniya, these are signs of God's wrath. Jāts, Bhāts, caterpillars and widows—all these should be kept hungry; if they eat their fill they are sure to do harm. When a buffalo is full she refuses oil cake; when a Baniya is well off he gives time to his debtors; when a Jāt is flourishing he starts a quarrel; when your banker is in a bad way he fastens upon you. When the Jāt prospers he shuts up the path (by ploughing over it); when the Karār (money-lender) prospers he shuts up the Jāt.

Loot the Baniya if you meet him, but let the Pathān go on his way. Better have no friends at all than take up with an Afghān, a Kamboh, or a rascally Kaṣhmīri. The crow, the Kamboh, and the Kalāl cherish their kin; the Jāt, the buffalo, and the crocodile devour their kin. All castes are God's creatures, but three castes are ruthless, the Ahīr, the Baniya, the Kasbi; when they get a chance they have no shame.

There are three careless knaves, the washerman, the barber, and the tailor. "The goldsmith's acid and the tailor's tag." This highly-condensed saying requires explanation; it is a proverb of delay, the suggestion being that the Sonār tells you that your ornament is ready, all but the final cleaning with acid; while the Darzi says that your coat is ready and only the tags for fastening it have to be sewn on. The Teli knows all about oil-seeds; the Shimpi (Kanarese tailor) all about lies; the village watchman all about thieves; the Lingāyat all about everything. The washerman knows who is poor in the village; the goldsmith knows whose ornaments are of pure gold.

Bābhans, dogs, and Bhāts are always at war with their kin. Seven Chamārs are not as mean as one Bābhan, and seven Bābhans are not as mean as one Nuniyār Baniya. In no man's land one makes friends with Gūjars and Gaddis. The Gareri got drunk when he saw the Ahīr in liquor. The Kāchhi is not a good caste; there is no virtue in a Māli; and the Lodhā is a poor creature who ploughs with tears in his eyes.

We may pass from these *genre* pictures of the standard types of Indian village life to groups defined by religion rather than by caste, but which nevertheless are regarded as castes by popular usage. Conspicuous among these are the Pārsis, concerning whom many proverbs are current in Gujarāt, the country where they first appeared after leaving Persia. Considering how much the Pārsis have done for Bombay, both by their spirit of enterprise and by their munificent donations to public purposes, it is a little surprising to find them so savagely attacked in the proverbs of their earliest home in India. The Pārsi, it is said, loses no time in breaking his word; a Pārsi youth never tells the truth; a bankrupt Pārsi starts a liquor shop, and celebrates the day of Zoroaster by drinking brandy. Domestic scandal is hinted at in the punning proverb, "All is dark (*andhyārā*) in a house where you find an *andhyāru* or Pārsi priest." "Oh, Dastūrji," says a supposed penitent, "how shall my sins be forgiven?" "First present a gold cat and a silver necklace, and then we will see." The proverb, "If a Pārsi grows rich he takes a second wife," has ceased to be applicable since the reproach of polygamy has been removed by the Pārsi Marriage Act, a self-denying ordinance passed at the instance of the Pārsis themselves. The influence of their Indian environment on the Pārsis is illustrated by the saying, "The Pārsi woman offers a cocoanut at the Holi," and by the curious fact that the mitre-shaped hat worn by old-fashioned Pārsis is merely a pasteboard copy of a Gujarāti pagri or turban. It is interesting and characteristic to find the Pārsis asserting their own superiority in retaliatory proverbs. "Crows your uncles and Pārsis your fathers" is their rejoinder, in the suggestive style

The Parsi.

of Oriental innuendo, to the Hindus who call them crows on account of their custom of exposing their dead. "The Hindu worships stones," say the Pārsis, "the Musalmān bows down to saints; the Pārsi religion is as pure as the water of the Ganges." Finally, we have the quaint saying, "A Pārsi's stroke, like a cannon ball," which one would like to trace to the hard-hitting achievements of Pārsi cricketers.

The Ascetics.

In India, as in mediæval Europe, the hypocrisy, the immorality and the shameless rapacity of ascetics and religious mendicants move the indignation of the proverbial philosopher. Mendicancy is the veil that covers the lion. An ascetic's friendship spells ruin to his friends. Money will buy the most pious of saints. When a man cannot get a wife he turns ascetic. When his crop has been burnt the Jāt becomes a fakīr. When fish are in season the Jogi loses his head. One widow has more virtue than a hundred Dandis. The Jogi and the profligate pass sleepless nights. "She went to the fakīr to learn morals; the holy man stripped off her trousers." A sect mark on his forehead and ten rosaries round his neck—in appearance a saint, but at heart in love with a prostitute. Promise a Brāhman nothing, but promise a mendicant less. The local Jogi gets no alms. "Reverend father, what a crowd of disciples!" "They will vanish, my son, as soon as they are hungry." "What has a saint to do with dainties?" "If there is no butter-milk I can manage with curds." "Oh, mother, give me some sweets; they are very good for the eyes." "My son, if you have a taste for milk and cream you should turn Nānakshāhi." "As soon as the ducks lay eggs the devotees eat them up."

In examining the proverbs relating to village life, no attempt has been made to group the material by provinces. The atmosphere of rural society is very much the same all over India, and the sayings which emanate from it breathe everywhere much the same spirit and partake of the same general character. Except in Sind, Baluchistan and the North-West Frontier Province, where the Hindus form an insignificant minority, the proverbial philosophy of the village takes its cue from Hinduism, and everywhere vents its spleen on the familiar figures of the extortionate priest, the greedy mendicant, the grasping money-lender, the garrulous barber, the pilfering goldsmith, the knavish washerman, the foolish weaver—all of them Hindus or Muhammadans grouped in occupational castes of the Hindu type.

The Muhammadans.

But in dealing with the specific proverbs which depict the foibles of Muhammadans it will be convenient to adopt a provincial arrangement. The bulk of the material is considerable, and it can hardly be grouped on any other principle; and the geographical distribution of Muhammadans happens to correspond pretty closely with the vital distinction noticed in an earlier chapter, between the Muhammadan who claims distinguished foreign descent and the native Indian converts who, in Bengal at any rate, were recruited from the dregs of the Hindu community, and embraced Islam as a short cut to social promotion.

In Baluchistan and North-West Frontier Province.

The proverbs of Baluchistan and the North-West border furnish plentiful illustrations of the amenities current in a primitive tribal society, the members of which are endowed with a pretty sense of allusive humour and addicted to the vigorous prosecution of all conceivable forms of vendetta. The Afghān is faithless (*Afghān be īmān*). A Pashtun's self-will will bring him to hell. A saint one moment, a devil the next, that is the Pathān. A Pathān's enmity is like a dung fire. The Pathāns took the village and the Behnas (cotton carders) got swollen heads. A Pathān's mouth waters the moment his hands are dry, *i.e.* he is hungry directly he has washed his hands after a meal. The weak antithesis of my rendering is a poor substitute for the crisp rhyme of the original, *Hāth sūkhā Pāthān bhūkhā.* "Be a thief, be a thief!" say the Afrīdi parents to their child as they pass it from one to the other through a hole in a wall, and thus baptize it in burglary. An Achakzai is a thief who will steal an empty flour bag. Here comes the Kākar besmeared with filth; when you meet him hit him with a stick; kick him out of the mosque and you will save trouble all round. A Masezai has no hope of God, and God has no hope of a Masezai. Though a Kāsi become a saint, he will still have a strain of the devil in him. A Khatak can ride, but he is a man of but one charge; so say the enemies of the Khataks, the Marwāts. The Khataks retaliate with the pleasant saying, "Keep a Marwāt to look after asses, his stomach well filled and his feet well worn." "A hundred Bhitanni ate a hundred sheep, so thriftless were they." Hold up a rupee and you may see any Mohmand, whether man or woman.

"Blood for blood" is the watch-word of the Baloch, a tribe recruited from all sorts of masterless men, and held together mainly by the bond of the blood-feud. Of themselves they say in poetical strain: "The hills are the fortress of the Baloch; for a steed he has white sandals; for a brother his sharp sword"; and of the chief of Las Bela, "Though the Jām be the Jām, yet is he by descent a Jadgal (converted Jāt) and therefore not the equal of the princely race of Baloch." To these vapourings their neighbours have the vulgar retort, "There goes a Baloch with his trousers full of wind," a reflexion at once on the boastfulness and on the expansive nether garments of the average Baloch tribesman. The democratic spirit of the Baloch is illustrated by the saying, "One Sanni and seven chiefs." To common honesty they are strangers. "The Baloch who steals gains paradise for his ancestors even unto seven generations." Wisdom begged in vain for mercy from the Rinds (the conquering tribe of Balochistan) and decency from the Meds (the seafaring people of the Makrān Coast). The black-faced Meds are like tamarisk sparks, without any glow of courage. The Med sailor lives by the wind and by the wind he dies. The Med is wrapped up in his voyage, and his wife is wrapped up with her lover.

No one seems to have a good word for the Brāhūi. He is no man's friend; he is the striped snake that bit the Prophet; he is always coveting other people's property; he will quarrel over an inheritance even with his mother, against whom he enforces the tribal custom by which Brāhūi women are excluded from succession. If you have never seen an ignorant lump come and look at a Brāhūi; he is the tail of a dog and his good is evil. (The word *sharr* which means "good" in Arabic means "evil" in Brāhūi.) The Jhalāwāns of Khuzdār are without honour; the Kalātis have ever been faithless; the army of the Kurds vanishes like the spark of a burning juniper; the Muhammad Shāhi are blood-suckers; the Raisāni usurers; if you ask a jackass whether he has any relations, he will tell you that the Sāssoli boast of being his cousins. The Mengals eat half-cooked meat, and "a Mengal's roast" is a proverbial synonym for an immature scheme. The Lahri alone escape general condemnation; their honesty is rated so high that in a country where promises are ratified by shaking hands "a Lahri's two fingers" ranks as a typical guarantee of faithful performance.

In Sind and Gujarāt the pretentious poverty and the domestic squabbles of the Miyān or petty Musalmān landholder are a favourite subject of ridicule. The Miyān is passing rich on a mat and a tooth-brush ; the pole of his carriage is spliced with string, and he stops at every grog-shop on the road. The Miyān's mare could only carry him to the end of the village. Look at the Miyān's new fashion : his coat is tied up in three places! The Miyān swaggers abroad but is meek as a mouse at home; when he comes back from tinning pots and pans, Bībī, his wife, combs his beard; he is only a *ser* and she is a *ser* and a quarter. A cheerful couple, Miyān and Bībī! when he broke his stick on her, she smashed the water-jar. The Bībī cries for sweets and the Miyān licks the lamps in the mosque. The Miyān cannot get it and the Bībī does not like it (sour grapes). The Miyān has no shoes to beat his wife with. The Miyān's beard on fire, and Bībī thinks he is warming himself. Miyān a fop and Bībī sweeping the house. The Miyān killed a crow and swore that he had shot a tiger. A Miyān's talk, like a kick from a fly. The Miyān is ripe for the grave and the Bībī is ripe for the bridal bed. (January and May.) "Why weeping, Miyān?" "My wife died to-day." "Why laughing, Miyān?" "I marry a new one to-day." God is straight, but the Miyān is crooked: if he is going north he says he is going south. "Time to get up, Miyān!" "All right, give me a hand." When Miyān goes to Mecca, Bībī goes to Mālwa. A Miyān's cat; a Miyān's cow buffalo. (Both half-starved.)

In Sind and Gujarāt.

The Jāt Musalmān cultivator of Sind is a person of dirty habits; two blankets and a half last him a lifetime. If you are civil to him he will knock you down. He is a merciless and importunate creditor—"the Jāt's farthing will break the skin while the Baniya's hundred rupees will not hurt you." If you rely on the word of a Jāt you will come to grief, yet sometimes he meets his match: his wife soaked the yarn to make it heavy, but the Baniya weighed it with false weights. Educate a Jāt and he becomes a nuisance to gods and men.

In the Punjab.

Throughout Northern India the Mullā (priest) and the Kāzi (marriage registrar and judge) fare badly at the hands of the popular oracle. The face of a Mullā conceals the heart of a butcher. The Kāzi will drink if he gets the liquor for nothing. The Mullā was drowned because he had never given anything to anybody, and could not bear to give his hand even to save his life.

A Kāzi's verandah is a place to sit in after meals, when you do not mind waiting for a decision long delayed, and "a Kāzi's judgment" is a synonym for injustice. Yet during his life all men honour the Kāzi; his bitch may give pups where she pleases, and when she dies the whole town is at the funeral. But when the Kāzi himself dies, not a soul follows his coffin to the grave. So every one strokes the Mullā's cow until the Mullā dies from a surfeit of milk and parched rice. Your love, it is said, is like that of the Mullā who feeds fowls in order to eat them. A Mullā's outing takes him as far as the mosque where he looks for alms. The horse kicked him off, but the Mullā boasted of his ride. The Mullā is a thief and the Banga who calls to prayer is his witness. Half a doctor is a danger to life; half a Mullā is a danger to faith.

In the United Provinces.

In the United Provinces they say, "A Musalmān, a wasp and a parrot are no man's friends; in time of trouble they will turn on you and sting or bite." When rich, a Mīr; when poor, a Fakīr; when dead, a Pīr. Sesamum, molasses, and the love of a Musalmān are sweet at first but afterwards turn to bitterness. Here and in the ironical question, "Since when has the Bībī become a Brāhmani," the allusion is to the facilities for divorce among Muhammadans. Where there are Musalmāns there is population; but their love is the friendship of a snake; even two families of them cannot agree. A Musalmān takes back the gift he has given, a reference to the practice of resuming a married daughter's dowry at her death. The true Musalmāns lie buried in their graves, and their faith lies buried in their books. A Musalmān convert cries "Allah! Allah!" all day long. Mīrsāhib is indeed of high family with his smooth cheeks and his empty stomach. "Mīrsāhib! Times are hard; you must hold on your turban with both hands."

In Behar.

From Behar we get the following: A real Miyān is a Miyān indeed but some Miyāns are Pinjāras (cotton teasers). When the Miyān (family tutor) is at the door it is a bad look-out for the dog. A farthing's worth of soap makes the Miyān a Bābu.

In Madras.

The south of India also treats the subject from the Hindu point of view. The country that has no crows has no Musalmāns. What does a beef-eater know of decent language? If girls are sold for a farthing a-piece, don't buy a Musalmāni. A Musalmān ascetic's butter-milk is toddy.

A curious series of proverbs is occupied with the delineation, in none too polished language, of provincial and local characteristics. "Never make friends with a Deccani," say the

Gujarātis, "he is as false as a latrine is foul; put not your faith in a three-cornered *pagri* (turban)." The Marāthas' retort courteous is: "The fool of a Gujarāti, kick him first and then he may understand what you want." "A Dravidian's nose-scratching" is another Marātha proverb aimed at the devious and insincere ways of the Dravidian Brāhman who is represented as scratching his nose by putting his hand round the back of his neck.

Provincial and local Proverbs.

As has been mentioned in an earlier chapter, the strong sense of family and racial obligations, and the remarkable capacity for adapting themselves to modern conditions of life which distinguish the Bengalis have led to their diffusion all over Northern India, where they exercise considerable influence in certain circles. But these domestic and public virtues, while they have gained for Bengalis a share in all grades of salaried employment proportionate to their industry and ability, have somehow, possibly for this very reason, failed to endear them to the other Indian races; and the supposed characteristics of this type, the most marked and the most provincial in India, are glanced at in a series of needlessly spiteful proverbs. Their dark complexion and the habit imputed to them of chewing betel incessantly are referred to in the guise of a traveller's observation:—"I have seen the land of Bengal, where teeth are red, and faces black." There is nothing to show that Bengalis chew betel more assiduously than other Indians. But both betel and areca nut grow well in Bengal; the province is very rich and very lightly taxed, and the people are able to indulge in small luxuries. "Bengal is the home of magic and the women are full of witchery," and "If a Bengali is a man what is a devil" serve to illustrate the suspicion which attaches to people who live in a distant country far away from the great centres of religious orthodoxy and social propriety, and may perhaps be a specific allusion to the debased forms of Tantric worship alleged to be current in Bengal. "A hungry Bengali cries 'Rice, rice'"—is the gibe of the fighting races at a diet associated in their minds with effeminacy and cowardice. "Twelve Bengalis cannot cut off a goat's ear" imputes feebleness and timidity in more direct terms. "An Eastern donkey with a Western bray" is a hit at the Bengali Bābus who affect European manners and dress. The Assamese, a type closely akin to the Bengali, are attacked for their vanity and social pretensions. "A pagri on his head and nakedness below, the

Assamese wishes to lead the way." These ill-natured witticisms savour of the malice of the unsuccessful competitor, the idle apprentice who in a well-regulated world would be debarred from manufacturing proverbs for general consumption. While making general accusations of cowardice they take no account of the proficiency of the educated Bengalis of the present day in football and hockey, games not unaccompanied with hard knocks. They forget that, in the Eastern districts of Bengal, the monotony of rural existence is relieved by Homeric battles in which the favourite weapon is a heavy fish spear made by splitting a bamboo into a cluster of branches, each of which is armed with formidable steel barbs. People who fight half-naked with these appalling implements can afford to disregard the charge of personal timidity. Worse still, the proverbs ignore such instances of conspicuous gallantry on the part of Bengalis as was furnished a few months ago by a Calcutta undergraduate, Nafar Chandra Kundu, who let himself down into a sewer reeking with poisonous gas in the almost hopeless attempt to rescue three municipal coolies who were lying there insensible and whose fate he himself shared. Courage of this order is rare anywhere in the world.

The swagger of the ubiquitous Mārwāri money-lender, who pretends that he is a Rājā in his own country, is thus ridiculed: "For houses hurdles of madār; for hedges heaps of withered thorn; millet for bread, horse-peas for pulse; this is thy kingdom, Rājā of Mārwār!" Another proverb alludes to the shape of their *pagris* and their capacity for getting on in the world. "The three-tufted ones (Mārwāris), the red-faced ones (Europeans), and the cactus plant cannot live without increasing."

General Proverbs.

Throughout this chapter the endeavour has been to arrange the material on inductive lines, so that the reader of what to many people will be strange sayings from an unknown world shall be led by easy stages from the particular to the general, from the concrete to the abstract, from reflexions on the vices and foibles of individual castes to the larger criticism of Indian life, as viewed through the medium of caste ideas and prepossessions, which is put forth in some of the more philosophical proverbs. Commencing, therefore, with a gallery of village portraits, we proceeded to examine the proverbs which combine and compare the various types, passing on to those which deal with the larger groupings of sect and religion and the wider field of local and provincial characteristics. The series may now be closed with some instances of the most general type of Indian proverbs, those which are concerned with the caste system as a whole and illustrate the extent of its influence. Proverbs of this kind are not numerous, and one would gladly have more of them, for they breathe a tolerant spirit which contrasts pleasantly with the spiteful malevolence of some of the rural portraits.

The authority of caste is of course uncompromisingly asserted. "When plates are interchanged," that is to say, when members of different castes intermarry, is a proverb of the impossible. "The high-born man mourns the loss of his caste as he would the loss of his nose," and "The caste killeth and the caste maketh alive," seem to refer to the vital issues involved in the decisions of caste tribunals which may make or mar the lives of those who come before them. In view of these grave possibilities, the discreet advice is given, "Having drunk water from his hands, it is foolish to ask about his caste." To take water from low-caste people is to incur ceremonial pollution, entailing expulsion from caste pending submission to a disagreeable purificatory ritual and the payment of a heavy fine; the least said, therefore, the soonest mended. "A low-caste man is like a musk-rat, if you smell him you remember it." "As the ore is like the mine, so a child is like its caste." "The speech fits the caste as the peg fits the whole;" the idea being that you can tell a high-caste man by his refined language and accent. "I have sold my limbs not my caste," says a servant to his master when he is asked to do something derogatory to his caste.

Along with these sayings affirming the supremacy of the modern doctrine of the necessity and inviolability of caste, we find others which seem to recall an earlier order of ideas when castes were not so rigidly separated, when members of different castes could intermarry, and when, within certain limits, caste itself was regarded as a matter of personal merit rather than of mere heredity. "Love laughs at caste distinctions." "Caste springs from actions not from birth." "Castes may differ; virtue is everywhere the same." "The Vaisyas and Sūdras must have come first, and it was from them that Brāhmans and Kshatriyas were made." "Though your caste is low, your crime is none the less." "Every uncle says that his caste is the best." In others again we hear the croaking tone of the *laudator temporis acti* to whom all change is a stumbling-block and a reproach. "The Hindu gods have fled to Dwārka; the Musalmān saints to Mecca; under British rule the Dheds shove you about." The Dheds, as has been explained above, are one of the scavenger castes of Bombay, whose mere touch is pollution. "Nowadays money is caste." "In old times men looked to caste when they married their children, now they look only to money." "The Pandit reads his Scriptures and the Mullā his Qurān; men make a thousand shows yet find not God." "To the Hindu Rām is dear, to the Musalmān Rahīm; they hate with a deadly hatred but know not the reason why."

No useful purpose would be served by attempting a comparative study of the Indian proverbs relating to caste and the European proverbs regarding trades and professions. Where the environment and the point of view differ so widely, there is really little opening for comparison between the two series of sayings. The Indian proverbs here collected stand by themselves; they centre round caste; and caste, as elaborated in India, is a unique phenomenon. It would be possible to pick out from the mass of material a few parallels between the shortcomings of tailors, barbers and shoemakers in Europe and in India; but neither the contrasts nor the correspondences are specially interesting, and two trades which figure largely in European proverbial literature—those of the miller and the baker—are conspicuous for their absence from the Indian group of portraits. In the East people grind their own corn and bake their own bread, and have no occasion to sharpen their wit on the rascals who steal the one and adulterate the other.

It is more instructive to note the difference between the popular conception of the Brāhman as illustrated by the proverbs and the ideal picture of him presented in the Institutes of Manu—the moral text-book of the orthodox Hindu. Here we read how the Brāhman is by right the lord of the whole creation, since through his mouth the gods continually consume the sacrificial viands and the manes receive the offerings made for the benefit of the dead. Other mortals subsist through his benevolence; he can create new worlds and new guardians of the world, and can deprive the gods of their divine station. Though Brāhmans employ themselves in all sorts of mean occupations, they must be honoured in every way; for each of them is a very great deity. To slay a Brāhman is mortal sin; whoever threatens him with physical violence will wander for a hundred years in hell; the man who seizes his property will feed in another world on the leavings of vultures. Even the cardinal duty of veracity is dispensed with in the interest of the Brāhman. In the chapter on witnesses the obligation to tell the truth is strongly insisted on and is enforced by the most terrible penalties. "Naked and shorn, tormented with hunger and thirst and deprived of sight, shall the man who gives false evidence go with a potsherd to beg food at the door of his enemy." Yet it is also written: "No crime, causing loss of caste, is committed by swearing falsely to women the objects of one's desire, at marriages, for the sake of fodder for a cow, or of fuel, and in order to show favour to a Brāhman." *

BIBLIOGRAPHY OF INDIAN PROVERBS.

ADAMS, LIEUT.-COL. A. *The Western Rajputana States*, 2nd ed. London, 1900.

CHELAKESAVARAYĀ MUDALIĀR, T. *Parallel Proverbs, Tamil and English.* Madras, 1903.

CHRISTIAN, J. *Bihar Proverbs.* London, 1891.

CROOKE, W. *A Rural and Agricultural Glossary for the North-West Provinces and Oudh.* Calcutta, 1880.

CROOKE, W. *Tribes and Castes of the North-West Provinces and Oudh.* Calcutta, 1896.

ELLIOT, SIR H. M. *Memoirs on the History, Folklore, and Distribution of the Races of North-West India*, ed. J. Beames, London, 1869.

FALLON, S. W. *Hindustani English Dictionary.* Benares, 1879.

FALLON, S. W. *Dictionary of Hindustani Proverbs*, ed. Sir R. Temple. Benares, 1886.

GANESH NĀRĀYAN DESHPANDE. *A Dictionary of Marāthi Proverbs.* Poona, 1900.

GANGĀ DATT UPRETI PANDIT. *Proverbs and Folklore of Kumaun and Garhwal.* Lodiana, 1894.

GĀNGADHAR GOVIND SĀPKAR. *Marathi Proverbs.* Poona, 1872.

GRAY, J. *Ancient Proverbs from the Burmese.* London, 1886.

GRIERSON, G. A. *Bihār Peasant Life.* Calcutta, 1885.

GURDON, CAPT. P. R. *Some Assamese Proverbs.* Shillong, 1896.

IBBETSON, D. C. J. *Punjab Ethnography.* Calcutta, 1883.

ISHUREE DASS. *Domestic Manners and Customs of the Hindus of Northern India.* Benares, 1866.

JAMJETJEE PETIT. *Collection of Gujarati Proverbs.* Bombay.

JENSEN, REV. H. *A Classified Collection of Tamil Proverbs.* Madras, 1897.

LAL BIHARI DAY. *Bengal Peasant Life.* London, 1878.

LAWRENCE, SIR W. R. *The Valley of Kashmir.* London, 1895.

LONG, REV. J. *Eastern Proverbs and Emblems.* London, 1881.

---

* *The Laws of Manu* translated by G. Bühler, I, 93, 95, 101; IV., 165; VIII., 93, 112; IX., 235, 315, 319; XI., 26.

LYALL, J. B. *Report on the Land Revenue Settlement of the Kangra District, Punjab.* Lahore, 1865–72.

MACONACHIE, J. R. *Agricultural Proverbs of the Panjab.* Lahore, 1890.

MANWARING, REV. A. *Marathi Proverbs, collected and translated.* Oxford, 1899.

NĀRĀYAN DĀMODAR CHHATRE. *Marāthi Practical Proverbs.* Poona, 1871.

NATESA SĀSTRI, PANDIT. *Familiar Tamil Proverbs.*

NESFIELD, J. C. *A Brief View of the Caste System of the North-West Provinces and Oudh.* Allahabad, 1885.

PERCIVAL, P. *Tamil Proverbs, with their English Translation*, 3rd ed. Madras, 1874.

PRABODH PRAKĀS SEN GUPTA. *Dictionary of Proverbs.* Calcutta, 1899.

PURSER, W. E. and FANSHAWE, H. C. *Settlement Report of the District of Rohtak.* Lahore, 1880.

RAYIPATI GURUVAYA GURU. *A Collection of Telugu Proverbs*, translated by Capt. M. W. Carr. Madras, 1868.

ROCHIRĀM GAJUMAL. *Handbook of Sindhi Proverbs.* Karachi, 1895. *Tamil Sayings and Proverbs on Agriculture.* Madras.

UPENDRO KRISHNA BONERJEA. *Handbook of Proverbs*, English and Bengali. Calcutta, 1891.

WILSON, J. *Grammar of Western Panjabi.* Lahore, 1898.

CHAPTER IV

CASTE AND MARRIAGE

> Das Ewig-Weibliche
> Zieht uns hinan.
>
> GOETHE. *Faust II.*

> Nous ne dépendons point des constitutions ni des chartes, mais des instincts et des mœurs.
>
> ANATOLE FRANCE.

AMONG the various causes which contribute to the growth of a race or the making of a nation by far the most effective and persistent is the *jus connubii*—the body of rules and conventions governing intermarriage. The influence of these rules penetrates every family; it abides from generation to generation, and gathers force as time goes on. The more eccentric the system, the more marked are the consequences which it tends to produce. With men, as with animals, artificial selection is more potent and works more rapidly than natural selection. In no department of life is the contrast sharper between the East and the West, the stationary and the progressive societies, the races of India and the nations of Europe. The first point which strikes an observer is the almost universal prevalence of the married state. In Europe sentiment and prudence hold divided sway, and the tendency on the whole is rather towards a decline in the number of marriages. In India neither of these motives comes prominently into play. Religion on the other hand, which in the West makes in the main for celibacy, throws its weight in India almost wholly into the other scale. A Hindu man must marry and beget children to perform his funeral rites, lest his spirit wander uneasily in the waste places of the earth. If a high-class Hindu maiden is unmarried at puberty, her condition brings social obloquy on her family, and on a strict reading of certain texts entails retrospective damnation on three generations of ancestors. But the general obligation

Contrasts between India and Europe.

to marry is hampered by numerous conditions. In the West the field from which a man can choose his wife is practically unlimited. The restrictions based on consanguinity are few, and all but an insignificant number of marriages are determined by the free choice of persons who have attained physical maturity, and believe that they know their own minds. In India, throughout the ever widening area dominated by Hindu tradition or influence, one set of rules contracts the circle within which a man must marry; another set artificially expands the circle within which he may not marry; a third series of conventions imposes special disabilities on the marriage of women. A fourth injunction, not as yet universal but constantly gaining ground, forbids a widow to marry again. Under the regime of infant marriage, wedded life too often commences before physical maturity has set in, and the children thus united make their first acquaintance when they are already husband and wife. Polygamy tempered by poverty, and two forms of polyandry, both tending to disappear under the influence of popular disapproval, complete the series of contrasts between Indian and European marriage customs. We shall consider later on how far the dry figures of the census bear witness to the far-reaching consequences of these restrictions on the natural tendencies of the human race. But before examining the statistics it will be of interest to describe more fully the customs alluded to above. Two of these, endogamy and exogamy, are common to all primitive societies. Polyandry and polygamy are found in several societies which are not primitive. Infant marriage, and the prohibition of widow remarriage are, I believe, peculiar to India.* Hypergamy, though it is met with in other countries, is probably more fully developed in India than anywhere else in the world. In describing these rules it is impossible to avoid constant reference to the social groups—tribes, castes and the like—by which their operation is determined. Marriage is the most prominent factor in the caste system, and the customs which regulate marriage can only be described in terms of caste or of some tribal unit which closely resembles a caste or represents a stage in the process by which caste has been evolved. The only people to whom this remark does not apply are the Burmese and other races of further India. The

* [The custom of infant marriage and the prohibition of remarriage of widows prevail in other countries besides India (E. Westermarck, *The History of Human Marriage*, 1891, p. 213 *et seq.*, 127.)]

Muhammadans in most parts of India have been affected in various degrees by the example of Hindu marriage usage; and Indian Christians have not always escaped the same pervading influence.

Endogamy.

The terms endogamy and exogamy—*passablement barbares* as M. Senart has called them—were introduced more than forty years ago by the late Mr. J. F. McLennan in his well-known essay on *Primitive Marriage.* The laws governing marriage which these terms denote were then unnamed. Mr. McLennan was, I believe, the first to draw attention to them, and the names devised by him have been adopted by all who have since written on the subject. Endogamy, or "marrying in," is the custom which forbids the members of a particular social group to marry any one who is not a member of the group. An endogamous division, therefore, is a group within which its members must marry. The following types of endogamous divisions may be distinguished. The enumeration is probably not exhaustive, but it will serve to illustrate the lines on which the principle of endogamy works in India:—

I. *Ethnic* groups consisting of compact tribes like the Indo-Aryan Rajputs of Rajputana and the Dravidian Mūndās, Orāons and Santāls of Chutia Nagpur, and also including tribes, like the Bhūmij, who have adopted Hinduism and transformed themselves into a caste. In the case of the latter, the assumption of a common origin is borne out by what is known of the history and affinities of the tribe, but after having become a caste, its members set to work to strip themselves of all customs likely to betray their true descent. At the same time the substantial landholders, if there are any among the tribe, usually break off from the rest and set up as Rajputs, a designation which outside of Rajputana proper does not necessarily imply any race distinction, and frequently means nothing more than that the people using it have or claim to have proprietary rights in land. The local Rājā of the Bhūmij country pretends to be some kind of Rajput, and the smaller landholders of the tribe tend to follow his example. The change of style does not take long to effect, and it is no one's business to challenge its validity. I have known a man who habitually posed as a Sūrajbansi Rajput file in court and lay immense stress upon a document in which his grandfather wrote himself down a Bhūmij. His composure was not materially disturbed when the anomaly was pointed out to him.

II. *Linguistic or Provincial* groups, such as Tamil, Telugu, Bengali, Oriya, and Paschima or Bihari Brāhmans. These classes are very large, and include whole castes which in their turn are broken up into endogamous sub-castes. Such groups arise partly from the fiction which assumes that men who live in a different part of the country and speak a different language must be of a different race, and probably also in some measure from the inclusion of different stocks under a single caste-name. It can hardly be doubted, for example, that the large and miscellaneous groups included under the name Brāhman have been recruited to some extent from the local priests of tribes which adopted Hinduism.

III. *Territorial or Local* groups not corresponding to any distinction of language, such as the Rārhi and Bārendra Brāhmans, the Uttariya and Dakshini (north and south of the Ganges) Doms of Bihar, the Tamāria and Sikharbhūmi Bhūmij of Manbhum, and numerous others. It is curious to observe that in some cases these groups are called after ancient territorial divisions, such as Rārh, Bārendra, Sikharbhūm, etc., which appear on no map, and the names of which may possibly throw some light upon the early history of India.*

IV. *Functional or Occupational* groups, such as the Mecho and Hālia or Helo sub-castes of Kaibartta, of whom the former sell fish, while the latter, who have now given themselves brevet rank as Māhishyas, confine themselves to cultivation; and the Dulia, Machhua, and Matiāl sub-castes of Bāgdis who are distinguished respectively by carrying palanquins, fishing, and labouring as tank-diggers and earth-workers. Writing about the Hālia sub-caste of Kaibartta in 1891, I ventured on the conjecture that "this sub-caste will rise in social estimation and will altogether sink the

* The position of most of these ancient territorial divisions is now fairly well known. Amongst recent writers on the subject may be mentioned Mr. Pargiter, late of the Indian Civil Service, and Mahāmahopādhyāya Hāra Prasād Sāstri.

Kaibartta." The forecast has come true. They now call themselves Māhishyas, a name unheard of ten years ago, and pose as a distinct caste. The claim has not yet been fully recognized, but that is merely a question of time and importunity.*

V. *Sectarian* groups like the Bishnois of Northern India, and the Lingāyats of Bombay. These were originally religious sects which have now closed their ranks to outsiders and marry only among themselves. As a rule, however, groups based upon religious differences within the range of Hinduism do not tend to become endogamous, and the evolution of a caste from a sect is a comparatively rare phenomenon.

VI. *Social* groups marked off by abstaining from or practising some particular social or ceremonial usage. Thus the Sagāhut sub-caste of Sūnris (traders and liquor sellers) in Bihar allow their widows to re-marry by the maimed rite of *sagāi*, while another sub-caste of Sūnris forbid widow marriage, and designate themselves *biyāhut*, "the married one," from *biyāh*, the full-blown wedding ceremony which no woman can go through twice.

In theory all the members of each of the numerous groups included in these classes are regarded as forming a body of kindred, though in any particular instance their pedigree may be extremely obscure. In the first or ethnic class, the racial tie which binds the members together and distinguishes them from other tribes forming part of the same class is palpable and acknowledged, and various legends are current which purport to account for it. In the other classes the tendency towards sub-division, which is inherent in Indian society, seems to have been set in motion by the fiction that men who speak a different language, who dwell in a different district, who worship different gods, who observe different social customs, who follow a different profession, or practice the same profession in a slightly different way, must be of a fundamentally different race. Usually, and in the case of sub-castes invariably, the fact is that there is no appreciable difference of blood between the newly-formed group and the larger aggregate from which it has broken off.

For reasons which need not be entered upon here, complete statistics of these countless divisions are never likely to be

---

* See p. 118, *supra*.

available. But many of them are known to be exceedingly small, and even the larger ones, when distributed over a large area of country, may be so scantily represented in a given locality that the number of possible marriages open to their members must be inconveniently restricted.

The disintegrating influence of the constant creation of separate connubial groups has not escaped the notice of Indian social reformers. In an able paper on the fusion of sub-castes in India Lāla Baijnāth Lāl, Judge of the Court of Small Causes in Agra, has pointed out the harm which they do "physically by narrowing the circle of selection in marriage, intellectually by cramping the energies, and morally by destroying mutual self-confidence and habits of co-operation." The writer goes on to propose that social reformers should use their influence "to make those sub-sections of a caste which inter-dine (*sic*) also intermarry." The suggestion is sound in itself and is put forward with conspicuous moderation. Its author wisely refrains from advocating intermarriage between members of different castes, and lays stress on the expediency of proceeding gradually and commencing with the smallest groups. But clearly his plan will only meet those cases where the *jus convivii* is wider than the *jus connubii*. Ordinarily, no doubt, when people will not eat together, still less will they intermarry. But this is not always the case. Among the Agarwāls, for instance, members of different religious sects intermarry but do not eat together. At marriage the wife is formally admitted into her husband's sect, and must in future have her food cooked separately when she stays with her own people. A well-known proverb says of the Kanaujia Brāhmans of the United Provinces—*Tīn Kanaujia terah chūlhā*, "Three Kanaujias want thirteen kitchens," implying that their notions on the subject of ceremonial purity are so extreme that they will hardly eat even with their nearest relations. Of these people Lāla Baijnāth remarks that "the smallness of their various clans causes the greatest difficulty in obtaining husbands for girls except on payment of extortionate sums of money." Mr. Burn, however, informs me that, although their usages are not sufficiently defined to be capable of clear description, the groups which cannot eat together are much smaller than those which cannot intermarry. In both cases, therefore, the change suggested would aggravate the very evil which it is intended to cure. Both serve to illustrate the diversity and intricacy of social usage in India and the dangers which beset the path of any one who seeks to introduce what at first sight may seem to be a most obvious reform.

An interesting case has recently been published by Mr. Burn, tending to show how the most modern and enlightened movements, so far from promoting the consolidation of social groups, merely encourage the instinct of separation which is the governing principle of the caste system. Among the mercantile castes of the United Provinces are two large groups known as Bārahseni and Chauseni, the members of which do not intermarry. The former are shop-keepers and confectioners, and pride themselves on not allowing widows to marry again. The Chauseni are usually regarded as an illegitimate or outcast branch of the Bārahseni, but they are endeavouring to improve their status and, as a means to that end, an important section of them "has refused to recognize widow marriage, and even the rest of the group look on the practice with growing disfavour." Some members of the Bārahseni community have recently joined the modern reformers of the Ārya Samāj, "and a marriage was lately celebrated between a Bārahseni man and a widow of the same group. When the project was announced, the orthodox Hindus held a meeting and endeavoured to stop further proceedings, but without success. Two days after the marriage another meeting was held, and the married couple and those who aided them were solemnly excommunicated. A printed notice has been widely circulated directing all Bārahsenis to avoid dining, marrying, drinking, or holding any communication with those outcasted. A large feast was subsequently held, at which about 4,000 orthodox Bārahsenis were present, but to which none of the guilty members were invited. The feeling has gone so far that some men whose sons had previously married into families now outcasted have recalled their daughters-in-law, and refuse to let them visit their parents. Others have turned their own daughters out of their houses as they are married to outcasts." *

These proceedings give rise to the awkward question, what is to become of all the people thus expelled from their own society. The Chausenis will not receive them, because they have offended against a rule which the Chausenis themselves are beginning to observe. Nor would the outcasts consent to enter the lower group, since they insist on the entire legality of the marriages which have been contracted. The result is

* *J. A. S. B.*, Vol. I., No. 10, 1905.

that at present they belong to no caste at all, and, arguing from analogy, it seems probable that they may be driven to set up a new caste of their own.

Exogamy, or "marrying out," is the custom which forbids the members of a particular social group, usually supposed to be descended from a common ancestor, or to be associated with a certain locality, to marry any one who is a member of the same group. An exogamous division, therefore, is a group outside of which its members must marry.

Exogamy.

The following classes of exogamous divisions are found in India:—

I. *Totemistic*, being the names of animals, plants, etc., such as *Hānsda*, wild goose, *Hemron*, betel palm. A man of the Hānsda division may not marry a woman of that division, and so on. These totemistic divisions are confined for the most part to tribes and castes of Dravidian descent.

II. *Eponymous*, the ancestor who gives his name to the group being either a Vedic saint (as with the Brāhmans and the castes who imitate them), or a chief of comparatively modern date, as with the Rājputs and others.

III. *Territorial*, referring either to some very early settlement of a section or to the birthplace of its founder; prevalent among the Rājputs and the trading castes supposed to be allied with them, and found also among the Kandhs of Orissa and the Nāgas of Assam in a very primitive form, the sept there residing in the local area whose name it bears.*

IV. *Local, communal, or family* sections of small size and comparatively recent origin.

V. *Titular, or nickname* groups referring to some personal peculiarity or adventure of the founder of the sept, or to some office which he is supposed to have held.

Besides these we also find castes which have no sections of any kind, or, which comes to the same thing, have only one section and habitually marry within it, and simply reckon prohibited degrees in much the same way as we do ourselves.

We have seen that endogamy restricts intermarriage in one direction by creating a number of artificially small groups within which people must marry. Exogamy brings about the same result by artificially enlarging the circle within which

[* T. C. Hodson, *The Nāga Tribes of Manipur*, 1911, p. 71.]

they may not marry. Here again no complete statistics are available. But in certain proceedings held in Madras in connection with the classification of the Kamalākar caste of immigrants into Tanjore from the Deccan, who call themselves Saurāshtra Brāhmans, it was stated that each of their exogamous divisions contained about 2,000 persons. A somewhat similar result may be arrived at by calculation for the subcastes of Brāhmans in Bombay. Compare these figures with the largest number of persons that can be imagined to be excluded by our own table of prohibited degrees and the contrast is sufficiently striking. The calculation, however, understates the case. As has often been pointed out, exogamy is one-sided in its operation. In no case may a man marry into his own group, but the name of the group goes by the male side, and consequently, *so far as the rule of exogamy is concerned*, there is nothing to prevent him from marrying his sister's daughter, his maternal aunt, or even his maternal grandmother.* Alliances of this kind are barred by a separate set of rules, which usually overlap the exogamous rule to some extent. Marriage with any person descended in a direct line from the same parents is universally forbidden. In order to simplify the calculation of collateral relationship—a complicated business which severely taxes the rural intellect—the following formula is in use throughout Bihar :—*Chacherā, mameru, phuphera, musera, ye chār nātā bachāke shādi hotī hai,* "the line of paternal uncle, maternal uncle, paternal aunt, maternal aunt, these four relationships are to be avoided in marriage." Here the first point to notice is that in the first generation the whole of the paternal uncle's descendants, both male and female, are excluded by the rule prohibiting marriage within the section. In the second and subsequent generations agnates are barred, but descendants through females are not. For the paternal uncle's daughters must have married out of the section, so that their children must belong to some other section, and thus second cousins are able to marry. Another

[* In Southern India cousin marriage is common (W. H. R. Rivers, "The Marriage of cousins in India," *Journal Royal Asiatic Society*, July, 1907, p. 611 *et seq.*). "It is a prevalent custom throughout Southern India that a girl's father's sister's son has the first right to her hand in marriage. The Malayālam word for son-in-law (*maru makan*) means nephew. If a stranger should marry a girl, he is also called nephew. But the unmarried nephew, having the first admitted right to the girl, must be paid eight annas, or two fanams, before he will allow her to be taken away" (E. Thurston, *Castes and Tribes of Southern India*, 1909, vol. vii., p. 60; cf. J. G. Frazer, *Totemism and Exogamy*, 1910, vol. ii., p. 331 *et seq.*; *Census Report*, *Central Provinces*, 1911, vol. i., p. 134). For cross-cousin marriage among Muhammadans in Northern India, see *Census Report*, *Kashmir*, 1911, vol. i., p. 139.]

point is that the formula does not state the number of generations to which the prohibition extends, and that different castes supply this omission in different ways. The Dravidian races generally incline to laxity. The Santāls, for example, in the Santāl Parganas, are said to make up for their sweeping prohibition on the father's side by allowing very near alliances on the mother's side—a fact well illustrated in their proverb "No man heeds a cow-track, or regards his mother's sept." Many castes, again, exclude a smaller number of generations on the female side, while others profess to prohibit intermarriage so long as any relationship, however remote, can be traced between the parties.

Hypergamy.

Hypergamy, or "marrying up," * is the custom which forbids a woman of a particular group to marry a man of a group lower than her own in social standing, and compels her to marry in a group equal or superior in rank. A hypergamous division, therefore, is a group forming part of a series governed by the foregoing rule. The men of the division can marry in it or below it; the women can marry in it or above it.

The following are instances of hypergamous divisions :—

(*a*) The four original classes (*varnas*) as depicted in the somewhat contradictory utterances of the law books, which seem to deal with a period of transition when caste was being gradually evolved out of a series of hypergamous classes. Thus one set of passages in Manu, Baudhāyana, Vishnu and Nārada allows a Brāhman to marry in succession a woman of each of the four castes; while other texts from the same authorities forbid him to marry a Sūdra woman. According to Baudhāyana, Gautama, and Usanas marriages in which the wife was only one grade below the husband are freely admissible and the children take the rank of the father, so that the son of a Vaisya by a Sūdra woman was counted a Vaisya.† On the other hand, all authorities agree in reprobating marriages between men of lower classes and women of higher.

---

* This is what the term was intended by its inventor to mean. He alone is responsible for the etymology. [Sir D. Ibbetson, *Census Report*, *Punjab*, 1881, vol. i., p. 356.]

[† Manu, *Laws*, iii., 12-13, ix. 85-87, with the references quoted by G. Bühler, *Sacred Book of the East*, xxv., 1886, pp. 77, 342. A. A. Macdonell, A. H. Keith, *Vedic Index of Names and Subjects*, 1913, i. 476.]

(*b*) The groups Kulin, Siddha-Srotriya, Sādhya-Srotriya, and Kāshta-Srotriya among the Rārhi Brāhmans of Bengal as organized by Ballāl Sen. The rule was that a man of the Kulin class could marry a woman of his own class or of the two higher Srotriya classes; a Siddha-Srotriya could marry in his own group or in the Sādhya group; but the Sādhya and Kāshta-Srotriyas might take wives only within the limits of their own classes. Conversely, women of the Sādhya-Srotriya class could marry in their own class or the two classes above them; Siddha-Srotriya women in their own class or in the Kulin class; while Kulin women at one end of the scale and Kāshta women at the other were restricted in their choice of husbands to the Kulin and Kāshta groups.

(*c*) Among the Marāthas families belonging to groups such as Kadam, Bānde, Bhosle, Powār, Nimbālkar, etc., whose ancestors rose to power during the Marātha ascendancy, will not give their daughters in marriage to Marāthas of lower social position.* In some cases intermarriage has been entirely broken off; and the group is converting itself into a caste which claims descent from the traditional Kshatriyas.

(*d*) A curious development of hypergamy has taken place of recent years among the Pods, a cultivating and fishing caste very numerous in the districts near Calcutta. Those Pods who have taken to English education and become clerks, pleaders, doctors, and the like, refuse to give their daughters in marriage to their agricultural and fishing-caste fellows though they still condescend to take brides from the latter. The case is closely parallel to that of the Māhisya Kaibarttas mentioned above, and is of interest as exhibiting an earlier stage in the process of caste-making. The educated Pods, it will be observed, have not completely separated from the main body of their caste; they have merely set up for themselves a special *jus connubii*, the right of taking girls without giving them in return, like the three higher classes in the traditional Indian system. Their number being comparatively small, they probably have not women

[* This restriction is now being relaxed, *Ethnological Survey*, *Central Provinces*, Part IX., 1911, p. 127.]

enough to meet their own needs. But this will right itself in course of time, and they will then follow the classical precedent of the twice-born classes and will marry only within their own group. Later on they will start a distinctive name, probably a pretentious Sanskrit derivative, and will disclaim all connexion with the Pods. They will then have become a caste in the ordinary acceptation of the word, and in a generation or two their humble origin will be forgotten.

The examples given above show the custom of hypergamy to be of great antiquity, and to prevail in India over a very wide area at the present day. Its theoretical working is perhaps best illustrated by the following diagram. Let X

represent a caste divided into the three hypergamous groups, A, B, and C. Within each group, the capital letters stand for the marriageable men, and the small letters for the marriageable women of the group. The horizontal and diagonal lines connecting the capitals with the small letters show what classes of men and women can intermarry. It will be seen that a man of the A group can marry a woman of his own or of the two lower groups; a man of B can marry into B or C, while a man of C is confined to his own class, and cannot marry a woman from either of the classes above him. Conversely, a woman of the C class can get a husband from A, B, or C, and a woman of the B class from A or B; but a woman of the A class cannot find a husband outside of her own group. Excluding polygamy and polyandry,

Influence of hypergamy.

and supposing the women of each group to be evenly distributed among the groups they are entitled to marry into, the result of the first series of marriages would be to leave two-thirds of the women in the A group without husbands, and two-thirds of the men in the C group without wives. Of course in practice the system does not work in this mechanical fashion. Husbands are at a premium in the upper groups and become the object of vigorous competition; the bride-price of early usage disappears, and is replaced by the bridegroom-price now paid among most of the higher castes in India. The rich get their daughters married above their proper rank; poorer people are driven to reckless borrowing or, in the last resort, to other means, if they would avoid the disgrace of letting their daughters grow up unmarried. There are, unhappily, several ways of redressing the unequal proportions of the sexes and putting artificially straight what has been artificially made crooked. One approved way is for the parents to kill, or to make no attempt to keep alive, all female infants except those for whom they can make sure of finding husbands. This is what the Rajputs of Northern India used to do until a law was passed making things unpleasant for any village which could not show a respectable proportion of girls. The practice seems to be as old as the Yajur Veda, which speaks of female infants being exposed when born; while the remark in the Atharva Veda, that the birth of a daughter is a calamity, may perhaps imply that then, as now, infanticide was connected with the difficulty of getting daughters suitably married.*

Another method is that of wholesale polygamy, such as was practised by the Kulin Brāhmans of Bengal a couple of generations ago. Several middle-aged Kulins are known to have had more than a hundred wives, and to have spent their lives on a round of visits to their mothers-in-law. For each wife they had received a handsome bridegroom-price, diminishing in amount with the number of wives they had at the time of the marriage; they made what they could out of each periodical visit; and they asked no questions about the children. Nearly forty years ago Babu Abhaya Chandra Das described this scandalous state of things in a paper read before the Dacca Institute. He said: "I know of two Kulins, one of whom married about 60 wives, and the other had upwards of 100; each of these men had a book in which he entered the names of villages where he married as well as the names of the fathers of the wives married. At the commencement of the cold weather, each would start on his connubial tour, if I may so express it, with his memo-book, and after collecting money from each wife visited according to her father's pecuniary circumstances, return home at the beginning

[* A. A. Macdonell, *A History of Sanskrit Literature*, 1900, p. 163. An interesting attempt by the poorer classes in Western India to obviate the difficulty, under the system of hypergamy, of finding husbands for their daughters, is reported among the Kunbīs. Groups of villages have been formed, the residents of which refuse to marry their girls to the wealthier residents in towns. (*Census Reports*, *Baroda*, 1911, vol. i., p. 136 *et seq.*; *Bombay*, 1911, vol. i., pp. 118 *et seq.*, 200 *et seq.*, 280.) A similar revolt against hypergamy is reported among the Khatrīs and the Brāhmans, who serve them, in the Panjab (H. A. Rose, *Glossary of the Tribes and Castes of the Punjab and North-Western Province*, 1911, vol. ii., pp. 126, 514).]

of the summer to spend the rest of the year in his village. It is not infrequently the case that fathers and sons and husbands and wives meet as perfect strangers to one another, and become overwhelmed with shame when their mutual relations are known. I heard also of one case in which a Kulin, by mistaking the name, visited the daughter of a certain Bangsaj, who was glad to receive his supposed son-in-law, but a few days afterwards, the real son-in-law paid his visit, and the mistake was then found out to the utter amazement of the father"—and, one would think, to the consternation of the daughter.

The system, I am informed, has even now not wholly died out, but it prevails on a less outrageous scale; a connubial touring season is not so much in evidence; and educated opinion condemns it forcibly. According to a recent writer,* however, "it is still in full force in East Bengal, where such an abominable practice of having many wives still exists." And an actual case was mentioned to me recently of a Kulin Brāhman living in the neighbourhood of Calcutta who has more than fifty wives, duly entered in a register, whom he visits, for a consideration, during the cold weather. The same writer gives an interesting account of a modern development of the principle of hypergamy which has arisen from the demand for graduate husbands in the marriage market of Bengal.

"Education instead of stifling or mitigating the baneful effects of Kulinism has gone in a horrible degree to strengthen them. In fact, the University standard has become a more powerful engine of oppression for the girl's father than the so-called Ballāli Kulinism. A Bachelor of Arts, if he is also a bachelor in life, even if he is a homeless pauper living upon his friends' bounty, and be he a Kulin or a Maulik or Achal, must have, besides 'a wingless nymph,' as goes the Bengali adage, for his spouse adorned with jewelry and gold ornaments from head to foot, a cash demand of at least Rs. 4000, besides the personal dower for the bridegroom's embellishment called *barābharan*, from a girl's father of ordinary means, say a Deputy Magistrate or a Sub-Judge. If the father has the misfortune to possess a girl of somewhat dark complexion

* *The Brahmans and Kayasthas of Bengal*, by Babu Girindranath Dutt, B.A., M.R.A.S., M.S.A., Madras, 1906 [for recent instances of Kulin polygamy see *Census Report, Bengal*, 1911, vol. i., p. 327].

or in any way ugly or deformed, the demand may run up to Rs. 15,000. Add to this the numerous other items of expenditure to be incurred by the bride's father on, before, and after the marriage, and the result is simply ruinous to him, to say the least. We have personal knowledge of an incident where the bridegroom's party, composed of educated men and headed by an M.A., a renowned professor of a Government College, had demanded after the marriage from the bride's father, who had already paid double the demand contracted, a blackmail which he agreeably termed *barayātramaryādā* (honorarium to bridegroom's party) for each member, whether Kulins or Mauliks, composing the bridegroom's party, for partaking food in the bride's house. The most ridiculous feature in the whole affair was that the names of the bridegroom, his brother and his father, who had already received a handsome honorarium for his position as the boy's father, were also enlisted in this general list of bridegroom's party to exact double honorarium. The bride's father having refused to comply with this unjust demand as an insult, innovation and contrary to family custom, he was asked to remit this demand immediately by telegraphic money-order on pain of having his little girl detained in a forlorn and far-off country in case of default. In the majority of cases, the bridegroom's party now demands the whole amount in cash in advance, and many even stoop to the meanness of demanding a registered document binding the bride's father in a contract so that he may not defraud hereafter. The least causes of dissatisfaction, however frivolous (and these could be easily picked up), subject the poor little girl-wife to all sorts of ill-treatment in her strange father-in-law's house, so long as she does not grow old enough to assert her independence there. Threats to remarry the bridegroom at once if the bride's party would not soon suitably make amends for such frivolous omissions and commissions are also in some cases realized to wreak vengeance. The miserable position of a girl's father is very well depicted in the Bengali adages which say that 'he has hanging over his head a chain of shoes to strike him at every turn,' and that 'bride's father is soil and bridegroom's father is peg' (*meyer bāp māti chheler bāp khūnti*). In view of the increasing difficulties in daughters' marriages which are being occasioned in consequence of the daily rising and multiplicity of the items of demand, thoughtful men have already rightly apprehended, that if matters go on in this stride, there would soon be a time when girls' fathers would be compelled to have recourse to secret infanticide." *

Mr. Dutt's view of the matter is confirmed by a remarkable speech delivered in Bengali by the Hon'ble Mr. Justice Mittra of the Calcutta High Court and published in the *Kāyasth Patrika*.

"Look at the present situation. I have heard that in Rajputana daughters used to be killed as soon as they were born, because bridegrooms could not be had easily. In these disastrous days of ours, in our country also, in order to rid ourselves of the troubles of a daughter's marriage, we might also be tempted to do the same at her birth. Now, as it is, the faces of the parents grow lean as soon as a girl is born to them. The birth of a daughter is considered to be the penalty of sins committed in a former state of existence. It is needless to dwell on the present state of Hindu society, as it is too well known. Led by avarice or vanity, though many shut their eyes and raise the plea that there is nothing wrong in 'committing highway robbery on a thief,' they fully understand what a disaster has been the effect. Hundreds of girls' fathers have to sell or mortgage their residential houses; thousands of girl-wives have to suffer in patience maltreatment like prisoners under their fathers-in-laws' roofs in consequence of their fathers' inability to meet unjust demands. Placed in a strange house for the first time, the poor girl-wives sorely feel the absence of their fathers, mothers, brothers, and sisters; they are constantly tormented by the abusive epithets heaped on their parents and they are themselves subjected to intolerable personal ill-usage. These circumstances drive us to the conclusion that it would be far better to kill girls as soon as they are born or to keep them in life-long maidenhood regardless of religion and morality. ******* A boy's father, who has not even a house of his own and lives in a hired lodging where he has brought up his son, now aspires to become the possessor of a two-storied house and Govt. Promissory paper on his son's marriage. Perhaps he is over head and ears in debt and he intends to liquidate that by his son's marriage. He wants to send his son to England to become a Civilian,

[* "Educational qualifications put up the price of a bridegroom, not so much because of any belief in education as an advantage *per se*, but because the bridegroom is more likely to get remunerative employment. The possession of a degree may even change the whole situation and cause a bridegroom-price to be paid instead of a bride-price." Instances are given of the monstrous demands made by the parents of sons thus qualified. (*Census Report, Bengal*, 1911, vol. i., p. 316.)]

he has no money, so he must get it by his son's marriage. * * * * * Punishments for theft and robbery are provided in the Indian Penal Code, but there is no provision in it for punishing such a father, although his offence is just as bad, and because there is no such provision, he can ruïn the girl's father with absolute impunity."

These bitter complaints relate to the state of things among the Dakhin-Rārhi sub caste of Kāyasths in Bengal. But they are not confined to that sub-caste. A case has been brought to my notice which shows that the Uttar-Rārhi Kāyasths are involved in similar difficulties arising out of the rule of hypergamy. A gentleman belonging to the Kulin sub-division of this sub-caste had two daughters. For the elder he was unable to find a Kulin husband, so he married her to a Maulik, an offence for which the community made him pay a heavy fine. Shortly before his death, he managed, after much haggling, to arrange a marriage for the second girl with a Kulin boy of suitable pedigree, for whom he had to pay a bridegroom price of Rs. 1000, which was deposited with one of the boy's relatives under an agreement that it should be spent on his education. The girl was married when she was nine years old, her husband being then fourteen, but she remained with her own family until she had completed her twelfth year, the statutory age for cohabitation. Soon after she joined her husband it came out that his people had made away with the Rs. 1000, and they demanded from the girl's brother, a clerk on a small salary, a regular payment of Rs. 10 a month for the education of her husband, who had just passed the Matriculation examination of the Calcutta University. When the brother protested his inability to meet this unreasonable demand, the mother-in-law, following the example of Mr. Wackford Squeers, repeatedly beat the helpless child-wife so severely that she fainted from pain. Fortunately the girl had been taught to write and she managed to post a letter describing her sufferings, whereupon a stalwart relative intervened and took her away by force. She is now with her own people, and I understand that they intend to keep her until she is big enough to bid defiance to her mother-in-law.

It seems at first sight surprising that two highly cultivated representatives of the chief literate caste in the most advanced province in India should gravely refer to female infanticide as a solution of matrimonial difficulties arising from a demand for English education which is itself hardly two generations old.

Nor is it less remarkable to find the primitive belief that a girl unmarried at puberty is a disgrace to her family, and an offence against religion, surviving in undiminished force side by side with vigorous competition for the modern luxury of a graduate bridegroom. But so long as these conditions prevail, the danger of a reversion to barbarous usages, such as the writers quoted above apprehend, cannot be wholly excluded. The truth of course is—and the sooner it is realized the better—that the development of the literate classes in modern India has proceeded on irregular and one-sided lines. Intellectual and political ideals have assumed undue prominence, while the social and moral reforms without which no wholesome national life is possible have been thrust into the background. History affords no warrant for the belief that the enthusiasm of nationality can be kindled in sordid and degenerate surroundings. Wherever that sentiment has displayed any real vitality, it has been fostered and stimulated by the influence of the women of the race. A society which accepts intellectual inanition and moral stagnation as the natural condition of its womankind cannot hope to develop the higher qualities of courage, devotion, and self-sacrifice which go to the making of nations.

The voluminous literature relating to female infanticide in India contains many indications that where the practice is not merely sporadic, resulting from the pressure of starvation, but has hardened into a recognized usage, it may be traced to the operation of two distinct causes. In certain stages of tribal society, the practice of killing females seems to be connected with the rule of exogamy. The late Mr. J. F. McLennan observed long ago that the two usages often existed side by side. In the theory of exogamy put forward in his essay on Primitive Marriage, he argued that female infanticide as practised by savages disturbed the balance of the sexes and drove men to capture their wives from other tribes—a custom which in course of time resolved itself into the systematic observance of exogamy. This view was open to the obvious rejoinder that if all tribes killed their female infants at an equal rate, there would soon be no women to capture, and the race would die out. Even without pressing this point, it was difficult to see why primitive man should prefer the dangerous and inconvenient process of capturing a wife from a hostile tribe to the simpler method of marrying a girl belonging to his own local community. Given, however, an adequate cause inducing people to practise

Female infanticide and exogamy.

exogamy—a cause as effective as the influence of natural selection would unquestionably be—and it becomes easy to understand that in certain states of society a tendency to female infanticide would be a natural consequence, not as McLennan supposed a *cause*, of the custom of exogamy. For if men were restrained by inexorable usage from marrying the girls born in the sept or local group of blood kindred, the temptation to kill these *bouches inutiles* would probably be very strong. Not only would girls be useless to the men of the tribe as wives, but the more of them there were, the more would the tribe be preyed upon by neighbours in quest of wives. As a matter of fact, this was very much the view that the Khonds took of the question. In 1842 they told Major Macpherson in so many words that it was better to destroy girls in their infancy than to allow them to grow up and become causes of strife afterwards.* I am indebted to the late Sir John Edgar, K.C.I.E., C.S.I., for a parallel instance from the Nāgas with whom, as with the Khonds, the local exogamous clan is the unit of tribal society. It seems that on a tour through the Nāga country, Colonel McCulloch, Political Agent for Manipur, came across a village which struck him as remarkably destitute of female children. On making inquiries he found that there was not a single girl in the place, for the simple reason that the people killed all that were born in order to save themselves from the annoyance of being harried by wife-hunting parties from a stronger clan. Colonel McCulloch got hold of the mothers, and managed to induce them to spare their girls in future, on the understanding that their neighbours should stop raiding and adopt a more peaceable method of wooing. By a judicious mixture of threats and persuasion, the other clan was led to agree to the arrangement, and many years after, while staying in Manipur, Sir John Edgar was present, when a troop of Nāga girls from the weaker group paid a visit of ceremony to Colonel McCulloch, bearing an offering of cloth of their own weaving in token of their gratitude to the man who had saved their lives.†

[* S. C. Macpherson, *Memorials of Service in India*, 1865, p. 132 *et seq.* The superstition reported from Bengal, that one of the causes of female infanticide among the Khonds was the belief that the souls of girl children killed in this way would not be born again, and hence that the number of female children would decrease, does not seem to prevail among the tribe in the Central Provinces or Bengal. (*Census Report, Central Provinces*, 1911, vol. i., p. 160; *Id. Bengal*, 1911, vol. i., p. 330.)]

[† T. C. Hodson (*Nāga Tribes of Manipur*, 1911, p. 98, note) discredits the existence of female infanticide among Nāgas at the present day. It certainly prevailed in comparatively recent times. (*Census Report, Assam*, 1891, p. 120, note.)]

Instances of this sort, vouched for by competent observers and drawn from tribes dwelling so far apart and belonging to such widely different stocks as the Dravidian Khonds of Orissa and the Mongoloid Nāgas of Assam, may be regarded as crucial in their bearing on the question of the relation of female infanticide to the custom of exogamy. They seem to show that the practice of killing female infants is a consequence, not a cause, and assuredly not *the* cause, of the rule that a man may not marry a woman of his own tribe. This consequence, moreover, ensues only so long as society is in a savage state; and tends to die out, as it has died out among both Khonds and Nāgas, directly a régime of violence is succeeded by a régime of law. As soon as this change has been effected, the value of women tends to rise. They become a saleable commodity, which neighbouring tribes will buy with a price, and the inducement to kill them in infancy ceases to exist. In short, savage infanticide is an incident of the primitive struggle for bare existence which disappears when the severity of the struggle is mitigated by peace.

Female infanticide and hypergamy.

There is, however, another form of infanticide, which is connected not with exogamy but with hypergamy, and which requires to be carefully distinguished from the savage type. Given a tribe like the Rājputs of Northern India, divided into a number of exogamous septs, and strongly impressed with the idea of purity of blood and the importance of correct ceremonial observances, it follows of necessity that in course of time some groups will drop behind the others and will come to be regarded as socially inferior to the rest. To these septs the superior groups refuse to give their daughters in marriage and there arises the state of things illustrated by the diagram on page 165. The balance of the sexes is disturbed; the superior groups find themselves embarrassed with a surplus of girls; and the bridegroom-price tends to rise until it presses severely on the means of families unfortunate enough to have several daughters to marry. Family pride, religious prescription, and the necessity of avoiding scandals, render it impossible to let girls grow up with the prospect of remaining old maids; convents and sisterhoods are unknown; and the only way out of the difficulty, as it presents itself to the Rājput father, is to permit no more girls to arrive at maturity than can certainly be provided with husbands. The ultimate result no doubt is much the same as among savage people like Nāgas and Khonds, but it is arrived at in a different way and springs from a different principle. The Nāga kills his daughter lest a stronger man than he should desire her, and in effecting her capture should take her father's head as an incidental trophy. The Rājput makes away with his daughter in the belief that no one will be anxious to marry her, and that the family will be disgraced if she grows up an old maid. In the one case husbands are too scarce; in the other they are obtrusively plentiful. It may be added that this refined form of infanticide is far more difficult to suppress than the savage form. The one dies out of itself as the forcible capture of wives falls into disuse, and life generally becomes easier; the other tends to spread with the growth of family pride and personal luxury, and may even offer substantial resistance to the attempt to stamp it out by penal legislation.

It may be asserted with confidence that the savage form of infanticide no longer exists in India. For many years past tribal raids in quest of wives or of heads have been very effectually discouraged, and the usage has died out with the removal of the cause. Whether the refined or sumptuary form, where a daughter's life is sacrificed to save the *dot* demanded by family pride, has entirely disappeared is a question on which there is room for difference of opinion. That it prevailed on a large scale up to comparatively recent times there is only too much reason to believe, and it seems to have been most persistent where one would least expect to find it—side by side with the otherwise chivalrous traditions of the warlike Indo-Aryan races of Upper India.

In 1881 Mr. Coldstream, Deputy Commissioner of Hoshyār-pur in the Punjab, wrote on the subject as follows:—

"Forty years ago probably many hundreds of female children were annually buried in this district immediately after birth. When several female children were born in succession, the destruction of the last born was carried out with the following observance—a piece of *gur* (molasses) was placed in the mouth of the child, a skein of cotton was laid on her breast, and the following incantation recited two or three times:—

> "Eat gur, spin your thread,
> We don't want you, but a brother instead."

The infants were usually put into *gharras* or waterpots and buried in the ground. . . . Illustrating the subject of the small proportional number of females, I will quote some remarks by a highly educated native officer, a Hindu. He writes as follows:—

"Infanticide has not quite disappeared. I am quite sure that in certain old families, those who by custom must spend much money on the marriage of daughters, and are poor, it is still practised. They either suffocate them or give the juice of the *āk* plant (*Calatropis gigantea*) in the *gurthi*, the first nourishment given to a newborn child."

More recondite methods were also sometimes adopted. A Panjābi friend of mine, a member of a tribe which followed the custom of hypergamy, with whom I was discussing the subject of female infanticide, told me that when he was eight years old he was summoned to his mother's bedside to sanction and assist at the murder of a newborn girl. His father being away from home, he was called upon to exercise the *patria potestas* as the eldest male member of the household then present. The child was given him to hold, and the midwife poured over her head two large jars of water, chilled almost to freezing by being put out on the roof during a December night. Her face instantly turned black and she died in the arms of her terrified brother. All the girls that were born met with a similar fate. The mother complied reluctantly with the barbarous usage of the family, but the horror of the thing was with her through life, and when she was dying her remorse conjured up a ghastly vision of the spirits of her murdered children, standing at her bed-side armed with iron hooks and crying vindictively to the soul still lingering in her body, "Come out, come out that we may tear you in pieces." This, however, happened nearly fifty years ago, and my friend assures me that in his tribe at any rate systematic infanticide has disappeared under the influence of popular education, and that twenty girls may now be seen where in his boyhood hardly one could be found.

Official opinion seems to incline, on the whole, to the comfortable belief that these crude manifestations of paternal authority have of late years fallen into disuse. No one has the least desire to unveil the mysteries of high caste households, and there is something to be said for the cynical view that it is better to wink at the secret murder of an uncertain number of babies than to face the certain odium of repressive legislation enforced by the domiciliary visits of an Asiatic police. Hardly any one, however, is prepared to go the length of asserting that infanticide is now nothing more than a dim tradition of the dreadful past. On the contrary the practice is definitely stated to continue, though in a modified, more subtle, and, as some may think, less merciful form. According to the writers of the last three Census Reports, all of whom seem to have taken much trouble to arrive at the truth, the mental attitude of the average Panjābi parent towards superfluous daughters may be summed up in Clough's couplet:

> "Thou shalt not kill, but need'st not strive
> Officiously to keep alive."

Writing in 1883 Sir Denzil Ibbetson quotes Mr. Coldstream's remark that "there is, I think, some indication given in the statistics of the existence of a certain popular depreciation of female child life," and goes on to say, "this last sentence appears to me exactly to express the existing state of affairs. That infanticide is practised at all generally I do not believe; that it is habitual with any class, I doubt; and if with any, it is, I think, only with some exceedingly limited sections of the community, such as perhaps the Bedi families of Gurdaspur, and even there takes the form of intentional neglect rather than actual murder. But there is not the slightest doubt that the life of a girl is less valued and worse cared for than that of a boy; chiefly indeed, among the hypergamous classes who cannot find husbands for them, the higher castes of the Eastern Punjab who will not sell their daughters, and the Hindus who spend much money on their marriage and account it shameful to leave them unmarried; but also in a less degree and as a relic of the old fighting days, and perhaps from the contagion of Hindu ideas, among all other classes of the Punjab people without distinction of race, religion, or locality."

Ten years later we find Mr. Maclagan, who conducted the Census of 1891, stating his conclusions as follows:—

"It is notorious that in this country female life is less cared for at all ages, and more especially in infancy, than that of males. Whether the neglect of female life in early youth is intentional or not, and whether infant girls are actually killed, are questions to which our statistics can scarcely give more than a very slight clue. The general impression, doubtless, is that in the province at large there is a certain amount of customary neglect which can scarcely be called intentional; but that in certain areas and among certain classes the evil assumes a more serious form. And the statistical returns may be found of some slight value in indicating the localities and the castes which are most open to suspicion on this account." *

Mr. Rose, the Superintendent of the Census taken in 1901, writes thus:

[* *Census Report*, 1891, vol. i., p. 217. *Census Report, India*, 1911, vol. i., p. 215.]

"On the whole, I should be inclined to think that deliberate female infanticide is rare, and that when perpetrated, it is due to a combination of causes. If it was felt that the child was likely to cause misfortune, *and* that her marriage would be difficult, it may be that she would be killed. But such cases cannot be numerous. To this the Jāts, Hindu and Sikh, are a possible exception, and the only solution of the problem in their case is that infanticide is a barbarous form of Malthusian practices. This idea was suggested many years ago by Major Goldney, as Deputy-Commissioner of Ludhiana, the district in which the data are the most inexplicable. Even less easy is it to account for the mortality amongst girl-children after the age of infancy. No one who has seen the peasantry, especially the Jāt peasantry, in their villages, at fairs and the like, could for a moment suggest that women and girls in this province are treated, generally, with cruelty or intentional neglect. Sikhs, especially, treat women well. One can only say that ignorance and an unconscious ill-treatment of females at all ages may result from the low estimation in which savage and backward races hold women. Of all the data obtained the most significant is the mortality among female infants in years of famine." *

The statistics of the subject certainly present some remarkable features. It is difficult to offer any plausible explanation of the fact that the proportion of girls to boys among children under five ranges in British territory from 96 per cent. among Muhammadans, and 92 per cent. among Hindus, to 76 per cent. among Sikhs, while the Sikh figure in one district is no more than 70, and in a particular tribe falls as low as 62 per cent. The idea has been thrown out that the practice of killing female infants, if persevered in for many generations, might induce among the surviving women a hereditary tendency to bear more boys than girls. Darwin's authority has been cited in support of this conjecture, which was first put forward by Colonel Marshall in explanation of the preponderance of males among the Todās of the Nilgiri hills.† There is obviously no means of testing the speculation,

[* *Census Report*, 1901, vol. i., p. 216. Pandit Harikishan Kaul, while recognizing that female infanticide now prevails only among certain families or groups of families, points out that female infants suffer largely from neglect (*Census Report*, 1911, vol. i., p. 230 *et seq.*, 243 *et seq.*).]

[† C. Darwin, *The Descent of Man*, 2nd ed., 1889, p. 255 *et seq.* W. E. Marshall, *A Phrenologist among the Todas*, 1873, p. 111. W. H. R. Rivers, the latest and best authority on the tribe, shows that while infanticide at one time prevailed widely, it has but in 1891 Mr. Maclagan observed that "castes, such as the Gakkhars and semi-Rājput tribes, such as the Dhunds and Rāthis, which used to practise or to be suspected of practising infanticide have now a larger proportion of women than the average; and this fact so far tends to damage the theory that female infanticide leads to a hereditary incapacity to produce female children." In an earlier paragraph of the same report Mr. Maclagan writes: "It has been suggested to me that the methods of dressing young children (when they are dressed at all) may have something to do with the different rates of death among girls and boys. In the centre of the province it is customary to find young girls dressed in petticoats only, and young boys in jackets only; and as the latter is undoubtedly the sounder method from a sanitary point of view, the boys have a better assurance of life than the girls." He does not himself accept this explanation, which is open to the obvious criticism, first, that in other parts of India where the custom in the matter of children's dress is the same, no such marked disproportion between the sexes is observed; and, secondly, that when children are under five, even this exiguous raiment is deemed superfluous, and both sexes run about impartially naked. Seeing then, that neither natural selection nor fashion can be appealed to in explanation of the Punjab statistics, we can but take refuge in the sage and comprehensive remark of the latest continental writer on the problem of sex that the question is "involved in the profoundest obscurity." Only one thing is certain—if legislation cannot compel a man to love his neighbour like himself, still less can it compel him to love his daughter as much as his son. The people themselves must cure the evil, if evil there be. The tradition of ages which leads to the neglect of female children will only give way to a general rise in the standard of domestic ethics. That no doubt will come in time as the spread of education, especially of female education, brings about a higher conception of the position and influence of women in the Eastern world.

Origin of hypergamy.

The origin of the custom of hypergamy is obscure. We find it in full force at the time of the law-books, the earliest of which are believed by Bühler to be somewhat anterior to the fourth and fifth centuries B.C., and it has been shown to be quite alive and

now greatly diminished, and at the present day exists chiefly, owing to their conservatism, among the priestly classes. (*The Todas*, 1906, pp. 478, 691.)]

continually assuming new forms at the present day. It is curious that a practice which extends over so long a period, and is so intimately connected with the evolution of caste, should have escaped the notice of all modern writers on the early history of marriage. The authors of the law-books give no account of the causes which produced it, nor would one expect them to do so. They merely say that marriages between men of a higher class and women of a lower class are according to the order of nature (*anuloma* "with the hair"), while marriages of the converse type are *pratiloma*, "against the hair" or unnatural. The usage seems to be one which might arise wherever an invading race, bringing with it comparatively few women, took captives from among the people whose territory they occupied. Captured women would become the wives or concubines of their captors; male captives, if not slain offhand, would be kept as slaves, and would in no case be accepted as husbands for the daughters of the conquering race. One may say, indeed, that wherever slavery has prevailed, or wherever one race has established a marked political ascendency over another, there hypergamy has necessarily established itself. The mixed or coloured races of America, Mulattoes, Quadroons, Mestizos, and the like were, in the first instance at any rate, the offspring of hypergamous unions, corresponding to the *anuloma* marriages of the Indian law-books. The fathers were Spaniards or Englishmen, the mothers Indians or Negresses. In Rajputana, on the other hand, hypergamy appears to be associated with territorial sovereignty and the possession of landed property. In theory all Rajputs are equal within the tribe, but ruling chiefs will only give their daughters to men of their own class, and a land-owning Rajput, deeming himself no doubt a chieftain in a small way, will not accept a landless man as his son-in-law. A curious story, which seems to belong to the same order of ideas, is told in the Punjab to account for the hypergamous status of one of the Jāt clans. One day, it is said, as the Emperor Akbar was out hunting, he came suddenly upon a Jāt woman who was standing by a well with a heavy jar of water on her head and a full-grown buffalo and its calf on either side of her. The Emperor's cavalcade frightened the animals and they prepared to break away. But the sturdy Jātni was equal to the emergency. With one hand she seized the buffalo and held it by a horn, with the other she steadied the jar of water on her head, while she secured the calf by putting her foot on its tethering rope.

Seeing this display of strength and presence of mind the Emperor exclaimed, "A woman like that should be the mother of heroes," and shortly afterwards took her to wife in due form. Her people had places of honour given them in the Imperial Darbār, and the clan has been known ever afterwards as Akbari or Darbāri Jāts, ranking at the top of the hypergamous system of the tribe, taking wives from other clans, but giving their daughters to none.*

A singularly complete parallel to the Indian usage of hypergamy occurs in Madagascar, where the Antimerina or patrician caste is divided into six classes, each of which claims descent from a royal ancestor and regards itself as a group of blood relations. According to M. Arnold Van Gennep,† the latest authority on the subject, these groups are endogamous in theory, but a man of a higher class may marry a woman of a lower class. On the other hand, a woman of higher rank is prohibited by strict taboo from marrying beneath her; and if she should so far demean herself as to marry a commoner, she loses her title of nobility and is disowned by her family.

Here one is tempted to hazard the conjecture that the matrimonial relations between patricians and plebeians in Rome before the Lex Canuleia (B.C. 445), may have been regulated by the custom of hypergamy, patricians taking wives from among the plebeians but not giving their daughters in return. This seems to be in accordance with the traditional origin of the plebeians. Had the two groups been as absolutely separate as the imaginary debate reported in the fourth book of Livy seems to imply, it is difficult to understand how the *jus connubii* could have been granted as readily as is alleged to have been the case, or why the plebs should have been so anxious to obtain the concession. When distinct castes have once been formed, the sentiment of the lower groups as well as of the higher is usually opposed to amalgamation. I surmise, therefore, that at the time of the passing of the Lex Canuleia, the plebs and the patriciate had not actually hardened into castes,‡ and that marriages between patrician men and plebeian women did actually take place, possibly by an inferior grade of ritual. What the plebs wanted and what the law gave them, it is

[* Akbar certainly did not marry a Jāt girl; the tale is told by more than one Jāt sept. (H. A. Rose, *Glossary of the Tribes and Castes of the Punjab and N.W. Frontier Province*, vol. ii., 1911, pp. 220 note, 236, 377.)]

† *Tabou et Totemisme à Madagascar*, Arnold Van Gennep, Paris, 1904.

‡ Ortolan speaks of them as "two radically distinct castes between the members of which a Roman marriage could never take place." (*History of Roman Law*, p. 585.)

suggested, was the right for plebeian men to marry patrician women. This conjecture seems to derive some support from Livy's account of the transaction. He says in one place that the denial of *connubium* to the plebs dated only from the time of the decemvirs; while in another passage he puts into the mouth of the advocate of the plebeian cause an argument which is only intelligible on the assumption that marriages between patricians and plebeians were not wholly unknown. The patrician orator argues that the change will introduce confusion into the system of clans; that no one will know to what *gens* he belongs; and that the religious observances (*sacra gentilicia*) incumbent on these family groups will come to be neglected. To this the plebeian replies that the status of the father will determine that of the child (*patrem sequuntur liberi*), and that the appeal to religion is a mere attempt to prejudice the case. Now if the plebs and patriciate had been distinct castes in the strict Indian sense of the term, no intermarriage would have been possible, and the question of the offspring of mixed marriages belonging to their father's group could not have arisen. The argument *patrem sequuntur liberi* would have appealed to no one had it not been a statement of fact with which the audience were familiar. And it cannot have meant that if a plebeian man married a patrician woman the children ranked as plebeians, for if that had been so, there would have been full *connubium* and no legislation would have been required. It seems to follow that the statement expressed the fact that when a patrician man married a plebeian woman, the children were reckoned as patricians and belonged to the *gens* of the father—that the relations between the two groups were what we call hypergamous.

Whatever may have been the origin of the custom, whether slavery, conquest, racial superiority, political or plutocratic domination, or territorial supremacy gave it the first impulse, it is clear that, in any locality where it got started, the principle would be likely to extend itself, by the operation of imitative fiction, to the connubial relations of all classes not absolutely equal in rank. This is what seems to have happened in several parts of India, where the influence of hypergamy may be traced in the disturbance of the balance of the sexes, and the prevalence of polygamy or female infanticide.

Of all the peculiar usages which are associated with marriage in India none have impressed themselves so distinctly on the census statistics as the custom which prohibits the second marriage of a widow, and the convention enjoining the marriage of a daughter before she attains physical maturity. In the case of the higher castes both of these usages may claim a respectable antiquity. In the lower strata of society, on the other hand, they appear to have been developed, in the form which they now assume, at a comparatively recent date under the pressure of peculiar social conditions. Both, again, are looked upon by the people who observe them as badges of social distinction, and to the fact that they are regarded in this light is mainly due their rapid extension within the last two or three generations. No excuse therefore is needed for examining their prevalence and its causes in some detail.

Widow and infant marriage.

For the ultimate origin of the prohibition of widow marriage among the higher castes we must look back, far beyond the comparative civilization of the Vedas, to the really primitive belief that the dead chief or head of the family will need human companionship and service in that other world which savage fancy pictures as a shadowy copy of this. To this belief is due the practice of burning the widow on the funeral pile of her dead husband, which is referred to as an "ancient custom" (*purānā dharma*) in the Atharva Veda.* The directions given in the Rig Veda for placing the widow on the pile with her husband's corpse, and then calling her back to the world of life, appear, as Tylor † has pointed out, to represent "a reform and a reaction against a yet more ancient savage rite of widow sacrifice, which they prohibited in fact, but yet kept up in symbol." The bow of the warrior and the sacrificial instruments of the priest were thrown back upon the pile to be consumed; the wife, after passing through the mere form of sacrifice, was held to have fulfilled her duties to her husband and was free to marry again. A passage in the Rig Veda quoted by Zimmer ‡ shows that in some cases, at any rate, the widow married her husband's younger brother (*devar*); and it is not unreasonable to suppose that her obligations in this respect were very much what we now find among the castes which permit widow marriage.

Prohibition of widow marriage unknown in Vedic times.

---

* *Atharva Veda*, 18, 3, 1, quoted by Zimmer, *Altindisches Leben*, p. 331.

† *Primitive Culture*, i., 466.

‡ *Altindisches Leben*, p. 329. See also Oldenberg, *Die Religion des Veda*, 575, and Macdonell, *History of Sanskrit Literature*, 126. Jolly, *Recht und Sitte*, 59, seems to take a different view.

At this point the historical record, such as it is, breaks off, and conjecture alone can divine the precise motives which induced the Brāhmans of a later age to revive that custom of primitive savagery which their ancestors had expressly condemned. Closer contact with more barbarous races; the growth of the sacerdotal spirit; the desire, as Sir Henry Maine has suggested, to get rid of the inconvenient lien which the widow held over her husband's property;—all these motives may have contributed to the result. But when widow-sacrifice had been thus re-introduced, it is *primâ facie* unlikely that it should have been enforced with that rigid consistency which distinguishes the true savage; and, in fact, the texts prescribe for the widow the milder alternative of a life of ascetic self-denial and patient waiting to join the husband who has gone before. According to some authorities, they also recognize, though as a less excellent path than the two former, the alternative of re-marriage.

Causes of its revival.

I will not attempt to enter upon the controversy as to the precise meaning of the passage in Parāsara's Institutes, on which the modern advocates of widow marriage rely, still less to discuss its applicability to the present age of the world. It seems more profitable to state the causes which, irrespective of isolated texts, would in any case have favoured the growth of the modern custom which forbids the widows of the highest castes to marry again, and which shows signs of extending itself far beyond its present limits and finally of suppressing widow marriage throughout the entire Hindu community. Some, at any rate, of these causes are not far to seek. In the first place, the anxiety of the early Hindu law-givers to circumscribe a woman's rights to property would unquestionably tend to forbid her to join her lot to a man whose interest it would be to assert and extend those rights as against the members of her husband's family. At the same time the growth of the doctrine of spiritual benefit would require her to devote her life to the annual performance of her husband's *srāddh*.* Technical obstacles to her re-marriage also arise from the Brahmanical theory of marriage itself. That ceremony being regarded as a sacrament ordained for the purification of women, and its essential portion being the gift of the woman by her father to her husband, the effect of the gift is to transfer

Considerations of property, of spiritual benefit, of sacramental doctrine.

* *Tagore Law Lectures*, 1879, pp. 187, 188.

her from her own *gotra* or exogamous group into that of her husband. The bearing of this transfer on the question of her re-marriage is thus stated by an orthodox Hindu at pages 276–277 of the *Papers relating to Infant Marriage and Enforced Widowhood*, published by the Government of India:—

"Her father being thus out of the question, it may be said that she may give herself in marriage. But this she cannot do, because she never had anything like disposal of herself. When young, she was given away, so the ownership over her (if I may be permitted to use the phrase) vested then in the father, was transferred by a solemn religious act to the husband, and he being no more, there is no one to give her away: and since Hindu marriage must take the form of religious gift, her marriage becomes impossible."

The argument seems academic, but in the atmosphere of pedantry which pervades Indian society an academic argument is as good as any other.

Influence of hypergamy.

Some influence must also have been exerted in the same direction by the competition for husbands resulting from the action of hypergamy. Widows certainly would be the first to be excluded from the marriage market, for in their case the interests of the individual families would be identical with those of the group. The family would already have paid a bridegroom-price to get their daughter or sister married, and would naturally be indisposed to pay a second, and probably higher price to get her married again. The group, in its turn, would be equally adverse to an arrangement which tended to increase the number of marriageable women. Members of the higher castes, indeed, have frequently told me that these reasons of themselves were sufficient to make them regard with disfavour the modern movement in favour of widow marriage. For, said one of them, we find it hard enough already to get our daughters married into families of our own rank, and things will be worse still if widows enter the competition with all the advantages they derive from having got over their first shyness, and acquired some experience of the ways of men. The sentiments of Mr. Weller sounded strange in the mouth of a Kulin Brāhman, but the argument was used in entire good faith, and was backed up by much lamentation over the speaker's ill-luck in being the father of four daughters, all unmarried.

Practice of lower castes.

The considerations stated above are entitled to whatever support they may derive from the fact that the Muhammadans, and those Hindu castes which permit widows to remarry, know nothing of the custom of hypergamy, and as a rule pay for brides, not for bridegrooms. Among these groups the normal proportion of the sexes, whatever that may be at the age of marriage, has not been affected by any artificial divisions, and there is every reason to believe that widows who are in other respects eligible have no particular difficulty in finding husbands. Polygamy prevails on a limited scale, and a certain proportion of the men have two wives, the second wife being often a young widow chosen by the man himself for her personal attractions, after the first wife, whom his parents selected for him, has lost her looks and become little more than a household drudge. Another point is that the lower castes seem to have a greater capacity than the higher for throwing off sub-castes. Deviations from caste usage, trivial changes of occupation, settlement outside the traditional habitat of the caste, and a variety of similar causes, which in the higher castes would, as a rule, merely affect the standing of certain families in the scale of hypergamy, tend in the lower castes to form endogamous groups, the members of which intermarry only among themselves. The difference is important, as the latter process does not disturb the balance of the sexes, and the former does.

Feeling of the people as to extension of widow marriage.

The present attitude of the Hindu community towards proposals to recognize and extend the practice of widow marriage may, I think, be briefly stated somewhat to the following effect :—The most advanced class of educated men sympathize in a general way with the movement, but their sympathy is clouded by the apprehension that any considerable addition to the number of marriageable women would add to the existing difficulty and expense of getting their daughters married. Below these we find a very numerous class who are educated enough to appreciate the prohibition of widow marriage supposed to be contained in certain texts, and who have no desire to go behind that or any similar injunction in support of which tolerably ancient authority can be quoted. Then come the great mass of the uneducated working classes, with rather vague notions as to the scriptures, but strong in their reverence for Brāhmans, and keen to appreciate points of social precedence. To them widow marriage is a badge of social degradation, a link which connects those who practise it with Doms, Bunas, Bāgdis and "low people" of various kinds. Lastly, at the bottom of society, as understood by the average Hindu, we find a large group of castes and tribes of which the lower section is represented by pure non-Aryan tribes practising adult marriage and widow re-marriage, while the upper section consists of castes of doubtful origin, most of whom, retaining widow marriage, have taken to infant marriage, while some have got so far as to throw off sub-castes distinguished by their abstention from widow marriage.*

It is not suggested that the groups indicated above can be marked off with absolute accuracy. But without insisting upon this, it is clear that the tendency of the lower strata of Hindu society is continually towards closer and closer conformity with the usages of the higher castes. These alone present a definite pattern which admits up to a certain point of ready imitation, and the whole Brahmanical system works in this direction. Of late years, moreover, the strength of the Hinduising movement has been greatly augmented by the improvement of communications. People travel more, pilgrimages can be more easily made, and the influence of the orthodox section of society is thus much more widely diffused. Railways in particular, which are sometimes represented as a solvent of caste prejudices, have in fact enormously extended the area within which those prejudices reign supreme.

The practice of infant marriage has spread much further and taken root more deeply among the lower castes than its social complement, the prohibition of widow marriage. Both customs, the positive as well as the negative, have been borrowed from the higher castes, and are now regarded as paths leading towards social distinction. But the one is much easier to follow than the other. A man must get his daughter married at latest when she is fourteen or fifteen years old. To marry her five or six years earlier causes him no particular inconvenience, and confers on him whatever consideration may attach to religious orthodoxy and social propriety. On the other hand, to stop the re-marriage of widows, in castes where the balance of the sexes has not been disturbed by hypergamy, must at starting cause some practical inconvenience. Among the lower castes women are much more of a power than they are among the higher; they assert themselves freely on a variety of public occasions, and in many cases they have secured for themselves the right to initiate proceedings for divorce. One can

Prevalence of infant marriage.

[* In Baroda the attitude of the people towards widow marriage is described as "passive sympathy on the part of the educated and blind opposition on the part of the ignorant." A recent Act permits a girl widow under sixteen to re-marry with the consent of her guardian; if she is above sixteen she can marry again if she pleases (*Census Report*, 1911, vol. i., p. 158 *et seq.*).]

hardly doubt that their influence would be exercised in favour of widow marriage, and that it would tend on the whole towards keeping that institution alive. Some allowance must also be made for the fact that the lower castes do not keep their women in seclusion. A good-looking widow shut up in the family zenana can be more easily sacrificed to notions of social propriety than a woman who goes out and meets possible suitors every day of her life. To whatever cause the difference may be due, it is certain that of two customs, both adopted under pressure of the same motives, the one—infant marriage—is almost universal, while the other—the prohibition of widow marriage—has at present only a comparatively limited currency. Infant marriage in fact is now so widely diffused as to have almost entirely displaced adult marriage within the limits of the caste system proper. The Dravidian races of Chutiā Nāgpur, the Central Provinces and the Madras hills, the Mongoloid tribes of the Himalayan region, Assam and Burma, still maintain a system of courtship and marriage between full-grown youths and maidens which has been minutely described by several sympathetic observers. Directly we leave these tolerably compact tribes and pass on to the less definite groups which form a debatable land between the tribe and the caste, we find either infant marriage in undisputed possession or a mixed system prevailing, which tolerates adult marriage as a resource open to those who cannot afford to do anything better for their children, but at the same time enjoins the more respectable custom of infant marriage for all parents whose circumstances admit of it.

Origin of infant marriage.

In the case of the lower castes there is little room for doubt that the custom of infant marriage has been consciously borrowed from the higher castes in obedience to that tendency to imitation which we may almost describe as an ultimate law of the caste system. But how did the higher castes come by a custom which is without a parallel, at any rate on so large a scale, elsewhere in the world, and which cannot be referred to any of those primitive instincts which have usually determined the relations of the sexes? Neither sexual passion nor the desire for companionship and service can be called in to account for a man marrying a girl at an age when she is physically incapable of fulfilling any of the duties of a wife. Primitive man knows nothing of infant marriage, nor is it easy to conceive how such an institution could have arisen in the struggle for existence out of which society has been evolved. The modern savage woos in a summary and not over delicate fashion a sturdy young woman who can cook his food, carry baggage, collect edible grubs, and make herself generally useful. To his untutored mind the Hindu child-bride would seem about as suitable a helpmate as a modern professional beauty. If, then, infant marriage is in no way a normal product of social evolution, and in fact is met with only in India, to what causes shall we look for its origin? The standard Brahmanical explanation is palpably inadequate. It represents marriage as a sort of sacrament, of which every maiden must partake in order that she may cleanse her own being from the taint of original sin, that she may accomplish the salvation of her father and his ancestors, and that she may bring forth a son to carry on the domestic worship (*sacra privata*) of her husband's family. So far as marriage itself goes, all this is intelligible enough as a highly specialized development of certain well-known ancient ideas. But it does not touch the question of age. Granted that the begetting of a son is essential for the continuance of the *sacra privata*, as Greek and Roman examples teach us, why should the householder on whom this solemn duty devolves go out of his way to defer its fulfilment by marrying a girl who has not yet attained the age of child-bearing? The Brāhman will reply that the earlier in a girl's life she accomplishes her mystical functions the better. But this clearly belongs to the large class of *ex post facto* explanations of which sacerdotal and legal literature is in all ages and countries so full. The priests and lawyers who compile the text-books find certain customs in force, and feel bound to invent reasons for their existence. Being unfettered by the historical sense, and disposed to give free play to their inner consciousness, it is hardly surprising that their reasons should be as often false as true.

Mr. Nesfield's theory.

An explanation of a more scientific character, put forward by Mr. Nesfield in 1885, seeks to connect the custom with communal marriage and the practice of capturing wives. On this theory infant marriage was consciously introduced with the object of protecting the child-wife from the stain of communism within the tribe and from the danger of being forcibly abducted by a member of an alien tribe. It was, in fact, a revolt against primitive usages which the moral sense of a more civilized generation had begun to condemn. The argument is ingenious, but it does not fit the facts we have to deal with. The society depicted in the Rig and Atharva Vedas must have got far beyond the stage of communal marriage and forceful abduction of wives. Courtship of a very modern tpye was fully recognized, and the consent of the girl's father or brother was sought only after the young people had themselves come to an understanding. As an additional and conclusive indication that the kind of marriage contemplated by the Vedas was the *individual* marriage of comparatively advanced civilization, I may refer to a remarkable custom, traces of which have survived in modern Italy—the lustration of the bride's night-dress after the wedding night.* Such a custom is clearly incompatible with communal marriage, and could only have arisen in a society which set a high value on female chastity and had left primitive communism (if, indeed, such a condition ever existed) ages behind.

Antiquity of the custom; its possible causes.

The change from this Arcadian state of things to a regime of infant marriage seems to have taken place at a very early date. According to Baudhāyana a girl who is unmarried when she reaches maturity is degraded to the rank of a Sūdra, and her father is held to have committed a grave sin by having neglected to get her married. This rule is common to all the law-books, and many of them go further still and fix a definite age for the marriage of girls. The later the treatise, the earlier is the age which it prescribes. According to Manu,† a man of thirty should marry a girl of twelve, and a man of twenty-four a girl of eight. Later writers fix the higher limit of age in such cases at ten years or eight years, and reduce the lower limit to seven, six, and even four years. What induced people already practising a rational system of adult marriage to abandon it in favour of a rigid and complicated system of infant marriage? In the nature of things no confident answer can be given; the whole question belongs to the domain of conjecture. One can only surmise that the growth of the patriarchal power of the head of the family must have been adverse to any assertion of independence on the part of its female members, and

---

* Zimmer, *Altindisches Leben*, p. 314, Gubernatis, *Usi Nuziali*, p. 432. [Marriage in the early Vedic texts appears essentially as the union of two persons of full development. Child-wives first occur regularly in the Sūtra period, though it is still uncertain to what extent the rule of marriage before puberty then obtained. (A. A. Macdonell, A. B. Keith, *Vedic Index of Names and Subjects*, 1913, i. 475 *et seq.*)]

[† *Laws*, IX. 94.]

more especially to their exercising the right of choosing their husbands for themselves. Where family interests were involved, it may well have seemed simpler to get a girl married before she had developed a will of her own, than to court domestic difficulties by allowing her to grow up and fall in love on her own account.* The gradual lowering of the position of women from the ideal standard of Vedic times, and the distrust of their virtue induced by the example of pre-matrimonial license set by the Dravidian races must also have had its effect, and, as is not obscurely hinted in the literature of the subject, a girl would be married as a child in order to avert the possibility of her causing scandal later on.

Apart from these general causes, a powerful influence must also have been exerted by the custom of hypergamy, which, as has been explained above, limits the number of possible husbands for the girls of the higher classes and thus compels the parents to endeavour to secure appropriate bridegrooms as soon as possible. That this motive operates strongly at the present day is plainly stated by one of the writers in the official publication already referred to,† who says:—

> "Under these circumstances, when, in the case of a daughter, parents see that, unless they marry her at once, the one or two bridegrooms that there are open for their selection would be availed of by others, and that they would be disabled from marrying her before the eleventh year, and that they would thereby incur a religious sin and social degradation as regards the caste, they would seize that opportunity to marry their daughter, quite disregardful of the evil effects of infant marriages."

Again, when the custom of infant marriage had once been started, under pressure of social necessity, by the families of the highest group, who had the largest surplus of marriageable daughters, a sort of fashion would have been set and would be blindly followed through all the grades. Two forces are thus at work in the same direction, both tending to disturb the balance of the sexes and to produce abnormal matrimonial relations between the members of different social groups. Enforced competition for husbands on the part of the higher groups, and the desire to imitate their superiors which animates the lower groups combine to run up the price of husbands in the upper classes; while the demand for wives by the men of the lowest class, which ought by rights to produce equilibrium, is artificially restricted in its operation by the rule that they can in

[* A further extension of the practice is shown in the custom of betrothing unborn children which is reported among the Kunbis of Western India, and the Uppara salt-makers of Madras (*Census Report*, *Baroda*, 1911, vol. i., p. 148; *Central Provinces*, 1911, vol. i., p. 137).]

† *Papers relating to Infant Marriage and Enforced Widowhood in India*, p. 178.

no circumstances marry a woman of the classes above their own. These men, therefore, are left very much out in the cold, and often do not get wives until late in life. An unmarried son does not disgrace the family, but there is no greater reproach than to have a daughter unmarried at the age of puberty. Husbands are bought for the girls, and the family gets its money's worth in social estimation. Bargains, however, must be taken when they are to be had; and no father dares run the risk of waiting till his daughter is physically mature. He is bound to be on the safe side, and therefore he gets her married, child as she may be, whenever a good match offers.*

Many hard things have been said of infant marriage, and the modern tendency is to assume that a population which countenances such a practice must be in a fair way towards extreme moral degradation, if not to ultimate extinction. An Indian apologist might reply that much of the criticism is greatly exaggerated, and is founded on considerable ignorance of the present conditions and future possibilities of oriental life. He might point out that, in fact, excluding the poetical view that marriages are made in heaven, two working theories of the institution are at present in existence—one which leaves marriages to make themselves by the process of unrestricted courtship, and another which requires them to be made by the parents or guardians of the persons who are to be married. The first, which may perhaps be called the method of natural selection, is accepted and more or less acted up to by all Western nations, except those who follow the French custom of *mariages de convenance.* The second, a system of avowedly artificial selection, is in force, with few exceptions, throughout

[* In the Central Provinces "infant marriage is not, so far as can be inferred from the present practices, an indigenous custom among the tribes, but has sometimes been adopted by those of them who have been brought into contact with Hindu ideas, and are attempting by adopting Hindu customs, to raise their status. . . . It would seem to have had its origin in the increasing demand for women's labour as life changed from nomadic to more settled conditions, together with the growing sense of individual property, and the altered view of the position of woman which accompanied the development of the patriarchal system" (*Census Report*, *Central Provinces*, 1911, vol. i., p. 137 *et seq.*). Mr. Gait regards the theory that infant marriage was borrowed from Hinduism as untenable: "Like others of the same kind, it ignores the important part played by the aborigines in the development of Indian religious ideas and social practices" (*Census Report*, *India*, 1911, vol. i., p. 264). In parts of Bengal, Behār and Darbhanga the prevalence of infant marriage is attributed to the teaching and influence of the Maithil Brāhmans, to whom the celebration of the marriage ceremony is a source of profit (*Census Report*, *Bengal*, 1911, vol. i., p. 339).]

the East, and assumes its most rigid form in the usages of Hindu society. He might further observe that in entering upon this subject we must dismiss from our minds all those ideas of love and courtship with which, for most Europeans, the institution of marriage is associated. Whether such ideas will ever gain a footing in India is a question on which it would be rash to hazard an opinion. To fancy it possible to introduce them on a large scale now would argue an ignorance of the elementary conditions of Eastern life rivalling that of the famous undergraduate who told the examiner that John the Baptist was beheaded because he *would* dance with Herodias' daughter. The dream of an Indian Hermann and Dorothea wandering hand in hand through the ripening rice-fields, and plighting their troth in the odorous stillness of the palm-grove, would be an equally grotesque misapplication of Western ideas to Eastern surroundings. Here and there, amongst the Hinduised Unitarians of the Brahmo-Samāj, or in the group of Anglicised Indians who, having finished their education in England and adopted more or less completely European clothes and European manners, seem now to be on the high-road to form a new caste, it may be that marriage will be preceded by courtship of the European type. But even within these narrow circles such cases will for a long time to come be rare, and will be confined to those families which are afflicted with a surplus of daughters and find a difficulty in getting them married under normal conditions. For all Hindus, except the relatively small number who are influenced by European ideas on the subject of marriage, the bare idea that a girl can have any voice in the selection of her husband is excluded by the operation of three inexorable sanctions—by the ordinances of the Hindu religion, by the internal structure of the caste system, and by the general tone and conditions of social life in India. Religion prescribes that, like the Roman bride of early days, a Hindu girl shall be given (*tradita in manum*) by her father into the power of her husband; caste complications demand that the ceremonial portion of the transfer shall be effected while she is still a child; while the character of society, the moral tone of the men, the seclusion of the women, the immemorial taboos and conventions of family etiquette, render it impossible that she should be wooed and won like her European sister. To persons of a romantic turn of mind the suggestion that infant marriage in some shape

The case for infant marriage.

must be accepted as an ultimate fact of the Hindu social system will sound like a final abandonment of all hope of reform. But an orthodox Hindu may justly reply that there is more to be said for the custom than appears at first sight. He may fairly argue that if any sort of controlling authority is to make people's marriages for them, the earlier it commences and completes its operations the better. Where the choice of a husband must in any case be undertaken by the parents, it is clearly tempting Providence for them to defer it until their daughter has grown up, and may have formed an embarrassing attachment on her own account. As for love, that may come—and, from all that one hears and reads of Hindu unions, usually does come—as readily after marriage as before, provided that opportunities for falling in love with the wrong man are judiciously withheld.

When we have shown that a custom is ancient and that it is deeply rooted in the constitution of Indian society, it may seem that there is not much more to be said. But the physiological side of the question cannot be left wholly out of account. Looked at from this point of view, what does infant marriage really mean and what are its ultimate tendencies? Now, the first point to realize is, that in different parts of India infant marriage prevails in two widely different forms, one of which is at least free from physiological objections, while the other deserves, from every point of view, the strongest condemnation. The former usage, which is current in the Punjab, is thus described by Sir Denzil Ibbetson, a high authority on the usages and domestic life of that part of India:—

The physiological side of the question.

"Wherever infant marriage is the custom, the bride and bridegroom do not come together till a second ceremony called *muklāwa* has been performed, till when the bride lives as a virgin in her father's house. This second ceremony is separated from the actual wedding by an interval of three, five, seven, nine, or eleven years, and the girl's parents fix the time for it. Thus it often happens that the earlier in life the marriage takes place, the later cohabitation begins. For instance, in the eastern districts, Jāts generally marry at from five to seven years of age, and Rajputs at fifteen or sixteen, or even older; but the Rajput couple begins at once to cohabit, whereas the parents of the Jāt girl often find her so useful at home as she grows up that some pressure has to be put upon them to give her up to her husband, and the result is that, for practical purposes, she begins married life later than the Rajput bride."

No one who has seen a Punjābi regiment march past, or has watched the sturdy Jāt women lift their heavy water-jars at the village well, is likely to have any misgivings as to the effect of their marriage system on the *physique* of the race. Among the Rajputs both sexes are of slighter build than the

Jāts, but here again there are no signs of degeneration. The type is different, but that is all.

As we leave the great recruiting ground of the Indian army, and travel south-eastward along the plains of the Ganges, the healthy sense which bids the warrior races keep their girls at home until they are fit to bear the burden of maternity seems to have been cast out by the demon of corrupt ceremonialism, ever ready to sacrifice helpless women and children to the tradition of a fancied orthodoxy. Already in the United Provinces we find the three highest castes—the Brāhman, the Rajput, and the Kāyasth—permitting the bride, whether *apta viro* or not, to be sent to her husband's house immediately after the wedding; although it is thought better, and is more usual, to wait for a second ceremony called *gauna*, which may take place one, three, five or seven years after the first, and is fixed with reference to the physical development of the bride.

What is the exception in the United Provinces tends unhappily to become the rule in Bengal. Here the influence of woman's tradition (*strī-āchār*) has overlaid the canonical rites of Hindu marriage with a mass of senseless hocus-pocus (performed for the most part in the women's apartments at the back of the courtyard, which in India, as in ancient Greece, forms the centre of the family domicile), and has succeeded, without a shadow of textual authority, in bringing about the monstrous abuse that the girls of the upper classes commence married life at the age of nine years, and become mothers at the very earliest time that it is physically possible for them to do so. How long this practice has been in force no one can say for certain. Nearly a century ago, when Dr. Francis Buchanan made his well-known survey of Bengal, embracing, under the first Lord Minto's orders, "the progress and most remarkable customs of each different sect or tribe of which the population consists," he wrote as follows of one of the districts in Bihar, the borderland between Bengal and the United Provinces:—

Abuses in Bengal.

"Premature marriages among some tribes are, in Shahabad, on the same footing as in Bengal, that is, consummation takes place before the age of puberty. This custom, however, has not extended far, and the people are generally strong and tall. The Pamār Rajputs, among whom the custom of early consummation is adopted, form a striking proof of the evils of this custom; for among them I did not observe one good-looking man, except the Raja Jaya Prakās, and most of them have the appearance of wanting vigour both of body and mind. This custom, so far as it extends, and the great number of widows condemned by rank to live single, no doubt prove some check upon population." *

[* M. Martin, *Eastern India*, 1838, vol. i., p. 472.]

In another place Dr. Buchanan says that in respect of marriage customs, Patna—

> "is nearly on a footing with Bhagalpur, but here (in Bihar) the custom of premature marriage is not so prevalent: and it must be observed that in these districts this custom is by no means such a check on population as in Bengal, for there the girl usually is married when she is ten years of age, but in this district the girl remains at her father's house until the age of puberty, and of course her children are stronger and she is less liable to sterility.*

At the beginning of this century, then, we find the premature inception of conjugal relations described by a peculiarly competent observer as an established usage in Bengal, which was beginning to extend itself among the high castes in Bihar. Concerning the state of things at the present day, a highly educated Hindu gentleman, one of the ablest and most energetic of our native officials in Bengal, wrote to me some years ago as follows:—

> "It is the general practice—as indefensible as reprehensible under the Hindu scriptures—for husband and wife to establish cohabitation immediately after marriage. Parents unconsciously encourage the practice and make it almost unavoidable. . . . On the second day after marriage is the flower-bed ceremony; the husband and wife—a boy and girl, or generally, nowadays, a young man and a girl—must lie together in the nuptial bed. . . . Within eight days of her marriage the girl must go back to her father's house and return to her father-in-law's, or else she is forbidden to cross her husband's threshold for a year. In a few families the bride is not brought in for a year; but in the majority of cases this is considered more inconvenient than the necessities of the case would require, and the eight days' rule is kept, so as not to bar intercourse for a year. It would cost nothing worth the reckoning, and the good would be immense, if the one-year rule were strictly enforced in all cases; or better, if the interval were increased from one to two years, and the subsidiary eight days' rule expunged from the social code. . . . The evil effects of the pernicious custom, which not only tolerates, but directly encourages unnatural indulgence, need no demonstration. Among other things, it forces a premature puberty, and is thus the main root of many of the evils of early marriage, which may be avoided without any affront to religion."

This opinion—the opinion of an orthodox Hindu of high caste, who has not permitted his English education to denationalize him—marks the social and physiological side of infant marriage in Bengal.

The matter is one to be handled with discretion. No one would wish to kindle afresh the ashes of an extinct agitation. Happily there is reason to believe that the leaders of Indian society are fully alive to the disastrous consequences, both to the individual and the race, which arise from premature cohabitation and are anxious to use their influence to defer the commencement of conjugal life until the wife has attained the full measure of physical maturity requisite to fit her for child-bearing. Here the great

Reform in Rajputana.

[* *Ibid.*, vol. i., p. 112 *et seq.*]

clans of Rajputana have set an example which deserves to be followed throughout India. Themselves among the purest representatives of the Indo-Aryan type, they have revived the best traditions of the Vedic age and have established for themselves the ordinance that no girl shall be married before she is fourteen years old and that the marriage expenses shall in no case exceed a certain proportion of the father's yearly income. That, I venture to think, is the aim which those who would reform society should, for the present, set before themselves If they succeed in doing for India what Colonel Walter did for Rajputana, they will achieve more than any Indian reformer has yet accomplished. To bring back the Vedas is no unworthy ideal.

The Rajputana movement is so remarkable in itself and contains the germs of such high promise that it calls for fuller notice. Nearly twenty years ago, at the suggestion of Colonel Walter, then Agent to the Governor-General in Rajputana, all the Sardārs of the various States of Rajputana assembled at Ajmer for the purpose of discussing arrangements for regulating the expenses incurred on the occasion of marriages, deaths, etc., among Rajpūts of all ranks except the ruling chiefs. By the unanimous decision of these leaders of Rajput society, a series of observances were prescribed which, revised from time to time, have now assumed the form of definite rules enforced by the influence of a society known, in grateful commemoration of its founder, as the Walterkrit Rajputra Hitakārini Sabhā. The chief Political Officer in Rajputana is the President of the Society, and in every State a committee is appointed, consisting of a Sardār, an official and members of the Chāran and Rāo castes, to make arrangements for carrying out the regulations regarding marriages and deaths and other instructions embodied in the rules.

Rules of the Walterkrit Sabha.

Under the head of marriage expenses, if the marriage is that of a Thākur himself or of an eldest son, sister or daughter, the limit of expenditure is fixed on the following scale: When the value of the State is below Rs. 1,000, not more than two-thirds of the annual income may be spent at the marriage; for values between Rs. 1,000 and Rs. 10,000 the proportion is reduced to half; for incomes between Rs. 10,000 and 20,000, to one-third, and for incomes above Rs. 20,000 to one-fourth. In the case of marriages of sons other than the eldest, or nephews and nieces and brothers of the

As to Expenses.

Thākur who are dependent for support upon him, the expenditure may not exceed one-tenth of that admissible in the cases stated above. The abuses attendant on the extravagant largess which used to be distributed among bards and musicians on the occasion of marriages have been got rid of by limiting this expenditure to a percentage of Rs. 6-12-0 on the annual income of the State, and by further restrictions limiting the number of those who may claim such presents to the residents of the territory in which the marriage takes place. Only the father of the bridegroom is liable to make such payments; the father of the bride cannot be charged.

As to betrothal.

In the old days in Rajputana the ceremony of *tīkā* or betrothal was performed with great pomp and show, and the presents made to the bridegroom's father included elephants, horses, and camels. It was on this ceremony that the reputation of the bride's father more especially depended, and the fortunes lavished upon it not only reduced a number of Rajputs to poverty but were also, as the Sabhā are careful to point out, "detrimental to the future happiness of the marrying couple." The expenditure on *tīkā* represented in fact the price of an eligible bridegroom, and the various social considerations affecting the market value of husbands gave rise to unseemly haggling between the parties to the bargain. The Committee have therefore decided that the sending of *tīkā* or betrothal presents should be altogether stopped. The customary presents of opium, betel leaves and other articles of trifling value are allowed to continue, but the betrothal is to be arranged by letter only. The rules lay down that "the usual mark or *tīkā* shall be made on the intended bridegroom's forehead, and betel leaves and cocoanut together with cash not exceeding one gold mohur and not less than one rupee shall be placed in his hand; presents of such fruits as are usual shall be placed on his lap; the people present on the occasion shall also receive opium and sweetmeats or fruits." Servants and others who have hitherto been entitled to receive presents are to be paid according to rates varying from Rs. 5 for a State worth less than Rs. 1,000, to Rs. 100 for States worth more than Rs. 50,000. But even this is not obligatory, and it is expressly stated that anybody may spend less if he likes.

As has been pointed out above, the expense involved in getting a daughter married has everywhere been the main factor in bringing about the evils which have grown up, and this explains the prominence given in the rules to the question of expenditure. The Society, however, did not stop there. They plainly stated their opinion that, "as a rule, boys and girls are married at an early age, notwithstanding that the evils of such a custom are well known to all and need no description." They then proceeded to lay down that boys and girls should not be married before the ages of 18 and 14 respectively, and in order to guard against evasions of this rule, they provided that a half-yearly register of births, deaths and marriages should be kept up and submitted to the special committees at the capitals of the different States through the district officials or Nizāmats. A further rule prescribes that "whereas in this country marriage contracts are not made by the girl's choice, her guardians being entrusted with that duty, it is advisable that girls be not kept unmarried above the age of twenty years." With the object of discouraging polygamy, it has been ruled that no second marriage should take place during the life-time of the first wife unless she is afflicted with an incurable disease or has no offspring. As regards widowers, it is laid down that when a widower has attained the age of 45 years and has a son living, he should not contract another marriage; but if he is healthy and strong, he can marry a second wife, provided that the bride is above the age prescribed by the rules. Where, however, a widower of 45 years has an infant child by his deceased wife and it is difficult for him to bring up the child as well as to look after the household affairs, the State Committee can make a special exception to the rule after satisfying itself that it is proper to do so.

As to Age.

Marriage expenses are controlled by the rule that the number of persons accompanying a wedding party may not exceed twenty, except in the case of marriages on a large scale when it is to be determined at the rate of two men for every hundred rupees that may be spent by the girl's father. The marriage procession is to arrive at the house of the bride's father on the day fixed for the marriage, stay there for two days and take leave on the fourth or on the fifth day at the latest, if the fourth day is considered inauspicious for departure.

The poverty of some classes of Rajputs has led to their obtaining the necessary funds for their daughter's marriage from the bridegroom's father. This the Society condemns as "a most objectionable practice, and one that is opposed to the Dharma Shāstrās." In the case, however, of those Rajputs who have neither land nor maintenance and only earn their livelihood as cultivators, it is permissible to take a bride-price of not more than Rs. 100 from the bridegroom's father and to spend that sum upon the marriage.

The reports submitted by the Society during the last eighteen years show a progressive improvement in respect of compliance with the rules. The scale on which their beneficent influence is now being exercised may be gathered from the fact that out of 5,038 marriages performed among Rajputs in 1903, the rules regarding age were complied with in 4,928 cases and were violated only in 110, of which 55 occurred in the State of Udaipur, where the tendency to stand upon the ancient ways is probably more marked than in other parts of Rajputana. Out of this large number of marriages the rules were infringed in 25 cases in respect of expenditure, in 17 cases in respect of presents to bards and musicians, and in 65 cases in respect of the numbers of the marriage-party. When it is borne in mind that the operations of the Society have the sanction of no criminal law and that their success depends solely upon the influence that can be exercised by the State Committees, most people, I venture to think, will hold that the Walterkrit Sabhā has not only attained most remarkable results within its own sphere of activity, but has set to the rest of India a striking example of what can be done by patriotic combination to promote the cause of social reform.*

Legislation. Mr. Ghose's scheme.

Attempts have also been made to attain the same end by legislative action. More than fourteen years ago Mr. Manmohan Ghose, a Bengali barrister in large criminal practice, put forward a proposal that a general law should be passed for British India "declaring that no marriage shall be valid if either of the contracting parties at the time of celebrating their marriage is below a certain minimum age," which he proposed to fix for the present at twelve years. He admitted that such a measure involved interference with the supposed marriage laws of the Hindus, and was certain to be opposed by a great many orthodox people on that ground. But he pointed out that some doubt existed as to what was the true Hindu law on the subject, and he observed that so eminent a Sanskrit scholar as Dr.

[* "Polygamy is said to be on the decrease in Karauli; this is ascribed partly to the increased cost of living, and partly to the influence of the Walterkrit Hitakārini Sabhā . . . The principles underlying the rules of this Society are said to be slowly leavening some of the other castes in Rajputana" (*Census Report*, 1911, vol. i., p. 184).]

Bhandārkar had held that there was really nothing in law or in the Hindu scriptures to make it obligatory upon a Hindu to marry his daughter before she is twelve. He added that if Dr. Bhandārkar were right, the prevailing idea in Bengal and elsewhere that a girl must be married before a certain period in her life irrespective of her age was erroneous, while the fact that the highest class of Brāhmans (Kulins) frequently do not marry their girls before they are past the age of twenty-one pointed to a similar conclusion. Mr. Manmohan Ghose considered that such a measure would have the effect of putting down the pernicious custom of child-marriage with its concomitant evils; that it would meet with no serious opposition in the advanced province of Bengal; and that it need not be extended to backward provinces until in the opinion of the Local Government they were ripe for such a measure. His views found no support among his countrymen in Bengal.

The Mysore Act.

Three years after the publication of Mr. Manmohan Ghose's proposal, the Mysore State introduced a regulation to prevent infant marriages among the Hindus in the territory of Mysore. The scope of this enactment falls far short both of the Rajputana practice and of Mr. Manmohan Ghose's restricted suggestion, for it defines an infant girl as a girl who has not completed eight years of age. Any person who causes the marriage of an infant girl or aids or abets such a marriage, and any man over eighteen years of age who marries an infant girl, is liable on a prosecution sanctioned by the Government to be punished with simple imprisonment up to six months. It is obvious, however, that so far as the great majority of marriages are concerned, the Mysore law only touches the fringe of the evil, since a boy under eighteen can, if his people choose to run the risk of a prosecution, be married to a girl under eight, and no restriction at all is placed upon infant marriages between the ages of eight and fourteen. The law, indeed, seems to be mainly aimed at the practice of aged widowers marrying child-wives. Here it enacts that any man who having completed fifty years of age marries a girl who has not completed fourteen years of age, shall be punished with imprisonment of either description for a term which may extend to two years or with fine or with both. Seeing that at the age of fourteen most girls are already married, it follows that a man over fifty can have very little chance of securing a wife.

The Mysore Government points to the increase of aged

widowers in the recent census as illustrating the effect of its legislation. This, however, seems to be its sole effect. For the census figures show that the proportion of married girls under ten to 1,000 of the female population had varied between 1891 and 1901 only from 8 to 3, while on the other hand the proportion of girls unmarried at that age had declined in the same period from 281 to 275. The utmost that can be said, therefore, is that the law passed in 1894 may have reduced the proportion of girls married under ten by about five per thousand.*

The Baroda Act.

The Early Marriage Prevention Act passed by the State of Baroda in July, 1904, is designed, as appears from the preamble, "to draw the increased attention of the public towards physical training, whereby the future progeny may be healthy and long-lived." It defines a minor girl as one who has not completed her twelfth year, and a minor boy as one who has not completed his sixteenth year. If the guardians of a minor girl, whose age is above nine, desire to get her married, they must apply to a tribunal consisting of the local sub-judge and three assessors of the petitioners' caste. If the tribunal is satisfied that in the event of the marriage not taking place on the date proposed, it will probably not take place at all or not within one year of the bride attaining her majority, or that the parents and guardians of the girl are not likely, owing to old age and infirmity, to survive until she comes of age, and that she has no other guardian, or that inevitable difficulties of a similar nature are likely to occur, they may grant permission for the marriage to take place. If the sub-judge disagrees with the assessors, the case is referred to the district judge, whose decision appears to be final. The following comments on the working of the Act appear in the Baroda Administration Report for 1904–5:—

"People living outside the limits of this State have an inadequate conception of the degree to which public opinion influences legislation in Baroda. The utmost consideration is shown to such opinion; and His Highness the Mahārāja consented to reduce the limit of age for the marriage of girls from 14 to 12 in deference to the popular wish. Other modifications

[* During the past sixteen years (1895-6—1910-1) the total number of cases prosecuted under the Regulation was 202, of which 175 resulted in the conviction of 475 persons. "The present piece of legislation in Baroda is much more advanced than in Mysore, and much further ahead of current notions and practices among the people at large. It has already been pointed out that, as regards early marriage, the recent Census figures are more favourable to Mysore than to Baroda" (*Census Report, Mysore*, 1911, vol. i., p. 97.)]

were also made in the original Bill, so as to make it less obnoxious to orthodox communities.

"*Results of the Early Marriage Prevention Act.*—It is now over a year since the Act for the Prevention of Early Marriages came into operation, and it would not be without interest to take stock of the results achieved during this first year of its operation. That freedom to contract marriages within the prohibited limits of age, with the permission of the Civil Courts, has been freely availed of, would appear from the fact that no less than 695 applications were presented for such license; and the circumstance that such permission was accorded to 68 per cent. of such petitions, shows a liberal and sympathetic solicitude on the part of the Courts for the religious and social susceptibilities of the people. Some leniency was desirable in the first year of the execution of this law, to which the people had not been accustomed. At the same time it was necessary to enforce the new law, so that it might not be regarded as a dead letter; and 718 offenders were punished with fines, in sums ranging from one rupee to twenty-five rupees, during the year in the whole State. Seventy-eight per cent. of the fines inflicted under this Act fell below five rupees, and only four per cent. exceeded ten rupees. No better proof can be afforded of the indulgence with which offences against this special enactment have been dealt with.

Its practical working.

"The Act has already had a wholesome educative effect on the higher classes of the Hindu society; for we find that the percentage of convictions among the three higher castes did not exceed five. The largest number of offenders belonged to the Dhed and Bhangi classes, which had no less than 39 per cent. of convictions against them. The Kunbis or the cultivating classes had only 11 per cent., while the artisan classes had also an equal number. The percentage among Brahmans and Banias was less than two, and that among Mahomedans was about four—a circumstance which clearly proves that it is only custom, and no religious behest or scriptural text, which supports the practice of early marriages. And when once the force of usage is broken, the progress of the desired reform is smoothed and accelerated even beyond our most sanguine expectations."*

[* The results of this Act during the last decade in Baroda have proved unsatisfactory. The slight decrease in the number of infant marriages "may be attributed to the progress of education and enlightened ideas." Numerous applications for exemption from its provisions

The latest scheme for reforming the marriage usages of India by means of legislation is that put forward by Sardār Arjun Singh of Kapurthala at a meeting of the East India Association held in London on the 31st July, 1905, and published in the *Asiatic Quarterly Review* for October, 1905. The Sardār sums up his proposals in the following words:—

Sardār Arjun Singh's Scheme.

"Allowing that the Government interference is not desirable, has not the Government got other means to eradicate, or at least to mitigate, the custom of early marriages, and thus save the female children, or, at least a proportion of them, from improper widowhood?

"Let the Government pass an Act, the operative part of which may be somewhat in the following form:—

"1. This Act shall apply (*a*) to those persons only who belong to such caste, out-caste, religion, or community, which, after holding public meetings, pass a resolution to come under the protection of this Act; (*b*) to those districts only in which such meetings shall have been held for such purpose.

"2. Under this Act, no marriage shall have the legal force, unless at the date of marriage the husband has completed his twelfth and the wife her tenth year.

"Let the Government also exert its influence on different castes and communities in every district to hold meetings and come to a definite conclusion.

"By such an action on the part of the Government we may be sure that almost every caste, every religion, and every community in the whole of India, by the influence of the Government and under the leadership of educated people, will, with great pleasure, place itself under this Act.

"The Government will do immense good to the well-being

---

were made, and the result of them proves that "the Courts are very indulgent in their treatment of applications for exemption, which may be said to be practically given for the asking." On the introduction of the Act "there was unusual activity in hurrying up marriage before the expected restraint was imposed . . . Probably it is yet too premature to judge of the salutary effects of this beneficent enactment" (*Census Report, Baroda*, 1911, vol. i., p. 154 *et seq.*). To this may be added the remarkable custom of the Kadvā Kunbīs of Gujarāt, who, in order to reduce marriage expenses, celebrate the marriages of the whole caste on a single day (*Census Reports, Baroda*, 1911, vol. i., pp. 173, 290, 307; *Bombay*, 1911, vol. i., p. 242), A similar custom prevails among the Nambutiri Brāhmans of South India, who marry two or three girls to a single man so as to avoid payment of the heavy bridegroom-price, and some Konkanī Brāhmans now invest the dowry in the name of the bride, and thus prevent waste at the marriage celebration (L. K. Anantha Krishna Iyer, *Cochin Tribes and Castes*, vol. ii., 1912, pp. 210, 354; E. Thurston, *Castes and Tribes of Southern India*, 1909, vol. ii., p. 93).]

of the whole country, save 115,285 girls from child-widowhood every ten years, and shall win the hearts of the people."

This *projet de loi* met with a rather chilling reception from the Indian speakers at the meeting. One Hindu gentleman "thought it was high time the Government interfered. If the matter was to be left at the option of the people, it would require centuries before the position of the Indian woman would be uplifted and the custom of early marriages obliterated. It would be a pity to wait so long when the same thing could be done by Government in a shorter time." A Muhammadan followed with the pertinent observation that "every one who had received English education agreed that the custom was pernicious; every one would like to see it abolished; but many friends of his, who had studied at the Universities, when they went back to India, were entirely unable to stem the tide of public opinion. Why was that? It was because the ladies of the house did not agree with them, and they did not carry female opinion with them." This led him to the conclusion that "it would be far better to have no legislation on the subject, but to work out their own ideas, and to feel that they had been the authors of their own salvation." It was now the turn of a Hindu to point out that the Ārya Samājists were even more advanced in this matter than the Brahmos and had "declared that any marriage of a boy under twenty-five and a girl under sixteen was unauthorized by law, was against religion, and was to a certain extent immoral;" while the authorities of the Central Hindu College at Benares "had ruled that no married boy would be admitted to their school." The speaker expressed himself as opposed to legislation, and was supported in this by a Muhammadan who took the opportunity of protesting against the lecturer's conjecture that infant marriage was devised by the Hindus to secure their young women from the outrages of invaders from Central Asia. Finally, the Chairman, Sir Lepel Griffin, summed up the debate in a speech of admirable discretion, in the course of which he admitted that it was news to him to hear that the Mysore and Baroda States had legislated on the subject, and intimated a doubt whether the lecturer's proposal to fix the minimum age at twelve for boys and ten for girls would not be "almost a retrogade step."

Indian Views of it.

It is perhaps a little surprising that a meeting of this kind, with a distinguished ex-political officer in the chair, should not have been aware that the very problem which they were engaged in discussing had been successfully approached in Rajputana nearly twenty years ago. In the face of that illustration of what people can do for themselves we may be absolved from discussing in detail the scheme for permissive legislation propounded by Sardār Arjun Singh. Few persons will share its author's belief, so characteristic of the modern Indian, in the efficacy of a public meeting as an instrument of social reform; while no one can fail to be struck by the pathetic admission of one of his critics that young men brought up on English history and literature, and more or less imbued with European ideas of domestic morality, find their worst foes in the ladies of their own households. The fact, of course, is that in matters of this kind the Anglicised middle classes are hardly in a position to give a decisive lead. Their social standing is not such as to command universal respect, and their orthodoxy is often open to suspicion. The people who can exercise a real influence and set an example that will be followed are, in the first place, the ancient aristocracy of India, the men who in Rajputana have created and carried on the Walterkrit Sabhā. Below them, as the working agents who will transmit to the masses the impulsive proceeding from their natural leaders, come the *panchāyats* or caste councils, the caste and clan Brāhmans, the genealogists and astrologers, the village barbers, and the professional match makers, male and female, who conduct the elaborate process of haggling by which Hindu marriages are put on the market. The influence of the *ghataks* or marriage brokers is very great. Five hundred years ago a famous *ghatak* remodelled for matrimonial purposes the highest sub-caste of Bengal Brāhmans, and his classification holds good to the present day. The caste councils, which bear a sort of resemblance to a club committee, are equally powerful, and perhaps more accessible than the *ghataks* to liberal ideas. Both have the utmost respect for the Hindu scriptures coupled with the scantiest knowledge of their contents, and reforms on the Rajputana lines might with equal regard for truth and expediency be presented to their minds as a revival of pristine usage making for ceremonial righteousness.*

Prospects of reform.

[* "A society, called the Hindu Marriage Reform League, has been started by Hindu gentlemen in Calcutta with the object of raising the age, at which girls can be given in marriage, to 16 years. Till recently such attempts have been made only by the higher castes, but the

In favour of legislation, some people will doubtless urge that in the East where so many things are, according to Western ideas, upside down, the relations between positive law and positive morality are also reversed. In Europe, one is told, morality must always be in advance of law. It took generations of quibbles and all the efforts of Bentham and Romilly to lift the English criminal law to a level approaching that of the conventional ethics of the day. In India, it will be said, if law is to wait until popular morality is ready, things will remain as they are until the end of time. To this it may be replied first, that in Rajputana the end in view is being attained without the intervention of the State; secondly, that the Mysore and Baroda laws hardly rise above the level of popular usage, and may well have the effect of impeding reform by stereotyping the very conditions which it is desirable to improve; thirdly, that there is very little to show that these enactments are not a dead letter; fourthly, that any law dealing with this subject cannot, in the nature of things, be restricted to a particular class. Its operation must be general, and it would be liable to be defeated by the ancient and familiar device of boycotting the advocates of premature reform. Exclusive dealing in husbands cannot be put down by law. It may or may not be possible to compel a Tipperary grocer to sell sugar to a man who has taken a boycotted tenement; it would certainly be impossible to compel an Indian father to give his son to a girl whose parents had forgotten to get her married at the proper time.

Difficulties of legislation.

Two forms of polyandry are recognized in the literature of the subject: the fraternal, where a woman becomes the joint wife of several brothers; and the matriarchal, where she has a number of husbands who are not necessarily related to each other. The essential feature is that the woman lives with several men *at the same time.* If her husbands are not synchronous but successive, if she lives with one husband for a year or so and then takes another, the arrangement may

---

movement is spreading downwards. A general conference of the Namasudras held in 1908, resolved that any one marrying a son under 20 or a daughter under 10 years of age should be excommunicated. This resolution has had some effect, for it is reported in the Narail sub-division of Jessore, the age of a bride varies from 8 to 11, and that of a bridegroom from 16 to 20. In this sub-division it has further been determined that no Namasudra parent shall take more than Rs. 30 for a daughter, and, if he is in affluent circumstances, nothing at all" (*Census Report, Bengal,* 1911, vol. i., p. 319).]

be morally reprehensible, but it is not what is meant by polyandry. Under both systems there is necessarily extreme uncertainty as to the parentage of the joint wife's children. Where the matriarchal form of polyandry prevails, this uncertainty affects the law of succession to property, since it is impossible to prove that a man living in a polyandrous group has ever had any children of his own. Consequently inheritance is traced through females, and a man's ordinary heir-at-law is his sister's son. Where fraternal polyandry is in fashion, the problem of paternity is equally obscure, and it is impossible to say for certain which of the brothers is the father of a particular child. But for working purposes it is assumed that one of them must be, and therefore the children belong to the same exogamous group as their fathers and inheritance to the joint property is reckoned in the male line.

The two forms of polyandry.

There is abundant evidence to prove that matriarchal polyandry was at one time an established custom among the Nāyars of the Malabar coast. Thus Cæsar Fredericke, who travelled in those parts in the year 1563, writes of them:

"These men go naked from the girdle upwards, with a clothe rolled about their thighs, going barefooted, and having their haire very long and rolled up together on the toppe of their heads, and alwayes they carrie their Bucklers or Targets with them and their swordes naked, these Nairi have their wives common amongst themselves, and when any of them goe into the house of any of these women, he leaveth his sworde and target at the doore, and the time that he is there, there dare not be any so hardie as to come into that house. The King's children shall not inherite the kingdom after their father, because they hold this opinion, that perchance they were not begotten of the King their father, but of some other man, therefore they accept for their King one of the sonnes of the King's sisters, or of some other woman of the blood roiall, for that they be sure that they are of the blood roiall." *

Matriarchal polyandry.

The Portuguese traveller, Fernão Lopes de Castanheda, says much the same:† "By the laws of this country these Nāyars cannot marry, so that no one has any certain or

* The voyage and travell of M. Cæsar Fredericke, Marchant of Venice, into the East India and beyond the Indies: translated out of Italian by Mr. Thomas Hickocke. Hakluyt, *Voyages*, V., 394.

† *Historia de descobrimento e conquista da India pelos Portuguezes*, 1551–1561.

acknowledged son or father; all their children being born of mistresses, with each of which three or four Nāyars cohabit by agreement among themselves. Each one of this confraternity dwells a day in his turn with the joint mistress, counting from noon of one day to the same time of the next, after which he departs, and another comes for the like time. They thus spend their lives without the care or trouble of wives and children, yet maintain their mistresses well, according to their rank. Any one may forsake his mistress at his pleasure, and in the like manner the mistress may refuse admittance to any one of her lovers when she pleases. These mistresses are all gentlewomen of the Nāyar caste, and the Nāyars, besides being prohibited from marrying, must not attach themselves to any woman of a different rank. Considering that there are always several men attached to one woman, the Nāyars never look upon any of the children born of their mistresses as belonging to them, however strong a resemblance may subsist, and all inheritances among the Nāyars go to their brothers or the sons of their sisters born of the same mothers, all relationship being counted only by female consanguinity and descent. This strange law prohibiting marriage was established that they might have neither wives nor children on whom to fix their love and attachment and that, being free from all family cares, they might the more willingly devote themselves to warlike service."

A series of observers, among whom may be mentioned Alexander Hamilton (1744), Jonathan Duncan (1792), Francis Buchanan (1807), James Forbes (1813), and the Lutheran Missionary Graul (1849–1853), confirm the accounts given by the travellers of the sixteenth century. During the last fifty years, however, polyandry in the strict sense of the term seems to have fallen into disuse. Mr. Fawcett, of the Madras police, writing in 1901, says that he has "not known any admitted instance of polyandry amongst the Nāyars of Malabar at the present day," * and twenty years earlier Mr. Wigram wrote in his treatise on "*Malabar Law and Custom*," as follows:—

"Polyandry may now be said to be dead, and although the issue of a Nāyar marriage are still children of their mother rather than of their father, marriage may be defined as a contract based on mutual consent, and dissoluble at will. It has been well said (by Mr. Logan) that nowhere is the marriage tie, albeit informal, more rigidly observed or respected than it

[* *Bulletin Madras Government Museum*, vol. iii., No. 3, p. 241.]

is in Malabar: nowhere is it more jealously guarded, or its neglect more savagely avenged."

It is a peculiar and characteristic feature of Nāyar matrimonial usage that every woman goes through two forms of marriage. The first, *tāli kettu* or tying of the *tāli*, is purely ceremonial, and must take place before a girl attains puberty. Its essential incident consists in the nominal husband tying round her neck a tiny plate of gold shaped like the leaf of the Indian fig tree. The accompanying ritual is costly, and to neglect it entails social ostracism. Consequently, for economical reasons, one man is often engaged to tie the *tāli* on a number of girls of all ages from three months to twelve years. Having played his part in the ritual and received the customary fee, the ceremonial husband goes his way and is never heard of again. His functions are purely formal, and he has no conjugal rights over any of the girls whom he has technically married. Opinions differ as to the origin of the *tāli kettu* marriage, and some observers regard it as a Brāhman innovation of comparatively recent date. A different explanation is suggested by Capt. Hamilton's statement that "when the Zamorin marries, he must not cohabit with his bride till the Nambourie, or chief priest, has enjoyed her, and, if he pleases, may have three nights of her company, because the first fruits of her nuptials must be an holy oblation to the god she worships. And some of the nobles are so complaisant as to allow the clergy the same tribute, but the common people cannot have that compliment paid them, but are forced to supply the priests' places themselves."* It seems possible that the ceremony may be a survival of a primitive taboo on virginity which has in course of time become purely formal and has been overlaid by observances borrowed from Hindu sources. This view derives some support from the fact that the ritual resembles in certain respects that which is used for the consecration of a *Deva-Dāsi* or temple prostitute.

The ceremonial husband.

On attaining physical maturity a Nāyar girl contracts a second marriage variously known as *Sambandham* (association); *guna dosham* (for better for worse); *pudavamuri* (the giving of a cloth); *kitakoram* (the marriage of the bed). The ceremony is of the simplest kind and consists mainly in the bridegroom presenting betelnut, clothes, and money to the bride at night in the

The actual husband.

[* Ed. 1744, vol. i., p. 310.]

bridal chamber before her female relatives. As to the negotiations which precede it opinions seem to differ. One authority describes it as "generally effected with mutual consent," while another says that "in most cases the bride and bridegroom are utter strangers to each other until this night." All agree that *Sambandham* is followed by consummation, and that it is terminable at the will of either party. Frivolous divorces, however, are said to be rare and to be discouraged by public opinion and by the influence of the *karnavan*, the autocratic head of the Malabar *tarwād*, a joint family tracing its descent in the female line from a common ancestress. Where the husband can afford it, his wife lives with him; in other cases she lives with her *tarwād* and he visits her there—a plain survival of the earlier conditions described above. The children are usually educated by the *tarwād*.

Taking the evidence as a whole, it seems to point to the conclusion that within the last two or three generations the refining influence of higher education has induced the Nāyars to abandon the practice of polyandry and to attach to the *Sambandham* connexion the full sanctity of a monogamous union. Their marriage ritual and their law of inheritance still retain unmistakable traces of polyandrous usage, but the tendency is to relegate these to the background. A series of judicial decisions have given to any member of a Malabar joint family the absolute disposal during his lifetime of property acquired by himself, and recent legislation has enabled him to bequeath such property by will to his children by his *Sambandham* wife.

Fraternal polyandry in Tibet and Sikkim.

In the Himalayan region where fraternal polyandry is in vogue, there are no indications of any moral revolt against the system, unless indeed the germs of such a feeling may be traced in the slight shyness which people are apt to display when questioned on the subject, and in their manifest preference for discussing the connubial arrangements of some family other than their own. In Western Tibet even these faint signs of grace are wanting, and the account given by the latest observer points to the prevalence of considerable sexual depravity.

"Each household contains for all practical purposes three or four families,* and one can imagine the atmosphere in which the children are brought up with polyandry all round them, and when the time comes for a girl to enter another similar household, and be the bride of numerous brothers, it may truly

* Charles A. Sherring, *Western Tibet and the British Borderland*, 1906, p. 190.

be said that there is no modesty left in her. Merchants and officials from Lhasa can anywhere get women throughout Western Tibet to live with them temporarily for the mere asking, even of the best local families."

At the time of the last Census polyandry as practised in Sikkim and Eastern Tibet was enquired into by Mr. Earle, then Deputy-Commissioner of Darjeeling, on the basis of a set of questions drawn up by me in 1891. The information collected was carefully verified and may be regarded as substantially correct.

"If the eldest of a group of brothers marries a woman, she is regarded as the common wife of all the brothers. It does not, however, necessarily follow that she will cohabit with all the younger brothers. She exercises much liberty in this respect, and it will depend upon her pleasure as to whether she will cohabit with any particular younger brother. If the eldest brother (*i.e.*, the real husband) dies, the wife passes to one of the younger brothers according to her own selection. Should her choice fall on the next brother, she will still be the common wife of the younger brothers. Should, however, she select any of the younger brothers, she will be the common wife only of those younger than him, and, if he be the youngest, she will be his wife only. If the eldest brother of a group of brothers does not marry, but the second or third brother does so, then the wife will be the common wife of such second or third brother and his younger brothers only. Elder brothers, in such cases, will separate and leave the family, having no claim on the wives of the younger brothers. Cousins, both on the father's and mother's side, and half-brothers may be admitted as members of the group of brothers only if the husband agrees and has no brothers of his own. Several cousins cannot take a wife between them except in the instance just quoted. There are instances in the Darjeeling district, but apparently not in Sikkim or Tibet, of a number of men, not brothers or near relations, taking a wife between them, but this appears to be a novel practice introduced for purposes of economy. There appears to be no tradition of any such custom in Sikkim and Tibet in former times." Property descends in the male line, and there are no traces of inheritance through a sister's son. The eldest brother counts as the father of the joint wife's children and the other brothers are spoken of as their uncles.

When asked about the origin of the custom, people usually

give sumptuary reasons recalling those which have given rise to the suspicion that fraternal polyandry was not unknown among the Venetian nobility of the sixteenth century. One is told that a man who is too particular to share a wife with his brethren must pay for the luxury of a household of his own in the form of a separate assessment to revenue; that polyandry keeps the family property together, that it promotes harmony among the brothers, and so forth. I have never heard it assigned to a scarcity of women, and there is no reason to believe that the proportion of the sexes in Sikkim and Tibet is not fairly equal.* Religious zeal, however, encourages professed celibacy especially among the men, and according to Mr. Earle "superfluous women become nuns or prostitutes or remain single." †

Origin of polyandry.

We may conclude this chapter with a brief glance at the statistics of the subject which are alive with human interest. From the point of view of the European old maid India seems at first sight a sort of connubial paradise, where the selfishness of male celibacy is condemned by religion and discouraged by fashion, and every girl who is not physically disqualified for marriage may count with certainty upon finding a husband. Of the entire female population between the ages of fifteen and twenty, four out of every five are married, while in the more critical period from twenty to thirty only one woman out of seven remains single. The Eden so easily won is, however, quickly lost; even in India males marry later than females, and the disparity of ages finds expression in the figures, which show that among women of all ages more than one in six is a widow, while in the case of men the corresponding proportion is only

Statistics of marriage.

[* Ladākh Proper, and the other Mongoloid races in Kashmir show the highest proportion of women in the State (*Census Report*, 1911, vol. i., p. 125).]

[† Comparing the Bahimi of Central Africa with the Todas of India, Sir J. Frazer (*Totemism and Exogamy*, 1910, vol. ii., p. 539 *et seq.*) suggests that "there is something in the pastoral life which favours the growth of abnormal relations between the sexes. . . . The superstition which debars these people from a vegetable diet not only impoverishes them, and retards economic progress by presenting a serious obstacle to the adoption of agriculture; it affects society in another and curious way by fostering a type of marriage which effectually checks the growth of population, and which can hardly fail to be injurious to the women and thereby to their offspring." On the other hand, E. S. Hartland (*Primitive Paternity*, vol. ii., 1910, p. 162 *et seq.*) denies that polyandry results from economic causes, "in face of the evidence from all parts of the world of indifference to what the civilized peoples of Europe generally regard as womanly virtue." He believes that it results from the general absence of marital jealousy among backward races, and he suggests that women exercise a powerful influence in support of the customs. For further discussion of the question see *Census Report*, *India*, 1911, vol. i., p. 238 *et seq.*]

one in eighteen. In England, where from three-fifths to two-thirds of both sexes are single and not more than a third are married, the proportion of the widowed is only one in thirty for males and one in thirteen for females. The actual number of widows in India in 1901 was nearly twenty-six millions, while the widowers numbered only eighteen millions. Between the ages of forty and sixty every other woman is a widow, and even at the earlier period of from thirty to forty, one woman in five finds herself in the same unfortunate condition.

Among Hindus.

These general characteristics—the universality of marriage, the prevalence of early marriage, and the frequency of premature widowhood—are in the case of Hindus accentuated by the influence of religion or inviolable usage. Both sexes marry earlier than is the case with the population at large, and of the unmarried girls only one in every fourteen has turned her fifteenth year. Nearly half of the girls between the ages of ten and fifteen are married, while of those between fifteen and twenty only one-fifth have failed to find husbands. This vision of domestic felicity is clouded by the fact that one in every five Hindu women is a widow. Many of them are condemned to a life of penance and humiliation at a comparatively early age, while some are mere infants who have never known their husbands and have had no chance of bearing a child.

Among Muhammadans.

Judged by a European standard, the matrimonial relations of the Muhammadans are less abnormal than those of the Hindus. Marriage is a civil function; its cost is not swollen by the demands of a swarm of greedy priests; the field of selection is larger and is less affected by artificial restrictions relating to social status; and there is no bar to widows marrying again. The males marry later in life, and the pitiful spectacle of a struggling student hampered by a wife and children while he is still cramming for University examinations is less frequent than among Hindus. In the case of females the contrast is still more marked. Among Muhammadan girls between the ages of five and ten only seven per cent. are married compared with twelve per cent. among Hindus; while between ten and fifteen the proportion of child-wives is thirty-nine for Muhammadans and forty-seven for Hindus. The marriage expenses are on a less extravagant scale; bridegrooms are not bought and sold for fantastic prices; and the balance of the sexes is not disturbed by the pernicious custom of hypergamy.

In respect of widowhood the Muhammadans are also more favourably situated. It is true that the descendants of Hindu converts, and especially the Jolāha weavers and Dhuniya wool-carders, are not free from the Hindu prejudice against the re-marriage of widows. But this feeling finds no support from the religion and traditions of Islam and is rebuked by the example of the Prophet himself. It is therefore weaker and less general than among Hindus, and unions between widowers and widows are recognized as legitimate and even appropriate. These influences are reflected in the statistics, which show only ten per cent. of widows among women between fifteen and forty, while in the case of Hindus the proportion is as high as fourteen.

P.S.—Since this chapter was in type public attention has been drawn to the subject of Kulin polygamy by an animated correspondence in the columns of the *Times*. Those who are curious in these matters will find in Appendix VIII some extracts from letters by Sir Henry Cotton, Sir George Birdwood, Sir G. Grierson, Mr. John Christian, and Mr. Bernard Shaw, together with the report of the Committee appointed in 1867 by the Bengal Government to inquire into the subject with reference to a proposal for legislation which was made by the Mahārāja of Burdwan and the well-known Hindu reformer, Iswar Chandra Vidyasāgar.

Without following Mr. Bernard Shaw in his rather advanced suggestions for the breeding of the Super-Man, any one who approaches the question from a scientific point of view may be permitted to join with him and Sir George Birdwood in condemning as insular and inappropriate the tone of virtuous indignation that appears in some of the letters in the *Times*. The merest glance at the vast literature which is occupied with the origin of human marriage ought to convince most reasonable people that all sorts of connubial permutations and combinations have been in vogue in different times and places, and that these have resulted, not from any innate depravity on the part of those who practised them, but from the action of some overmastering social force which disturbed the balance of the sexes and brought about matrimonial connexions which we now regard as more or less abnormal. If, then, Kulin polygamy is nothing more than an unhappy but inevitable consequence of exaggerated hypergamy, is it quite rational to denounce the unfortunate victims of a perverted system for preferring a fractional share in an itinerant husband to the reproach of having no husband at all and to the painful repression of the craving for maternity which is nowhere stronger than in India? To treat the symptom does not necessarily cure the disease, although it may induce new symptoms. Supposing Kulin polygamy to be effectively abolished by repressive legislation or social disapproval, the surplus of marriageable girls resulting from hypergamy would still remain. What is to become of them? European experience suggests that enforced celibacy on a large scale is not invariably an ideal condition. If, therefore, a fresh set of evils is to be avoided, the reformers would do wisely to follow Mr. Girindra Nath Dutt's advice and strike boldly at hypergamy, whatever form it may assume. This they can only deal with themselves, since legislation on the subject would plainly be futile. Indigenous complaints demand indigenous remedies.

Whatever may be the case in Bengal, the following extract from the recently published *District Gazetteer* seems to be conclusive as to the existence of polygamy among the Brāhmans of Muzaffarpur, a district forming part of the ancient tract of Mithila, whence, according to Mr. Girindra Nath Dutt, the system of Kulinism was borrowed some centuries ago by the Brāhmans of Bengal. Most of the Muzaffarpur Brāhmans belong to the Maithil or Tirhutiyā sub-caste, which is divided into five hypergamous groups—Srotriya or Sote, Jog, Pānjibaddh, Nagar and Jaiwār. The men of each group may take wives from the groups ranking below it in this scale of social precedence, but the women can only marry in their own or in a higher group.

"Polygamy," says Mr. O'Malley, the author of this interesting volume, "is practised among these Brāhmans by the Bikauwā or 'Vendor'—a class of Maithil Brāhmans who derive their name from the practice of selling themselves, or more rarely their minor sons, to the daughters of the lower groups of the series given above. Some have as many as forty or fifty wives, who live with their own parents and are visited at intervals by their husbands. Bikauwā Brāhmans who have married into the lower classes are not received on equal terms by the members of their own class, but the women whom they marry consider themselves raised by the alliance. The price paid for a Bikauwā varies according to the class to which he belongs and the means of the family of the girl whom he is to marry. It may be as little as Rs. 20: it has been known to rise as high as Rs. 6,000." *

[* On polygamy in Bengal see *Census Report*, 1911, vol. i., p. 326 *et seq.*]

CHAPTER V

CASTE AND RELIGION

> Notre vie est du vent tissu.
>
> JOUBERT.

> Alles Vergängliche
> Ist nur ein Gleichniss.
>
> GOËTHE.

IN India, as in the greater part of the East, religion is still a power for good or for evil, and has over the minds of men an empire which in modern Europe has long passed out of its hands. Assisted by the kindred agency of fiction, it exercises a subtle influence on family ritual and domestic usage, and through these tends insensibly to modify and transform the internal structure of Indian society. At the risk of driving patient analogy too hard, we may perhaps venture to compare the social gradations of the Indian caste system to a series of geological deposits. The successive strata in each series occupy a definite position, determined by the manner of their formation, and the varying customs in the one may be said to represent the fossils in the other. The lowest castes preserve the most primitive usages, just as the oldest geological formations contain the simplest forms of organic life. Thus the totems or animal-names by which the animistic races regulate their matrimonial arrangements, give place, as we travel upwards in the social scale, to group-names based upon local and territorial distinctions, while in the highest castes kinship is reckoned by descent from personages closely resembling the eponymous heroes of early Greek tradition. Even the destructive agencies, to which the imperfection of the geological record is attributed, have their parallel in the transforming influences by which the two great religions of modern India, Hinduism and Islam, have modified the social order. A curious contrast may be discerned

Stratification of caste.

in their methods of working and in the results which they produce.

Hinduism and Islam.

Islam is a force of the volcanic sort, a burning and integrating force, which, under favourable conditions, may even make a nation. It melts and fuses together a whole series of tribes, and reduces their internal structure to one uniform pattern, in which no survivals of pre-existing usages can be detected. The separate strata disappear; their characteristic fossils are crushed out of recognition; and a solid mass of law and tradition occupies their place. Hinduism, transfused as it is by mysticism and ecstatic devotion, and resting ultimately on the esoteric teachings of transcendental philosophy, knows nothing of open proselytism or forcible conversion, and attains its ends in a different and more subtle fashion, for which no precise analogue can be found in the physical world. It leaves existing aggregates very much as they were, and so far from welding them together, after the manner of Islam, into larger cohesive aggregates, tends rather to create an indefinite number of fresh groups; but every tribe that passes within the charmed circle of Hinduism inclines sooner or later to abandon its more primitive usages or to clothe them in some Brahmanical disguise. The strata, indeed, remain, or are multiplied; their relative positions are, on the whole, unaltered; only their fossils are metamorphosed into more advanced forms. One by one the ancient totems drop off, or are converted by a variety of ingenious devices into respectable personages of the standard mythology; the fetish gets a new name, and is promoted to the Hindu Pantheon in the guise of a special incarnation of one of the greater gods; the tribal chief sets up a family priest, starts a more or less romantic family legend, and in course of time blossoms forth as a new variety of Rajput. His people follow his lead, and make haste to sacrifice their women at the shrine of social distinction. Infant-marriage with all its attendant horrors is introduced; widows are forbidden to marry again; and divorce, which plays a great, and on the whole, a useful part in tribal society, is summarily abolished. Throughout all these changes, which strike deep into the domestic life of the people, the fiction is maintained that no real change has taken place, and every one believes, or affects to believe, that things are with them as they have been since the beginning of time.

It is curious to observe that the operation of these tendencies has been quickened, and the sphere of their action enlarged, by the great extension of railways which has taken place in India during the last few years. Both Benares and Manchester have been brought nearer to their customers, and have profited by the increased demand for their characteristic wares. Siva and Krishna drive out the tribal gods as surely as grey shirtings displace the less elegant but more durable hand-woven cloth. Pilgrimages become more pleasant and more popular, and the touts, who sally forth from the great religious centres to promote these pious excursions, find their task easier and their clients more open to persuasion than was the case even twenty years ago. A trip to Jagannāth or Gaya is no longer the formidable and costly undertaking that it was. The Hindu peasant who is pressed to kiss the footprints of Vishnu, or to taste the hallowed rice that has been offered to the Lord of the World, may now reckon the journey by days instead of months. He need no longer sacrifice the savings of a lifetime to his pious object, and he has a reasonable prospect of returning home none the worse for a week's indulgence in religious enthusiasm. Even the distant Mecca has been brought, by means of competing lines of steamers, within the reach of the faithful in India; and the influence of Muhammadan missionaries and returned pilgrims has made itself felt in a quiet but steady revival of orthodox usage all over the country.

Railways and religion.

Rapidly as these levelling and centralizing forces do their work, a considerable residue of really primitive usage still resists their transforming influence. The oldest of the religions recorded in the last Census, if indeed it can be called a religion at all, is the medley of heterogeneous and uncomfortable superstitions now known by the not entirely appropriate name of Animism. The difficulty of defining this mixed assortment of primitive ideas is illustrated by the fact that there is no name for it in any of the Indian languages. For Census purposes, therefore, recourse must be had to the clumsy device of instructing the enumerators that in the case of tribes who are neither Hindus nor Muhammadans, but have no word for their religious beliefs, the name of the tribe itself must be entered in the column for religion. Thus one and the same religion figures in the original returns of the Census under as many different designations as there are tribes professing it. On turning to the European literature of the subject we find that even among scientific observers the curiously indeterminate character of the beliefs in question has given rise to considerable diversity of nomenclature. Three different names, each dwelling on a different aspect of the subject, have obtained general acceptance, and an attempt has been made to introduce a fourth which seeks to accentuate characteristics overlooked by the rest.

The earliest and best-known name, Fetishism, was first brought into prominence by Charles de Brosses, President of the Parliament of Burgundy, who published in 1760 a book called *Du Culte des Dieux Fétiches, ou Parallèle de l'ancienne Religion de l'Egypte avec la Religion actuelle de la Nigritie.* De Brosses was a man of very various learning. He ranked high in his day among the historians of the Roman Republic; he wrote a scientific treatise on the origin of language; he is recognized as one of the founders of the modern school of anthropological mythology; and he is believed to have invented the names Australia and Polynesia. He did not, however, invent, nor was he even the first to use, the word fetish, which is a variant of the Portuguese *fetiço* or *fetisso*, an amulet or talisman, derived from the Latin *factitius*, "artificial," "unnatural," and hence "magical." It was employed, naturally enough, by the Portuguese navigators of the sixteenth century to describe the worship of stocks and stones, charms, and a variety of queer and unsavoury objects, which struck them as the chief feature of the religion of the negroes of the Gold Coast. Nor did de Brosses travel so far on the path of generalization as some of his followers. He assumed indeed that Fetishism was the beginning of all religion, since no lower form could be conceived; but he did not extend its domain like Bastholm, who in 1805 claimed as fetishes "everything produced by nature or art which receives divine honour, including sun, moon, earth, air, fire, water, mountains, rivers, trees, stones, images, and animals if considered as objects of divine worship."

Fetishism.

For some five and twenty years after Bastholm wrote, the term Fetishism lay buried in the special literature of anthropology, whence it seems to have been unearthed by Auguste Comte, who used it, in connexion with his famous *loi des trois états*, as a general name for all the forms of primitive religion which precede and insensibly pass into polytheism. Comte described the mental attitude of early man towards religion as "pure fetishism, constantly characterized by the free and direct exercise of our primitive tendency to conceive all external bodies whatsoever, natural or artificial, as animated by a life essentially analogous to our own, with mere differences of intensity." * His authority, combined with the natural attractions of a cleanly cut definition, gave wide currency to this extended sense of the word, and it is only of late years that it has been confined to the particular class of superstitions to which the Portuguese explorers originally applied it. In the light of our present knowledge, Fetishism may be defined as the worship of tangible inanimate objects believed to possess in themselves some kind of mysterious power. Thus restricted, the term marks out a phase of primitive superstition for which it is convenient to have a distinctive name.

Shamanism.

We have seen how Fetishism came to us from the west coast of Africa. For the origin of Shamanism we must look to Siberia. *Shaman* is the title of the sorcerer-priest of the Tunguz tribe of Eastern Siberia, between the Yenisei and Lena rivers. The word has been supposed to be a variant of the Sanskrit *Sramana*, Pāli *Samana*, which appears in the Chinese *sha-man* or *shi-man* in its original sense of a Buddhist ascetic, and may have passed into the Tunguz language through the Manchu form *Saman*. Ethnologists seem to have been introduced to it by the writings of the German explorer and naturalist, Peter Simon Pallas, who travelled through the Tunguz country up to the borders of China in 1772, and wrote a lengthy account of his wanderings.† The essence of Shamanism is the recognition of the

---

* Comte, *Philosophie Positive*, vol. v., p. 30, quoted by Tylor, *Primitive Culture*, vol. ii., 2nd ed., 1873, p. 144.

† Pallas uses the words *Schaman* and *Schamanin* (Zauberer and Zauberin) in his curious book, *Samlungen historischer Nachrichten über die Mongolischen Völkerschaften*, printed at St. Petersburg in 1776 by the Imperial Academy of Science. Chapter VII. of the second volume (1801) entitled, "Von den Gaukeleyen des Schamanischen Aberglaubens, Zaubereyen und Weissagerey unter den Mongolischen Völkern," deals with the survivals of Shamanism which Pallas found among the Kalmucks and Mongols "daubed over" as he says (übertüncht), "with a coat of the later Buddhistic doctrine." But he does not profess to treat of Shamanism at length, and remarks that this would be superfluous as full particulars are to be found in the Siberian Travels of the elder Gmelin and in Georg's Description of the Nations of the Russian Empire. The "Elder Gmelin" was Johann Georg, born 1709, who travelled in Siberia from 1743 to 1773 and published his *Reisen durch Siberien* in four octavo volumes at Gottingen in 1751–52. He became Professor of Botany at Tübingen in 1749, six years before his death. He was also the author of the *Flora Siberia*, two volumes of which were published during his life, while the remaining two were edited by his nephew, Samuel Gotlob Gmelin, who travelled with Pallas in Siberia. After leaving Pallas, Samuel went to the Crimea, where he was captured by the Khan, and died in prison at the age of thirty-one. I mention these particulars, for which I am indebted to my friend Lt.-Col. Prain, C.I.E., F.R.S., because it seems possible that the word "Shaman" may have been introduced not by Pallas, but by Johann Georg Gmelin. The Gmelins were a notable family, and no less than seven of them wrote books on botany at dates ranging from 1699 to 1866. None

Shaman, medicine man, wizard, or magician, as the authorized agent by whom unseen powers can be moved to cure disease, to reveal the future, to influence the weather, to avenge a man on his enemy, and generally to intervene for good or evil in the affairs of the visible world. The conception of the character of the powers invoked varies with the culture of the people themselves. They may be gods or demons, spirits or ancestral ghosts, or their nature may be wholly obscure and shadowy. In order to place himself *en rapport* with them, the Shaman lives a life apart, practises or pretends to practise various austerities, wears mysterious and symbolical garments, and performs noisy incantations in which a sacred drum or enchanted rattle takes a leading part. On occasion he should be able to foam at the mouth and go into a trance or fit, during which his soul is supposed to quit his body and wander away into space. By several observers these seizures have been ascribed to epilepsy, and authorities quoted by Peschel go so far as to say that the successful Shaman selects the pupils whom he trains to succeed him from youths with an epileptic tendency. It seems possible, however, that the phenomena supposed to be epileptic may really be hypnotic. In this and other respects there is a general resemblance between the Shaman and the spiritualist medium of the present day. Both deal in much the same wares, and spiritualism is little more than modernized Shamanism. Nevertheless, though the principle of Shamanism is proved, by these and other instances, to be widely diffused and highly persistent, it does not cover the entire field of primitive superstition, and it is misleading to use the name of a part for the purpose of defining the whole. Still less can we follow Lubbock in treating Shamanism as a necessary stage in the progress of religious development, or Peschel in extending the term to the priesthoods of organized religions like Buddhism, Brahmanism, and Islam. Traces of Shamanism may have survived in all of them, as in the witchcraft occasionally met with in modern Europe; but to call their

---

of their books are to be had in Calcutta, so I am unable to verify the conjecture thrown out above.

The copy of Pallas's *Samlungen* in the library of the Asiatic Society of Bengal appears from a note on the title page, to have been presented by the Czar of Russia in 1846. The second volume was published twenty-five years after the first, and bears the imprimatur of the St. Petersburg Censor which is wanting in the earlier volume. [Banzaroff derives *Shaman* from a Manchu root, and asserts that it is met with in Chinese writings of the seventh century, when North Mongolia was dominated by the Yuan-yuan, a people of Tungus-Manchu origin (J. Hastings, *Encyclopædia of Religion and Ethics*, vol. iii., 1910, p. 15.)]

hierarchy Shamanistic is to ignore historical development and to confuse the Yogi with the Brāhman, and the Fakīr with the Mulla.

The word Animism was first used to denote the metaphysical system of Georg Ernst Stahl, the originator of the chemical hypothesis of Phlogiston, who revived in scientific form the ancient doctrine of the identity of the vital principle and the soul. In his *Theoria medica vera* published at Halle in 1707, Stahl endeavoured, in opposition to Hoffman's theory of purely mechanical causation, to trace all organic functions to the action of an inherent immaterial substance or *anima*. In his great work on Primitive Culture Sir E. B. Tylor, transferred the term from metaphysics, where it had had its day, to ethnology, where it has taken root and flourished, and made the idea which it conveys the basis of his exposition of the principles underlying primitive religion. "It is habitually found," he writes, "that the theory of Animism divides into two great dogmas forming parts of one consistent doctrine; first, concerning souls of individual creatures, capable of continued existence after the death or destruction of the body; second, concerning other spirits, upward to the rank of powerful deities. Spiritual beings are held to affect or control the events of the material world, and man's life here and hereafter; and it being considered that they hold intercourse with men, and receive pleasure or displeasure from human actions, the belief in their existence leads naturally, and it might also be said inevitably, sooner or later to active reverence and propitiation. Thus Animism, in its full development, includes the belief in souls and in a future state, in controlling deities and subordinate spirits, these doctrines practically resulting in some kind of active worship." *

Animism.

Here for the first time we are presented with a name derived from careful comparison and analysis of a large body of facts, and purporting to express the central and dominant idea underlying primitive religion. The advance on the earlier terminology is immense. We have passed from the superficial to the essential, from the casual impressions of traders and travellers to the mature conclusions of a skilled observer. Although the term has not escaped criticism, it covers, if not the whole field, at any rate a large and conspicuous part of it; it has gained universal currency and is unlikely to be displaced.

The best term available.

* Tylor, *Primitive Culture*, i. 426.

It is indeed almost inconceivable that any name should be devised which would embody a precise conception of the confused bundle of notions wrapped up in savage religion; and most reasonable people will feel that haggling over terminology is a thankless and futile form of intellectual exercise.

Ideas underlying Animism.

While I entirely accept Animism, as the best name that we are likely to get, some objections to which it is liable may perhaps be mentioned. In the first place, it connotes, or seems to connote, the idea that gods are merely the ghosts or shadows of men, projected in superhuman proportions, like the spectre of the Brocken, on the misty background of the unknown, but still in their inception nothing but common ghosts. Definitions, of course, cannot be judged merely by etymology, but a name which appears to beg a controverted question is *pro tanto* not a good name. Moreover, this particular name, failing the explanations necessary to bring out its limitations, seems to have done some real dis-service to science, and that in a branch of investigation where a name counts for a great deal. One may almost say of Animism that it has given rise to a new bias, the anthropological bias. The theological or missionary bias we know, and are prepared to discount. It leads those who are possessed by it to regard all alien gods, in one case as devils, and in another as degenerate survivals of an original revelation or intuition. But the tutored anthropologist is worse than the untutored missionary. He knows the game only too well; he sees what his theory of origins allows him to see, and he unconsciously shapes the evidence in the collecting so as to fit the theory with which Mr. Tylor has set him up. Secondly, it admits of being confused with the idea, common to savages and children, that all things are animated, a notion not easy to reconcile with the ghost theory of religion, which is based on the assumption that primitive man was profoundly impressed by the difference between the dead and the living and evolved therefrom the conception of spirit. Thirdly, the name leaves out of account, or at any rate inadequately expresses, what may be called the impersonal element in early religion, an element which seems to me to have been rather overlooked. In touching on this point I am reluctant to add yet another conjecture to a literature already so prolific in more or less ingenious guesses. But I have had the good fortune, while settling a series of burning disputes about land, to have been brought into very intimate relations with some of the strongest and most typical Animistic races in India, and thus to have enjoyed some special opportunities of studying Animism in those forest solitudes which are its natural home. More especially in Chutia Nāgpur, where this religion still survives in its pristine vigour, my endeavours to find out what the jungle people really do believe have led me to the negative conclusion that in most cases the indefinite something which they fear and attempt to propitiate is not a *person* at all in any sense of the word. If one must state the case in positive terms, I should say that the idea which lies at the root of their religion is that of *power*, or rather of many powers. What the Animist worships, and seeks in strange ways to influence and conciliate, is the shifting and shadowy company of unknown powers or tendencies making for evil rather than for good, which reside in the primeval forest, in the crumbling hills, in the rushing river, in the spreading tree, which gives its spring to the tiger, its venom to the snake, which generates jungle fever, and walks abroad in the terrible guise of cholera, small-pox, or murrain. Closer than this he does not seek to define the object to which he offers his victim, or whose symbol he daubs with vermilion at the appointed season. Some sort of power is there, and that is enough for him. Whether it is associated with a spirit or an ancestral ghost, whether it proceeds from the mysterious thing itself, whether it is one power or many, he does not stop to enquire. I remember a huge Sāl tree (*Shorea robusta*) in a village not far from my head-quarters, which was the abode of a nameless something of which the people were mightily afraid. My business took me frequently to the village, and I made many endeavours to ascertain what the something was. There was no reluctance to talk about it, but I could never get it defined as a god, a demon, or a ghost. Eventually an Anglicised Hindu pleader from another district took a speculative lease of the village, and proceeded to enhance the rents and exploit it generally. One of the first things he did was to assert himself by cutting down the haunted tree. Strange as it may seem, no one was in the least alarmed at this sacrilegious act. The Hindu, they said, was a foreigner, so nothing could happen to him, while the villagers were blameless, for they had not touched the tree. What was supposed to have become of its mysterious occupant I never could ascertain. The instance is typical of the Animistic point of view, and has numberless parallels. All over Chutia Nāgpur there are many jungle-clad hills, the favourite haunts of bears, which beaters of the Animistic races steadfastly refuse to approach until the mysterious power which pervades them has been conciliated by the sacrifice of a fowl. Everywhere we find sacred groves, the abode of equally indeterminate beings, who are represented by no symbols and of whose form and functions no one can give an intelligible account. They have not yet been clothed with individual attributes; they linger on as survivals of the impersonal stage of early religion.

Impersonal elemental forces.

If we assume for the moment the possibility that some such conception, essentially impersonal in its character and less definite than the idea of a spirit, may have formed the germ of primitive religion, one can see how easily it may have escaped observation. The languages of wild people are usually ill-equipped with abstract terms, and even if they had a name for so vague and inchoate a notion, it would certainly have to be translated into the religious vocabulary of their anthropomorphic neighbours. A Santāl could only explain Marang Buru, "the great mountain," by saying that it was a sort of *Deo* or god. A Mech or Dhimāl could give no other account of the reverence with which he regards the Tista river, a frame of mind amply justified by the destructive vagaries of its snow-fed current. On the same principle a writer * of the 17th century says of the West African natives that "when they talk to whites, they call their idolatry *Fitisiken*, I believe because the Portuguese called sorcery *fitiso*." In Melanesia, according to Dr. Codrington, "plenty devil" is the standard formula for describing a sacred place, and the Fiji word for devil has become the common appellation of the native ghosts or spirits. So it is with the Animistic races of India. If they are questioned about their religion, they can only reply in terms of another religion, in Sanskrit derivatives which belong to a wholly different order of ideas. And when we find in Melanesia the very people who put off the inquisitive foreigner with the comprehensive word devil, still retaining the belief in incorporeal beings with neither name nor shape, round whom no myths have gathered, who are not and never have been human, who control rain and sunshine and are kindly disposed towards men, one is tempted to conjecture that the same sort of belief would be found in India by any one who could adequately probe the inner consciousness of the Animistic races.

* W. J. Müller, *Die Africanische Landschaft Fetu*, Nuremberg, 1675, quoted by Max Müller, *Anthropological Religion*, p. 120.

Origin of unworshipped supreme beings.

The hypothesis that the earliest beginnings of savage religion are to be sought in the recognition of elemental forces to which, in the first instance, no personal qualities are ascribed, may perhaps afford an explanation of a problem which has exercised several enquirers of late—the origin of the *fainéant* unworshipped Supreme Beings who figure in savage mythology almost all over the world. The existence of such personages does not fit in with some current theories of the origin of religion, nor are the facts readily explained away. Sir E. B. Tylor believes these beings to have been borrowed from missionary teaching; Mr. Andrew Lang holds that they "came, in some way only to be guessed at," first in order of evolution, and mentions, as "not the most unsatisfactory" solution of the problem, the hypothesis of St. Paul (Rom. i. 19). "Because that which may be known of God is manifest in them, for God hath showed it unto them." We find distinct traces of them in Indian Animism, but in India no one has been at the trouble of speculating about their origin. Now, if man began merely by believing in undefined powers which he attempted to control by means of magic, is it not conceivable that the powers whose activity was uniformly beneficial should, as time went on, receive less attention than those which on occasion were capable of doing mischief? When natural conservatism has to some extent spent its force, magicians and their clients must by degrees perceive, or must by accident discover, that the rising of the sun is in no way dependent upon the imitative magical rites designed to secure its recurrence, and these functions accordingly fall into disuse. When the monsoon current is fairly regular, the powers of the air tend to share the same fate, though the women of the tribe still preserve and occasionally practise the magic art of rain-making, stripping themselves naked at night and dragging a plough through the parched fields, as the Kochh women do this day in Rangpur. But he would be a bold man who would venture to neglect the destructive powers of nature, the diseases which strike without warning, and the various chances of sudden and accidental death. When the era of anthropomorphism sets in, and personal gods come into fashion, the active and passive powers of the earlier system are clothed in appropriate attributes. The former become departmental spirits or gods, with shrines and temples of their own and incessant offerings from apprehensive votaries. The latter receive sparing and infrequent worship, but are recognized, *en* *revanche*, as beings of a higher type, fathers and well-wishers of mankind, patrons of primitive ethics, maker of things who have done their work and earned their repose. The Santāl Marang Buru represents the one; the Bongās or godlings of disease are examples of the other. With the transformation of impersonal powers into personal gods, magic too changes its character. The materialistic processes which consist of imitating the outward and visible effects of natural forces give place to spells, incantations, and penances which are supposed to compel the gods to obey the commands of the magician. In course of time magic itself is ousted by religion, and banished to those holes and corners of popular superstition where it still survives in varying degrees of strength.*

Beginnings of Religion.

The theory carries us still further. It endeavours to account, by the operation of known processes of thought, not merely for what Mr. Lang calls "the high gods of low races," but also for the entire congeries of notions from which the beginnings of religion have gradually emerged. It supposes that early man's first contact with his surroundings gave him the idea of a number of influences, powers, tendencies, forces, outside and other than himself, which affected him in various ways. His dealings with these were at first determined by the rudimentary principle of association, common to men and other animals, that like causes like. In that early stage of his mental development the primitive philosopher did not impute personal attributes of any kind to the something not himself which made for his comfort or the reverse; nor did he suppose that the effects which the various somethings produced were brought about by the action of any individual even remotely resembling himself. Had he entertained any such idea, it is difficult to see how magic could ever have come into existence, still less how it could have preceded the development of what we call religion. For the essence of magic is compulsion. *Flectere si nequeo Superos, Acheronta movebo.* If certain operations are accurately gone though, certain results are bound to follow, as a mere sequence of effect and cause. The earliest type of such processes is what is called imitative magic, because it imitates the phenomena which it seeks to produce. Or, to put the case in another way, it attempts to set a cause in motion by mimicking its consequences. Fires are lighted to make the sun

[* For a discussion of this type of belief, now designated Pre-Animism or Teratism, see R. R. Marett, *The Threshold of Religion*, 1914, chap. i.]

shine in season; water is sprinkled in a shower of drops with the object of inducing rain. In either case the operation is of a quasi-scientific character, and the operator endeavours to control a natural force by imitating its manifestations on a small scale. His mental attitude is so far removed from our own that it would be futile to attempt to analyse it, but it seems to involve the same kind of instinctive or semi-conscious association of ideas, of which instances may be observed among intelligent animals such as monkeys and dogs.

The ghost theory.

On the other hand, if "in the beginning at least," as Mr. Grant Allen * affirms, "every god was nothing but an exceptionally powerful and friendly ghost—a ghost able to help, and from whose help great things may reasonably be expected," one can only wonder how people who desired to enlist his sympathy could have ventured to approach him in ways so inappropriate and disrespectful as those associated with magic. The greater the ghost, the more striking is the incongruity of the ritual. Take the case of a strong chief like the Zulu Chaka, who exercised the most absolute power in the most arbitrary fashion, and loomed so large in the consciousness of the tribe that he seemed to them none other than a god—how could they imagine that he who in life was so strong and so relentless should after death be at the beck and call of any medicine man who could mumble a formula correctly? Surely, apotheosis can never have involved degradation. If there is any force in this line of argument, it leads us to the following dilemma: Either we must abandon the view that magic has everywhere preceded religion; or we must throw over the theory that every god commenced life as a magnified ghost. But there is much in modern research that tends to confirm the former opinion, and it is hardly necessary to travel beyond the Vedas for proof of its validity. Vedic ritual is full of imitative or sympathetic magic, which almost everywhere appears as a palpable survival from older modes of worship.

Growth of Ancestor-worship.

The ancestral theory, on the other hand, or at any rate that extreme form of it with which we are now concerned, is less firmly established. No one of course disputes the existence of ancestor-worship, or denies that every Pantheon has been largely recruited from men, not always of the most respectable

[* *The Evolution of the Idea of God*, 1897, p. 71.]

antecedents, who have fascinated the popular imagination by their doings in life or by the tragic or pathetic fashion of their death. India can show a motley crowd of such divinities. Priests and princesses, pious ascetics and successful dacoits, Indian soldiers of fortune and British men of action, bridegrooms who met their death on their wedding day, and virgins who died unwed, jostle each other in a fantastic Walpurgis dance where new performers are constantly joining in and old ones seldom go out. How modern some of these personages are may be seen from a few illustrations. In 1884 Keshab Chandra Sen, the leader of one of the numerous divisions of the Brahmo Samāj, narrowly escaped something closely resembling deification at the hands of a section of his disciples. A revelation was said to have been received enjoining that the chair used by him during his life should be set apart and kept sacred, and the Legal Member of the Viceroy's Council was invited to arbitrate in the matter. Sir Courtenay Ilbert discreetly refused "to deal with testimony of a kind inadmissible in a Court of Justice;" the parties to the dispute arrived at a compromise among themselves; and the apotheosis of the famous preacher remained incomplete. In Bombay a personage of a very different type has been promoted to divine honours. Sivaji, the founder of the Marātha Confederacy, has a temple and image in one of the bastions of the fort at Malvan in the Ratnagiri district and is worshipped by the Gauda caste of fishermen. This seems to be a local cult, rather imperfectly developed, as there are no priests and no regular ritual. But within the last generation smaller men have attained even wider recognition. By the aid of railways and printing, the fame of a modern deity may travel a long way. Portraits of Yashvantrāo, a subordinate revenue officer in Khandesh, who ruined himself by promiscuous almsgiving, and sacrificed his official position to his reluctance to refuse the most impossible requests, are worshipped at the present day in thousands of devout households. Far down in the south of India, I have come across cheap lithographs of a nameless Bombay ascetic, the Swāmi of Akalkot in Sholapur, who died about twenty years ago. In life the Swāmi seems to have been an irritable saint, for he is said to have pelted with stones any ill-advised person who asked questions about his name and antecedents. As he was reputed to be a Mutiny refugee, he may have had substantial reasons for guarding his incognito. He is now revered from the Deccan to Cape Comorin as Dattātreya, a sort of composite incarnation of

Brahmā, Vishnu, and Siva, and has a temple and monastery of his own.

Facts such as these lead one to surmise that some students of the modern science of religion have been so impressed by the undeniable facility with which historical personages are transformed into gods that they have rather overlooked the stages by which ancestor-worship has grown up, and have assumed that its latest form was also its earliest. Now, in India at any rate, we can trace in the funeral ceremonies, both of the Hindus and the Animists, survivals of ideas which have every appearance of going back to a far older phase of the religious instinct than that which leads to the deification of famous men. In the Vedic ritual, for example, as given by Gobhila, a prominent feature is the banquet offered to the souls of the dead—a rite which is met with among primitive people all over the world. Here is no suggestion that the souls go to heaven; they abide on or under the earth near the dwellings of men, and wait for the living to supply them with food and clothes. These *pia munera* are offered at monthly intervals, but the motive which inspires them is plainly disclosed by the symbolical acts which accompany the offering. At the close of the ceremony the dead ancestors are bidden to depart to their ancient habitations deep under the earth; the footprints of the mourners are swept away with a branch lest the souls should track the living to their homes; every man shakes out the corners of his garments for fear an importunate spirit lurk somewhere in their folds; a stone or a clod of earth is set up to bar the soul's return; the funeral party step over running water which spirits cannot pass, and are careful not to look behind them on their way home. For the same reason the Mangars of Nepal obstruct the road leading from the grave with a barricade of thorns, through which the soul, conceived of as a miniature man, very tender and fragile, is unable to force its way. The Kol, the Orāon, and the Bhūmij are even now in the stage which appears in Vedic ritual as a mere survival. They do not *worship* their ancestors, in any intelligible sense of the word. That is to say, they do not pray to them as the Vedic people did, for male offspring, length of days, abundant flocks and herds, and victory over their enemies. It is true that they appease them with food, but this they do, partly from a kindly regard for their welfare, but mainly to deter them from coming back and making themselves unpleasant. None of their gods can be shown to be deified ancestors, nor do any of them bear personal names. There is another point which deserves notice. Among all these tribes memorial stones are set up to mark the spots where the ashes of the headmen of the village have been buried. Some of these stones are rounded off at the top into the rudimentary semblance of a head. Yet the stones are not worshipped, nor are similar stones erected in honour of the powers which *are* worshipped. If these powers were once upon a time ancestors or chiefs of the tribe, how did they come to lose the stones which were their due? Thus the usages of both Aryans and Dravidians point to a conception of the souls of the dead as neither immortal nor divine, and as depending for their subsistence on human ministrations, which are rendered more in fear than in affection, and are coloured throughout by the desire to deter these unwelcome guests from revisiting the abodes of the living. If these are the oldest ideas on the subject, as most authorities seem to hold, are we not justified in regarding with some suspicion the theory that everywhere and among all people the first step in the evolution of religion was the transformation of the *revenant* into a god? At any rate, the beliefs and practices of the most vigorous of the Dravidian races, the compact tribes of Santāls, Mūndās, Orāons, and Hos, seem, so far as they go, to lend some support to the hypothesis that the beginnings of religion are to be sought in the recognition of impersonal forces which men endeavour to coerce by magic; that personal gods, approached by prayer and sacrifice, are a later development; and that the deification of chiefs and ancestors is probably the latest stage of all—a stage reached, it may be, by means of the ambitious fiction which commenced by claiming certain gods as ancestors, and ended by transforming some ancestors into gods.

Animism in India.

We may now sum up the leading feature of Animism in India. It conceives of man as passing through life surrounded by a ghostly company of powers, elements, tendencies, mostly impersonal in their character, shapeless phantasms of which no image can be made and no definite idea can be formed. Some of these have departments or spheres of influence of their own: one presides over cholera, another over small-pox, and another over cattle disease; some dwell in rocks, others haunt trees, others again are associated with rivers, whirlpools, waterfalls, or with strange pools hidden in the depths of the hills. All of them require to be diligently propitiated by reason of the ills which proceed from them, and usually the land of the village provides the ways and means for this propitiation. In the Rānchi district of Chutia Nāgpur there is a tenure called *Bhūt-Kheta*, which may be interpreted Devil's Acre, under which certain plots of land are set apart for the primitive priest whose duty it is to see that offerings are made in due season, and that the villagers are protected from the malign influences of the shadowy powers who haunt the dark places of their immediate environment. The essence of all these practices is magic. If certain things are done decently and in order, the powers of evil are rendered innocuous in a mechanical but infallible fashion. But the rites must be correctly performed, the magic formulæ must be accurately pronounced, or else the desired effect will not be produced. It is, I think, unfortunate, that at the time when Sir E. B. Tylor's great book on *Primitive Culture* was written, the essential distinction between magic and religion had not been clearly defined. Had this been so, had we then known all that Sir J. G. Frazer has since told us, I venture to doubt whether the term Animism would ever have come into existence. Considerations of ritual and usage, rather than of mythologies, traditions, and cosmogonies, would have led Sir E. B. Tylor to the conclusion that the governing factor in these primitive religions is to be sought not in belief, not in any compact theory as to dreams, spirits, or souls, but in the magical practices which enter into the daily life of semi-civilized men.

Relation between Animism and popular Hinduism.

Premising then that when we speak of Animism what we really mean is that exceedingly crude form of religion in which magic is the predominant element, we may go on to consider what is the relation between Animism and popular Hinduism. Several definitions of Hinduism are contained in the literature of the subject. In his report on the Punjab Census of 1881 (para. 214), Sir Denzil Ibbetson described it as—

> "A hereditary sacerdotalism with Brahmans for its Levites, the vitality of which is preserved by the social institution of caste, and which may include all shades and diversities of religion native to India, as distinct from the foreign importations of Christianity and Islam, and from the later outgrowths of Buddhism, more doubtfully of Sikhism, and still more doubtfully of Jainism."

A few years later Babu Guru Prasād Sen said that Hinduism was "what the Hindus, or a major portion of them, in a Hindu community do." * Sir Athelstane Baines, who was Census Commissioner in 1891, proceeded by the method of exclusion,

[* *Introduction to the Study of Hinduism*, 1893, p. 9.]

and defined Hinduism as "the large residuum that is not Sikh, or Jain, or Buddhist, or professedly Animistic, or included in one of the foreign religions such as Islam, Mazdaism, Christianity, or Hebraism."* More recently, Sir Alfred Lyall,† the first living authority on the subject, roughly described it as "the religion of all the people who accept the Brahmanic Scriptures." He went on to speak of it as "a tangled jungle of disorderly superstitions." Finally, he called it "the collection of rites, worships, beliefs, traditions, and mythologies that are sanctioned by the sacred books and ordinances of the Brahmans and are propagated by Brahmanic teaching." The general accuracy of this newest definition is beyond dispute, but I venture to doubt whether it conveys to any one without Indian experience even an approximate idea of the elements out of which popular Hinduism has been evolved, and of the conflicting notions which it has absorbed. From this point of view Hinduism may fairly be described as *Animism more or less transformed by philosophy*, or, to condense the epigram still further, as *magic tempered by metaphysics.* The fact is that within the enormous range of beliefs and practices which are included in the term Hinduism, there are comprised entirely different sets of ideas, or, one may say, widely different conceptions of the world and of life. At one end, at the lower end of the series is Animism, an essentially materialistic theory of things which seeks by means of magic to ward off or to forestall physical disasters, which looks no further than the world of sense, and seeks to make that as tolerable as the conditions will permit. At the other end is Pantheism combined with a system of transcendental metaphysics.

Illustration of Animistic ideas.

I will give two simple illustrations of the lower set of ideas. In a small sub-divisional court, where I used once to dispense what passed for justice in the surrounding jungles, there was tied to the railings which fenced off the presiding officer from the multitude a fragment of a tiger's skin. When members of certain tribes, of whom the Santāls were a type, came into court to give evidence, they were required to take a peculiar but most impressive oath the use of which was, I believe, entirely illegal. Holding the tiger's skin in one hand, the witness began by invoking the power of the sun and moon, and, after asseverating his intention to speak the truth, he

* *Census Report, India*, 1891, p. 158.]
[† *Asiatic Studies*, 1899, vol. ii., p. 288.]

ended up by devoting himself to be devoured by the power of the tiger in case he should tell a lie. Some of the tribes who used to swear this weird oath have now been caught up in the wide-spread net of Hinduism, and have already parted with their tribal identity. Others again, like the Santāls, are made of sterner stuff, and still preserve an independent existence as compact and vigorous tribes. But the oath deserves remembrance as a vivid presentment of the order of ideas that prevails on the very outskirts of Hinduism. The reality of these ideas and the effectiveness of the sanction which they invoke, were sufficiently attested by the manifest reluctance of a mendacious witness to touch the magic skin, and by the zeal with which the court usher insisted upon his taking a firm grasp of it. The people who swore thus in fear and trembling, and having sworn usually told the truth according to their lights, were not in the least afraid of the mere physical tiger. On the contrary, they slew him without the smallest compunction, and carried off his corpse in triumph to claim the Government reward. Their most effective weapon was a very powerful bamboo bow, trained on the tiger's customary path, and carrying a poisoned arrow which was discharged by a string crossing the track. This string was called the *Kāl dori* or "thread of death." At a short distance on either side of it were two other strings, known as *dharm dori* or "threads of mercy." If these were touched, they twitched the arrow off its rest, and rendered the bow innocuous. They were set at such a height that a tiger would walk under them, while a man or a cow would be bound to run against them. If one asked how goats escaped, one was told that they were protected by certain magical spells. The point which this digression seeks to establish is that the oath sworn in court derived its sanction not from any reverence for the tiger in the flesh, nor from the fear of being eaten by him, but from the vague dread of a mysterious tiger-power or tiger-demon, the essence and archetype of all tigers, whose vengeance no man who swore falsely could hope to escape.

If we move a few grades further up in the social scale, we find the worship of various kinds of Fetishes which the Portuguese seamen observed in West Africa in the middle of the 15th century, still holding its own almost from the top to the bottom of Hindu society. Here, again, it is ritual rather than the theories of the books that gives the clue to the actual beliefs of the people. How tenacious these beliefs are, and in what curiously modern forms they frequently express themselves, may be gathered from the following instance, which, I believe, is now recorded for the first time. Every year when the Government of India moves from Simla to Calcutta, there go with it, as orderlies or *chaprāsis*, a number of cultivators from the hills round about Simla, who are employed to carry despatch boxes, and to attend upon the various grades of officials in that great bureaucracy. At the time of the spring equinox there is a festival called Sri Panchami, when it is incumbent on every religious-minded person to worship the implements or insignia of the vocation by which he lives. The soldier worships his sword; the cultivator his plough; the money-lender his ledger; the Thags had a picturesque ritual for adoring the pickaxe with which they dug the graves of their victims; and, to take the most modern instance, the operatives in the jute mills near Calcutta bow down to the Glasgow-made engines which drive their looms. Five years ago I asked one of my orderlies what worship he had done on this particular occasion, and he was good enough to give me, knowing that I was interested in the subject, a minute description of the ritual observed. The ceremony took place on the flat roof of the huge pile of buildings which is occupied by the secretariats of the Government of India. The worshippers, some thirty in number, engaged as their priest a Punjābi Brāhman, who was employed in the same capacity as themselves. They took one of the large packing cases which are used to convey office records from Simla to Calcutta, and covered its rough woodwork with plantain leaves and branches of the sacred *pīpal* tree. On this foundation they set up an office despatch box which served as a sort of altar; in the centre of the altar was placed a common English glass ink-pot with a screw top, and round this were arranged the various sorts of stationery in common use, pen-holders and pen-nibs, red, blue, and black pencils, pen-knives, ink erasers, foolscap and letter-paper, envelopes, postage stamps, blotting paper, sealing wax, in short, all the clerkly paraphernalia by means of which the Government of India justifies its existence. The whole was draped with abundant festoons of red tape. To the fetish thus installed each of the worshippers presented with reverential obeisance grains of rice, turmeric, spices, pepper and other fruits of the earth, together with the more substantial offering of nine copper

The Sri Panchami and Animism.

pice or farthings—"*numero deus impare gaudet*"—the perquisite of the officiating priest. The Brāhman then recited various cabalistic formulæ, supposed to be texts from the Vedas, of which neither he nor the worshippers understood a single word. When the ceremony was over, the worshippers attacked a vast mass of sweetmeats which had been purchased by a subscription of a rupee a head. The Brāhman ate as much as he could, and they finished the rest. I asked my informant, who is a small landowner in one of the hill states near Simla, what he meant by worshipping an imported ink-pot when he ought to have worshipped a country-made plough. He admitted the anomaly, but justified it by observing that after all he drew pay from the department; that the ink-pot was the emblem of the Government; and that he had left his plough in the hills. These are the lower aspects of Hinduism, survivals of magical observances which show no signs of falling into disuse.*

Sources of Animistic usages.

The Animistic usages of which we find such abundant traces in Hinduism appear, indeed, to have passed into the religion from two different sources. Some are derived from the Vedic Aryans themselves, others from the Dravidian races who have been absorbed into Hinduism. As to the first, Bergaigne has shown in his treatise on Vedic religion that the Vedic sacrifice, which is still performed by the more orthodox Hindus in various parts of India, is nothing more nor less than an imitation of certain celestial phenomena.† It is, in other words, merely sympathetic magic directed, in the first instance, to securing the material benefits of sunshine and rain in their appointed seasons. The Vedas themselves, therefore, are one source of the manifold Animistic practices which may now be traced all through popular Hinduism. They have contributed not only the imitative type of sacrifice, but also the belief, no less magical in its character, that by the force of penance and ascetic abnegation man may shake the distant seat of the gods

* The practice of worshipping office furniture seems to be older than I had supposed. I am indebted to the Honourable Mr. Miller, C.S.I., Member of the Viceroy's Council, for the following quotation: "All the working classes offer sacrifices and worship on stated days to the implements through which their subsistence is obtained; Sāhukārs and merchants to their ledgers and hoards of treasure; and revenue servants to the Daftar, or public records, of their departments." *Report on the Territories of the Rajah of Nagpore.* By Richard Jenkins, Esq., Resident at the Court of the Rajah of Nagpore, 1827, p. 53. [It is described by H. H. Wilson, *Essays and Lectures chiefly on the Religion of the Hindus*, 1862, vol. ii., p. 187; W. Crooke, *Popular Religion and Folk-lore of Northern India*, 2nd ed., 1896, vol. ii., p. 185 *et seq.*]

† *La Religion Védique*, 1, 125. See also Oldenberg, *Die Religion Des Veda.*

and compel them to submit themselves to his will. It would be fruitless to attempt to distinguish the two streams of magical usage—the Vedic and the Animistic. They are of mixed parentage like the people who observe them, partly Indo-Aryan and partly Dravidian.

Pantheism.

At the other end of the scale, in the higher regions of Hinduism, the dominant idea is "what is called Pantheism, that is, the doctrine that all the countless deities, and all the great forces and operations of nature, such as the wind, the rivers, the earthquakes, the pestilences, are merely direct manifestations of the all-pervading divine energy which shows itself in numberless forms and manners." * Of this doctrine the most eloquent and effective description is that given in the Sixth book of the *Æneid* (724–729)—a passage so transfused with Indian thought that it is hardly possible to doubt that its leading ideas are of Indian descent, though Virgil may have derived them from Ennius, and he again from the Pythagoreans of Magna Græcia.

> Principio cælum ac terras camposque liquentis
> Lucentemque globum Lunæ Titaniaque astra
> Spiritus intus alit, totamque infusa per artus
> Mens agitat molem et magno se corpore miscet.
> Inde hominum pecudumque genus vitæque volantum
> Et quæ marmoreo fert monstra sub æquore pontus.

Here we seem at first sight to have travelled very far from the chaos of impersonal terrors that forms the stuff of which primitive religion is made. Yet it is easier to trace Pantheism to the gradual consolidation of the multifarious forces of Animism into one philosophic abstraction than to divine how a host of personal gods could have been stripped of their individual attributes and merged in a sexless and characterless world-soul. In a word, Animism seems to lead naturally to Pantheism; while the logical outcome of Polytheism is Monotheism. The former process has completed itself in India; the latter may be yet to come.

Between these extremes of practical magic at the one end and transcendental metaphysics at the other, there is room for every form of belief and practice that it is possible for the human imagination to conceive. Worship of elements, of natural features and forces, of deified men, ascetics, animals, powers of life, organs of sex, weapons, primitive implements, modern machinery; sects which enjoin the sternest forms of

* Sir Alfred Lyall, *Hinduism; Religious Systems of the World*, p. 113.

asceticism; sects which revel in promiscuous debauchery; sects which devote themselves to hypnotic meditation; sects which practise the most revolting form of cannibalism—all of these are included in Hinduism and each finds some order of intellect or sentiment to which it appeals. And through all this bewildering variety of creeds there is traceable the influence of a pervading pessimism, of the conviction that life, and more especially the prospect of a series of lives, is the heaviest of all burdens that can be laid upon man. The one ideal is to obtain release from the ever-turning wheel of conscious existence, and to sink individuality in the impersonal spirit of the world.

Transmigration and Karma.

Pantheism in India is everywhere intimately associated with the doctrine of metempsychosis. The origin of this belief, deeply engrained as it is in all ranks of Indian society, is wholly uncertain. Professor Macdonell * tells us that "the Rig Veda contains no traces of it beyond the couple of passages in the last book which speak of the soul of a dead man as going to the waters or spirits," and he surmises that the Aryan settlers may have received the first impulse in this direction from the aboriginal inhabitants of India. To any Indian official who has served in a district where the belief in witchcraft is prevalent, the conjecture appears a peculiarly happy one, for in the course of exercising his ordinary magisterial functions, he will have come across abundant evidence of the widespread conviction among savage people, not only that the souls of the dead may pass into animals and trees, but that living people may undergo a similar temporary transformation. But if they borrowed transmigration from the Dravidian inhabitants of India, the Indo-Aryans lent to it a moral significance of which no trace is to be found among the Animists. They supplemented the idea of transmigration by the theory of self-acting retribution which is known as *Karma*. According to this doctrine every action, good or evil, that a man does in the course of his life, is forthwith automatically recorded for or against him, as the case may be. There is no repentance, no forgiveness of sins, no absolution. That which is done carries with it its inevitable consequences through the long succession of lives which awaits the individual soul before it can attain the Pantheistic form of salvation, and become absorbed in the world-essence from which it originally emanated. As the

[* *History of Sanskrit Literature*, 1900, p. 115.]

wheel of existence goes on turning and man, who is bound to it, passes from one life to another, at the close of each a balance is struck which determines his condition in the life that follows. If the balance is against him, he descends to a lower grade; if it is in his favour, he moves up higher and ultimately, when the system of self-working retribution has run its course, he may attain to the final goal of the absolute extinction of individual existence. As Virgil puts it, in a phrase which has puzzled most of his commentators, "*Quisque suos patimur manes.*" In the light of Indian speculation the meaning of the passage becomes clear. It embodies one of the leading ideas of *Karma*, that man through his actions is master of his fate. But the context discloses no trace of the characteristic Indian development that destiny is worked out by means of countless transmigrations. That doctrine seems at first sight to possess a fine moral flavour, and to harmonize with the teaching of the Greek dramatist δράσαντι παθεῖν. Unfortunately for the ethical aspects of *Karma*, consciousness does not continue through the whole series of lives; at the close of each life a curtain of oblivion descends, and the Brāhman whose sins have degraded him to the position of an over-tasked animal has no remembrance of the high estate from which he has fallen. The philosophic sinner, therefore, may eat his oysters in comfort, and console himself with the thought that, although undoubtedly a reckoning awaits him, he will have become somebody else by the time the bill is presented.

Lucian on Karma.

Lucian, with his characteristic sense of the practical application of theological dogmas, has given a dramatic illustration of the problem touched upon above in the concluding episode of one of his most telling dialogues—*The Shades at the Ferry or the Tyrant.* The scene opens with Charon waiting on the shore of Acheron for the daily consignment of souls which Hermes ought to have delivered. He complains to Clotho that he has not taken a penny all day, though the boat might have made three journeys if the passengers had only been up to time. At last Hermes appears puffing and blowing, drenched in sweat, and all over dust. He apologizes for being late, and explains how he took over from Atropos 1004 souls; but when Æacus came to check them with the invoice he found one short, and made unpleasant remarks about Hermes' thievish propensities and his talent for practical jokes. It was then discovered that one Megapenthes, the tyrant of a small Greek city, whom his courtiers had poisoned, had managed to slip away, and Hermes, aided by the shade of a sturdy philosopher armed with a club, had a sharp race to catch him just as he was regaining the light of day. Even when recaptured and dragged down to the boat, Megapenthes still struggles for a respite. He offers Clotho ten thousand talents and two golden mixing bowls, for which he had murdered his friend Kleokritus, as a bribe to let him live till he can complete his half-finished palace, or can at least tell his wife where his great treasure is buried. When this is refused, he makes what he calls the modest request to live long enough to conquer the Persians, to exact tribute from the Lydians, and to build himself a colossal monument. Eventually he is hustled into the boat, and the cobbler Micyllus is deputed to sit on his head and keep him quiet.

While crossing the ferry, Charon collects the fares from every one except the philosopher and the cobbler, neither of whom has an obolus to his name. On landing, the ghostly company are brought before Rhadamanthus; each one is stripped to show the brands which his past sins have stamped upon his soul (surely an artistic echo of the doctrine of *Karma*), and the cases proceed. The philosopher Cyniscus, who helped to catch Megapenthes, appears as his prosecutor; Hermes calls on the case. The tyrant pleads guilty to a variety of murders, but denies certain other counts in the indictment. The dialogue continues:—

"*Cy.*—I can bring witnesses to these points too, Rhadamanthus.

Rhad.—Witnesses, eh?

Cy.—Hermes, kindly summon his Lamp and Bed. They will appear in evidence, and state what they know of his conduct.

Her.—Lamp and Bed of Megapenthes, come into court. Good, they respond to the summons.

Rhad.—Now, tell us all you know about Megapenthes. Bed, you speak first.

Bed.—All that Cyniscus said is true. But really, Mr. Rhadamanthus, I don't quite like to speak about it; such strange things used to happen overhead.

Rhad.—Why, your unwillingness to speak is the most telling evidence of all! Lamp, now let us have yours.

Lamp.—What went on in the daytime I never saw, not being there. As for his doings at night, the less said the better. I saw some very queer things, though, monstrous queer. Many is the time I have stopped taking oil on purpose, and tried to go out. But then he used to bring me close up. It was enough to give any lamp a bad character.

Rhad.—Enough of verbal evidence. Now, just divest yourself of that purple, and we will see what you have in the way of brands. Goodness gracious, the man's a positive network! Black and blue with them! Now, what punishment can we give him? A bath in Pyriphlegethon? The tender mercies of Cerberus, perhaps?

Cy.—No, no. Allow me,—I have a novel idea; something that will just suit him.

Rhad.—Yes? I shall be obliged to you for a suggestion.

Cy.—I fancy it is usual for departed spirits to take a draught of the water of Lethe?

Rhad.—Just so.

Cy.—Let him be the sole exception.

Rhad.—What is the idea in that?

Cy.—His earthly pomp and power for ever in his mind; his fingers ever busy * on the tale of blissful items;—'tis a heavy sentence!

Rhad.—True. Be this the tyrant's doom. Place him in fetters at Tantalus' side,—never to forget the things of earth." †

One is tempted to wonder whether Lucian, himself an Asiatic and a singularly detached observer of the religious ideas of his day, can have realized the dilemma which his dialogue suggests, that immortality marred by old memories would be at best but a sorry boon, while, if purged of its memories, it would not be immortality at all. Achilles, as we see him in the *Odyssey* striding across the mead of asphodel, is haunted by heroic discontent; had he drunk the waters of Lethe, he would have purchased harmony with his surroundings at the price of his unique personality. Arguing from the experiences duly recorded by Homer and other classical authorities, it would seem that in order to find even Elysium a tolerable abode, the shade of a departed hero ought to be furnished with a discreetly eclectic memory, which would reject all things disagreeable, and would recall only the pleasant incidents of the vista of the past. Failing this alternative, which would have savoured too frankly of the miraculous to commend itself

* ἀναπεμπαζόμενος, "Counting over to himself on his fingers."

† *The Works of the Lucian of Samosata.* Translated by H. W. and F. G. Fowler. Clarendon Press, 1906. Vol. i., pp. 244–46.

to his critical temperament, one can imagine Lucian accepting, as a comfortable *pis-aller*, the Hindu solution or evasion of the problem by which the fatal gift of eternal reminiscence is bestowed only on those who have been so wise and virtuous as to have neither faults nor follies to forget.

Comparisons have frequently been drawn between various aspects of life under the later Roman Empire and corresponding phases of Indian society under British rule. In the domain of religion the resemblances and contrasts between the two sets of phenomena are close and striking. In both our attention is at once engaged by the bewildering multitude of deities embodying in human or animal form the visible powers of nature and the great operative principles that underlie them, birth and decay, death and regeneration, the cycle of conscious existence with its infinite variety, the lusts of the flesh, the pride of life, and the more subtle pride of ascetic renunciation. The motley crowd comprises gods who once were men, gods borrowed from strange people whose origin is a mystery, gods of hills and woods, rivers and streams, guardians of the collective life of the village, patrons of the family life that centres round the domestic hearth, kindly ancestors who watch over the destinies of their descendants, spiteful and malicious ghosts of those who came to a bad end, or were denied the appointed rites of sepulture. Of all these types of divinity there were countless instances in the Roman Empire of St. Augustine's time as in the India of to-day. In Rome too, as in India, the higher minds had risen under the influence of philosophy to the conception of one great central power, the unknown and perhaps unknowable reality hidden behind the crowd of symbolical gods and goddesses and the manifold fantastic illusions of the world of sense. In both countries the refining instincts of philosophy manifest themselves in the efforts made to explain away myths which are felt to be wanting in the quality of edification. To the Roman with a turn for metaphysical speculation "Saturn devouring his children is intelligence returning upon itself." * For the Hindu of similar tendencies the legend which recounts how Krishna in his riotous youth stole the clothes of certain milkmaids while they were bathing, retired with them up a tree, and made the unfortunate girls sue in person for the restitution of their garments, illustrates, in the

Ancient Paganism and modern Hinduism.

* Sir S. Dill, *Roman Society in the Last Century of the Western Empire*, 2nd ed., 1899, p. 104.

form of a gross popular tale, the struggles of the human spirit to attain to the beatific vision of absolute truth, naked and unadorned, stripped of the material raiment that conceals her from mortal eyes. The *lingam*, a phallic emblem of the *vis genetrix naturæ* believed by some to have been derived from Dravidian sources, is idealized as "the symbol of the great Pillar of Fire, which is the most characteristic manifestation of Mahādeva, the destroying element which consumes all dross but only purifies the gold." The churning of the sea of milk with the mountain Mandara and the serpent Vāsuki is an allegory expressing the modern theory of the genesis of the chemical elements.

Adaptiveness of Paganism.

Like Hinduism again, classical Paganism was surprisingly flexible and adaptive, and opened its doors with impartial hospitality to any god whose acquaintance the legionaries might have made in the course of travel or conquest. Even Julius Cæsar, whom one would credit with some critical faculty, discovers Mercury, Apollo, Mars, Jupiter, and Minerva among the deities of Gaul;* and in the vision of Lucius, described by Apuleius, Isis is made to reveal herself as one shape with many names worshipped in Phrygia as Cybele the mother of the gods; in Athens as Minerva; in Cyprus as the Paphian Venus; in Crete as Diana; in Sicily as Proserpina; and at Eleusis as Ceres. The Indian system of avatārs could hardly evolve a more comprehensive personality. Indeed, in this matter of borrowing other people's gods Hinduism appears to me hardly to have gone so far as Paganism. The latter, of course, had a far greater choice of religions to borrow from as the boundaries of the Empire were gradually extended, and it may well be that the narrow formalism of the early Roman religion predisposed its votaries to embrace the more emotional beliefs of the East. Sir S. Dill finds an illustration of this in the popularity of the worship of Mithra, a solar cult adopted about 70 B.C. from certain Cilician pirates conquered by Pompey. Mithraism seems to have appealed to the Roman world by the mystical character of its ritual, by its secret ceremonies of initiation into a close guild of devotees comprising many degrees of holiness, and by its promise of purification from sin which culminated in the Taurobolium or baptism to righteousness in the blood of a slaughtered bull. Nothing could well be more foreign to the ideas of the elder generation

* *De Bell. Gall.*, vi. 17.

of Romans, who looked upon religious observances as a sort of legal obligation towards the gods and discouraged as *superstitio* any excessive manifestation of devotion. Yet nothing brings out more clearly the innate adaptiveness of the Roman form of Paganism, which in this respect closely resembles Hinduism. It may be that Hinduism has borrowed more extensively than we know, but the foreign material has been so completely absorbed that its source can no longer be traced. This process must have been facilitated by the fact that, unlike some of the races conquered by Rome, the Dravidians themselves were anxious to adopt Hinduism, and were merged along with their tribal deities in a system which makes ample provision for both social and religious obligations.

On its metaphysical side Roman Paganism seems to have been hardly so well equipped as Hinduism. Apart from the dreams of a few mystics, it had behind it no definite philosophical system, no compact theory of life and destiny, such as Hinduism possesses in its doctrines of the world-soul whence all things arise and have their being, of the illusiveness of sensory phenomena, and of the cycle of retributive and purifying transmigration through which the human soul attains ultimate release by absorption into the primal essence. These ideas are not the monopoly of the learned: they are shared in great measure by the man in the street. If you talk to a fairly intelligent Hindu peasant about the *paramātma*, *karma*, *māyā*, *mukti*, and so forth, you will find, as soon as he has got over his surprise at your interest in such matters, that the terms are familiar to him, and that he has formed a rough working theory of their bearing upon his own future. The religious life of the bulk of the Roman people was passed on a lower plane. Involved in a dreary maze of trivial beliefs, petty superstitions, and minute observances, they were condemned, in the words of their own poet, "*Errare atque viam palantes quærere vitæ*," without the metaphysical clue to the riddle of existence which guides the thoughtful Hindu. The road which the latter must travel may not to our eyes offer an exhilarating prospect, but at least his path is clear.

Weaker than Hinduism in metaphysics and ethics.

In the department of ethics Paganism was equally weak. It had no dogmatic system to regulate personal conduct, and it lacked the moral tone and discipline which Christianity introduced into the world and infused with a spirit of enthusiasm and self-sacrifice. The Emperor Julian was keenly sensible of these defects. A prominent feature of his abortive revival of Paganism was his attempt to reform the priesthood itself and to regenerate the ancient worship "by borrowing a dogmatic theology from Alexandria, an ecstatic devotion from Persia, a moral ideal from Galilee."* Hinduism cannot be charged with indifference to moral ideals. Its sacred literature teems with pious reflexions on the vanity of human life, the glory of renunciation, the necessity of good works, the duty of sympathy with all living things, the beauty of forbearance, the hatefulness of revenge, and the power of man to determine his own fate by right conduct. It appeals both to the intellect and to the emotions, and it derives a certain measure of support from the social penalties imposed by the caste system.

Stronger in national sentiment.

In one direction only does Paganism seem to have the better of Hinduism as a national religion. Its intimate connexion with the corporate life of the community and its capacity for personifying abstract ideas enabled it to embody in the form of Roma Dea the conquering and organizing genius of the Latin race, the centuries of struggle and victory by which Rome had won the mastery of the world. Devotion to the goddess of the Imperial City was one of the strongest obstacles to the triumph of the Christian Church. Hinduism has never given rise to that sentiment of patriotism which in the last days of Rome still clung to the old gods as the symbols of the earlier régime, of the city that had lost its liberties, of the republic that had long been dead, of the Empire that was crumbling to pieces before the inroads of the barbarians. We may search in vain among the myriads of Hindu divinities for a Palladian Athena or a Capitoline Jupiter; the germs of a national cult are entirely wanting; there are no gods of cities or states; there is no nucleus of religion round which patriotic enthusiasm might rally and gather force.

It has been shown above that no sharp line of demarcation can be drawn between Hinduism and Animism. The one shades away insensibly into the other, and the most obvious test—the employment of priests who claim to be Brāhmans—is liable in practice to be defeated by the doubt whether these Brāhmans themselves are anything more than animistic soothsayers writ large. Taking the adherents of the two cults together, they number close on 216 millions, and comprise

* Dill, *loc cit.*, p. 100.

nearly three-fourths (73·3 per cent.) of the population of India. Islam comes next with 62½ millions or 21 per cent.; Buddhism counts nearly 9½ millions or three per cent.; Christianity has a little under 3 millions or 1 per cent. During the ten years preceding the Census of 1901, the Muhammadans increased by 9 per cent. and the Christians by nearly 28 per cent.* In the case of the other two religions, the facts are obscured by uncertainty as to the figures. The general position, however, is clear. Hinduism is the dominant religion of India; in all its developments it is intimately associated with caste, and the two sets of factors, the social and the religious, can hardly be considered apart. The two rival creeds, Christianity and Islam—for Buddhism may be left out of account—avowedly reject the principle of caste, and have been affected by its influence solely through their contact with Hinduism. So long as Hinduism shows no decline from its present strength, caste will preserve its ancient reign, and nothing short of a great accession of strength to either Islam or Christianity can materially modify the social and religious future of India. Are there any signs of a tendency in this direction? Can the figures of the Census of 1901 be regarded as in any sense the forerunners of an Islamic or Christian revival which will threaten the citadel of Hinduism? Or will Hinduism hold its own in the future as it has done through the long ages of the past?

Statistics of religion.

The statistics of the Census of 1901 show that during a decade of famine the Muhammadans in India increased by 9 per cent., while the population as a whole rose by only 3 per cent. No doubt these proportions were affected by the fact that the famines were most severe in those parts of the country where Muhammadans are relatively least numerous, but in the fertile and wealthy region of Eastern Bengal, which has never been touched by real famine, though people on small fixed incomes suffer from high prices, their rate of increase was 12·3 per cent. or nearly double that of the Hindus. The figures illustrating the proportion of children tell a similar tale, and indicate that in that part of India the Muhammadans are not only "more enter-

Increase of Muhammadans.

[* At the Census of 1911 Hindus, including Animists, numbered 227 millions (62 per cent. of the whole population); Muhammadans 66⅔ millions (21·2 per cent.); Buddhists 10⅔ millions (3·4 per cent.); Christians 3¾ millions (1·2 per cent.). The percentages of increase since 1901 were for Hindus 5 per cent.; Muhammadans 7 per cent.; Buddhists 13 per cent.; Christians 32 per cent. (*Census of India Report*, 1911, vol. i., p. 119 *et seq.*).]

prising and therefore better off than their Hindu neighbours," but also more prolific and more careful of their offspring. The reasons are not far to seek. The diet of the Muhammadans is more nourishing and more varied; they are free from the *damnosa hereditas* of infant marriage enforced by social ostracism; they are under no temptation to practise female infanticide; they marry their girls at a more reasonable age, and fewer females become widows while still capable of bearing children. The influence of the itinerant preachers of Islam in its original purity is fast eradicating any tendency to imitate the Hindu prohibition of widow marriage, and Muhammadan widows escape the trials and temptations which beset the Hindu woman who is so unfortunate as to lose her husband while she is still young and attractive. As is pointed out in the Census Report of 1901, "in the case of the intrigues in which widows so often indulge, the Hindu female who thus becomes *enceinte* resorts to abortion, while the Musalmāni welcomes the prospect of a child as means of bringing pressure upon her paramour and inducing him to marry her."

Influence of conversion.

Conversions from Hinduism to Islam must also contribute in some degree to the relatively more rapid growth of the Muhammadan population. Here no appeal to statistics is possible, but a number of specific instances of such changes of religion were extracted by Mr. Gait, C.I.E., from the reports of Hindu and Muhammadan gentlemen in twenty-four districts and published as Appendix II. to the Bengal Census Report of 1901.

The motives assigned in various cases—names and particulars are usually given—may be grouped somewhat as follows:—

(1) Genuine religious conviction of the purity and simplicity of Islam, derived from study of the Muhammadan scriptures or from the preaching of the Maulavis who go round the villages. The conversion of high-caste Hindus, Brāhmans, Rājputs, Kāyasths and the like is commonly ascribed to this cause. We hear, for example, from a Hindu source, of a wealthy Kāyasth landholder of Eastern Bengal, who was suspected of holding unorthodox views, and consequently found difficulties in getting his daughter married. Indignant at what he deemed persecution, he openly embraced Islam, assumed a Muhammadan name, and testified to his zeal by sacrificing cows "in the precincts of the very building where his father had worshipped the Hindu gods." Muhammadan society gave him a cordial welcome, and his daughter married into a high-class family.

His wife, however, refused to change her religion and went back to her own people.

(2) The growing desire on the part of the lower Hindu castes to improve their social position leads individuals among them to embrace a creed which seems to offer them a fair chance in life. Mālis, Kahārs, Goālās, Nāpits, Kāns, Beldārs and other castes of similar status furnish numerous illustrations of this tendency.

(3) The proverb "Love laughs at caste" accounts for a large number of conversions. Hindus of all ranks of society succumb to the charms of good-looking Musalmāni girls, and Muhammadans show themselves equally susceptible to the attractions of Hindu maidens. Hindu widows seek a refuge from their dreary lot in marriage with Muhammadans, while Hindu men who have been caught out in liaisons with girls of lower caste—an affair with a pretty gipsy is one of the instances cited—and find themselves socially stranded, prefer the respectability of Islam to the mixed company of some dubious Vaishnava sect. In all such cases Islam gains and Hinduism loses, for caste rules are rigid and no individual can become a Hindu. These irregular attachments sometimes give rise to embarrassing situations. A Hindu gentleman of Eastern Bengal relates how a high-caste Hindu physician saw in the course of his practice a very handsome Muhammadan girl and fell so hopelessly in love that he wanted to marry her. Her father insisted that he must turn Muhammadan, but after he had done so refused to give him the girl. Meanwhile he had of course been cast off by his own people and had become a social derelict.

(4) Causes connected with taboos on food and drink and with various caste misdemeanours have also to be taken into account. Hindus in sickness or distress are tended by Muhammadans and take food and water from their hands; the caste excommunicates them and they join the ranks of a more merciful faith.

It is needless to observe that none of these causes, nor all of them taken together, exercise an influence wide or potent enough to bring about a great Islamic revival in India. The day of conversions *en masse* has passed, and there are no signs of its return. Nevertheless certain tendencies are discernible which may add materially to the number of individual conversions. On the one hand, the Muhammadans may raise their standard of education, they may organize and consolidate their influence, they may establish their claim to larger representation in the Legislative Councils and in Government service, and they may thus come to play in Indian public life a part more worthy of the history and traditions of their faith. On the other hand, the spread of English education among the middle and lower ranks of Hindus may lead to a revolt against the intolerance of the higher castes, and in particular against their virtual monopoly of place and power. In Southern India whole castes have been known to become Muhammadans because the Brāhmans would not allow them to enter Hindu temples and compelled them to worship outside. It is conceivable that other castes in other parts of India will some day realize that for the low-born Hindu the shortest road to success in life, whether at the bar or in the public service, may lie through the portals of Islam.

Influence of Christianity on the low castes.

Faithful to its earliest traditions, Christianity in India has from the first devoted itself to the poor and lowly, and its most conspicuous successes have been attained among the Animists and the depressed castes on the margin of Hinduism. To the Animist haunted by a crowd of greedy and malevolent demons ever thirsting for blood, like the ghosts that flocked round Ulysses, Christianity opens a new world of love and hope. To the Pariah, the Mahār, the Dher and a host of other helots it promises release from the most searching and relentless form of social tyranny—the tyranny of caste; it offers them independence, self-respect, education, advancement, a new life in an organized and progressive society. "These people," says Mr. Francis,* writing of the Pariahs of the South, "have little to lose by forsaking the creed of their forefathers. As long as they remain Hindus they are daily and hourly made to feel that they are of commoner clay than their neighbours. Any attempts which they may make to educate themselves or their children are actively discouraged by the classes above them: caste restrictions prevent them from quitting the toilsome, uncertain and undignified means of subsistence to which custom has condemned them, and taking to a handicraft or a trade: they are snubbed and repressed on all public occasions: are refused admission even to the temples of their gods; and can hope for no more helpful partner of their joys and sorrows than the unkempt and unhandy maiden of the *pārācheri*† with her very primitive notions of comfort and cleanliness.

[* *Census Report*, *Madras*, 1901, vol. i., p. 41 *et seq.*]

† The ghetto of the typical South Indian village where the Pariahs herd together in irregular clusters of squalid palm-leaf huts.

"But once a youth from among these people becomes Christian his whole horizon changes. He is as carefully educated as if he was a Brahman; he is put in the way of learning a trade or obtaining an appointment as a clerk; he is treated with kindness and even familiarity by missionaries who belong to the ruling race; he takes an equal part with his elders and betters in the services of the church; and in due time he can choose from among the neat-handed girls of the Mission a wife skilled in domestic matters and even endowed with some little learning. Nowadays active persecution of converts to Christianity is rare. So those who hearken to its teaching have no martyr's crown to wear, and sheltered, as they often are, in a compound round the missionary's bungalow, it matters little to its adherents if their neighbours look askance upon them. The remarkable growth in the numbers of the Native Christians thus largely proceeds from the natural and laudable discontent with their lot which possesses the lower classes of the Hindus, and so well do the converts, as a class, use their opportunities that the community is earning for itself a constantly improving position in the public estimation."

In the face of this testimony can any one say that Christian Missions have been a failure in India? To me at any rate it seems beyond question that the Missions which have devoted themselves to the Animists and the Helots chose their field wisely and worked it well. The fruit, no doubt, has not yet been brought to perfection, but if due allowance is made for the inherited tendencies of the converts, and the conditions in which they live, those who are responsible for this branch of missionary effort in India have no reason to be ashamed of their labours. They have been guided by the spirit of the apostolic age; they have achieved much and they may yet accomplish more. There are, however, other missions which have worked on more ambitious lines and have set before themselves the ideal of converting the higher castes among the Hindus, in the hope that Christianity would filter downwards through the masses in the same way as Brahmanism, and thus would ultimately bring about the fulfilment of M. Saint Hilaire's anticipation, "*que l'Inde finira par être Chrétienne tout entière.*" It is to these missions that my friend the Bishop of Madras refers when he says in a recent number of *The Nineteenth Century* that the Missionary "attacks which have been made for the last fifty years upon positions of almost impregnable strength . . .

Causes of its failure with the high castes.

undoubtedly have failed so far as the main purpose of Christian missions is concerned, viz. the winning of converts to faith in Christ and the building up of the Christian Church." The Bishop ascribes this failure to the operation of two causes. "The advance of higher education," he says, "has perceptibly increased the friction and antagonism between Europeans and Indians, and this has necessarily reacted strongly upon the attitude of educated Indians towards Christianity." The second cause is the influence of caste. The Bishop says—"The great obstacle to the conversion of the upper ranks of society is the impenetrable barrier of caste. The social system inflicts such tremendous penalties on conversion to Christianity that a convert from the higher castes is truly a miracle."

All this is unquestionably true, but I am not sure that it is the whole truth. The antagonism to Europeans as such is a tendency of comparatively recent growth, and I should prefer to attribute it to the shortcomings of educational methods in India rather than to regard it as a necessary consequence of higher education itself. May we not hope that this phase will pass away and that wider culture and freer social intercourse will bring with them a larger faith and will lead at any rate to wise tolerance of the small body of European fellow-workers in a common cause to whose honest if sometimes unsympathetic efforts the educated classes in India owe the position that they now occupy and the privileges that they enjoy? Intellectual self-consciousness on the one side and racial aloofness on the other are defects which time and mutual forbearance may be expected to cure. The old order of things is visibly passing away; much will depend upon the tact and discretion of the leaders of both races by whom the new order is introduced.

The Bishop rightly dwells on the essential antagonism between the spirit of caste and the spirit of Christian teaching. The enthusiasm of humanity can make no terms with the principle of hereditary taboo. Not only are there no signs of any *rapprochement* between the two sets of ideas, but the inducement to seek in Christianity a refuge from the tyranny of caste has of late years been sensibly weakened by the modern tendency to relax those minor restrictions relating to food, drink, and travel which weighed heavily upon the educated classes. Within certain wide limits an advanced Indian can now do pretty much what he pleases in respect of such matters, and the probability of his turning Christian in order to escape vexatious social penalties has thereby become appreciably more remote.

While admitting the validity of the reasons assigned by the Bishop for the failure of Christianity to attract the upper classes of India, I may perhaps be permitted to suggest that other and less obvious causes have contributed to the result. Caste, after all, is a fluid and variable institution which is ready enough to adapt itself to circumstances when called upon to surrender in sufficiently imperative terms. Had Christianity been presented in a form more congenial to the mystical Indian temperament, with the Logos as a humanized version of the *paramātma*, one can imagine that it might have stood a better chance of success. Caste certainly would not have permanently blocked its path, any more than it succeeded in arresting the progress of Islam. Why then has Hinduism, hampered as it is, at any rate to outward view, by an unedifying mythology, a grotesque Pantheon, a burdensome ritual, a corrupt priesthood, and above all by the taint of palpable idolatry, retained its sway over the higher minds to whom a simpler and purer faith might have been expected to offer irresistible attractions? The main reason seems to be that to the educated Hindu religion is largely a matter of the intellect. He demands from it not merely spiritual comfort but philosophical conviction. A religion which rests upon no metaphysical basis, and which in his view does not even attempt to solve the great problems of life, cannot expect to command his acceptance. With all its shortcomings of precept and practice, Hinduism at least has behind it a philosophy which, in spite or perhaps because of its indolent pessimism, satisfies the Eastern mind and has fascinated some of the leading intellects of the West. To despair with Goëthe and Schopenhauer is to despair in good company. In the domain of religion mere temperament counts for a good deal, and the Indian whose critical sense rejects as incredible the evidences of the Christian revelation finds no difficulty in accepting by intuition the Pantheistic dream which underlies his own philosophy. Nor does the strength of Hinduism lie only in its metaphysics. There are those who hold that the idea of *karma*, the theory that on each sin as it is committed there is passed a judgment from which there is no appeal, stands on a higher plane and exercises a greater moral influence than the Christian doctrines of repentance and the forgiveness of sins. The belief in a spiritual backstairs does not necessarily make for righteousness.

These seem to be among the leading motives that tend to deter the educated Hindu from seeking in Christianity a solution of the problems with which his speculative temperament has for centuries been occupied. Of late years their strength has been greatly enhanced by the growth of the idea of an Indian nationality. Indefinite and rudimentary as this idea is, it nevertheless inspires the small body of men who are possessed by it with the strongest antipathy to anything of foreign origin that is not absolutely indispensable, whether it be a particular religion or a particular form of textile manufactures. It is a notable fact that the Hindu sectarian movement which appeals most strongly to the educated classes is bitterly opposed to Christianity, and lays itself out not merely to counteract the efforts of missionaries, but to reconvert to Hinduism high-caste men who have become Christians.

Nationalism and the Ārya Samāj.

The Ārya Samāj, founded about 1875 by Dāyananda Sāraswati on the basis of the infallibility of the four Vedas, stands out at the present time as the most conspicuous movement within the vast miscellany of beliefs and superstitions which go to make up the religion of the Hindus. It may, indeed, almost be described as a nationalist development of Hinduism. Taking their stand upon the Vedas, as the divinely inspired scriptures of the Indo-Aryan race, the Āryas discover in them, by a liberal method of symbolical interpretation, not merely an ample store of moral and spiritual guidance, but "the germ of all modern knowledge including physical science." * They seek to revive Vedic practice in the matter of marriage, and hold that a girl should on no account be married before thirteen, and would do better to wait till she is fourteen or even sixteen. Young men ought not to marry before eighteen at the earliest. Widows are allowed to marry again, and several such marriages have taken place in high-caste Ārya families. One of the primary duties of the sect is to "diffuse knowledge and dispel ignorance," and in pursuance of this precept they have already founded a number of educational institutions, the most important of which is the Dayanand Anglo-Vedic College at Lahore.

The Ārya movement has undoubtedly derived a great accession of force from its intimate association with the Khatris, whom Sir George Campbell described more than forty years ago as "one of the most acute, energetic, and

* *Report on the Census of the N.-W. P. and Qudh*, 1901, by R. Burn, I.C.S., vol. i., p. 91.

remarkable races in India," and as being in the Punjab "all that Maratha Brāhmans are in the Maratha country, besides engrossing the trade which the Maratha Brāhmans have not. They are not usually military in their character, but are quite capable of using the sword when necessary." It is hardly an exaggeration to discover in the Khatris an epitome of the three twice-born castes of the traditional Hindu system. By founding the Sikh religion, and by continuing to furnish its priests, they have exercised within a sphere of some importance an influence elsewhere confined to the Brāhmans. Their record of administrative and military success as ministers to the Mughal Emperors, as governors of Multan, Peshawar, and Badakhshan, and as generals in the Sikh army, is appealed to in support of their claim to be the modern representatives of the ancient Kshatriyas; while by their activity in trade and their prominence in the ranks of the legal profession they have more than absorbed the functions of the ancient Vaisyas.

The Samāj and the Khatris.

A movement of this type, promoted by such influential supporters, seems to be of high promise, and may even contain the germ of a national religion. The Āryas start with a definite creed resting upon scriptures of great antiquity and high reputation; their teaching is of a bold and masculine type and is free from the limp eclecticism which has proved fatal to the Brahmo Samāj; they have had the courage to face the vital question of marriage reform; and finally, they recognize the necessity of proselytism and do not hesitate to say "those who are not with us are against us." These are elements of strength, and the movement seems likely to gather to itself many adherents among the educated classes. Whether it will spread beyond the relatively small circle of literates seems to depend upon the reception that it meets with from the Brāhmans who cater for the spiritual needs of the masses of the people.* Seeing that the Āryas condemn offerings to idols, pilgrimages, and bathing in sacred rivers, it seems doubtful whether the priests who live by promoting

[* In Bengal, "unlike the United Provinces, where the Samāj is largely recruited from the educated classes, the Aryas of Patna are mostly members of the lower castes, such as Kurmis, Kahars, etc.; its doctrines have found favour with only a limited number of Hindus and Musalmans of the higher classes. The explanation is that the theory of the submergence of caste in the Arya community appeals most to the lower classes, who regard the new system as improving their position and bringing them on a level with the upper classes. Moreover, the custom of widow marriage was already an established custom with many of them, and the sanction given to this practice by the new faith was no small attraction" (*Census Report, Bengal*, 1911, vol. i., p. 211).]

these modes of propitiating the gods will regard the new movement with favour. No signs of such a tendency are at present visible. But within its own sphere of influence the movement has achieved remarkable success. It offers to the educated Hindu a comprehensive body of doctrine purporting to be derived from Indian documents and traditions, and embodying schemes of social and educational advancement without which no real national progress is possible. In this revival of Hinduism, touched by reforming zeal and animated by patriotic enthusiasm, Christianity is likely to find a formidable obstacle to its spread among the educated classes.

It follows from what has been already said that the supremacy of Hinduism as the characteristic religion of India is not as yet seriously threatened. The Animistic hem of the garment may, indeed, be rent off, and its fragments parted among rival faiths. But the garment itself, woven of many threads and glowing with various colours, will remain intact and will continue to satisfy the craving for spiritual raiment of a loose and elastic texture which possesses the Indian mind.

The future of Hinduism.

It has often been said that the advance of English education, and more especially of the teaching of physical science, will make short work of the Hindu religion, and that the rising generation of Hindus is doomed to wander without guidance in the wilderness of agnosticism. This opinion seems to lose sight of some material considerations. Science, no doubt, is a powerful solvent of mythology and tradition, and the "seas of treacle and seas of butter" over which Macaulay made merry in his famous Minute are not likely to resist its destructive influence. But the human mind is hospitable and the Indian intellect has always revelled in the subtleties of a logic which undertakes to reconcile the most manifestly contradictory propositions. Men whose social and family relations compel them to lead a double life, will find little difficulty in keeping their religious beliefs and their scientific convictions in separate mental compartments. Putting aside, however, casuistry of this kind, an inevitable feature of a period of transition, it may fairly be said, in justice to the adaptability of Hinduism, that a religion which has succeeded in absorbing Animism is not likely to strain at swallowing science. The doctrine of *Karma*, which in one of its aspects may be regarded as a sort of moral totalisator infallibly recording the good and bad actions of men, admits of being represented, in another aspect, as an ethical anticipation of the modern determinist doctrine that character and circumstance are the lords of life; that the one is a matter of heredity and the other a matter of accident, and that the idea of man being master of his fate is no better than a pleasing fiction conjured up by human fantasy to flatter human egotism. Nor is this the last refuge of Hinduism. If it appeals to the intellect by its metaphysical teaching, it also touches the emotions by the beatific vision which it offers to the heart and the imagination. Sir G. Grierson * may or may not be right in holding that the doctrine of *bhakti* or ecstatic devotion, which has played so large a part in the later developments of Hinduism, was borrowed by Chaitanya from Christian sources. To some minds the evidence in support of this view may appear rather conjectural. But whatever may have been its origin, the idea has now taken its place among the characteristic teachings of Hinduism; it has been absorbed in the fullest sense of the word. And a religion which rests both on philosophy and on sentiment is likely to hold its ground until the Indian temperament itself undergoes some essential change.

[* See Art. *Bhakti-mārga*, in J. Hastings' *Encyclopædia of Religion and Ethics*, vol. ii., 1909, p. 539 *et seq.*]

CHAPTER VI

THE ORIGIN OF CASTE

Les dieux jaloux ont enfoui quelque part les témoignages de la descendance des choses.—*De Guérin.*

No one can have studied the literature of social origins which has been so prolific of late years without feeling the force of Sir Henry Maine's remark that theories of primitive society are apt to land the enquirer in a region of "mud banks and fog." More especially is this the case in India, where the palæological data available in Europe hardly exist at all, while the historical value of the literary evidence is impaired by the uncertainty of its dates, by the sacerdotal predilections of its authors, by their passion for wire-drawn distinctions and symmetrical classifications, and by their manifest inability to draw any clear line between fact and fancy, between things as they are and things as they might be, or as a Brāhman would desire them to be. All these points are obvious at a glance; they merely reflect the idiosyncrasies of the Indian intellect, its phenomenal memory, its feeble grasp of questions of fact, its subtle manipulation of impalpable theories, its scanty development of the critical faculty. Its strength lies in other lines of mental activity, in a region of transcendental speculation which does not lead to the making of history.

The origin of caste.

These general grounds, which any enquirer can verify for himself at the shortest notice, might be thought to justify us in putting aside, as an insoluble and unprofitable conundrum, the much-discussed question of the origin of caste. But the Indian tradition as to the origin of caste is so inextricably mixed up with the most modern developments of the system; its influence is so widely diffused; and it forms so large a part of the working consciousness of the Hindu population of India that it can hardly be left out of account merely because it has no foundation in fact. It is indeed a fact in itself, a belief which has played, and continues to play, a large part in the shaping of Indian society, and whose curious vitality throws an instructive light on the inner workings of the Indian mind. To endeavour to understand the people of India, to enter into their point of view, and realize how things strike them, is the first condition of successful administration. As the work of Government becomes more complex and touches the life of the people at a greater number of points, as new interests spring up and old interests assume novel forms, the stronger is the obligation to know as much as possible of the society which our rule is insensibly but steadily modifying. The study of the facts is therefore essential, and we must take the theories, whether Indian or European, along with them. The search for origins, like the quest of the Sangreal, possesses endless fascination, and if it does not yield any very tangible results, it at least has the merit of encouraging research.

Several theories of the origin of caste are to be found in the literature of the subject. The oldest and most famous is accepted as an article of faith by all orthodox Hindus, and its attraction extends, as each successive Census shows, through an ever-widening circle of aspirants to social distinction. It appears in its most elaborate form in the tenth chapter of that curious jumble of magic, religion, law, custom, ritual, and metaphysics, which is commonly called the Institutes of Manu. Here we read how the *Anima Mundi*, the supreme soul which "contains all created beings and is inconceivable," produced by a thought a golden egg, in which "he himself was born as Brahman, the progenitor of the whole world." Then "for the sake of the prosperity of the worlds, he caused the Brāhmana, the Kshatriya, the Vaisya, and the Sūdra to proceed from his mouth, his arms, his thighs, and his feet," and allotted to each of these their distinctive duties. The Brāhman was enjoined to study, teach, sacrifice, and receive alms; the Kshatriya to protect the people and abstain from sensual pleasures; the Vaisya to tend cattle, to trade, to lend money, and to cultivate land; while for the Sūdra was prescribed the comprehensive avocation of meekly serving the other three groups. Starting from this basis, the standard Indian tradition proceeds to trace the evolution of the caste system from a series of complicated crosses, first between members of the four original groups and then between the descendants of these initial unions. The men of the three higher groups might marry women of any of the groups below

The Indian theory.

them, and if the wife belonged to the group next in order of precedence the children took her rank, and no new caste was formed. If, however the mother came from a group lower down in the scale, her children belonged neither to her group nor to their father's, but formed a distinct caste called by a different name. Thus the son of a Brāhman by a Vaisya woman is an Ambastha, to whom belongs the art of healing; while if the mother is a Sūdra, the son is a Nishāda and must live by killing fish. The son of a Kshatriya father and a Sūdra mother is "a being called Ugra, resembling both a Kshatriya and a Sūdra, ferocious in his manners and delighting in cruelty." In all of these the father is of higher rank than the mother, and the marriages are held to have taken place in the right order (*anuloma*, or "with the hair"). Unions of the converse type, in which the woman belongs to a superior group, are condemned as *pratiloma*, or "against the hair." The extreme instance of the fruit of *pratiloma* relations is the Chandāl, the son of a Sūdra by a Brāhman woman, who is described as "that lowest of mortals," and is condemned to live outside the village, to clothe himself in the garments of the dead, to eat from broken dishes, to execute criminals, and to carry out the corpses of friendless men. But the Ayogavas, with a Sūdra father and a Kshatriya mother, are not much better off, for the accident of their birth is sufficient to brand them as wicked people who eat reprehensible food. Alliances between the descendants of these first crosses produce among others the Sairandhra, who is "skilled in adorning his master" and pursues as an alternative occupation the art of snaring animals; and "the sweet-voiced Maitreyaka, who, ringing a bell at the appearance of dawn, continually praises great men." Finally, a fresh series of connubial complications is introduced by the Vrātya, the twice-born men who have neglected their sacred duties and have among their direct descendants the Malla, the Licchivi, the Nata, the Karana, the Khasa, and the Drāvida, while each of these in its turn gives rise to further mazes of hypothetical parentage.

Its historic elements.

It is small wonder that European critics should have been so impressed by the unreal character of this grotesque scheme of social evolution, that some of them have put it aside without further examination as a mere figment of the systematizing intellect of the ingenious Brāhman. Yet, fantastic as it is, it opens indirectly and unconsciously an instructive glimpse of pre-historic society in India. It shows us that at the time when Manu's treatise was compiled, probably about the second century A.D., there must have existed an elaborate and highly developed social system, including tribal or national groups like the Māgadha, Vaideha, Malla, Licchivi, Khasa, Drāvida, Saka, Kirāta, and Chandāl; and functional groups such as the Ambastha, who were physicians, the Sūta, who were concerned with horses and chariots, the Nishāda, and the Märgavas, Dāsas, or Kaivartas who were fishermen, the Ayogava, carpenters, the Kārāvara and Dhigvansa, workers in leather, and the Vena, musicians and players on the drum.* It is equally clear that the occupations of Brāhmans were as diverse as they are at the present day, and that their position in this respect was just as far removed from that assigned to them by the traditional theory. In the list of Brāhmans whom a pious householder should not entertain at a *srāddha* † we find physicians; temple-priests; sellers of meat; shopkeepers; usurers; cowherds; actors; singers; oilmen; keepers of gambling houses; sellers of spices; makers of bows and arrows; trainers of elephants, oxen, horses or camels; astrologers; bird-fanciers; fencing-masters; architects; breeders of sporting dogs; falconers; cultivators; shepherds; and even carriers of dead bodies. The conclusions suggested by the passages cited from Manu are confirmed by Dr. Richard Fick's instructive study ‡ of the structure of society in Bihār and the eastern districts of the United Provinces at the time of Buddha. Dr. Fick's work is based mainly upon the Jātakas or "birth-stories" of the southern Buddhists, and from these essentially popular sources, free from any suggestion of Brahmanical influence, he succeeds in showing that, at the period depicted, the social organization in the part of India with which his authorities were familiar did not differ very materially from that which prevails at the present day. Then, as now, the traditional hierarchy of four castes had no distinct and determinate existence; still less had the so-called mixed castes supposed to be derived from them; while of the Sūdras in particular no trace at all was to be found. Then, as now, Indian society was made up of a medley of diverse and heterogeneous groups, apparently not so strictly and uniformly endogamous as the castes of to-day, but containing within

* *Laws of Manu*, G. Bühler, X, 22, 34, 36, 44.

† *Laws of Manu*, III, 151—166.

‡ *Die Sociale Gliederung im Nordöstlichen Indian zu Buddha's Zeit.* Von Dr. Richard Fick, Kiel, 1897. [T. W. Rhys Davids, *Buddhist India*, 1903, p. 32 *et seq.*; *Journal Royal Asiatic Society*, 1901, p. 868.]

themselves the germs out of which the modern system has developed by natural and insensible stages. That development has been furthered by a variety of influences which will be discussed below.

Its probable origin.

Assuming that the writers of the law-books had before their eyes the same kind of social chaos that exists now, the first question that occurs to one is:—From what source did they derive the theory of the four castes? Manu, of course, as Sir Henry Maine has pointed out, is a relatively modern work; but the traditional scheme of castes figures in earlier law-books, such as Baudhāyana and Āpastamba, and it seems probable that for them it was not so much a generalization from observed facts as a traditional theory, derived from still older authorities, which they attempted to stretch so as to explain the facts. The Indian pandit does not take kindly to inductive methods, nor is it easy to see how he could have arrived by this road at a hypothesis which breaks down directly it is brought into contact with the realities of life. But it is possible that the Brahmanical theory of castes may be nothing more than a modified version of the division of society into four classes—priests, warriors, cultivators, and artisans—which appears in the sacerdotal literature of ancient Persia.* It is true, no doubt, that the Iranian groups, with the exception of the Athravans or priests, appear not to have been endogamous, and to have observed none of the restrictions on marriage which are so prominent in the Indian system. But we know very little about them, and it is possible that their matrimonial relations may have been governed by the practice of hypergamy which is apt to arise under a regime of classes as distinguished from castes. Let me make my meaning clear. It is not suggested that the Iranian legend of four classes formed part of the stock of tradition that the Aryans brought with them into India. Had this been so, the myth relating to their origin would have figured prominently in the Vedas, and would not have appeared solely in the Purusha Sūkta, which most critics agree in regarding as a modern interpolation. The conjecture is that the relatively modern compilers of the law-books, having become acquainted with the Iranian legend, were fascinated by its assertion of priestly supremacy, and made use of it as the basis of the theory by which they attempted to explain the manifold

---

* Spiegel, *Eranische Alterthumskunde*, III, 547—670.

complexities of the caste system. The procedure is characteristic of Brahmanical literary methods, and is in itself no more absurd than the recent attempt on the part of the Ārya Samāj to discover in the Rig Veda an anticipation of the discoveries of modern science, and to interpret the horse sacrifice in Sūkta 162 as an allegorical exposition of the properties of heat or electricity.*

The Indian and Iranian classes.

The resemblance between the two schemes is striking enough to suggest that it can hardly be the result of a mere accidental coincidence, but that the Indian theory must have been modelled on the Iranian.† The differences in the categories are trifling, and admit of being accounted for by the fact that India has, what Persia had not, a large aboriginal population differing from the Indo-Aryans in respect of religion, usages, and physical type, and more especially in the conspicuous attribute of colour. These people had somehow to be brought within the limits of the scheme; and this was done by the simple process of lumping them together in the servile class of Sūdras, which is sharply distinguished from the twice-born groups and has a far lower status than is assigned to the artizans in the Iranian system. Thus the four *varnas*, or colours, of the Indian myth seem to occupy an intermediate position between the purely occupational classes of ancient Persia and Egypt and the rigidly defined castes of modern India. In the Persian system only the highest group of Athravans or priests was endogamous, while between the other three groups, as between all the groups of the Egyptian system (excluding the swineherds if we follow Herodotus), no restrictions on intermarriage appear to have been recognized. Moreover, as is implied by the distinction between the twice-born classes and the Sūdras, and by the prominence given to the element of colour (*varna*), the Indian system rests upon a basis of racial antagonism of which there is no trace in Persia and Egypt. Yet in the stage of development portrayed in the law-books the system has not hardened into the rigid mechanism

---

* R. Burn, *Census Report of the United Provinces*, 1901, vol. i., p. 91.

[† "There is no probability in the view of Senart or Risley (*Imperial Gazetteer of India*, I, 336—348), that the names of the old classes were later super-imposed artificially on a system of castes that were different from them in origin. We cannot say that the castes existed before the classes, and that the classes were borrowed by India from Iran, as Risley maintains, ignoring the early Brāhmana evidence for the four Varnas, and treating the transfer as late." A. A. Macdonald, A. B. Keith, *A Vedic Index of Names and Subjects*, 1912, II, 270.]

of the present day. It is still more or less fluid; it admits of intermarriage under the limitations imposed by the rule of hypergamy; it represents caste in the making, not caste as it has since been made. This process of caste-making has indeed by no means come to an end. Fresh castes are constantly being formed, and wherever we can trace the stages of their evolution they seem to proceed on the lines followed in the traditional scheme. The first stage is for a number of families, who discover in themselves some quality of social distinction, to refuse to give their women in marriage to other members of the caste, from whom nevertheless they continue to take wives. After a time, when their numbers have increased, and they have bred women enough to supply material for a *jus connubii* of their own, they close their ranks, marry only among themselves, and pose as a superior sub-caste of the main caste to which they belong. Last of all, they break off all connexion with the parent stock, assume a new name which ignores or disguises their original affinities, and claim general recognition as a distinct caste. The educated Pods of Bengal are an illustration of the first stage; the Chāsi Kaibartta of the second; the Māhisya of the third.

Sir Denzil Ibbetson's theory.

We may now pass from the pious fictions of Manu and the Rāmāyana to those modern critical theories which, whether they carry conviction or not, at least start from and give full weight to the facts, and make an honest attempt to work out a scientific solution of the problem. Among these Sir Denzil Ibbetson's description* of caste in the Punjab contains the most vivid presentment of the system in its everyday working, of the various elements which have contributed to its making, and of the surprising diversity of the results which have been produced. The picture is an admirable piece of open-air work; it has been drawn on the spot; it is full of local colour; and it breathes throughout the quaint humour of the peasantry of the Punjab, the manliest and most attractive of all the Indian races. From this wealth of material it is not altogether easy to disentangle the outlines of a cut-and-dried theory, and it may well have been the intention of the writer to leave the question more or less open, and to refrain from the futile endeavour to compress such infinite variety within the limits of any formula. The following passage sums up the leading features of the

* *Report on the Census of the Punjab*, 1881, pp. 172—341.

hypothesis, but the exposition of its working requires to be studied as a whole, and I have, therefore, reproduced in Appendix V the greater part of the section dealing with the evolution of caste. The report which I quote has long been out of print, and foreign ethnologists enquire for copies in vain.

"Thus, if my theory be correct, we have the following steps in the process by which caste has been evolved in the Punjab:—(1) the tribal divisions common to all primitive societies; (2) the guilds based upon hereditary occupation common to the middle life of all communities; (3) the exaltation of the priestly office to a degree unexampled in other countries; (4) the exaltation of the Levitical blood by a special insistence upon the necessarily hereditary nature of occupation; (5) the preservation and support of this principle by the elaboration from the theories of the Hindu creed or cosmogony of a purely artificial set of rules, regulating marriage and intermarriage, declaring certain occupations and foods to be impure and polluting, and prescribing the conditions and degree of social intercourse permitted between the several castes. Add to these the pride of social rank and the pride of blood which are natural to man, and which alone could reconcile a nation to restrictions at once irksome from a domestic and burdensome from a material point of view; and it is hardly to be wondered at that caste should have assumed the rigidity which distinguishes it in India."

M. Senart's criticism * of this theory is directed to two points. He demurs, in the first place, to the share which he supposes it to assign to Brahmanical influence, and challenges the supposition that a strict code of rules, exercising so absolute a dominion over the consciences of men, could be merely a modern invention, artificial in its character and self-regarding in its aims. Secondly, he takes exception to the disproportionate importance which he conceives Sir Denzil Ibbetson to attach to community of occupation, and points out that, if this were really the original binding principle of caste, the tendency towards incessant fission and dislocation would be much less marked: the force that in the beginning united the various scattered atoms would continue to hold them together to the end. Both criticisms appear to miss an essential feature in the scheme, the influence of the idea of kinship, which is certainly

* *Les Castes dans l'Inde*, p. 191.

the oldest and probably the most enduring factor in the caste system, and which seems to have supplied the framework and the motive principle of the more modern restrictions based upon ceremonial usage and community of occupation.

Mr. Nesfield * is a theorist of quite a different type. He feels no doubts and is troubled by no misgivings. Inspired by the systematic philosophy of Comte, he maps out the whole confused region of Indian caste into a graduated series of groups and explains exactly how each has come by the place that it occupies in the scheme. He assumes as the basis of his theory the essential unity of the Indian race, and appeals to "physiological resemblance" to prove that "for the last three thousand years at least no real difference of blood between Aryan and aboriginal" has existed "except perhaps in a few isolated tracts." In his opinion the conquering Aryan race was absorbed by the indigenous population as completely as the Portuguese of India have already become absorbed into Indians, so that no observer could now distinguish members of the higher castes from the scavengers who sweep the roads. The homogeneous people thus formed are divided by Mr. Nesfield, in the area to which his researches relate, the United Provinces of Agra and Oudh, into the following seven groups, among which he distributes the 121 castes enumerated in the census of 1881 :—

Mr. Nesfield's theory.

- I. Casteless tribes.
- II. Castes connected with land—
  - A. Allied to hunting state.
  - B. Allied to fishing state.
  - C. Allied to pastoral state.
  - D. Agricultural.
  - E. Landlords and warriors.
- III. Artisan castes—
  - A. Preceding metallurgy.
  - B. Coeval with metallurgy.
- IV. Trading castes.
- V. Serving castes.
- VI. Priestly castes.
- VII. Religious orders.

The classification, it will be observed, is based solely upon occupation, and it expresses Mr. Nesfield's conviction that "function, and function only, as I think, was the foundation upon which the whole caste system of India was built up." The order of the groups is determined by the principle that "each caste or group of castes represents one or other of those progressive stages of culture which have marked the industrial development of mankind not only in India, but in every other country in the world wherein some advance has been made from primeval savagery to the arts and industries of civilized life. The rank

* *Brief View of the Caste System of the North-Western Provinces and Oudh*, pp. 3, 4, 75, 88, 129—132.

of any caste as high or low depends upon whether the industry represented by the caste belongs to an advanced or backward stage of culture; and thus the natural history of human industries affords the chief clue to the gradations as well as to the formation of Indian castes." At the bottom of the scale are the more or less primitive tribes—Thārus, Kanjars, Doms, and Nats—"the last remains and sole surviving representatives of the aboriginal Indian savage, who was once the only inhabitant of the Indian continent, and from whose stock the entire caste system, from the sweeper to the priest, was fashioned by the slow growth of centuries." Then come the hunting Baheliyas, the Mallāhs, and Dhīmars (boatmen and fishermen), the pastoral Ahīrs and Gadariyas, and the great mass of agriculturists, while above these Mr. Nesfield finds in the Chattri or Rajput the sole representative of the landlord and warrior caste. The artisan castes are subdivided with reference to the supposed priority of the evolution of their crafts. The basket-making Bānsphors, the weavers (Kori and Jolāhā), the potters (Kumhār), and the oilmen (Teli) fall within the more primitive group antecedent to metallurgy, while blacksmiths, goldsmiths, tailors, and confectioners are placed in the group coeval with the use of metals. Above them again come the trading and the serving castes, among whom we find in rather odd collocation the scavenging Bhangi, the barber (Nāpit or Nāi), the bard and genealogist (Bhāt), and the Kāyasths, who are described as estate managers and writers. The Brāhmans and the religious orders complete the scheme. But the mere classification obviously offers no solution of the real problem. How did these groups, which occur in one form or another all over the world, become hardened into castes? Why is it that in India alone their members are absolutely forbidden to intermarry? Mr. Nesfield replies without hesitation that the whole series of matrimonial taboos which constitute the caste system are due to the initiative of the Brāhmans. According to him, they introduced for their own purposes, and in order to secure the dignity and privileges of their own caste, the rule that a Brāhman could only marry a Brāhman, and all the other classes, who up to that time had intermarried freely, followed their example "partly in imitation and partly in self-defence." The proposition recalls the short way that writers of the eighteenth century were apt to take with historical problems, and reminds one of Bolingbroke's easy assertion that the sacred literature of Egypt was invented by the priests. Detailed criticism would be out of place here: the main object of this chapter is to lay stress on precisely those factors of evolution which Mr. Nesfield ignores; but I may observe that a theory which includes in the same categories the Dom and the Teli, the Banjāra and the Khatri, the Bhangi and the Kāyasth must, in the race for acceptance, lose a good deal of ground at the start.

M. Senart's theory.

After examining the views propounded by Sir Denzil Ibbetson and Mr. Nesfield, and by myself in *The Tribes and Castes of Bengal*, M. Senart passes on to formulate his own theory of the origin of caste. In his view caste is the normal development of ancient Aryan institutions, which assumed this form in the struggle to adapt themselves to the conditions with which they came into contact in India. In developing this proposition he relies greatly upon the general parallelism that may be traced between the social organization of the Hindus and that of the Greeks and Romans in the earlier stages of their national development. He points out the close correspondence that exists between the three series of groups—*gens*, *curia*, tribe at Rome; family, φρατρία, φυλή in Greece; and family, *gotra*, caste in India.* Pursuing the subject into fuller detail, he seeks to show from the records of classical antiquity that the leading principles which underlie the caste system form part of a stock of usage and tradition common to all branches of the Aryan people. In the department of marriage, for example, the Athenian γένος and the Roman *gens* present striking resemblances to the Indian *gotra*. We learn from Plutarch that the Romans never married a woman of their own kin, and among the matrons who figure in classical literature none bears the same gentile name as her husband. Nor was endogamy unknown. At Athens in the time of Demosthenes membership of a φρατρία was confined to the offspring of the families belonging to the group. In Rome, the long struggle of the plebeians to obtain the *jus connubii* with patrician women belongs to the same class of facts; and the patricians, according to M. Senart, were guarding the endogamous rights of their order—or should we not rather say the *hypergamous* rights, for in Rome, as in Athens, the primary duty of marrying a woman of equal rank did not exclude the possibility of union with women of humbler origin, foreigners or liberated slaves. Their children, like those of a Sūdra in the

[* "To assume, with Senart, that the family system was the basis of caste is difficult in face of the late appearance of words for family and of stress on family." A. A. Macdonell, A. B. Keith, *Vedic Index of Names and Subjects*, 1912, I, 281 *et seq.*]

Indian system, were condemned to a lower status by reason of the gulf of religion that separated their parents. We read in Manu how the gods disdain the oblations offered by a Sūdra: at Rome they were equally offended by the presence of a stranger at the sacrifice of the *gens*. Marriage itself is a sacrifice at which husband and wife officiate as priests, and their equality of status is attested by their solemnly eating together. The Roman *confarreatio* has its parallel in the *got kanāla* or "tribal trencher" of the Punjab, the connubial meal by partaking of which the wife is transferred from her own exogamous group to that of her husband.

As with marriage so with food. The prohibition, which strikes us as so strange, on eating with members of another caste or partaking of food prepared by a man of lower caste, recalls the religious significance which the Aryans attached to the common meal of the household. Cooked at the sacred fire, it symbolized the unity of the family, its life in the present, its ties with the past. In Rome as in India, daily libations were offered to ancestors, and the funeral feasts of the Greeks and Romans (περίδειπνον and *silicernium*) correspond to the *srāddha* of Hindu usage which, in M. Senart's view, represents an ideal prolongation of the family meal. He seems even to find in the communal meals of the Persians, and in the Roman *charistia*, from which were excluded not only strangers but any members of the family whose conduct had been unworthy, the analogue of the communal feast at which a social offender in India is received back to caste. The exclusion from religious and social intercourse symbolized by the Roman interdict *aqua et igni* corresponds to the ancient Indian ritual for expulsion from caste, where a slave fills the offender's vessel with water and solemnly pours it out on the ground, and to the familiar formula *hukka pāni band karna*, in which the modern luxury of tobacco takes the place of the sacred fire of the Roman excommunication. Even the caste *panchāyat* that wields these formidable sanctions has its parallel in the family councils which in Greece, Rome, and ancient Germany assisted at the exercise of the *patria potestas*, and in the chief of the *gens* who, like the *mātabar* of a caste, decided disputes between its members and gave decisions which were recognized by the State.

How was it that out of this common stock of usage there were developed institutions so antagonistic in their nature as the castes of India and the nations of Europe? To what causes is it due that among the Aryans of the West all the minor groups have been absorbed in the wider circle of national unity, while the Indian Aryans have nothing to show in the way of social organization but a bewildering multitude of castes and sub-castes? M. Senart suggests a cause, but makes no attempt to follow out or to illustrate its workings. He says, "L'Inde ne s'est élevée ni à l'idée de l'État ni à l'idée de la Patrie. Au lieu de s'étendre, le cadre s'y resserre. Au sein des républiques antiques la notion des classes tend à se résoudre dans l'idée plus large de la cité; dans l'Inde elle s'accuse, elle tend a se circonscrire dans les cloisons étroites de la caste. N'oublions pas qu'ici les immigrants se répandaient sur une aire immense; les groupements trop vastes étaient condamnés a se disperser. Dans cette circonstance les inclinations particularistes puisèrent un supplément de force."

Distribution over a wide area, tending to multiply groups; contact with the aborigines, encouraging pride of blood; the idea of ceremonial purity, leading to the employment of the indigenous races in occupations involving manual labour, while the higher pursuits were reserved for the Aryans; the influence of the doctrine of metempsychosis, which assigns to every man a definite status determined by the inexorable law of *karma*; the absence of any political power to draw the scattered groups together; and the authority which the Brahmanical system gradually acquired—these seem to be the main factors of M. Senart's theory of caste. It may be urged in favour of his view of the subject that evolution, especially social evolution, is a gradual and complex process, that many causes work together to produce the final result, and that the attempt to reduce them to a single formula carries with it its own refutation. On the other hand, as Dr. Fick * has pointed out, if caste were a normal extension of the ancient Aryan family system, the absence of any traces of this tendency in the Vedas is hardly accounted for by the statement that development proceeded so slowly, and was based on such primitive and instinctive impulses, that we could hardly expect to find any tangible indication of it in a literature like that of the hymns.

Caste not merely occupation. The guilds of mediæval Europe.

Before proceeding further we may dispose of the popular notion that community of occupation is the sole basis of the caste system. If this were so, as M. Senart has effectively pointed out, the institution "aurait montré moins de tendance à se morceler, à se disloquer; l'agent qui l'aurait

* *Loc. cit.*, p. 3.

unifiée d'abord en aurait maintenu la cohésion." To put it in another way, if the current idea were correct, all cultivators, all traders, all weavers, ought to belong to the same caste, at any rate within the same area; but every one knows that this is not the case; that the same occupation embraces a whole crowd of castes, each of which is a close corporation, though the members of each carry on in exactly the same way the avocation that is common to them all. Several writers have laid stress on the analogy between Indian caste and the trade guilds of mediæval Europe. The comparison is misleading. In the first place, the guild was never endogamous in the sense that a caste is: there was nothing to prevent a man of one guild from marrying a girl of another guild. Secondly, there was no bar to the admission of outsiders who had learned the business: the guild recruited smart apprentices, just as the Baloch and Brāhūi open their ranks to a fighting-man who has proved his worth. The common occupation was a real tie, a source of strength in the long struggle against nobles and kings, not a symbol of disunion and weakness like caste in India. If the guild had been a caste, bound by rigid rules as to food, marriage, and social intercourse, and split up into a dozen divisions which could not eat together or intermarry, the wandering apprentice who was bound to travel for a year from town to town to learn the secrets of his art, and who survives, a belated but romantic figure, even at the present day, could hardly have managed to exist; still less could he have discharged, like Quintin Matsys and a host of less famous craftsmen, the traditional duty of marrying his master's daughter. It seems, indeed, possible that the decadence and sterility of Indian art at the present day may be due in some measure to the trammels by which the caste system has checked its natural growth. A guild may expand and develop; it gives free play to artistic inspiration; and it was the union of the guilds that gave birth to the Free Cities of the Middle Age. A caste is an organism of a lower type; it grows by fission; and each step in its growth detracts from its power to advance or even to preserve the art which it professes to practise.

Caste under the Roman Empire.

A curious illustration of the inadequacy of occupation alone to generate and maintain the instinct of caste as we see it at work in India is furnished by certain ordinances of the Theodosian Code. In the early part of the fifth century, when the Western Roman Empire was fast falling to pieces and the finances had become disorganized, an attempt was made, from purely fiscal motives, to determine the status and fix the obligations of all classes of officials. In his fascinating account of the constitution of society in those days Sir S. Dill tells us how "an almost Oriental system of caste" had made all public functions hereditary, "from the senator to the waterman on the Tiber or the sentinel at a frontier post."* The Naviculari who maintained vessels for transport by sea, the Pistores who provided bread for the people of Italy, the Pecuarii and Suarii who kept up the supply of butcher's meat, were all organized on a system as rigid and tyrannical as that which prevails in India at the present day. Each caste was bound down to its characteristic occupation, and its matrimonial arrangements were governed by the curious rule that a man must marry within the caste, while if a woman married outside of it, her husband thereby acquired her status and had to take on the public duties that went with it. This surprising arrangement was not a spontaneous growth, like caste in India, but owed its existence to a law enforced by executive action.

"One of the hardest tasks of the Government," says Sir S. Dill, "was to prevent the members of these guilds from deserting or evading their hereditary obligations. It is well known that the tendency of the later Empire was to stereotype society, by compelling men to follow the occupation of their fathers, and preventing a free circulation among different callings and grades of life. The man who brought the grain of Africa to the public stores at Ostia, the baker who made it into loaves for distribution, the butchers who brought pigs from Samnium, Lucania, or Bruttium, the purveyors of wine and oil, the men who fed the furnaces of the public baths, were bound to their callings from one generation to another. It was the principle of rural serfdom applied to social functions. Every avenue of escape was closed. A man was bound to his calling not only by his father's but by his mother's condition.† Men were not permitted to marry out of their guild. If the daughter of one of the baker caste married a man not belonging to it, her husband was bound to her father's calling. Not even a dispensation obtained by some means from the imperial

* *Roman Society in the last Century of the Western Empire*, Book iii, Chap. i, 1899, p. 228.

† C. Th. xiv, 4, 8, "ad munus pristinum revocentur, tam qui paterno quam materno genere inveniuntur obnoxii"; [*Dill, op. cit.*, p. 233.]

chancery, not even the power of the Church, could avail to break the chain of servitude." There was even a caste of *curiales* or, as we should say in India, municipal commissioners, of whom we read that at a certain time all of them were ordered back to their native cities, and were forbidden to evade their hereditary obligations by entering any branch of the government service. As the Empire broke up, the caste system vanished with it. Men hastened to shake off all artificial restrictions and to choose wives and professions for themselves. But on the current theory, that community of function is the sole causative principle of caste, that is the last thing that they ought to have done. They should have hugged their chains and proceeded to manufacture new castes or sub-castes to fit every new occupation that sprung up. If the principle had been worth anything, it should have operated in Europe as effectually as it does in India. No one can say that the Theodosian Code had not given it a good start.

Castes not merely developed tribes.

But, it will be asked, if the origin of caste is not to be found in the trade guild, may we not seek it in the more primitive institution of the tribe? Early society, as far back as we can trace it, is made up of a network of tribes, and in India it is easy to observe the process of the conversion of a tribe into a caste. The conjecture seems at first sight plausible; but a glance at the facts will show that the transformation in question is confined to those tribes which have been brought into contact with the regular caste system, and have adopted its characteristic usages from religious or social motives. The Manipuris, for example, were converted from Nāgas into Hindus only a century or two ago; and I am informed that the family archives of the Rāja contain an account of the process by which the change was effected. The Bhūmij, again, were a tribe at a still more recent date, and retain plentiful traces of their origin. On the other hand, the races of Baluchistan, where Hindu influence is practically non-existent, show no inclination to follow the example of the Indian Muhammadans and organize themselves on the model of caste. The primitive tribe, in fact, wherever we find it, is not usually endogamous, and, so far from having any distaste for alien marriages, makes a regular business of capturing wives. This practice has given rise to one of the forms of infanticide and may well have been the cause of the extinction of whole tribes in the early struggle for existence. In short, when tribes are left to themselves, they exhibit no inborn tendency to crystallize into castes. In Europe, indeed, the movement has been all in the opposite direction. The tribes consolidated into nations; they did not sink into the political impotence of caste.

The genesis of caste: the basis of fact.

As I have said above, speculation concerning the origin of things is mostly vanity. Sooner or later in the course of our researches into the past we run up against the dead wall of the unknown, which is often also the unknowable. In the case of a complex phenomenon such as caste, to the formation of which a number of subtle tendencies must have contributed, all that we can hope to do is to disentangle one or two leading ideas and to show how their operation may have produced the state of things that actually exists. Following out this line of thought, it seems possible to distinguish two elements in the growth of caste sentiment: a basis of fact and a superstructure of fiction. The former is widespread if not universal; the latter is peculiar to India. Whenever in the history of the world one people has subdued another, whether by active invasion or by gradual occupation of their territory, the conquerors have taken the women of the country as concubines or wives, but have given their own daughters in marriage only among themselves. Where the two peoples are of the same race, or at any rate of the same colour, this initial stage of what we have called hypergamy soon passes away, and complete amalgamation takes place. Where, on the other hand, marked distinctions of race and colour intervene, and especially if the dominant people are continually recruited by men of their own blood, the course of evolution runs on different lines. The tendency then is towards the formation of a class of half-breeds, the result of irregular unions between men of the higher race and women of the lower, who marry only among themselves and are to all intents and purposes a caste. In this literal or physiological sense caste is not confined to India. It occurs in a pronounced form in the Southern States of the American Commonwealth, where negroes intermarry with negroes, and the various mixed races, mulattoes, quadroons, and octoroons, each have a sharply restricted *jus connubii* of their own and are absolutely cut off from legal unions with white races. Similar phenomena may be observed among the half-breeds of Canada, Mexico, and South America, and among the Eurasians of India, who do not intermarry with natives and only occasionally with pure-bred Europeans. In each of these cases the facts are well-known. The men of the dominant race took to themselves women of the subject race, and the offspring of these marriages intermarried for the most part only among themselves. The Eurasians of Ceylon, who are known locally as "Burghers," are a notable example of the formation of a caste in the manner here described. During the Dutch occupation of Ceylon (1656—1795) very few Dutch women settled in the island. This fact, combined with the tremendous penalties imposed by the puritanical Dutch laws on the sin of fornication, induced many of the colonists to marry Cingalese women of the higher castes. The descendants of these marriages ranked as Dutch citizens, and very soon crystallized into a caste, disdaining further alliances with the natives and marrying only among themselves. Conscious of their legitimate parentage and proud of a title which recalls their Dutch ancestry, the Burghers of Ceylon now form a distinct and independent class, standing apart from both Europeans and natives, and holding a position far superior to that of the Eurasians in India. Illustrations of the same process may be observed in the Himālayas, where, if anywhere in India, the practices recorded with exaggerated precision in the Indian law books still survive. The Dogras of the Kāngra Hills and the Khas of Nepal are believed to be the offspring of alliances between conquering Rajputs and women of more or less Mongoloid descent. In the case of Nepal, Hodgson has described at length the conditions of these unions, which correspond in principle with those of the traditional system of Manu. Working from this analogy it is not difficult to construct the rough outlines of the process which must have taken place when the second wave of Indo-Aryans first made their way into India through Gilgit and Chitral. At starting they formed a homogeneous community, scantily supplied with women, which speedily outgrew its original habitat. A company of the more adventurous spirits set out to conquer for themselves new domains among the neighbouring Dravidians. They went forth as fighting men, taking with them few women or none at all. They subdued the inferior race, established themselves as conquerors, and captured women according to their needs. Then they found themselves cut off from their original stock, partly by the distance and partly by the alliances they had contracted. By marrying the captured women they had, to some extent, modified their original type; but a certain pride of blood remained to them, and when they had bred females enough to serve their purposes and to establish a distinct *jus connubii*, they closed their ranks to all further intermixture of blood. When they did this, they became a caste like the castes of the present day. As their numbers grew, their cadets again sailed forth in the same way, and became the founders of the Rajput and pseudo-Rajput houses all over India. In each case complete amalgamation with the inferior race was averted by the fact that the invaders only took women and did not give them. They behaved, in fact, towards the Dravidians whom they conquered in exactly the same way as some planters in America behaved to the African slaves whom they imported. This is a rough statement of what may be taken to be the ultimate basis of caste, a basis of fact common to India and to certain stages of society all over the world. The principle upon which the system rests is the sense of distinctions of race indicated by differences of colour: a sense which, while too weak to preclude the men of the dominant race from intercourse with the women whom they have captured, is still strong enough to make it out of the question that they should admit the men whom they have conquered to equal rights in the matter of marriage.

The genesis of caste: the influence of fiction.

Once started in India, the principle was strengthened, perpetuated, and extended to all ranks of society by the fiction that people who speak a different language, dwell in a different district, worship different gods, eat different food, observe different social customs, follow a different profession, or practise the same profession in a slightly different way must be so unmistakably aliens by blood that intermarriage with them is a thing not to be thought of. Illustrations of the working of this fiction have been given above in the description of the various types of caste and might be multiplied indefinitely. Its precise origin is necessarily uncertain. All that can be said is that fictions of various kinds have contributed largely to the development of early societies in all parts of the world, and that their appearance is probably due to that tendency to vary, and to perpetuate beneficial variations, which seems to be a law of social no less than of physical development. However this may be, it is clear that the growth of the caste instinct must have been greatly promoted and stimulated by certain characteristic peculiarities of the Indian intellect—its lax hold of facts, its indifference to action, its absorption in dreams, its exaggerated reverence for tradition, its passion for endless division and sub-division, its acute sense of minute technical distinctions, its pedantic tendency to press a principle to its furthest logical conclusion, and its remarkable capacity for imitating and adapting social ideas and usages of whatever origin. It is through this imitative faculty that the myth of the four castes—evolved in the first instance by some speculative Brāhman, and reproduced in the popular versions of the epics which the educated Hindu villager studies as diligently as the English rustic used to read his Bible—has attained its wide currency as the model to which Hindu society ought to conform. That it bears no relation to the actual facts of life is, in the view of its adherents, an irrelevant detail. It descends from remote antiquity; it has the sanction of the Brāhmans; it is an article of faith; and every one seeks to bring his own caste within one or other of the traditional classes. Finally, as M. Senart has pointed out, the whole caste system, with its scale of social merit and demerit and its endless gradations of status, is in remarkable accord with the philosophic doctrine of transmigration and *karma*. Every Hindu believes that his spiritual status at any given time is determined by the sum total of his past lives: he is born to an immutable *karma*, what is more natural than that he should be born into an equally immutable caste?

Summary. The ethnological conclusions which the foregoing chapters seek to establish may now be summed up. They are these:—

(1) There are seven main physical types in India, of which the Dravidian alone is, or may be, indigenous. The Indo-Aryan, the Mongoloid, and the Turko-Iranian, types are in the main of foreign origin. The Aryo-Dravidian, the Mongolo-Dravidian, and the Scytho-Dravidian are composite types formed by crossing with the Dravidians.

(2) The dominant influence in the formation of these types was the physical seclusion of India, involving the consequence that the various invaders brought few women with them and took the women of the country to wife.

(3) To this rule the first wave of Indo-Aryans formed the sole exception, for the reasons given on pages 49—55.

(4) The social grouping of the Indian people comprises both tribes and castes. We may distinguish three types of tribe and seven types of caste.

(5) Both tribes and castes are sub-divided into endogamous, exogamous, and hypergamous groups.

(6) Of the exogamous groups a large number are totemistic.

It is suggested that both totemism and exogamy are traceable to the general law of natural selection.

(7) Castes can be classified only on the basis of social precedence, but no scheme of classification can be framed for the whole of India.

(8) The Indian theory of caste was perhaps derived from Persia. It has no foundation in fact, but is universally accepted in India.

(9) The origin of caste is from the nature of the case an insoluble problem. We can only frame more or less plausible conjectures, derived from the analogy of observed facts. The particular conjecture now put forward is based—firstly, upon the correspondence that can be traced between certain caste gradations and certain variations of physical type; secondly, on the development of mixed races from stocks of different colour; and thirdly, on the influence of fiction.

CHAPTER VII

CASTE AND NATIONALITY

Rien n'est bête que de bouder l'avenir.

Anatole France.

So sind sie Particularisten von Natur: das nationale Bewusstsein erscheint bei ihnen erst als Erzeugniss der fortschreitenden Bildung.

Von Sybel, 1890.

It will be seen from the picture imperfectly outlined in the preceding chapters that caste in India is something more than what is called a social system, something beyond a mere mode of grouping the loose atoms of humanity which the wheel of circumstance has created and a turn of the same wheel may destroy or transform. We should rather conceive of it as a congenital instinct, an all-pervading principle of attraction and repulsion entering into and shaping every relation of life. For Hindus caste is bound up with their religion, and its observance is enforced by the authority of the priests; its influence is conspicuous in the social usages of most Indian Muhammadans; and it extends even to the relatively small communities of Christians. Thus it forms the cement that holds together the myriad units of Indian society. In the words of Sir K. Sheshadri Iyer, the great Dewan of Mysore, "the whole social fabric of India rests upon caste." Were its cohesive power withdrawn or its essential ties relaxed, it is difficult to form any idea of the probable consequences. Such a change would be more than a revolution; it would resemble the withdrawal of some elemental force like gravitation or molecular attraction. Order would vanish and chaos would supervene. Yet we are told from time to time, in tones of settled conviction, that the bonds of caste are being burst asunder by the disruptive force of modern ideas and that the Indian spirit is now about to be liberated from this prison-house of the past Such facile

European idea that caste is breaking up.

assurances proceed for the most part from philanthropic Englishmen who have seen little of India beyond the Presidency towns, who know none of the vernacular languages, and who derive their impressions from the small body of Anglicized Indians whom Sir Henry Cotton describes, with rather needless acidity, in one place as "a disorganised class within the community," and in another as "an artificial and exotic product." *

Let it be admitted, however, that there is some excuse for those who, in their just and natural admiration for the educated Indian, leave out of view the people of India and the governing principle of Indian society—caste. Any one who has the curiosity to glance at the second chapter of this book will see that from the sixteenth century onwards almost all observers have been struck by the prohibitions on food and drink, and the rules about personal contact which caste entails, and have hardly noticed its restrictions upon marriage. Both sets of rules are, of course, inherent in the system. But they do not stand upon the same footing, and the penalties attached to their violation differ widely. A marriage, or even a *liaison*, with a member of another caste *ipso facto* involves final and irremediable excommunication. A slip in the matter of food can within limits be expiated by penance. Moreover, the rules about diet and contact with other castes rest upon a metaphysical theory of ceremonial pollution which admits of many exceptions. Ever since the time of Manu it has been recognized that the devout traveller, when in danger of starvation, must pocket his caste scruples and satisfy his hunger as best he can. In modern times, and especially since the introduction of railways, this comfortable doctrine has been developed and elaborated by Brahmanical casuistry. It has long been held, for example, that sweetmeats, a generic and elastic term which includes all the promiscuous messes sold on the railway platforms, may be taken from almost anybody. Nice enquiries about the caste of itinerant vendors of sweetstuff cannot be prosecuted from the window of a third-class carriage during a short stoppage, and a modern proverb sums up the position in the practical query—"You have eaten the food he gave you, why ask about his caste?" On the same principle the wise man finds it convenient to forget that ice was once water, that

Founded on misconceptions of fact.

* *New India*, p. 260.

soda water, before it found its way into a cunningly contrived bottle, owned the same humble origin and did not necessarily come straight from the Ganges; that certain essences and extracts used for medical purposes bear an ascertainable relation to beef, and that imported biscuits must have passed in their making through the hands of all sorts of casteless folk. Nor is he so indiscreet as to enquire at how many paces' distance his neighbour can convey pollution, when he must in any case rub shoulders with him in a railway carriage for twelve hours on end.

The every-day occurrences which an observant tourist may notice in the course of his cold-weather progress through India manifestly conflict with his preconceived notion of caste as a rigid system of unalterable prohibitions. To people who do not understand all that is implied in the cry of *Pāni Pānre,* which one hears at each halt of a train in Northern India, the apparent difference between the theory of the guide-book and the practice of the people may well seem marked enough to warrant the belief that English education, modern civilization, the growth of industries, the march of progress, and all the rest of it are making short work of an ancient and famous institution for which the Indian world has no longer any use. Yet what the tourist sees from his railway carriage comprises only the accidents of caste, which may change from year to year as convenience or fashion may dictate. The substance of the system lies hidden from the eye of the globe-trotter (and scarcely perceptible even to those who are not globe-trotters) in the hard and fast rules which regulate marriage. In this department of life, where the fact or fiction of community of blood has continually to be reckoned with, there are no signs of compromise or concession. People must marry within the caste or sub-caste in which they were born, or must take the consequences. Even the most advanced of modern Indians have had occasion to discover that exclusive dealing in husbands is a formidable weapon to use against a family man, and that the frivolous foreigner who defined caste as "a turnpike to matrimony" had, at any rate, hit off an aspect of it which comes home to the father of marriageable daughters. As for the mass of the people, all that they know or care to know is that whoever kicks over the connubial traces is promptly turned out of his caste, and must either become a Muhammadan or must join some dubious sect which offers a sympathetic welcome to persons caught out in sexual delinquencies. The idea that any properly constituted Hindu should *wish* to marry outside his caste would seem to them too preposterous to be worth discussing. As long as the people think thus, so long will caste endure, whatever philanthropists may say.

Quite apart, moreover, from caste developments many things are happening in the India of to-day which tend to bewilder an observer recently arrived from Europe, and unable to command a wider outlook than is afforded by his own immediate surroundings. It is hardly possible to imagine a more startling series of contrasts than is disclosed directly one penetrates below the mere surface of Indian society. One sees there a sort of disordered kaleidoscope in which the oldest and the newest ideas of the human spirit whirl round together in the most bewildering fashion. Science and religion, expediency and prescription, contract and status, the Western enthusiasm of humanity, the Eastern carelessness of human life—all these mighty opposites are mixed and jumbled up together in a fantastic medley out of which a benevolent despotism, controlled in the last resort by a distant but not unwise democracy, is constantly attempting to evolve an order of things which, while satisfying the comparatively simple wants of oriental life, shall not fall too conspicuously short of European ideals of progress and prosperity. An illustration or two will show at a glance how great a gulf is fixed between the educated minority and the great body of the Indian people, and what savage impulses throb behind the deceptive veil of apparent culture. Not very long ago, while a talented Bengali professor, well known to the scientific world of London, was lecturing to crowded audiences on the transcendental properties of metals under the influence of electricity, widows were being burnt alive in Bihar, incidents curiously suggestive of human sacrifice were occurring in Orissa, and in Calcutta, the *soi-disant* centre of light and leading, a large section of the population, shrewd enough in the business of daily life, were deterred from going out after dark by their dread of a mysterious personage who was believed to be hunting for heads to cement the foundations of the Victoria Memorial Hall. In the face of such vigorous survivals of ideas far more primitive than caste itself, we may be excused for receiving with some scepticism the argument that because a few archaic taboos on food, drink, and personal contact have been relaxed, therefore the entire fabric of caste, undermined by European science, must be tottering to its fall.

Sir Henry Cotton takes a more just view of the general situation when he writes :—

"The country recoils from such a social revolution as our Western civilisation has thrust upon it. It still needs the hierarchical leadership of caste. The tendency to reduce the power of the dominant classes and to destroy, if possible, all distinction between the different strata of society is much in vogue among headstrong administrators, who are too apt to transplant the radical associations of our democracy into a country altogether unsuited to their growth. But there is no more patrician *milieu* in the world than that which has for centuries flourished in India and is still vigorous, in spite of attacks upon it."

Not shared by Sir Henry Cotton.

"Those reformers who are in the habit of describing caste as the root of all evils in Hindu society overlook the impossibility of uprooting an institution which has taken such a firm hold on the popular mind. They forget that the attempt to abolish caste, if successful, would be attended with the most dangerous consequences, unless some powerful religious influence were brought to bear upon the people in its place. They forget also that caste is still stronger as a social than as a religious institution, and that many a man who has entirely lost his belief in his religion, is zealous and tenacious of his position as a high-caste man, and scrupulously performs all customary rites and ceremonies. Caste is now the framework which knits together Hindu society; it is the link which maintains the existing religious system of Hinduism in its present order. The problem of the future is not to destroy caste, but to modify it, to preserve its distinctive conceptions, and to gradually place them upon a social instead of a supernatural basis." *

The late Babu Guru Prasād Sen, a native of Eastern Bengal, who practised as a pleader in Patna, and wrote an instructive little book on Hindu social life, lays equal stress on the necessity of retaining caste unless Indian society is to fall utterly to pieces. He dwells upon its value as the guardian of a proper *esprit de corps* among the groups to which it gives rise, and notices the wholesome influence which it exercises by maintaining unbroken the traditions of remote ancestry; by preserving the distinct existence of the Hindu people; and by enforcing the due subordination of the various parts of society to the whole.

The opinion held by Sir Henry Cotton and Babu Guru Prasād Sen that caste, so far from being moribund, still maintains its ancient place in the Indian social system, receives striking confirmation from the returns of the last Census. It may be said with confidence that the tendency to rebel against the prescriptions of caste has not spread beyond the relatively small circle of those who, in Mr. Gokhale's words, "have come under the influence of some kind of English education." † Outside those limits caste, with all its restrictions, is regarded as the natural law governing human society. Now the male adults who described themselves in the Census of 1901 as being

* *New India*, pp. 225 and 252.

† Presidential address to National Indian Congress, 1905.

able to read and write English—a test not necessarily representing a high standard of English education—numbered in the whole of India just 707,000, or less than one per cent. of the male adult population.* Even if the whole of this company of *literati*, scattered over all the provinces and states of India, were banded together to beleaguer the citadel of caste, many generations must pass before their attack could effect a practicable breach. The walls of immemorial usage will not crumble at the first blast of the trumpet of reform. But how many even of the advanced members of the literate class seriously contemplate the disruption of the social régime under which they live? So far as can be gathered from the various sources of information available, the number of such iconoclasts is extremely small, while their ranks are mainly recruited from among those who, for one reason or another, have become alienated from their own people and have lost touch with Indian society. Nor does English education of itself, at any rate in its present state of development, necessarily incline an Indian patriot to enter upon the uncongenial task of demolishing indigenous institutions and reconstructing them on a foreign model. On the contrary, with the growth of national or provincial self-consciousness which has manifested itself within the last few years, the opposite tendency may be observed, and Indian religion, philosophy, usage, and family life are extolled as intrinsically superior to anything that the Western World has succeeded in producing.

Whose views are confirmed by statistics and by the best Indian opinion.

If then the régime of cast, with all that it implies, is likely to survive for an indefinite period in India, what influence may it be expected to have over the growth of the modern idea of an Indian nationality? At first sight the two things appear to be antagonistic and incompatible: the principle of separation conflicts with the principle of consolidation. This, indeed, seems to be the deliberate opinion of two competent Indian critics. The disordered state of things arising from particularism in India was vividly described a few months ago by an advanced Bengali politician in a letter to a Calcutta newspaper: "We must not forget that India is not yet a nation; we must not forget that it is a congeries of races, which are not always friendly to each other: we must not forget the ancient hate, the

[* In the whole of India in 1911, 1·7 million persons were found to be literate in English. Of every ten thousand persons of each sex, ninety-five males and ten females possessed this knowledge (*Census of India Report*, 1911, vol. i., p. 299).]

ancient prejudice, the ancient clashing of castes and creeds which still hold India under their vice-like grip." * A serious student of social problems in India, who stands aloof from politics, and approaches the subject of reform from the firmer ground of religion and philosophy, writes in an equally despondent tone. After referring to the high ideals of public and private life that prevailed in ancient India, he goes on to say :—" Truth (satya) and duty (dharma), the good old rule of not doing to others what was disagreeable to one's own self, was held up as the ideal by the sages of those times, and many tried to live it. And it is because we have lost that ideal, that we present the spectacle of a people rent asunder by mutual dissensions, divided into thousands of castes and sub-castes, sects and subsects, with all spirit of nationality crushed out, weak in body and mind and slaves of circumstances." † Yet clearly Sir Henry Cotton and Babu Guru Prasād Sen do not regard the matter in the same light as the most recent observers on the spot. For both of them look forward with enthusiasm to the birth of an Indian nation; and the latter, while asserting with some emphasis that "there was no Indian nation at the date of Vikramāditya, or at any period of past Indian history," goes on to quote with approval Comte's reference to caste as "a necessary preparation" for the wider sentiment of patriotism. Sir Henry Cotton ‡ dips even further into the future, and does not hesitate to sketch, in terms which recall the seventh book of the Mahābhārata, the main outlines of the political organization in which the national spirit will find its appropriate embodiment and expression. "What is required," he says, "in the absence of an emasculating foreign army, is an organization of small States, each with a prince at its head, and a small body of patrician aristocracy interposing between him and the lower orders of working-men. For such an arrangement the country appears to be eminently adapted; the United States of India should be bound together by means of some political organization other than the colonial supremacy of England. The basis of internal order is to be found in the recognition of a patriciate accustomed by hereditary associations to control and lead,"—in other words a Council of Nobles.

Apparent antagonism of Caste and Nationality.

* Hon. Babu Bhupendra Nath Basu of the Bengal Legislative Council.—*Statesman*, 28th May, 1907.

† *Hinduism: Ancient and Modern*, by Rai Bahadur Lala Baij Nath, B.A., District and Sessions Judge, Ghazipur. New edition, 1905, p. 104.

‡ *New India*, p. 227.

In an interesting essay in the *Empire Review* for September, 1907, Mr. A. M. T. Jackson has shown how the theory of the traditional Hindu Kingship—the political ideal which the genius of the warrior Sivaji sought to revive and which the intriguing spirit of the Brāhman Peshwas effectually shattered—was rooted in caste. At the head of it stands the King, the one absolute and responsible ruler, uniting in his own person all legislative, judicial, and executive functions, but assisted in their exercise by a purely advisory Council consisting of members appointed by himself in certain proportions from among the leading castes. Subject to the orders of the King, whose duty it is to enforce the rules of the various castes, "each of the functions required in a civilised community is discharged by a separate section of the people. The worship of the gods is the business of one caste, banking of another, shoe-making of another, and so on. By analogy the business of government is also assigned to one particular section, instead of being the common business of all as it is usually held to be in Europe. In India, this arrangement reacted upon the body politic in two ways. Firstly, the exclusion of most of the castes from politics left little room for the growth of feelings of common interest and public spirit; secondly, the efficiency of the governing section became of immense importance. Only if this section were strong could it perform its function of keeping each caste to its proper duties, and thereby combine the parts into an organic whole; while if it were weak, society would fall apart into disconnected atoms. Anarchy is the peculiar peril of a society that is organized on the basis of caste, and the dread of anarchy leads to monarchy as the strongest defence against it. Indian thinkers were well aware of the weakness of divided counsels, holding that one person should be appointed to one task, and not two or three. 'It is always seen that several persons, if set to one task, disagree with one another.'" *

Caste and Monarchy.

Under the rule of the model King depicted in the Mahābhārata, of whom it is written that "he should always have the rod of chastisement uplifted in his hands," the forces of caste were kept under proper control, and the system was prevented from degenerating into an organized tyranny. Monarchy seems to have guarded against this danger; would a democracy of the modern type be able to do the same? In considering how

* *Mahābhārata* VII., p. 258.

such a democracy would work in India, it must not be forgotten that caste would provide the party in power, the party that had spoils to divide, with what Americans call a "machine" surpassing in efficiency the wildest dream of the most ingenious wire-puller. It already possesses a ready-made system of standing caucuses each under the control of a "boss" or a committee of "bosses." Once organized for political purposes, it could whip up voters *en masse* and could secure the adoption of any conceivable ticket. Men would be compelled to vote solid by penalties compared with which the Papal interdict that drove an Emperor barefoot to Canossa was a clumsy and ineffectual instrument. In a society where every one is peculiarly dependent on his neighbours, the recalcitrant voter would speedily find himself cut off not merely from the amenities, but also from the barest necessaries of life. No one would eat with him, drink with him, smoke with him, or sell him food; the barber would not shave him; the washerman would decline to wash his clothes; the Brāhman would deny him the offices of religion; no man would marry his daughter; and the attendants of the dead would refuse him the accustomed funeral rites. These are some of the blessings which popular government, controlled and directed by caste organization, would confer upon the subjects committed to its charge. Whatever future centuries may have in store for the people of India it may be hoped that they will be spared the misfortune of government by social ostracism.

Caste and democracy.

The discussion of speculative constitutions is a futile pursuit. But the relation between caste and nationality, between the idea of a rigidly exclusive matrimonial group and the idea, whether realized or not, of a wider community embracing many such groups—has taken rudimentary shape in India before now and may yet make itself felt on a larger scale. If what might have been the germ of a nation can shrink into a caste, as we have seen in the case of the Marāthas and the Newārs, may not the converse process be possible and a number of castes, without sacrificing their individual characteristics, draw together into that larger aggregate which we call a nationality? For the answer to this question no antecedent experience can be appealed to, since the institution of caste is peculiar to India, and the historical causes by which certain Teutonic tribes (which under different conditions might have hardened into

Caste and nationality.

castes) were converted into nations can hardly be expected to repeat themselves here at the present day. It seems of interest, however, to attempt to determine to what extent the continuance of caste is in itself favourable or adverse to the growth of a consciousness of common nationality among the people of India.

In the first place, let us endeavour to make clear what is meant by *nationality*. This abstract term, originally denoting the fact of belonging to a particular nation (as we speak of the "nationality" of a ship), has within the last fifty years acquired a concrete meaning implied rather than expressed in such phrases as "oppressed nationalities." The standard literature of the subject approaches the question from the European standpoint, and the development of the idea of nationality in Asia has as yet received no exhaustive treatment. As the word is ordinarily used, it seems to imply that the persons composing a nationality are keenly conscious, and may even be passionately convinced, that they are closely bound together by the tie of common interests and ideals, that in a special and intimate way they belong to one another, and that the moral force and enthusiasm by which their sentiment of unity is inspired render it independent of the government or governments under which they may happen to live. This feeling of self-consciousness gives to a body of men a sort of personality, so that they become "a moral unity with a common thought." The idea is not necessarily associated with democratic tendencies; it may equally arise from loyalty to a dynasty. Nor is it invariably directed towards consolidation; it can be seen at work as a disintegrating force which fastens upon a particular racial, linguistic or geographical group and seeks to detach it from the political system of which it forms part. When a homogeneous multitude of men, animated by this complex sentiment, are united under a single government expressing their common aspirations and carried on by themselves, they are no longer described as a nationality, but are recognized as a nation. Thus we speak of the Polish, Finnish and Bohemian nationalities, and of the Greek, German, and Italian nations. The factors which go to the making of a national consciousness are of somewhat indefinite character and have been variously described. The most precise enumeration of them is perhaps that given by Sidgwick in *The Elements of Politics*. He notices the following:—The belief in a common origin; the possession

The factors of nationality.

of a common language and literature; the pride that is felt in common historic traditions, in the memories of a common political history, and of common struggles against foreign foes; community of religion; community of social customs. The last factor is in India so closely associated with religion that it need not be specially considered.

Belief in a common origin, frequently traced back to a mythical ancestry, figures largely in the inherited traditions of most European nations. Into the foundations of such beliefs it would be unkind to enquire too narrowly: in the nebulous domain of national sentiment a picturesque legend carries higher value than the most authentic historical documents. If people can succeed in persuading themselves that they come of the same stock, they will not thank any one for showing that their descent is extremely mixed, and that pure races exist only in theory. It may perhaps be argued that in these respects the general position in India is not altogether dissimilar to that in Europe, and that the diffusion of patriotic fiction may in either case be expected to bring about much the same result. But in India we have to reckon with the existence of a number of distinct physical types, the contrasts between which strike the most superficial observer; and these types not only occupy widely different stages of intellectual advancement and general culture, but are organized in a social system which tends to stereotype and perpetuate their hereditary or acquired characteristics. Can we look forward to a time when these antagonistic masses will be animated by the conviction of their common origin, and will sink their natural antipathies in the idea of a united nationality? Can we suppose, for example, that the Muhammadans will readily surrender their cherished tradition of descent from Arab and Moghul conquerors, that the Rājputs will claim kinship with the Bengalis, or that the millions of Dravidian and Mongoloid people will be recognized as owning the same parentage as the Brāhmans of Benares and Ajodhya? No student of ethnology will ignore the influence that has been exercised by fiction in forging imaginary affinities between people of very different origin, but in India this influence has hitherto been directed towards separation rather than consolidation, and even when that tendency has been reversed, an immense amount of leeway will still have to be made up.

Community of origin.

There are at present no indications that the factor of language, which has done so much to promote national movements in Europe, is likely to play the same part in India. At the last Census of the Empire no less than 147 distinct languages were recorded, 22 of which were spoken by more than a million people.* The situation, therefore, so far as language is concerned, is even more complex and chaotic than it is in the Austrian dominions, where the Parliamentary oath may have to be administered in eight different languages. It is perhaps conceivable that one of the many dialects of Hindustani might in course of time become established as the vernacular of the whole of Northern India, though the linguistic jealousies of Hindus and Muhammadans as to the script and vocabulary of the language will not readily be appeased. But to suppose that the Dravidians of Southern India will ever abandon Tamil and Telugu in favour of some form of Indo-Aryan speech, or that the peasantry of Bengal and Orissa, Mahārāshtra and Gujarāt will change their characteristic languages and alphabets, requires almost as large an effort of the imagination as the dream that English itself may in the remote future become the *lingua franca* of the three hundred millions who inhabit the Indian Empire. Speculations of this kind pay but a sorry tribute to the vitality of the Indian vernaculars and the attractions of the valuable literature which they possess—a literature which appeals to the most intimate feelings of the people and is closely bound up with their religious beliefs and their social obligations. The day is far distant when the Rāmāyana of Tulsi Dās will lose its hold over the peasantry of Upper India; and when the hymns of Tukārām will cease to be household words in the Marātha country. Nor do the classical languages of India supply a bond of union which may form the basis of a common nationality. The tendencies of Sanskrit writings are hierarchical rather than national, while their contemplative and metaphysical tendencies are absolutely at variance with the actively militant spirit of the Arabic and Persian classics on which Indian Muhammadans are brought up. It is difficult to imagine any form of symbolical interpretation or intellectual compromise by which the quietist philosophy characteristic of the Hindu scriptures could be reconciled with the fiery dogmatism of the Koran, or to conceive how two races looking back to such widely different literatures could be brought to regard them as the common heritage of one united nationality. We

Language.

[* In 1911 220 languages (including 38 minor dialects) spoken by 313 millions, were recorded (*Census of India Report*, 1911, vol. i., p. 321).]

can only conclude therefore that in India, so far as can be at present foreseen, the development of the national idea is not likely to derive much support from popular speech or learned tradition.

It is possible indeed—distant as the prospect now appears—that English may after all stand the best chance of becoming the national language of India. Its adoption would at any rate avoid the antipathies and antagonisms with which any Indian vernacular would have to contend. English is already the medium of communication for the upper classes, at any rate on certain subjects, all over India. As the men of the elder generation, who prefer the vernacular, die off, and English comes to be the language of the family as well as the language of public life, it may spread in Northern India as it has spread in the south and may extend to classes which are not now touched by it. This process would be greatly expedited, and at the same time the development of nationality promoted, if the modern "direct" method of teaching were introduced and colloquial English were taught to British Indian children as thoroughly as colloquial French is taught in Pondicherry and Chandernagore. There would then be less temptation to mix the two languages, taking the structure of the sentence from one and the vocabulary from the other. This, I believe, is more common in Upper India than in Madras. When such expressions as "*āpnār* theatricals *bŏrŏ* tedious *hŏbe*" can be heard in the best Indian society, one feels that those who use them are hardly on the right road to a real command of either language.

We may look back in vain through India's stormy past for memories of a common political history and common struggles against foreign foes. Wave after wave of conquest or armed occupation has swept over the face of the country, but at no time were the invaders confronted with resistance organized on a national basis or inspired by patriotic enthusiasm. If here and there a local chieftain fought for independence, as Porus opposed Alexander and Prithirāj resisted Muhammad Ghori, his nearest rivals hastened to offer their swords to the foreign enemy. Tribal jealousies, dynastic intrigues, internal disunion

Political history.

combined to create a political vacuum which the first comer who knew his own mind was irresistibly impelled to fill. Even the Marātha confederacy, which to some may have seemed stable enough to form the nucleus of a national dominion, was broken up by the personal disputes which arose among its leaders. The Sikh league, held together for a time by the masterful personality of Ranjit Singh, began to fall to pieces at his death. Illustrations might be multiplied without limit, but it is an unwelcome task to dwell upon a picture of general discord and confusion. The facts are beyond dispute, and they point to the inevitable conclusion that national sentiment in India can derive no encouragement from the study of Indian history.

In the series of lectures published under the title, "*The Expansion of England*," the late Sir John Seeley speaks of religion as "the strongest and most important of the elements which go to constitute nationality," and throws out the idea that Hinduism may prove to be the germ from which that sentiment may be developed in India. He then draws attention to the failure of the Hindus to organize a national resistance to the advance of the Muhammadan invaders, and of the Marātha confederacy, which he describes as "an organization of plunder," to inspire Hinduism with the spirit of active patriotism. There he leaves the subject, after a passing glance at the "facile comprehensiveness of Hinduism" which in his judgment "has enfeebled it as a uniting principle," and rendered it incapable of generating true national feeling. It may be admitted that the flame of patriotic enthusiasm will not readily arise from the cold grey ashes of philosophic compromise, and that before Hinduism can inspire an active sentiment of nationality, it will have to undergo a good deal of stiffening and consolidation. The Ārya Samāj seems to be striking out a path which may lead in this direction, but the tangled jungle of Hinduism bristles with obstacles, and the way is long. Meanwhile, it is curious to observe that Sir John Seeley's forecast leaves Islam entirely out of account, though in an earlier lecture he dwells on the fact that the population of India is "divided between Brāhmanism and Muhammadanism." His general proposition as to the influence of religion upon nationality seems, moreover, to lose sight of the historical fact that while community of religion strengthens and consolidates national sentiment, religious differences create distinct types within a nation and tend to perpetuate separate and antagonistic interests. This difficulty has not escaped the observation of Sir Henry Cotton, who rightly points out that "it is impossible to be blind to the general character of the relations between Hindus and Muhammadans; to the jealousy which exists and manifests itself so

Religion.

frequently, even under British rule, in local outbursts of popular fanaticism; to the kine-killing riots and to the religious friction which occasionally accompanies the celebration of the Ram Lila or the Bakr Id or the Muharram." * Sir Theodore Morison † approaches the question from a different point of view. Writing of the educated Muhammadans, he says:—"The possibility of fusion with the Hindus, and the creation by this fusion of an Indian nationality, does not commend itself to Muhammadan sentiment. The idea has been brought forward only to be flouted; the pride of Muhammadans revolts at such a sacrifice of their individuality." But in the same article he seems to admit the possibility of the conception of territorial nationality, irrespective of race or creed, taking hold of the Indian Muhammadans and bringing them into the same political fold with the Hindus. In the case of the most advanced Muhammadans such a *rapprochement* is perhaps conceivable. But even with them it will take a long time to effect, and great changes of religious feeling and practice will have to take place before they can induce the main body of their co-religionists to follow their lead. The problem is a difficult one. As long as Muhammadans are accustomed to kill for food or sacrifice the animal deemed sacred by the Hindus, occasions for deadly strife are bound to arise when the passion of religious animosity will overpower the weaker sentiment of common nationality.

It will be observed that the right of free intermarriage, the *jus connubii* which played so large a part in the growth and progress of the Roman Empire, finds no place in Sidgwick's catalogue of the essential characteristics of nationality. No one writing in Europe would imagine that people who were capable of conceiving the idea of national unity had not long ago passed the stage at which restrictions on intermarriage could form part of their code of social custom. Yet this, which may be called the physiological aspect of the question, is one of the first points that strike an observer in India. It was referred to, as long ago as 1889, by Sir Comer Petheram, Chief Justice of Bengal, in an address delivered by him as Vice-Chancellor of the Calcutta University:—

Intermarriage.

"Above all," he said, "it should be borne in mind by those who aspire to lead the people of this country into the untried regions of political life, that all the recognized nations of the world have been produced by the freest possible intermingling and fusing of the

* *New India*, p. 228.

† *Quarterly Review*; April 1906.

different race stocks inhabiting a common territory. The horde, the tribe, the caste, the clan, all the smaller separate and often warring groups characteristic of the earlier stages of civilization, must, it would seem, be welded together by a process of unrestricted crossing before a nation can be produced. Can we suppose that Germany would ever have arrived at her present greatness, or would indeed have come to be a nation at all, if the numerous tribes mentioned by Tacitus, or the three hundred petty princedoms of last century, had been stereotyped and their social fusion rendered impossible by a system forbidding intermarriage between the members of different tribes or the inhabitants of different jurisdictions? If the tribe in Germany had, as in India, developed into the caste, would German unity ever have been heard of? Everywhere in history we see the same contest going forward between the earlier, the more barbarous instinct of separation, and the modern civilizing tendency towards unity, but we can point to no instance where the former principle, the principle of disunion and isolation, has succeeded in producing anything resembling a nation. History, it may be said, abounds in surprises, but I do not believe that what has happened nowhere else is likely to happen in India in the present generation."

The view there stated is borne out by Rivier's * observation.

"Ou ne peut guère douter que ce ne soit en grande partie aux mélanges infinis qui, durant des siècles, ont pétri et trituré les Européens d'aujourd'hui, qu'est du la suprématie *mondiale* actuelle de notre continent."

So long as a regime of caste persists, it is difficult to see how the sentiment of unity and solidarity can penetrate and inspire all classes of the community, from the highest to the lowest, in the manner that it has done in Japan where, if true caste ever existed, restrictions on intermarriage have long ago disappeared. It may be said on the other hand that the caste system itself, with its singularly perfect communal organization, is a machinery admirably fitted for the diffusion of new ideas; that castes may in course of time group themselves into classes representing the different strata of society; and that India may thus attain, by the agency of these indigenous corporations, the results which have been arrived at elsewhere through the fusion of individual types. The problem is a novel one, but so are the conditions which give rise to it, and the ferment of new ideas acting upon ancient institutions may bring about a solution the nature of which cannot now be foreseen.

The basis of Indian nationality.

We have seen that the factors which in other countries are regarded as essential to the growth of national sentiment either do not exist at all in India, or tend to produce separation rather than cohesion. We have also observed that the influence of caste seems at first sight to favour particularist rather than nationalist tendencies. Are we then to conclude

---

* Rivier: *Principes du Droit des Gens.*

that the conception of an Indian nationality rests upon no substantial or even intelligible basis, and may be brushed aside as a figment of the prolific oriental imagination stimulated by its recent contact with Western thought? Such a conclusion would, I think, be premature. Indian national sentiment is, indeed, at present in rather a fluid condition, but its existence within a certain section of the community can hardly be denied, and the causes which have led to its development are plainly discernible. They may be said to be two in number:—

(1) The consciousness of a certain community of intellectual pursuits and aspirations, derived from the common study of the history and literature of England, and from the common use, for certain special purposes, of the English language in addition to a provincial vernacular.

(2) The consciousness of being united and drawn together by living under a single government, by taking part in the administration of a common system of laws, and by sharing in the material benefits of a common civilization.

Here one naturally looks for some instance in history of a genuine nationality arising from the partial adoption of a foreign language and the partial assimilation of a few foreign institutions. Within the modern period the search for such a parallel would be fruitless. The modern theory of nationality figured prominently among the original doctrines of the French Revolution, but in the hands of Napoleon it speedily became an instrument of territorial aggrandisement, and it can hardly be said to have attained general recognition in Europe before about 1830. Long before that time all the peoples affected by it had formed their own languages, had made their own history, and had developed characteristic institutions to which they were passionately attached. Even the oppressed nationalities, whom other powers were trying to absorb, cherished these feelings in unabated strength. Going back some centuries earlier it may perhaps be thought that the common use of Latin by the learned classes of Europe as a medium of communication on political and literary subjects offers a resemblance to the common use of English by the educated class in India. But the survival of Latin as the language of diplomacy, science and scholarship down to the middle of the 18th century did no more towards developing any consciousness of common nationality among Europeans as such than the remotely analogous fact that under the rule of the Moghuls in India Hindu officials

Has it any parallel in history?

were in the habit of addressing their conquerors and of transacting public business in Persian. In neither case did the practice of the learned give rise to any community of political sentiment either among them or among the people at large.

The example of Gaul.

If we travel still further back in the history of Europe an approach to a precedent of the kind we are in search of seems at first sight to be furnished by the intellectual and social development of Gaul under Roman rule. In B.C. 38 when Julius Cæsar, yielding to the entreaties of the Gauls for aid against the Helvetii, entered upon the shortest of Roman wars,* he found the country between the Rhine and the Pyrenees in the possession of about eighty independent political communities (*Civitates*). These were united by no federal tie; they recognized no superior authority; they had not risen to the idea of a common country or a national life; and their local patriotism was bounded by their own little territories, and inspired by hatred of their immediate neighbours. Most of them were in form aristocratic republics governed by Senates in which the educated classes had a decided preponderance. But they were torn by internal factions ever ready to call in a foreign ally, and were in constant danger of being overthrown by any ambitious chief who was rich enough to gather round himself a small army of rudely equipped retainers Independent Gaul was a chaos of disorderly local jealousies aggravated by perpetual war. When the Romans appeared on the scene, some of the States hastened to make terms; others offered a fitful and ineffectual resistance under leaders whose real object was to set up tyrannies of their own. With an army consisting mainly of Gallic levies, drilled and disciplined on the Roman system and stiffened by a few Italian legions, Cæsar subdued the country in five campaigns, and substituted a single Roman supremacy for a confused medley of local supremacies. On the establishment of the *pax Romana* an era of civilization commenced which resulted in the development of political and religious unity.

The influence of language was the chief factor in the change. From the first century onwards all the inscriptions that have been discovered, whether dedications to the gods, family epitaphs, or municipal decrees are without exception in Latin.

---

* Si cuncta bella recenseas nullum breviore spatio quam adversus Gallos confectum. Tac. Ann XI, 24.

Among the common people the ancient Celtic dialect seems to have survived down to the middle of the third century and then to have died out so completely that in the fifth century, when Gaul was converted to Christianity by Latin-speaking missionaries, no trace of the original language remained.* As Coulanges observes, when two peoples are in contact, it is not always the less numerous that gives up its language; it is rather the one that has the most need of the other. Here the need was all on the side of the Gauls. Their own language was poor and was unable to express the new ideas that came in with advancing civilization. They had no literature and no art of their own. They borrowed both from Roman sources and they founded schools all over Gaul to teach poetry, rhetoric, mathematics, the entire harmony of studies which the Latins called humanity. Religion, law, social usage followed in the same path, and in all departments of life Gallic culture perished and Latin culture took its place. Yet the result of this process of assimilation was not to produce an independent Gallic nationality, but to merge the people of Gaul in the Roman nation. The Gauls ceased to be Gauls in any but a geographical sense and became Romans with a Gallic tinge. The process is a remarkable one, and many of its incidents seem almost to have repeated themselves in the history of India. But it throws no direct light on the problems connected with the idea of an Indian nationality.

The example of Japan.

It is in no way surprising that the imagination of the Indian nationalists should have been deeply touched by the rise of Japan, or even that some of the more ardent spirits among them should have formed the opinion that if forty years of contact with European thought could make a nation of the Japanese, more than a century of similar experience ought to have done the same for the people of India. Here there seems to be some misconception of the facts. Japan has many lessons for the Indians of to-day, but when they begin to study her history they will assuredly not learn from it that Japanese nationalism was the work of two generations, or that it owed anything at all to foreign culture or influence. Centuries before Commodore Perry landed in Yokohama the various race elements out of which the Japanese people have been formed, had been

* Here I follow Coulanges, *La Gaule Romaine*. Mommsen, in *The Provinces of the Roman Empire*, takes a different view of the scanty evidence available.

crushed together and consolidated by the sternest discipline that any nation has ever undergone. In all the stages of this process religion was the dominant influence. *Shinto* or "The way of the gods," a form of Animism coloured and idealized by the belief that the dead are ever present with the living and take an unseen but active share in the fortunes of their descendants, lent itself to a social regime of extraordinary stringency. Under the rule of the dead no man could call his soul his own. His actions, his words, his demeanour, his thoughts, his emotions were perpetually watched by a ghostly company of ancestors, who were grieved at any wrong conduct and visited it on the family at large. Thus the rights of the dead came to be enforced by the living, and formed the basis of a domestic despotism of the most searching kind. Even the quality of a smile was defined by inviolable convention, and to smile at a superior so broadly as to show the back teeth was reckoned as a mortal offence.

The minute regulations promulgated in 681 A.D. by the Emperor Temmu, and expanded, a thousand years later, by the great Shogun Iyéyasu, afford many illustrations of the coercion employed. "Every member of a Kumi,"* says one of these, "must carefully watch the conduct of his fellow members. If any one violates these regulations without due excuse, he is to be punished; and his *Kumi* will also be held responsible." Behind the Kumi was the clan, then came the community, then the tribe—a hierarchy of groups, ruled by the "Heavenly Sovereign," the divinely incarnate Mikado, and all working together to suppress independent personality and to produce a uniform type of character for the service of the nation. The ordinances cover every incident of life from marriage to the material or cut of a dress, or the value of a birthday present to a child. They lay infinite stress on obedience to parents and superiors, respect for elders, faithful service to masters, and friendly feelings towards all members of the community. Intrigue, party spirit, the formation of cliques, competition for leadership, appeals to the passions of the ignorant—in short, all forms of political selfishness are condemned in scathing terms. The patriot must put aside personal vanity and may not play for his own hand. Breaches of the rules were punished by social ostracism, by flogging, by torture, and in

* A *Kumi* was a group of five or more households under a Kumi-gashira or group-chief who was responsible for the conduct of the *Kumi* and of each of its members.

the last resort by banishment for life or for a term of years. In old Japan the banished man was dead to human society. Even the outcast classes would not receive him; without permission he could not become a Buddhist monk; and the last resource of selling himself as a slave was withdrawn from him by the later Shoguns. The religion of loyalty could make no terms with the rebel or the renegade. It demanded absolute submission as the first condition of national unity.

The centuries of coercion which the Japanese passed through produced in them a superb heredity, moulded by discipline and instinct with loyalty. When the new era opened and the Mikado resumed his temporal power, he found ready to his hand a nation that moved like one man, and was inspired through all its ranks with the single sentiment of devotion to the country and to the ever-present ancestors of the race. The world is still wondering at the achievements of the last fifty years. But these were rendered possible by the training of the ages that had gone before. Japanese nationalism did not originate in the theoretical sentiment of a literate class which may or may not work down to the lower strata of society. It is rooted in the popular religion and bound up with the life of the race. To my mind the most striking among the many evidences of the diffusion of the spirit of unity in Japan is to be found in the extraordinary secrecy maintained during the war with Russia. The correspondents of foreign papers, ready to pay any price for news, saw one Division after another vanish into space, but no foreigner could find out where the troops embarked, where they would land, or what was their ultimate destination. At a time when the issue of the contest hung upon the command of the sea two great battleships were lost by misadventure, and the disaster was concealed until its disclosure could no longer imperil the national existence. These things were known to thousands, but the secret was safe, because all classes were inspired by the passionate enthusiasm and self-devotion which the Shinto religion has developed into an instinct, so that the low-born coolie is as fine a patriot as the *Samurai* of ancient descent. When India can rise to these heights of discipline and self-control, India may rival Japan. But those who cherish that lofty ideal must bear in mind that in the region of evolution there is no such thing as a short cut.

Having brought the enquiry to this point and having attempted to show what factors have and what have not contributed to the growth of national sentiment in India, one is left with the uncomfortable feeling that one has by no means got to the root of the matter. Analysis has its limits and a people, like an individual, is something more than a bundle of tendencies. The mysterious thing called personality, the equally mysterious thing called national character, has in either case to be reckoned with. Beneath the manifold diversity of physical and social type, language, custom and religion which strikes the observer in India, there can still be discerned, as Mr. Yusuf Ali has pointed out, a certain "underlying uniformity of life from the Himalayas to Cape Comorin." There is in fact an Indian character, a general Indian personality, which we cannot resolve into its component elements. How is this character to be inspired and transfused by that consciousness of common interests and ideals which is the predominant feature of the sentiment of nationality? The question admits of being answered either on idealist or on evolutionary lines—in the light of Indian theory or of European or Japanese experience. It may be said on the one hand that the idea of nationality is in itself nothing more than an impalpable mental attitude, a subjective conviction which may subsist independently of any objective reality, a fine flower of sentiment, springing from an unknown germ and nourished on Māyā or illusion. But once planted on Indian soil it may spread far and wide as its seeds are blown hither and thither by the breath of popular imagination. We have seen how the legend of the four original castes, evolved in the active brain of some systematizing pandit, has filtered downwards, has taken hold of the mind of the people, and has become almost an article of faith with the general body of Hindus. No one cares to enquire whether it rests on any basis of fact, yet it holds its ground, it gains constantly wider currency, and it undoubtedly does in a way influence practice in matters of social usage. It is conceivable that the idea of nationality may run a similar course, that it may possess the mind of the upper classes and may be diffused thence through wider circles until it reaches the rank and file of the Indian people. The process will take time, and even when it is completed, the result will be wanting in substance and vitality. If on the other hand we look to the history of Europe, and more especially to the history of Japan, we shall see that wherever genuine nationalities have arisen, they have been the product of character and circumstances—common character and common

The future of Indian Nationalism.

experience acting and reacting on each other through a long period of time. There is no doubt that the common character exists in India, if only in the rather shadowy and undeveloped form in which Mr. Yusuf Ali depicts it. It has still to undergo the common experience necessary to mould it into national character. This apprenticeship, if it is to be of any real effect, must be based upon facts, not upon fancies, and must extend to the masses of the people. A mere top-dressing of idealism will not make a nationality. How then are the people to be reached? Japan supplies the answer—by the development of indigenous beliefs and institutions. The vast majority of the people of India are as yet untouched by the idea of nationality. This cannot be impressed upon them through their own vernaculars, the influence of which would make for separatism rather than for unity. Nor can they be reached through English, at least not for many generations. But they might be drawn together by the common interests which would be created by a genuine form of popular self-government. This should be built up from the bottom on the basis of two indigenous institutions—the village community and the village council—the common property of the Aryan people both in Europe and in India. Reconstruction on these lines offers the best prospect of realizing the national ideal, and of controlling the separatist tendencies of caste. It may be that in the first instance the process will produce not an Indian nationality, but a number of provincial nationalities. But history shows this to be the natural course of evolution. Everywhere particularism has come first, just as crystallisation takes place by centres, and nationalities have been formed by the agglomeration of the particularist units into a larger whole.

Let us now try to draw together the threads of this discussion. The standard elements of nationality either do not exist in India or make for diversity rather than uniformity. Caste in particular, an institution peculiar to India, seems at first sight to be absolutely incompatible with the idea of nationality, but the history of the Marāthas suggests that a caste or a group of castes might harden into a nation, and that the caste organization itself might be employed with effect to bring about such a consummation. The factors of nationality in India are two—the common use of the English language for certain purposes and the common employment of Indians in English administration. At present these factors affect only a limited group of persons, among whom the Muhammadans have hitherto stood rather aloof. The masses have not been affected at all. They cannot be reached through language, but they might be reached through the agency of self-governing institutions. The orderly development of the indigenous germs of such institutions ought to be the immediate object of the Indian nationalists. In this direction and, I believe, in this direction alone, is it possible to advance towards real political representation. Progress will in any case be slow, but nothing will retard it more certainly than the "impatient idealism" which insists upon beginning at the wrong end.

APPENDIXES

APPENDIX I

CASTE IN PROVERBS AND POPULAR SAYINGS

BRĀHMAN.

(PRIEST.)

BEFORE the Brāhman is in want the king's larder will be empty. Like the cat in a Brāhman's house (No risk of being killed). The Brāhman's house smells sweet (He burns sandal wood in the sacred fire). Only he is a true Brāhman who comforts those who come to him for help. Like priest, like people. The riches of the Brāhman are in the Veda; help him who teaches it (A Brāhman's advice). Will the new moon wait till the Brāhman comes? The Brāhman is in a hurry, the temple must be decorated. Like killing a cow and making shoes for a Brāhman of her hide! (An unsuitable present.) He feeds Brāhmans, but his own mother starves. Even an Aiyangar (title of Brāhmans) can give you a contagious disease. A Brāhman's Tamil and a Vellāla's Sanskrit are equally bad. When the Brāhman was at the point of death, his wife wept for his scalp lock. Leading an ass and feeding a fire. (The allusion is to the tale of a certain king whose barber could shave him while he slept without waking him. To reward his skill the king made his priests turn the barber into a Brāhman, which was done by leading him round a sacrificial fire. Next day the king saw his Vizier busily engaged in leading a donkey round a fire and asked what he was doing. The Vizier replied that as the priests had made a Brāhman out of a barber he was making a horse out of an ass.) The priest will, after all, be obliged to eat the gram cakes. (Here the Brāhman is supposed to be angry with his wife for giving him gram instead of wheat: at first he refuses his food, but hunger drives him to eat what is put before him.) What signifies the knowledge of the *shāstras* to him who fails to practise virtue? If I say this, it is as bad as killing a Brāhman; if I say that, it is as bad as killing a cow. Betel nut in the hand of a priest. A girl must be married at ten even if to a Pariah (A gibe at infant marriage among Brāhmans). A Nāgar will always lie; if he speaks the truth his *guru* (spiritual teacher) must have been a fool. You will not get the better of a Nāgar; if you do, he must be a Hajjām. To get a Nāgar wife you must pay a jar full of money. (The Nāgar bride-price is high.) You may see a Nāgar bride naked. (She will bear inspection.)

What is a Brāhman? A thing with a string round its neck. Does the thread make the Brāhman? A saint, a cook, a water carrier, and an ass? (Aimed at the multifarious occupations of the modern Brāhmans.) A priest by appearance, a butcher at heart. There are three blood-suckers (butchers) in this world—the bug, the flea, and the Brāhman. The Brāhman and the vulture look out for corpses. Flaunting a rosary and hiding a knife, you chant the Divine Song, O Brāhman, exhorting others but sinning yourself. A Chaube set out to become a Chhabbe, but returned a Dube. (Chaube and Dube are Brāhman titles denoting in theory that the holders know four Vedas or two Vedas respectively. The irony of the saying is directed at the ignorant Brāhman who wants to know *six* Vedas when there are only four.) What is in the Brāhman's book is on the Brāhman's tongue. Bathe in the Ganges and lend to a Brāhman. (If you are drowned or lose your money you get salvation as a set-off.) A Brāhman need only prophesy ; a bullock must plough his furrow. Every Brāhman has his own moral code. A Brāhman is damned by his own teaching. Follow a Brāhman's precepts, not his practice. A learned Brāhman dies of hunger. A Brāhman's wisdom—after the event. One old woman is worth a hundred Joshis. (Brāhman astrologer.) The gods are false and the Brāhmans impure. A Brāhman washes his sacred thread, but does not cleanse his inner man. A Brāhman with hair to his waist. (To show his piety.) Though the Brāhman prostrate himself (in penance) he will not be saved. Be the Brāhman never so vile, he still rules the three worlds. (A gibe at priestly infallibility and popular credulity.) Whatever a Brāhman pours out is holy water. Trace not the source of a river, nor the parentage of a Brāhman : the one is mud, the other dirt. When a Chaube dies he becomes a monkey ; when a monkey dies he becomes a Chaube. Who is fairer than the faithless Kashmiri Brāhman : the leper. When the Brāhman drowns he drags his clients down. A Bāgar, a south-east Panjābi, brings famine ; a Brāhman brings bad luck. The absent-minded Brāhman ate beef and said, "By God, never again!" Three Kanaujiās and thirteen fireplaces. (A skit on the fuss that the Kanaujiā Brāhmans make about ceremonial observances, especially in the matter of cooking.)

To invite a Brāhman is to open your door to an enemy. Strain water before you drink it and test a Brāhman before you make him your family priest. When we are by ourselves he is my family priest. (He is too disreputable to associate with in public.) Waste not your breath on a Brāhman, nor converse with an ascetic. Better have leprosy than a Brāhman for a neighbour. A Brāhman and a goat are a nuisance to their neighbours. The Brāhman next door brews a quarrel and settles it (for a consideration). A village with a Brāhman is like a tank full of crabs. Keep clear of a Brāhman as you would of a horse's hind legs. A Srimāli or West Indian Brāhman is best asleep ; he carries a plague in his pocket. One Nāgar Brāhman, nine hundred devils ; two, God knows what is coming ; three, certain disaster ; four, sudden death. Trust a Pariah in ten things, a Brāhman in none. When the gods give, beware of the Brāhman. A Brāhman has no pity, not even if his brother dies in his house. A Brāhman, a dog, and a barber growl at their own kith and kin. A hungry Brāhman will sell his gods. God knows right from wrong ; the Brāhman only knows *dāl* (pulse) from rice. Walk among snakes but steer clear of Vaishnava Brāhmans. Kill a cat, kill a Brāhman. Set a Brāhman to kill a snake. (If he is bitten no one will miss him.) If a Brāhman is at hand, why swear by your child? (The person on whom a false oath is taken is supposed to die.) May you be cursed with a Brāhman servant. Guruji (priest) is always to the fore, except when there is a river to be crossed. (Post of danger.) Twelve Brāhmans have the strength of a goat. A Brāhman's wife will speak you fair. Why do you look like a Brāhman to whom a daughter has been born? Give a Brāhman's daughter money, and she will say the Muhammadan creed. (Will stick at nothing.) A Brāhman has no sense ; he will sell his cow buffalo (which gives milk) and buy a mare (which he cannot ride). A Brāhman out of work will worship his *Patla* (the stool on which he keeps his sacrificial implements). Client sorry, Brāhman merry. (He will be paid to propitiate the powers that bring the misfortune.) "Brāhman, why don't you marry?" "Thanks, my village perquisites satisfy me" (Droits de seigneur?). Is that stump a stalk for me, and the cocoanut for the Nambutri Brāhman? (The Nambutris in Malabar get the pick of the Nāyar girls.) I was just combing my beard when he brought me here and called me a Brāhman. (An Assam proverb, apparently alluding to the manufacture of Brāhmans from Bengali Muhammadans.) He posed as a Brāhman, but his name was Pīroz Khān. The Ahīr's (herdsman's) belly is deep; but the Brāhman's is a bottomless pit. The Brāhmans' bellies are full; they lie about like gorged buffaloes. A Brāhman has faith only after a meal. A Brāhman risks everything for a dinner. A scanty loin-cloth and an empty stomach; by these you may know the Brāhman. Rice on his plate and his sacred thread in his hand. When the Brāhman's stomach is over-full a dish of curds sets it aching. Life is dear to us Brāhmans; we have eaten our fill; give us money to take us home. Other people's flour and butter, what do they cost the Brāhmans? The Brāhman gets cake to eat; the children of the house may lick the mill-stone. The pony grows fat in Asārh (June–July, when it is too hot to ride), the Brāhman in Bhādra (July–August, when ancestors are worshipped and Brāhmans fed). The Brāhman wanted both Hindu sweets and Muhammadan loaves, and got neither. You will repent, Brāhman, and eat the same pulse after all. A hungry Brāhman is like a tiger. Vishnu gets the empty litany; the Brāhman takes the sacred food. (The offerings to Hindu idols are eaten by the priests.) "Brāhman, Brāhman, here is uncooked food for your dinner." "That will do to take home, but first give me a dinner here." After dinner a Brāhman rubs his belly and a Jogi (ascetic) his head. The vegetables are rotten, give them to the Brāhman. A degraded Brāhman, give him a dead cow. The Brāhman wore flowers and the gardens were stripped bare. A Brāhman's cow eats little, but gives much milk. O God, let me not be born a Brāhman, who is always begging and is never satisfied. A Brāhman will beg with a *lākh* (Rs. 100,000) in his pocket. A one-eyed cow for the Brāhman (Give him what is useless). A black cow for the Brāhman (Give him of your best, as the scriptures enjoin). Vultures and Brāhmans spy out corpses. What is written in the Brāhman's book (the duty of alms-giving) is tied up in his wife's shawl. The Brāhman asks, the Baniya pays. The Brāhman's son lives by begging. To a clerk a bribe, to a Brāhman a gift. A cat that will not lap milk, and a Brāhman who refuses a bribe. A Brāhman's hand and an elephant's trunk are never at rest. A Brāhman will wriggle and twist till he has done you out of both interest and principal. Give the Brāhman a corner of your veranda and he will soon have the whole house. Is the ridge-pole of the Brāhman's house made of bamboo? (Proverb of the improbable.) The trader has lost his capital: the Brāhman claims his percentage of the profits. (Baniyas in western India set apart a pice in the rupee of their profits to give to Brāhmans.) The Patel (village headman) and his wife may die, but the Brāhman must have his fee. The son of the house cannot afford a wife, but his father must pay for the wedding of the Brāhman's son.

Ask a Brāhman for alms. (Blood from a stone.) If you dine with a Brāhman, you go away hungry. A Brāhman's servant is worked like an oil-presser's bullock, and gets nothing but stale bread. A Brāhman out of work lives on pulse. Give a Brāhman waste flour or bran, and he will make bread with it. When four Brāhmans meet, they dine off sweets or starve (Caste scruples and ceremonial observances). It is poison to a Brāhman to dine at home. A Brāhman's guest; a prostitute's wedding. If a sheep comes into a Brāhman village each one will get a hair. The pulse is in the market (not yet bought), but the Brāhman beats his wife and asks "will you make it thick or thin?" The Sūdra prostrated himself: the Brāhman dunned him for his father's debt.

BHĀT.

(Bard and Genealogist.)

What is the use talking to a Bhāt: he smacks his lips like a camel. A hungry Bhāt will set the village on fire. A Bhāt, a Chāran, and a dog will sit at the door; they will not go away when you have fed them and they will feel no shame. (Alludes to the practice of sitting *dharna* at a man's door to recover a debt.) A Bhāt went into business and made his hundred into thirty. Bhāts, Bhatiyārās and harlots are a bad lot: when you come in they are civil: when you leave they don't care.

RĀJPUT.

(Warrior and Landholder.)

The Rājput is in the front of the fight. The wall may give way; the Rājput will stand fast. It is ill dealing with a Rājput; sometimes you get double value, sometimes nothing at all. Let him alone when he is full: do not meddle with him, when he is empty: a Rāngar (Muhammadan Rājput) is only bearable in his own house or in his grave. The Rāngar and Gūjar are two; the cat and dog are two; but for these four one might sleep with open doors. A Rāngar is best in a wine shop, or in prison, or on horseback (as a trooper), or at the bottom of a deep hole. The Rāngar and the devil are enemies of religion; they sin themselves and tempt others to sin. The Baniya lives on air, the Hora swings himself, the Rājput drinks *kusambhā* (a decoction of opium), and a woman plays tricks. Rājput and Miyān—braggarts both. Gossip for the Baniya, for the Rājput a song, sweets for a Brāhman and music for a ghost. A Rājput is bred in poverty. At a Rājput wedding there is nothing to eat and you must sleep in the open. A Rājput wedding is like a fire of maize stalks; there is plenty of drumming and very little dinner. Grudge not the *ghi*; the horse will be useful in battle. (Rājput's answer to his wife when she demurred to his wasting ghi on his horse, while antelopes did very well on grass.) He ought to be grateful to me: I married his female relations. (Allusion to the difficulties of Rājputs in finding husbands for their girls.) He starves himself but keeps a Bhāt to sing his exploits at his door. (Rājput pride.)

You can no more make an ascetic out of a Rājput than a bow out of a pestle. The Rājput says, "I have been suckled at the breast of a Rājputni." There is no end to the clans of Rājputs and the varieties of rice. The Baghel and the Gohel (clans of Rājputs) are fierce as steel. When asleep a Rājput, when awake a fool. Rājputs live on dried-up crusts; they have to grind corn, and when they beg for butter-milk they hide the cup. The Rājput is your friend only so long as it pays him. The marriages of Rājputs are full of pomp and splendour, but meals are to be had only from heaven.

MEO.

(Cultivator and Freebooter.)

When a Meo gives his daughter in marriage he gets from the bridegroom a mortar full of silver. (Referring to the high bride-price paid by the Meos.) The Meo's son will nurse his revenge for twelve years.

BAIDYA.

(Physician.)

Let no man fix his abode where there is no wealth, no divine teacher, no magistrate, no river, and no physician. Sect marks on his forehead, and "Govind, Govind" on his lips, he pretends to be a physician. He cannot even find the pulse, yet he doctors every one ; what is it to the Baidya if his helpless patient dies? The disease has eaten the Bej's (quack-doctor's) nose. Rising and falling is the Baidya's lot, provided the original stock remains sound. (The allusion is to the complicated rules of inter-marriage among the Baidyas of Bengal, under which the social status of a family is determined by the marriages of the daughters.)

KĀYASTH.

(CLERK.)

A Kāyasth is a man of figures (A theorist). Trust not a Kāyasth, a crow, or a snake without a tail. A young Kāyasth is as cunning as an old gipsy. Whoso thinks he can jockey a Kāyasth is a great fool. The pen is the Kāyasth's weapon. A Kāyasth's son should be either learned or dead : an ignorant Kāyasth is as an oil-presser's bullock. The youngest amongst Kāyasths. (The fag of the family.) The son of a Kāyasth lives by the point of his pen. In a Kāyasth's house even the cat learns two letters and a half. The strings of a sieve, a bit without a bridle, and a Kāyasth servant are three useless things. Half a loaf is enough ; I am a Kāyasth, not a beast. Drinking comes to a Kāyasth with his mother's milk. Beware of the Kāyasth who wears a gold necklace. (The suggestion is that a Kāyasth money-lender is a merciless creditor.) They will die if you touch them, but still they crawl and bite—where have these two creatures, bugs and Kāyasths, come from? A Kāyasth who can pay cash is the devil; he is an angel when deep in debt. Wherever three Kāyasths are gathered together a thunderbolt is sure to fall. When honest men fall out the Kāyasth gets his chance. Kāyásths, crows, and *roras* (loose ponies) are much of a muchness. Where there are no tigers the Kāyasth will become a shikāri. The Kāyasth was eleven months in his mother's womb, yet he did not bite her : why? he had no teeth.

JĀT.

(PUNJAB CULTIVATOR.)

No kindness in a Jāt, no weevil in a stone. A Jāt is your friend as long as you have a stick in your hand. Bind up a wound, tie up a Jāt. To be civil to a Jāt is like giving treacle to a donkey. Kill the Jāt ; let the snake go. When a Jāt runs wild it takes God to hold him. A Jāt's laugh would break an ordinary man's ribs.

What does a Jāt know about dainties? he might as well be eating toad-stools. When a Jāt becomes refined there is a great run on the garlic : when a Jāt learns manners he blows his nose with a door-mat. If a Hindki cannot harm you he will leave a bad smell as he goes by. Wheedle a Pathān, but heave a clod at a Hindki. (Pathāns calls the Jāts Hindki.)

The Jāt's *damri* (half a pie) draws blood : the Baniya's hundred does not break the skin. (If you borrow half a pie from a Jāt he will dun you for it as much as a Baniya would for Rs. 100.) If a Jāt gives you butter-milk he will put a rope round your neck. The Jātni wetted her thread : the Karār put a stone in the scale. A good sort is the Jātni ; hoe in hand she weeds the fields with her husband. When it is sowing time with the Jāt (and help is needed) every one is his aunt or his sister-in-law ; when the crop is ripe he does not know his own sister. The Jāt's baby has a plough-handle to play with. The Jāt stood on his corn-heap and called out to the King's elephant-drivers, "Hi, there, what will you take for those little donkeys?"

Doubt the solvency of a Jāt who wears white clothes and eats chicken. If a Jāt stops ploughing in *Srāvan*, one of the months in the rainy season, he ruins himself ; if an old man marries, he puts his beard in the fire. There is little to choose between a Jāt and a pig ; but the Jāt weighs more, and grubs up a whole acre while the pig is grubbing a hole. Says the Jāt, "Come, my daughter, join hands and circle the marriage fire; if this husband dies, there are plenty more." (Jāts allow widows to marry.) Put not your trust in *ghi* kept in an earthen pot, in a Hindu's beard, in a father of many daughters, or in a debt due from a Jāt. (The *ghi* will taste of the pot; the Hindu may shave his beard; the father's means will be exhausted in getting his daughters married; and the Jāt will repudiate his debt.) In a company of Jāts there is ceaseless chatter. A scythe has no sheath, a Jāt has no learning. Saith the Jāt, "Listen, wife, we have got to live in this village; if the folks say a cat walked off with a camel we must chime in." A whole family and one wife between them. (Allusion to the fraternal polyandry believed to prevail *sub rosa* among the Jāts.) O Jāt, abandon your neighbour's couch. You may fathom the acrobat's art, but not the wit of a Jāt. (The reference is to a Rabelaisian tale of how a king had sworn a rash oath to make over his kingdom to a female acrobat (Natni) if no one could defeat her. Whereupon a Jāt climbed the Natni's pole, sat on the top and besprinkled the spectators after the manner of Gulliver in Lilliput. The Natni could not compete with this, and so the kingdom was saved.)

KUNBI OR KURMI.

(CULTIVATOR.)

No month without a day; no village without a Kunbi. Better a solvent Kurmi than a bankrupt millionaire. The Kunbi is always planting, whether his crop lives or dies. Rain in Hathiya gladdens the Kunbin's heart. (An asterism in which rain is specially beneficial to the autumn crops.) Rain in September brings the Kurmin golden earrings. A basket on her head and a child on each hip—by this you may know the Kunbin. Kunbis and flour improve with pounding. You will as soon grow a creeper on a rock as make a Kurmi your friend. A Kunbi has no sense; he forgets whatever he learns. A Kunbi with a stye on his eyelid is as savage as a bull. A Kunbi is as crooked as a sickle, but you can beat him straight. The Kunbi is so obstinate that he plants thorns across the path. The Kunbi went cowherding and earned an earthen pot. A Kunbi does not know an upright from a cross. The master sits at home and the field is full of thorns. A Konkani ghost pounds rice. (A gibe at the cowardice of the Kunbi of the Konkan, the rice-growing country between the western Ghāts and the sea.) The Kunbi's son has nothing but a loin-cloth, but is great at giving alms. A Kunbi's bounty —you must beat him first.

ARAIN.

(MARKET GARDENER.)

A cow is a good beast, and an Arain is a good cultivator. If you trust in God, put no trust in an Arain. Kill the Arain and the Chandar bird: the one will slander you, the other will eat your grapes.

GIRTH.

(PUNJAB CULTIVATOR.)

When the rice is bending with its own weight the Girth looks round and swaggers. You cannot make a saint of a Girth or teach a buffalo modesty. You cannot make a widow of a Girthni or change a bull-buffalo into a barren cow. (Girths allow widows to marry, and the women are credited with making free use of the privilege.)

REDDI.

(MADRAS CULTIVATOR.)

The Reddi fed his dog like a horse and barked himself. The Reddi who had never been on a horse sat with his face to the tail. When the clumsy Reddi got into a palankin it swung from side to side. The envious Reddi ruined the village while he lived and was a curse to it when he died.

AHOM AND BHUIYA.

(ASSAM LANDHOLDERS.)

For the Ahom the *chalang*, for the Hindu the *bei;* I am in your hands, do with me what you will. (The *chalang* is the Ahom form of marriage; *bei* the Hindu form. The proverb purports to express the feelings of a newly-married bride.)

Be it torn, be it crumpled, it is still a silk scarf: be he young, be he old, he is still a Bhuiya's son. (Social position of landholders.)

VELLĀLA.

(MADRAS CULTIVATOR.)

The agriculture of the Vellāla of to-day is no agriculture. The Vellāla was ruined by adornment, the harlot by finery.

BANIYA.

(TRADER AND MONEY-LENDER.)

A Baniya's heart is no bigger than a coriander seed. A friendly Baniya, a chaste courtesan. (Proverb of the impossible.) The faith of a Komati. (*Punica fides.* The Komati is the trader of the Telugu country.)

The grain merchant turns pice into lakhs or lakhs into pice. Shāh first, Bādshāh afterwards. (The Baniya's progress.) A timid Baniya loses both principal and interest. A Baniya has credit, a thief has none. A well-known Baniya prospers; a well-known thief gets hanged. A Baniya robs his friend, a thief his acquaintance. First beat the Baniya, then the thief. Four thieves robbed eighty-four Baniyas. (Cowardice and disunion.) In a full boat the Baniya is a dead-weight. Trust neither the Baniya nor the ferryman. If a Sūd (Amritsar Baniya) is on the other side of the river, leave your bundle on this side. The Chetti (Madras Baniya) and the goldsmith. (*Arcades ambo.*) No one knows what a Chetti is worth till he is dead. The outside of his turban is white, but inside it is all rags. Profit may be made by a rise of rates, but not by using false weights. The Gandhi (grocer or druggist) buys a basketful for a rupee and sells it for a rupee per tola. Gandhis and doctors are close friends. You cannot set up as a Gandhi with one bit of ginger. A petty ginger-seller and wants news of the steamer! (As if he expected a large consignment.) Hīra Dalāl, with a pice worth of nuts, calls himself a merchant (his name means "diamond"). To-day a Baniya, to-morrow a Potdār (coin-tester). The mouse found a rag and set up as a cloth merchant. The grocer steals his own sugar. (To keep his hand in.) Spilt salt is doubled. (By picking up dust.) A Baniya's five-*ser* weight! (Typical illustration of fraud.) What can the poor Baniya do? the scales tip themselves! The simple Baniya weighed in some pice with the cloves. (And thus gave short weight.) The Jāt's wife soaked her yarn (to make it heavy), but the Baniya's weights were light. The Chetti cut the price; the weaver cut the width. A frightened Baniya gives full weight. To recover five the Baniya spends fifty. (Litigation for bad debts.) A Baniya short of a job will weigh his own weights or shift rice from one barn to another. A Baniya will start an auction in a desert. An insolvent Baniya keeps his accounts on the wall. (Where he can rub them out.) A bankrupt Baniya sets up as a broker; a bankrupt Pārsi as a liquor-seller. When a Baniya talks of old times you may know that he is in a bad way. When a buffalo is full she refuses oil cake; when a Baniya is well off he gives time to his debtors; when a Jāt prospers he starts a quarrel; when your banker is in a bad way he fastens upon you. When the Jāt does well he shuts up the path (by ploughing it); when the Kirār (money-lender) does well, he shuts up the Jāt. A bankrupt Baniya puts on the robe of the mendicant and begs from door to door. Even when insolvent a Chetti is a Chetti; silk is silk though never so torn. Your debt to a Baniya grows like a rubbish heap. A Baniya's account, a horse's gallop. The Baniya has him by the scalp-lock. A Baniya is no one's friend: if he takes a walk it is only for gain. If a Baniya's son tumbles down he is sure to pick something up. Trust not a drowning Baniya; he is not going down stream for nothing; let him sink or swim. Only a madman is wiser than a Baniya; only a leper is whiter than an Englishman. If four Baniyas meet they rob the whole world. When the merchant started adorning himself the whole town was plundered. The Baniya has taken the field and the village is full of relations. (Poverty and obligations.) A Baniya for neighbour is like a boil in the armpit. I tilled the field; the Baniya filled his granary. The Baniya nets the wise; the Thag strangles the fool. The Dom borrowed ten from the Baniya and repaid a hundred. You can't pass a false coin on a Baniya. A Baniya's terms are indefinite; he says one thing at night and another in the morning. Trust a tiger, a scorpion, a snake, but a Baniya's word you can never take. (Cradle song in Gujarāt.) The Baniya's urine breeds scorpions. He has the jaws of an alligator and a stomach of wax. A Baniya and a drum are made to be beaten. The Baniya's greeting is a message from the devil. There are three shameless ones—the Baniya, the Ahīr and the whore. A crow, a Kirār (shopkeeper) and a dog; trust them not even when asleep. Father a Baniya, son a Nawāb. Better a leprous forehead than a Modh Baniya for your neighbour. There is no stopping a child or a Saukār. (The idea is that a money-lender demands payment as persistently as a child clamours for something which it wants.) He won't lend money and he won't advance grain: what does he mean by calling himself a Sāh (village money-lender and shopkeeper)? What the Baniya writes God alone can read. (In most parts of India the trading castes keep their accounts in a special character which is very difficult to read.)

The dogs starve at a Baniya's feast. Will a Baniya eat *ghi* and *khichri* every day: not he, he eats his own treacle in fear and trembling. A Baniya's wedding is run on the cheap. He chooses the bride for her skill in cooking, but every one stares at her when she goes to the well. (For her good looks and her ornaments.) The Baniya's wife spent a farthing on betel-nut: quoth he, "We shall soon be ruined." Call a Baniya father and he will give you treacle. One Bhuinhār is meaner than seven Chamārs; one Nuniār (Baniya) is meaner than seven Bhuinhārs. The Mahesri buys sugar; if the price falls he will sell his wife. The Sarāogi cooks rice, but gives parched gram to his friends. Scales with a long beam and short strings, and a *ser* that weighs only three-quarters: by these you may know the true-born Baniya. The Agarwāl swaggers; his mother a Bhatiyāri (cook), his father a Kalāl (distiller). The Baniya does not trouble to curl his moustache. Here comes the grain-dealer with a basket in his hand and a rosary round his neck. (Affected piety.)

The Baniya bought up rotten grain and sold it dear: the beam of his scales broke and his weights were worn thin: he flourished and the Jāt perished: first died the weavers (Jolāhā), then the oilmen (Teli): a rupee was worth only eight annas: millet sold at the price of pistāchio nuts, and wheat at the price of raisins:

the carts lay idle, for the bullocks were dead; and the bride went to her husband without the accustomed rites. (A picture of famine.) Wheat jumped from sixteen *sers*, the rupee to thirty-two: "Oh, wheat, how hast thou dealt with me," cries the dealer, beating his breast in the shop; "as sure as I am a Khatri, no more wheat for me. Oh! that I had had my money made up into necklaces and beads." (A picture of plenty.)

A Komati's evidence. (The story is that a Komati, being called in to identify a horse about which a Hindu and a Musalmān were quarrelling, said that the front part of it looked like the Musalmān's horse and the hind part like the Hindu's.) A monkey's death, a Komati's adultery. (Both secret.) The Mudaliar's pride wastes lamp-oil. The Mudaliar has only a pound of rice; but his pot is big enough for a bushel. (Ostentation.)

A bamboo cannot fruit, a Khatri cannot plough. (When a bamboo flowers it dies, if a trader takes to agriculture he is ruined.) When frost has killed the sugar-cane, the money-lender pretends to be bankrupt: the Jāt goes to borrow (to pay his land revenue), the Khatri puts him off. A hundred goldsmiths make one Thag, a hundred Thags make one brass-worker (Thathera), a hundred Thatheras make one Khatri. Says the Khatri: "The thieves were four and we eighty-four; the thieves came on and we ran away." Minced Khatri makes Khoja. A Khoja is poison hidden in honey; he goes in like a needle and comes out like a sword. From that sort of itch may the Lord deliver us. (Play on the word *khujli*, the itch, and *Khoja.*) A mouthful in the morning is better than ten in the evening; one Khoja without experience is better than ten Kirārs with it.

A crow, a Kirār, and a dog, trust them not even when asleep. You can no more make a friend of a Kirār than a *sati* of a courtesan. A Kirār sleeps only to steal. The nine Kirārs felt all alone when they met the Rāthi with a hoe in his hand. The Jātni wetted the thread; the Kirār put a stone in the scale.

BĀBHAN.

(BIHAR LANDHOLDER.)

Rice and the Bābhan share the same lot. (Both should be pounded, and of both there are many varieties.) If Hararias, Kodarias, and Bhusbharats (sections of the Bābhan caste) would die, Tirhut would be purged of its sin. Trust not a Bābhan, not even if he stand in the Ganges and swear by the ammonite, by the life of Krishna, and by his own son.

NĀPIT OR HAJJĀM.

(BARBER.)

The crow among birds, the barber among men. Among men most deceitful is the barber, among birds the crow, among creatures of the water the tortoise. The Hajjām shaves all, but none shaves the Hajjām. Barbers, doctors, pleaders, prostitutes, all must have cash down. The barber, the washerman, the tailor—all three rogues. Stick to your barber, change your washerman. The bridegroom gets a wife and the barber burns his fingers. (The barber lights the lamps at the wedding.) Here comes the barber with his razor; not a hair will be spared. (A reference to the custom of shaving a man completely when he performs penance for a breach of caste rules.) The razor is sharp, mother, what are you crying about? (Addressed to a newly-made widow about to have her head shaved, the disfiguring custom of western India.) The Brāhman blessed the barber, and the barber showed his glass. (Diamond cut diamond, both castes living by fees.) Vain as a barber. A barber by birth, with a Pārsi name. Arrogant as a barber, affected as a washerman. A man to carry the barber's bag!

A slave under a slave and under him a barber. At a barber's wedding all are lords. (In Bihar the barber is ironically called Thākur.) A clumsy barber wants many razors. (A bad workman quarrels with his tools.) To shave like a hill barber. A barber learns by shaving fools. A barber out of work bleeds the wall, shaves a footstool, a buffalo, a cat, his shaving pot, etc. As the idol so the burner of incense; as the barber so the strop. The barber's rubbish heap does not lack hair. What cares the barber if he cuts the child's head? If the washerman's son dies the barber cares not a hair. Beat a barber on the head with a shoe, you will not make him hold his tongue. Touching barbers and their gossip, the wise say, "Throw a dog a morsel to stop his mouth." (Choke off a reporter with a scrap of news.) A Hajjām found a purse and all the world knew it. The riches of a Hajjām! An elephant in a Hajjām's house! (Proverbs of the impossible.) A burglary at a Hajjām's; stolen, three pots of combings! The tailor's to-morrow never comes, but the barber must be up to time. The barber and the washerman never come in time. The tailor steals your cloth, and the goldsmith your gold; the barber can steal nothing but your hair. The barber is so rich that he asks for a virgin bride! The barber's son-in-law has his moustache shaved at his wedding. If you go back four generations you will find that your uncle was a barber. (Suggests that the barber is unduly intimate with the women of the household.) In a Palle village the barber is the schoolmaster. (Palle, a low fishing caste in Madras.) A barber, a dog, and a hawk are no good when full; a bullock, a Baniya and a king are no good when empty. Three useless things—a king with no subjects, a he-goat with no flock, a barber with no customers. What can a bald man owe to the barber's mother? A Dom made friends with a barber and got shaved for nothing. A barber's penny. (All profit and no risk.) A barber with bamboo nail-scissors. (Inexperience.) The barber's son learns to shave, the wayfarer gets cut. Nails grow at the sight of the barber. A barber's wit has sixteen sides. When a girl talks cleverly you may know she is a barber's daughter.

SONĀR.

(GOLDSMITH.)

The goldsmith, the tailor, the weaver are too sharp for the angel of death: God alone knows where to have them. Trust not the goldsmith; he is no man's friend, and his word is worthless. If you have never seen a tiger, look at a cat; if you have never seen a thief, look at a Sonār. The goldsmith's ear-boring does not hurt. Break up old ornaments, order new ones, and the Sonār is happy. No thief like the goldsmith; no bumper crop but in irrigated land. The wearer has the bracelet, the Sonār has the gold. The Sonār will ruin your ornaments (by mixing base metal with the gold supplied to him) and will clamour for wages besides. A Sonār will rob his mother and sister; he steals gold even from his wife's nose-ring; if he does not steal, his belly will burst with longing. A little goes in hammering, a little goes in melting, and there is no gold left. (A Sonār's methods.) One goldsmith and one who sifts his ashes. (Two rogues.) The Sonār works in gold and his wife dies of hunger. Buying or selling, the goldsmith is always content. (He makes a profit whether he buys old ornaments or sells new ones.) If a Sonār comes to the other bank of the river, keep an eye on your bundle on this side. In an out-of-the-way village the goldsmith's wedding party will stay for seven days. (Shameless sponging.) The fool who made friends with the goldsmith. Only a goldsmith knows a goldsmith's tricks. Is the goldsmith's dog afraid of the sound of the hammer?

KUMHĀR.

(POTTER.)

A potter is always thinking of his pots. The clay is on the wheel; the potter may shape it as he will. The clay said to the potter, "Now you trample on me; one day I shall trample on you." (When you are dead.) Turned on the wheel, yet no better for it. (Persistent ill luck.) Praise not the pot till it has been fired. You bought the pot; do you think the potter will change it? A wife is no earthen pot that you can change at will. (What can't be cured must be endured.) If all the pots that are made lasted and all the children that are born lived, there would be no room left on the earth. The potter eats from broken pots. As the potter so the pot; like father like son. The potter will not ride his ass if you tell him to. The potter's wives fell out, and the donkey's ears were twisted. A Kumhār in a temper with his wife pulls his donkey's ears. The wrath of the potter's wife falls on her ass. The Kumhār's ass runs after any one with muddy breeches. Sooner or later the potter's daughter-in-law must come to the refuse heap. (Kumhārs burn refuse in their kilns and cannot afford to seclude their women.) The Kumhārin has become *sati* for the death of the Teli's ox. (Proverb of the meddlesome.) To the potter a year, to the cudgel a minute. (The making and breaking of pots.) The Kumhār can sleep sound; no one will steal his clay.

If you are civil to a potter he will neither respect you nor sell you pots. The potter's bride must come to the kiln. Like selling pots in potters' street. A dearth of pots in a potter's house. (Proverb of the impossible.) The proof of the kiln is in the firing of the pots. In a deserted village even a potter is a scribe. (Kumhārs are supposed to be very stupid.)

CHŪRIHĀR.

(BANGLE-MAKER.)

If the bangle-maker drops his load he wants a basket to pick up the bits. (The bangles are of glass.) The bangle-maker can squeeze a girl's arm under her husband's nose. (Bangles must be fitted, even in the zanana.)

LOHĀR, KĀMĀR, ETC.

(BLACKSMITH.)

One stroke of a blacksmith is worth a goldsmith's hundred. Seven strokes by a carpenter equal one by a Lohār. The Lohār is a bad friend; he will either burn you with fire or stifle you with smoke. Sparks are the lot of a blacksmith's legs. Do not sit near a carpenter or near a blacksmith's forge. (For fear of chips from the one and sparks from the other.) If you live with a blacksmith your clothes will be burned. To sell a needle in the Lohār's quarter (Coals to Newcastle). If the bull must be branded let the Lohār do it. A blacksmith's shop—like the place where donkeys roll. A monkey saw the good nature of the Kallān and asked him to make it a pair of anklets. Don't buy the smith's pet *maina* even if you can get it for a pice. (The bird will mimic the noise of his hammer.) When a child is born to a Kallān, sugar is distributed in the street of the dancing-girls.* To keep house like a Kammālan (Said of slovenly management). If you buy a cow from a Kammālan cut its ears first. The Kammālan's cloth—so thin that the hair on his legs shows through, and so dirty that it will not burn. They met the Kāmār on the road and wanted him to make them a *dāo*. (When he had no tools with him.) Before the smith can make a screw he must learn how to make a nail.

BARHAI, SUTĀR.

(CARPENTER.)

When the work is done who remembers the carpenter? For long things a Sutār, for short ones a Lohār. (The former cuts up planks, the latter hammers out bits of iron and makes them longer.) The carpenter's face! (Not to be seen when he promised to come.) The Sutār cuts the wood but saves the chips. (For fuel.) Do not sit near the Sutār. (His chips fly.) A whore's oath and a Sutār's chip. The Sutār's adze is as sharp as the gibe of the first wife at the second. The Sutār thinks of nothing but wood, and his wife walks and talks in time to the plane. A carpenter out of work planes his friends' buttocks. The fool of a Barhai has neither chisel nor adze and wants to be the village carpenter.

Lifelong drudgery, like the carpenter, who can never stop making spoons of cocoanut shell. A carpenter knows all sorts of wood, but cannot cut down a tree. Will you find curds in the house of the carpenter or boiled rice in the house of the niggard? The carpenter wants his wood too long, and the blacksmith wants his iron too short.

BHARBHŪNJA.

(GRAIN-PARCHER.)

A Bharbhūnja's (grain-parcher's) daughter, and saffron on her forehead! (Proverb of presumption.)

BHATIĀRA.

(INN-KEEPER.)

Will the children of a Bhatiāra die of hunger. The mother a cook, the son a fop. The Bhatiāra's platter is licked clean. The cook is dead; the constable weeps.

HALWAI.

(CONFECTIONER.)

A confectioner's daughter and a butcher's mistress.

MĀLI.

(GARDENER.)

The Māli may water the trees, but the season brings the flowers. The jackals quarrel over the Māli's Indian corn. In famine the Māli; in plenty the weaver. (Food comes before clothes.) Mother an oilwoman, father a Māli; their son a Muhammadan and calls himself Sujān Ali. (Reflexion on liaisons between members of different castes.) Offend a Māli; he will take your flowers but not your life.

PANSĀRI.

(DRUGGIST.)

A mouse found a bit of turmeric and set up as a Pansāri.

TELI.

(OILMAN.)

What will an oilman do if you set him to weave? Two Telis and foul talk. Whose friend is the Teli; he earns a rupee and calls it eight annas. An oilman sits at ease while his mill goes round. The Ghānchi's bullock walks miles and gets no further. (He goes round and round in the mill.) A Ghānchi's bullock crushed in the oil-mill. (Over-work.) Don't be a Brāhman's servant or an oil-presser's bullock. The oil-presser lost his bullock and is still looking for the peg to which it was tied. The Teli's bullock is always blind. What does an oilman know about the savour of musk? An oilman's daughter, and she climbs up a *siras* tree and sits on the top branch! A Ghānchi's daughter and has never heard of oil-cake! The mother a day labourer, the father an oilman, and the son a "bunch of flowers." (Parvenu's swagger.) The Telin saves a little oil whenever she serves, but God takes all at once. (She gives short measure, but loses all when the jar breaks.) A woman who quarrels with her Telin must sit in the dark. A woman who marries a Teli need never wash her hands with water. The Red-book (Qāzi) up and spoke, "What made the ox fight? The oil-cake you fed it on; so give me the ox and pay a fine into the bargain."

AHĪR, GOLA, ETC.

(COWHERD.)

You will get good out of an Ahīr when you get butter out of sand. Can a crust be dainty, can an Ahīr teach religion? An Ahīr's wealth; an earthen pot. The churner is worth more than the pail.

Koshi (the head of the Ahīrs) has fifty brick houses and several thousand swaggerers. An Ahīr, however clever, can sing nothing but his Lorik song. (A tribal ballad of the origin of the Ahīrs.)

Better be kicked by a Rājput, or stumble uphill, than hope for anything from a jackal, from spear-grass, or from an Ahīr. The Ahīr's business has been done and he won't stand us even a draught of butter-milk. See the perversity of the Ahīr's wife: she takes out the grain and serves the husks. The barber's son learns to shave on the Ahīr's head. (A clown for a shaving-block.) As long as a Musahar (a gipsy-like menial) lives, the Ahīr will get no good out of his cows. A Gola, a drum beater and a procurer are nobody's friends. A Gola's heart is as hollow as a bamboo. Never be civil to a Gola; he is full of vices; his mother is a bad lot and he counts his fathers by the dozen. The cow is in league with the milkman and lets him milk water into the pail. A Gola's quarrel. (Drunk at night and friends in the morning.) For a Gola the court is always next door. (Litigiousness.) The Gola and his wife fall out and their donkey gets his ears cropped. The Gola was guilty, but the Ghānchi lost his bullock. A donkey has more sense than a Gola. Calls himself a Gola but eats *kānji*. (Rice gruel made with water.) If I have to pay for my curds, what do I gain by flirting with the milkmaid? A milkman would not give pure milk even to his father.

GŪJAR.

(CULTIVATOR.)

When you see a Gūjar hammer him. You cannot tame a hare, or make a friend of a Gūjar. Dogs, monkeys and Gūjars change their minds at every step. When all other castes are dead make friends with a Gūjar. A house in ruins is better than a village full of Gūjars. It will remain waste unless a Gūjar takes it. (Said of poor land.) The Rāngar and Gūjar are two, the cat and dog are two; but for these four you might sleep with open doors. A Gūjar's daughter is a box of gold. (The bride-price is high among Gūjars.) A Dom made friends with a Gūjar; the Gūjar looted his house. We have caught the Gūjar's wife; fetch a large basin to hold the ransom. Sense for a Gūjar; a sheath for a harrow. (Two impossibles.) In no man's land one makes friends with Gaddis and Gūjars.

GARERI, BHARWĀD.

(SHEPHERD.)

However good a shepherd be is still a bit of a fool. The shepherd looks for his sheep while he has it on his shoulders. The shepherd who trusted a bear! The shepherd said that the sheep would bite him and hid himself in a pot. For one thing she is a Garerin; for another she stinks of garlic. The Gareri got drunk when he saw the Ahīr in liquor. If you have never seen a ghost (*bhūt*), look at a Bharwād. A squint-eyed Bharwād has seven hundred friends. (Every one knows him by his squint.)

BANJĀRA.

(CARRIER AND NOMAD.)

The Banjāras are honest and never steal. The Banjāra's mother watches the seasons (for her son's return from his periodical journeys). Watch for the home-coming of a servant, a thief, a Thag and a Banjāra. Strip off her shell, O Banjāra, and put it on some one more worthy. (Refers to the shell bracelets worn by married women, and to the reputation of the Banjāris.)

GADHVI.

(NOMAD AND CATTLE DEALER.)

However far the Gadhvi goes he is always at home. "Whither bound, Gadhvi?" "The beast that goes furthest will carry me." The Gaddi is a good-natured sort of fool; ask him for a cap and he will give you a coat.

DARZI.

(TAILOR.)

Tailors, goldsmiths, and weavers are too sharp for the angel of death: God only knows where to have them. The tailor's "this evening" and the shoe-maker's "next morning" never come. A tailor's finishing, a goldsmith's polishing take many days. However sharp his sight a Darzi is blind. (He sees nothing but his work.) A Darzi's son is a Darzi and must sew as long as he lives. A Darzi steals your cloth and makes you pay for sewing it. When four tailors meet they talk about want of work. When a tailor is out of work he sews up the mouth of his son. Sāi, Merāi, and Darzi, these be three; "with our yards, scissors and thread," say they, "we be six." A tailor's needle, now in embroidery and now in canvas. What is it to a tailor whether he march or halt? (He has only needle and thread to carry.) A snake in a tailor's house; who wants to kill it?

DHOBI.

(WASHERMAN.)

Every one has his clothes washed, but the Dhobi is always unclean (ceremonially). Change your Dhobi as you change your clothes. The washerman cries for his wages; the master for his clothes. A Dhobi's dog; neither at home nor at the washing-place (A rolling stone). As many changes of linen as a Dhobi. The king's scarf is used as the Dhobi's loin-cloth. At a Dhobi's wedding they all walk on cloth. (The customers' clothes are used as a carpet.) The Dhobi's son is the swell of the village. The Dhobi's son is always smart on a whistle and a bang. (The Dhobi whistles at his work and bangs the clothes on a stone to drive the water through them. He then gives them to his son to wear.) A washerman's finery is never his own. The Dhobi's house is robbed, and the neighbours lose their clothes. The Dhobi's stone is his brother. Had you been born a stone you might have been of use to a Dhobi. (Proverb of a worthless fellow, good only to beat clothes on.) No soap is used unless many Dhobis live together. (Effect of competition.) The Dhobi takes care not to tear his father's clothes. A donkey has but one master and a washerman has but one steed. Steal the Dhobi's donkey and give it to the Dom. (Rob Peter to pay Paul.) At the Dhobi's wedding the donkeys have a holiday. The mother a laundress and the son a draper. In a Koiri village the Dhobi is the accountant. (He is the only man who can count.) To see a Dhobi the first thing in the morning brings bad luck. The washerman knows when the village is poor; the orderly knows when his master has been degraded. Though a washerman were dying of thirst rain would kill him straight off. A washerman who has learnt his letters throws away his washing-board. A new washerman washes with care. The washerman had a drum beaten when he started washing. (Directed at the arrogance of washermen.) If a washerman is sick he gets well at the washing-stone. (He cannot stop work.) What cares the washerman for one who wears no clothes? The desire of the washerman is for the washerwoman; the desire of the washerwoman is for her donkey. A washerman's donkey. (Proverb of overwork.) Though its life is oozing out of its eyes the washerman's donkey must carry the linen home. Will ploughing with an ass make a farmer of the washerman? Was it the wind or the washerman that spoiled the cloth?

KALĀL.

(DISTILLER AND LIQUOR SELLER.)

Oil and bribes soften most things, but not a *kūpa*, a Kalāl, or a Musalmān. (A *kūpa* is a large leather bottle used for carrying *ghi*.) If you have never seen a Thag take a look at a Kalāl. Death may budge, but a Kalāl won't. The Kalāl's daughter went to drown herself, and the people said "she is drunk." The drunkard's evidence is in favour of the Kalāl. If you want to climb trees you must be born a Shānār. (A South Indian caste who tap palm trees for toddy.)

JOLĀHA.

(MUSALMĀN WEAVER.)

If he has a pot full of grain, a Jolāha thinks himself a Raja. A Jolāha's daughter and calls her sisters "Bubu." (In imitation of high caste people.) How should a weaver be able to reap barley? The fool of a Jolāha went out to cut grass when even the crows were going home. *Kodo* and *marua* are not real food grains; the Jolāha and Dhuniya are not real cultivators. The silly Jolāha has found the hind peg of a plough and wants to start farming on the strength of it. Last year I was a Jolāha; this year I am a Shekh; next year if prices rise I shall be a Saiyad. A weaver by caste and his name is Fateh Khān. (Lord of Victory.) God save us! The Jolāha going a-hunting! Pathāns the slaves of Jolāhas! (Proverb of the impossible.) The weaver steals a reel at a time, but God destroys whole bales. If a Jolāha leaves his loom and takes to travelling he is sure to be knocked about. The Jolāha went out to see the rams fight and got butted himself. If there are eight Jolāhas and nine *huqqās* they fight for the odd one. (None of them can count.) The Jolāha was one of twelve, he could only find eleven and went off to bury himself. (He had omitted to count himself and concluded that he must be dead.) A Jolāha will crack indecent jokes with his mother and sister. The Jolāha's wife will pull her own father's beard.

A Jolāha reckons time by his own standard. The ass eats the crop and the

Jolāha gets hammered. The Jolāha went to the mosque to get off his fasting, and was told to say prayers as well. *Īd* without a Jolāha! (Impossible.) The Jolāhas came to a field of linseed by moonlight; the leader said, "How blue the water is; I hope you all can swim." The Jolāha got into his boat, but forgot to pull up the anchor; after rowing all night he found himself where he was and wept at the thought that his native village could not bear to lose him and had followed him on his journey. A crow snatched a piece of bread from the Jolāha's child and flew with it to the roof: before he gave the child any more the Jolāha took away the ladder. The Jolāha listened to the priest reading the Qurān and delighted the reader by bursting into tears: on being asked what part affected him most, he explained that the old Mullā's wagging beard reminded him of the death of his pet goat. Even if you see the Jolāha brushing the newly woven cloth, do not believe him if he says it is ready: he is as big a liar as the Chamār. When his dogs barked at the tiger the weaver whipped his child. The weaver's wife was fool enough to wrestle with a camel. The Moghal and the Pathān have had their day; now even the Tānti learns Persian. The Tānti ruined himself by buying a pair of bullocks. (By taking to agriculture) A weaver in a small way of business took to weaving *tasar* silk. The thief was seized with colic, and the weaver sat down on a wasp. (Proverb of sudden misfortune.) The weaver digs a pit and falls into it himself. (His loom is sunk in the ground.) There is neither yarn nor cotton, yet the Kori (Sind weaver) beats his apprentice for not weaving cloth. What has a weaver to do with a sword? (Reputed cowardice.) The weaver weaves what he has in his mind.

DHUNIYA.

(COTTON CARDER.)

No one meddles with the tailor and carpenter; all comers beat the cotton carder.

MĀRIYA or THATHERA.

(BRAZIER.)

No one knows the mind of women, crows, parrots and Māriyas. When the Māriya meets his wife he beats her. One brazier swopping goods with another. (Greek meets Greek.) Two Thatheras cannot make a deal.

NUNIYA.

(EARTH-WORKER.)

A Nuniya's daughter gets no rest, neither in her father's house nor in her husband's.

KASĀI.

(BUTCHER.)

A Kasāi never tells the truth; if he did he would not be a Kasāi. Butchers have no human feelings. If you have not seen a tiger, you must have seen a cat; if you have not seen a Thag, you must have seen a Kasāi. To give a cow to a butcher. (Putting sheep in charge of the wolf.) A bad cow is best with the butcher. The righteous man is in trouble and the butcher prospers. Pen-butchers (clerks) are worse than cow-butchers. How can a Rāmdāsi (Hindu ascetic) live in a village of Kasāis? The butcher hunted for his knife when he had it in his mouth.

RANGĀRI RANGSĀZ.

(DYER.)

A dyer wants to paint the town red! (The point of the original is in the play on the Marāthi word *Ranga*, meaning both pleasure and colour.)

SALĀT or SILĀVAT.

(STONE CARVER.)

A Salāt out of work will cut stones.

NĀIKIN or DEVADĀSI.

(DANCING GIRL.)

The dancing girl who could not dance said the room was too small. Does a dancing girl's daughter need to be taught dancing?

ATTĀR.

(PERFUMER.)

An Attār's scent bottle is a juggler's bag of tricks. (He will call his one scent whatever the purchaser demands.)

MĀCHHI, KOLI, ETC.

(FISHERMAN.)

Better three clouts from an oil woman than three kisses from a fishwife. (The latter stinks of fish.) A fisherman's tongue (Billingsgate). The fisherman wears a rag, the Pantāri (fishmonger) has gold in his ears. What does a fisherman know about precious stones? If the fishmonger saw what the net sees he would die of joy. The Muhāno (Sind fisherman) has a stomach-ache and his donkey is branded. Sometimes the float is uppermost, sometimes the fisherman. (Fishermen float face downwards on earthen pots which occasionally capsize.) A Māchhi woman will go on talking even after she has been buried. A fishwife dead is better than an oil woman living. The buffalo and the Māchhi woman both lose flesh in Phālgun. (When the grass is dried up, and the stocks of grain have run short so that the services of the Māchhini as a professional grain parcher are not much in demand.) A cow to a fisherman, a boat to a herdsman. (Square peg in round hole.) A hungry Brāhman will set fire to a village; a hungry hill Koli will loot a house. The hill Koli digs a hole at night (in the mud wall of the house which he is robbing).

CHAMĀR, MOCHI, ETC.

(TANNER AND LEATHER WORKER.)

The Chamār and the jackal—both wily. The Chamār and the Dhed (birds of a feather). Slippery as a Chamār. The Chamār knows about his last: his curiosity goes no further. (*Ne sutor ultra crepidam.*) The Chamār always looks at your shoes (to see if they want mending). The shoemaker's wife goes barefoot. The shoemaker gets a smack in the face with a shoe of his own making. Offer old shoes to the shoemaker's god. (The shortest way with a Chamār is to beat him with a shoe.) The shoemaker sits on his awl and beats himself for stealing it. Stitch, stitch, in the shoemakers' quarter; stink, stink, in the tanners' quarter. The cobbler's dirt, the barber's wound are both hard to bear. The cobbler's shoe pinches; the barber's razor cuts. What profits a wayfarer by the best of food in a Chamār's house? (The caste is unclean.) Too many tanners spoil the hide. The

Chamārs quarrel and the Rāja's saddle is torn. The Mochi's knife does not ask where the leather comes from (*i.e.*, whether it is clean or unclean). May you die at a Mochi's door! (So that he may tan your skin.) The Mochi grieves at the sight of his own skin. (Because he can make no use of it.) The Mochi's wife runs away, but the Mochi goes on sewing. The good-looking Chamārin prides herself on her complexion. A Chamār's daughter and her name is Rāja Rāni! The Chamār's daughter does *begār* (compulsory unpaid labour) even in heaven. The Mochi's aunt has smart clothes given to her, but his wife and mother go bare. (A reflexion on the morals of the aunt.) If sandal-wood fell into the hands of a Chamār and he used it to pound leather, what could the poor sandal-wood do? (Unwilling association with low people.) The Chamār said to the village headman: "How is that buffalo of yours?" (The skins of dead cattle are the perquisite of the village Chamār, who is supposed to resort to poison to secure his rights.) Even a Chakkali girl and the ear of the millet are beautiful when ripe (*i.e.*, when the girl has attained puberty). The spoiled child of the shoemaker made her dinner off shoes: though she did not digest them they did her no harm. To buy leather from a shoemaker. (Proverb of the inappropriate, as the shoemaker keeps leather to make up into shoes.) A shoemaker's wife and a blacksmith's mare are always the worst shod. She is a shoemaker's wife, but her feet burn for want of shoes. My affairs are like Nandan's kingdom. (Nandan was a Chamār, who became a king for three hours, and issued leather coin.) Now that Chamārs may drink from the Ganges the righteous die and the wicked live. (Formerly Chamārs were not allowed to touch the Ganges.) There is no hiding the belly from the midwife. (Said of people who make a mystery of what is well known.)

DOM.

(SCAVENGER.)

The Dom is the lord of death. (He provides the wood for cremating a corpse.) Doms, Brāhmans, goats—no good in time of need. Carts, boats and Doms—all three run crooked. A Dom is a bad servant and a fiddle-bow a bad weapon. A Dom met a barber; one beat his drum, the other held up his mirror. (Demanding their fees.) A Dom made friends with a barber and got shaved for nothing. A Dom made friends with a weaver and got clothed for nothing. A Dom made friends with a Baniya; he borrowed ten and repaid a hundred. A Dom sang for a Jāt and got as much milk as he could drink. A Dom made friends with a Rānghar and found no worse thief than he. A Dom made friends with a Gūjar; the Gūjar looted his house. A Dom made friends with a Kanjar; the Kanjar stole his dog. (Kanjars are gipsies and professional thieves and are said to be fond of dogs.) A Dom his father and a Dom his grandfather, yet he boasts of his noble birth. (After conversion to Islam.) Behind your back, the Dom is a king. Encourage a Domni and she will bring her whole family and sing out of tune. If donkeys could excrete sugar, Doms would not be beggars. A Dom in a palanquin and a Brāhman on foot. (Society upside down.) If a Dom strips himself naked, what can you do to him? (Shamelessness.) The fool of a Domni put the antimony on her nose (Instead of on her eyelids.) A Domni's slave. (Expression of contempt.) The fisherman Dom has seven wives and never a bed for one. The Domni lifted the load without polluting it. The absent-minded Domni took a net for a basket and called her husband *kakāi* (elder brother) in the dark. At the Dom's wedding the Dom may call the tune. The Domni's son betrays his caste by drinking from an earthen pot. The Chandāl licks the platter, he leaves neither hair nor flies.

BHĪL.

The Bhīl is the king of the jungle; his arrow flies straight. The Bhīl is always ready for the prey. With a Bhīl for escort your life is safe. If you please him he is a Bhīl; if not, he is the son of a dog. Bhīls are very shifty; one buttock bare, the other clothed. Bhīls and Berads have no lack of children. What is an aunt to a Māng or a niece to a Bhīl. (Reflexion on their morality.) As noisy as a company of Bhīls. There is no dawdling in a Bhīl's house. (Referring to their wandering habits.)

DHED.

(SCAVENGER.)

Dheds are friends only with Dheds. When a Dhed dies the world is the cleaner. Riches in the hands of a Dhed. (Put to a bad use.) To eat like a Dhed. (To eat unlawful food.) A Dhed's tamarind, be it sweet or sour! (It is anyhow untouchable.) A Dhed looked at the water jar and thus polluted it. A Dhedni's foster son. (A low fellow.) The Havāldār (steward) sent for a Dhedni and she polluted the whole village. If a Dhed runs up against you, you must go off and bathe. Even a Dhedni's feet are red for four days. (Until the henna applied at her marriage has worn off.) Who will marry a Dhed's daughter? Who would father a Dhed's children? Annoy a Dhed and he throws up dust. (In sweeping the road.) He went to the Dhed's quarter and found only a heap of bones.

PARIAH.

Every village has its hamlet of Pariahs (outside its limits). The work of a Pariah is only half done. If you teach a Pariah, will he unlearn his brogue? A palm tree casts no shade, a Pariah has no caste rules. The flower of a bottle gourd stinks, a Pariah's song is unsavoury. If an ox grows fat, it will not stay in the stall; if a Pariah grows rice he will not sit on a mat. Not even a Pariah will plough on a full moon day. If a Pariah offers boiled rice, will not the god accept it? He that breaks his word is a Pariah at heart.

MAHĀR.

(VILLAGE MENIAL.)

The Mahār is dead; he no longer defiles. The Mahār only meddles with you at the village gate. (He is the gate-keeper of the walled villages in the Marātha country.) Why is the Mahār's wife so stuck up? She has got a cow's horn full of grain. Why is the Mahār so stuck up? He is holding the headman's horse. Be it crooked or straight, the bread comes from the village. (The Mahār is said to have fifty-two perquisites. One of them is the right to collect bread from house to house.) To the Mahār's god the offering is an old blanket. The Mahār's child has bones for playthings. (Animals that die in the village are the perquisite of the Mahār.) Let the Chamār run away with the Mahār's mother.

MĀNG.

Trust not a Māng; he will say anything. Māngs watch the forest-paths as cobras watch treasure. (It is believed that each site of hidden treasure has its keeper reborn in the form of a cobra.) What is an aunt to a Māng or a niece to a Bhīl? (Neither has any morals.)

PĀRSI.

A Pārsi! He loses no time in breaking his word. Pārsis are educated and yet they sell oil. (Considered rather a low occupation.) A Pārsi out of work goes to Pārdhi. (*Græculus esuriens in cœlum jusseris ibit.*) Why follow after Bezon Surti? (A notable Pārsi swindler and hypocrite.) A Pārsi's son; the urine of an ass. A Pārsi youth never tells the truth. (*Pārsi bachchā, kabhi na bole sachchā.*) Grāsias are not dirty, and Pārsis are not outcasts. A bankrupt Baniya turns broker; a bankrupt Pārsi starts a liquor shop. The day of Zoroaster; open the box and get out the brandy. If a Pārsi gets rich, he takes a second wife, or buys his neighbour's house. (Dating from before the Pārsi Marriage Act by which at the instance of the Pārsis themselves the reproach of polygamy was removed from their community.) Spectacles to the blind, sweets to the sick, a Pārsi at a Hindu's table. (Orthodox Hindus cannot eat with Pārsis.) The Māli waters the jasmine, the Bhisti looks for a well, the Andhyāru (Pārsi priest) peers for a rich man's death. (In quest of fees.) All dark in a house where you find an Andhyāru. (Suggestion of scandal; notice the pun.) If a Dastūr (priest) speaks, he will dishonour his beard.

"Oh, Dastūrji, how shall my sins be forgiven?" "Present a gold cat, and a silver necklace, and then we will see." The Pārsi woman offers a cocoanut at the Hindu Holi. Crows your uncles and Pārsis your fathers. (Pārsi repartee, in the usual style of Oriental innuendo, to those who call them crows because they expose their dead to be eaten by crows and vultures.) A Pārsi's stroke—like a cannon ball. (A Pārsi saying which one would like to trace to the achievements of Pārsi cricketers.) The Hindu worships stones; the Musalmān saints; the religion of the Pārsi is as pure (from idolatry) as the water of the Ganges.

ASCETICS & DEVOTEES.

Who can identify a drug that has been powdered and an ascetic whose head has been shorn? (Jogis do not say, and often do not know, what caste they originally belonged to.) Who cares what was a Jogi's caste. Money will buy the most pious of saints. In old days the Bhakats used to wash their firewood before cooking; now they do not even wash their feet. Penance alone does not make a saint. You may put on saintly garb, O Jogi, but the ashes will cover no evil deeds. A sect mark on his forehead and ten rosaries round his neck, in appearance a saint, but at heart in love with a prostitute. An ascetic of yesterday, and matted hair down to his knees. A naked woman will tempt a saint. When fish are in season the Jogi loses his head. She went to the Fakīr to learn morals; the holy man tore off her trousers. Follow your preceptor's precepts, not his practice. One Sannyāsi is as good as a hundred Brāhmans. One widow has more virtue than a hundred Dandis (Saivite ascetics who carry clubs). When a man cannot get a wife he turns ascetic. When his crop has been burnt up, the Jāt turns Fakīr. As soon as the ducks lay eggs the Bhakats eat them up. Is the pestle of the *dhenki* heavier than the demands of the Bhakat?

An ascetic's friendship spells ruin to his friends. A king, a Jogi, fire, and water are not to be trusted. Whether the bitch die on the road or by the river, the Jogi will say "see how my words have come true." It is a bad sign if a Saiyad blows a horn (like a Fakīr) or a Brāhman wears a dagger. When the Fakīr goes mad he burns his own hut. Though the mountain may move, the Fakīr won't. The Fakīr is happy in his old blanket. Better the rice of a mendicant Brāhman than the rice of a king riding on an elephant. Promise a Brāhman nothing, but promise a mendicant less. Even ascetics observe caste and religious distinctions. Among shepherds no Saivas, among potters no Vaishnavas. A Sannyāsi's alms in Musalmān street. (Going to the wrong shop.)

A Fakīr's bag contains everything. Who can stop a Fakīr's tongue? A Fakīr's inn is where night overtakes him. To a Fakīr a blanket is a shawl. A Fakīr, a borrower and a child are all devoid of understanding. What has a Fakīr to do with fighting? Mendicancy is the veil that covers the lion. (Concealed rapacity.) The Jogi and the profligate pass sleepless nights.

"Reverend father, what a crowd of disciples!" "They will vanish, my son, as soon as they are hungry." "What has a saint to do with dainties? If there is no butter-milk I can manage with curds." "Oh, mother, give me some sweets; they are very good for the eyes." "My son, if you have a taste for milk and cream you should turn Nānakshāhi." The local Jogi gets no alms. Too many ascetics spoil the feast of Jagannāth.

The Dhundia is neither Hindu nor Musalmān; neither Jogi nor Jati; he is a stupid fellow. If you follow the Dhundia's religion ill luck will follow you. The Dhundia has an ebony walking-stick with a silk tassel, but for all that he is an arrant knave. The Ganges is spotless, the Jangam is childless. What has a Jangam to do with a sacred thread or a Brāhman with trade? Company ruined the Jangam; solitude ruined the Domba (strolling clown).

MISCELLANEOUS.

The human race is a mixed crowd: some are Bhānds and some Bhangis; but Bhānds are better than Bhāts. A Rānd (prostitute), a Bhānd and a Bhainsa (buffalo) are dangerous if they turn against you. If a Bhānd will hold his tongue I will give him a buffalo. He cultivated with a Bhānd for his partner; the Bhānd took all the crop and said he had earned it by his music. What caste has the sweeper, what credit the liar? A Mochi (leather dresser) marries a Bhangi (sweeper) and does not stay the night. A big charger and a sweeper riding it. God takes care of the Dublā. A Dublā eats what he earns and leaves his funeral to God. What will you get by robbing a Dublā? A Dublā will do no work while a grain is left in the pot. Dogs and Dublās never lose their way. A Dublā girl married to a Desāi. (Social promotion.) When Thags are being registered the whole village turns ascetic. When a Thag dines with a Thag the dinner consists of high words. In the company of artisans, bow-makers, and clothiers you will hear plenty of lies; if you want more try the Mirāi. Trustees, devils, Rājputs, widows, and Mirāsis make an outward show of friendship, but inside are full of deceit. The Nāga's wife has a baby; the Nāga takes the medicine. (Is this a reminiscence of the *couvade?*) Do not abuse the boatman until you are over the ferry. A broken cart, an old buffalo, and a Pachāda for a friend; avoid these or they will devour you. A Bhābhā (Bhāttiya) is no man's friend. They buried the Bhāttiya seven yards deep and still he did not die. Have you ever seen a dead monkey or a dead Kuravan? Beat not a barking dog, nor tempt the mouth of a Tigālā woman. (The Tigālās, market gardeners of Mysore, are notoriously quarrelsome.) Two Mahatam huts and calls itself Luckville (Khairpur). Does the son of an Irulan starve when field rats are scarce? An acrobat's son is always turning somersaults. The Tartar who lives in a city feels himself in prison. Make a Wāghia a Pāgia (Captain), he will still cry *Elkot.* (The story goes that a Wāghia who had been dedicated as a child at the temple of Khandoba near Poona rose to command a squadron of Maratha cavalry. One day his horse shied and threw him, forcing from him the cry of "*Elkot*" with which the Wāghias demand alms.) He killed his own buffalo to save it from the Wāghri. When a bat is near death, it flies to the Wāghri's house.

MUHAMMADANS.

The country that has no crows has no Musalmāns. In a village where there are no Musalmāns the cotton cleaner calls himself Saiyad Miyān. (An impossible name made up of two distinguished titles.) What does a beef-eater know of decent language? If girls are sold for a pie a piece don't take a Musalmāni. Can a Musalmān become a Dāvari by going to Tirupati? (A famous Hindu temple in the Madras Presidency.) A Musalmān ascetic's buttermilk is toddy. Even a Qāzi (Muhammadān judge) will drink spirits if he gets it for nothing.

The Afghān is faithless. Be a thief, be a thief. (Injunction of Afrīdi parents to a child while passing him backwards and forwards through a hole in a wall—the ordinary method of burglarious entry in India.) Blood for blood. (The sanctity of the vendetta.) The Baloch who steals gains Paradise for his ancestors even unto seven generations. Who marries not an Ishāqī girl deserves an ass for a bride. (The Ishāqī clan of the Bannūchi is noted for the beauty of its women.) You may know the Chishti by his squint. (A sign of rascality.)

The Mullā preferred to be drowned rather than give his hand. (Proverb of avarice.) The Niāzi love a quarrel. A Pathān's enmity is like a dung-fire. A saint one moment; a devil the next; that is the Pathān. The Pathān boy and his brother took a short cut and fell over the cliff. (Impatience.) Hold up a rupee and you may look at any Mohmand whether man or woman. (Venality.) The Pathāns conquer the city and the Jolāhas get the benefit. (By serving them.) The Shekh came out with a shoe in his hand; the Pathān ran into his house. The Pathān is hungry as soon as his hands are dry. (When he has washed his hands after eating. The brevity of the original—*hāth sukhā Pathān bhūkhā*—disappears in translation.)

A Khatak is like a hen; if you seize him slowly he sits down; if suddenly he clucks. Make friends with any one but a Khatak—may the devil take him! Though the Khatak is a good horseman yet he is a man of but one charge. (Proverb of the Marwāts, the enemies of the Khataks.) Keep a Marwāt to look after asses; his stomach well filled and his feet well worn. (Proverb of the Khataks.)

The drum was beating in the plains and the Bitanni were dancing in the hills. (Stupidity.) A hundred Bitanni ate a hundred sheep. (Thriftlessness.) A dead Kundi is better than a live one. By caste a cotton carder (Behna), by name Nawāb. The Pathāns took the village and the Behnas got swollen head. A swaggering Behna loaded a hen with his drum.

A Musalmān takes back the alms he has given. (Allusion to the practice of resuming the dowry when a married daughter dies.) Even two families of Musalmāns cannot agree. A Musalmān convert cries "Allah! Allah!" all day long. A Dom his father; a Dom his grandfather; yet he talks of his noble birth. The mother a Panhāri, the father a Kanjar, and the son Mīrza Sangar.

When Mīr comes the Pīrs retire. When rich, a Mīr; when poor, a Fakīr; when dead, a Pīr. Mīrsāhib is indeed of high family with his smooth cheeks and his empty stomach. Mīrsāhib! Times are hard, you must hold on your turban with both hands.

When two hearts agree what can the Qāzi do? The Red-book (Qāzi) up and spoke, "Oilman, what made the ox fight? The oil cake you gave him, so I must have the ox and a fine into the bargain." The Hindu who is hauled up before a Qāzi does not find it a feast. A Qāzi's judgment (Proverb of injustice). "Qāzi, why so thin?" "The city's cares wear me within." The fowl killed by the Qāzi is lawful meat. The Qāzi's bitch may give pups anywhere. When the Qāzi's beard is on fire he must put it out himself. When the Qāzi's bitch died the whole town was at the funeral; when the Qāzi himself died not a soul followed his coffin. Though a Qāzi become a saint he will still have a strain of the devil. To trust a Qāzi is to court misfortune. The will of God but the act of a Qāzi. You get nothing from a Qāzi save by force or fraud.

If you are well off you are a Shekh; if not you are a Jolāha. Don't put a peg into a sack or a Shekh into a regiment. (Low-caste converts make bad soldiers.) A Shekh can deceive even a crow.

A Turk, a parrot, and a hare; these three are never grateful. Do not provoke a hungry Turk; he will hunt you to death. The sons of a slave-girl are a faithless brood.

The true Musalmāns lie buried in their graves and their faith lies buried in their books. Where there are Musalmāns there is population. There should be no reserve among Musalmāns. (Addressed to one who declines an invitation to a meal.) The love of Musalmāns is the friendship of a snake. A Musalmān, a wasp, and a parrot are no man's friends; in time of difficulty they will turn and sting or bite. Sesamum, molasses and the love of a Musalmān are sweet at first and afterwards bitter. (Allusion to ease of divorce among Musalmāns.)

Half a doctor and a danger to life: half a Mullā and a danger to faith. You love like the Mullā, who feeds fowls to eat them. A real Miyān is a Miyān indeed, but some Miyāns are Pinjārās (cotton teasers). When the Miyānji (family tutor) is at the door it is a bad look-out for the dog. A Miyānji's walk is only as far as the mosque. (He is always begging, either at people's houses or at the mosque.) A farthing's worth of soap makes the Miyān a Bābu. Since when has the Bībi become a Brāhmani? (Allusion to the looseness of the marriage tie among Muhammadans.)

Calls himself a Saiyad and will steal even a nose-stud. A Bohra is never straight; he will cringe to you when he wants something and cut you when he has got it.

When salt loses its savour then will the Mopla cease to cheat.

A Pashtūn will go to hell through his own self-will. To see a Mullā is to see misfortune.

The camel calf of uncle Achak. (The reference is to certain Achakzāis who mistook the remains of a Hindu who had been cremated outside the city gates for a camel calf roasted by some robbers and made a hearty meal of it. The proverb is aimed at their ignorance and stupidity and may be regarded as the Baloch analogue of the story of the Thames bargees who ate the puppy pie under Marlow bridge.) The Achakzāi is a fellow who will steal an empty flour-bag. A wicked son of Achak—if you see him, fly from him. If the father makes friends with Achak, the son should not follow suit. The Kākar besmeared with filth—if you see him hit him with a stick: expel him from the mosque and you will save trouble. A Masezāi has no hope of God; and God has no hope of a Masezāi.

The hills are the forts of the Baloch: better are they than double-storied houses with wind-sails: his steed is a pair of white sandals: his brother is his sharp sword. The beauty of the night is in the stars: and that of the desert in the Baloch. Though a Jām be a Jām, yet he is Jadgal by descent; and therefore not the equal of the princely race of Baloch. A Baloch with his trousers full of wind. (Referring to his boastfulness and the wide trousers that he wears.) All the sandal-wearing Baloch are brothers. (Illustrating their democratic spirit.) Whose friend is the black snake of a Gichki? his words are sweet, but his heart is poison. When all is said and done a Gichki is a Hindu at bottom. (Gichkis are supposed to be Hindu immigrants from India.) One Sanni and seven chiefs. On this side sixty and on that side fifty: all shared the fate of the chameleon. (The story is that a boy of the Burfat tribe chased a chameleon in the house of a Kalmati and killed it there. The wife of the Kalmati complained to her husband that the sacred right of sanctuary had been violated and he killed three Burfat boys in revenge. Thus arose a blood feud, lasting a hundred years, in the course of which sixty Kalmatis and fifty Burfats were killed) The precipice of the Kalmati. (Foolish pride. On his way from Pasni to Kech a Kalmati asked the road from a stranger who pointed out the track. The Kalmati, however, insisted on going straight on into the hills, with the result that his camel broke its neck. Thereupon he and the stranger fought to the death and were both slain.)

The Kulānchi's sheep and the Med's cauldron. (Habit of exaggeration. A Kulānchi told a Med of a huge mountain sheep which he had seen standing on a high hill and grazing in a distant valley. The Med retorted by describing a cauldron being made in Bombay on which forty thousand coppersmiths were employed, and when asked by the Kulānchi how such a thing was possible, replied: In what other utensil could your sheep be cooked?) Wisdom has begged in vain for mercy from the Rinds: and for decency from the Meds. The black-faced Meds are like tamarisk sparks without even a glow of courage. (Tamarisk embers soon die down.) The Med's livelihood depends upon the wind: and his death comes from the wind. The Med busy on his voyage: and his wife busy with her lover. (The Meds are engaged in sea-faring.) The Mīr of the Rinds and the throne of Delhi. (Democratic spirit. According to Baloch traditions, when Mīr Chākar, the Rind, took Delhi in the 15th century and sat upon the throne, his brethren, jealous of his position, sat all round, on the arms and elsewhere, and one of them not to be outdone, climbed upon the canopy, when the whole fell down and he was impaled by the spike on the top.)

Whose friend is the misguided Kurgāl? he is the striped snake who bit the Prophet: he is always coveting other people's property: he even quarrels for it with his mother. (*Kurgāl* is a term used among the Jāts of the plains for the Brāhūis. It is possibly a corruption of *Kurd-gal, i.e.* Kurd folk. The last line refers to the tribal custom by which Brāhūi women are excluded from inheritance.) If you have never seen ignorant hobgoblins and mountain-imps, come and look at the Brāhūi. What people are these? their *good* is evil. (A play upon the Brāhūi word *Sharr*, which means good in Brāhūi but evil in Arabic.) The Brāhūis and self-will. The Brāhūis are the tail of a dog.

A Mengal's roast. (The Mengals eat half-cooked meat and this expression is used of any immature plan.)

Man, are you a Nichāri? You may not win, but you will not lose. (Slimness.)

One asked a jackass: "Have you any relations?" It replied: "The Sassoli boasts of being my cousin." (Ignorance.)

Talk of loans in Zahri: and the dead will rise. You a Zarakzāi, and I a Zarakzāi: who will light the fire?

A Meman will be faithless though he read seventy *Qurāns*. (Meman is the local name of the Khojas.)

When the Lori gets up, he says: "O God, give me a funeral or wedding to-day." (The Loris perform duties connected with these ceremonies.)

The face of a Mullā but heart of a butcher. The Miyān's (Mahomedan zamindār) whole stock of wealth is a mat and a tooth brush. Even if the Meman (Mahomedan shopkeeper) goes to Mecca for pilgrimage he will steal a pair of scales and weights. When the Meman becomes a lunatic, he throws his clothes on his own relations. The Miyān is fit for the grave and the *bībi*, his wife, is fit for the bridal bed. The Khatija enjoys the earnings, her daughter bears the blows. (Sale of girls among Mahomedans.) The Jāt's (Mahomedan cultivator's) age is 2½ *kamlis* or blankets. (Measured by the time it takes him to change his blanket—dirty habits.) If the Jāt peasant is educated, heaven will be in a fix.

The Fakīr pockets the alms and the monkey gets but blows. The degenerate Moghul beats the ladies of his harem. When the Moghuls come the Persian language is forgotten. (The local people do not speak Persian in their presence because they cannot speak it pure.)

A Musalmān takes time to bathe and a Hindu takes time to eat his dinner.

A Meman and a fish go against the stream. Miyān and Mahādeo will never agree.

If Miyān and Bībi are willing what can the Qāzi do? When the Miyān broke his stick, the Bībi broke the jar of water. (When beaten she broke the pot out of revenge.) A Miyān's carriage! the yoke tied up with palm fibre: he will stop at the nearest grog-shop. A Miyān's friendship will last till he reaches your gate! Miyān returns from work and his Bībi combs his beard! Miyān dies, and the Masjid is lit up. Miyān licks the floor of the Masjid and the Pīr wants goats. Miyān licks the lamps in the Masjid and his wife wants dainties. Although Miyān falls his legs are up. A Miyān was not well and drank *bhang* (hemp). (Confusion worse confounded.) Miyān goes on striking and cuts down the corn. (Recklessness.) Miyān a pigmy, and his beard a foot long. Miyān a *seer*, but Bībi a *seer* and a quarter. (The gray mare the better horse.) A Miyān has killed a crow, and coming to the town he shouts out that he killed a tiger. The Miyān's mind after a prostitute and the Bībi's mind after the cooking pots. If the Miyān has to go to the north, he will say he goes to the south. Think him mad who tries to be wiser than the Miyān. The Miyān can beat his Bībi (wife) with shoes if he only has them on his feet. (Poverty and pride.)

The Miyān's mare went only as far as the boundary of the village. The Miyān's beard on fire, and the Bībi thinks he is warming himself. A Miyān's cat. (A poor and meek person.) The Miyān cannot get it, and the Bībi does not like it. (Sour grapes.) "What are you doing, oh Miyān?" "I have not a minute's leisure and yet I do not earn even a *pie*." "Why do you cry, Miyān?" "My wife died to-day." "Why do you laugh, Miyān?" "I got another wife to-day." "Get up, Miyān!" He will say, "Give me your hand (to raise me)." Miyān goes to Mecca, Bībi goes to Mālwa. Miyān a fop and Bībi does the dusting. A Miyān will live anyhow, but how will the Bībi live?

Every one strokes the Mullā's cow. The horse kicked him off, but the Mullā boasted of his riding.

PROVINCIAL CHARACTERISTICS.

Never make friends with a Deccani; he is as false as a latrine is filthy. Put not your faith in a three-cornered *pagri* (turban). (Gujarāt proverbs of the Marāthas.)

A Dravidian's nose-holding. (Circumlocution. A Dravidian is said to hold his nose for ceremonial purposes by putting his hand round the back of his neck.) A prosperous Telugu is no good to any one.

The fool of a Gujarāti, kick him first and then he may understand you (*cf.* the similar saying about the Chattīsgarhi cited above).

For houses hurdles of *madār;* for hedges heaps of withered thorn; millet for bread, horse peas for pulse; this is thy kingdom, Rāja of Mārwār. (Aimed at Mārwāri money-lenders who pretend to be great people in their own country.)

I have seen the land of Bengal where teeth are red and faces black. (Referring to the dark complexion of Bengalis and their supposed fondness for chewing betel.) If a Bengali is a man what is a devil? The Dacca Bengalis have not so much as an earthen pot between them. Bengal is the home of magic and the women are full of witchery. An Eastern donkey with a Western bray. (Aimed at the Bābus who affect European manners.) A hungry Bengali cries "Rice, rice!" Twelve Bengalis cannot cut off a goat's ear. (Gujarāt proverb of the weakness and cowardice of Bengalis.)

A *pagri* (turban) on his head and nakedness below, the Assamese wishes to lead the way. (The vanity of a pauper.) The worthless has three wives, the worthy one. (Undeserved luxury.)

COMPARISONS BETWEEN CASTES.

The Mullā, the Bhāt, the Brāhman, the Dom; these four were not born on giving day. When a Jāt is well off he kicks up a row; when a buffalo is gorged he refuses to plough; when a Khatri gets rich he still cringes; when a Brāhman has money he quarrels. A Jāt, a son-in-law, a nephew, a shepherd, and a goldsmith are always ungrateful. A Khatri woman brings forth sons always; a Brāhman woman only sometimes. (Possibly aimed at the practice of female infanticide imputed to the Khatris). Brāhmans are made to eat, Bhavaiyās to play and sing, Kolis to commit robbery, and widows to mourn. A meddlesome Brāhman gives advice; a guileless Baniya gives short weight. Brāhman and Jati; mother-in-law and daughter-in-law; wheat and the mill; a modest woman and a prostitute—none of these agree. You can rob a Brāhman but beware of a Grāsia. (He will show fight.) The field belongs to the Miyān, not to a Brāhman widow. The hungry Brāhman sets the village on fire; the hungry Koli (his accomplice) plunders the houses. The Kunbi died from seeing a ghost, the Brāhman from wind in the stomach, the goldsmith from bile. (The first is superstitious: the second over-eats himself; the third sits too long over his fire.) A Brāhman begs, a Kunbi ploughs; after all old things are best. Mahārudra (Siva in his terrible aspect) trembles at the sight of a black Brāhman and a fair Sūdra. A black Brāhman, a fair Sūdra, an undersized Musalmān, a *ghar-jamāi*, an adopted son—all birds of a feather. (A *ghar-jamāi* is a son-in-law who lives with his father-in-law and is supported by him.) A dark Brāhman, a fair Chūhra, a woman with a beard—these three are contrary to nature. Do not cross a river with a black Brāhman or a fair Chamār. Trust not a black Brāhman, nor a fair Holeya. (One of the lowest castes in Southern India supposed, like the Chandāls in Bengal, to be descended from Sūdra fathers and Brāhman mothers.) The Brāhman works for the *pinda* (rice cake offered to the dead), the Holeya works for drink.

A Brāhman met a barber; "God be with you" said the one, but the other showed his looking-glass. (Each expecting a fee for services rendered.) Laughing Brāhmans, coughing thieves, and illiterate Kāyasths are the destroyers of their race. There are three careless ones—the washerman, the barber, and the tailor. Pipe, tobacco, courtesans, the Gūjar and the Jāt, all are one as in the race from Father Jagannāth. (At the festival of Jagannāth there is no distinction of castes.) There is no escape from a Baniya's guile and a Jogi's curse. A Brāhman for minister, a Bhāt for favourite, and the Rāja's fate is sealed. Baniyas improve their property; Jāts ruin theirs; Doms, poets and Bhāts live by flattery. The Gūjar finds joy in the steppe; the mendicant in the *Dhāk* tree; the Brāhman in rice and milk. (The Gūjars are herdsmen; the *Dhāk* is a sacred tree; and Brāhmans are proverbially greedy.) Better a barren field than a Gūjar; a desert than a Mīna. The Brāhman is lord of the water; the Rājput lord of the land; the Kāyasth lord of the pen; and the Khatri lord of the back, *i.e.*, a coward. The youngest among Brāhmans, the eldest among Mukuvans (fishermen), are the drudges of the family.

The Chāsā (cultivator) goes to plough; the Brāhman goes to sleep. Loot the Baniya if you meet him, but let the Pathān go on his way (or you will catch a Tartar). Beware of these three—a goldsmith, a tailor, and a village clerk. The goldsmith steals gold and the tailor cloth; the poor carpenter has only a log to shape, and can steal nothing. The goldsmith's acid and the tailor's tag. (Proverb of delay; the one tells you that the ornament is ready, all but the cleaning with acid; the other that the clothes have been made, but the tags have to be sewn on.) The goldsmith, the tailor, the Baniya will cheat even their own father. The Teli knows all about oil seeds; the Shimpi (tailor) all about lies; the village watchman all about thieves; the Lingāyat all about everything.

Vellāla chief among cultivators; Kallār chief among thieves. Trust not a black Brāhman nor a fair Pariah. Like a Pariah and a Brāhman (oil and vinegar). The tricks of a goldsmith and a weaver are nothing to those of a washerman. The washerman knows who is poor in the village; the goldsmith knows whose ornaments are of pure gold. The goldsmith and the Chetty. (Both rascals.) Only an albino is fairer than a Khatri; only an adulterer is sharper than a Kāyasth. Qāzis, Kasbis, Kasāis, and Kāyasths—the four bad K's. Kāyasths, Khatris and cocks support their kin; Brāhmans, Doms, and Nāis destroy theirs. Qāzis, crows, and Kāyasths stand by their kindred. Ahīrs, Gareris (shepherds) and Pāsis (fowlers)—a poisonous crew. A Dhobi's stone and a potter's donkey; both get plenty of beating. The Rājput and the Jāt are like bows made of pestles; they will break but never bend. If a Tāmboli (betel-seller) does the oilman's work he will set the house on fire. The oilman's cheeks are smooth and shining; the grain parcher's burnt brown. Bābhans, dogs, and Bhāts are always at war with their kin. Seven Chamārs are not as mean as one Bābhan, and seven Bābhans are not as mean as one Noniyār Baniya. Only the Nāus (barbers) and the Kewats help their own caste; the others merely pretend. Oh King sneeze! let go the Brāhman and keep the Jati; and should you meet a Baniya never let him off. A Dhobi is better than a Kāyasth; a Sonār is better than a cheat; a dog is better than a deity; and a jackal better than a Pandit.

The Gareri got drunk when he saw the Ahīr in liquor. Ahīr, Dafāli, Dhobi, Dom—these are the four castes that sing. A prodigal Baniya, a weak King, a Baidya with an ignorant son, a silent Bhāt, an unclean harlot, these, saith Ghāg, will come to no good. There be three that dance in other people's houses—the Kāyasth, the Baidya, and the *dalāl.* (Profit by the misfortunes of others. The *dalāl* is the lawyer's tout who promotes litigation and flourishes exceedingly in modern India.) The Baniya can trade; others can only imitate. The oilman trades without capital; the grain parcher's stock is a broken pot. When the salt dealer's salt is upset he gains; when the oilman spills his oil he loses. (The salt picks up sand, the oil soaks into the ground.) The Baniya's speech is polished, the Kumhār's is rough, the Sikligar (cutler) is honest and the Chamār a rogue. Dine with a Brāhman and Jogi and let a Karār make the fourth. (The two former have a reputation as gourmets, the latter is said to be good company.) A Dom, a Brāhman, and a goat are of no use in time of need. A Māli wants clouds, a Dhobi sun, a slanderer will talk, and a thief will hold his tongue. In no man's land one makes friends with Gūjars and Gaddis.

Provoke not the Meo at his ferry or the Karār in his shop; if you beard the Jāt in his field he will break your head. When a buffalo is full she refuses oil-cake; when a Baniya is well off he gives time to his debtors; when a Jāt is prosperous he begins to quarrel; when your banker is in a bad way he fastens upon you.

Better have no friends at all than take up with an Afghān, a Kamboh or a rascally Kashmīri. The crow, the Kamboh and the Kalāl cherish their kin; the Jāt, the buffalo and the crocodile devour their kin. Kāyasths, birds, and pandits (Deccanis) befriend their kin; Baniyas, dogs and Brāhmans are hostile to their kin.

When the Jāt prospers he shuts up the path (by ploughing over it); when the Karār (money-lender) prospers, he shuts up the Jāt. Jāts, Bhāts, caterpillars and widows—all these should be kept hungry; if they eat their fill they do harm. Hope, dice, a courtesan, Thag, Thakar, Sonār, monkey, Turk and Kalāl—these nine are no good. Give me an Arāin for work, and give the Khatīk a cow. A cucumber is not a vegetable; a *king* (one-stringed guitar) is not a musical instrument; a Labāna is not a Hindu, and a Meo cannot be a friend.

Bribe a Kāyasth, feed a Brāhman, water paddy and betel, but kick a low caste man. You may know a good Kāyasth by his pen; a good Rājput by his moustache;

and a good Baidya by his searching medicine. A Turk wants toddy, a bullock wants grain, a Brāhman wants mangoes, and a Kāyasth wants an appointment. If you cannot ruin yourself by keeping a Brāhman servant, taking money from a Kasāi, or begetting too many daughters, you will do it by going to law with bigger men.

The Jāt, the Gūjar, the Ahīr and the Gola ; these four are much of a muchness. All castes are God's creatures, but three castes are ruthless—the Ahīr, the Baniya, the whore ; when they get a chance they have no shame.

When the tax collector is a Jāt, the money-lender a Brāhman, and the ruler of the land a Baniya, these are signs of God's wrath. A barber, a dog, and a hawk are useless when full ; a money-lender, a bullock, and a king are useless when empty. To the wine merchant early ; to the butcher late. (In the former case you get fresh toddy, in the latter you avoid yesterday's remnants which the butcher mixes up with his first sales on the next day.) The Māli waters the jasmine; the waterman looks for a well ; and the Pārsi priest peers round to see if a rich man is dead. Kāchhi is not a good caste, there is no virtue in a Māli, and the Lodha is a poor creature who ploughs with tears in his eyes. The Lodha is very hasty, the Kunbi a good farmer, the Brāhman a great liar who begs his bread from door to door. Four Lodhas and silly talk ; four Kāchhis and sensible talk. The three tufted ones (Mārwāris), the red-faced ones (Europeans), and the cactus plant cannot live without increasing. Mārwāris, crows, and Pārsi liquor shops you see wherever you go.

CASTE IN GENERAL.

A highborn man mourns the loss of his caste as he would the loss of his nose. The caste killeth and the caste maketh alive. (Referring to the effect of the decisions of caste tribunals.) When plates are interchanged. (When different castes intermarry ; proverb of the impossible.) Caste springs from actions not from birth. The Vaisyas and Sūdras must have come first and it was from them that Brāhmans and Kshatriyas were made.

Love laughs at caste distinctions. Let your love be as a Hindu wife ; with you in life and with you in death.

Having drunk water from his hands, it is foolish to ask about his caste. (Water is the most potent vehicle of ceremonial pollution. Moral—the least said the soonest mended.) When on a journey you should act like a Sūdra and take food from any one.

A low-caste man is like a musk rat; if you smell him you remember it. His father pounded parched rice ; his grandfather coriander seed. In old days men looked to caste, now they look to money. (Aimed at modern Indian match-making.)

As the ore is like the mine, so a child is like its caste. Scholars adorn a caste. As caste hates caste, so does one agnate hate another. A slipper in the mouth of caste cost money to all. (One man's offence dishonours the whole caste.) The speech fits the caste as the peg fits the hole. (Refined language is a sign of good caste.) Castes may differ, virtue is everywhere the same. Every uncle says that his caste is the best.

Though your caste is low, your crime is none the less. Nowadays money is caste. Half-castes are the scum of the earth.

"I have sold my limbs, not my caste." (Supposed to be said by a servant whose master has asked him to do something injurious to his caste.)

The Hindu gods have fled to Dwārka ; the Musalmān saints to Mecca ; under British rule the Dheds shove you about. (The Dheds are a low caste of Bombay whose touch is pollution.) Rākhāls and Chāsās handle the ammonite. (This and the preceding proverb refer to the decline of religion in modern times.) The Pandit reads his scriptures and the Mullā his Qurān ; men make a thousand shows, yet find not God. Spectacles for the blind, sweets for the sick, a Pārsi at a Hindu's table. (A Hindu cannot entertain a Pārsi.) Musalmāns go mad at *tābūts* (the miniature tombs carried in procession at the Muharram festival), women at marriages, Hindus at the *Holi*. To the Hindu Rām is dear, to the Musalmān Rahīm ; they hate with a deadly hatred, but know not the reason why. The Hindu bows down to stones (idols), the Musalmān worships saints ; but the Pārsi's religion is pure as Ganges water. (Pārsi proverb of the freedom of their religion from the stain of idolatry.) A superstitious Pārsi woman offers a cocoanut at the Holi. (Illustrating the common tendency to observe other people's festivals.) An ass is unclean ; a *chotliwālā* is no friend. (Pārsi proverb : *chotli* is the Gujarāti name for the scalp-lock worn by Hindus.) A Musalmān takes time to bathe ; a Hindu takes time to eat (Muhammadan saying).

APPENDIX II

MAPS OF CASTES

NOTE.—In these Maps the four Sub-Provinces of Bengal have been shown separately, and Sind has been dealt with apart from the rest of the Bombay Presidency.

[These Maps have not been prepared for the Census of 1911. They have been reprinted in the present edition, as, with some minor differences, they represent the caste distribution as it prevails at present.]

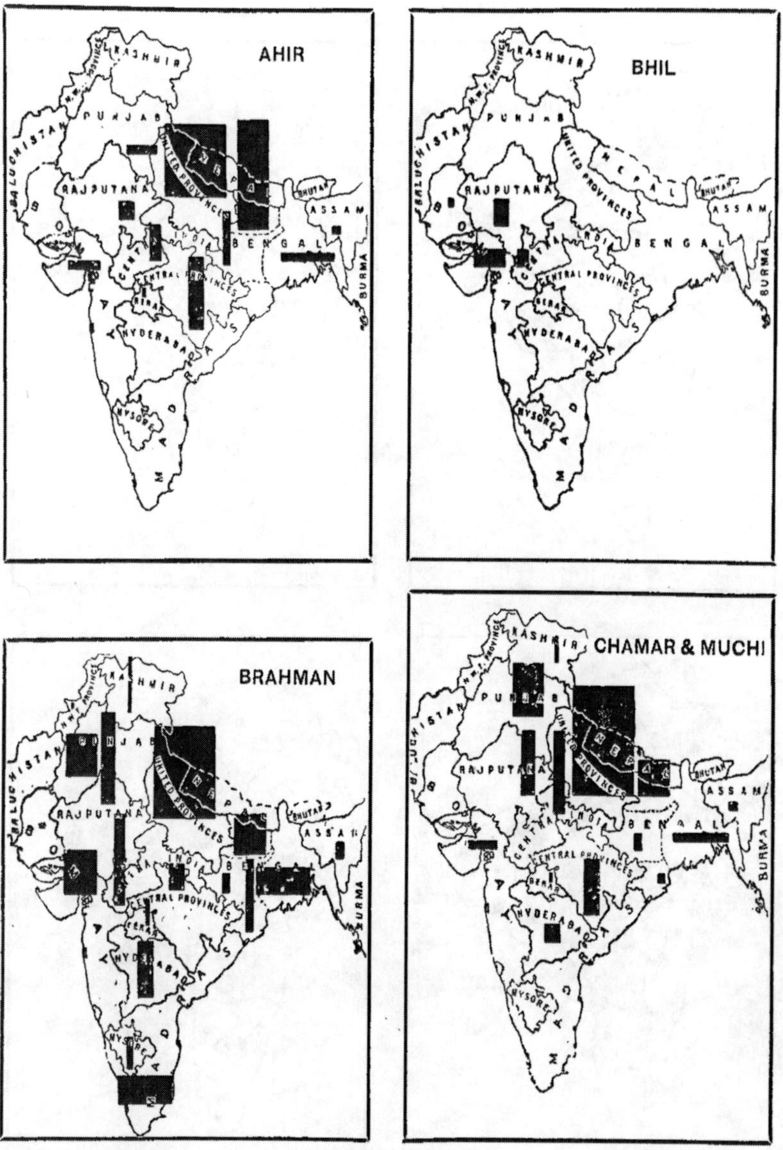

THE AREA OF EACH RECTANGLE SHOWS THE STRENGTH OF THE CASTE IN EACH PROVINCE ■ 300,000

THE BASE OF EACH RECTANGLE INDICATES THE POPULATION OF THE PROVINCE.................. 0 MILLION, 10, 20, 30

THE HEIGHT SHOWS THE PROPORTION WHICH THE CASTE BEARS TO THE POPULATION OF THE PROVINCE 5 P.C., 3 " ", 1 " ", 0 " "

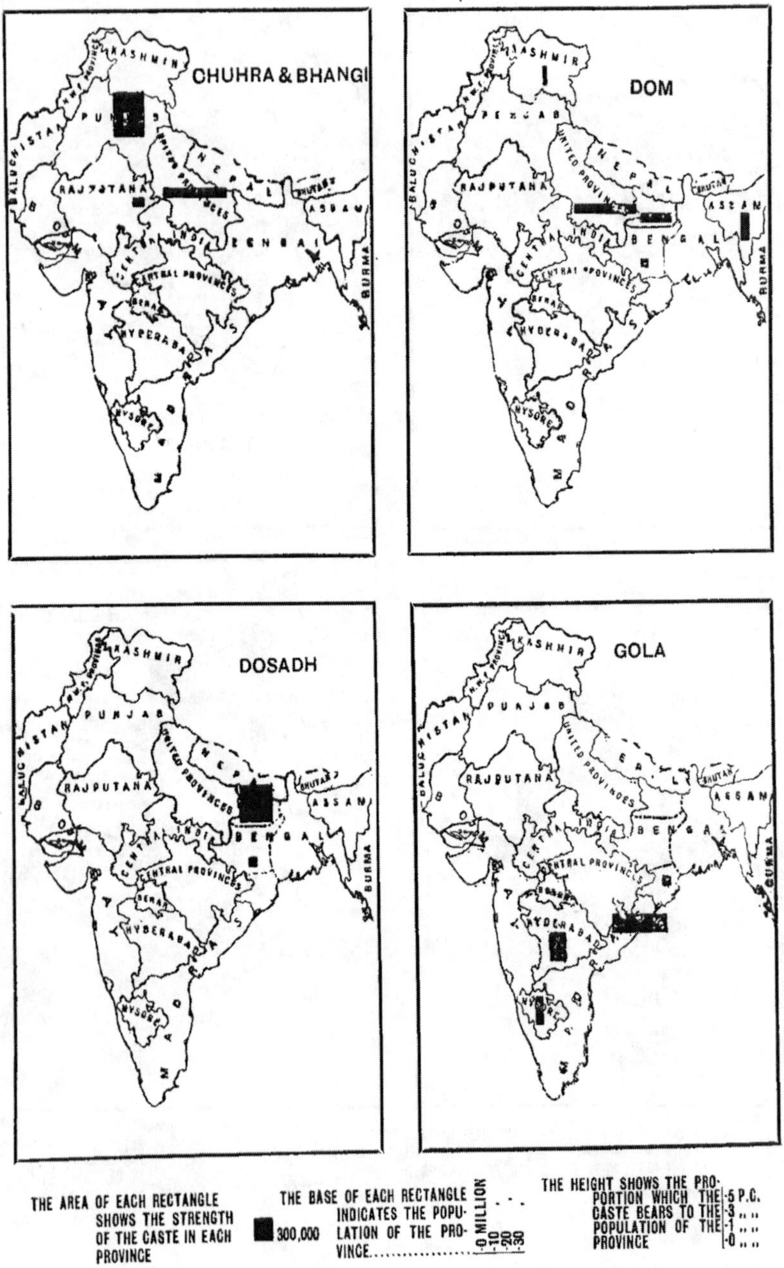
CHUHRA & BHANGI
DOM
DOSADH
GOLA
KASHMIR
PUNJAB
BALUCHISTAN
RAJPUTANA
NEPAL
BHUTAN
ASSAM
UNITED PROVINCES
BENGAL
CENTRAL INDIA
CENTRAL PROVINCES
BURMA
BERAR
HYDERABAD
MYSORE
MADRAS
BOMBAY
THE AREA OF EACH RECTANGLE SHOWS THE STRENGTH OF THE CASTE IN EACH PROVINCE
300,000
THE BASE OF EACH RECTANGLE INDICATES THE POPULATION OF THE PROVINCE
0 MILLION
10
20
30
THE HEIGHT SHOWS THE PROPORTION WHICH THE CASTE BEARS TO THE POPULATION OF THE PROVINCE
·5 P.C.
·3 „ „
·1 „ „
·0 „ „

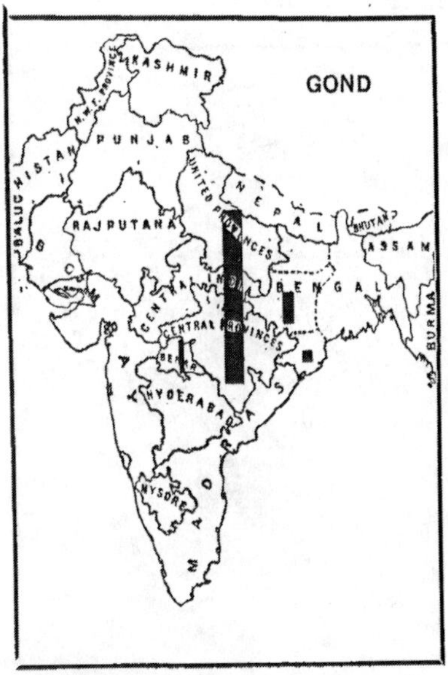

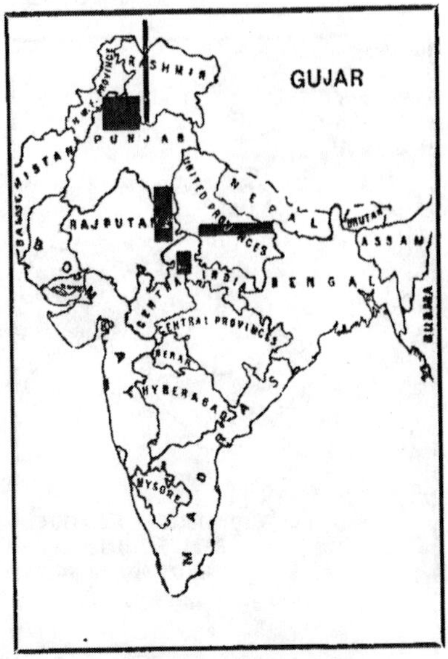

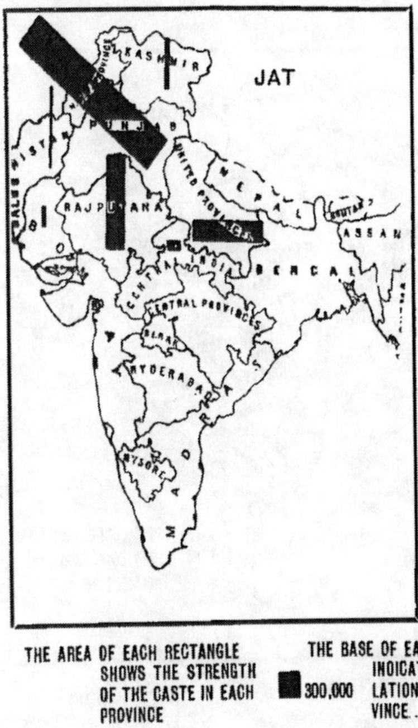

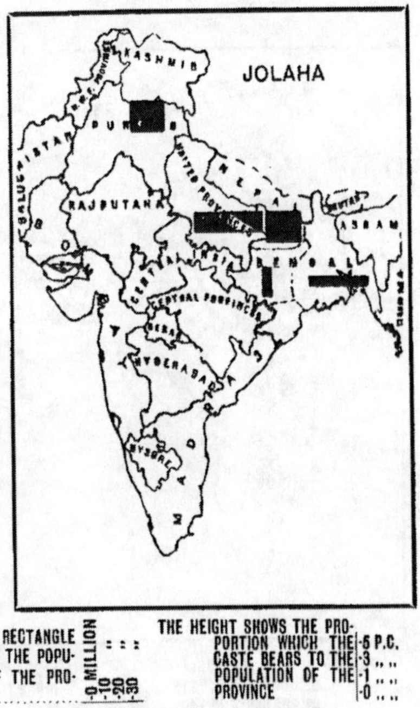

THE AREA OF EACH RECTANGLE SHOWS THE STRENGTH OF THE CASTE IN EACH PROVINCE ■ 300,000

THE BASE OF EACH RECTANGLE INDICATES THE POPULATION OF THE PROVINCE: 0 MILLION, 10, 20, 30

THE HEIGHT SHOWS THE PROPORTION WHICH THE CASTE BEARS TO THE POPULATION OF THE PROVINCE: 5 P.C., 3 " ", 1 " ", 0 " "

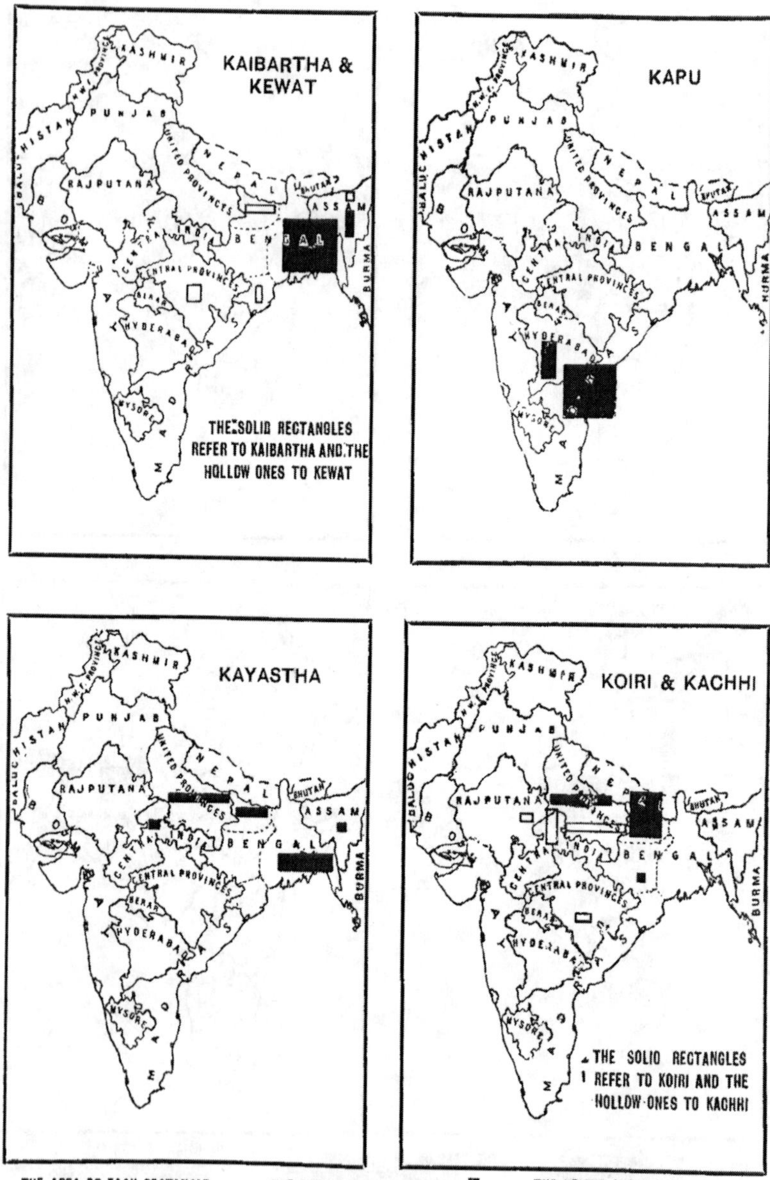

THE AREA OF EACH RECTANGLE SHOWS THE STRENGTH OF THE CASTE IN EACH PROVINCE ■ 300,000

THE BASE OF EACH RECTANGLE INDICATES THE POPULATION OF THE PROVINCE .... 0 10 20 30 MILLION

THE HEIGHT SHOWS THE PROPORTION WHICH THE CASTE BEARS TO THE POPULATION OF THE PROVINCE 5 P.C. 3 " " 1 " " 0 " "

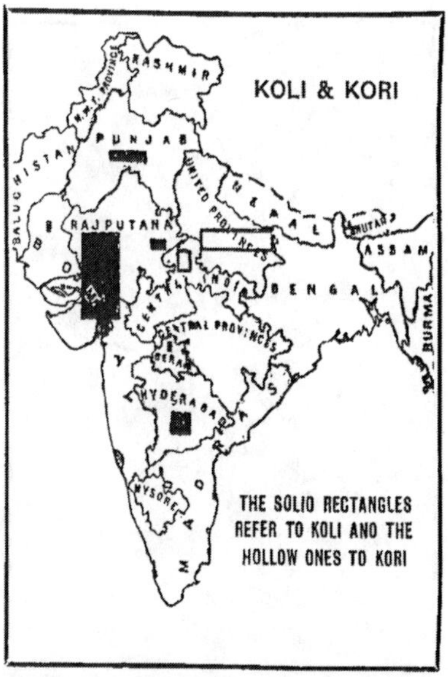

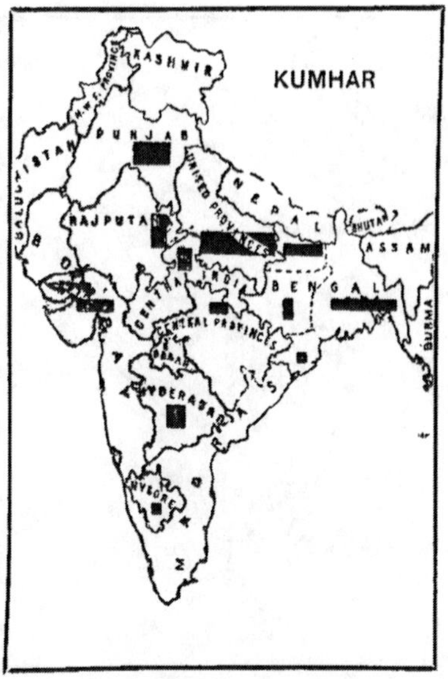

THE AREA OF EACH RECTANGLE SHOWS THE STRENGTH OF THE CASTE IN EACH PROVINCE ■ 300,000

THE BASE OF EACH RECTANGLE INDICATES THE POPULATION OF THE PROVINCE.................. ·0 MILLION ·10 ·20 ·30

THE HEIGHT SHOWS THE PROPORTION WHICH THE CASTE BEARS TO THE POPULATION OF THE PROVINCE ·5 P.C ·3 ,, ,, ·1 ,, ,, ·0 ,, ,,

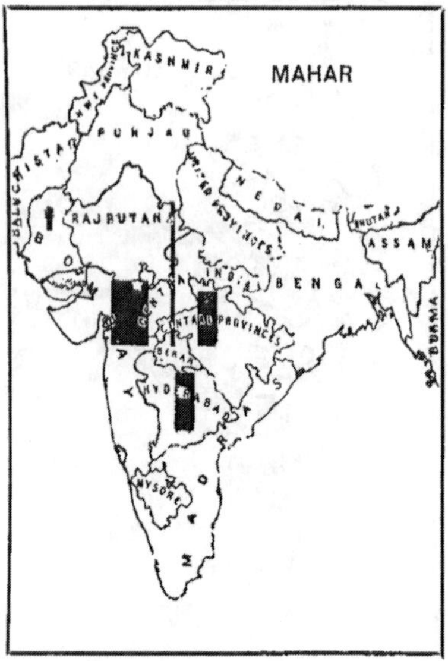

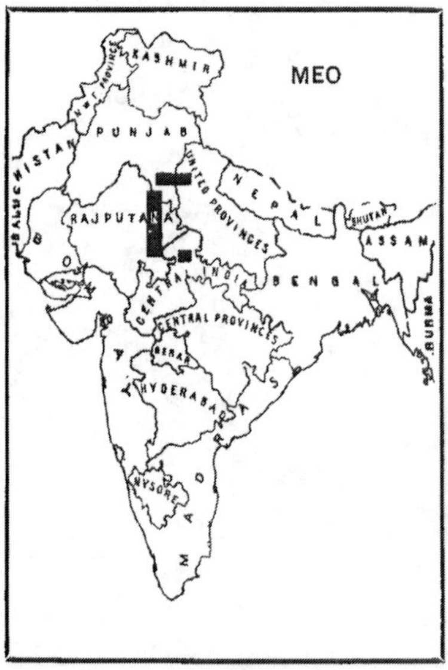

THE AREA OF EACH RECTANGLE SHOWS THE STRENGTH OF THE CASTE IN EACH PROVINCE ■ 300,000

THE BASE OF EACH RECTANGLE INDICATES THE POPULATION OF THE PROVINCE .... 0 MILLION · 10 · 20 · 30

THE HEIGHT SHOWS THE PROPORTION WHICH THE CASTE BEARS TO THE POPULATION OF THE PROVINCE ·5 P.C. ·3 „ „ ·1 „ „ ·0 „ „

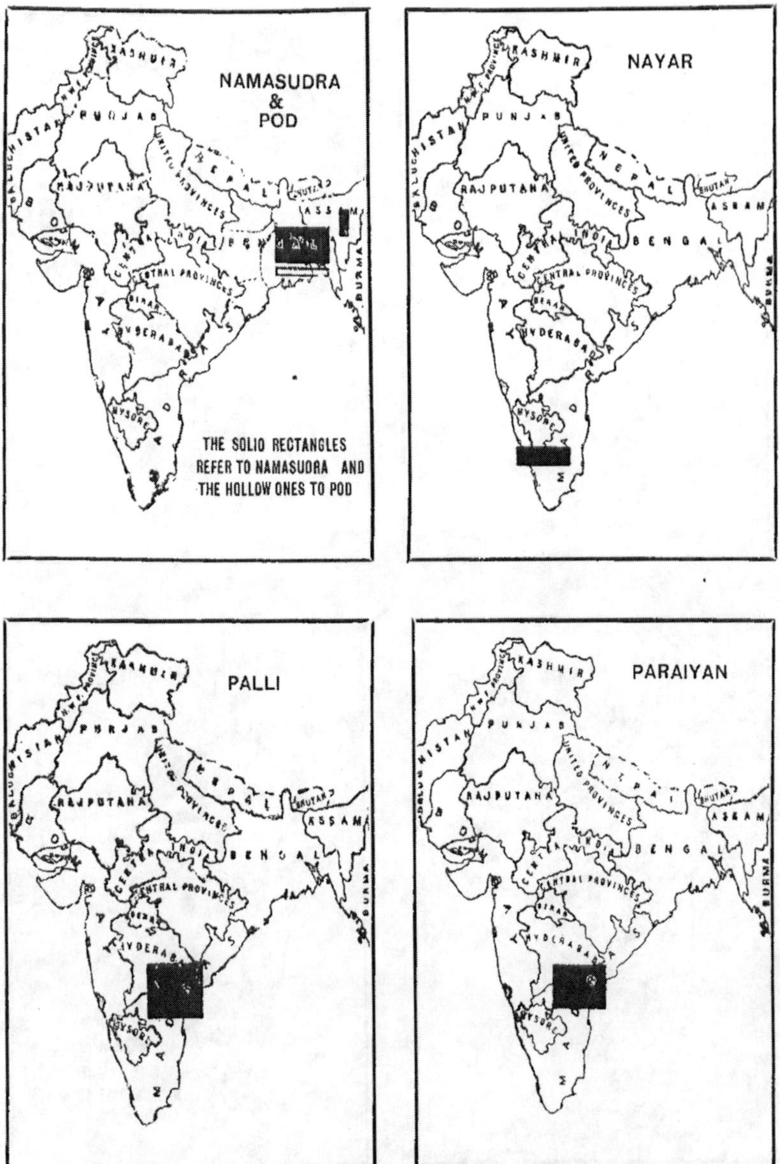

THE AREA OF EACH RECTANGLE SHOWS THE STRENGTH OF THE CASTE IN EACH PROVINCE ■ 300,000

THE BASE OF EACH RECTANGLE INDICATES THE POPULATION OF THE PROVINCE .... 0 MILLION, 10 ,, 20 ,, 30 ,,

THE HEIGHT SHOWS THE PROPORTION WHICH THE CASTE BEARS TO THE POPULATION OF THE PROVINCE 5 P.C., 3 ,, ,, 1 ,, ,, 0 ,, ,,

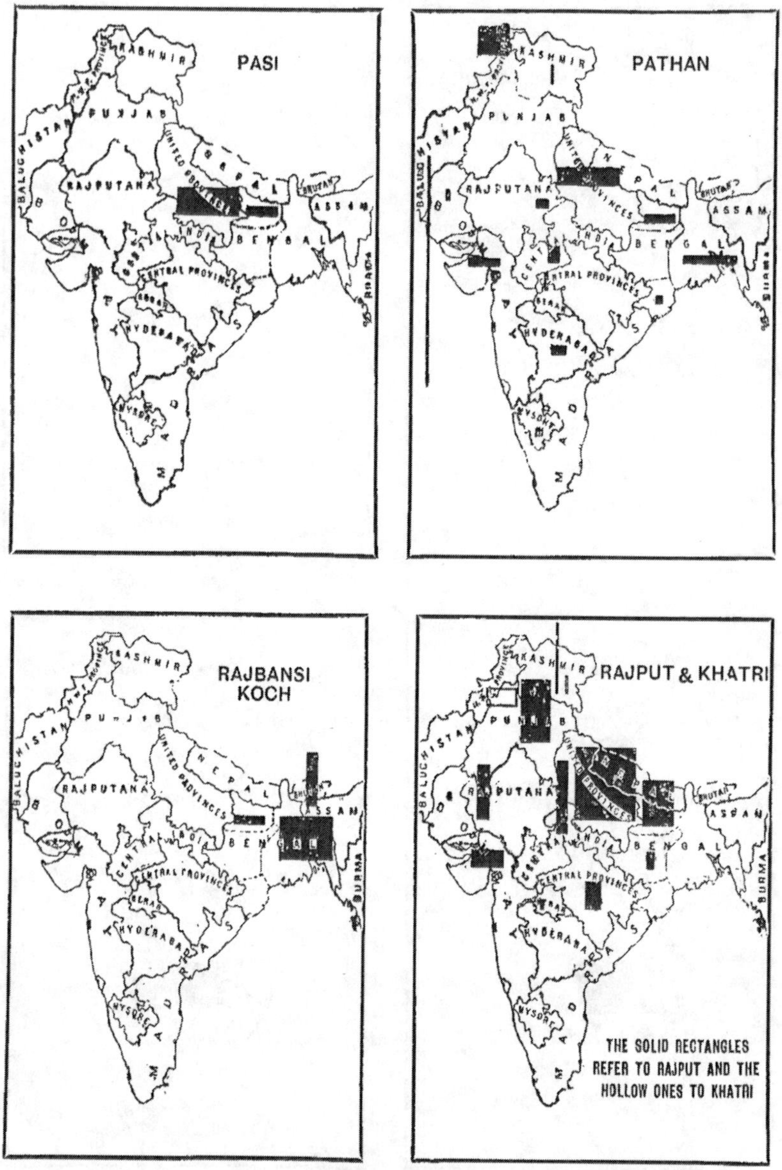

THE AREA OF EACH RECTANGLE SHOWS THE STRENGTH OF THE CASTE IN EACH PROVINCE ■ 300,000

THE BASE OF EACH RECTANGLE INDICATES THE POPULATION OF THE PROVINCE .... 0 MILLION, 10, 20, 30

THE HEIGHT SHOWS THE PROPORTION WHICH THE CASTE BEARS TO THE POPULATION OF THE PROVINCE: 5 P.C., 3 ,, ,,, 1 ,, ,,, 0 ,, ,,

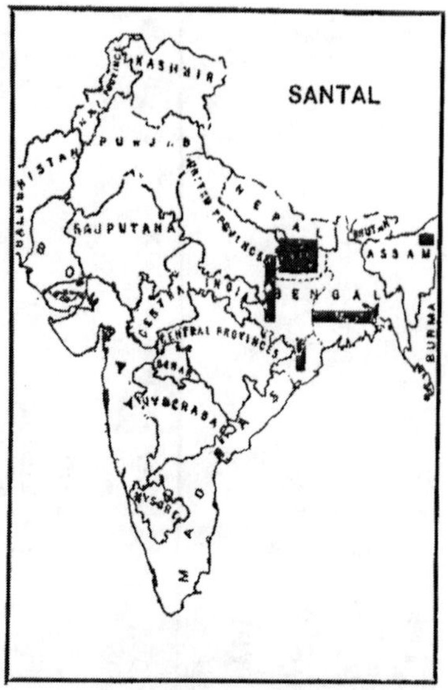

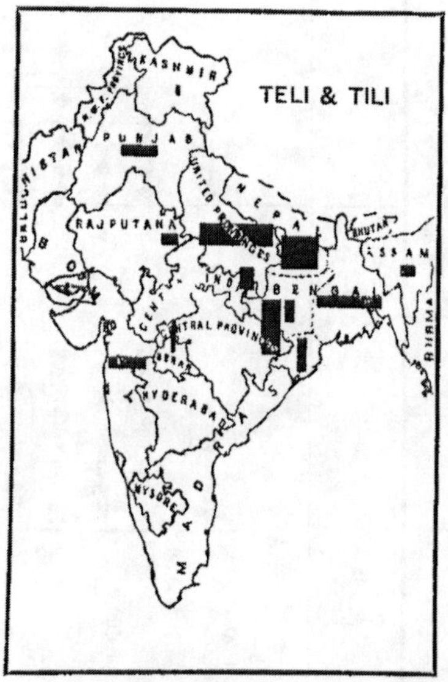

THE AREA OF EACH RECTANGLE SHOWS THE STRENGTH OF THE CASTE IN EACH PROVINCE ■ 300,000

THE BASE OF EACH RECTANGLE INDICATES THE POPULATION OF THE PROVINCE........ 0 MILLION, 10, 20, 30

THE HEIGHT SHOWS THE PROPORTION WHICH THE CASTE BEARS TO THE POPULATION OF THE PROVINCE 5 P.C., 3 " ", 1 " ", 0 " "

APPENDIX III

ANTHROPOMETRIC DATA

SERIATIONS.

TURKO-IRANIAN TYPE.

Type Specimen: Jāt.

PROPORTIONS OF HEAD. (Cephalic Index.)		PROPORTIONS OF NOSE. (Nasal Index.)		RELATIVE PROMINENCE OF ROOT OF NOSE. (Orbito-Nasal Index.)	
Average	79·8	Average	63·1	Average	125
Maximum	92	Maximum	84	Maximum	143
Minimum	70	Minimum	42	Minimum	104
Range	22	Range	42	Range	39

Indices.		Number of subjects.	Percentage on number of subjects.
HEAD.			
VERY LONG HEADS (Hyper-dolicho-cephalic).	Under 70	2	2
LONG HEADS (Dolicho-cephalic).	70 and under 72·5	4	4
	72·5 and under 75	6	6
MEDIUM HEADS (Meso-cephalic).	75 and under 77·5	13	13
	77·5 and under 80	17	17

Broad heads (Brachy-cephalic).	80 and under 82·5 .	32
	82·5 and under 85 .	18
	85 and under 87·5 .	6
	87·5 and over . .	2
NOSE.		
Fine noses (Leptorrhine).	Under 50 . . .	2
	50 and under 55 .	8
	55 and under 60 .	21
	60 and under 65 .	32
	65 and under 70 .	17
Medium noses (Mesorrhine).	70 and under 75 .	15
	75 and under 80 .	2
	80 and under 85 .	3
ROOT OF NOSE.		
Platy-opic (Flat).	Under 110 . .	2
Pro-opic (Prominent).	113 and under 116	2
	116 and under 119 .	6
	119 and under 122 .	11
	122 and under 125 .	24
	125 and under 128 .	30
	128 and over . .	25

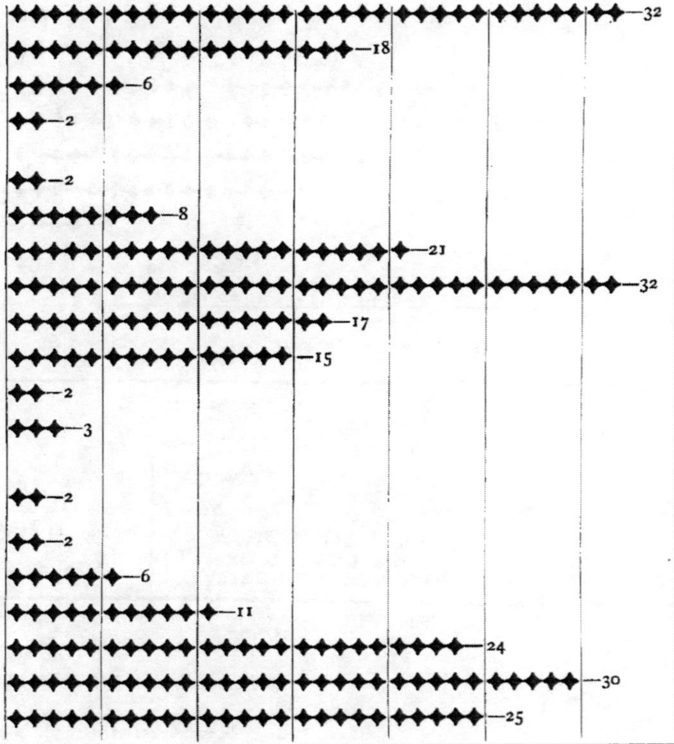

SERIATIONS.

TURKO-IRANIAN TYPE.

Type Specimen: Baloch.

Consisting of Marri, Bugti and Rind, etc., from the country round Sibi.

PROPORTIONS OF HEAD. (Cephalic Index.)		PROPORTIONS OF NOSE. (Nasal Index.)		RELATIVE PROMINENCE OF ROOT OF NOSE. (Orbito-Nasal Index.)		STATURE.	C.M.
Average	80·4	Average	72·5	Average	118·4	Average	167·8
Maximum	90	Maximum	94	Maximum	128	Maximum	180·5
Minimum	70	Minimum	57	Minimum	111	Minimum	150·6
Range	20	Range	37	Range	17	Range	34·4

Indices.		Number of subjects.	Percentage on number of subjects.
HEAD.			
LONG HEADS (Dolicho-cephalic).	70 and under 72·5	4	1
	72·5 and under 75	12	4
MEDIUM HEADS (Meso-cephalic).	75 and under 77·5	38	14
	77·5 and under 80	62	23
BROAD HEADS (Brachy-cephalic).	80 and under 82·5	70	26
	82·5 and under 85	59	22
	85 and under 87·5	21	8
	87·5 and under 90	5	2

NOSE.			
FINE NOSES (Leptorrhine).	Under 60	5	2
	60 and under 65	41	15
	65 and under 70	57	21
MEDIUM NOSES (Mesorrhine).	70 and under 75	76	28
	75 and under 80	58	21
	80 and under 85	32	9
BROAD NOSES (Platyrrhine).	85 and over	11	4
ROOT OF NOSE.			
MESOPIC (Medium).	110 and under 113	12	5
PRO-OPIC (Prominent).	113 and under 116	56	21
	116 and under 119	93	34
	119 and under 122	74	27
	122 and over	36	13
STATURE. Centimetres.			
SHORT	Under 160 5′ 3″	29	11
BELOW MEAN	160 and under 165 5′ 3″—5′ 5″	50	18
ABOVE MEAN	165 and under 170 5′ 5″—5′ 7″	94	35
TALL	170 and under 175 5′ 7″—5′ 9″	64	24
	175 and over 5′ 9″	34	12

SERIATIONS.

TURKO-IRANIAN TYPE.

Type Specimen: *Mir Jats.*

PROPORTIONS OF HEAD. (Cephalic Index.)		PROPORTIONS OF NOSE. (Nasal Index.)		RELATIVE PROMINENCE OF ROOT OF NOSE. (Orbito-Nasal Index.)	
Average	81·2	Average	61·7	Average	124·6
Maximum	96	Maximum	75	Maximum	137
Minimum	73	Minimum	40	Minimum	111
Range	23	Range	35	Range	26

Indices.		Number of subjects.	Percentage on number of subjects.
HEAD.			
LONG HEADS (Dolicho-cephalic).	72·5 and under 75	5	10
MEDIUM HEADS (Meso-cephalic).	75 and under 77·5	6	12
	77·5 and under 80	8	17

Broad heads (Brachy-cephalic).	80 and under 82·5 .	9	19
	82·5 and under 85 .	9	19
	85 and under 87·5 .	7	15
	87·5 and under 90 .	2	4
	90 and over . .	2	4
NOSE.			
Fine noses (Leptorrhine).	Under 50 . . .	2	4
	50 and under 55 .	4	8
	55 and under 60 .	11	23
	60 and under 65 .	15	32
	65 and under 70 .	8	17
Medium noses (Mesorrhine).	70 and under 75 .	5	10
	75 and under 80 .	3	6
ROOT OF NOSE.			
Mesopic (Medium) .	110 and under 113 .	1	2
Pro-opic (Prominent).	113 and under 116 .	1	2
	116 and under 119 .	2	4
	119 and under 122 .	11	23
	122 and under 125 .	16	33
	125 and under 128 .	6	13
	128 and over . .	11	23

SERIATIONS.

TURKO-IRANIAN TYPE.

Type Specimen: Dehwar.

PROPORTIONS OF HEAD. (Cephalic Index.)		PROPORTIONS OF NOSE. (Nasal Index.)		RELATIVE PROMINENCE OF ROOT OF NOSE. (Orbito-Nasal Index.)		STATURE.	C.M.
Average	81·7	Average	74·3	Average	118	Average	164·2
Maximum	91	Maximum	98	Maximum	130	Maximum	180·8
Minimum	72	Minimum	60	Minimum	109	Minimum	148·8
Range	19	Range	38	Range	21	Range	32

Indices.		Number of subjects.	Percentage on number of subjects.
	HEAD.		
LONG HEADS (Dolicho-cephalic).	Under 75	8	4
MEDIUM HEADS (Meso-cephalic).	75 and under 77·5	22	11
	77·5 and under 80	30	15
BROAD HEADS (Brachy-cephalic).	80 and under 82·5	50	25
	82·5 and under 85	54	27
	85 and under 87·5	26	13
	87·5 and under 90	8	4
	90 and over	2	1

NOSE.			
FINE NOSES (Leptorrhine).	Under 65	22	11
	65 and under 70	32	16
MEDIUM NOSES (Mesorrhine).	70 and under 75	50	25
	75 and under 80	44	22
	80 and under 85	40	20
BROAD NOSES (Platyrrhine).	85 and over	12	6
ROOT OF NOSE.			
PLATY-OPIC (Flat).	Under 110	2	1
MES-OPIC (Medium).	110 and under 113	16	8
PRO-OPIC (Prominent).	113 and under 116	36	18
	116 and under 119	70	35
	119 and under 122	56	28
	122 and over	20	10
STATURE. Centimetres.			
SHORT	Under 160 5′ 3″	34	17
BELOW MEAN	160 and under 165 5′ 3″—5′ 5″	76	38
ABOVE MEAN	165 and under 170 5′ 5″—5′ 7″	62	31
TALL	170 and over 5′ 7″	28	14

SERIATIONS.

TURKO-IRANIAN TYPE.

Type Specimen: Kakar.

PROPORTIONS OF HEAD. (Cephalic Index.)		PROPORTIONS OF NOSE. (Nasal Index.)		RELATIVE PROMINENCE OF ROOT OF NOSE. (Orbito-Nasal Index.)		STATURE.	C.M.
Average	81·9	Average	69·6	Average	116·6	Average	168
Maximum	90	Maximum	88	Maximum	124	Maximum	188·2
Minimum	74	Minimum	60	Minimum	107	Minimum	157·0
Range	16	Range	28	Range	17	Range	31·2

Indices.		Number of subjects.	Percentage on number of subjects.
HEAD.			
Long heads (Dolicho-cephalic).	Under 75	2	2
Medium heads (Meso-cephalic).	75 and under 77·5	6	5
	77·5 and under 80	18	16
Broad heads (Brachy-cephalic).	80 and under 82·5	40	36
	82·5 and under 85	22	20
	85 and under 87·5	19	17
	87·5 and over	5	4

	NOSE.		
FINE NOSES (Leptorrhine).	Under 65	22	20
	65 and under 70	38	34
MEDIUM NOSES (Mesorrhine).	70 and under 75	33	29
	75 and under 80	10	9
	80 and under 85	8	7
BROAD NOSES (Platyrrhine).	85 and over	1	1
	ROOT OF NOSE.		
PLATY-OPIC (Flat).	Under 110	2	2
MES-OPIC (Medium).	110 and under 113	13	12
PRO-OPIC (Prominent).	113 and under 116	33	29
	116 and under 119	36	32
	119 and under 122	20	18
	122 and over	8	7
	STATURE. (Centimetres.)		
SHORT	Under 160 5′ 3″	9	8
BELOW MEAN	160 and under 165 5′ 3″—5′ 5″	25	23
ABOVE MEAN	165 and under 170 5′ 5″—5′ 7″	34	30
TALL	170 and under 175 5′ 7″—5′ 9″	35	31
	175 and over 5′ 9″	9	8

SERIATIONS.

TURKO-IRANIAN TYPE.

Type Specimen: *Med.*

PROPORTIONS OF HEAD. (Cephalic Index.)		PROPORTIONS OF NOSE. (Nasal Index.)		RELATIVE PROMINENCE OF ROOT OF NOSE. (Orbito-Nasal Index.)	
Average	82·0	Average	68·1	Average	127·3
Maximum	92	Maximum	92	Maximum	140
Minimum	72	Minimum	53	Minimum	113
Range	20	Range	39	Range	27

Indices.		Number of subjects.	Percentage on number of subjects.
HEAD.			
LONG HEADS (Dolicho-cephalic).	70 and under 72·5	1	1
	72·5 and under 75	1	1
MEDIUM HEADS (Meso-cephalic).	75 and under 77·5	5	6
	77·5 and under 80	13	16
BROAD HEADS (Brachy-cephalic).	80 and under 82·5	25	32
	82·5 and under 85	18	23
	85 and under 87·5	10	13
	87·5 and over	6	8

NOSE.

Class	Index	No.	Diagram
Fine noses (Leptorrhine).	50 and under 55	6	7
	55 and under 60	3	4
	60 and under 65	11	14
	65 and under 70	24	30
Medium noses (Mesorrhine).	70 and under 75	19	24
	75 and under 80	12	15
	80 and under 85	2	3
Broad noses (Platyrrhine).	85 and over	2	3

ROOT OF NOSE.

Class	Index	No.	Diagram
Mes-opic (Medium).	110 and under 113	1	2
Pro-opic (Prominent).	116 and under 119	1	2
	119 and under 122	8	14
	122 and under 125	8	14
	125 and under 128	14	25
	128 and under 131	10	17
	131 and under 134	9	16
	134 and under 137	4	7
	137 and over	2	3

SERIATIONS.

INDO-ARYAN TYPE.

Type Specimen: Rājput.

PROPORTIONS OF HEAD. (Cephalic Index.)		PROPORTIONS OF NOSE. (Nasal Index.)		RELATIVE PROMINENCE OF ROOT OF NOSE. (Orbito-Nasal Index.)		STATURE.	C.M.
Average	72·4	Average	71·6	Average	117·9	Average	174·8
Maximum	81	Maximum	91	Maximum	129	Maximum	192·4
Minimum	64	Minimum	53	Minimum	107	Minimum	165·4
Range	17	Range	38	Range	22	Range	27

Iodices.		Number of subjects.	Percentage on number of subjects.
HEAD.			
VERY LONG HEADS (Hyper-dolicho-cephalic).	Under 70	71	17
LONG HEADS (Dolicho-cephalic).	70 and under 72·5	151	36
	72·5 and under 75	108	26
MEDIUM HEADS (Meso-cephalic).	75 and under 77·5	65	15
	77·5 and under 80	19	5
BROAD HEADS (Brachy-cephalic).	80 and over	6	1

NOSE.			
FINE NOSES (Leptorrhine).	Under 60	11	3
	60 and under 65	39	9
	65 and under 70	98	23
MEDIUM NOSES (Mesorrhine).	70 and under 75	136	32
	75 and under 80	79	19
	80 and under 85	44	11
BROAD NOSES (Platyrrhine).	85 and over	13	3
ROOT OF NOSE.			
PLATY-OPIC (Flat).	Under 110	2	1
MES-OPIC (Medium).	110 and under 113	26	6
PRO-OPIC (Prominent).	113 and under 116	90	22
	116 and under 119	144	34
	119 and under 122	102	24
	122 and over	56	13
STATURE.—Centimetres.			
ABOVE MEAN	165 and under 170 5′ 5″—5′ 7″	58	14
TALL	170 and under 175 5′ 7″—5′ 9″	159	38
	175 and under 180 5′ 9″—5′ 11″	156	37
	180 and over 5′ 11″ and over	47	11

SERIATIONS.

INDO-ARYAN TYPE.

Type Specimen: Chuhra.

PROPORTIONS OF HEAD. (Cephalic Index.)		PROPORTIONS OF NOSE. (Nasal Index.)		RELATIVE PROMINENCE OF ROOT OF NOSE. (Orbito-Nasal Index.)		STATURE.	C.M.
Average	73·4	Average	75·2	Average	115·3	Average	166·6
Maximum	82	Maximum	94	Maximum	123	Maximum	180·3
Minimum	68	Minimum	60	Minimum	108	Minimum	152·4
Range	14	Range	34	Range	15	Range	27·9

Indices.		Number of subjects.	Percentage on number of subjects.
HEAD.			
VERY LONG HEADS (Hyper-dolicho-cephalic).	Under 70	8	10
LONG HEADS Dolicho-cephalic).	70 and under 72·5	0	25
	72·5 and under 75	29	36
MEDIUM HEADS (Meso-cephalic.)	75 and under 77·5	17	22
	77·5 and under 80	5	6
BROAD HEADS (Brachy-cephalic).	80 and over	1	1

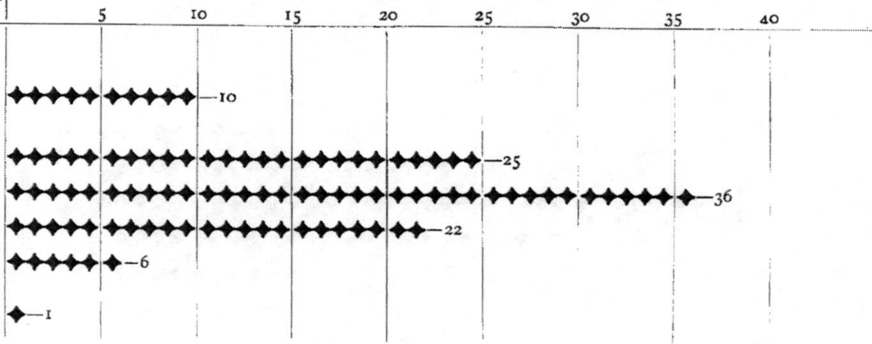

NOSE.			
FINE NOSES (Leptorrhine).	Under 60	1	1
	60 and under 65	3	4
	65 and under 70	7	9
MEDIUM NOSES (Mesorrhine).	70 and under 75	34	42
	75 and under 80	12	15
	80 and under 85	20	25
BROAD NOSES (Platyrrhine).	85 and over	3	4
ROOT OF NOSE.			
PLATY-OPIC (Flat).	Under 110	3	4
MES-OPIC (Medium).	110 and under 113	17	21
PRO-OPIC (Prominent).	113 and under 116	26	33
	116 and under 119	26	33
	119 and under 122	7	8
	122 and over	1	1
STATURE. Centimetres.			
SHORT	Under 160 / 5′ 3″	8	10
BELOW MEAN	160 and under 165 / 5′ 3″—5′ 5″	17	30
ABOVE MEAN	165 and under 170 / 5′ 5″—5′ 7″	24	31
TALL	170 and under 175 / 5′ 7″—5′ 9″	25	21
	175 and under 180 / 5′ 9″—5′ 11″	4	5
	180 and over / 5′ 11″	2	3

SERIATIONS.

SCYTHO-DRAVIDIAN TYPE.

Type Specimen: Nagar Brahman.

PROPORTIONS OF HEAD. (Cephalic Index.)		PROPORTIONS OF NOSE. (Nasal Index.)		RELATIVE PROMINENCE OF ROOT OF NOSE. (Orbito-Nasal Index.)		STATURE.	C.M.
Average	79·7	Average	73·1	Average	116·7	Average	164·3
Maximum	90	Maximum	90	Maximum	124	Maximum	178·8
Minimum	71	Minimum	57	Minimum	108	Minimum	151·3
Range	19	Range	33	Range	16	Range	27·5

Indices.		Number of subjects.
HEAD		
LONG HEADS (Dolicho-cephalic).	70 and under 72·5	4
	72·5 and under 75	11
MEDIUM HEADS (Meso-cephalic).	75 and under 77·5	13
	77·5 and under 80	26
BROAD HEADS (Brachy-cephalic).	80 and under 82·5	22
	82·5 and under 85	10
	85 and under 87·5	11
	87·5 and over	3
NOSE.		
FINE NOSES (Leptorrhine).	under 65	13
	65 and under 70	20

Percentage on number of subjects.

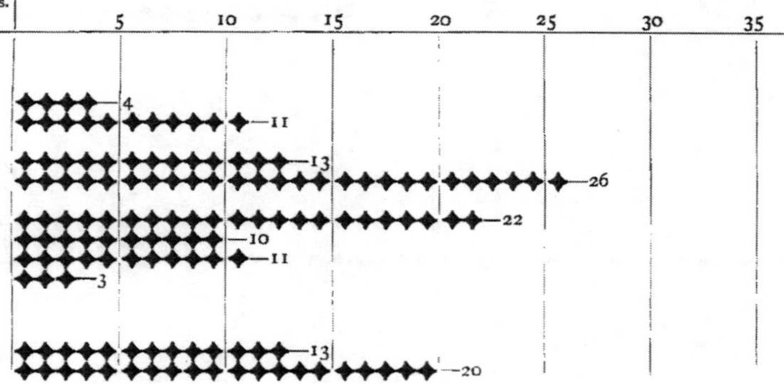

MEDIUM NOSES (Mesorrhine).	70 and under 75	25	
	75 and under 80	16	
	80 and under 85	20	
BROAD NOSES (Platyrrhine).	85 and over	6	
ROOT OF NOSE.			
PLATY-OPIC (Flat).	107 and under 110	2	
MES-OPIC (Medium).	110 and under 113	9	
PRO-OPIC (Prominent).	113 and under 116	29	
	116 and under 119	34	
	119 and under 122	21	
	122 and over	5	
STATURE. Centimetres.			
SHORT	Under 155 5′ 1″	3	
	155 and under 160 5′ 1″—5′ 3″	23	
BELOW MEAN	160 and under 165 5′ 3″—5′ 5″	33	
ABOVE MEAN	165 and under 170 5′ 5″—5′ 7″	22	
TALL	170 and under 175 5′ 7″—5′ 9″	16	
	175 and over 5′ 9″	3	

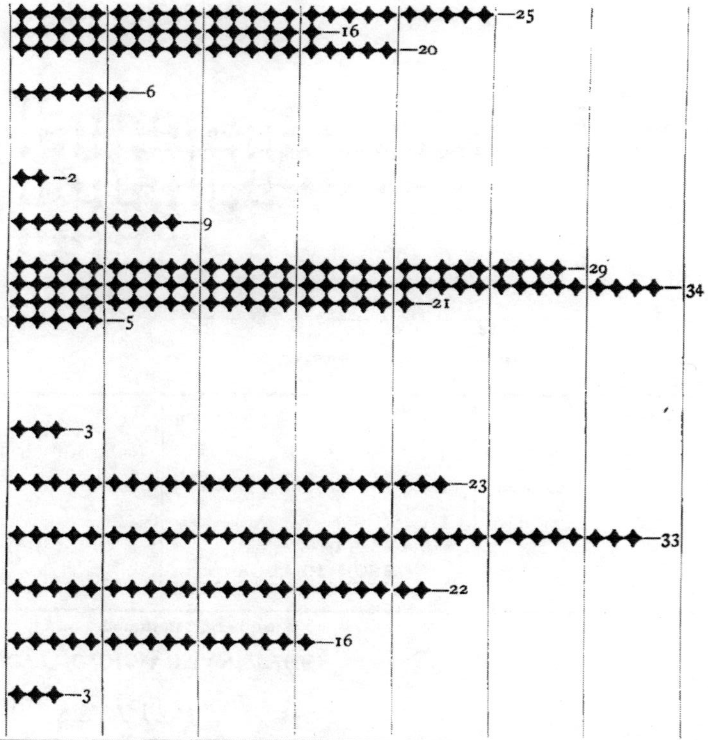

SERIATIONS.

SCYTHO-DRAVIDIAN TYPE.

Type Specimen: Prabhu.

PROPORTIONS OF HEAD. (Cephalic Index.)		PROPORTIONS OF NOSE. (Nasal Index.)		RELATIVE PROMINENCE OF ROOT OF NOSE. (Orbito-Nasal Index.)		STATURE.	C.M.
Average	79·9	Average	75·8	Average	113·4	Average	162·7
Maximum	89	Maximum	93	Maximum	121	Maximum	181·4
Minimum	70	Minimum	60	Minimum	106	Minimum	150·4
Range	19	Range	33	Range	15	Range	31

Indices.		Number of subjects.
HEAD.		
LONG HEADS (Dolicho-cephalic).	70 and under 72·5	3
	72·5 and under 75	8
MEDIUM HEADS (Meso-cephalic).	75 and under 77·5	13
	77·5 and under 80	24
BROAD HEADS (Brachy-cephalic.)	80 and under 82·5	25
	82·5 and under 85	17
	85 and under 87·5	8
	87·5 and over	2
NOSE.		
FINE NOSES (Leptorrhine).	60 and under 65	6
	65 and under 70	13

Percentage on number of subjects.

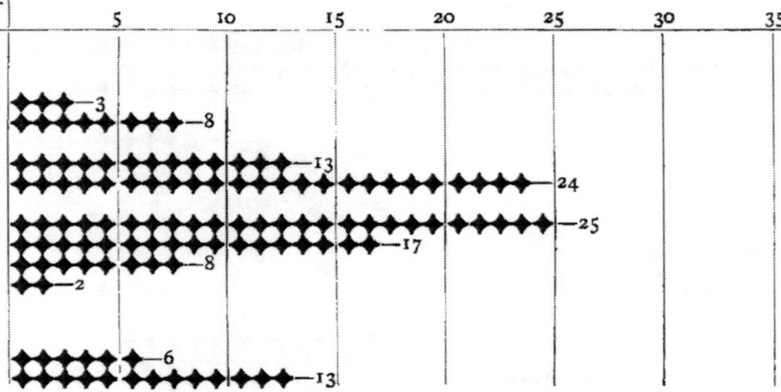

MEDIUM NOSES (Mesorrhine).	70 and under 75	29	
	75 and under 80	23	
	80 and under 85	17	
BROAD NOSES (Platyrrhine).	85 and under 90	7	
	90 and over	5	
ROOT OF NOSE.			
PLATY-OPIC (Flat).	Under 107	1	
	107 and under 110	14	
MES-OPIC (Medium).	110 and under 113	30	
PRO-OPIC (Prominent).	113 and under 116	35	
	116 and under 119	15	
	119 and under 122	5	
STATURE. Centimetres.			
SHORT	Under 155 5′ 1″	9	
	155 and under 160 5′ 1″—5′ 3″	27	
BELOW MEAN	160 and under 165 5′ 3″—5′ 5″	21	
ABOVE MEAN	165 and under 170 5′ 5″—5′ 7″	33	
TALL	170 and under 175 5′ 7″—5′ 9″	8	
	175 and over 5′ 9″	2	

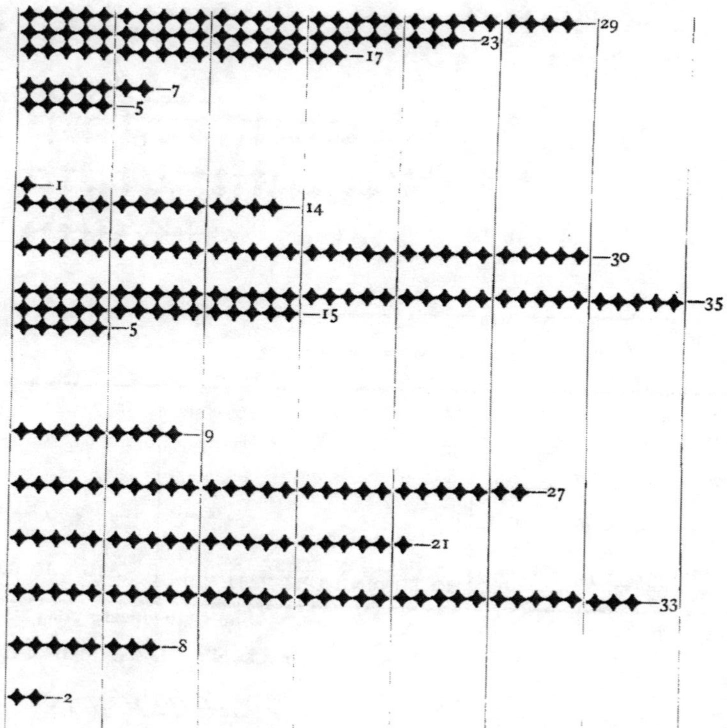

SERIATIONS.

SCYTHO-DRAVIDIAN TYPE.

Type Specimen: Coorg.

PROPORTIONS OF HEAD. (Cephalic Index.)		PROPORTIONS OF NOSE. (Nasal Index.)		RELATIVE PROMINENCE OF ROOT OF NOSE. (Orbito-Nasal Index.)		STATURE.	C.M.
Average	79·9	Average	72·0	Average	120	Average	168·7
Maximum	89	Maximum	86	Maximum	130	Maximum	182·0
Minimum	74	Minimum	61	Minimum	108	Minimum	158·0
Range	15	Range	25	Range	22	Range	24·0

Indices.		Number of subjects.
HEAD.		
LONG HEADS (Dolicho-cephalic).	72·5 and under 75	3
MEDIUM HEADS (Meso-cephalic).	75 and under 77·5	6
	77·5 and under 80	9
BROAD HEADS (Brachy-cephalic).	80 and under 82·5	6
	82·5 and under 85	5
	85 and over	3
NOSE.		
FINE NOSES (Leptorrhine).	60 and under 65	2
	65 and under 70	10

Percentage on number of subjects.

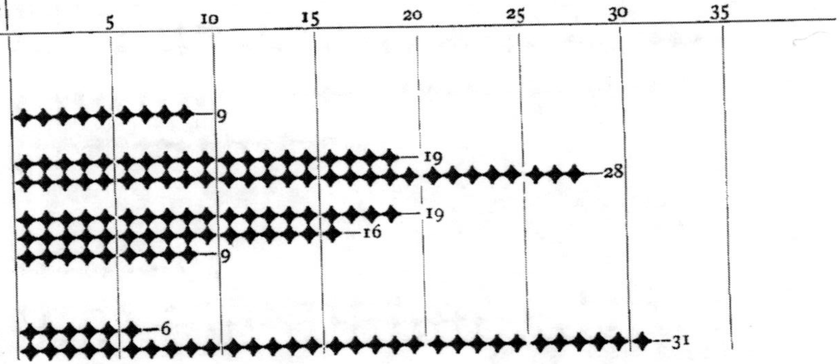

MEDIUM NOSES (Mesorrhine).	70 and under 75	11	35
	75 and under 80	6	19
	80 and under 85	2	6
BROAD NOSES (Platyrrhine).	85 and over	1	3
ROOT OF NOSE.			
PLATY-OPIC (Flat).	107 and under 110	2	6
MES-OPIC (Medium).	110 and under 113	1	3
PRO-OPIC (Prominent).	113 and under 116	4	13
	116 and under 119	7	22
	119 and under 122	5	16
	122 and under 125	7	22
	125 and under 128	4	12
	128 and over	2	6
STATURE. Centimetres.			
SHORT	Under 160 / 5′ 3″	2	6
BELOW MEAN	160 and under 165 / 5′ 3″—5′ 5″	7	22
ABOVE MEAN	165 and under 170 / 5′ 5″—5′ 7″	10	31
TALL	170 and under 175 / 5′ 7″—5′ 9″	5	16
	175 and under 180 / 5′ 9″—5′ 11″	7	22
	180 and over / 5′ 11″	1	3

SERIATIONS.

DRAVIDIAN TYPE: S. INDIA.

Type Specimen: Vellala (Good Sudra).

PROPORTIONS OF HEAD. (Cephalic Index.)		PROPORTIONS OF NOSE. (Nasal Index.)		STATURE.	C.M.
Average	74·1	Average	73·1	Average	162·4
Maximum	81·1	Maximum	91·5	Maximum	172·8
Minimum	67·9	Minimum	60·8	Minimum	153·2
Range	13·2	Range	30·7	Range	19·6

Indices.		Number of subjects.	Percentage on number of subjects.
HEAD.			
VERY LONG HEADS (Hyper-dolicho-cephalic).	Under 70	2	5
LONG HEADS (Dolicho-cephalic).	70 and under 72·5	12	30
	72·5 and under 75	13	32
MEDIUM HEADS (Meso-cephalic).	75 and under 77·5	9	23
	77·5 and under 80	2	5

Broad heads (Brachy-cephalic).	80 and under 82·5	2	5
NOSE.			
Fine noses (Leptorrhine).	Under 70	14	35
Medium noses (Mesorrhine).	70 and under 75	10	25
	75 and under 80	12	30
Broad noses (Platyrrhine).	85 and under 90	3	8
	90 and under 95	1	2
STATURE.	Centimetres.		
Short	Under 155 (5′ 1″)	3	7
	155 and under 160 (5′ 1″—5′ 3″)	11	28
Below mean	160 and under 165 (5′ 3″—5′ 5″)	12	30
Above mean	165 and under 170 (5′ 5″—5′ 7″)	11	28
Tall	170 and over (5′ 7″)	3	7

SERIATIONS.

DRAVIDIAN TYPE: S. INDIA.

Type Specimen: Mukkuvan.

PROPORTIONS OF HEAD. (Cephalic Index.)		PROPORTIONS OF NOSE. (Nasal Index.)		STATURE.	C.M.
Average	75·1	Average	81·0	Average	163·1
Maximum	83·5	Maximum	104·8	Maximum	177·8
Minimum	68·6	Minimum	62·5	Minimum	150·8
Range	14·9	Range	42·3	Range	27·0

Indices.		Number of subjects.	Percentage on number of subjects.
HEAD.			
VERY LONG HEADS (Hyper-dolicho-cephalic).	Under 70	1	3
LONG HEADS (Dolicho-cephalic).	70 and under 72·5	7	18
	72·5 and under 75	10	25
MEDIUM HEADS (Meso-cephalic).	75 and under 77·5	12	30
	77·5 and under 80	8	20
BROAD HEADS (Brachy-cephalic).	80 and under 82·5	1	2
	82·5 and under 85	1	2

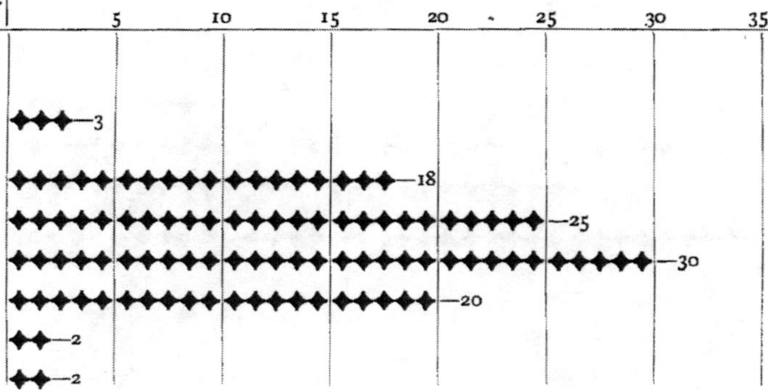

NOSE.

Fine noses (Leptorrhine).	Under 70	3	7
Medium noses (Mesorrhine).	70 and under 75	6	15
	75 and under 80	9	23
	80 and under 85	11	28
Broad noses (Platyrrhine).	85 and under 90	6	15
	90 and under 95	2	5
	95 and under 100	1	2
	100 and over	2	5

STATURE.

Centimetres.

Short	Under 155 (5′ 1″)	2	5
	155 and under 160 (5′ 1″—5′ 3″)	9	23
Below mean	160 and under 165 (5′ 3″—5′ 5″)	12	30
Above mean	165 and under 170 (5′ 5″—5′ 7″)	14	35
Tall	170 and over (5′ 7″)	3	7

SERIATIONS.

DRAVIDIAN TYPE: RAJPUTANA.

Type Specimen: Bhil.

PROPORTIONS OF HEAD. (Cephalic Index.)		PROPORTIONS OF NOSE. (Nasal Index.)		STATURE.	C.M.
Average	76·5	Average	84·1	Average	162·9
Maximum	84	Maximum	105	Maximum	176·4
Minimum	68	Minimum	63	Minimum	147·6
Range	16	Range	42	Range	28·8

Indices.		Number of subjects.	Percentage on number of subjects.
HEAD.			
VERY LONG HEADS (Hyper-dolicho-cephalic).	Under 70	3	2
LONG HEADS (Dolicho-cephalic).	70 and under 72·5	20	10
	72·5 and under 75	56	28
MEDIUM HEADS (Meso-cephalic).	75 and under 77·5	48	24
	77·5 and under 80	37	18
BROAD HEADS Brachy-cephalic).	80 and under 82·5	28	14
	82·5 and under 85	8	4

NOSE.

Fine noses (Leptorrhine).	Under 70	5	3
Medium noses (Mesorrhine).	70 and under 75	9	4
	75 and under 80	42	21
	80 and under 85	53	26
Broad noses (Platyrrhine).	85 and under 90	43	22
	90 and under 95	29	14
	95 and under 100	16	8
	100 and over	3	2

STATURE.

Centimetres.

Short	Under 155 5′ 1″	17	8
	155 and under 160 5′ 1″—5′ 3″	33	17
Below mean	160 and under 165 5′ 3″—5′ 5″	84	42
Above mean	165 and under 170 5′ 5″—5′ 7″	43	22
Tall	170 and over 5′ 7″	23	11

SERIATIONS.

DRAVIDIAN TYPE: CHUTIA NAGPUR.

Type Specimen: Santāl.

PROPORTIONS OF HEAD. (Cephalic Index.)		PROPORTIONS OF NOSE. (Nasal Index.)		STATURE.	C.M.
Average	76·1	Average	88·8	Average	161·4
Maximum	88	Maximum	110	Maximum	177·0
Minimum	69	Minimum	74	Minimum	151·0
Range	19	Range	36	Range	26·0

	Indices.	Number of subjects.
HEAD.		
VERY LONG HEADS (Hyper-dolicho-cephalic).	Under 70	1
LONG HEADS (Dolicho-cephalic).	70 and under 72·5	11
	72·5 and under 75	25
MEDIUM HEADS (Meso-cephalic).	75 and under 77·5	28
	77·5 and under 80	21

Percentage on number of subjects.

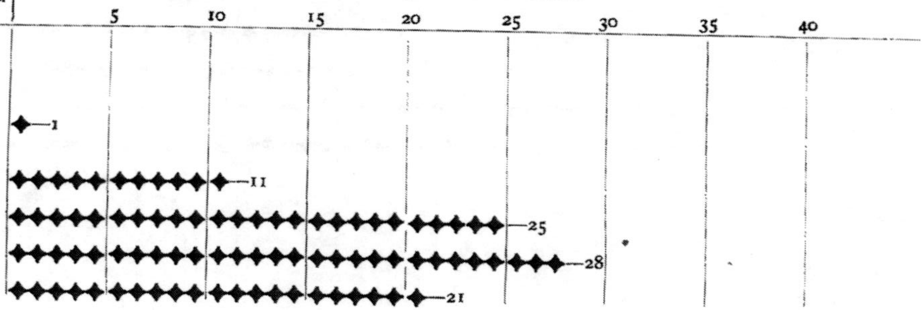

Broad heads (Brachy-cephalic).	80 and under 82·5	8
	82·5 and under 85	5
	85 and over .	1
NOSE.		
Medium noses (Mesorrhine).	70 and under 75 .	1
	75 and under 80 .	10
	80 and under 85 .	20
Broad noses (Platyrrhine).	85 and under 90 .	26
	90 and under 95 .	16
	95 and under 100	15
	100 and over .	12
STATURE. Centimetres.		
Short . .	Under 155 . . 5′ 1″	12
	155 and under 160 5′ 1″—5′ 3″	25
Below mean .	160 and under 165 5′ 3″—5′ 5″	43
Above mean	165 and under 170 5′ 5″—5′ 7″	17
Tall . . .	170 and over . 5′ 7″	3

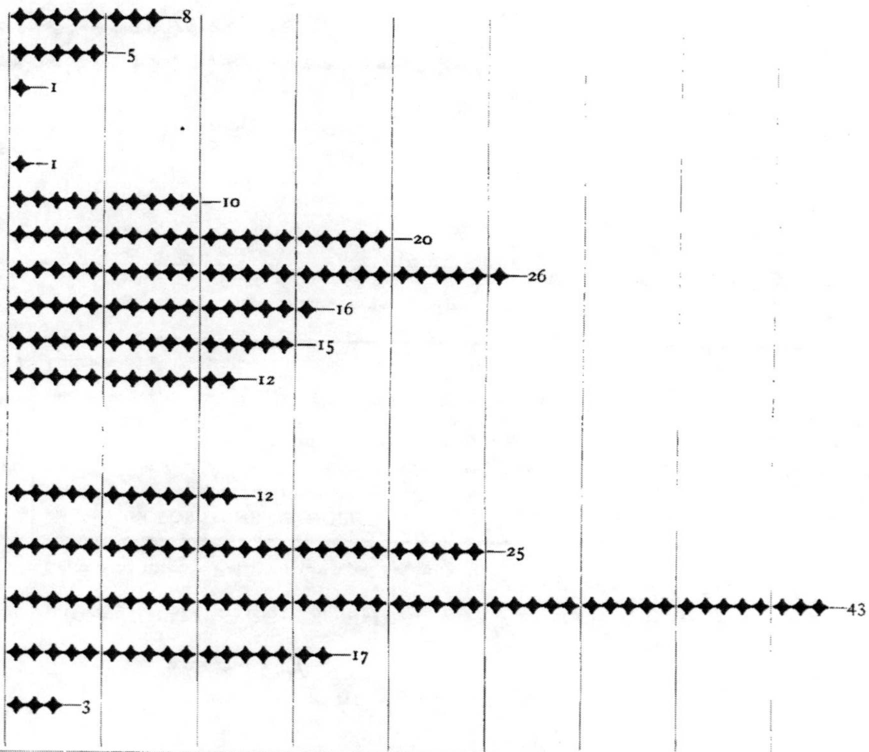

SERIATIONS.

DRAVIDIAN TYPE: S. INDIA.

Type Specimen: Paniyan (Jungle Tribe).

PROPORTIONS OF HEAD. (Cephalic Index.)		PROPORTIONS OF NOSE. (Nasal Index.)		STATURE.	C.M.
Average	74·0	Average	95·1	Average	157·4
Maximum	81·1	Maximum	108·6	Maximum	171·6
Minimum	68·4	Minimum	72·9	Minimum	152·0
Range	12·7	Range	35·7	Range	19·6

Indices.		Number of subjects.	Percentage on number of subjects. (scale 5–50)
HEAD.			
VERY LONG HEADS (Hyper-dolicho-cephalic).	Under 70	2	8
LONG HEADS (Dolicho-cephalic).	70 and under 72·5	8	32
	72·5 and under 75	5	20

MEDIUM HEADS (Meso-cephalic.)	75 and under 77·5	8	32
	77·5 and under 80	1	4
BROAD HEADS (Brachy-cephalic).	80 and under 82·5	1	4

NOSE.

MEDIUM NOSES (Meso-rrhine).	70 and under 75	1	4
	80 and under 85	2	8
BROAD NOSES (Platy-rrhine).	85 and under 90	3	12
	90 and under 95	4	16
	95 and under 100	5	20
	100 and over	10	40

STATURE.

Centimetres.

SHORT	Under 155 5′ 1″	6	24
	155 and under 160 5′ 1″—5′ 3″	13	52
BELOW MEAN	160 and under 165 5′ 3″—5′ 5″	5	20
TALL	170 and over 5′ 7″	1	4

SERIATIONS.

ARYO-DRAVIDIAN TYPE.

Type Specimen: Brahman of the United Provinces.

PROPORTIONS OF HEAD. (Cephalic Index.)		PROPORTIONS OF NOSE. (Nasal Index.)		STATURE.	C.M.
Average	73·1	Average	74·6	Average	165·9
Maximum	84	Maximum	100	Maximum	187·9
Minimum	66	Minimum	60	Minimum	142·2
Range	18	Range	40	Range	45·7

Indices.		Number of subjects.	Percentage on number of subjects.
HEAD.			
VERY LONG HEADS (Hyper-dolicho-cephalic).	Under 70	16	16
LONG HEADS (Dolicho-cephalic).	70 and under 72·5	24	24
	72·5 and under 75	34	34
MEDIUM HEADS (Meso-cephalic).	75 and under 77·5	15	15
	77·5 and under 80	9	9

Broad heads (Brachy.-cephalic).	80 and over	2
NOSE.		
Fine noses (Leptorrhine).	60 and under 65	10
	65 and under 70	17
Medium noses (Mesorrhine).	70 and under 75	25
	75 and under 80	24
	80 and under 85	13
Broad noses (Platyrrhine).	85 and under 90	5
	90 and under 95	4
	95 and under 100	1
	100 and over	1
STATURE.		
Centimetres.		
Short	Under 160 / 5′ 3″	12
Below mean	160 and under 165 / 5′ 3″—5′ 5″	18
Above mean	165 and under 170 / 5′ 5″—5′ 7″	37
Tall	170 and over / 5′ 7″	33

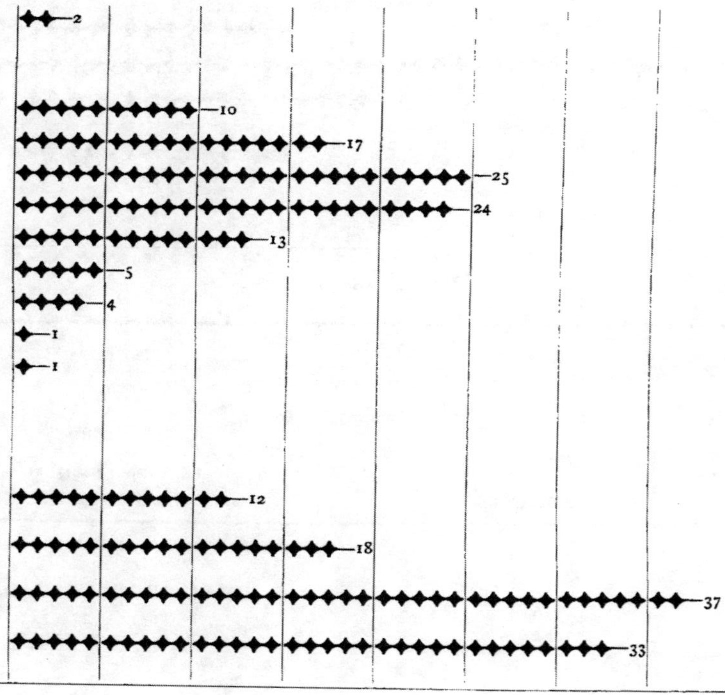

SERIATIONS.

ARYO-DRAVIDIAN TYPE.

Type Specimen: Chamār of the United Provinces.

PROPORTIONS OF HEAD. (Cephalic Index.)		PROPORTIONS OF NOSE. (Nasal Index.)		STATURE.	C.M.
Average	72·8	Average	86·0	Average	163·0
Maximum	81	Maximum	109	Maximum	176·5
Minimum	67	Minimum	64	Minimum	152·4
Range	14	Range	45	Range	24·1

Indices.		Number of subjects.
HEAD.		
VERY LONG HEADS (Hyper-dolicho-cephalic).	Under 70	17
LONG HEADS (Dolicho-cephalic).	70 and under 72·5	23
	72·5 and under 75	38
MEDIUM HEADS (Meso-cephalic).	75 and under 77·5	15
	77·5 and under 80	5

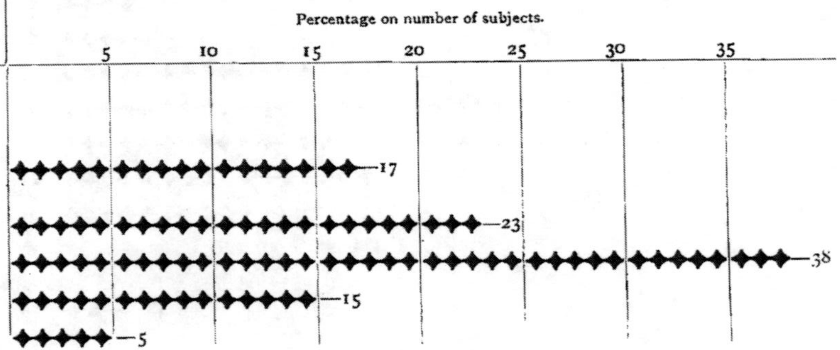

BROAD HEADS (Brachy-cephalic).	80 and over	2

NOSE.

FINE NOSES (Leptorrhine).	Under 65	1
	65 and under 70	1
MEDIUM NOSES (Mesorrhine).	70 and under 75	5
	75 and under 80	13
	80 and under 85	19
BROAD NOSES (Platyrrhine).	85 and under 90	25
	90 and under 95	27
	95 and under 100	3
	100 and over	6

STATURE.

Centimetres.

SHORT	Under 160 5′ 3″	11
BELOW MEAN	160 and under 165 5′ 3″—5′ 5″	32
ABOVE MEAN	165 and under 170 5′ 5″—5′ 7″	39
TALL	170 and over 5′ 7″	18

SERIATIONS.

MONGOLO-DRAVIDIAN TYPE.

Type Specimen: Kochh.

PROPORTIONS OF HEAD. (Cephalic Index.)	Risley.	Waddell.	PROPORTIONS OF NOSE. (Nasal Index.)	Risley.	Waddell.	RELATIVE PROMINENCE OF ROOT OF NOSE. (Orbito-Nasal Index.)	Risley.	Waddell.	STATURE.	Risley.	Waddell.
Average	75·2	76·7	Average	76·6	80·0	Average	110·8	110·0	Average	160·7	159·1
Maximum	84	87	Maximum	92	109	Maximum	121	121	Maximum	174·6	169·5
Minimum	68	71	Minimum	61	67	Minimum	104	93	Minimum	144·0	150·2
Range	16	16	Range	31	42	Range	17	28	Range	30·6	19 3

RISLEY . . . . .
WADDELL . . . . .

Indices.		Number of subjects.
HEAD.		
LONG HEADS (Dolicho-cephalic).	Under 72·5	19
		12
	72·5 and under 75	25
		34
MEDIUM HEADS (Meso-cephalic).	75 and under 77·5	32
		20
	75·5 and under 80	16
		15
BROAD HEADS (Brachy-cephalic).	80 and over	8
		7

Percentage on number of subjects.

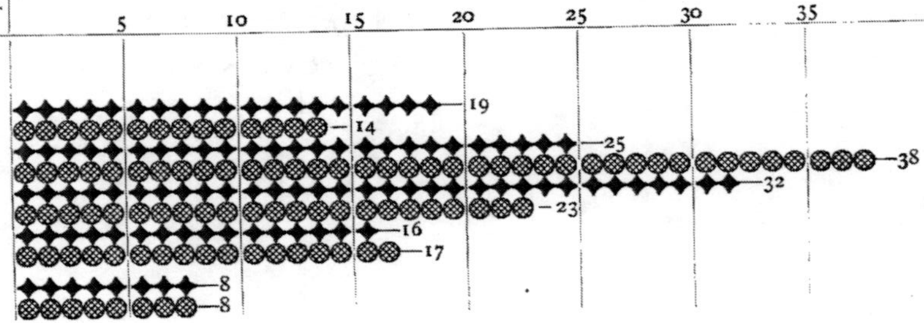

	NOSE.		
FINE NOSES (Leptorrhine).	60 and under 65 .	1	1
	65 and under 70 .	12	12
		5	6
MEDIUM NOSES (Mesorrhine).	70 and under 75 .	23	23
		8	9
	75 and under 80 .	31	31
		19	21
	80 and under 85 .	25	25
		29	33
BROAD NOSES (Platyrrhine).	85 and under 90 .	5	5
		13	15
	90 and over .	3	3
		14	16
	ROOT OF NOSE.		
PLATY-OPIC (Flat).	Under 101 . .	4	5
	101 and under 104	2	2
	104 and under 107	8	8
		15	17
	107 and under 110	30	30
		24	27
MES-OPIC (Medium).	110 and under 113	40	40
		27	31
PRO-OPIC (Prominent).	113 and under 116	19	19
		10	11
	116 and over .	3	3
		6	7
	STATURE.—Centimetres.		
SHORT . .	Under 155 5′ 1″ . .	13	13
		13	15
	155 and under 160 5′ 1″—5′ 3″	30	30
		31	35
BELOW MEAN . .	160 and under 165 5′ 3″—5′ 5″	33	33
		26	30
ABOVE MEAN	165 and under 170 5′ 5″—5′ 7″	21	21
		18	20
TALL . . .	170 and over . 5′ 7″	3	3

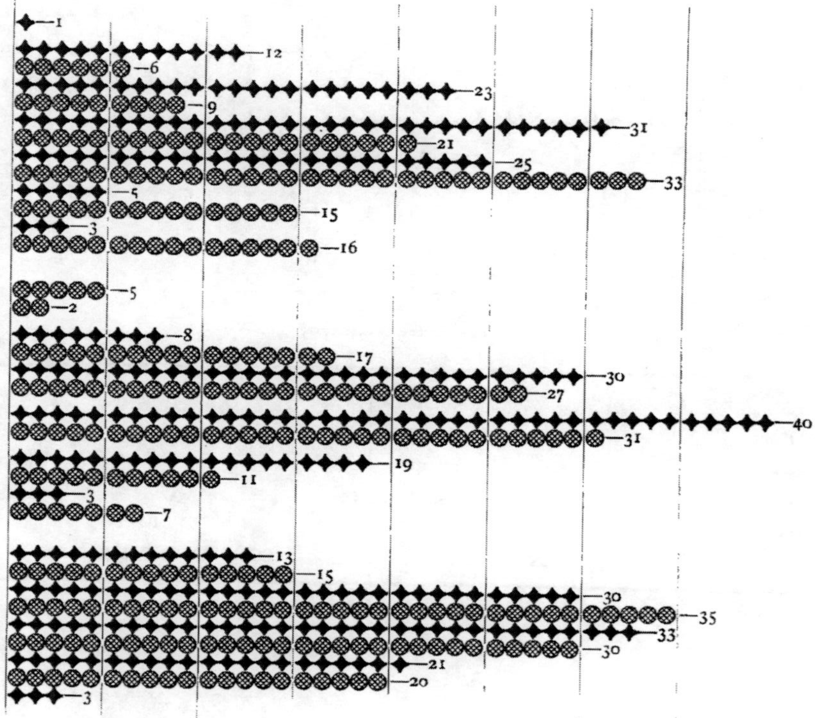

SERIATIONS.

MONGOLO-DRAVIDIAN TYPE.

Type Specimen: Brahman of East Bengal.

PROPORTIONS OF HEAD. (Cephalic Index.)		PROPORTIONS OF NOSE. (Nasal Index.)		STATURE.	C.M.
Average	79·0	Average	70·3	Average	165·3
Maximum	88	Maximum	85	Maximum	179·2
Minimum	70	Minimum	56	Minimum	147·4
Range	18	Range	29	Range	31·8

	Indices.	Number of subjects.	Percentage on number of subjects.
	HEAD.		
LONG HEADS (Dolicho-cephalic).	70 and under 72·5	1	1
	72·5 and under 75	8	12
MEDIUM HEADS (Meso-cephalic).	75 and under 77·5	14	21
	77·5 and under 80	21	31
BROAD HEADS (Brachy-cephalic).	80 and under 82·5	12	18
	82·5 and under 85	9	13
	85 and over	3	4

NOSE.

Fine noses (Leptorrhine).	Under 60	4	6
	60 and under 65	8	12
	65 and under 70	19	28
Medium noses (Mesorrhine).	70 and under 75	20	29
	75 and under 80	14	21
	80 and under 85	2	3
Broad noses (Platyrrhine).	85 and over	1	1

STATURE.

	Centimetres.		
Short	Under 155 (5′ 1″)	2	3
	155 and under 160 (5′ 1″—5′ 3″)	8	12
Below mean	160 and under 165 (5′ 3″—5′ 5″)	22	32
Above mean	165 and under 170 (5′ 5″—5′ 7″)	22	32
Tall	170 and under 175 (5′ 7″—5′ 9″)	12	18
	175 and over (5′ 9″)	2	3

SERIATIONS.

MONGOLOID TYPE.

Type Specimen: Chakma.

PROPORTIONS OF HEAD. (Cephalic Index.)		PROPORTIONS OF NOSE. (Nasal Index.)		RELATIVE PROMINENCE OF ROOT OF NOSE. (Orbito-Nasal Index.)		STATURE.	C.M.
Average	84·3	Average	84·5	Average	106·4	Average	159·5
Maximum	96	Maximum	105	Maximum	112	Maximum	169·6
Minimum	77	Minimum	70	Minimum	102	Minimum	149·0
Range	19	Range	35	Range	10	Range	20·6

Indices.		Number of subjects.
HEAD.		
MEDIUM HEADS (Meso-cephalic).	77 and under 77·5	3
	77·5 and under 80	15
BROAD HEADS (Brachy-cephalic).	80 and under 82·5	16
	82·5 and under 85	21
	85 and under 87·5	19
	87·5 and under 90	18
	90 and over	8

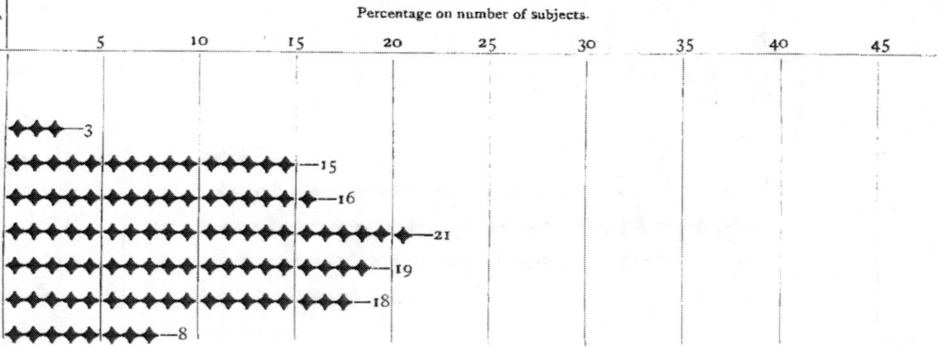

NOSE.

MEDIUM NOSES (Meso-rrhine).	70 and under 75	2
	75 and under 80	28
	80 and under 85	20
BROAD NOSES (Platy-rrhine).	85 and under 90	31
	90 and under 95	9
	95 and under 100	6
	100 and over .	4

ROOT OF NOSE.

PLATY-OPIC (Flat).	101 and under 104	14
	104 and under 107	45
	107 and under 110	37
MES-OPIC (Medium).	110 and under 113	4

STATURE.

Centimetres.

SHORT . .	Under 155 . . 5′ 1″	19
	155 and under 160 5′ 1″—5′ 3″	33
BELOW MEAN	160 and under 165 5′ 3″—5′ 5″	33
ABOVE MEAN	165 and under 170 5′ 5″—5′ 7″	15

SERIATIONS.

MONGOLOID TYPE.

Type Specimen: Lepcha.

PROPORTIONS OF HEAD. (Cephalic Index.)		PROPORTIONS OF NOSE. (Nasal Index.)		RELATIVE PROMINENCE OF ROOT OF NOSE. (Orbito-Nasal Index.)		STATURE.	C.M.
Average	79·9	Average	67·2	Average	108·1	Average	157·0
Maximum	90	Maximum	83	Maximum	113	Maximum	169·0
Minimum	73	Minimum	59	Minimum	103	Minimum	149·0
Range	17	Range	24	Range	10	Range	20·0

Indices.		Number of subjects.
HEAD.		
LONG HEADS (Dolicho-cephalic).	72·5 and under 75	2
MEDIUM HEADS (Meso-cephalic).	75 and under 77·5	4
	77·5 and under 80	18
BROAD HEADS (Brachy-cephalic).	80 and under 82·5	16
	82·5 and under 85	10
	85 and over	7

Percentage on number of subjects.

Indices.	Percentage
72·5 and under 75	3
75 and under 77·5	7
77·5 and under 80	32
80 and under 82·5	28
82·5 and under 85	18
85 and over	12

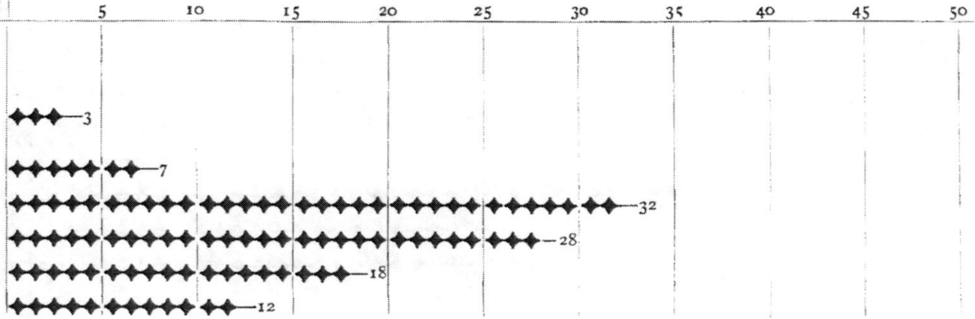

NOSE.			
FINE NOSES (Lepto-rrhine).	Under 60 . .	1	2
	60 and under 65	8	14
	65 and under 70	19	33
MEDIUM NOSES (Meso-rrhine).	70 and under 75	19	33
	75 and under 80	4	7
	80 and under 85	6	11
ROOT OF NOSE.			
PLATY-OPIC (Flat).	101 and under 104	2	4
	104 and under 107	14	26
	107 and under 110	27	50
MES-OPIC (Medium).	110 and under 113	11*	20
STATURE. Centimetres.			
SHORT .	Under 150 . 4′ 11″	3	5
	150 and under 155 4′ 11″—5′ 1″	14	25
	155 and under 160 5′ 1″—5′ 3″	18	32
BELOW MEAN	160 and under 165 5′ 3″—5′ 5″	16	28
ABOVE MEAN	165 and under 170 5′ 5″—5′ 7″	6	10

* Three cases without data have been omitted.

SERIATIONS.

MONGOLOID TYPE.

Type Specimen: KASIA.

LT.-COL. WADDELL.

PROPORTIONS OF HEAD. (Cephalic Index.)		PROPORTIONS OF NOSE. (Nasal Index.)		RELATIVE PROMINENCE OF ROOT OF NOSE. (Orbito-Nasal Index.)		STATURE.	C.M.
Average	78·6	Average	86·3	Average	108·4	Average	156·9
Maximum	84	Maximum	108	Maximum	119	Maximum	170·0
Minimum	72	Minimum	73	Minimum	101	Minimum	141·7
Range	12	Range	35	Range	18	Range	28·3

Percentage on number of subjects.

Indices.		Number of subjects.	Percentage
HEAD.*			
LONG HEADS (Dolicho-cephalic).	70 and under 72·5	2	3
	72·5 and under 75	5	6
MEDIUM HEADS (Meso-cephalic).	75 and under 77·5	22	28
	77·5 and under 80	36	45
BROAD HEADS (Brachy-cephalic).	80 and under 82·5	9	11
	82·5 and under 85	6	7

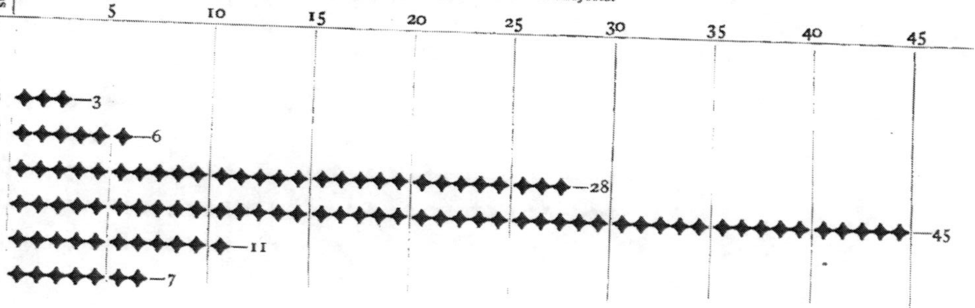

NOSE.

MEDIUM NOSES (Mesorrhine).	70 and under 75	2	3
	75 and under 80	18	22
	80 and under 85	13	16
BROAD NOSES (Platyrrhine).	85 and under 90	14	17
	90 and under 95	16	20
	95 and under 100	12	15
	100 and over .	6	7

ROOT OF NOSE.†

PLATY-OPIC (Flat).	101 and under 104	4	8
	104 and under 107	16	34
	107 and under 110	8	17
MES-OPIC (Medium).	110 and under 113	17	35
PRO-OPIC (Prominent).	113 and under 116	1	2
	116 and over .	2	4

STATURE.

Centimetres.

SHORT . .	Under 150 . . 4′ 11″	4	5
	150 and under 155 4′ 11″—5′ 1″	20	25
	155 and under 160 5′ 1″—5′ 3″	33	40
BELOW MEAN	160 and under 165 5′ 3″—5′ 5″	20	25
ABOVE MEAN	165 and under 170 5′ 5″—5′ 7″	3	4
TALL . .	170 and over . 5′ 7″	1	1

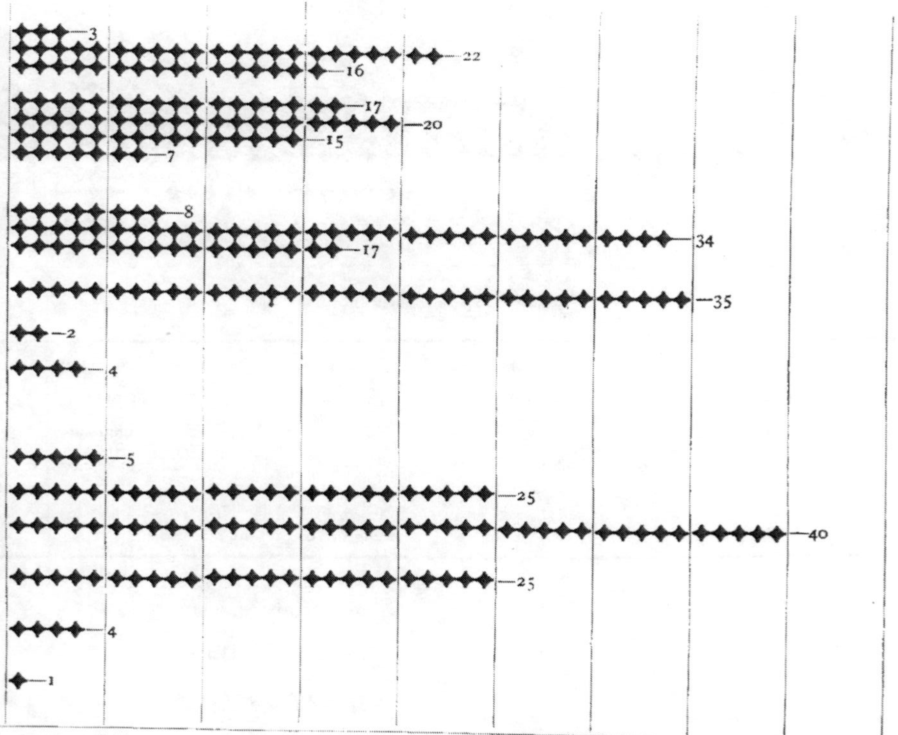

* 80 Measurements availabl

† Only 48 Measurements available.

SERIATIONS.

NEGRITO TYPE.

North Andamans.

MALE ✦ AND FEMALE ⊗ SERIES.

PROPORTIONS OF HEAD. (Cephalic Index.)	Male.	Female.	PROPORTIONS OF NOSE. (Nasal Index.)	Male.	Female.	STATURE.	C.M. Male.	C.M. Female.
Average	82·0	81·9	Average	92·5	94·3	Average	148·6	138·5
Maximum	88	88	Maximum	115	113	Maximum	156·8	150·0
Minimum	78	78	Minimum	77	77	Minimum	140·0	127·7
Range	10	10	Range	38	36	Range	16·8	23·3

Indices.		Number of subjects.	Percentage on number of subjects.
HEAD.			
MEDIUM HEADS (Meso-cephalic).	77·5 and under 80	11	22
		7	14
BROAD HEADS (Brachy-cephalic).	80 and under 82·5	21	42
		25	50
	82·5 and under 85	12	24
		14	28
	85 and under 87·5	5	10
		3	6
	87·5 and under 90	1	2
		1	2

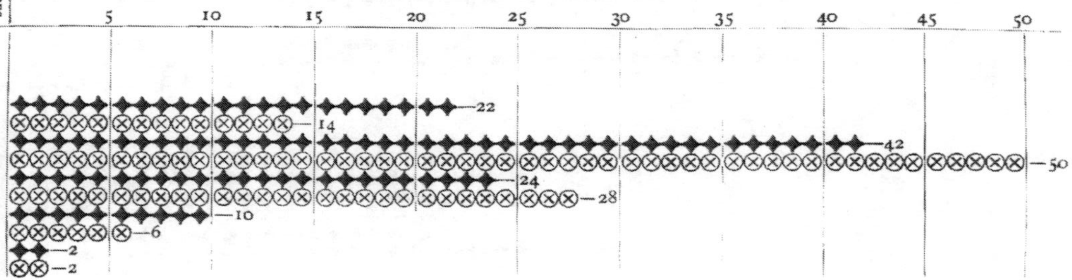

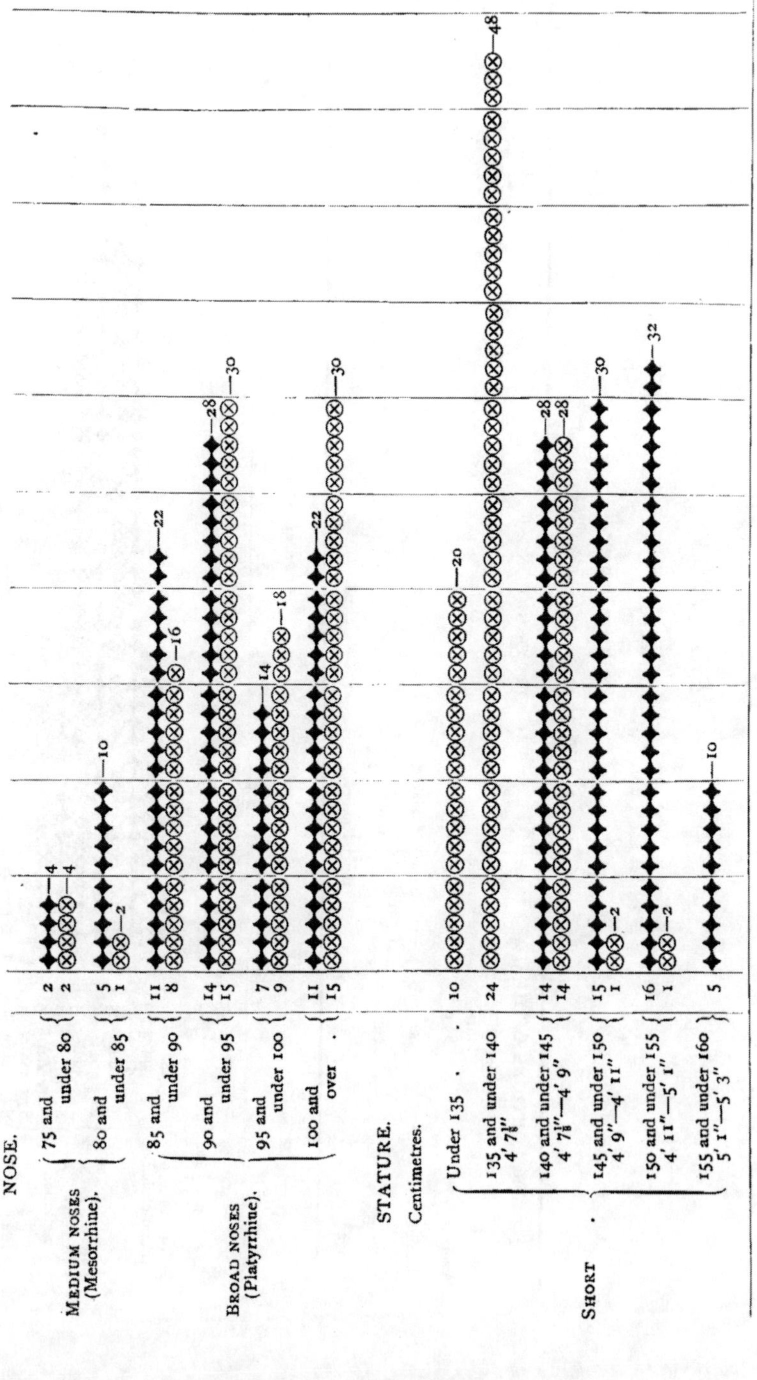
NOSE.
MEDIUM NOSES (Mesorrhine).
75 and under 80
2
2
4
4
80 and under 85
5
1
10
2
85 and under 90
11
8
22
16
BROAD NOSES (Platyrrhine).
90 and under 95
14
15
28
30
95 and under 100
7
9
14
18
100 and over
11
15
22
30
STATURE.
Centimetres.
Under 135
10
20
135 and under 140
4' 7⅛"
24
48
140 and under 145
4' 7⅛"—4' 9"
14
14
28
28
SHORT
145 and under 150
4' 9"—4' 11"
15
1
30
2
150 and under 155
4' 11"—5' 1"
16
1
32
2
155 and under 160
5' 1"—5' 3"
5
10

SERIATIONS.

NEGRITO TYPE.

South Andamans.

MALE ✦ AND ⊗ FEMALE SERIES.

PROPORTIONS OF HEAD. (Cephalic Index.)	Male.	Female.	PROPORTIONS OF NOSE. (Nasal Index.)	Male.	Female.	STATURE.	C.M. Male.	C.M. Female.
Average	83·0	82·7	Average	88·2	89·4	Average	148·2	140·2
Maximum	90	87	Maximum	102	113	Maximum	159·4	148·5
Minimum	79	79	Minimum	74	70	Minimum	138·0	129·1
Range	11	8	Range	28	43	Range	21·4	19·4

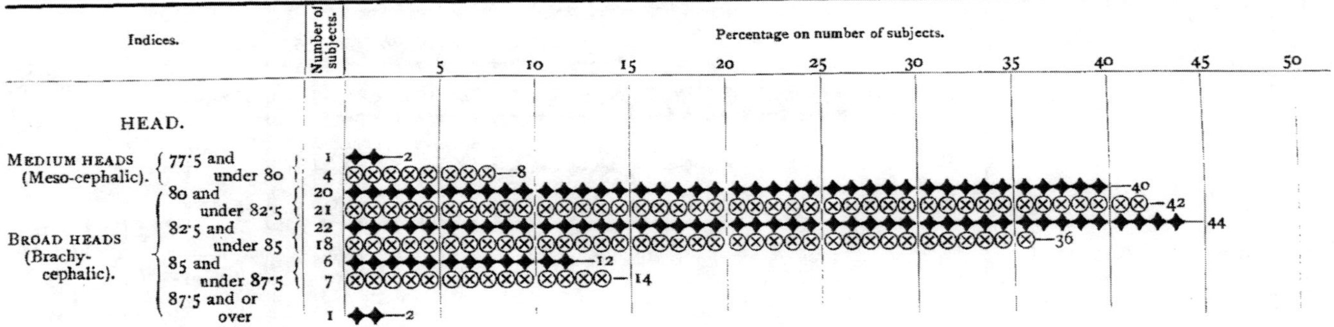

NOSE.

Class	Index	No.	Total
Fine noses (Leptorrhine).	65 and under 70	1	2
	70 and under 75	1	2
		1	2
Medium noses (Mesorrhine).	75 and under 80	3	6
		7	14
	80 and under 85	15	30
		6	12
Broad noses (Platyrrhine).	85 and under 90	10	20
		8	16
	90 and under 95	8	16
		12	24
	95 and under 100	8	16
		2	4
	100 and over	5	10
		13	26

STATURE.

Centimetres.

Class	Stature	No.	Total
Short.	Under 135	6	12
	135 and under 140, 4′ 7⅛″	2	4
		16	32
	140 and under 145, 4′ 7⅛″—4′ 9″	8	16
		22	44
	145 and under 150, 4′ 9″—4′ 11″	25	50
		6	12
	150 and under 155, 4′ 11″—5′ 1″	12	24
	155 and under 160, 5′ 1″—5′ 3″	3	6

APPE…

SUMMARY OF

TURKO-IR…

WESTERN PUNJAB, NORTH-WESTERN FRONTIER PR…

Number of subjects.	Name of Tribe or Caste.	Language or Dialect.	Locality.	Dimensions of Head. Length (Glabello-occipital). Average.	Maximum.	Minimum.	Breadth (Extreme). Average.	Maximum.	Minimum.	P… C… Average.
								WESTERN PUI		
7	Nāgar . .	Burusharki .	Nāgar . .	190·7	198	180	143·8	151	142	75·4
80	Pathān . .	Western Punjābi	North-Western Punjab	185·2	203	165	141·7	152	133	76·5
6	Kāfir . . .	Ashkun .	Kāfirstān . .	194·6	199	191	149·6	160	143	76·9
9	Hunza . .	Burusharki .	HuNza . .	192·8	200	181	152·0	165	144	78·8
60	Baloch (mixed) .	Western Punjābi	Western Punjab .	179·2	197	155	143·5	152	133	80·0
200	Hazāra . .	Persian .	Afghanistan .	179·6	202	160	152·8	168	140	85·0
58*	Lori . . .	Brāhūi and Gypsy (Mokāki)	Quetta and Saruna	177·6	192	158	139·5	152	130	78·[illegible]
100*	Makhiāni (Pathān)	Pashto .	Harnai, Thal Chotiali	181·0	200	163	142·1	159	130	78·5
59*	Wanechi (Pathān)	Do. . .	Babihan, Thal Chotiali	178·1	195	161	141·2	155	126	79·2
76*	Dehwār . .	Dehwāri .	Mastung . .	179·4	200	165	142·2	155	130	79·2
100*	Jāt . . .	Jadgali .	Sibi . . .	177·8	196	160	141·9	155	130	79·8
100	Pani (Pathān) .	Pashto .	Do. . . .	183·9	198	168	147·4	158	139	80·1
271	Baloch . .	Balochi .	Mārri and Bugti Hills and Kacchi	181·8	205	161	146·2	159	131	80·4
24*	Dehwār . .	Dehwāri .	Kālāt. . .	178·5	183	168	144·4	160	133	80·8
100	Achakzāi (Pathān)	Pashto .	Chaman, Quettā Pishin	187·7	210	175	152·4	171	140	81·1
48*	Mir Jāts .	Jatki . .	Sibi . . .	180·1	200	162	146·4	158	135	81·2
198	Brāhūi . .	Brāhūi.	Sarawan Country	182·0	197	166	148·4	165	135	81·5
200	Dehwār . .	Dehwāri .	Mastung . .	179·4	198	165	146·6	159	131	81·7
112	Kākar (Pathān) .	Pashto .	Quetta and Zhob	184·7	202	170	151·4	169	140	81·9
79*	Med . . .	Makrāni Balochi	Pasni, Gwadur, Chahar and Ormara	181·4	200	170	148·9	160	136	82·0
77*	Mengal (Brahūi) .	Brāhūi .	Saruna . .	179·5	190	161	148·7	162	130	82·[illegible]
100	Tārin (Pathān) .	Pashto .	Pishin . .	182·1	199	165	150·9	170	138	82·[illegible]
13	Ghulām (Slaves) .	Balochi .	Baluchistan. .	179·0	188	170	150·2	159	141	83·9
33*	Chhutta . .	Jadgāli .	Hinidan Levy Tracts	176·1	190	162	150·2	162	140	85·2
35*	Bandija . .	Do. . .	Kila do. .	174·6	190	162	152·0	162	144	87·[illegible]

* Mr. B. …

MEASUREMENTS.

NIAN TYPE.

)VINCE AND BALUCHISTAN. (In order of Cephalic Index.)

OPOR- NS OF EAD.		DIMENSIONS OF NOSE.						PROPOR- TIONS OF NOSE.			STATURE.			RELATIVE PROMINENCE OF ROOT OF NOSE.				
PHALIC IDEX.		HEIGHT.			BREADTH.			NASAL INDEX.						AVERAGE DIMENSIONS.		ORBITO-NASAL INDEX.		
Maximum.	Minimum.	Average.	Maximum.	Minimum.	Average.	Maximum.	Minimum.	Average.	Maximum.	Minimum.	Average.	Maximum.	Minimum.	External orbital breadth (average).	Bi-orbito nasal arc (average).	Average.	Maximum.	Minimum.
IAB & N.-W. F. PROVINCE.																		
79	72	58·4	64	52	37·0	40	35	63·3	69	55	1648	1690	1606	103·0	116·8	113·3	124	108
87	69	50·0	59	45	34·2	40	30	68·4	80	56	1687	1866	1562	115·9	135·9	117·1	131	108
82	73	54·1	58	52	37·3	39	36	68·9	72	64	1671	1738	1560	107·0	124·3	116·1	118	113
84	76	53·2	62	50	38·5	40	37	72·3	78	65	1708	1800	1648	109·0	123·7	113·4	119	109
95	72	49·4	58	45	34·3	40	30	69·4	87	57	1662	1803	1524	113·8	134·2	117·9	129	110
99	74	46·3	56	37	37·3	45	31	80·5	111	63	1684	1806	1525	114·0	126·8	111·2	120	103
ALUCHISTAN.																		
90	71	56·4	66	44	35·1	44	26	62·2	85	48	..	..	..	98·7	119·5	121·0	133	105
87	65	57·4	64	46	34·0	43	29	59·2	78	48	..	..	..	99·3	124·0	124·8	134	113
89	70	56·9	66	48	33·7	45	28	59·2	87	47	..	..	..	99·2	121·8	122·7	133	114
88	68	54·9	68	45	34·1	40	28	62·1	80	47	..	..	..	98·3	119·2	121·2	133	107
92	70	56·1	64	44	35·4	46	25	63·1	84	42	..	..	..	98·0	122·5	125·0	143	104
90	75	50·9	58	43	37·2	43	32	73·0	90	55	1677	1852	1560	112·0	132·0	117·8	126	111
90	70	52·4	61	45	38·0	46	32	72·5	94	57	1678	1850	1506	112·8	133·6	118·4	128	111
88	73	59·5	70	53	34·7	40	30	58·3	67	48	..	..	..	100·0	122·2	122·2	133	113
91	74	55·3	63	48	37·8	47	31	68·3	90	55	1722	1862	1602	116·4	136·4	117·1	125	111
96	73	57·3	86	48	35·4	45	30	61·7	75	40	..	..	..	99·6	124·2	124·6	137	111
92	72	51·3	65	41	36·4	45	30	70·9	98	55	1659	1794	1526	110·9	130·9	118·0	128	110
91	72	48·4	59	42	36·0	45	30	74·3	98	60	1642	1808	1488	107·6	127·0	118·0	130	109
90	74	53·4	61	·46	37·2	44	32	69·6	88	60	1683	1882	1570	114·9	134·0	116·6	124	107
92	72	55·9	68	44	38·1	46	30	68·1	92	53	·	..	..	117·3	149·4	127·3	140	113
93	70	57·8	68	41	34·4	43	30	59·5	83	50	..	..	..	108·0	130·3	120·6	135	103
93	74	54·1	62	45	36·7	49	30	67·8	86	54	1683	1928	1533	114·7	133·6	116·4	127	111
88	75	51·2	56	46	39·3	46	35	76·7	92	66	1642	1706	1526	109·3	126·6	115·8	123	110
95	80	60·0	70	50	35·2	40	30	58·6	71	50	..	..	..	111·2	138·3	124·3	134	111
94	81	59·4	70	54	35·0	42	28	58·9	71	47	..	..	..	115·1	141·2	122·6	139	110

Gupte, F.Z.S.

SUMMARY OF

INDO-ARY

PUNJAB AND RAJPUTANA.

Number of subjects.	Name of Tribe or Caste.	Language or Dialect.	Locality.	Dimensions of Head. Length (Glabello-occipital). Average.	Maximum.	Minimum.	Breadth (Extreme). Average.	Maximum.	Minimum.	Pro tion He Cep Ind Average.
19	Māchhi . .	Punjābī . .	Punjāb . .	188·4	196	182	136·3	147	127	72·3
120	Rājput . .	Rājasthāni .	Rajputānā	192·5	213	180	139·4	151	127	72·4
13	Gūjar . .	Punjābī . .	Punjāb . .	192·6	205	185	139·6	148	133	72·4
27	Arora . .	Ditto . .	Ditto .	190·7	206	177	138·6	149	130	72·6
80	Sikh (Jāt) . .	Ditto . .	Ditto .	190·2	203	172	138·4	152	127	72·7
100	Meo . . .	Rājasthāni .	Rajputānā .	189·5	204	178	138·4	147	126	73·0
100	Mīna Zamindār .	Ditto . .	Ditto . .	192·4	207	174	140·6	155	132	73·0
100	Mīna Chaukidār .	Ditto . .	Ditto . .	189·9	207	176	139·1	150	130	73·2
80	Chuhra . .	Punjābī . .	Punjāb . .	186·7	200	171	137·1	152	127	73·4
60	Khatri . .	Ditto . .	Ditto . .	185·7	200	172	137·5	150	128	74·0
33	Awān . .	Ditto . .	Ditto . .	188·8	201	175	140·5	147	130	74·4

DIX III

MEASUREMENTS.

AN TYPE.

(In order of Cephalic Index.)

POR-S OF AD.		DIMENSIONS OF NOSE.						PROPORTIONS OF NOSE.			STATURE.			RELATIVE PROMINENCE OF ROOT OF NOSE.				
HALIC EX.		Height.			Breadth.			Nasal Index.								Orbito-Nasal Index.		
Maximum.	Minimum.	Average.	Maximum.	Minimum.	Average.	Maximum.	Minimum.	Average.	Maximum.	Minimum.	Average.	Maximum.	Minimum.	External orbital breadth (average).	Bi-orbito nasal arc (average).	Average.	Maximum.	Minimum.
76	68	49·8	53	46	34·9	41	31	70·0	82	62	1699	1828	1600	112·1	131·0	116·8	125	110
81	64	51·2	61	43	36·7	44	31	71·6	91	53	1748	1924	1654	108·5	128·0	117·9	129	107
78	68	50·3	55	47	33·7	39	31	66·9	78	60	1703	1778	1650	112·7	130·6	115·8	123	111
81	67	49·7	54	47	35·4	42	30	71·2	81	60	1658	1803	1574	111·5	129·5	116·1	121	110
81	66	50·1	61	45	34·5	41	30	68·8	85	56	1716	1905	1625	113·6	132·5	116·6	125	110
81	67	50·4	60	43	38·1	46	32	75·5	92	59	1690	1852	1536	106·4	121·2	113·9	123	107
83	67	51·2	59	41	38·1	44	32	74·4	91	61	1713	1850	1606	108·0	124·4	115·1	123	107
81	61	51·0	59	44	37·8	44	32	74·2	96	61	1703	1820	1570	108·5	125·4	115·5	125	107
82	68	48·0	56	45	36·1	45	31	75·2	94	60	1666	1803	1524	112·2	129·4	115·3	123	108
86	66	48·8	58	44	35·7	42	30	73·1	95	59	1662	1803	1574	111·9	126·6	113·1	122	106
80	70	50·7	57	44	34·9	39	30	68·8	79	55	1706	1828	1600	113·0	131·3	110·1	125	110

APP

SUMMARY OF

SCYTHO-D

BOMBAY AND COORG

Number of subjects.	Name of Tribe or Caste.	Language or Dialect.	Locality.	Dimensions of Head.						
				Length (Glabello-occipital).			Breadth (Extreme).			
				Average.	Maximum.	Minimum.	Average.	Maximum.	Minimum.	
100	Deshasth Brāhman	Marathi . .	Poona, Satara, Ahmednagar	185·4	198	170	142·7	157	131	7
100	Mahār . .	Marathi . .	Poona . .	181·6	195	165	140·0	152	129	7
100	Kokanasth Brāhman (Chitpāvan)	Marathi . .	Bombay and Poona	186·4	202	170	144·2	155	122	[illegible]
100	Kunbi . .	Marathi . .	Poona . .	180·1	197	165	139·4	156	130	[illegible]
100	Koli (Sōn) . .	Koli Dialect .	Thana . .	185·0	201	171	143·5	159	134	[illegible]
100	Marātha . .	Marathi . .	Poona . .	181·3	195	166	142·1	158	127	[illegible]
100	Shenvi Brāhman .	Marathi . .	Bombay city .	186·2	201	170	147·1	160	132	[illegible]
127	Vania . . .	Gujerati . .	Ahmedabad .	183·0	202	170	145·2	156	135	[illegible]
100	Nāgar Brāhman .	Gujerati . .	Ahmedabad .	184·4	202	151	147·1	166	132	[illegible]
100	Prabhu . .	Marathi . .	Satara, Poona, Bombay (city), Thana	184·2	198	170	147·2	158	131	[illegible]
32	Coorg* . .	Kodagu . .	Coorg . .	184·0	195	168	147·0	154	138	[illegible]
							Dravidian For			
	Kātkari . .	Kātkari . .	Thana . .	178·8	199	160	133·0	143	126	[illegible]

* T. H. H

EASUREMENTS.

VIDIAN TYPE.

in order of Cephalic Index.)

POR-IS OF EAD.		DIMENSIONS OF NOSE.						PROPOR-TIONS OF NOSE.			STATURE.			RELATIVE PROMINENCE OF ROOT OF NOSE.				
HALIC DEX.		Height.			Breadth.			Nasal Index.						External bi-orbital Breadth (average).	Bi-orbito nasal arc (average).	Orbito-Nasal Index.		
Maximum.	Minimum.	Average.	Maximum.	Minimum.	Average.	Maximum.	Minimum.	Average.	Maximum.	Minimum.	Average.	Maximum.	Minimum.			Average.	Maximum.	Minimum.
88	68	48·9	56	42	38·8	44	34	79·3	98	69	1642	1750	1486	116·6	135·6	116·2	127	105
88	69	47·2	53	41	38·7	46	33	81·9	96	70	1634	1792	1490	113·9	130·6	114·6	125	108
85	70	49·3	57	41	37·8	43	31	76·6	93	60	1655	1813	1512	116·0	134·2	115·6	124	103
92	69	47·9	54	40	37·9	42	33	79·2	93	67	1600	1776	1420	113·2	129·5	114·5	124	104
85	71	49·6	57	42	37·9	47	31	76·4	93	62	1601	1760	1482	114·5	129·5	113·1	122	104
89	69	47·8	57	38	38·3	48	33	80·1	108	66	1632	1770	1476	114·9	133·1	115·8	132	107
92	71	50·3	59	42	37·6	43	33	74·7	95	63	1648	1774	1481	112·9	129·5	114·7	124	104
88	70	49·9	59	35	37·8	49	31	75·7	10	61	1612	1732	1489	113·1	131·5	116·2	128	108
90	71	50·7	61	44	37·1	44	31	73·1	90	57	1643	1788	1513	114·1	133·2	116·7	124	108
89	70	50·1	58	44	38·0	45	32	75·8	93	60	1627	1814	1504	113·0	128·2	113·4	121	106
89	74	51·5	57	46	37·0	40	32	72·0	86	61	1687	1820	1580	110·0	132·0	120·0	130	108

Nomads in Scytho-Dravidian Tract.

32	68	44·0	52	37	38·7	45	31	88·0	111	70	1584	1690	1438	107·8	121·2	112·4	121	104

A.R.C.S., F.G.S.

SUMMARY OF

SCYTHO-DR

MADRAS (DECCAN).

[E. THU

Number of subjects.	NAME OF TRIBE OR CASTE.	Language or Dialect.	Locality.	DIMENSIONS OF			
				LENGTH (GLABELLO-OCCIPITAL).			
				Average.	Maximum.	Minimum.	Average.
40	Madiga	Telugu	Bellary	183	200	172	14(
25	Brāhman (Deshasth)	Canarese	Bellary	187	202	180	144
30	Mala	Telugu	Bellary	184	198	168	142
25	Sadaru Lingāyat	Canarese	Bellary	182	200	170	141
25	Komati	Canarese	Bellary	182	194	170	143
40	Bidar	Telugu	Bellary	184	200	168	143
30	Linga Banjigaru	Canarese	Bellary	182	194	166	142
30	Padma Sale	Telugu	Bellary	178	190	165	141
50	Kuruba	Canarese	Bellary	181	196	170	142
30	Jangam (Lingāyat)	Canarese	Bellary	181	196	166	143
30	Rangāri	Marāthi	Bellary	181	198	168	145
30	Togata	Telugu	Bellary	177	190	162	142
20	Ganiga	Canarese	Bellary	180	191	166	144
20	Devanga	Canarese	Bellary	180	196	170	145
30	Suka Sale	Marāthi	Bellary	177	188	166	145
30	Sukun Sale	Marāthi	Bellary	176	190	160	144

DIX III

EASUREMENTS.

IDIAN TYPE.

order of Cephalic Index.)

ɴ, Esquire.]

AD.		PROPORTIONS OF HEAD.			DIMENSIONS OF NOSE.						PROPORTIONS OF NOSE.			STATURE.		
ADTH REME).		Cephalic Index.			Height.			Breadth.			Nasal Index.					
Maximum.	Minimum.	Average.	Maximum.	Minimum.	Average.	Maximum.	Minimum.	Average.	Maximum.	Minimum.	Average.	Maximum.	Minimum.	Average.	Maximum.	Minimum.
54	130	76·5	83·3	68·0	46	51	40	35	39	32	77·5	91·1	66·7	1629	1734	1522
52	132	77·0	83·4	71·0	48	54	44	36	42	32	75·8	87·2	66·0	1634	1750	1514
48	134	77·1	85·9	70·3	48	52	44	36	41	34	76·2	93·2	66·7	1639	1750	1538
52	134	77·7	87·0	65·0	48	53	42	35	40	32	73·4	88·9	60·4	1658	1745	1522
52	133	77·9	88·2	72·2	47	53	43	36	43	32	77·8	100·0	65·3	1610	1683	1532
52	132	78·1	85·3	70·8	46	48	43	36	40	34	79·4	91·0	65·2	1654	1766	1560
50	134	78·3	87·9	73·7	47	52	43	35	38	31	74·6	86·4	61·5	1656	1730	1578
51	132	78·7	86·2	72·8	47	53	41	35	38	32	73·2	83·7	61·5	1599	1714	1538
54	134	78·9	88·4	72·9	47	52	41	35	42	30	74·9	92·2	63·3	1627	1754	1474
52	132	79·1	86·8	70·4	47	52	42	35	38	31	74·5	88·1	64·7	1651	1736	1576
54	138	79·8	92·2	70·7	49	52	46	36	41	33	73·6	84·1	63·5	1613	1684	1544
48	136	80·0	88·1	73·7	47	50	42	36	46	33	77·5	93·9	68·8	1605	1689	1514
52	140	80·5	86·7	74·5	48	53	44	35	38	32	73·7	84·4	62·7	1643	1724	1550
55	136	80·8	87·1	74·7	47	52	43	35	38	32	74·6	80·9	65·3	1618	1686	1546
50	134	81·8	88·2	76·1	47	51	43	35	40	32	74·8	86·1	62·3	1611	1700	1478
54	136	82·2	90·0	73·9	47	52	41	35	38	31	74·8	84·4	61·5	1603	1676	1525

SUMMARY OF MEASUREMENTS.

DRAVIDIAN TYPE.

MADRAS, CHOTA NAGPUR, MEWAR AND CEYLON. (In order of Nasal Index.)

Number of subjects.	Tribe or Caste.	Language or Dialect.	Locality.	Dimensions of Head. Length (Glabello-occipital). Average.	Maximum.	Minimum.	Breadth (Extreme). Average.	Maximum.	Minimum.	Proportions of Head. Cephalic Index. Average.	Maximum.	Minimum.	Dimensions of Nose. Height. Average.	Maximum.	Minimum.	Breadth. Average.	Maximum.	Minimum.	Proportions of Nose. Nasal Index. Average.	Maximum.	Minimum.	Stature. Average.	Maximum.	Minimum.
40	Lambādi	Gujerāthi	Mysore	184	197	166	139	148	128	75·4	83·5	68·7	49	55	43	34	39	29	69·1	83·7	59·2	1645	1768	1520
...	Kannādiyan (Lingāyat)	Canarese	Chingleput	184	200	166	140	156	128	76·3	90·4	69·0	47	53	40	34	38	29	71·5	88·9	60·0	1631	1724	1504
30	Syrian Christians, Southern	Malayālam	Travancore	189	202	179	141	150	130	74·8	81·8	69·3	49	53	42	35	40	30	71·6	88·9	60·0	1648	1724	1560
40	Syrian Christians, Northern	Malayālam	Travancore	187	200	172	143	152	130	76·3	82·8	72·6	49	52	43	35	40	31	72·3	87·0	62·3	1653	1780	1540
40	Muhammadan: Shekh	Hindustāni: Tamil	Madras City	183	200	167	138	145	128	75·6	81·6	71·5	48	54	44	35	40	30	72·4	87·0	60·0	1646	1748	1538
40	Muhammadan: Pathān	Hindustāni: Tamil	Madras City	185	196	172	142	152	133	76·2	83·1	71·1	48	53	42	35	42	30	73·0	88·1	57·7	1644	1776	1556
40	Vellāla	Tamil	Madras City	186	196	177	138	146	131	74·1	81·1	67·9	47	51	42	34	43	30	73·1	91·5	60·8	1624	1728	1532
40	Muhammadan: Saiyad	Hindustāni: Tamil	Madras City	185	196	172	140	150	131	75·6	84·9	68·2	48	56	43	36	42	32	74·0	91·3	61·2	1644	1853	1538
40	Agamudaiyan	Tamil	Chingleput	188	200	178	139	146	128	74·0	80·9	66·7	48	53	43	35	43	30	74·2	88·9	60·0	1658	1756	1536
40	Tiyan	Malayālam	Malabar	189	203	178	137	149	126	73·0	78·7	68·5	47	52	42	35	40	31	75·0	85·7	61·5	1641	1716	1552
40	Mappila (Moplah)	Hindustāni: Malayālam	Malabar	189	200	180	137	140	130	72·8	78·5	68·0	48	53	42	36	40	32	75·1	88·1	64·0	1648	1744	1450
40	Badaga	Canarese	Nilgiri Hills	189	202	180	136	145	128	71·7	77·5	66·1	46	51	41	34	39	32	75·6	88·4	62·7	1641	1802	1540
25	Brāhman: Deshastha	Canarese	Bellary	187	202	180	144	152	132	77·0	83·4	71·0	48	54	44	36	42	32	75·8	87·2	66·0	1634	1750	1514
25	Brāhman: Pattar	Malayālam	Malabar	188	203	172	140	151	131	74·5	81·4	69·1	47	51	42	36	41	32	76·5	95·3	64·7	1643	1750	1534
40	Brāhman: Tamil (poorer classes)	Tamil	Madras City	186	199	173	142	152	127	76·5	84·0	69·0	47	55	41	36	39	30	76·7	95·1	60·0	1625	1746	1530
175	Nāyar	Malayālam	Malabar	192	206	170	141	155	129	73·2	80·4	65·0	47	55	40	36	44	29	76·7	102·3	56·9	1651	1808	1511
60	Cheruman	Malayālam	Malabar	184	319	171	135	144	123	73·4	81·9	67·7	45	51	40	35	40	29	77·2	88·9	63·3	1566	1674	1458
25	Kota	Canarese	Nilgiri Hills	192	202	183	142	151	134	74·1	79·1	69·9	45	50	41	35	4	31	77·2	92·9	64·0	1619	1742	1555
40	Palli	Tamil	Chingleput	186	204	174	138	144	126	74·2	78·6	69·1	46	50	41	35	41	32	77·3	90·5	68·3	1625	1716	1498
50	Malaiāli	Tamil	Shevaroy Hills	183	193	170	137	144	130	74·4	82·8	61·0	46	52	39	35	41	30	77·8	100·0	63·8	1639	1732	1532
40	Palli	Tamil	Madras City	186	196	174	136	146	121	73·0	80·0	64·4	46	51	41	36	41	31	77·9	95·1	60·8	1625	1694	1510
...	Chakkiliyan	......	......	186	198	176	139	152	130	74·7	80·9	70·4	46	52	40	36	41	32	78·2	97·6	64·0	1622	1745	1503
100	Shānan Karukupattayar	Tamil	Tinnevelly	189	198	176	145	154	134	76·6	85·4	70·4	47	52	41	37	43	33	79·3	104·9	68·0	1701	1828	1586
25	Pulaiyan	Malayālam	Travancore	183	193	170	139	150	130	76·3	83·0	72·3	44	50	40	35	40	30	79·3	92·7	68·0	1530	1626	1434
30	Shānan Nattati	Tamil	Tinnevelly	189	198	178	144	156	137	76·8	83·2	70·8	46	52	41	37	40	33	79·8	93·0	70·8	1701	1808	1622
40	Parayan (Pariah)	Tamil	Madras City	186	197	170	137	145	130	73·6	78·3	64·8	45	51	41	36	45	31	80·0	91·8	66·0	1621	1714	1494
40	Irula	Tamil	Chingleput	184	196	170	135	144	128	73·1	78·6	68·4	45	50	40	36	41	32	80·9	90·5	70·0	1599	1668	1502
40	Mukkuvan	Malayālam	Malabar	190	204	176	142	152	134	75·1	83·5	68·6	47	51	42	38	44	32	81·0	104·8	62·5	1631	1778	1508
25	Kanikar	Malayālam	Travancore	185	194	178	136	142	130	73·4	78·9	69·1	44	47	39	37	43	34	84·6	105·0	72·3	1552	1703	1502
25	Irula	Tamil	Coimbatore	180	191	170	137	143	131	75·8	80·9	70·8	44	48	41	37	43	32	84·9	100·0	72·3	1598	1680	1520
25	Māla Vedar	Malayālam	Travancore	185	196	174	136	146	130	73·4	80·9	69·8	43	47	38	36	40	32	84·9	102·6	71·1	1542	1638	1408
23	Malasar	Tamil	Coimbatore	182	192	173	135	144	124	74·5	80·0	70·0	43	48	40	38	42	34	87·2	102·4	75·4	1612	1705	1528
22	Yeruva	Canarese	Coorg	182	193	164	134	140	125	73·6	82·0	67·0	45	51	37	40	45	37	89·6	103·0	81·0	1587	1680	1500
25	Kadia	Tamil	Anaimalai Hills	184	194	172	134	138	125	72·9	80·0	69·1	43	48	38	39	45	32	89·8	115·4	72·9	1577	1694	1486
25	Paniyan	Malayālam	Malabar	183	193	175	136	149	130	74·0	81·1	68·4	43	48	33	38	42	32	95·1	108·6	72·9	1574	1716	1520
	Ceylon and Southern India.																							
22	Moormen	......	Ceylon and Southern India	182	193	169	144	[illegible]	131	79·1	90·0	70·0	48	52	42	39	42	31	80·7	95·0	62·0	1625	1752	1510
	Rajputana.																							
200	Bhil	Bhil	Mewar (Rajputana)	181·3	198	166	138·7	149	130	76·5	84	68	44·8	52	37	37·7	45	30	84·1	105	63	1629	1764	1476
	Chota Nagpur and Western Bengal.																							
20	Dom	Bihāri	Lohardaga	184·7	194	173	140·4	148	130	76·0	84	69	48·9	55	43	38·7	41	36	79·1	91	72	1626	1720	1540
100	Kurmi	Karmali: Bengali	Manbhum	185·6	202	167	140·5	151	128	75·7	83	66	47·2	53	38	39·0	47	35	82·6	98	69	1608	1720	1500
20	Bauri	Bengāli	Western Bengal	185·0	195	174	138·9	144	129	75·0	81	71	46·1	51	40	38·8	44	31	84·1	98	66	1603	1716	1500
9	Tānti	Bihāri	Lohardaga	184·3	190	180	140·6	146	134	76·2	81	73	45·5	48	43	38·8	44	36	85·2	94	78	1562	1670	1490
2	Birhor	Kharia	Ranchi	185·5	186	185	142·0	148	136	76·5	80	74	47·5	49	46	40·5	41	40	85·2	87	84	1643	1680	1606
29	Chik	Bihāri	Lohardaga	187·6	197	179	138·5	148	131	73·8	80	69	46·2	51	42	39·7	46	36	85·9	103	78	1589	1734	1460
100	Orāon	Kurukh	Lohardaga	184·6	198	165	139·3	158	131	75·4	87	67	46·2	53	38	39·8	47	34	86·1	113	70	1621	1744	1480
100	Bhūmij	Bhumij: Bengali	Manbhum	185·9	203	162	139·6	150	130	75·0	84	67	46·7	53	40	40·4	47	35	86·5	113	72	1592	1782	1460
73	Lohār	Bihāri	Lohardaga	186·1	202	173	140·3	151	131	75·3	84	70	45·9	55	39	39·8	49	33	86·7	113	64	1621	1730	1488
4	Chero	Bihāri	Lohardaga	190·7	195	186	138·2	143	136	72·4	74	70	43·5	50	39	38·0	39	37	87·3	95	76	1584	1680	1500
8	Binjhia	Bihāri	Lohardaga	182·7	186	174	137·3	140	130	75·1	81	70	43·3	45	40	38·2	42	35	88·2	98	80	1594	1646	1510
78	Kharia	Kharia	Lohardaga	184·4	198	170	137·4	150	130	74·5	86	69	45·3	51	33	40·1	45	35	88·5	118	77	1601	1700	1480
100	Bhuiya	Bihāri	Lohardaga	183·0	197	167	139·1	148	128	76·0	85	67	44·6	51	37	39·6	45	35	88·7	113	69	1577	1700	1470
100	Santāl	Santāli	Santal Parganas	184·8	201	171	140·7	153	131	76·1	88	69	45·7	53	40	40·6	48	35	88·8	110	74	1614	1770	1510
100	Kharwār	Bihāri	Lohardaga	185·7	200	173	140·2	150	130	75·5	87	68	45·0	52	39	40·4	47	31	89·7	113	69	1605	1700	1466
100	Mānda	Mundāri	Lohardaga	185·9	200	169	138·6	150	130	74·5	81	69	44·7	50	36	40·2	50	33	89·9	112	74	1589	1718	1446
21	Korwa	Korwāri	Lohardaga	185·2	194	172	137·8	145	130	74·4	81	69	44·0	48	41	40·7	48	36	92·5	109	79	1595	1680	1480
100	Mal Pahāria	Bengāli	Santal Parganas	183·4	200	169	139·1	147	129	75·8	82	71	44·1	55	36	41·0	48	35	92·9	110	71	1577	1726	1450
100	Māle	Mālto	Santal Parganas	183·6	198	166	137·5	149	127	74·8	82	69	43·9	49	38	41·5	49	35	94·5	113	77	1577	1708	1470
2	Asur	Asur or Agaria	Lohardaga	187·0	193	181	138·5	141	136	74·0	75	73	42·5	47	38	40·5	42	39	95·9	103	89	1630	1656	1604

SUMMARY OF

ARYO-DRA

UNITED PROVINCES, BEHAR AN

Number of subjects.	Name of Tribe or Caste.	Language or Dialect.	Locality.	Dimensions of Head. Length (Glabello-occipital). Average.	Maximum.	Minimum.	Breadth (Extreme). Average.	Maximum.	Minimum.	Propo tions Hea Cepha Inde Average.	Maximum.
26	Bhuinhār	Eastern Hindi	United Provinces	187·2	198	178	137·4	144	128	73·3	77
67	Brāhman	Bihari	Behar	187·8	202	171	140·8	156	130	74·9	84
59	Bābhan	Do.	Do.	187·8	201	176	144·1	161	130	76·7	9[illegible]
100	Brāhman	Eastern Hindi	United Provinces	187·5	202	170	137·2	152	127	73·1	84
100	Kāyasth	Western Hindi	Do.	186·4	200	174	135·4	154	124	72·6	8[illegible]
100	Goāla	Bihari	Behar	185·4	202	171	141·4	160	128	76·2	87
100	Chhatri	Eastern Hindi	United Provinces	188·3	203	172	137·6	152	123	73·0	84
103	Kanjar	Western Hindi	Do.	181·8	195	165	135·9	149	120	74·7	82
15	Khatri	Eastern Hindi	Do.	188·0	195	175	035·2	141	130	71·9	79
71	Kurmi	Bihari	Behar	186·9	202	167	141·5	152	133	75·7	83
100	Kurmi	Eastern Hindi	United Provinces	184·0	200	170	134·9	147	125	73·3	81
65	Thāru	Do.	Do.	184·0	205	166	136·0	145	128	73·9	83
80	Bania	Do.	Do.	187·2	200	175	133·5	150	124	71·3	84
56	Kahār	Bihari	Behar	186·1	203	173	141·7	154	132	76·1	83
33	Barhi	Western Hindi	United Provinces	185·4	197	175	133·3	140	125	71·8	78
100	Goāla	Eastern Hindi	Do.	185·2	202	170	135·2	145	125	73·0	85
100	Kewat	Do.	Do.	184·3	198	170	134·0	145	124	72·7	8[illegible]
100	Bhar	Do.	Do.	185·5	197	170	136·4	147	120	73·5	81
100	Maghya Dom	Bihari	Behar	186·3	203	171	142·1	154	132	76·2	87
13	Bind	Do.	Do.	184·6	192	176	136·7	146	125	74·0	81
32	Kol	Eastern Hindi	United Provinces	183·1	195	170	132·6	140	120	72·4	81
100	Dosādh	Bihari	Behar	184·8	201	168	141·8	155	130	76·8	85
45	Lohār	Western Hindi	United Provinces	184·9	200	170	134·7	145	120	72·8	82
100	Guria	Eastern Hindi	Do.	184·7	207	169	133·8	147	123	72·4	80
56	Sinhalese	Sinhalese	Ceylon	183·4	202	171	143·9	155	133	78·4	87
62	Chamār	Bihari	Behar	184·4	198	168	140·3	154	128	76·0	88
100	Kāchhi	Western Hindi	United Provinces	184·6	198	172	133·2	149	122	72·1	81
100	Dom	Eastern Hindi	Do.	182·7	204	170	136·8	148	124	74·8	84
100	Lodha	Western Hindi	Do.	185·2	201	170	334·5	145	123	72·6	81
100	Koiri	Do.	Do.	185·2	197	170	133·6	145	120	72·1	81
100	Pāsi	Eastern Hindi	Do.	185·0	206	169	134·4	146	126	72·6	80
100	Chamār	Do.	Do.	185·1	196	166	134·9	147	123	72·8	81
18	Musahar	Do.	Do.	181·7	197	170	134·8	145	130	74·1	79
77	Musahar	Bihari	Behar	183·0	200	171	138·6	150	130	75·7	84

IX III

EASUREMENTS.

IAN TYPE.

EYLON. (In order of Nasal Index.)

Dimensions of Nose.						Proportions of Nose.			Stature.			Relative Prominence of Root of Nose.				
Height.			Breadth.			Nasal Index.								Orbito-Nasal Index.		
Average.	Maximum.	Minimum.	Average.	Maximum.	Minimum.	Average.	Maximum.	Minimum.	Average.	Maximum.	Minimum.	External orbital breadth (average).	Bi-orbito nasal arc (average).	Average.	Maximum.	Minimum.
47·2	52	40	34·5	41	31	73·0	91	61	1660	1727	1574	...	...	...	...	...
49·3	56	40	36·1	43	31	73·2	93	63	1661	1790	1544	...	...	...	...	...
50·5	58	42	37·4	43	33	74·0	90	62	1662	1760	1540	...	...	...	...	...
46·5	53	35	34·7	41	28	74·6	100	60	1659	1879	1422	...	...	...	...	...
46·6	52	32	34·9	44	30	74·8	102	58	1648	1792	1498	...	...	...	...	...
48·5	56	41	37·2	45	29	76·7	100	58	1642	1780	1502	...	...	...	...	...
45·8	53	38	35·6	43	29	77·7	97	58	1661	1803	1498	...	...	...	...	...
43·7	54	32	34·1	40	28	78·0	106	59	1636	1778	1498	...	...	...	...	...
45·7	53	40	35·7	39	33	78·1	93	64	1623	1727	1524	...	...	...	...	...
47·6	56	40	37·4	42	30	78·5	98	60	1630	1764	1520	...	...	...	...	...
43·9	52	39	34·8	41	30	79·2	98	60	1642	1966	1349	...	...	...	...	...
45·4	59	40	36·1	46	31	79·5	102	61	1614	1752	1524	114·0	130·0	114·0	119·0	109·0
44·7	54	35	35·6	41	30	79·6	106	65	1642	1816	1473	...	...	...	...	...
48·0	56	40	38·3	45	30	79·7	103	63	1624	1760	1510	...	...	...	...	...
42·9	48	37	34·7	42	31	80·8	105	67	1637	1727	1574	...	...	...	...	...
43·1	52	35	34·9	42	29	80·9	108	60	1628	1752	1447	...	...	...	...	...
43·2	52	32	35·2	42	29	81·4	100	62	1626	1752	1498	...	...	...	...	...
44·4	55	33	36·4	46	30	81·9	109	60	1612	1790	1473	...	...	...	...	...
48·0	55	40	39·5	48	32	82·2	98	62	1648	1770	1496	112·6	128·7	114·2	125·0	103·0
45·0	52	38	37·0	40	35	82·2	100	71	1612	1686	1534	111·9	125·9	112·5	112·0	107·0
44·0	49	41	36·2	40	30	82·2	93	64	1650	1779	1549	...	...	...	...	...
46·8	56	40	38·6	44	33	82·4	100	64	1620	1728	1494	134·5	132·1	115·3	126·0	105·0
43·4	52	35	35·8	43	29	82·4	114	60	1636	1826	1498	...	...	...	...	...
42·1	52	33	34·8	41	28	82·6	103	60	1627	1752	1473	...	...	...	...	...
47·7	52	41	39·2	46	34	82·6	100	68	1625	1730	1499	99·5	112·3	112·8	118·0	106·0
46·0	52	39	38·1	44	32	82·8	95	65	1612	1840	1480	...	...	...	...	...
41·7	50	33	34·6	42	29	82·9	117	60	1642	1821	1485	...	...	...	...	...
45·4	55	37	37·7	45	32	83·0	122	62	1655	1778	1524	...	...	...	...	...
41·6	49	34	34·7	42	30	83·4	109	65	1628	1778	1536	...	...	...	...	...
42·7	51	35	35·7	43	30	83·6	111	60	1628	1752	1511	...	...	...	...	...
41·2	52	33	35·2	42	27	85·4	115	66	1639	1778	1524	...	...	...	...	...
41·0	50	34	35·3	41	30	86·0	109	64	1630	1765	1524	...	...	...	...	...
42·5	47	37	36·6	43	32	86·1	103	73	1598	1701	1498	...	...	...	...	...
45·5	52	38	40·4	49	34	88·7	113	72	1591	1696	1500	108·3	121·8	112·4	121·0	105·0

APPI

SUMMARY OF

MONGOLO-

BENGAL AND ORISSA

Number of subjects.	Name of Tribe or Caste.	Language or Dialect.	Locality.	Dimensions of Head.						PF TI(I
				Length (Glabello-occipital).			Breadth (Extreme).			Ce I
				Average.	Maximum.	Minimum.	Average.	Maximum.	Minimum.	Average.
100	Kochh (Rājbansi)	Rājbansi	N.-E. Bengal	186·2	202	166	140·2	153	127	75·2
88*	Kochh (Rājbansi)	Do.	Do.	181·0	202	165	139·0	152	131	76·7
99	Bāgdi	Bengali	Bengal	182·7	201	172	139·5	153	130	76·3
12	Māl	Do.	Western Bengal	183·0	191	166	141·3	146	135	77·2
41	Goāla	Do.	Eastern Bengal	183·8	198	170	142·1	153	131	77·3
100	Kaibarta	Do.	Do.	182·3	198	166	141·1	152	129	77·3
48	Sadgop	Do.	Bengal, 24-Parganas	182·6	190	168	142·1	150	132	77·6
27	Muchi	Do.	Eastern Bengal	182·9	198	170	142·0	151	133	77·6
100	Pod	Do.	Bengal, 24-Parganas	183·2	198	172	142·4	155	130	77·7
185	Muhammadan	Do.	Eastern Bengal	182·8	199	168	142·7	156	131	78·0
67	Chandāl	Do.	Do.	183·2	201	166	143·1	151	131	78·1
100	Kāyastha	Do.	Bengal	182·4	195	169	142·8	155	129	78·2
32	Brāhman	Do.	Western Bengal	182·2	195	171	142·6	151	135	78·2
68	Brāhman	Do.	Eastern Bengal	181·5	195	170	143·4	151	134	79·0
20	Rājbansi Magh	Magh	Chittagong	178·6	192	166	148·4	157	140	83·0
43	Karan	Oriya	Puri	186·1	197	174	142·0	152	130	76·2
26	Niāri	Do.	Cuttack	185·0	193	170	141·5	151	131	76·4
45	Teli	Do.	Puri	184·0	196	166	140·8	150	129	75·6
59	Chāsa	Do.	Cuttack	183·9	196	169	141·9	151	129	77·1
52	Shashan Brāhman	Do.	Puri	182·9	195	171	141·2	155	128	77·1
38	Kewat	Do.	Cuttack	183·4	198	173	141·9	157	131	77·3
40	Khandait	Do.	Do.	183·6	197	171	142·0	153	133	77·3
40	Bauri	Do.	Do.	180·4	193	165	139·6	149	130	77·3
40	Mastān Brāhman	Do.	Puri	183·8	197	169	142·7	154	132	77·6
40	Pān	Do.	Cuttack	182·2	193	161	141·5	154	130	77·6
41	Gaura	Do.	Do.	182·8	198	166	142·1	151	130	77·7
41	Panda Brāhman	Do.	Puri	183·3	195	171	142·7	152	132	77·8
41	Kandra	Do.	Cuttack	182·6	198	168	143·3	157	133	78·4
40	Guria	Do.	Puri	182·9	204	163	143·5	167	135	78·4

* Lt.-

IEASUREMENTS.

RAVIDIAN TYPE.

(In order of Cephalic Index.)

R- OF B.	DIMENSIONS OF NOSE.						PROPORTIONS OF NOSE.			STATURE.			RELATIVE PROMINENCE OF ROOT OF NOSE.				
... L.	Height.			Breadth.			Nasal Index.								Orbito-Nasal Index.		
Minimum.	Average.	Maximum.	Minimum.	Average.	Maximum.	Minimum.	Average.	Maximum.	Minimum.	Average.	Maximum.	Minimum.	External orbital breadth (average).	Bi-orbito nasal arc (average).	Average.	Maximum.	Minimum.
Bengal.																	
68	48·9	57	44	37·5	45	32	76·6	92	61	1,607	1,746	1,440	103·7	115·0	110·8	121	104
71	45·0	52	37	36·0	49	30	80·0	109	67	1,591	1,695	1,502	100·0	110·0	110·0	121	93
68	46·7	55	39	37·6	45	30	80·5	100	62	1,603	1,722	1,434	106·0	119·0	112·2	118	106
71	47·2	50	42	40·0	46	33	84·7	100	70	1,622	1,730	1,520	...	...	...	...	...
71	49·0	58	43	36·4	40	31	74·2	87	62	1,646	1,746	1,500	...	...	...	...	...
70	48·0	55	37	36·6	43	32	76·2	103	63	1,629	1,770	1,490	...	...	...	...	...
72	49·6	55	42	36·7	49	30	73·9	98	55	1,633	1,780	1,510	...	...	...	...	...
72	49·1	54	42	36·8	43	32	74·9	88	63	1,641	1,742	1,536	...	...	...	...	...
70	49·1	56	41	37·4	43	32	76·1	91	63	1,625	1,850	1,490	99·6	111·1	111·5	118	104
70	49·4	58	40	38·3	45	32	77·5	96	64	1,634	1,760	1,500	113·2	128·6	113·6	121	106
70	49·6	56	43	36·7	42	30	73·9	89	62	1,619	1,734	1,472	112·3	128·1	114·0	121	106
70	50·2	58	42	35·3	41	29	70·3	89	56	1,636	1,810	1,544	...	...	...	...	...
72	48·5	54	40	34·9	40	29	71·9	100	58	1,670	1,734	1,550	...	...	...	...	...
70	49·9	59	36	35·1	42	28	70·3	85	56	1,653	1,792	1,474	...	...	...	...	...
74	51·0	57	43	38·2	46	33	74·9	88	63	1,645	1,750	1,542	106·6	118·3	110·9	115	105
Orissa.																	
68	47·7	55	39	38·8	44	32	81·3	100	66	1,638	1,792	1,486	109·8	127·7	116·3	126	102
70	46·8	53	39	37·7	42	32	80·5	100	70	1,611	1,756	1,469	107·9	122·8	113·8	120	107
71	47·1	56	39	36·5	42	31	77·4	95	65	1,619	1,794	1,500	107·8	124·8	115·7	123	108
70	47·5	53	41	37·7	42	33	79·3	95	67	1,615	1,752	1,450	108·2	123·5	111·4	121	109
67	48·4	57	41	37·2	47	32	76·8	93	59	1,635	1,748	1,498	109·2	127·4	116·6	123	110
71	47·0	59	40	38·7	45	34	82·3	98	66	1,611	1,716	1,500	108·3	123·7	114·2	121	109
69	48·0	55	40	37·8	44	33	78·7	98	67	1,645	1,728	1,529	109·5	126·9	115·8	123	108
70	45·5	56	38	38·3	44	33	85·1	113	68	1,585	1,686	1,476	110·3	124·2	112·6	117	104
69	67·9	55	40	38·0	48	31	79·3	100	63	1,642	1,755	1,468	110·6	129·5	171·0	120	112
68	46·6	54	39	38·3	45	33	82·1	100	66	1,607	1,748	1,462	110·0	124·1	112·8	119	107
70	48·4	55	42	37·2	43	27	76·8	96	60	1,627	1,748	1,510	110·3	126·0	114·2	122	108
70	47·9	55	41	37·1	44	32	77·4	100	66	1,642	1,750	1,558	109·5	126·9	115·8	124	107
69	47·6	54	40	37·9	42	33	79·6	100	70	1,625	1,722	1,506	111·7	127·8	114·4	121	110
69	47·0	55	41	37·3	45	31	79·3	93	63	1,606	1,724	1,476	108·9	125·6	115·3	122	107

I. Waddell.

SUMMARY OF

MONGOI

EASTERN HIMALAYA, CHITTAGONG HILL TRACT

Number of subjects.	Name of Tribe or Caste.	Language or Dialect.	Locality.	Dimensions of Head. Length (Glabello-occipital). Average.	Maximum.	Minimum.	Breadth (Extreme). Average.	Maximum.	Minimum.	PF TIC I — C I Average.
17	Kuki . . .	Rangkhol	Rangamati . .	187·2	200	179	142·8	156	136	76·2
11	Kuki *	Rangkhol	Rangamati . .	187·0	195	176	143·0	151	137	76·4
100	Chakma . .	Tipura .	Rangamati . .	177·9	195	162	150·0	161	134	84·3
8	Chakma * . .	Tipura	Chittagong . .	181·0	186	177	144·0	156	135	79·5
17	Ao * . . .	Ao .	Naga Hills . .	179·0	187	170	144·0	153	137	80·4
50	Limbu . .	Limbu .	Nepal . . .	181·4	193	170	153·1	167	140	84·3
80	Magh . .	Magh .	Rangamati . .	182·1	198	170	148·5	161	136	81·5
32	Khambu . .	Kiranti (Khambu)	Nepal . . .	182·4	194	169	147·8	160	130	81·0
11	Kiranti * . .	Kiranti .	Ilam (E. Nepal) .	176·0	182	171	145·0	153	138	82·3
7	Khamti (Tai) * .	Khamti	Dibrugah (Assam) Bor-khamli	187·0	196	180	148·0	151	144	79·1
58	Tipra . . .	Tipura .	Rangamati . .	181·4	193	167	146·1	160	136	80·5
18	Ar-leng (Mikir) *	Mikir .	Kamrup (Assam) .	181·0	193	172	141·0	151	138	77·9
57	Lepcha . .	Lepcha .	Sikkim . . .	185·0	195	174	146·7	161	136	79·9
36	Lepcha (Rong) * .	Rangor Lepcha	Sikkim . . .	180·0	193	167	145·0	157	133	80·5
81	Kasia * . .	Kasi .	Kasia Hills (Assam)	183·0	193	171	144·0	151	133	78·6
5	Murung . .	Mrung Tipura	Chittagong . .	185·4	189	182	142·0	152	135	76·5
35	Mangor . .	Magar .	Nepal . . .	183·6	201	163	145·2	156	136	79·0
7	Dafla * . .	Dafla .	N. Lakhimpur (Assam)	183·0	189	178	141·0	146	138	77·0
65	Murmi . .	Murmi .	Nepal and Darjeeling	188·0	196	169	149·6	161	134	79·5
9	Bhotanese * .	Bhotia .	Pato (E. Himalaya)	183·0	188	176	147·0	157	140	80·3
108	Tibetans . .	Bhotia .	Eastern Himalaya .	186·9	207	172	151·4	168	141	81·0
8	Tibetans * . .	Bhotia .	Kong-bu (E. Himalaya)	182·0	189	173	148·0	161	143	81·3
10	Mech . . .	Mech .	Goalpara (Assam) .	185·0	203	171	147·0	153	143	79·0
33	Bodo (Kachari) *	Bodo .	Kamrup (Assam) .	181·0	195	171	142·0	152	135	78·4
28	Gurung . .	Gurung .	Darjeeling and Nepal	181·3	202	169	148·1	168	141	81·6
7	Abor . . .	Abor .	Dihong valley .	184·0	192	172	142·0	147	135	77·1
13	Newār . .	Newar .	Nepal . . .	181·9	193	169	148·3	156	142	81·5
25	Mi-shing (Miri) *	Miri .	Sibsagar (Assam) .	178·0	199	169	144·0	153	139	80·8
27	Sin-teng (Jaintia) *	Khasi .	Jantia Hills . .	192·0	199	176	140·0	149	134	72·9
13	Ching-po (Singpho) *	Singpho	Bisha (Assam) .	185·0	192	173	140·0	146	137	75·6
19	Ahom * . .	Ahom .	Sibsagar (Assam) .	176·0	185	161	145·0	154	137	82·3
12	Rabha (Datiyal Kachari) *	Kachari	Kamrup (Assam) .	182·0	197	170	142·0	149	135	78·0
34	Mande (Garo) * .	Mande .	Garo Hills (Assam)	183·0	193	174	139·0	150	134	75·9
3	Chutiya * . .	Chutiya	Sibsagar (Assam) .	182·0	183	182	143·0	145	142	78·5
30	Kanet † . .	Lahauli .	Lahoul . . .	189·0	199	179	147·0	155	138	77·5
16	Anga-mi * . .	Angami	Ta-bo-pi-si-mi .	183·0	194	170	144·0	152	135	78·6
4	Kyon-Tsu ("Lhota" "Naga") *	Lhota .	Woka (Assam) .	187·0	200	178	144·0	154	141	77·0
60	Kanet † . .	Kulu .	Kulu . . .	192·0	204	181	143·0	154	132	74·3
6	Kolita * . .	Kachari	Gauhati (Assam) .	181·0	187	170	139·0	148	134	76·7

* Lt.-Col. Waddell, C.I.E.

NDIX III

MEASUREMENTS.

OID TYPE.

AND ASSAM. (In order of Orbito-Nasal Index—Risley.)

…S OF HEAD.		DIMENSIONS OF NOSE.						PROPORTIONS OF NOSE.			STATURE.			RELATIVE PROMINENCE OF ROOT OF NOSE.				
…		Height.			Breadth.			Nasal Index.								Orbito-Nasal Index.		
Maximum.	Minimum.	Average.	Maximum.	Minimum.	Average.	Maximum.	Minimum.	Average.	Maximum.	Minimum.	Average.	Maximum.	Minimum.	External orbital breadth (average).	Bi-orbital nasal arc (average).	Average.	Maximum.	Minimum.
81	71	46·7	52	43	39·7	43	34	85·0	93	74	1566	1650	1506	99·5	105·7	106·2	110	102
82	74	45	49	41	41	45	38	91·1	100	84	1587	1670	1508	110·0	121·0	110·0	113	105
96	77	47·2	53	41	39·9	46	30	84·5	105	70	1595	1696	1490	101·3	107·8	106·4	112	102
87	74	44	49	39	40	45	38	90·9	102	80	1597	1639	1546	103·0	117·0	113·5	121	107
85	76	44	49	37	36	41	31	81·8	100	70	1566	1648	1504	104·0	111·0	106·7	112	101
94	76	50·2	57	37	37·2	43	33	74·1	111	64	1603	1734	1450	109·1	116·7	106·9	113	104
95	73	47·5	55	38	39·4	48	34	82·9	102	68	1599	1710	1522	101·0	108·0	106·9	113	102
93	75	50·0	57	45	38·3	42	33	76·6	91	63	1571	1656	1416	107·2	115·0	107·1	113	103
88	77	42	44	39	36	40	35	85·7	98	82	1586	1606	1512	...	...	...	...	...
83	75	47	51	44	38	41	36	80·8	91	75	1641	1695	1575	105·0	113·0	107·6	110	105
92	74	47·1	59	40	39·9	45	35	84·7	105	68	1611	1712	1486	100·0	107·6	107·6	112	103
82	74	47	58	42	40	47	34	85·1	102	67	1633	1703	1558	103·0	111·0	107·7	114	104
90	73	51·6	60	42	34·7	41	33	67·2	83	59	1570	1690	1490	106·4	115·1	108·1	113	103
88	73	46	51	40	36	42	32	78·2	91	67	1584	1684	1449	102·0	108·0	105·8	119	92
84	72	44	52	36	38	45	33	86·3	108	73	1569	1700	1417	106·0	115·0	108·4	119	101
82	73	49·0	51	47	37·6	40	36	76·1	81	73	1582	1636	1536	100·2	108·8	108·5	115	103
91	72	49·6	56	40	38·0	44	34	76·6	98	61	1587	1680	1508	106·4	115·7	108·7	116	103
81	73	44	48	40	37	42	33	84·0	93	78	1606	1708	1532	103·0	112·0	108·7	114	104
89	73	49·7	57	41	37·4	43	32	75·2	100	63	1669	1760	1490	111·5	121·5	108·9	113	105
[illegible]	75	48	54	41	37	41	36	77·0	88	73	1672	1747	1611	110·0	120·0	109·0	115	105
[illegible]	73	51·8	59	38	38·3	47	31	73·9	103	58	1633	1760	1520	119·8	130·8	109·1	120	103
[illegible]	78	45	49	42	37	41	36	82·2	91	76	1634	1748	1570	106·0	112·0	105·6	109	102
[illegible]	71	43	45	42	39	43	38	90·6	100	84	1643	1722	1852	104·0	114·0	109·6	114	104
[illegible]	73	42	50	35	37	49	33	88·0	118	72	1608	1734	1483	103·0	113·0	109·7	116	103
[illegible]	73	48·9	58	38	38·4	43	34	78·5	102	65	1698	1746	1476	117·0	128·6	109·9	114	105
[illegible]	75	43	49	41	39	41	36	81·6	100	80	1579	1628	1490	108·0	119·0	110·1	115	107
[illegible]	76	50·7	57	44	37·2	42	34	73·3	81	64	1614	1706	1470	108·6	119·7	110·2	116	104
[illegible]	73	44	51	40	37	41	34	84·0	100	75	1564	1700	1518	105·0	116·0	110·4	119	103
[illegible]	69	45	52	39	37	42	32	82·2	100	68	1612	1713	1505	107·0	119·0	111·2	119	102
[illegible]	74	47	56	40	38	42	29	80·8	95	60	1605	1695	1528	104·0	116·0	111·5	128	104
[illegible]	75	44	49	38	36	41	33	81·8	90	73	1589	1720	1490	103·0	115·0	111·6	124	104
[illegible]	74	43	49	37	39	44	36	90·6	105	73	1605	1695	1528	102·0	114·0	111·7	128	104
[illegible]	71	41	47	36	39	43	35	95·1	117	83	1588	1679	1512	102·0	114·0	111·7	119	102
[illegible]	78	44	48	38	36	38	35	81·8	95	76	1591	1607	1582	110·0	124·0	112·7	119	106
	72	53	59	47	35	39	32	66·4	76	57	1618	1750	1450	99·0	112·0	112·9	123	105
[illegible]	71	45	52	42	37	40	36	82·2	91	73	1639	1693	1539	103·0	117·0	113·5	120	105
	75	43	47	38	34	38	34	79·0	100	72	1620	1690	1580	103·0	118·0	114·5	117	108
	68	51	59	45	37	44	30	74·1	96	56	1654	1760	1560	101·0	117·0	115·5	129	107
	74	43	47	38	36	40	31	83·7	97	66	1628	1666	1568	101·0	118·0	116·8	124	113

† T. H. Holland, Esq., A.R.C.S., F.G.S.

APPENDIX IV

INFANT MARRIAGE LAWS, MYSORE AND BARODA

REGULATION No. X OF 1894.

(PASSED ON THE 5TH DAY OF OCTOBER, 1894.)

A Regulation to prevent Infant Marriages in the Territories of Mysore.

Preamble.

WHEREAS it is expedient to prevent Infant Marriages in the Territories of Mysore: His Highness the Maharajah is pleased to enact as follows:—

Short title.

1. This Regulation may be called "The Mysore Infant Marriages Prevention Regulation."

Extent and commencement.

(2) It shall extend to the whole of the territories of Mysore, but it shall apply only to marriages among the Hindus. It shall come into operation at the expiration of six months from the date of its publication in the official Gazette.

Definition.

2. For the purposes of this Regulation, an "Infant Girl" means a girl who has not completed eight years of age.

Punishment for causing or abetting infant marriages.

3. Any person who causes the marriage of an infant girl, or who knowingly aids and abets within the meaning of the Indian Penal Code such a marriage, and any man who having completed eighteen years of age marries an infant girl, shall be punished with simple imprisonment for a term which may extend to six months, or with fine, or with both.

Punishment for a man more than fifty years of age marrying a girl under fourteen years of age.

4. Any man who having completed fifty years of age marries a girl who has not completed fourteen years of age, shall be punished with imprisonment of either description for a term which may extend to two years, or with fine, or with both.

Punishment for abetment of offence provided against in section 4.

5. Any person who causes the marriage of a girl who has not completed fourteen years of age, with a man who has completed fifty years of age, and any person who knowingly aids and abets, within the meaning of the Indian Penal Code, such a marriage, shall be punished with simple imprisonment for a term which may extend to six months, or with fine, or with both.

Offences under the Regulation by whom triable.

6. No offence punishable under this Regulation shall be tried by any Court inferior to that of a Magistrate of the District.

Validity of marriages notwithstanding the penalties provided by the Regulation.

7. No marriage which has actually taken place, shall be deemed to be invalid, on the ground of the penalties provided by this Regulation.

No prosecution to be instituted without the previous sanction of Government.

8. No prosecution under this Regulation shall be instituted without the previous written sanction of the Government accorded after such enquiry as the Government may deem fit to make.

ABSTRACT TRANSLATION OF

ACT No. VII OF SAMVAT 1960.

PASSED BY THE BARODA DURBAR.

(*Received the assent of His Highness the Maharajah Sahib on Ashad Sudi 2nd*, i.e., *the 15th of July*, 1904.)

THE EARLY MARRIAGE PREVENTION ACT.

Preamble.

WHEREAS it is expedient to draw the increased attention of the public towards physical training, whereby the future progeny may be healthy and long-lived, His Highness the Gaekwar has been pleased to rule as under :—

Title.

1. This Act shall be called "The Early Marriage Prevention Act."

Commencement.

2. This Act shall come into force on Ashad Sudi 9th Samvat 1960, *i.e.*, the 21st July, 1904.

Definitions.

3. In this Code, the following words have the following meanings :—

(1) "Minor" means—

(*a*) In case of a girl, one who has not completed her 12th year of age.

(*b*) In case of a boy, one who has not completed his 16th year.

(2) "Early marriage" means the marriage of a minor girl or of a minor boy. The word "marriage" does not include a "Baybar" marriage or a marriage with a ball of flowers, or such other nominal marriages.

(3) "Nyayadhish" means Nyayadhish of a Mahal, or who may be from time to time invested with the powers (of that officer).

(4) The term "Wahivatdar" includes Mahalkari also.

What authorities of the State are to be applied to for permission to allow an early marriage.

4. Whoever wishes to marry his minor son or daughter, or the minor girl or boy under his guardianship, shall submit a petition in writing to the Nyayadhish of the Taluka where he may be residing, or to that of the Taluka in which the intended marriage is to take place, for permission to allow the marriage.

Explanation.—There is no objection to a joint petition being submitted by both the parties in cases in which the girl and the boy are both minors.

The value of stamp on the application.

5. The petitions alluded to in the preceding Section must be written on a (Court-fee) stamped paper of Rs. 2.

Particulars to be embodied in the petition.

6. The petition mentioned in Section 4 must contain the following particulars :—

(*a*) the names, age, and caste of the bride and the bridegroom ;

(*b*) the names of their father or guardian ;

(*c*) the date and place of the marriage, and

(*d*) the mention, in full, of the difficulties likely to crop up in case the marriage does not take place.

Procedure to be followed on receipt of the application.

7. The Nyayadhish, on receipt of the application, shall take steps as under :—

(*a*) he shall fix a date, within the period of 15 days, for the hearing of the petition ;

(*b*) shall appoint three gentlemen of the petitioner's caste, as assessors ; and

(*c*) shall issue summonses for their appearance in the Court, on the appointed date.

Enquiries in connection with the application.

8. On the date of hearing, the Nyayadhish, assisted by the assessors, shall enquire into the petition, recording all such evidence as may be produced in its support, and shall dispose of the same by the end of the day.

(2) If the Nyayadhish and all the assessors present or any two of them be satisfied that in the event of the marriage not taking place on the appointed date,

(*a*) there is no probability of its celebration within one year after the bride or the bridegroom comes to age or that it will not take place at all, or

(*b*) it is likely that the parents or the guardian of the girl whose marriage is to be celebrated by them will not, owing to old age or infirmity, survive till she comes to age, and there is none else fit to take care of her besides them, or

(*c*) that unavoidable difficulties of a like nature are likely to crop up, the Nyayadhish shall grant written permission for the celebration of the marriage under his own seal and signature in accordance with the form laid down in the first schedule annexed to this Act.

Explanation.—The permission to be granted for reasons mentioned in sub-sections (*b*) and (*c*) should only be granted if the girl's age is above nine years.

(3) If permission for the celebration of an early marriage of a girl whose betrothal has taken place before this Act comes into force, be asked within three months after the passing thereof, the Nyayadhish should grant the necessary permission after satisfying himself only that the betrothal has taken place before this Act came into force.

Physical examination not compulsory.

9. In course of an enquiry held, or investigations made, for the purposes of this Act, neither the bride nor the bridegroom will be compelled to be present for bodily examination or the bride for any other examination.

Procedure to be followed when the Court does not agree with the assessors.

10. (*a*) If the Nyayadhish does not agree with the assessors or with any two of them, the proceedings shall be referred with their opinions and reasons therefor, by the Nyayadhish to the District Judge.

(*b*) The District Judge shall dispose of the same within a week, and if he thinks that permission should be given, the same shall be given by him in writing as laid down in Section 8.

The Suba to be supplied with a copy of the document granting the permission.

11. The Nyayadhish granting the permission shall, within eight days, forward to the Suba of the District, a copy of the document by which the permission applied for was granted by him.

Punishment.

12. Whoever celebrates or aids to celebrate an early marriage, which has not been given the required permission as laid down in Sections 8 and 10, shall be punished with a fine which may not exceed Rs. 100.

Exception—This provision does not extend to the bride and the bridegroom.

Period of time during which the offence can be tried. 13. None of the offences provided for by this Act shall be tried by the Court, after two years from the date of the marriage.

The registration of marriages. 14. In all the towns, kasbas and villages of the Baroda State, the officials mentioned below shall keep a register of marriages as per the Schedule No. 2 and fill in the particulars as required by Section 15:

(*a*) In the city of Baroda ... ... The Municipal Inspectors.
(*b*) In the kasbas ... ... The Sudhrai Kamdar.
(*c*) In the villages or kasbas where there is no municipality. Village or villages administered in any other way ... ... The Mulki Patel.
(*d*) In Inam village or villages administered in any other way ... ... The Mukhi, or Inamdar, or Administrator.

(2) A copy of the registration (sub-section 1) shall be submitted before the 10th of the next month by the officials concerned to the Suba, through the Taluka Wahivatdar. Immediate information regarding marriages celebrated against the provision of this Act, shall be given to the Nyayadhish having jurisdiction.

(3) The Suba on receipt of the copy (sub-section 2) shall submit annually a statement (Schedule No. 3) to the Sar Suba. It should be despatched within two months after the expiration of each year.

(4) In the absence of any other orders, the Nyayadhish, to whom a copy of the register of marriages is sent according to sub-section 2, should understand that a complaint has been laid before him according to Section 12 of this Act and shall proceed to try the offence summarily in accordance with the provisions of the Code of Criminal Procedure. The case, however, should not be handed over to the Police for investigations under Section 56 of the Criminal Procedure Code.

(5) At the termination of the enquiries (sub-section 4) if any punishment be awarded, the same shall be communicated (as per Schedule No. 4) to the Suba within eight days.

All marriages must be reported. 15. The father or the guardian of the bride shall report the marriage to the officials concerned within eight days after its celebration and shall obtain from them particulars, as per the Schedule No. 5.

Punishment for not getting the marriages registered. 16. If the father or the guardian of the bride fails to give the information about the marriage as required by the preceding section, or gives false information in connection with the same, he shall be punished with a fine which may not exceed Rs. 10.

Responsibilities in connection with the registration of marriage. 17. The responsibilities for the proper registration of marriages, as laid down in Section 14, shall rest with the Wahivatdar of the Mahal.

The marriage cannot be set aside. 18. An early marriage, if once celebrated, cannot be set aside.

APPENDIX V

MODERN THEORIES OF CASTE

*MR. NESFIELD'S THEORY.**

If it were possible to compress into a single paragraph a theory so complex as that which would explain the origin and nature of Indian caste, I should attempt to sum it up in some such words as the following: A caste is a marriage union, the constituents of which were drawn from various different tribes (or from various other castes similarly formed), in virtue of some industry, craft or function, either secular or religious, which they possessed in common. The internal discipline, by which the conditions of membership in regard to connubial and convivial rights are defined and enforced, has been borrowed from the tribal period which preceded the period of castes by many centuries, and which was brought to a close by the amalgamation of tribes into a nation under a common sceptre. The differentia of *caste* as a marriage union consists in some community of function; while the differentia of *tribe* as a marriage union consisted in a common ancestry, or a common worship, or a common totem, or in fact in any kind of common property except that of a common function. Long before castes were formed on Indian soil, most of the industrial classes, to which they now correspond, had existed for centuries, and as a rule most of the industries which they practised were hereditary on the male side of the parentage. These hereditary classes were and are simply the concrete embodiments of those successive stages of culture which have marked the industrial development of mankind in every part of the world. Everywhere (except at least in those countries where he is still a savage), man has advanced from the stage of hunting and fishing to that of nomadism and cattle-grazing, and from nomadism to agriculture proper. Everywhere has the age of metallurgy and of the arts and industries which are coëval with it been preceded by a ruder age, when only those arts were known or practised which sufficed for the hunting, fishing, and nomad states. Everywhere has the class of ritualistic priests and lettered theosophists been preceded by a class of less cultivated worshippers, who paid simple offerings of flesh and wine to the personified powers of the visible universe without the aid of an hereditary professional priesthood. Everywhere has the class of nobles and territorial chieftains been preceded by a humbler class of small peasant proprietors, who placed themselves under their protection and paid tribute or rent in return. Everywhere has this class of nobles and chieftains sought to ally itself with that of the priests or sacerdotal order; and everywhere has the priestly order sought to bring under its control those chiefs and rulers under whose protection it lives. All these classes, then,

---

* *Brief view of the Caste System of the N.-W. P. and Oudh*, by John C. Nesfield, M.A., Oxon, pp. 114—116, para. 195.

had been in existence for centuries before any such thing as caste was known on Indian soil; and the only thing that was needed to convert them into castes, such as they now are, was that the Brāhman, who possessed the highest of all functions —the priestly—should set the example. This he did by establishing for the first time the rule that no child, either male or female, could inherit the name and status of Brāhman, unless he or she was of Brāhman parentage on *both* sides. By the establishment of this rule the principle of marriage unionship was superadded to that of functional unionship; and it was only by the combination of these two principles that a caste in the strict sense of the term could or can be formed. The Brāhman therefore, as the Hindu books inform us, was "the first-born of castes." When the example had thus been set by an arrogant and overbearing priesthood, whose pretensions it was impossible to put down, the other hereditary classes followed in regular order downwards, partly in imitation and partly in self-defence. To a nation mesmerised by Brāhmans and blinded with superstition and ignorance no other course was open. Immediately behind the Brāhman came the Kshatriya, the military chieftain or landlord. He therefore was the "second-born of castes." Then followed the bankers or upper trading classes (the Agarwāl, Khattri, etc.); the scientific musician and singer (Kathak); the writing or literary class (Kāyasth); the bard or genealogist (Bhāt); and the class of inferior nobles (Taga and Bhuinhār) who paid no rent to the landed aristocracy. These, then, were the third-born of castes. In all communities, such classes must stand rather high in the scale of social respectability, since the stages of industry or function which they represent are high in proportion; but in India their rank was more precisely defined than elsewhere by the fact that they made a nearer approach than the castes below them to the Brāhmanical ideal of personal dignity and purity. Next in order came those artisan classes, who were coëval with the age and art of metallurgy; the metallurgic classes themselves; the middle trading classes; the middle agricultural classes, who placed themselves under the protection of the Kshatriya and paid him rent in return (Kurmi, Kāchhi, Māli, Tāmboli); and the middle serving classes, such as Nāpit and Baidya, who attended to the bodily wants of their equals and superiors. These, then, were the fourth-born of castes; and their rank in the social scale has been determined by the fact that their manners and notions are further removed than those of the preceding castes from the Brāhmanical ideal. Next came the inferior artisan classes, those which preceded the age and art of metallurgy (Teli, Kumhār, Kalwār, etc.); the partly nomad and partly agricultural classes (Jāt, Gūjar, Ahīr, etc.); the inferior serving classes, such as Kahār; and the inferior trading classes, such as Bhunja. These, then, were the fifth-born of castes, and their mode of life is still further removed from the Brāhmanical ideal than that of the preceding. The last born, and therefore the lowest, of all the classes are those semi-savage communities, partly tribes and partly castes, whose function consists in hunting or fishing, or in acting as butcher for the general community, or in rearing swine and fowls, or in discharging the meanest domestic services, such as sweeping and washing, or in practising the lowest of human arts, such as basket-making, hide-tanning, etc. Thus throughout the whole series of Indian castes a double test of social precedence has been in active force, the Industrial and the Brāhmanical; and these two have kept pace together almost as evenly as a pair of horses harnessed to a single carriage. In proportion as the function practised by any given caste stands high or low in the scale of industrial development, in the same proportion does the caste itself, impelled by the general tone of society by which it is surrounded, approximate more nearly or more remotely to the Brāhmanical ideal of life. It is these two criteria combined which have determined the relative ranks of the various castes in the Hindu social scale.

Outside the caste system altogether stand the few and shattered remains of those aboriginal tribes, out of which the whole series of caste was fashioned by slow degrees, through the example and under the guidance of the Brāhmanical priesthood. Had the Brāhman never come into existence and had his arrogance proved to be less omnipotent than it did, the various industrial classes would never have become stereotyped into castes, and the nation would then have been spared a degree of social disunion to which no parallel can be found in human history. There seems to be no likelihood of caste being banished from Indian soil until Brāhmanism itself—the *fons et origo mali*—has died a natural death by the rise of the scientific spirit, and the fallacy of its pretensions has become an object of general scorn. As soon as the Brāhman begins to disappear, the rest will follow.

*SIR DENZIL IBBETSON'S THEORY.**

The popular conception of caste.

An old agnostic is said to have summoned up his philosophy in the following words :—"The only thing I know is that I know nothing; and I am not quite sure that I know that." His words express very exactly my own feelings regarding caste in the Punjab. My experience is that it is almost impossible to make any statement whatever regarding any one of the castes we have to deal with, absolutely true as it may be as regards one part of the Province, which shall not presently be contradicted with equal truth as regards the same people in some other district. Yet I shall attempt to set forth briefly what seem to me the fundamental ideas upon which caste is based; and in doing so I shall attempt partly to explain why it is that the institution is so extraordinarily unstable, and its phenomena so diverse in different localities. What I propound in the following paragraphs is simply my working hypothesis as it at present stands; but I shall not stop to say so as I write, though almost every proposition made must be taken subject to limitations, often sufficiently obvious, and not unfrequently involved in some other proposition made in the very next paragraph. My views are of little weight so long as they are not illustrated and supported by instances drawn from actually existing fact. Such instances I have in great abundance, and they will be found in part in the detailed description of castes which follow this discussion. But I have leisure neither to record all my evidence, nor to marshal what I have recorded; and I give my conception of caste with a crudeness of exposition which lack of time forbids me to modify, not because I think that it is anything even distantly approaching to the whole truth, but because I believe that it is nearer to that truth than is the generally received theory of caste as I understand it.

The popular and currently received theory of caste I take to consist of three main articles :—

(1) that caste is an institution of the Hindu religion, and wholly peculiar to that religion alone;

(2) that it consists primarily of a fourfold classification of people in general under the heads of Brāhman, Kshatriya, Vaisya, and Sudra;

(3) that caste is perpetual and immutable, and has been transmitted from generation to generation throughout the ages of Hindu history and myth without the possibility of change.

Now I should doubtless be exaggerating in the opposite direction, but I think that I should still be far nearer to the truth if, in opposition to the popular conception thus defined, I were to say—

(1) that caste is a social far more than a religious institution; that it has no necessary connection whatever with the Hindu religion, further than that under that religion certain ideas and customs common to all primitive nations have been developed and perpetuated in an unusual degree; and

* Report on the Census of the Punjab, 1881, pp. 172—6.

that conversion from Hinduism to Islam has not necessarily the slightest effect upon caste :

(2) that there are Brāhmans who are looked upon as outcasts by those who under the fourfold classification would be classed as Sudras ; that there is no such thing as a Vaisya now existing ; that it is very doubtful indeed whether there is such a thing as a Kshatriya, and if there is, no two people are agreed as to where we shall look for him ; and that Sudra has no present significance save as a convenient term of abuse to apply to somebody else whom you consider lower than yourself ; while the number of castes which can be classed under any one or under no one of the four heads, according as private opinion may vary, is almost innumerable :

(3) that nothing can be more variable and more difficult to define than caste ; and that the fact that a generation is descended from ancestors of any given caste creates a presumption, and nothing more, that that generation also is of the same caste, a presumption liable to be defeated by an infinite variety of circumstances.

The hereditary nature of occupations.

Among all primitive peoples we find the race split up into a number of tribal communities held together by the tie of common descent, each tribe being self-contained and self-sufficing, and bound by strict rules of marriage and inheritance, the common object of which is to increase the strength and preserve the unity of the tribe. There is as yet no diversity of occupation. Among more advanced societies, where occupations have become differentiated, the tribes have almost altogether disappeared ; and we find in their place corporate communities or guilds held together by the tie of common occupation rather than of common blood, each guild being self-contained and self-governed, and bound by strict rules, the common object of which is to strengthen the guild and to confine to it the secrets of the craft which it practises. Such were the trades-guilds of the middle ages as we first meet with them in European history. But all modern inquiry into their origin and earlier constitution tends to the conclusion—and modern authorities on the development of primitive institutions are rapidly accepting that conclusion—that the guild in its first form was, no less than the tribe, based upon common descent ; and that the fundamental idea which lay at the root of the institution in its inception was the hereditary nature of occupation. Now here we have two principles, community of blood and community of occupation. So long as the hereditary nature of occupation was inviolable, so long as the blacksmith's son must be, and nobody else could be, a blacksmith, the two principles were identical. But the struggle for existence is too severe, the conditions of existence too varied, and the character and capacity of individuals too diverse to permit of this inviolability being long maintained ; and in any but the most rudimentary form of society it must, like the socialist's dream of equal division of wealth, cease to exist from the very instant of its birth. And from the moment when the hereditary nature of occupation ceases to be invariable and inviolable, the two principles of community of blood and community of occupation become antagonistic. The antagonism still continues. In every community which the world has ever seen there have been grades of position and distinctions of rank ; and in all societies these grades and distinctions are governed by two considerations, descent and calling. As civilization advances and the ideas of the community expand in more liberal growth, the latter is ever gaining in importance at the expense of the former ; the question what a man is, is ever more and more taking precedence of the question what his father was. But in no society that the world has yet seen has either of these two considerations ever wholly ceased to operate ; in no community has the son of the coal-heaver been born the equal of the son of the nobleman, or the man who dies a trader been held in the same consideration as he who dies a statesman; while in all the son has begun where the father left off. The communities of India in whose midst the Hindu religion has been developed are no exceptions to this rule; but in their case special circumstances have combined to preserve in greater integrity and to perpetuate under a more advanced state of society than elsewhere the hereditary nature of occupation, and thus in a higher degree than in other modern nations to render identical the two principles of community of blood and community of occupation. And it is this difference, a difference of degree rather than of kind, a survival to a later age of an institution which has died out elsewhere rather than a new growth peculiar to the Hindu nation, which makes us give a new name to the old thing and call caste in India what we call position or rank in England.

Occupation the primary basis of caste.

The whole basis of diversity of caste is diversity of occupation. The old division into Brāhman, Kshatriya, Vaisya, Sudra, and the Mlechchha or outcast, who is below the Sudra, is but a division into the priest, the warrior, the husbandman, the artisan, and the menial; and the more modern development which substituted trader for husbandman as the meaning of Vaisya or "the people" did not alter the nature of the classification. William Priest, John King, Edward Farmer, and James Smith are but the survivals in England of the four *varnas* of Manu. But in India, which was priest-ridden to an extent unknown to the experience of Europe even in the middle ages, the dominance of one special occupation gave abnormal importance to all distinctions of occupation. The Brāhman who could at first claim no separate descent by which he should be singled out from among the Aryan community, sought to exalt his office and to propitiate his political rulers, who were the only rivals he had to fear, by degrading all other occupations and conditions of life. Further, as explained in the sections just referred to, the principle of hereditary occupation was to him as a class one of the most vital importance. As the Brāhmans increased in number, those numbers necessarily exceeded the possible requirements of the laity so far as the mere performance of priestly functions was concerned, while it became impossible for them to keep up as a whole even the semblance of sacred learning. Thus they ceased to be wholly priests, and a large proportion of them became mere Levites. The only means of preserving its overwhelming influence to the body at large was to substitute Levitical descent for priestly functions as the basis of that influence, or rather perhaps to check the natural course of social evolution which would have substituted the latter for the former; and this they did by giving the whole sanction of religion to the principle of the hereditary nature of occupation. Hence sprang that tangled web of caste restrictions and distinctions, of ceremonial obligations, and of artificial purity and impurity, which has rendered the separation of occupation from descent so slow and so difficult in Hindu society, and which collectively constitutes what we know as caste. I do not mean that the Brāhmans invented the principle which they thus turned to their own purpose; on the contrary, I have said that it is found in all primitive societies that have outgrown the most rudimentary stage. Nor do I suppose that they deliberately set to work to produce any craftily designed effect upon the growth of social institutions. But circumstances had raised them to a position of extraordinary power; and naturally, and probably almost unconsciously, their teaching took the form which tended most effectually to preserve that power unimpaired.

Indeed, in its earlier form, neither caste nor occupation was even supposed in India to be necessarily or invariably hereditary. It is often forgotten that there are two very distinct epochs in the post-Vedic history of the Hindu nations, which made respectively contributions of very different nature to that body of Hindu scriptures which we are too apt to confuse under the generic name of the Shastras, and which affected in very different manners the form of the Hindu religion. The earlier is the epoch of the Brāhmanas and the Upanishads, while Hinduism was a single and comparatively simple creed, or at most a philosophical abstraction; and the later is the epoch of the Puranas and Tantras, with their crowded Pantheon, their foul imaginings, their degraded idolatry, and their innumerable sects. The former may be said to end with the rise, and the latter to begin with the growing degeneracy of Buddhism. In the earlier Hinduism we find that, while caste distinctions were primarily based upon occupation, considerable license in this respect was permitted to the several castes, while the possibility of the individual rising from one caste to another was distinctly recognised. This was the case even as late as the age of Manu, by which time the caste system had assumed great strictness, and the cardinal importance of occupation had become a prominent part of the Brāhmanical teaching, though its hereditary nature had not yet been so emphatically insisted on. It was in the dark ages of Hindu history, about the beginning of an era during which Brāhmanism was substituted for Hinduism, and the religion became a chaos of impure and degraded doctrine and sectarian teaching, that the theory of the necessarily hereditary nature of occupation seems to have taken its present form. In the earlier epoch the priest was always a Brāhman; in the later the Brāhman was always a priest.

But if occupation was not necessarily transmitted by descent, and if caste varied with change of occupation in the earlier era of Hinduism, it is no less true that this is the case in the present day; though under caste restrictions as they now stand, the change, in an upward direction at least, is infinitely slower and more difficult than then, and is painfully effected by the family or tribe in the course of generations instead of by the individual in the course of years. The following pages will contain numerous instances of the truth of this assertion, and the whole body of tribal and caste tradition in the Punjab supports it. I have not always thought it necessary to state their traditions in discussing the various castes; and I have seldom stopped to comment on the facts. But the evidence, imperfect as it is, will be found to possess no inconsiderable weight; while the very fact of the general currency of a set of traditions, groundless as they may be in individual instances, shows that the theory of society upon which they are based is at least not repugnant to the ideas and feelings and even practice of the people who believe them. Indeed, for the purposes of the present enquiry it would almost be allowable to accept traditional origin; for though the tradition may not be true, it might have been, or it would never have arisen. Instances of fall in the social scale are naturally more often met with than instances of rise, for he who has sunk recalls with pride his ancestral origin, while he who has risen hastens to forget it.

The political and artificial basis of caste.

But before proceeding to give specific instances of recent change of caste, I must adopt a somewhat extended definition of occupation, and must take a somewhat wider basis than that afforded by mere occupation, even so defined, as the foundation of caste.

In India the occupation of the great mass of what may be called the upper or yeoman classes is the same. Setting aside the priests and traders on the one hand and the artisans and menials on the other, we have left the great body of agriculturists who constitute by far the larger portion of the population. This great body of people subsists by husbandry and cattle-farming, and so far their occupation is one and the same. But they are also the owners and occupiers of the land, the holders of more or less compact tribal territories; they are overlords as well as villains; and hence springs the cardinal distinction between the occupation of ruling and the occupation of being ruled. Where the actual calling of every-day life is the same, social standing, which is all that caste means, depends very largely upon political importance, whether present or belonging to the recent past. There is the widest distinction between the dominant and the subject tribes; and a tribe which has acquired political independence in one part of the country, will there enjoy a position in the ranks of caste which is denied it in tracts where it occupies a subordinate position.

Again, the features of the caste system which are peculiar to Brāhmanical Hinduism, and which have already been alluded to, have operated to create a curiously artificial standard of social rank. There are certain rules which must be observed by all at the risk of sinking in the scale. They are, broadly speaking, that widow-marriage shall not be practised, that marriages shall be contracted only with those of equal or nearly equal standing; that certain occupations shall be abstained from which are arbitrarily declared to be impure, such as growing or selling vegetables, handicrafts in general, and especially working or trading in leather and weaving; that impure food shall be avoided; and that no communion shall be held with outcasts, such as scavengers, eaters of carrion or vermin, and the like. There are other and similarly artificial considerations which affect social standing, such as the practice of secluding the women of the family, the custom of giving daughters in marriage only to classes higher than their own, and the like; but these are of less general application than those first mentioned. Many of these restrictions are exceedingly irksome. It is expensive to keep the women secluded, for others have to be paid to do their work; it is still more expensive to purchase husbands for them from a higher grade of society, and so forth; and so there is constant temptation to disregard these rules, even at the cost of some loss of social position.

Thus we have as the extended basis of caste, first occupation, and within a common occupation political prominence and social standing, the latter being partly regulated by a set of very arbitrary rules which are peculiar to Indian caste, and which are almost the only part of the system which is peculiar to it. It is neither tautology nor false logic to say that social standing is dependent upon caste and caste upon social standing, for the two depend each upon the other in different senses. The rise in the social scale which accompanies increased political importance will presently be followed by a rise in caste; while the fall in the grades of caste which a disregard of the arbitrary rules of the institution entails, will surely be accompanied by loss of social standing.

Instances of the mutability of caste.

The Brāhmans are generally husbandmen as well as Levites, for their numbers are so great that they are obliged to supplement the income derived from their priestly office. But when a Brāhman drops his sacerdotal character, ceases to receive food or alms as offerings acceptable to the gods, and becomes a cultivator pure and simple, he also ceases to be a Brāhman, and has to employ other Brāhmans as priests. Witness the Taga Brāhmans of the Delhi division, who are Tagas, not Brāhmans, because they have "abandoned" (*tāg dena*) their priestly character. Indeed, in the hills the very practice of agriculture as a calling or at least the actual following of the plough is in itself sufficient to deprive a Brāhman of all but the name of his caste; for Mr. Lyall points out that in the following quotation from Mr. Barnes, "ploughing" should be read for "agriculture" or "husbandry," there being very few even of the highest Brāhman families, who abstain from other sorts of fieldwork.

"It will afford a tolerable idea of the endless ramification of caste to follow out the details of even the Sārsut tribe as established in these hills. The reader acquainted with the country will know that Brāhmans, though classed under a common appellation, are not all equal. There are primarily two great distinctions in every tribe claiming to be of such exalted origin as the Brāhmans—*viz.* those who follow and those who abstain from agriculture. This is the great touchstone of their creed. Those who have never defiled their hands with the plough, but have restricted themselves to the legitimate pursuits of the caste, are held to be pure Brāhmans; while those who have once descended to the occupation of husbandry retain indeed the name, but are no longer acknowledged by their brethren, nor held in the same reverence by the people at large."

So again if a Brāhman takes to handicrafts he is no longer a Brāhman, as in the case of the Thāvis of the hills, some of whom were Brāhmans in the last generation. The Dharukras of Delhi are admittedly Brāhmans who have within the last few generations taken to widow-marriage ; and the Chamarwa Sādhs and the whole class of the so-called Brāhmans who minister to the outcast classes, are no longer Brāhmans in any respect beyond the mere retention of the name. The Mahā Brāhman, so impure that in many villages he is not allowed to enter the gates, the Dakaut and Gujrāti, so unfortunate that other Brāhmans will not accept offerings at their hands, are all Brāhmans, but are practically differentiated as distinct castes by their special occupations. Turning to the second of Manu's four great classes, we find the Mahājan a Mahājan in the hills so long as he is a merchant, but a Kāyasth as soon as he becomes a clerk ; while the Dasa Banya of the plains who has taken to the practice of widow-marriage is a Banya only by name and occupation, not being admitted to communion or intermarriage by the more orthodox classes who bear the same title. The impossibility of fixing any line between Rājpūts on the one hand, and Jāts, Gūjars, and castes of similar standing on the other, is fully discussed in the subsequent parts of this Chapter, in the paragraphs on the Jāt in general, on the Rājpūts of the Eastern Hills, and on the Thakar and Rāthi. I there point out that the only possible definition of a Rājpūt, in the Punjab at least, is he who, being the descendant of a family that has enjoyed political importance, has preserved his ancestral status by strict observance of the caste rules enumerated above. The extract there quoted from Mr. Lyall's report sums up so admirably the state of caste distinctions in the hills that I make no apology for repeating it. He says :—

> Till lately the limits of caste do not seem to have been so immutably fixed in the hills as in the plains. The Raja was the fountain of honour, and could do much as he liked. I have heard old men quote instances within their memory in which a Raja promoted a Girth to be a Rāthi, and a Thākur to be a Rājpūt, for service done or money given ; and at the present day the power of admitting back into caste-fellowship persons put under a ban for some grave act of defilement is a source of income to the Jagirdar Rajas.
>
> I believe that Mr. Campbell, the present Lieutenant-Governor of Bengal, has asserted that there is no such thing as a distinct Rājpūt stock ; that in former times, before caste distinctions had become crystallized, any tribe or family whose ancestor or head rose to royal rank became in time Rājpūt.
>
> This is certainly the conclusion to which many facts point with regard to the Rājpūts of these hills. Two of the old royal and now essentially Rājpūt families of this district, *viz.* Kotlehr and Bangahal, are said to be Brāhman by original stock. Mr. Barnes says that in Kangra the son of a Rājpūt by a low-caste woman takes place as a Rāthi ; in Seoraj and other places in the interior of the hills I have met families calling themselves Rājpūts, and growing into general acceptance as Rājpūts, in their own country at least, whose only claim to the title was that their father or grandfather was the offspring of a Kānetni by a foreign Brāhman. On the border line in the Himalayas, between Tibet and India Proper, any one can observe caste growing before his eyes ; the noble is changing into a Rājpūt, the priest into a Brāhman, the peasant into a Jāt ; and so on down to the bottom of the scale. The same process was, I believe, more or less in course in Kangra proper down to a period not very remote from to-day.

And Kangra is of all parts of the Punjab the place in which the proudest and most ancient Rājpūt blood is to be found. As Captain Cunningham says in his *History of the Sikhs*: "It may be assumed as certain that, had the conquering Moghals and Pathans been without a vivid belief and an organised priesthood, they would have adopted Vedism and become enrolled among the Kshatriya or

Rājpūt races." In Sirsa we have instances of clans who were a few generations ago accounted Jāt being now generally classed as Rājpūts, having meanwhile practised greater exclusiveness in matrimonial matters, and having abandoned widow-marriage; while the reverse process is no less common. So the Chauhans of Delhi are no longer recognised as Rājpūts since they have begun to marry their widows. Finally, we have the whole traditions of the Punjab tribes of the Jāt and Gūjar status to the effect that they are descended from Rājpūts who married below them, ceased to seclude their women, or began to practise widow-marriage; and the fact that one and the same tribe is often known as Rājpūt, where it has, and as Jāt where it has not, risen to political importance.

But it is possible for Rājpūts and Jāts to fall still lower. The Sahnsars of Hushyarpur were admittedly Rājpūts till only a few generations ago, when they took to growing vegetables, and now rank with Arains. Some of the Tarkhāns, Lohars, and Nais of Sirsa are known to have been Jāts or Rājpūts, who within quite recent times have taken to the hereditary occupations of these castes; and some of the Chauhans of Karnal, whose fathers were born Rājpūts, have taken to weaving and become Shekhs. So too the landowning castes can rise. A branch of the Wattu Rājpūts of the Sutlej, by an affectation of peculiar sanctity, have in the course of a few generations become Bodlas, and now deny their Rājpūt and claim Qureshi origin; and already the claim is commonly admitted. A clan of Ahirs in Rewari has begun to seclude their women and abandon widow-marriage; they no longer intermarry with the other Ahirs, and will presently be reckoned a separate caste; and there is a Kharral family lately settled in Bahawalpur, who have begun to affect peculiar holiness and to marry only with each other, and their next step will certainly be to claim Arab descent. The process is going on daily around us, and it is certain that what is now taking place is only what has always taken place during the long ages of Indian History. The ease with which Saiyads are manufactured is proverbial, and some of our highest Rājpūt tribes are beginning in the Salt-range to claim Moghal or Arab origin. On the frontier the dependence upon occupation of what there most nearly corresponds with caste, as distinct from tribe, is notorious. A Machhi is a Machhi so long as he catches fish, and a Jāt directly he lays hold of a plough. There are no Rājpūts because there are no Rajas; and those who are notoriously of pure Rājpūt descent are Jāts because they till the land.

Among the artisan and menial tribes the process is still more common, and the chapter on this section of the community abounds with instances. One Chamār takes to weaving instead of leather-working and becomes a Chamār-Julaha; presently he will be a Julaha pure and simple: another does the same and becomes a Rangreta or a Bania: a Chuhra refuses to touch night-soil and becomes a Musalli or a Kutana. Within the castes the same process is observable. The Chandar Chamar will not eat or marry with the Jatia Chamar, because the latter works in the hides of impure animals; one section of the Kumhārs will hold no communion with another, because the latter burn sweepings as fuel; a third section has taken to agriculture and looks down upon both. In all these and a thousand similar instances the sections are for all practical purposes distinct castes, though the caste name, being based upon and expressive of the hereditary occupation, is generally retained where the main occupation is not changed. Indeed, I have my doubts whether, setting aside the absolutely degrading occupations, such as scavengering, the caste does not follow the occupation in the case of even each individual among these artisan and menial castes much more generally than we suppose. We know next to nothing about their organisation, and I do not pretend to make anything more than a suggestion. But it it is certain that these lower castes have retained the organisation of the guild in extraordinary completeness long after the organisation of the tribe or caste has almost completely died out among the landowning classes whom they serve. And it may be, especially in towns and cities, that this organisation is meant to protect the craft in the absence of the bond of common descent, and that men belonging by birth to other castes and occupations may, on adopting a new occupation, be admitted to the fraternity which follows it.

The nature and evolution of the institution of the caste.

Thus we see that in India, as in all countries, society is arranged in strata which are based upon differences of social or political importance, or of occupation. But here the classification is hereditary rather than individual to the persons included under it, and an artificial standard is added which is peculiar to caste and which must be conformed with on pain of loss of position, while the rules which forbid social intercourse between castes of different rank render it infinitely difficult to rise in the scale. So, too, the classification being hereditary, it is next to impossible for the individual himself to rise; it is the tribe or section of the tribe that alone can improve its position, and this it can do only after the lapse of several generations, during which time it must abandon a lower for a higher occupation, conform more strictly with the arbitrary rules, affect social exclusiveness or special sanctity, or separate itself after some similar fashion from the body of the caste to which it belongs. The whole theory of society is that occupation and caste are hereditary; and the presumption that caste passes unchanged to the descendants is exceedingly strong. But the presumption is one which can be defeated, and has already been and is now in process of being defeated in numberless instances. As in all other countries and among all other nations, the graduations of the social scale are fixed; but society is not solid but liquid, and portions of it are continually rising and sinking and changing their position as measured by that scale; and the only real difference between Indian society and that of other countries in this respect is that the liquid is much more viscous, the friction and inertia to be overcome infinitely greater, and the movement therefore far slower and more difficult in the former than in the latter. This friction and inertia are largely due to a set of artificial rules which have been grafted on to the social prejudices common to all communities by the peculiar form which caste has taken in the Brāhmanical teachings. But there is every sign that these rules are gradually relaxing. Sikhism did much to weaken them in the centre of the Punjab, while they can now hardly be said to exist on the purely Mahomedan frontier; and I think that we shall see a still more rapid change under the influences which our rule has brought to bear upon the society of the Province. Our disregard for inherited distinctions have already done something, and the introduction of railways much more, to loosen the bonds of caste. It is extraordinary how incessantly, in reporting customs, my correspondents note that the custom or restriction is fast dying out. The liberty enjoyed by the people of the Western Punjab is extending to their neighbours in the east, and especially the old tribal customs are gradually fading away. There cannot be the slightest doubt that in a few generations the materials for a study of caste as an institution will be infinitely less complete than they are even now.

Thus, if my theory be correct, we have the following steps in the process by which caste has been evolved in the Punjab—(1) the tribal divisions common to all primitive societies; (2) the guilds based upon hereditary occupation common to the middle life of all communities; (3) the exaltation of the priestly office to a degree unexampled in other countries; (4) the exaltation of the Levitical blood by a special insistence upon the necessarily hereditary nature of occupation; (5) the preservation and support of this principle by the elaboration from the theories of the Hindu creed or cosmogony of a purely artificial set of rules, regulating marriage and intermarriage, declaring certain occupations and foods to be impure and polluting, and prescribing the conditions and degree of social intercourse permitted between the several castes. Add to this the pride of social rank and the pride of blood which are natural to man, and which alone could reconcile a nation to restrictions at once irksome from a domestic and burdensome from a material point of view; and it is hardly to be wondered at that caste should have assumed the rigidity which distinguishes it in India.

*M. SENART'S THEORY.**

Longtemps on a cru, sur le témoignage de Platon et d'Hérodote, que l'Egypte aurait été régie par le système des castes. C'est une vue abandonnée aujourd'hui par les juges les plus autorisés. Elle parait décidément contredite par les monumens indigènes. Les Grecs, peu accoutumés à de vastes organismes héréditaires reliés par le privilège du rang ou la communauté de la fonction, pouvaient aisément, là où ils en rencontraient des types plus ou moins stricts, en exagérer l'importance ou l'étendue. Jusqu'à présent, l'Inde a seule révélé un régime universel des castes, au sens où nous l'avons constaté et défini. Tout au plus trouve-t-on ailleurs des traces accidentelles, des germes d'institutions analogues; elles ne sont nulle part généralisées ni coordonnées en système.

La Grèce a connu, à Lacédémone et ailleurs, plusieurs cas des fonctions et des métiers héréditaires. Malgré les incertitudes qui en obscurcissent l'interprétation, les noms que portent les quatres tribus (*phylé*) ioniennes de l'Attique sont bien des noms professionnels: soldats, chevriers, artisans.† Ce ne sont assurément pas des castes. L'exemple prouve au moins que la tradition âryenne pouvait, sous l'empire d'une situation favorable, incliner vers la caste. L'enseignement est bon à retenir.

Un fait social qui domine un pays immense, qui s'enchevêtre dans tout son passé, a nécessairement plus d'une cause. A l'enfermer dans une déduction unique, trop précise, on s'égare à coup sûr. Des courans si puissans sont faits d'affluens nombreux. L'explication vraie doit, j'en suis convaincu, faire sa part à chacun des agens qu'on a tour à tour poussés au premier plan, dans un esprit trop systématique et trop exclusif. Il est bien d'autres pays où une race immigrante s'est trouvée juxtaposée à des occupans qu'elle a vaincus et dépossédés, et cette situation n'y a pas fait naître la caste. D'autres populations ont connu de fortes distinctions de classes, et la caste leur est demeurée étrangère. La théocratie s'accommode d'autres cadres. Il faut donc que le régime résulte dans l'Inde de l'action combinée de plusieurs facteurs. J'espère avoir discerné les principaux.

Tâchons d'embrasser d'un coup d'œil le raccourci de cette histoire.

Nous prenons les âryens à leur entrée dans l'Inde. Ils vivent sous l'empire des vieilles lois communes à toutes les branches de la race. Ils sont divisés en peuplades, clans et familles: plus ou moins larges, les groupes sont également gouvernés par une organisation corporative dont les traits généraux sont pour tous identiques, dont le lien est une consanguinité de plus en plus étroite. L'âge de l'égalité pure et simple de clan à clan, de tribu à tribu, est passé. Le prestige militaire et le prestige religieux ont commencé leur œuvre. Certains groupes, rehaussés par l'éclat des prouesses guerrières, fiers d'une descendance plus brillante ou mieux assurée, enrichis plus que d'autres par la fortune des armes, se sont solidarisés en une classe nobiliaire qui revendique le pouvoir. Les rites religieux se sont compliqués au point de réclamer, soit pour l'exécution des cérémonies, soit pour la composition des chants, une habileté spéciale et une préparation technique: une classe sacerdotale est née, qui appuie ses prétentions sur les généalogies plus ou moins légendaires qui rattachent ses branches à des sacrificateurs illustres du passé. Le reste des âryens est confondu dans une catégorie unique au sein de

---

* Senart, *Les Castes dans l'Inde*, pp. 243-257.
† Schömann, *Griech. Alterth.*, éd. 1861, I, p. 327 suiv.

laquelle les divers groupes se meuvent dans leur autonomie et sous leurs lois corporatives. Des notions religieuses dominaient dès l'origine toute la vie ; le sacerdoce dejà puissant double ici le prestige et la rigueur des scrupules religieux.

Les âryens s'avancent dans leur nouveau domaine. Ils se heurtent à une race de couleur foncée, inférieure en culture, qu'ils refoulent. Cette opposition, le souci de leur sécurité, le dédain des vaincus, exaltent chez les vainqueurs l'exclusivisme natif, renforcent toutes les croyances et tous les préjugés qui protègent la pureté des sectionnements entre lesquels ils se répartissent. La population autochtone est rejetée dans une masse confuse que des liens de subordination assez lâches rattachent seuls à ses maîtres. Les idées religieuses qu'apportent les envahisseurs y descendent plus ou moins avant, jamais assez pour la relever à leur niveau. Cependant, en s'étendant sur de vastes espaces où leurs établissemens ne sont guère cantonnés par aucunes limites naturelles, les envahisseurs se dispersent ; ébranlés par les accidens de la lutte, les groupemens primitifs se disjoignent. La rigueur du principe généalogique qui les unissait en est compromise : les tronçons, pour se reformer, obéissent aux rapprochements géographiques ou à d'autres convenances.

Peu à peu se sont imposées les nécessités d'une existence moins mouvante. C'est dans des villages d'industrie pastorale et agricole que se fixe la vie devenue plus sédentaire ; et c'est d'abord par parentés qu'ils se fondent ; car les lois de la famille et du clan conservent une autorité souveraine ; on continue d'observer les usages traditionnels que sanctionne la religion. Les habitudes plus fixes développent les besoins et les métiers d'une civilisation qui est mûre pour plus d'exigences. Les corps d'état sont à leur tour enveloppés dans le réseau, soit que la communauté de village entraîne la communauté d'occupation, soit que les représentans dispersés d'une même profession dans des lieux assez voisins obéissent à une nécessité impérieuse en se modelant sur le seul type d'organisation usité autour d'eux.

Avec le temps deux faits se sont accusés : des mélanges plus ou moins avoués se sont produits entre les races ; les notions âryennes de pureté ont fait leur chemin dans cette population hybride et jusque dans les populations purement aborigènes. De là deux ordres de scrupules qui multiplient les sectionnements, suivant l'impureté plus ou moins forte, soit de la descendance, soit des occupations. Si les principes anciens de la vie familiale se perpetuent, les facteurs de groupements se diversifient : fonction, religion, voisinage, d'autres encore, à coté du principe primitif de la consanguinité dont ils prennent plus ou moins le masque. Les groupes s'acroissent et s'entre-croisent. Sous la double action de leurs traditions propres et des idées qu'elles empruntent à la civilisation âryenne, les tribus aborigènes elles-mêmes, au fur et à mesure qu'elles renoncent à une vie isolée et sauvage, accélèrent l'afflux des sectionnemens nouveaux. La caste existe dès lors. On voit comment elle s'est, dans ses diverses dégradations, substituée lentement au régime familial dont elle est l'héritière.

Un pouvoir politique eût pu subordonner ces organismes aux ressorts d'un système régulier. Nulle constitution politique ne se dégage. L'idée même n'en naît pas. Comment s'en étonner? La puissance sacerdotale n'y peut être favorable, car elle en serait diminuée ; ou son action est très forte et très soutenue ; elle paralyse même dans l'aristocratie militaire l'exercice du pouvoir. Le relief du pays ne constitue pas de noyaux naturels de concentration ; toute limite est ici flottante. La vie pastorale a longtemps maintenu un esprit de tradition sévère ; aucun goût vif de l'action ne l'entame. La population vaincue est nombreuse ; refoulée plus qu'absorbée, elle est envahie lentement par la propagande sacerdotale plutôt que soumise par une brusque conquête. Avec quelques tempéramens elle garde, là surtout où elle se cantonne et s'isole, beaucoup de son organisation ancienne. Par sa masse qu'elle interpose, par l'exemple de ses institutions très rudimentaires, par la facilité même avec laquelle ces institutions se fondent dans l'organisation assez sommaire des immigrans, elle oppose un obstacle de plus à la constitution d'un pouvoir politique véritable. Donc nul rudiment d'État.

Dans cette confusion, la classe sacerdotale a seule, en dépit de ses fractionnemens, gardé un solide esprit de corps ; seule elle est en possession d'un pouvoir tout moral, mais très efficace. Elle en use pour affermir et pour étendre ses privilèges ; elle en use aussi pour établir, sous sa suprématie, une sorte d'ordre et de cohésion. Elle généralise et codifie l'état de fait en un système idéal qu'elle s'efforce de faire passer en loi. C'est le régime légal de la caste. Elle y amalgame la situation actuelle avec les traditions tenaces du passé où la hiérarchie des classes a jeté les fondemens de sa puissance tant accrue depuis.

Sorti d'un mélange des prétentions arbitraires et des faits authentiques, ce système devient à son tour une force. Non seulement les brâhmanes le portent comme un dogme dans les parties du pays dont l'assimilation se fait à une date tardive ; partout, grâce à l'autorité immense qui s'attache à ses patrons, il réagit par les idées sur la pratique. L'idéal spéculatif tend à s'imposer comme la règle stricte du devoir. Mais, des faits à la théorie, il y avait trop loin pour qu'ils aient pu jamais se fondre complètement.

Ce qui nous intéresse c'est le chemin qu'a suivi l'institution dans sa croissance spontanée. Je puis donc m'arrêter ici.

La caste est, à mon sens, le prolongement normal des antiques institutions âryennes, se modelant à travers les vicissitudes que leur préparaient les conditions et le milieu qu'elles rencontrèrent dans l'Inde. Elle serait aussi inexplicable sans ce fond traditionnel qu'elle serait in intelligible sans les alliages qui s'y sont croisés, sans les circonstances qui l'ont pétrie.

Que l'on m'entende bien ! Je ne prétends pas soutenir que le régime des castes, tel que nous l'observons aujourd'hui, avec les sections infinies, de nature et de consistance diverses qu'il embrasse, ne contienne que le développement logique, purement organique, des seuls élémens âryens primitifs. Des groupes d'origine variée, de structure variable, s'y son introduits de tout temps et s'y multiplient encore : clans d'envahisseurs qui jalonnent la route des conquêtes successives ; tribus aborigènes sorties tardivement de leur isolement farouche ; fractionnemens accidentels soit de castes proprement dites, soit des groupes assimilés. Il y a plus ; ces mélanges qui, aggravés de combinaisons multiples, donnent à la caste de nos jours une physionnomie si déconcertante, si insaisissable, se sont, à n'en pas douter, produits de bonne heure. S'ils ont été en s'accusant, ils ont commencé dés l'époque où le régime se formait. Je l'ai dit déjà, je le répète à dessein : à condenser en une formule sommaire une conclusion générale, on risque de paraître outrer son principe ; effort de précision ou séduction de nouveauté, on risque de fausser, en l'étendant à l'excès, une pensée juste. Je ne voudrais pas que l'on me soupçonnât d'un entraînement contre lequel je suis en garde.

Ce que j'estime, c'est que, quelques influences qu'ils aient pu subir du dehors, quelques troubles qu'aient apportés les hasards de l'histoire, les âryens de l'Inde ont tiré de leur propre fonds les éléments essentiels de la caste, telle qu'ils l'ont pratiquée, conçue et finalement coordonnée. Si le régime sous lequel l'Inde a vécu n'est ni une organisation purement économique des métiers, ni un chaos barbare des tribus et des races étrangères et hostiles, ni une simple hiérarchie des classes, mais un mélange de tout cela, unifiée par l'inspiration commune qui domine, dans leur fonctionnement, tous les groupes, par la communauté des idées et des préjugés caractéristiques qui les rapprochent, les divisent, fixent entre eux les préséances, cela vient de ce que la constitution familiale, survivant à travers toutes les évolutions, gouvernant les âryens d'abord, puis pénétrant avec leur influence et s'imposant même aux groupemens d'origine indépendante, a été le pivot d'une ente transformation.

Qu'elle ait été traversée d'élémens hétérogènes, je n'ai garde de l'oublier. D'ailleurs une fois achevée dans ses traits essentiels, elle a, cela va sans dire, comme tous les systèmes vieillissans où la tradition ne se retempe plus dans une conscience vivante des origines, subi l'action de l'analogie. Les principes qu'on a cru y découvrir, l'arbitraire même, armé de faux prétextes y ont fait leur œuvre. Pour être accidentelles ou secondaires, ces altérations n'ont pas laissé que de jeter quelque désarroi dans la physionomie des faits. Je n'y insiste pas cependant. On en retrouvera au besoin les sources dans les détails que j'ai eu l'occasion de signaler en passant.

Même à nous enfermer dans la période de formation, combien nous souhaiterions de fixer des dates ! Ce que j'ai dit de la tradition littéraire expliquera que je n'en aie pas des précises à offrir. Des institutions anciennes ne s'imprègnent que par progressions insensibles d'un esprit nouveau ; des mouvements qui peuvent, suivant les circonstances, marcher d'un pas inégal dans des régions diverses, ne se manifestent dans les témoignages que lorsque l'ordre antérieur est devenu tout à fait méconnaissable. Ils sont obscurs parce qu'ils sont lents. Ils ne supportent pas de dates rigoureuses. Tout au plus pourrait-on se flatter de déterminer à quel moment le système brâhmanique, qui régit théoriquement la caste, a reçu sa forme dernière. La prétention serait encore trop ambitieuse. Nous pouvons nous en consoler ; nous n'en serions pas beaucoup plus avancés, s'il est vrai que ce système résume l'idéal de la caste dominante plus qu'il ne reflète la situation vraie.

Même en ce qui concerne le Véda, la valeur des indices qu'il apporte n'est rien moins que définie. Il faudrait savoir s'il épuise bien l'ensemble des faits contemporains, s'il les rend intégralement et fidèlement. C'est ce dont je n'estime pas du tout que nous soyons certains. Ce qui est sûr c'est qu'on y voit saillir encore en un plein relief cette hiérarchie de classes qui s'est plus tard résolue dans le régime des castes. Il est pourtant indubitable que, dès la période védique, les causes avaient commencé d'agir qui, par leur action combinée et suivie, devaient sur le vieux tronc âryen greffer un ordre nouveau.

Les âryens de l'Inde et les âryens du monde classique partent des mêmes prémisses. Combien les conséquences sont de part et d'autre différentes !

A l'origine, les mêmes groupes, gouvernés par les mêmes croyances, les mêmes usages. En Grèce et en Italie, ces petites sociétés s'associent et s'organisent. Elles s'étagent en un système ordonné. Chaque groupe conserve dans sa sphère d'action sa pleine autonomie ; mais la fédération superieure que constitue la cité embrasse les intérêts communs et régularise l'action commune. Le chaos prend forme sous la main des Grecs. Les organismes disjoints se soudent en une unité plus large. Au fur et à mesure qu'elle s'achève, l'idée nouvelle qui en est l'âme latente, l'idée politique s'ébauche. Comme la caste, la cité est issue de la constitution primitive commune ; jetée dans le moule des mêmes règles religieuses, des mêmes traditions, mais inspirée par des necessités nouvelles, elle dégage un principe nouveau d'organisation. Elle se montre capable de s'élargir, de s'affranchir des barrières qui ont soutenu, mais aussi contenu ses premiers pas. Plus tard, elle suffira, en se transformant, aux besoins des révolutions de mœurs et de pouvoir plus profondes.

Dans l'Inde la caste continue les antiques coutumes ; elle les développe même à plusieurs égards dans leur ligne logique ; mais elle perd quelque chose de l'impulsion qui avait créé les groupes primitifs et elle n'en renouvelle pas l'esprit. Des notions diverses se mêlent ou se substituent ici au lien généalogique qui avait noué les premières sociétés. En se modifiant, en devenant castes, elles ne trouvent pas en elles-mêmes de principe régulateur ; elles s'entrecroisent, chacune isolée dans son autonomie jalouse. Le cadre est immense, sans limites précises, sans vie organique ; masse confuse de sociétés indépendantes, courbées sous un niveau commun.

La langue classique de l'Inde se distingue des langues congénères par une singularité frappante. Le verbe fini a peu de place dans la phrase ; la pensée s'y déroule en composés longs, de relation souvent indécise. Au lieu d'une construction syntactique solide où le dessin s'accuse, où les incidences se détachent elles-mêmes en propositions nettement arrêtées, la phrase ne connaît guère qu'une structure molle où les éléments de la pensée, simplement juxtaposés, manquent de relief. Les croyances religieuses de l'Inde ne se présentent guère en dogmes positifs. Dans les lignes flottantes d'un panthéisme mal défini, les oppositions et les divergences ne se soulèvent un moment que pour s'écrouler comme un remous instable dans la masse mouvante. Les contradictions se résolvent vite en un syncrétisme conciliant où s'énerve la vigueur des schismes. Une orthodoxie accommodante couvre toutes les dissidences de son large manteau. Nulle part de doctrine catégorique, liée intransigeante. Sur le terrain social, un phénomène analogue nous apparâit dans le régime de la caste. Partout le même spectacle d'impuissance plastique.

Quelque sève qu'il empruntée aux circonstances extérieures et historiques, c'est bien le fruit de l'esprit hindou. L'organisation sociale de l'Inde est à la structure des cités antiques ce qu'est un poème hindou à une tragédie grecque. Aussi bien dans la vie pratique que dans l'art, le génie hindou se montre rarement capable d'organisation, c'est-à-dire de mesure, d'harmonie. Dans la caste tout son effort s'est épuisé à maintenir, à fortifier un réseau de groupes fermes, sans action commune, sans réaction reciproque, ne reconnaissant finalement d'autre moteur que l'autorité sans contrepoids d'une classe sacerdotale qui a absorbé toute la direction des esprits. Sous le niveau du brâhmanisme, les castes s'agitent, comme les épisodes se heurtent désordonnés dans la vague unité du récit épique. Il suffit qu'un système artificiel en masque théoriquement le décousu.

Les destinées de la caste sont, à y bien regarder, un chapitre instructif de la psychologie de l'Inde.

APPENDIX VI

SIR HENRY COTTON AND OTHERS ON KULIN POLYGAMY

TO THE EDITOR OF "THE TIMES."

SIR,—More important still, though perhaps not so intentionally offensive, is the review in your *Literary Supplement* of Mr. Oman's book on "The Brāhmans, Theists, and Muslims of India." I have not yet seen this book, but my impression of it derived from a review by Sir Alfred Lyall in the *Nation* is very different from that put forward by your reviewer. I cannot believe that Mr. Oman's work is a mere *réchauffé* of the onslaught on Hinduism which was elaborated by Mr. James Mill and by the missionary Ward at the beginning of the last century. That is the impression your review conveys and your leading article repeats in stronger language. Mill's, Ward's, and Wilford's attacks on Hinduism were replied to at the time they were made, but, whatever truth they may have then contained, every one who knows anything of the subject is aware that the abominations to which you refer, and especially the privileges of the Kulin Brāhmans, "including the most outrageous and degrading form of polygamy," have no existence at the present day. You go so far as to say that "it is a notable fact that the spread of enlightenment as we conceive it among educated Hindus has not been accompanied by any serious attempt to do away with social anomalies such as child marriages, the seclusion of child widows, or the abominations practised by the Kulin Brāhmans." I reply that the very contrary is the fact. So-called child marriages among the educated classes are now of the rarest occurrence, and polygamy among Kulin Brāhmins is absolutely non-existent. My personal experience extends over a period of 40 years, and I never heard of a case of Kulin polygamy. The practice had died out before I went to India. I do not know whether Mr. Oman says it still exists. I doubt whether he has any personal knowledge of Bengal, and in any case I deprecate in the strongest possible manner the tone and character of the observations in your leading article on this subject, which are apparently based on Mr. Oman's book.

I am, Sir, yours faithfully,
HENRY COTTON.

DIEPPE, *September 14th*, 1907.

SIR,—While I desire to avoid even the appearance of controversy on matters capable of argument, I would ask permission to correct one serious misapprehension on a matter of fact that is to be found in Sir Henry Cotton's letter as printed in your issue of the 24th. He says, "Polygamy among Kulin Brāhmans is absolutely non-existent. My personal experience extends over a period of 40 years, and I never heard of a case of Kulin polygamy." Sir Henry Cotton has been very fortunate in his experience. Mine has been painfully different. I went to India after him; nevertheless, during my career in the Indian Civil Service, I heard of numerous instances of Kulin polygamy both in Bengal and (under another name) in Bihar. I have been personally acquainted with men who practised it, and have discussed the question with them. About the year 1878 I was connected with a movement to stop it, which was got up by natives who were not Kulins, and which was admittedly a failure. I have before me a book entitled "The Brāhmans and Kayasthas of Bengal," written by Babu Girīndranáth Dutt, who, as his name implies, is a Bengali. It was published in 1906, after appearing in serial form in a Calcutta magazine. The author in his preface says, "I have described at length the fictitious origin and the pernicious effects of this vicious system (*i.e.* Kulinism)." Elsewhere he says, "The only possible and practical means to extirpate the manifold vicious effects of Kulinism—*e.g.*, polygamy, ruinous marriage demands, matrimonial difficulties, etc., is to abolish the cause, Kulinism, from every section of the community."

I am, Sir, yours faithfully,
GEORGE A. GRIERSON.

CAMBERLEY, *September 25th*, 1907.

SIR,—I desire to offer my experience of Kulin polygamy in contradiction of Sir Henry Cotton's statement. I entered the Bengal Civil Service about 12 years before Sir H. Cotton, and my service in Bengal overlapped his in its termination.

In 1866 the Government of Bengal appointed a committee to inquire into and report on Kulin Polygamy. It was thus moved by a learned Brahmin Pundit, at whose instance a few years before the Legislature had passed the Hindu Widows' Remarriage Act. Sir Charles Hobhouse, who is still alive, was president of that committee, and I was a member and its secretary. Our inquiries showed that Kulin polygamy was very prevalent in Bengal, and that there were instances of Brahmins having nearly 100 wives, many of whom they had never seen since their marriage with them as girls. That was about the year before Sir H. Cotton came to Bengal. His statement, therefore, that "in my personal experience, extending over a period of 40 years, I never heard of a case of Kulin polygamy" shows singular ignorance of the social habits and customs of the country amongst the people of which he so long lived. His experience is evidently derived from association with Bengalis whose Western education no doubt may have tended to induce them to abandon it. But it would not be to such men that this pernicious system would have much attraction. Profit in a pecuniary sense, and not sensuality, is its stronghold. The father of a girl is obliged by Hindu law and the custom of the country to marry her before she attains puberty; she must marry in her own caste; and he has to buy a suitable husband for her. Kulin polygamy, it can be easily understood, appeals to Brahmins of the mendicant and priestly classes of small means. Education may have done much to reduce its sphere; but education has not reached such classes, and obviously they will be the last to come within its influence.

I do not desire to attempt to discuss or explain at length the marriage system amongst Hindus in Bengal; but I would point out that though education may have done something to mitigate its evils, it cannot claim to have done much to reduce the rates payable in the marriage market. The usual rate demanded by one who has taken the degree of Bachelor of Laws in the Calcutta University is, I was credibly informed not many years ago, Rs. 10,000, or nearly £700. It may be asked, Why does not the Congress which professes to act as a body anxious to reform all matters to the benefit of the people of India apply itself to such social matters of the highest importance? Why does it not commence its work at home before it stirs up matters of political controversy? The answer which suggests itself is obvious. Because it does not suit the aims of its leaders. Alas! that it should be so.

September 27th, 1907. H. T. PRINSEP.

Sir,—Sir Henry Prinsep misapprehends my letter to you on this subject. I never said that when I went to India 40 years ago there were no survivors of the old system of Kulin polygamy. On the contrary there were many, and Vidyasagar's committee appointed in 1866, to which Sir Henry Prinsep refers, proved the fact. My point was that during my time I never heard of a case of polygamous marriage being contracted among Kulins. I know it was common enough in old days. But I say that the practice for many years past has completely died out. There may, of course, have been isolated cases, but I am sure they are exceedingly few, and I never heard of one. Sir Henry Prinsep does not say that he has heard of any cases since 1866, and he admits that educated Bengalis have abandoned the practice. After all, the last word on this subject cannot be spoken by English officials, however great their experience may be, but must be said by the Indian members of the community concerned; and I am glad to think that the prominence given by you to this correspondence in your columns will lead to that result.

I am, yours faithfully,
HENRY COTTON.

October 1, 1907.

[*Editorial Note.*—In his letter to us of September 14 Sir Henry Cotton wrote:—"The practice [Kulin polygamy] had died out before I went to India." Yet, as Sir Henry Prinsep pointed out in his letter to us of September 27, the practice was still so prevalent about the time Sir H. Cotton went out to India that a committee had only recently been appointed to inquire into it.]

Sir,—Having very recently come from India and having a life-long acquaintance with that country, I am perhaps able to throw some light on the subject of Kulinism, which is being discussed just now in the columns of your paper. It is hard to kill a social custom when bound up and interwoven with the material interest of still a very influential class. Polygamy among Kulin Brahmans is certainly not dead. It is not as rampant as it was, say, half a century ago; but it still flourishes, or is still in vogue, in certain dark corners of the two provinces of Bengal and Behar, chiefly among the more bigoted classes of Hindus, who adhere to the abhorrent practice with a grim steadfastness which can scarcely be reconciled with the advanced and progressive state of certain other sections of Hindu society. Of course, the reason for the upkeep of this hateful custom is the burning desire of the parents (not uncommon in other parts of the world) to get their daughter married to a man on a somewhat higher social level, as regards the scale of castes, which is again bound up with their religion.

Dr. G. A. Grierson (than whom I scarcely know of a higher authority either in Indian literature or social practices and customs as they exist in the present day) is quite accurate in saying that polygamy is still prevalent among the people of Bengal and Behar—in Behar among the Ojhas, Dubes, and Chaubes principally. I knew of an Ojha family (a fairly well-to-do zemindar) whose three daughters, varying in age from 19 to 14 years, were married to one Brahman of about treble the age of the eldest girl. When I expostulated with the father, he said he could not possibly get his daughters married to husbands on a lower scale of caste, as it would for ever ruin the standing of his family, and it was hopeless to find a younger man, as it would be equally ruinous to his family from a pecuniary point of view.

Among the Bengalis too, who are more advanced, in a general sense, than the Beharis, fear of lowering the caste *status* still holds a tyrannical sway. A father who is a bigoted Hindu would not, if he can possibly avoid it, allow his daughter to get married to one whose *status* in caste is lower than his; he would much rather get her wedded to a polygamous husband.

I am, Sir, yours faithfully,
JOHN CHRISTIAN.

SIR,—Referring to the letters of Sir Henry Cotton, Dr. George Grierson, and "A retired Bengal Official" in *The Times* of the 24th, 27th, and 28th ultimo, respectively, I would like to add that the crushing reply to Sir Henry Cotton is the official report on "Kulinism" in the *Gazette of India* of February 7, 1867, signed by S. Ghosal, C. P. (now Sir Charles) Hobhouse, H. T. (now Sir Henry) Prinsep, D. Mitra, J. K. Mookerjea, I. C. Surma, and R. Tagore. Of these five Bengali signatories the last three (including the Theistic reformer Ramnath Tagore) add the statement that "Kulinism"—*i.e.* the *Kula-dharma* or "(religious) observance of race (purity)"—prevailed to a less extent in 1867 than a few years previously; but even with this qualification the report is an all-sufficing and dramatically effective answer to Sir Henry Cotton. My day in India began 13 years before his, and was all spent in Western India, and I always hesitate to speak of anything in India, beyond the Mahratta Ditch, and I generally keep strictly within "the Manor of Grenawic"; but even in far-off Bombay that report made an immense impression; and, surely, it is a record in Lethe'd obliviousness that Sir Henry Cotton, who, I see from the "India Office List," landed in Calcutta October 29, 1867, should never once "have heard of a case of Kulinism." I was possibly more interested in the report because some years earlier in the widely—in India—regenerative sixties I was visited by a wealthy Vaishnava, as a representative of other wealthy Vaishnavas, all of the Vallabhāchārya sub-sect, who, with passionate insistence, demanded the exposure of an immemorial religious rite of the sect, which gradually, under the influence of Western ideals, had become intolerable to them as husbands and, in all "the thoughts and intents of the heart," English gentlemen. This was, indeed, the beginning of the great action for libel the High Priest of the Vallabhāchārya was at length compelled, by the force of public opinion, to bring against *The Times of India;* and Sir Joseph Arnold's memorable judgment in the case, with Mr. Chisholm Anstey's speech for the plaintiff, and the evidence given, is the richest storehouse known to me of the authenticated facts of esoteric Hinduism accessible to English readers.

But what I desire, with your indulgence, to accentuate is not this latest and most bewildering example of Sir Henry Cotton's "lethargized discernings," but the inconsiderateness and unreasonableness of all three of your distinguished correspondents under comment in tacitly stigmatizing the *Kula-dharma* as outrageous and degrading because this peculiar form of regulated polygamy happens to be opposed to our own conventions on such relations. "Kulinism" is not with the Hindus, as with us, a "mystery of iniquity," but a "mystery of godliness"; and so long as it has the consent of their consciences, and is regarded as a high and religious obligation, it cannot be, and is not, morally degrading to them, although it does not tend to their physical elevation, and the development of their virility, as the one sure foundation of the manly virtues. Therefore, while always speaking and writing my mind freely in private to Hindus on such matters as the *ras-mandli* of Western India and the *Kula-dharma* of Eastern Bengal, I have never in public spoken or written in "moral indignation" on such freaks in morality, or rather, sociology. What is the history of "Kulinism"? The Sanscrit word *Kula*, clipt to *Kul*, means "race," "tribe," "family," and if not allied to, may be compared with, the words Kelt or Celt and Cul-dee ("the family," *i.e.* priest of God); and the word *Kulina* or *Kulin* means, primarily, "of good family"; while *Kula-dharma* means primarily a binding observance, of gradually growing religious import, arising out of the natural instinct to preserve in pristine purity the blue Aryan blood of that section of the Bengali Brahmans who, on quite inadequate grounds, regard themselves as superior to all other Brahmans, not only in Bengal, but throughout India, in the integrity of their illustrious descent. These primitive *Kulin* of Bengal are represented by the widely, and, let it be added, well-famed family names of Bonnerjee, Chatterjee, Gangully, and Mookerjea; while the great family names of Bose, Dutt, Ghose, and Mitra represent the Hindus who became attached to these *Kulin* families on their original immigration into Anga-Banga. And these *Kulin* are most honourable men; so that the word *Kulin* has at last come to be an honorific title, the equivalent of our "The Honourable," or "The Right Honourable," as it came to be in our earlier history with the words Kelt and Culdee. They happen also, for the most part, to be of fine physique; for after all polygamy may be less conducive to excess than monogamy, and Bengali Kulinism is largely nominal. Though for the greater part ignorant of English, they are learned Sanscritists and often accomplished Persian scholars, and they strictly maintain the tradition of the stately old Hindu manners and social customs, and are always the most excellent good company.

I am not worthy to "bow to the shadow of" Mr. Oman's "shoe tie," but in view of Sir Henry Cotton's obliquitous attack on his recent profoundly significant work, I will only say that I could confirm some of the strangest things in it from my own personal experience in the Canarese country among the Vira-Saiva *lingavant* and *lingadhari*.

I have the honour to be,
Sir,
Your most obedient servant,
GEORGE BIRDWOOD.

October 1, 1907.

SIR,—Will you allow me, as a subject of the British Empire, to join Sir George Birdwood in his protest against the gross insularity with which the subject of *Kulin* polygamy has been discussed in your columns since Sir Henry Cotton, by putting his denial of its existence in the form of a defence of Indian morality, assumed that the test of morality is simply conformity to English custom? In this all your correspondents except Sir George have followed him, the only difference being that his intentions were civil, and theirs openly offensive. To an Indian that can hardly weigh as a difference at all. If (to illustrate) an Indian paper were to publish a controversy between two Bengalis, one holding up the Archbishop of Canterbury to the execration of all pious Hindus as a Christian, and the other defending him as a man of far too high character to be tainted with the Christian superstition, the Archbishop would hardly feel much more obliged to his defender than to his assailant.

If the Empire is to be held together by anything better than armed force—and we have neither energy nor money enough to spare from our own affairs for that—we shall have to make up our minds to bring the institutions and social experiments of our fellow-subjects to a very much higher test than their conformity to the customs of Clapham. It is true that mere toleration for its own sake is out of the question: we are not going to tolerate suttee or human sacrifice on any terms from anybody, if we can help it. We are far too tolerant as it is, if not of other people's abominations and superstitions, at all events of our own, which are numerous and detestable enough in all conscience. But before we begin to hurl such epithets as "revolting" and "abhorrent" at any customs of our Indian fellow-subjects, we had better consider carefully why we are shocked by them. Very few of us are trained to distinguish between the shock of unfamiliarity and genuine ethical shock. Kulin polygamy is unfamiliar: therefore it shocks us, and causes gentlemen of ordinary good breeding to use abusive and intemperate language in your columns. Under these circumstances, I, having ascertained that my opinion in this matter is representative enough to be of some importance, am emboldened to say that the institution of Kulin polygamy, as described by your correspondents, does not seem to me on the face of it an unreasonable one. Let me compare it with our own marriage customs. We are told first that the Bengalis do not marry out of their caste. To them, therefore, the promiscuity which we profess must be "revolting" and "abhorrent"; but we have the ready and obvious defence that our promiscuity is only professed and not real, as our Deputy-Lieutenant class and our commercial traveller class, for instance, do not intermarry. Further, the Bengalis hold that it is part of the general purpose of things that women should bear children, and that childlessness is a misfortune and even a disgrace. It will not be disputed, I think, that this, under the surface, is as much an occidental as an oriental view. Again, the Bengalis attach great importance to their children being well-bred. So do we. On all these points the only difference between India and England is that England holds her beliefs more loosely, less religiously, less thoughtfully, and is less disposed to let them stand in the way of pecuniary gain and social position.

How then do the parents of an English family, of the class corresponding to the Indian Brahman class, secure well-bred grandchildren for themselves and also for their nation? They use their social opportunities to put their daughters promiscuously in the way of young men of their own caste, in the hope that a marriage with some one or other will be the result. Frequently it is not the result: the daughter becomes an old maid, one of the wasted mothers of a nation which, as Mr. Sydney Webb and Professor Karl Pearson have warned us, is perishing for want of well-bred children. Even when chance is favourable, and the daughter finds a husband, she often refuses to become a mother because her religious and social training has taught her to regard motherhood as a department of original sin, and to glory, not in the possession of children, but of a husband; so that the childless woman with a husband despises the mother who has no husband.

What does the Bengali father do under the same circumstances according to Sir Henry Prinsep? He selects a picked man—a Brahman, representing the highest degree of culture and character in his class; and he pays him £700 to enable his daughter to become the mother of a well-bred child.

Now this may strike the parochial Englishman as unusual or, as he would put it, "revolting," "abhorrent," and so forth; but it is certainly not unreasonable and not inhuman. Far from being obviously calculated to degrade the race, it is, on the face of it, aimed at improving it. Sir George Birdwood has just told us in your columns that the *Kulin* "happen, for the most part, to be of fine physique." Sir George has no doubt also noticed that the products of our system happen, for the most part, not to be of fine physique. Is it quite clear that this is mere happening? Is it not rather what one would expect under the circumstances? And is the practice of taking deliberate steps to produce and reproduce men of fine physique really revolting and abhorrent to our British conscience as distinguished from our British prejudice?

Let us, however, do justice to our system, indefensible as it is in many respects. It secures what most men want: that is, a sharing out of the women among the men so that every Jack shall have his Jill, and the able men and attractive women shall not accumulate partners and leave mediocrity unprovided. If this were the end of public policy in the matter, and if the race might safely take its chance of degeneracy provided monogamy, even on the hardest conditions, were maintained, there would be nothing more to be said. But as the whole Imperial problem before us is fundamentally nothing else than to produce more capable political units than our present system breeds—in short, to breed the Superman—this is not a time to rail at experiments made by people who are not under the harrow of our prejudices, or to persist in calling the customs founded on those prejudices by question-begging names such as purity, chastity, propriety, and so forth, and to speak of a Brahman who is the father of a hundred children as a libertine with a hundred wives. Any man of thirty may have a hundred children without having a wife at all and still be positively ascetic in his temperance compared with an average respectable and faithful British husband of the same age. And if the hundred children "happen, for the most part, to be of fine physique," the nation will be more powerful and prosperous in the next generation than if these hundred children were replaced by a hundred others of indifferent physique, each having a different father, promiscuously picked up in a Clapham drawing-room.

A system which limits the fertility of its men of fine physique to the child-bearing capacity of one woman, and wastes the lives of thousands of first-rate maiden ladies in barrenness because they like to own their own houses and manage their own affairs without being saddled with a second-rate or tenth-rate man, must not take its own merits for granted. It may be the right system; it may be bound up with all that is best in our national life and fortunate in our national history; it may be all that our stupidest people unanimously claim for it. But then again it may not. The evidence on the other side is weighty; and the population question is pressing hard on us. The case must be argued, not assumed; and the final verdict will be that of history and not of our modern suburban villas with no nurseries.

Yours truly,
G. BERNARD SHAW.

10, ADELPHI-TERRACE, W.C.,
Oct. 3.

SIR,—I have only just arrived from India, and have followed with interest the correspondence relating to *Kulinism* in your columns.

I am a Bengali Brahmin, and in our family daughters used never to be married except to *Kulins*. Sir Henry Cotton quite correctly says that the practice of polygamy for many years past has completely died out in Bengal. In fact, it had died out when Mormonism was very much alive in America.

Yours faithfully,
A. CHAUDHURI, B.A. (Cantab.), 1884,
Bar.-at-law (1886), *Fellow of the Calcutta University.*

98, THE GROVE, EALING,
4th Oct.

SIR,—In a leading article which appeared in *The Times* of the 2nd instant, you have referred to the barbarous institution of *Kulin* polygamy as a factor to be considered in determining the character of the reformers and agitators of Bengal. May I ask you, in the interest of truth, to permit me to offer a few critical remarks on the subject?

I have two distinct grounds for entering into the controversy. First, I am a student of sociology, whose duty it is to see that sociological *data* are not perverted for the purpose of evoking racial or political antipathies; secondly, I have the fortune or misfortune to belong to that class of Brahmins known as *Kulins*, who have long possessed the unenviable privilege of polygamy.

You have, I fear, attached too little importance to Sir Henry Cotton's able refutation of the statements that appeared in your columns. I hold no brief for Sir Henry. I do not know him personally, nor, indeed, do I always agree with his public utterances with regard to Indian matters. But it is sheer justice to him to state that he knows more about the social life of East Bengal than the learned correspondents on whose assertions you base a generalization which is totally incorrect. *Kulin* though I am, I have the greatest horror of the monstrous custom of *Kulin* polygamy, and I have thought it my duty to inquire whether the custom still exists. Social customs die hard, and it is inevitable that one or two instances may occasionally occur to arouse the critical acerbity of the civilized West. But let me assure you that *Kulin* polygamy as a tolerated institution has long ceased to be.

Even, however, if it still existed, is it quite logical to draw general inferences as to the moral character of a whole community when it is remembered that the *Kulins* who practised polygamy formed a very small minority of the total population of Bengal? Mr. Bepin Chandra Pal, for example, is no *Kulin*, and his character bears no ratio, direct or inverse, to polygamous licences. It would be quite as rational to assert that, as adultery is not regarded as a crime by the law of England, it must follow that the English are a nation of adulterers.

It does no good whatever to make an isolated instance the basis of a stricture that cannot but make the work of government difficult. If *Kulinism* is dead, *requiescat in pace*. If it is not, is there any sense in making false assertions that must wound the pride of the Indian on the one hand, and rouse the unreasoning prejudices of the Englishman on the other?

Yours faithfully,

VIRENDRANATH CHATTOPADHYAYA.

43, THANET-HOUSE, STRAND, W.C.,
4th Oct.

SIR,—When I wrote the letter which appeared in your issue of September 27th I little thought that I should be accused of expressing an opinion as to the merits or demerits of *Kulin* polygamy on the ground that (to quote Sir George Birdwood) it is opposed to our conventions of such relations. Nothing could have been further from my intentions. My object was to correct a mistake of fact, and to do so mainly from the evidence of a native witness. My own experience is of small value. As, however, the charge has been made both by Sir George Birdwood and by Mr. Bernard Shaw, may I explain that, putting all questions of sexual morality to one side, whether the system is right or wrong in theory, in the practical working of its extreme forms it is an organized system of extortion, working the most cruel injustice upon its unhappy victims? *Pace* Mr. Shaw, it actually condemns numbers of girls to an unmarried life who would otherwise be married. These are questions of fact. If Mr. Shaw doubts my evidence, I can refer him to the work written by a native of Bengal from which I quoted in my last letter, or (for earlier years) to the report of the Commission mentioned by Sir Henry Prinsep and Sir George Birdwood.

Let me also make one other point quite clear. While I do not hesitate to say what I think about the evils of *Kulinism*, I should be disloyal to the affection which I bear to the people amongst whom I spent some of the best and happiest years of my life did I not openly dissociate myself from those who, because of the existence of this evil, or because some foolish and some wicked men are guilty of violence, denounce Hindus or Bengalis as a nation. Like all of us who have served in India, I have had my bad moments, and have been in tight places; nevertheless, looking back along the vista of not a few years, it is not these that dwell in my memory, but loyal friends that I made and innumerable tokens of the mutual regard which existed between my own people and those amongst whom our lot was cast.

Yours faithfully,
GEORGE A. GRIERSON.

CAMBERLEY,
5th Oct.

[*Editorial Note.*—The book referred to by Mr. Grierson is entitled "The Brahmans and Kayasthas of Bengal," by Babu Girindranath Dutt. It was published in 1906. The passage quoted was as follows :—"The only possible and practical means to extirpate the manifold vicious effects of Kulinism—*e.g.*, polygamy, ruinous marriage demands, matrimonial difficulties, etc.—is to abolish the cause, Kulinism, from every section of the community."]

REPORT OF THE COMMITTEE APPOINTED IN 1866 BY THE GOVERNMENT OF BENGAL TO REPORT ON THE NECESSITY OF LEGISLATING ON THE SUBJECT OF POLYGAMY AMONG THE HINDUS.

From C. HOBHOUSE, ESQ., and others,
To THE SECRETARY TO GOVT. OF BENGAL.

Dated the 7th February, 1867.

WE have the honour to acknowledge the receipt of your letters Nos. 1647 to 1651T, dated Darjeeling, 22nd August, 1866, to our respective addresses, and we beg to submit the following reply :—

We understand that the Hon'ble the Maharajah of Burdwan, and some 21,000 other Hindu inhabitants of Lower Bengal, prayed for an enactment to prevent the abuses attending the practice of polygamy amongst the Hindus in Lower Bengal; that His Honor the Lieutenant-Governor was in favour of the measure of bringing the said practice strictly within the limits of ancient Hindu Law; that, on the other hand, His Excellency the Governor-General in Council was of opinion that the Hindu inhabitants of Lower Bengal were not prepared, either for the suppression of the system of polygamy, or yet for that strict limitation of it which His Honor the Lieutenant-Governor of Bengal recommended, but desired only a remedy for the special abuses practised by the sect of Koolin Brahmins; that His Excellency would therefore be prepared to take into consideration any deliberate measure which His Honor the Lieutenant-Governor might in consultation with some of the ablest of the leading native gentlemen in Bengal, think fit to recommend for the suppression of the special abuses above named, provided that such measure had not, on the one hand, the effect of restricting the general liberty now possessed by all Hindus to take more than one wife, and that it did not, on the other hand, give the express sanction of English Legislation to the system of polygamy, and that to us has been committed the duty of reporting on the best means of giving practical effect to the wishes of His Excellency the Governor-General in Council, and of framing and submitting a Draft Bill for that purpose.

In order that it may be seen exactly what we understand that system to be, for which we are instructed to suggest a remedy, we think it necessary, briefly, to trace the history of Koolinism back; to state how it arose and what it was, and what we believe it to be, and what in the main are declared to be those evils to which it has given rise, and which it perpetuates.

In the Institutes of Manu, we do not find any distribution of the sect of the Brahmins into distinct denominational classes, but we find it declared that certain

Brahmins were by conduct and acquirements entitled to higher respect than other Brahmins whose conduct was not so strict, and whose learning was not so great, and this declaration may possibly have laid the foundation of that distribution of the Brahmins into denominational classes which subsequently was made.

It was not until the time of the Hindu King Bullal Sen, who reigned some 284 years before the Mahomedan conquest, or about 877 A.D., that any distribution into denominational classes took place. This distribution was confined to the descendants of those Brahmins who had migrated from Kanouj into Bengal on the invitation of the Rajah Adisur, and it is stated that the cause of this distribution was the fact that the sect of Brahmins generally had fallen off in knowledge and in practice of the strict Hindu Shastras.

There were two chief divisions of Koolins, *viz.* the Barendros of what was then known as the geographical division of Barendrobhoom, and the Rarhis of Burdwan and other places.

The Koolins of Barendrobhoom were divided into two classes:—

1st—Koolins; and

2ndly—Kaps;

but as it is not amongst the Barendro Koolins that any abuse of the system of polygamy exists, we shall not further refer to these Koolins.

The Rarhi Koolins were also divided into two classes, *viz.*:—

1st—The Koolins;

2nd—The Shrotryos;

and subsequently to these classes was added a third, the Bhongshojo, the origin of which is somewhat obscure.

The Koolin class was an order of merit, and was composed of those Brahmins who had the nine qualifications—

1st—Of observance of Brahmin duties;

2nd—Of meekness;

3rd—Of learning;

4th—Of good report;

5th—Of a disposition to visit holy places;

6th—Of devotion;

7th—Of the preservation of the custom of marriages and intermarriages amongst equals only;

8th—Of asceticism; and

9th—Of liberality.

The Shrotryo was composed of those Brahmins who were supposed to have eight only of the nine qualifications of the Koolins.

When the above classes were first created, a peculiar Code of Laws, the bulk of which has in process of time swelled, and which is called by the Koolins the Kooleena Shastras, was laid down for the guidance of the Koolins.

If it were possible, it would be superfluous to trace the history of the Koolins from the time above mentioned up to the present time; it is sufficient that we should now state, not in its numerous ramifications and complications, but in its main features only, what we believe to be the present condition of the Koolin class or of Koolins and Koolinism as best known by these terms. We are speaking of the Rarhi division of Brahmins, and we believe we are right in stating that the chief distinctive classes amongst them at the present day are four in number, and are these, *viz.*:—

The Koolins, or first class.

Bhongo Koolins, or second class.

Bhongshojo Koolins, or third class.

Shrotryo Brahmins, or fourth class.

The first class is composed of persons who are supposed to possess the nine qualifications of the order of merit, and who, at any rate, are presumed never to have forfeited their title to that order by inter-marriages out of their own class.

These men, it is said, usually marry two wives,—one out of their own class, and one out of the class of the Shrotryos, and they take a consideration from the bride on the occasion of all inter-marriages with the Shrotryos, and also of all inter-marriages amongst themselves, except in cases where there is an exchange of daughters.

The second class is composed of Koolins of the first class, who have fallen from this latter class by inter-marriages with daughters of families in the third class.

This second class is again subdivided into—

1st—Swakrito Bhongo Koolins ;

2nd—Bhongo Koolins of the second generation ;

3rd—Bhongo Koolins of the third generation ;

4th—Bhongo Koolins of the fourth generation.

The male members of the first and second subdivisions of this second class contract an unlimited number of marriages during the life-time of the first wife, and except in cases of exchange, whether these marriages are contracted with Koolin women of their own class, or with the daughters of parents in the inferior classes, a consideration is given by the parents or family of the bride to the bridegroom.

In the fifth generation after the first act by which a Koolin of the first class has fallen into the second class, *i.e.* has become a Bhongo Koolin, he falls into the third class, *i.e.* he becomes Bhongshojo, and the fourth class, the Shrotryo, is composed of persons who have never been Koolins at all.

It will be most convenient here to state that the marriages most sought after are marriages with Bhongo Koolins of the first and second subdivisional classes, *i.e.* the Swakrito and the Bhongo Koolin of the second generation, and that the daughters of the class Bhongo Koolins generally are not permitted without degradation to marry beneath their class.

We will now describe some of the main customs in the matter of marriage, which, on the authority of the statements made in petitions to the Legislative Council, and in some instances within the knowledge of more than one of the native gentlemen on our Committee, obtain amongst the Bhongo Koolins, and we will state what are declared in the papers to be the evil results of some of those customs.

1st—In addition to the presents usually given amongst all classes of Hindoos on the occasion of marriage, a Bhongo Koolin always, except when he gives his daughter to a brother Bhongo, and takes in exchange that brother Bhongo's daughter, exacts a consideration for marriage from the family of the bride.

2nd—A present is often given in addition on the occasion of any visit made to the house of the father-in-law.

3rd—If the daughters of the first and second subdivisional classes of Bhongo Koolins cannot be given in marriage to husbands of their own classes, they must remain unmarried.

4th—The number of wives, including those of the same class, is said to be often as many as 15, 20, 40, 50, and 80.

5th—Polygamy is said to be resorted to as a sole means of subsistence to many Bhongo Koolins.

6th—Marriage, it is said, is contracted quite in old age, and the husband often never sees his wife, or only at the best visits her once in every three or four years or so.

7th—As many as three and four marriages have been known to have been contracted in one day.

8th—Sometimes all a man's daughters and his unmarried sisters are given in marriage to one and the same individual.

9th—It is so difficult to find husbands in the proper class for Koolin women that numbers, it is said, remain unmarried.

10th—The married or unmarried daughters and the wives of Koolins are said to live in the utmost misery; and it is alleged that crimes of the most heinous nature, adultery, abortion and infanticide, and that prostitution are the common result of the system of Bhongo Koolin marriages generally.

11th—Cases are cited of men who have married 82, 72, 65, 60 and 42 wives, and have had 18, 32, 41, 25 and 32 sons, and 26, 27, 25, 15 and 16 daughters.

12th—Lists have been adduced of families in the Burdwan and Hooghly districts alone, showing the existence of a plurality of wives on the above scale, and in numerous cases.

13th—The principle on which Koolinism was perpetuated, *viz.* that of preventing inter-marriages between certain classes, is violated.

14th—Families, it is said, are ruined, in order to provide the large sums requisite to give a consideration on the occasion of their daughters' marriages, or are unable to marry their daughters at all for want of means to procure such consideration.

15th—Marriages are, it is said, contracted simply in order to this consideration, and the husbands do not even care to enquire what becomes of their wives, and have never even had any intention of fulfilling any one of the marriage duties.

16th—The crimes that are said to result from the Koolin system of marriage are said to be habitually concealed by the actors in them and by their neighbours, and this so as to baffle the efforts of the Police at discovery.

17th—No provision is made for the maintenance of one wife before marriage with an unlimited number of others.

The above are said to be some of the customs and are declared to be some of the evils said to result from the system of polygamy as practised by the sect of Bhongo Koolins, and the evils may thus be briefly summed up:—

1st, The practical deprivation of the indulgence of natural ties and desires in the female sex in a legitimate manner; 2nd, the virtual, sometimes the actual, desertion of the wife by her natural and legal protector, the husband; 3rd, the encouragement of the practice of celibacy amongst the female sex; 4th, the non-maintenance of the wife by the husband; 5th, the supersession or abandonment of the wife at the mere pleasure of the husband; 6th, the formation of the contract of marriage for money considerations simply; 7th, the denial of nuptial intercourse except upon special monetary consideration given; 8th, the ruin, in a property point of view, of families; 9th, the contraction of the marriage tie avowedly without any intention even on the part of the husband of fulfilling any one of the duties of that tie; 10th, the binding down the female sex to all the obligations of the marriage state whilst yet withholding from that sex every one of the advantages of that state; 11th, prostitution; and lastly, the encouragement of the actual crimes of adultery, abortion, and infanticide and of the habit and practice of the concealment of such crimes.

The customs detailed above, as obtaining amongst Bhongo Koolins in the matter of marriage, have, on the whole, we think, been accurately detailed. The evils said to result from these customs are, we have reason to believe, greatly exaggerated, and the abuse of the permission to take a plurality of wives is, we believe, on the decrease; yet we do not doubt but that great evils exist, and those evils divide themselves naturally into two classes: first, that class which is contrary to religion and morality, and second, that which is contrary to established law.

We think that the following extracts, containing a brief view of the Hindu system of religion and morality as applied to the marriage state, will show that the system of polygamy, to whatever extent it is abused by the Bhongo Koolins, is opposed to the ordinances of the Hindu code of religion and morality :—

Brahmins are to shun the allurements of sensual gratification. Indulgence in sensual pleasure incurs certain guilt ; abstinence from it heavenly bliss. Neither the Vedas, nor liberality, nor sacrifices, nor strict observances, nor pious austerities ever procure felicity for the man contaminated by sensuality. The husband is to approach his wife in due season ; he is to honour and adorn her ; when he honours her, the deities are pleased ; when he dishonours her, religious acts are fruitless ; a wife unless guilty of deadly sin, must not be deserted ; the husband who does not approach his wife in due season is reprehensible ; he is one person with her, and she cannot by desertion be separated from him ; once a wife is given in marriage and the step is irrevocable ; only after a wife has treated a husband with aversion for a whole year can he cease to cohabit with her ; immorality, drinking spirituous liquors, affliction with an incurable or loathsome disease, mischievousness, waste of property, barrenness after eight years' cohabitation, death of all children after ten years of cohabitation, the production of only female children after eleven years of cohabitation, and speaking unkindly are the sole grounds for supersession of a wife ; desertion of a blameless wife is penal ; subtraction of conjugal rights is denounced with heavy penalties ; supersession of the wife is justifiable on grounds which regard the temper, conduct or health of the wife, and is tolerated on other grounds ; where neither justified nor tolerated, it is illegal ; abandonment of a blameless and efficient wife, without cause given or without her consent, is illegal ; the principles peculiar to the Brahmin forms of marriage are those of equal consent and disinterested motives ; immemorial custom, regulating marriage in general and in its different forms, and the relations of husband or wife, is to be observed, and non-observance leads to forfeiture of the fruits of the Vedas.

Manu, Chapter I, 109, 110 to 115.
" " III, 45, 55 to 57.
" " VIII, 389.
" " IX, 4, 45 to 47, 77, 80, 81.
Strange, Chapter II, pp. 46, 47, 48, 52 to 54.
Macnaghten, Vol. I, 58, 60.

The above texts clearly seem to us to indicate that the Bhongo Koolins to what extent they marry out of motives of sensuality only, or do not cohabit with, or abandon without any cause or supersede or neglect, or do not maintain their wives, or disregard the sanctity of the marriage tie generally, act contrary to the plainest injunctions of the Hindoo Shastras.

To the extent that the system of inter-marriages amongst the Bhongo Koolins encourages celibacy amongst women, and exacts a consideration for the contract of marriage ; it is questionable whether there is any practice which is at variance with the letter at least of the Hindoo Shastras.

In the matter of celibacy, the whole tenor of the Hindoo system of marriage does certainly advocate the marriage of women even before they have arrived at puberty ; penalties are prescribed for those fathers and families who neglect to marry their daughters before they have arrived at puberty, and daughters had formerly even the privilege of giving themselves in marriage in case of protracted neglect on the part of others to give them in marriage, yet on the other hand, perpetual celibacy is inculcated rather than the act of giving the daughter in marriage "to a bridegroom void of excellent qualities."—Manu, Chapter IX, Section 89.

And again on this subject—a father is prohibited from receiving any gratuity, however small, for giving his daughter in marriage, on the principle that he who through avarice takes such a gratuity is a seller of his offspring.—Manu, Chapter III, Section 51.

The case, however, that we have to contemplate is that of a father who gives, not one who takes, a gratuity in order to the marriage of his daughter, and who is not actuated by avarice, but by what the Hindoo Law declares to be the laudable desire of marrying his daughter early in life, and to a Brahmin of excellent qualities, and there is no text that we know of that prohibits a person from taking a consideration on the occasion of marriage.

The utmost that can be said against the taking of this consideration is that it is contrary to the principle on which the four first forms of marriage, which are peculiar to the Brahmins, are based, *viz.* that both parties to the marriage should be actuated by disinterested motives.—Macnaghten, Vol. I, paragraphs 59, 60.

Looking at the subject generally, however, there cannot be a doubt but that the system of polygamy as practised by the Bhongo Koolins is opposed to the strict ordinances of the Hindoo Shastras, and it is also said to be productive of the special offences against the law which we have named, and we are instructed, if we can, subject to the restrictions imposed upon us by His Excellency the Governor-General in Council, to suggest a legislative measure by which the system may be suppressed.

The root of the evil is in that custom by which Bhongo Koolins of the inferior grades and Bhongshojo Koolins eagerly offer, and Bhongo Koolins of the higher grades as eagerly accept, valuable considerations for the marriage of a woman of the former classes to a man of the latter class.

A law could, of course, be passed, rendering such contracts illegal under penalties on both the contracting parties.

But in the first place it is not clear that the letter of Hindoo Law is not rather in favour of, than against such contracts; and in the second place, in a case such as this, where both parties are interested to conclude the contract in question, it is evident that either the provisions of any law prohibiting such contracts would be evaded, or that violations of any such law would be effectually concealed.

And evasion of such a law is all the more easy under that part of the Hindoo system of religion and morals which inculcates acceptance by the Brahmin sect of gifts from the virtuous, if they themselves are poor, and this as one of the means of subsistence.—Manu, Chapter X, Sections 75, 76.

Systems of registration of marriages, of fines increasing in amount for every marriage after the first, of certificates of all marriages after the first, to be taken out in the Civil Courts, and such like schemes have been suggested and have suggested themselves to us; but in all these schemes, even if they were not otherwise objectionable, there would, it seems to us, be an element which would, indirectly at least, affect that "general liberty which is now possessed by all Hindoos to take more than one wife" with which we are instructed not to interfere.

The scheme which has at first sight seemed most feasible is that of framing a Declaratory Law, setting forth what the law is on the subject of polygamy, and prohibiting any infraction of it under penalties.

Such a Declaratory Law would certainly "regulate polygamy amongst the Hindoo inhabitants of Lower Bengal generally," and we are not quite certain, therefore, that, in proposing such a law, we should not be transgressing that part of our instructions which forbids us to "give the express sanction of English legislation to the Hindoo system" of polygamy; but for the sake of considering the subject, we will suppose that we are not prohibited from proposing a Declaratory Law.

No such a law must, in our judgments, clearly be declaratory of what the Hindoo system of polygamy is, and nothing more and nothing less; if it be more or less, then it ceases to be simply declaratory, and becomes inactive.

The following is that which, after consultation of the best authorities, we find to be the law which, strictly taken, should regulate the practice of polygamy amongst the Hindoos.

We find that, according to one of the ordinances of Manu, a Brahmin is enjoined to marry one wife, and this a woman of his own caste; but that, if he be so inclined, he is permitted to marry more than one wife, during the lifetime of his first wife, and he is recommended to select a second, a third, and a fourth wife in the order of the classes, *viz.* out of the Kshatrya, the Vaisya, and the Sudra classes respectively and consecutively.—Manu, Chapter III, Sections 12, 13.

This was an ordinance of the time of Manu, but we are now in the iron age of the Hindoo system, and so a Brahmin is now forbidden to marry any but a woman of his own caste.

It is contended, however, by the advocates of polygamy that the permission to marry a plurality of wives, which formerly extended to women of all the four classes, is to be construed, not so as to abolish polygamy altogether, but simply so as to confine it to inter-marriages amongst the various classes.

To this opinion Strange so far seems to incline, in that he states that it does not appear how many wives a Hindoo is competent to have at one and the same time (Chapter II, p. 56); and in Section 204, Chapter VIII, Manu, there is a case in which it is evidently contemplated that a man may be the husband of two persons of the same caste at one and at the same time, though, in this instance, the permission was evidently only accorded under circumstances of an exceptional nature; and again, in Section 161, Chapter IV, there is a general maxim, a maxim allowing the widest margin conceivable, to the effect that any act, though it be not prescribed, and if it be not prohibited, is lawful provided that it gratifies the mind of him who performs it.

Macnaghten, on the other hand, points out the illogical nature of the deduction made from the texts quoted, and states that action taken in the matter of marriages from this deduction is considered by the Pundits to be reprehensible.—Volume I, pp. 58, 59.

In our view the texts 12, 13, Chapter III, Manu, relied on, must be held to be obsolete and inapplicable. Those texts refer to an era in the Hindoo system in which it was permitted to a Brahmin to marry out of his own sect and thus prescribed the order, and put no restraint upon the circumstances under which he might contract such marriages; but we are now presumed to be living in a purer era, when marriages of this looser kind, which were before permitted, are now prohibited, and the logical deduction seems to us to be that those texts, which had for their main object the regulation of such marriages, have, with the marriages themselves, become obsolete.

We turn, therefore, to those other authorities which seem to us to declare most definitely the Hindoo system of polygamy.

Immemorial custom, which is defined to be good usages long established, is declared to regulate the laws concerning marriage, and the relationship of husband and wife.—Manu, Chapter I, Sections 112, 115, and Chapter II, Section 18.

A Brahmin who has not violated the rules of his order, who has read certain portions of the Vedas, who has obtained the consent of his spiritual guide, and who has performed certain ceremonial ablutions, may then espouse a wife of the same class as himself, who is endowed with certain excellencies, and not marked by certain defects.—Manu, Chapter III, Sections 2 and 4, and 7 to 11.

On the decease of the wife, the husband may, after performance of sacrifice and the funeral rites, marry again.—Manu, Chapter V, Section 168.

If a wife drinks spirituous liquors, if she acts immorally, if she shows aversion to her husband, if she be afflicted with any loathsome or incurable disease, if she be mischievous, if she wastes her husband's property, if she be afflicted with a blemish of which the husband was not aware when he married her, if she have been given in marriage fraudulently, if before marriage she have been unchaste, if, after seven years of married life, she has remained barren, if, in the tenth year of marriage, her children be all dead, if, after ten years of marriage, she has produced only daughters, and if she has spoken unkindly to her husband, she may in some of those contingencies, be altogether abandoned, and in all superseded by her husband.—Manu, Chapter IX, Sections 72, 77, 80, 81.

But the wife who is beloved and virtuous, though she be afflicted with disease, may yet not be superseded by another wife without her own consent.—Manu, Chapter IX, Section 82.

These causes are accepted by Strange as those which lead to separation (Chapter II, p. 47), and he remarks upon the latitude which they give to the will and caprice of the husband, whenever there is in him the disposition to take advantage of the letter of the law.

And further on, he points out that, where suppersession of the wife is not justifiable nor permissible, under, we would suppose, any one of the above contingencies, there it is illegal; and he defines illegal supersession to be the abandoning, with a view to another wife, a blameless and efficient wife who has given neither cause nor consent.—Pp. 52 to 54, Chapter II.

If we have rightly quoted, and if Mr. Justice Strange has rightly interpreted the law, then in any Bill declaratory of law, we should have to propose to give the sanction of English legislation to supersession of a wife on grounds the most trivial and inadequate, to say that she might be superseded, because she was found blemished (perhaps within the meaning of Sections 7 to 11, Manu, Chapter III) or was mischievous (whatever that may mean), or had spoken unkindly, or was barren (and who is to say where the fault of barrenness lies, for if it is with the husband, then under Section 79, Chapter IX, Manu, there is no supersession), or for many other causes more or less ridiculous, or incapable of proof.

On these considerations, we find that it is not in our power to suggest the enactment of any Declaratory Law, neither can we think of any legislative measure that, under the restricted instructions given for our guidance, will suffice for the suppression of the abuses of the system of polygamy as practised by the Koolin Brahmins, and we beg to report to that effect.

C. P. Hobhouse.
H. T. Prinsep.
Sutto Churn Ghosal.
Ishwar Chandra Surma.
Ramanauth Tagore.
Joykissen Mookerjee.
Degumber Mitter.

While subscribing to the report generally, we deem it due to record our opinion separately on the following points:—

1.—It is stated in page 6, Clause 4, that among other evils, of Koolin polygamy the "number of wives is often as many as 15, 20, and 80." Whatever might have been the case in times gone by we can distinctly state that it is not so now. The rapid spread of education and enlightened ideas as well as the growth of a healthy public opinion on social matters among the people of Bengal, has so sensibly affected this custom that the marrying of more than one wife, except in cases of absolute necessity, has come to be looked upon with general reprobation. Even among Bhongo Koolins of the 1st and 2nd class, the number of wives nowadays seldom exceeds four or five except in very rare instances, but there is ample reason to believe that this class of people will settle into a monogamous habit like the other classes of the community, as education will become more general among them and the force of social opinion be more widely felt.

2.—From the report it will appear that polygamy, as an institution, is confined to a certain class of Rarhi Koolins called Bhongo of the 1st and 2nd order, and that at present the practice even amongst them obtains in a much more mitigated form than a few years before. We need not notice that the number comprised in that class forms but a fraction of the population of Bengal; the catalogue of crimes, therefore, given in page 6 of the report, even if their correctness were unimpeached, must, it can be easily imagined, be infinitesimally small, so far as the same are traceable to polygamy as their immediate cause. However much we deprecate polygamy and lament its abuse, we cannot still conceal from ourselves the fact that the evils which are plausibly enough inferred as inseparably associated with it are not wholly ascribable to it. They are seen to exist in full force even where polygamy is not known or is considered a crime, and would appear to be simply the natural consequence of an imperfect knowledge of social laws not confined to India alone. A legislative enactment, however stringent and rigidly enforced, might be effectual in diverting those evils from their original course, but it is quite powerless to stop the source from which they take their rise.

3.—Our countrymen are already awakened to a proper sense of the duties which they owe to themselves and to their offsprings, to be swayed by those considerations which rendered polygamy at one time an unavoidable necessity. We are accordingly of opinion that this question may, without injury to public morals, be left for settlement to the good sense and judgment of the people. The Government cannot directly interfere with it without producing serious harm in diverse ways. All that it can and ought to do is to assist in the spread of that enlightenment which has already so much advanced the desired reform.

Some explanation is due from Baboo Joykissen Mookerjee, who had signed the petition, praying for a law for restricting the practice of polygamy. He desires to say that he has always been against this custom, and that when the movement was initiated about ten years ago, he was strongly in favour of it from a belief that the evils flowing from it would not be rooted out without the force of law, and when it was revived last year, he also gave his adhesion. But he is now satisfied by enquiries instituted by himself, as well as from representations made to him by others, that a remarkable change in the opinion of his countrymen has, within the last few years, taken place on this subject, that with other signs of social progress not the least is that which marks with strong disapprobation the old custom of taking a plurality of wives as a means of a man's subsistence, and that it would consequently be in accord with the true interests of morality as well as of the cause of improvement for the State to abstain from interfering in the matter.

RAMANAUTH TAGORE.
JOYKISSEN MOOKERJEE.
DEGUMBER MITTER.

CALCUTTA:
The 1st February, 1867.

I sign this report with the following reservations:—

I am of opinion that the evils alluded to in pages 434–5 are not "greatly exaggerated," and that the decrease of these evils is not sufficient to do away with the necessity of legislation.

I would translate the term "speaking unkindly" in page 438 to mean "habitually abusing," and the term "mischievous" to mean "exceedingly cruel."

I do not concur in the conclusion come to by the other gentlemen of the Committee. I am of opinion that a Declaratory Law might be passed without interfering with that liberty which Hindoos now by law possess in the matter of marriage.

ISHWAR CHANDRA SURMA.
(VIDYASAGAR.)

The 22nd January, 1867.

APPENDIX VII

SANTAL.

Sonthāl, Saontār, a large Dravidian tribe, classed on linguistic grounds as Kolarian, which is found in Western Bengal, Northern Orissa, Bhāgalpur and the Santāl Parganās. According to Mr. Skrefsrud the name Santāl is a corruption of Sāontār, and was adopted by the tribe after their sojourn for several generations in the country about Sāont in Midnapur. Before they went to Sāont they are said to have been called Kharwār, the root of which, *khar*, is a variant of *hor*, "man," the name which all Santāls use among themselves. As regards the derivation of the name of the tribe from Sāont, an obscure village, somewhat off the main line of their recent migrations, it may be observed that Colonel Dalton suggested a doubt whether the name of the place may not have been taken from the tribe, and this view seems to derive some support from his discovery of a small tribe of Sāonts in Sarguja and Keunjhar. The point, however, is not one of great importance. At the present day when a Santāl is asked what caste he belongs to, he will almost invariably reply, "Mānjhi" (literally "village headman," one of the commonest titles of the tribe), adding "Santāl Mānjhi" if further explanation is demanded of him.

In point of physical characteristics the Santāls may be regarded as typical examples of the pure Dravidian stock. Their complexion varies from very dark brown to a peculiar, almost charcoal-like, black; the proportions of the nose approach those of the negro, the bridge being more depressed in relation to the orbits than is the case with Hindus; the mouth is large, the lips thick and projecting; the hair coarse, black, and occasionally curly; the zygomatic arches prominent, while the proportions of the skull, approaching the dolicho-cephalic type, conclusively refute the hypothesis of their Mongolian descent.

Santāl tradition traces back the origin of the tribe to a wild goose (*hasdak*) which laid two eggs. From those sprang Pilchu Haram and Pilchu Būrhi, the parents of the race, who begat the first seven sub-tribes. Their earliest abode was Hihiri or Ahiri Pipri, a name which Mr. Skrefsrud derives from *hir* origin, and which others identify with *pargana* Ahuri in Hazaribagh. Thence they went westward to Khoj-Kaman, where all of them were destroyed for their wickedness by a deluge of fire-rain, except a single pair who were saved in a cleft of the mountain Hara. From Hara they went to Sasangbera, a plain on the banks of a great river, and after that to Jarpi, where is the great mountain Marang Buru, through which they could find no pass. Here they offered sacrifices to the mountain god, and prayed him to let them through. After a while they found a pass leading into a country called Ahiri, where they dwelled for a time, passing on to Kendi, Chāi, and finally Champa. In Champa they sojourned many generations, and the present institutions of the tribe were formed. At last the Hindus drove them out of Champa, and they established themselves in Sāont, and ruled there for two hundred years. Again pressed by the Hindus, they wandered on under a

Raja called Hambir Singh to the eastern part of the Manbhum district near Pachet. Here after a while their Rajas adopted the Hindu religion and set up as Rajputs, so that at the present day they intermarry with the family of the Raja of Sarguja. But the people would not change their religion, so they left their chief to rule over Hindus, and wandered on to the Santāl Parganās, where they are settled now.

Neither as a record of actual wanderings nor as an example of the workings of the myth-making faculty does this story of the wandering of the Santāls appear to deserve serious consideration. A people whose only means of recording facts consists of tying knots in strings and who have no bards to hand down a national epic by oral tradition, can hardly be expected to preserve the memory of their past long enough or accurately enough for their accounts of it to possess any historical value. An attempt has indeed been made by Mr. Skrefsrud to prove from these legends that the Santāls must have entered into India from the north-west, just as Colonel Dalton uses the same data in support of his opinion that the tribe came originally from Assam. The one hypothesis is as tenable or as untenable as the other, and all that can be said is that there is not a fraction of substantial evidence in support of either. If, however, the legends of the Santāls are regarded as an account of recent migrations, their general purport will be found to be fairly in accord with actual facts. Without pressing the conjecture mentioned above, that Ahiri Pipri may be no other than *pargana* Ahuri in the north-west of Hazaribagh district, it is clear that a large and important Santāl colony was once settled in Parganās Chai and Champā in the same district. A tradition is noticed by Colonel Dalton of an old fort in Chai occupied by one Jaura, a Santāl Raja, who destroyed himself and his family on hearing of the approach of a Muhammadan army under Sayyid Ibrāhim Ali *alias* Malik Bayā, a general of Muhammad Tughlak's, who died in 1353. This tradition, so far as it refers to the existence of a Santāl fort in Chai Champā, is to some extent corroborated by the following passage from the legends of the Southern Santāls collected by the Revd. J. Phillips and published in Appendix G to *Annals of Rural Bengal*, ed. 1868:—"Dwelling there (in Chai Champā) they greatly multiplied. There were two gates, the Ahin gate and the Bahini gate, to the fort of Chai Champā." If, moreover, the date of the taking of this fort by Ibrāhim Ali were assumed to be about 1340 A.D., the subsequent migrations of which the tribal legends speak would fill up the time intervening between the departure of the Santāls from Chai Champā and their settlement in the present Santāl Parganās. Speaking generally, these recent migrations have been to the east, which is the direction they might *primâ facie* have been expected to follow. The earlier settlements which Santāl tradition speaks of, those in Ahiri Pipri and Chai Champā, lie on the north-west frontier of the tableland of Hazaribagh and in the direct line of advance of the numerous Hindu immigrants from Bihar. That the influx of Hindus has in fact driven the Santāls eastward is beyond doubt, and the line which they are known to have followed in their retreat corresponds on the whole with that attributed to them in their tribal legends.

The internal structure of the Santāl tribe is singularly complete and elaborate. There are twelve exogamous septs, (1) Hāsdak, (2) Murmu, (3) Kisku, (4) Hembrom, (5) Marndi, (6) Saren, (7) Tudu, (8) Baske, (9) Besra, (10) Pāuria, (11) Chore, (12) Bedea. The first seven are believed to be descended from the seven sons of Pilchu Haram and Pilchu Būrhi or Ayo. The five others were added afterwards. All are exogamous. In order that members of the various septs may recognize each other when they meet, each sept, except Pāuria, Chore, and Bedea, has certain pass-words peculiar to itself, which are supposed to be the names of the original homes of the septs in Champā or in one of the earlier settlements of the tribe. The pass-words are as follows:—(1) Hāsdak—Tatijhāri, Gangijauni,

Kārā Guja, Sohodoro; (2) Murmu—Champāgarh, Bagsumbha, Naran Mānjhi; (3) Kisku—Kundagarh; (4) Hembrom—Kunda, Khairigarh, Jalaghatia; (5) Marndi—Badoligarh, Jelen Sinjo, Dhano Mānjhi; (6) Saren—Anbali, Barha, Pero Parganā; (7) Tudo—Simgarh, Sukrihutup Baru Mānjhi; (8) Baske—Ranga, Chunukjhandu; (9) Besra—Dhokrapalania, Gulu, Phagu Mānjhi. These pass-words or shibboleths seem to serve among the Santāls the purpose for which Australian and North American savages tattoo the totem on the body. They preservé the memory of the tie of blood which connects the members of the sept, and thus furnish an additional security against unconscious incest. They further go to show that the sept in its earlier form must have been a group of purely local character analogous to the communal septs. If due allowance is made for the causes which must tend in course of time to scatter the members of any particular sept over a number of different villages, it will be seen to be a remarkable circumstance, not that so few local septs are now to be found, but that any traces of such an organization have survived to so late a period.

Concerning the origin of the five additional septs the following stories are told. The eighth tribe, Baske, at first belonged to the seven, but by reason of their offering their breakfast (*baske*) to the gods while the Santāls were still in Champā, they were formed into a separate sept under the name of Baske. The Besras (No. 9) were separated on account of the immoral behaviour of their eponym, who was called Besra, the licentious one. The tenth sept, Pāuria, are called after the pigeon, and the eleventh, Chore, after the lizard; and the story is that on the occasion of a famous tribal hunting party the members of these two septs failed to kill anything but pigeons and lizards, so they were called after the names of these animals. The twelfth sept, the Bedea, was left behind and lost when the Santāls went up out of Champā. They had no father, so the story goes—at least the mother of their first ancestor could not say who his father was, and for this reason they were deemed of lower rank than the other septs. This sept is believed to have arisen during the time of Mando Singh in Champā when the Santāls had begun to come in contact with the Hindus. Some Santāls say the father was a Rājput and the mother a girl of the Kisku sept. There would be nothing antecedently improbable in the conjecture that the well-known gypsy tribe of Bedea may owe its origin to the *liaison* of a Rājput with a Santāl girl; but the mere resemblance of the names is a slender foundation for any such hypothesis. Santāls are very particular about the honour of their women, so far at least as outsiders are concerned, and it is quite in keeping with their ideas that a sept formed by a *liaison* with a Hindu should have been looked down upon, and eventually banished from the community. Any way it seems to be clear that the legend need not be taken to indicate the prevalence of the custom of female kinship in the tribe.

No Santāl may marry within his sept (*paris*), nor within any of the sub-septs (*khūnt*) (shown below) into which the sept is divided. He may marry into any other sept, including the sept to which his mother belonged. A Santāl proverb says:—No one heeds a cow track or regards his mother's sept.

Although no regard is paid in marriage to the mother's sept, the Santāls have precisely the same rule as the Kandhs concerning the sub-sept or *khūnt*. A man may not marry into the sub-sept or *khūnt* to which his mother belonged, though it is doubtful whether the Santāls observe this rule for as many generations in the descending line as is customary among the Kandhs. Many of the sub-septs have curious traditional usages, some of which may be mentioned here. At the time of the harvest festival in January the members of the Sidup-Saren sub-sept set up a sheaf of rice on end in the doorway of their cattle-sheds. This sheaf they may not touch themselves, but some one belonging to another sub-sept must be got to take it away. Men of the Sādā-Saren sub-sept do not use vermilion in their marriage ritual; they may not wear clothes with a red border on such occasions, nor may they be present at any ceremony in which the priest offers his own blood to propitiate the gods. The Jugi-Saren, on the other hand, smear their foreheads with *sindūr* at the harvest festival, and go round asking alms of rice. With the rice they get they make little cakes which they offer to the gods. The Mānjhi-Khil-Saren, so called because their ancestor was a Mānjhi or village headman, are forbidden, like the Sādā-Saren, to attend when the priest offers up his own blood. The Nāiki-Khil-Saren, who claim descent from a *nāiki* or village priest, may not enter a house the inmates of which are ceremonially unclean. They have a *jahirthān* or sacred grove of their own, distinct from the common *jahirthān* of the village, and they dispense with the services of the priest who serves the rest of the village. The Ok-Saren sacrifice a goat or a pig inside their houses, and during the ceremony they shut the doors tight and allow no smoke to escape. The word *ok* means to suffocate or stifle with smoke. The Mundu or Badar-Saren offer their sacrifices in the jungle, and allow only males to eat the flesh of the animals that have been slain. The Māl-Saren may not utter the word *māl* when engaged in a religious ceremony or when sitting on a *panchāyat* to determine any tribal questions. The Jihu-Saren may not kill or eat the *jihu* or babbler bird, nor may they wear a particular sort of necklace known as *jihu mala* from the resemblance which it bears to the babbler's eggs. The *jihu* is said to have guided the ancestor of the sept to water when he was dying of thirst in the forest. The Sankh-Saren may not wear shell necklaces or ornaments. The Barchir-Saren plant a spear in the ground when they are engaged in religious or ceremonial observances. The Bitol-Saren are so called because their founder was excommunicated on account of incest.

Girls are married as adults mostly to men of their own choice. Sexual intercourse before marriage is tacitly recognized, it being understood that if the girl becomes pregnant the young man is bound to marry her. Should he attempt to evade this obligation, he would be severely beaten by the Jag-mānjhi, and in addition to this his father would be required to pay a heavy fine. It is curious to hear that in the Santāl Parganās, shortly after the rebellion of 1855, it became the fashion among the more wealthy Santāls to imitate the usages of high-caste Hindus and marry their daughters between the ages of eight and twelve. This fashion has, however, since been abandoned, and it is now very unusual for a girl to be married before she attains puberty. Polygamy is not favoured by the custom of the tribe. A man may take a second wife if his first wife is barren, or if his elder brother dies he may marry the widow. But in either case the consent of his original wife must be obtained to the arrangement. Instances no doubt occur in which this rule is evaded, but they are looked upon with disfavour.

There seem to be indications that fraternal polyandry may at some time have existed among the Santāls. Even now, says Mr. Skrefsrud, a man's younger brother may share his wife with impunity; only they must not go about it very openly. Similarly a wife will admit her younger sister to intimate relations with her husband, and if pregnancy occurs scandal is avoided by his marrying the girl as a second wife. It will of course be noticed that this form of polyandry need not be regarded as a survival of female kinship.

The following forms of marriage are recognized by the Santāls and distinguished by separate names:—(1) Regular marriage (*bapla* or *kiring behu*, literally bride-purchase); (2) *Ghardi jawae*; (3) *Itut*; (4) *Nir-bolok*; (5) *Sanga*; (6) *Kiring jawae* or husband-purchase. The negotiations antecedent to a regular marriage are opened by the father of the young man who usually employs a professional match-maker to look for a suitable girl. If the match-maker's proposals are accepted by the girl's parents, a day is fixed on which the girl, attended by two of her friends, goes to the house of the Jag-mānjhi or superintendent of morals, in order to give the bridegroom's parents an opportunity of looking at her quietly. A similar visit of inspection is made by the bride's parents to the bridegroom's house, and if everything is found satisfactory the betrothal is concluded and an instalment of the bride-price is paid. The ordinary price of a girl is Rs. 3, and the bridegroom must also present a cloth (*sāri*) to the girl's mother and to both her grandmothers if alive. If more than this is paid, the bridegroom is entitled to receive a present of a cow from his father-in-law. In the case known as a *golat* marriage, when two families, each having a daughter and a son of marriageable age, arrange a double wedding, one daughter is set off against the other, and no bride-price is paid by either party. For a widow or a woman who has been divorced the bride-price is only half the standard amount, the idea being, as the Santāls pointedly put it, that such women are only borrowed goods, and must be given back to their first husbands in the next world. As the second husband has the use of his wife only in this world, it is clearly fair that he should get her for half-price. In an early stage of the marriage ceremony both bride and bridegroom separately go through the form of marriage to a *mahua tree* (*Bassia latifolia*). In the case of the bride a double thread is passed three or five times from the little toe of her left foot to her left ear, and is then bound round her arm with some blades of rice and stems of *dūba* grass (*Cynodon dactylon*). The conjecture suggests itself that this may be a survival of some form of communal marriage, but from the nature of the case no positive evidence is available to bear out this hypothesis, or to throw any light upon the symbolism of the usage. The essential and binding portion of the ritual is *sindurdan*, the smearing of vermilion on the bride's forehead and on the parting of her hair. This rite, however, is supposed to have been borrowed from the Hindus. The original Santāl ceremony is believed to have been very simple. The couple went away together into the woods and on their return were shut up by themselves in a room. When they came out they were considered to be man and wife. A practice closely resembling this was found by Colonel Dalton to be in vogue among the Birhors, and it is quite in keeping with what is known of the doings of primitive man in the matter of marriage. The memory of it, however, only survives among the Santāls in the form of a vague and shadowy tradition upon which no stress can be laid. *Sindurdan*, on the other hand, is nothing but a refined and specialised form of the really primitive usage of mixing the blood of a married couple and making them drink or smear themselves with the mixture, and although it is possible that the Santāls may have borrowed *sindurdan* from the Hindus, there are certainly good grounds for believing that the Hindus themselves must have derived it from the Dravidian races.

The second mode of marriage, *ghardi jawae*, is resorted to when a girl is ugly or deformed and there is no prospect of her being asked in marriage in the ordinary way. An instance has been reported to me in which a girl who had on one foot more than the proper number of toes was married in this fashion. The husband is expected to live in his father-in-law's house and to serve him for five years. At the end of that time he gets a pair of bullocks, some rice and some agricultural implements, and is allowed to go about his business.

The third form, *itut*, is adopted by pushing young men who are not quite sure whether the girl they fancy will accept them, and take this means of compelling her to marry them. The man smears his fingers with vermilion or, failing that, with common earth, and, watching his opportunity at market or on any similar occasion, marks the girl he is in love with on the forehead and claims her as his wife. Having done this, he runs away at full speed to avoid the thrashing he may expect at the hands of her relations if he is caught on the spot. In any case the girl's people will go to his village and will obtain from the headman permission to kill and eat three of the offender's or his father's goats, and a double bride-price must be paid for the girl. The marriage, however, is legal, and if the girl still declines to live with the man, she must be divorced in full form and cannot again be married as a spinster. It is said that an *itut* marriage is often resorted to out of spite in order to subject the girl to the humiliation of being divorced.

The fourth form, *nirbolok* (*nir*, to run, and *bolok* to enter), may be described as the female variety of *itut*. A girl who cannot get the man she wants in the regular way takes a pot of *handia* or rice-beer, enters his house and insists upon staying there. Etiquette forbids that she should be expelled by main force, but the man's mother, who naturally desires to have a voice in the selection of her daughter-in-law, may use any means short of personal violence to get her out of the house. It is quite fair, for example, and is usually found effective, to throw red pepper on the fire, so as to smoke the aspiring maiden out; but if she endures this ordeal without leaving the house, she is held to have won her husband and the family is bound to recognize her.

The fifth form, *sanga*, is used for the marriage of widows and divorced women. The bride is brought to the bridegroom's house attended by a small party of her own friends, and the binding proportion of the ritual consists in the bridegroom taking a *dimbu* flower, marking it with *sindur* with his left hand, and with the same hand sticking it in the bride's back hair.

The sixth form, *Kiring jawae*, is resorted to in the comparatively rare case when a girl has had a *liaison* with, and become pregnant by, a man of her sept whom she cannot marry. In order that scandal may be avoided, some one is procured to accept the post of husband, and in consideration of his services he gets two bullocks, a cow, and a quantity of paddy from the family of the man by whom the girl is pregnant. The headman then calls the villagers together, and in their presence declares the couple to be man and wife, and enjoins the girl to live with, and be faithful to, the husband that has provided for her.

A widow may marry again. It is thought the right thing for her to marry her late husband's younger brother, if one survives him, and under no circumstances may she marry his elder brother. Divorce is allowed at the wish of either husband or wife. If neither party is in fault, the one who wants a divorce is expected to bear the expenses. The husband, for example, in such a case would not be entitled to claim a refund of the bride-price originally paid, and would also have to pay a fine and give the woman certain customary dues. If, on the other hand, it is the wife who demands a divorce without just cause, her father has to make good the bride-price in addition to a fine for her levity of behaviour. The divorce is effected in the presence of the assembled villagers by the husband tearing asunder three *sal* (*Shorea robusta*) leaves in token of separation, and upsetting a brass pot full of water.

In the matter of inheritance Santāls follow their own customs, and know nothing of the so-called codes which govern the devolution of property among Hindus. Sons inherit in equal shares; a daughter has no claim to a portion as of right, but usually gets a cow given to her when the property is divided. Failing sons, the father takes; failing him, the brothers; after them, the male agnates. Failing agnates, the daughter inherits with succession to her children. If a man dies leaving young sons, his widow manages the property till all the sons are old enough to divide and start separate households. She then takes up her abode with the youngest. Should the widow marry outside the family, the male agnates take the property in trust till the sons are of age, and she gets nothing. If a man has male relatives, he cannot give away his property even to a son-in-law. Wills are unknown.

According to Mr. Skrefsrud traces may be discerned in the background of the Santāl religion of a *faineant* Supreme Deity called Thākur, whom the Santāls have long ceased to worship for the sufficient reason that he is too good to trouble himself about anybody and does neither good nor ill to mankind. Some identify him with the Sun, whom the Santāls regard as a good god and worship every fifth or tenth year with sacrifices of slain goats. But this point is uncertain, and I am myself inclined to doubt whether a god bearing the Hindu name Thākur, and exercising the supreme powers which mark a comparatively late stage of theological development, can really have formed part of the original system of the Santāls. However this may be, the popular gods of the tribe at the present day are the following:—(1) Marang Buru, the great mountain or the high one, who now stands at the head of the Santāl Pantheon, and is credited with very far-reaching powers, in virtue of which he associates both with the gods and with the demons. (2) Moreko, fire, now a single god but formerly known to the Santāls under the form of five brothers. (3) Jāir Era, a sister of Moreko, the goddess of the sacred grove set apart in every village for the august presence of the gods. (4) Gosain Era, a younger sister of Moreko. (5) Parganā, chief of the Bongas or gods and more especially master of all the witches, by reason of which latter functions he is held in especial reverence. (6) Mānjhi, a sort of second-in-command to Parganā, a personage who is supposed to be particularly active in restraining the gods from doing harm to men. The two latter are clearly deities constructed on the model of the communal and village officials whose names they bear. The idea is that the gods, like men, need supervising officials of this sort to look after them and keep them in order. All the foregoing gods have their allotted place in the sacred grove (*jahirthān*), and are worshipped only in public. Marang Buru alone is also worshipped privately in the family.

Each family also has two special gods of its own—the Orak-bonga or household god and the Abge-bonga or secret god. The names of the Orak-bongas are (1) Baspahar, (2) Deswāli, (3) Sās, (4) Goraya, (5) Barpahar, (6) Sarchawdi, (7) Thuntatursa. The Abge-bongas are the following:—(1) Dharasore or Dharasanda, (2) Ketkomkudra, (3) Champa-denagarh, (4) Garhsinka, (5) Lilachandi, (6) Dhanghara, (7) Kudrachandi, (8) Bahara, (9) Duārseri, (10) Kudraj, (11) Gosāin Erā, (12) Achali, (13) Deswali. No Santāl would divulge the name of his Orak-bonga and Abge-bonga to any one but his eldest son; and men are particularly careful to keep this sacred knowledge from their wives for fear lest they should acquire undue influence with the *bongas*, become witches, and eat up the family with impunity when the protection of its gods has been withdrawn. The names given above were disclosed to Mr. Skrefsrud by Christian Santāls. When sacrifices are offered to the Orak-bongas the whole family partake of the offerings; but only men may touch the food that has been laid before the Abge-bongas. These sacrifices take place once a year. No regular time is fixed, and each man performs them when it suits his convenience.

There still lingers among the Santāls a tradition of a "mountain-god" (Buru-bonga) of unknown name, to whom human sacrifices used to be offered, and actual instances have been mentioned to me of people being kidnapped and sacrificed within quite recent times by influential headmen of communes or villages, who hoped in this way to gain great riches or to win some specially coveted private revenge.

These are not the motives which prompted human sacrifice among the Kandhs of Orissa, a tribe whose internal structure curiously resembles that of the Santāls. The Kandh sacrifice was undertaken for the benefit of the entire tribe, not in the interest of individual ambition or malevolence. It is curious to hear that one of the men credited with this iniquity was himself murdered during the Santāl rebellion of 1855, by being slowly hewn in pieces with axes, just as his own victims had been—a mode of execution which certainly recalls the well-known procedure of the Kandhs.

The chief festival of the Santāls is the Sohrai or harvest festival, celebrated in *Posh* (November-December), after the chief rice crop of the year has been got in. Public sacrifices of fowls are offered by the priest in the sacred grove; pigs, goats and fowls are sacrificed by private families, and a general saturnalia of drunkenness and sexual license prevails. Chastity is in abeyance for the time, and all unmarried persons may indulge in promiscuous intercourse. This license, however, does not extend to adultery, nor does it sanction intercourse between persons of the same sept, though even this offence, if committed during the Sohrai, is punished less severely than at other times. Next in importance is the *Baha puja* kept in *Phalgun* (February-March), when the *sal* tree comes into flower. Tribal and family sacrifices are held, many victims are slain and eaten by the worshippers, every one entertains their friends, dancing goes on day and night, and the best songs and flute-music are performed. A peculiar feature of this festival is a sort of water-bottle in which men and women throw water at each other until they are completely drenched.

Mention may also be made of Erok-sim, the sowing festival kept in *Asārh* (May-June); Hariar-sim, the feast of the sprouting of the rice in *Bhadra* (September-October); Trigundlinauai, the offering of the first fruits of the millets *iri* (Panicum millaceum) and *gundli* (Panicum frumentaceum) also in *Bhadra;* Janthar puja in *Aghran* (October-November), the first fruit of the winter rice crop, *Sankrant puja* on the 1st day of *Posh*, when bread and Chira and molasses are offered to dead ancestors; Māgh-sim in the month of *Magh*, when the jungle grass is cut. This is the end of the Santāl year. Servants are paid their wages and fresh engagements are entered into. On this occasion all the village officials, the Mānjhi Parāmānik, Jag-Mānjhi, Jag-pāramānik, Gorait, Nāiki, and Kudam-naiki go through the form of resigning their appointments, and all the cultivators give notice of throwing up their lands. After ten days or so the Mānjhi or headman calls the village together and says he has changed his mind and will stay on as *mānjhi* if the village will have him. His offer is accompanied with free drinks of rice-beer, and is carried by acclamation. One by one the other officials do the same; the ryots follow suit, and after a vast amount of beer has been consumed the affairs of the village go on as they did before. The Sima-bonga or boundary gods are propitiated twice a year with sacrifices of fowls offered at the boundary of this village where these gods are supposed to live. *Jomsim puja* is an offering of two goats, or a goat and a sheep, to the sun. Every Santāl ought to perform this sacrifice at least once in his life. After a year's interval it is, or ought to be, followed by *Kutam dangra*, when a cow is offered to the household god, and an ox to Marang Buru and to the spirits of dead ancestors. *Makmore puja*, literally "cut five," is the sacrifice of three goats and many fowls offered to More-ko, the god of fire, supposed to have been originally five brothers on occasions of public calamity, such as a failure of the crops, an outbreak of epidemic disease, and the like.

The communal organization of the Santāls is singularly complete. The whole number of villages comprising a local settlement of the tribe is divided into certain large groups, each under the superintendence of a *parganait* or circle headman. This official is the head of the social system of the inhabitants of his circle; his permission has to be obtained for every marriage, and he, in consultation with a *panchayat* of village headmen, expels or fines persons who infringe the tribal standard of propriety. He is remunerated by a commission on the fines levied, and by a tribute in kind of one leg of the goat or animal cooked at the dinner, which the culprits are obliged to give. Each village has, or is supposed to have, the following establishment of officials holding rent-free land:—

1. *Mānjhi*.—Headman, usually also *ijardar* where the village is held on lease under a zamindar, collects rents, and allots land among the ryots, being paid for this by the proceeds of the *man* land which he holds free of rent. He receives Re. 1 as *marocha* at each wedding, giving in return a full *handi* of rice-beer.

2. *Paramānik.*—Assistant headman, also holding some *man* land.

3. *Jag-Mānjhi.*
4. *Jag-Paramānik.* } Executive officers, respectively of the *manjhi* and the *paramanik* who, as the Santāls describe it, "sit and give orders," which the *Jag-Manjhi* and *Jag-Paramanik* carry out.

5. *Naiki.*—Village priest of the aboriginal deities.
6. *Kudam-Naiki.*—Assistant priest, whose peculiar function it is to propitiate the spirits (*bhūts*) of the hills and jungles by scratching his arms till they bleed, mixing the blood with rice, and placing it in spots frequented by the *bhūts.*
7. *Gorait.*—Village messenger, who holds *man* land and acts as peon to the headman. The *gorait* is also to some extent a servant of the zamindar. His chief duty within the village is to bring to the *manjhi* and *paramānik* any ryot they want.

The communal circles of the Santāls seem to correspond closely to the *mutas* of the Khands and the *parhas* of the Mūndas and Oraons. It is a plausible conjecture that among all these tribes this organization was once connected with marriage as it is among the Khands at the present day.

MŪNDA.

Mūra, Horo-hon, a large Dravidian tribe of Chota Nāgpur, classed on linguistic grounds as Kolarian, and closely akin to the Hos and Santāls, and probably also to the Kandhs. The name Mūnda is of Sanskrit origin. It means headman of a village, and is a titular or functional designation used by the members of the tribe, as well as by outsiders, as a distinctive name much in the same way as the Santāls call themselves Mānjhi, the Bhūmij Sardār, and the Khambu of the Darjeeling hills Jimdār. The general name Kol, which is applied to both Mūndas and Oraons, is interpreted by Herr Jellinghaus to mean pig-killer, but the better opinion seems to be that it is a variant of *horo,* the Mūndāri for man. The change of *r* to *l* is familiar and needs no illustration, while in explanation of the conversion of *h* into *k,* we may cite *hon,* the Mūndāri for "child," which in Korwa becomes *kon* and *koro,* the Muāsi form of *horo,* "a man." It may be added that the Kharias of Chota Nāgpur call the Mūndas Kora, a name closely approaching Kol.

The Mūnda myth of the making of mankind tells how the self-existent primeval deities Ote Borām and Sing Bonga created a boy and a girl and put them together in a cave to people the world. At first they were too innocent to understand what was expected of them, but the gods showed them how to make rice-beer, which inflames the passions, and in course of time their family reached the respectable number of twelve of either sex. As is usual in myths of this class, the children were divided into pairs; and Singa Bonga set before them various kinds of food for them to choose from before starting in the world. The fate of their descendants depended on their choice. Thus "the first and second pair took bullocks' and buffaloes' flesh, and they originated the Kols (Hōs) and the Bhūmij (Matkum); the next took of the vegetables only, and are the progenitors of the Brāhmans and Chhatris; others took goats and fish, and from them are the Sudras. One pair took shell-fish and became Bhuiyās; two pairs took pigs and became Santāls. One pair got nothing, seeing which the first pairs gave them of their superfluity; and from the pair thus provided spring the Ghāsis, who toil not, but live by preying on others."

The Mundas are divided into thirteen sub-tribes, several of which, such as Kharia-Mūnda, Mahili-Mūnda, Oraon-Mūnda, appear to be the result of crosses with neighbouring tribes, while others again, like Bhuinhār-Mūnda and Mānki-Mūnda have reference to the land and communal system of the tribe. The Mahili-Mūnda sub-tribe has the pig for its totem, and for them pork is tabooed. But appetite has proved stronger than tradition, and the taboo is satisfied by throwing away the head of the animal, the rest of the carcase being deemed lawful food. The septs or *kilis*, which are very numerous, are mainly totemistic, and the totem is taboo to the members of the sept which bears its name. A list of the septs is given below. If it were possible to identify them all, and to ascertain precisely to what extent and in what manner the taboo of the totem is observed by each, the information would probably throw much light upon the growth of yearly tribal societies.

A Mūnda may not marry a woman of his own sept. The sept-name goes by the father's side, and intermarriage with persons nearly related through the mother is guarded against by reckoning prohibited degrees in the manner common in Behār. Adult marriage is still in fashion and sexual intercourse before marriage is tacitly recognized, but in all respectable families matches are made by the parents, and the parties themselves have very little to say in the matter. The bride-price varies from ₹4 to ₹20. *Sindurdān*, or the smearing of vermilion on the bride's forehead by the bridegroom and on the bridegroom's forehead by the bride, is the essential and binding portion. The practice described by Colonel Dalton of marrying the bride to a *mahua* tree [*Bassia latifolia*] and the bridegroom to a mango seems now to have been abandoned. Traces still survive among the Māndas of a form of marriage, resembling the Santāli *nirȯolok*. It is called *dhuko era*, meaning a bride who has entered the household of her own accord. The children of a woman thus married seem to have an inferior status in respect of their rights to inherit the landed property of their father. The late Babu Rākhāl Dās Hāldār, Manager of the estate of the Maharāja of Chota Nāgpur, gave me an illustration of this fact. Some years ago the *mūnda* or headman of one of the villages of the Government estate of Barkagarh died, leaving an only son by a *dhuko era* wife, and a question was raised as to the latter's right to succeed. Under Colonel Dalton's orders, a number of headmen of villages were called together, and their opinions were taken. No decided results, however, could be arrived at. Some thought the son should get the whole property. Others proposed to exclude him altogether, and a third party considered him entitled to maintenance. Eventually the question was compromised by admitting the son's right to one-fourth of the land and the whole of the personal property. The case is a curious comment on the uncertainty of tribal custom. Widows may marry again by the ritual known as *sagāi* in which *sindurdān* is performed with the left hand. Divorce is allowed at the instance of either party, and divorced women are permitted to marry again. In cases of adultery the seducer is required to pay to the husband the full amount of the bride-price.

At the head of the Mūnda religion stands Sing-Bonga, the sun, a beneficent but somewhat inactive deity, who concerns himself but little with human affairs and leaves the details of the executive government of the world to the gods in charge of particular branches or departments of nature. Nevertheless, although Sing-Bonga himself does not send sickness or calamity to men, he may be invoked to avert such disasters, and in this view sacrifices of white goats or white cocks are offered to him by way of appeal from the unjust punishments believed to have been inflicted by his subordinates. Next in rank to Sing-Bonga comes Buru-Bonga or Marang-Buru, also known as Pāt-Sarnā, a mountain god, whose visible habitation is usually supposed to be the highest or most remarkable hill or rock in the neighbourhood. "In Chota Nāgpur," says Colonel Dalton, "a remarkable bluff, near the village of Lodhma, is the Marang-Buru or Maha-Buru for a wide expanse of country. Here people of all castes assemble and sacrifice—Hindus, even Mahomedans, as well as Kols. There is no visible object of worship; the sacrifices are offered on the top of the hill, a bare semi-globular mass of rock. If animals are killed, the heads are left there, and afterwards appropriated by the *pahan* or village priest." Marang-Buru is regarded as the god who presides over the rainfall, and is appealed to in times of drought, as well as when any epidemic sickness is abroad. The appropriate offering to him is a buffalo. Ikir Bonga rules over tanks, wells and large sheets of water; Garhāera is the goddess of rivers, streams and the small springs which occur on many hill sides in Chota Nāgpur; while Nāge or Nāga-era is a general name applied to the minor deities or spirits who haunt the swampy lower level of the terraced rice-fields. All of these are believed to have a hand in spreading disease among men, and require constant propitiation to keep them out of mischief. White goats and black or brown cocks are offered to Ikir Bonga and eggs and turmeric to the Nāge. Deswāli or Kārā-Sarnā is the god of the village, who lives with his wife Jāhir Burhi or Sarhul-Sarnā in the Sarna or sacred grove, a patch of the forest primeval left intact to afford a refuge for the forest gods. Every village has its own Deswali, who is held responsible for the crops, and receives periodical worship at the agricultural festivals. His appropriate offering is a *kara* or he-buffalo; to his wife fowls are sacrificed. Gumi is another of the Sarna deities whose precise functions I have been unable to ascertain. Bullocks and pigs are sacrificed to him at irregular intervals. Chandor appears to be same as Chando Omol or Chanala, the moon worshipped by women, as the wife of Sing-Bonga and the mother of the stars. Colonel Dalton mentions the legend that she was faithless to her husband, and he cut her in two, "but repenting of his anger he allows her at times to shine forth in full beauty." Goats are offered to her in the *Sarna*. Haprom is properly the homestead, but it is used in a wider sense to denote the group of dead ancestors who are worshipped in the homestead by setting apart for them a small portion of every meal and with periodical offerings of fowls. They are supposed to be ever on the watch for chances of doing good or evil to their descendants, and the Mūnda fully realize the necessity for appeasing and keeping them in good humour.

The festivals of the tribe are the following:—(1) Sarhul or Sarjum-Bābā, the spring festival corresponding to the Baha or Bah-Bonga of the Santāls and Hos in *Chait* (March-April) when the *sāl* [*Shorea robusta*] tree is in bloom. Each household sacrifices a cock and makes offerings of *sāl* flowers to the founders of the village in whose honour the festival is held. (2) Kadletā or Batauli in *Asārh* at the commencement of the rainy season. "Each cultivator," says Colonel Dalton, "sacrifices a fowl, and after some mysterious rites a wing is stripped off and inserted in the cleft of a bamboo and stuck up in the rice-field and dung-heap. If this is omitted, it is supposed that the rice will not come to maturity." (3) Nanā or Jom-Nana, the festival of new rice in Asin, when the highland rice is harvested. A white cock is sacrificed to Sing-Bonga, and the first fruits of the harvest are laid before him. Until this has been done, it would be an act of impiety to eat the new rice. (4) Khāria puja or Kolom Singh, called by the Hos Deswāli Bonga or Magh Parab celebrating the harvesting of the winter rice, the main crop of the year. Five fowls and various vegetables are offered to Deswāli, the god of the village at the *kalihan* or threshing floor. Among the Hos of Singbhum the festival is kept as a sort of *saturnale*, during which the people give themselves up to drunkenness and all kinds of debauchery. This is less conspicuously the case with the Mūndas of the plateau who live scattered among Hindu and Christian neighbours, and do not form a compact tribal community like the Hos of the Kolhān. The festival, moreover, is kept by the Mūndas on one day only, and is not spread over a month or six weeks, during which time the people of different villages vie with each other in dissipation, as they do in the Kolhān.

The funeral ceremonies of Mūndas do not differ materially from those of the Hos.

Succession among the Mūndas is governed by their own customs, which appear to have been little affected by the influence of Hindu law. Property is equally divided among the sons, but no division is made until the youngest son is of age. With them, as with the Santāls, daughters get no share in the inheritance; they are allotted among the sons just like the live stock. "Thus if a man dies, leaving three sons and three daughters and thirty head of cattle, on a division each son would get ten head of cattle and one sister; but should there be only one sister they wait till she marries and divide the *pan*," or bride-price, which usually consists of about six head of cattle. Among the Hos of Singhbhum the bride-price is higher than with the Mūndas, and the question of its amount has there been found to affect seriously the number of marriages.

According to ancient and universal tradition, the central tableland of Chota Nāgpur Proper was originally divided into *parhas* or rural communes, comprising from ten to twenty-five villages, and presided over by a divisional chief, called the *rāja* or *mūnda* of the *parha*. In 1839, titular *rājas* of the *parha* were still existing in the Fiscal Division of Khukrā near Rānchi, who retained considerable authority in tribal disputes, and at times of festival and hunting. But this element in the Mūnda village system has now fallen into decay, and survives only in the *jhandas* or flags of the *parha* villages, and in the peculiar titles bestowed on the cultivators themselves. The exclusive right to fly a particular flag at the great dancing festivals is jealously guarded by every Mūnda village, and serious fights not unfrequently result from the violation of this privilege. Besides this, individual villages in a *parha* bear specific titles, such as *rāja*, *dīwān kunwar*, *thakur*, *chhota lal*, etc., similar to those which prevail in the household of the reigning family, which obviously refer to some organization which no longer exists. I am informed that these officials still make the arrangements for the large hunting parties which take place at certain seasons of the year.

A Kol village community consists, when perfect, of the following officers:—*Mūnda*, *mahato*, *pahn*, *bhandari*, *gorait*, *goala*, and *lohar*. Washermen, barbers and potters have been added since 1839, and even now are only found near much frequented halting places, and in villages where the larger Hindu tenure-holders live. The Kols invariably shave themselves, and their women wash the clothes.

(1) *Mūnda*.—The *mūnda* is the chief of the *bhuinhārs*, or descendants of the original clearers of the village. He is a person of great consequence in the village and all demands from the *bhuinhārs*, whether of money or labour, must be notified by the owner of the village through the *mūnda*. He is remunerated for his trouble by the *bhuinhāri* land, which he holds at a low rate of rent, and receives no other salary. In *pargana* Lodhmā, and in the south-eastern portion of Lohardagā, he sometimes performs the *mahato's* duties as well as his own, and he then gets a small *jagir* of half a *pawa* of land rent-free.

(2) *Mahato*.—The functions of a *mahato* have been compared to those of a *patwāri* or village accountant, but he may be more aptly described as a rural settlement officer. He allots the land of the village among the cultivators, giving to each man a *goti* or clod of earth as a symbol of possession; he collects the rent, pays it to the owner, and settles any disputes as to the amount due from the *raiyats*; and, in short, manages all pecuniary matters connected with the land. He is appointed by the owner of the village, and receives one *pāwa* of *rajas* land rent-free as a *jāgīr* or service tenure. But the office is neither hereditary nor permanent, and the *mahato* is liable to be dismissed at the landlord's discretion. Dismissal, however, is unusual, and the *mahato* is often succeeded by his son. Where the *mahato* collects the rents, he almost universally receives a fee, called *batta*, of half an anna from each cultivator, or of one anna for every house in the village. In one village *batta* amounts to four annas and a half on every *pawa* of land. Occasionally, where there is no *bhandāri* or agent for the owner's rent-

paying land, the *mahato* gets three bundles (*karais*) of grain in the straw, containing from ten to twenty *seers* apiece, at every harvest. Thus during the year he would receive three bundles of *gondli* [*Sorghum vulgare*] from the cold weather crop, and the same amount from the *gora* or early rice, and the *don* or late rice. In *khālsa* villages, which are under the direct management of the Mahārājā, the *mahāto* often holds, in addition to his official *jagir*, a single *pawa* of land, called *kharcha* or *rozīna khet*, from the proceeds of which he is expected to defray the occasional expenses incurred in calling upon cultivators to pay their rent, etc.

The functions of the *mahato* are shown in greater detail in the following extract from Dr. Davidson's Report of 1839:—"On a day appointed, the *thikadar* or farmer proceeds to the *akhra* or place of assembly of the village, where he is met by the *mahato*, *pahn*, *ahandari*, and as many of the *raiyats* as choose to attend. He proceeds, agreeably to the dictation of the *mahato*, to write down the account of the cultivation of the different *raiyats* stating the number of *pawas* held and the rent paid by each. Having furnished this account, any new *raiyats* who may wish to have lands in the village, after having the quantity and rent settled, have a *goti* given to them. If any of the old *raiyats* require any new land, a *goti* is taken for that, but not for the old cultivation. The *mahato* collects the rent as the instalments become due, according to the above-mentioned account given to the farmer; and all differences as to the amount of rent payable by a *raiyat*, if any ever arise, which very seldom happens, are settled by the opinion of the *mahato*. So well does this mode answer in practice, that in point of fact a dispute as to the amount of rent owed by a *raiyat* is of rare occurrence. When a farmer wishes to cheat a *raiyat*, he accuses him of having cultivated more land than he is entitled to, or of owing him *maswar* or grain rent for land held in excess; and if such a thing as a dispute as to the amount of rent owed ever does arise, the *mahato's* evidence is generally considered conclusive by both parties."

(3) *Pahn.*—The importance of the *pahn*, or priest of the village gods, may be inferred from the current phrase in which his duties are contrasted with those of the *mahato*. The *pahn*, it is said, "makes the village" (*gāon banātā*), while the *mahato* only "manages it" (*gāon chalātā*). He must be a *bhuinhār*, as no one but a descendant of the earliest settlers in the village could know how to propitiate the local gods. He is always chosen from one family; but the actual *pahn* is changed at intervals of from three to five years by the ceremony of the *sūp* or winnowing-fan, which is used as a divining rod, and taken from house to house by the boys of the village. The *bhuinhār* at whose house the *sūp* stops is elected *pahn*. On the death of a *pahn*, he is frequently, but not invariably, succeeded by his son. Rent-free lands are attached to the office of *pahn* under the following names:—(1) *Pahni*, the personal *jāgīr* or service-tenure of the priest, generally containing one *pawa* of land. (2) *Dalikatāri*, for which the *pahn* has to make offerings to Jāhir Burhi, the goddess of the village. It is called *dalikatāri*, as it is supposed to defray the expenses of the *Karm* festival, when a branch (*dali*) of the *karma* tree is cut down and planted in the fields. (3) *Desauli*, a sort of *bhūtkheta* or devil's acre, the produce of which is devoted to a great triennial festival in honour of Desauli, the divinity of the grove. This land is either cultivated by the *pahn* himself, or by *raiyats* who pay him rent. (4) *Panbhara* and *tahalu* are probably the same. Lands held under these names are cultivated by the *pahn* himself or his near relations; and whoever has them, is bound to supply water at the various festivals.

(4) *Bhandāri.*—The *bhandāri*, or bailiff, is the landlord's agent in respect of the management of the village. He is usually a Hindu, and represents the landlord's point of view in village questions, just as the *pahn* is the spokesman of the *bhuinhārs* or original settlers. He generally holds one *pawa* of land rent-free from the owner, receiving also from every *raiyat* three *karais* or sheaves of each crop as

it is cut—one of *gondli*, one of early rice, and one of wet rice. Instead of the land, he sometimes gets Rs. 3 or Rs. 4 in cash, with 12 *kats*, or 4½ cwt. of paddy.

(5) *Gorait.*—The *gorait* is, in fact, the *chaukidār*, or village watchman. He communicates the owner's orders to the *raiyats*, brings them to the *mahato* to pay their rents, and selects coolies when required for public purposes. As a rule he holds no service land, but receives the three usual *karais*, or sheaves, from every cultivator.

(6) *Ahīr* or *Goāla.*—The *ahīr's* duty is to look after the cattle of the village, and to account for any that are stolen. He is remunerated by a payment of one *kat* of paddy for each pair of plough-bullocks owned by the cultivators whose cattle are under his charge. He also gets the three *karais*, or sheaves, at harvest time, besides an occasional *sūp* or winnowing-fan full of paddy. If cows are under the *ahīr's* charge, the milk of every alternate day is his perquisite. In the month of *Aghan* (December) he takes five seers of milk round to the cultivators, receiving in return *pakhira* or 20 seers of paddy as a free gift. He always pays the *abwāb* known as *dadani ghī*, and in some villages has to give the *baithawan ghi* as well. In a very few cases the *ahīr* holds half a *pawa* of land rent-free.

(7) *Lohār.*—The *lohār*, or blacksmith, gets one *kat* of paddy and the three *karais* for every plough in the village, and is also paid two or three *annas* for every new *phar* or plough-share; in a very few villages, he holds half a *pawa* of land rent-free.

The *kotwāl* or constable, and the *chaukidār* or watchman, do not belong to the genuine Munda village system, and need not be mentioned here.

In the Fiscal Division of Tori the bulk of the inhabitants belong to the Kharwār sub-tribe of Bhogtas, and the village system differs from that which prevails on the central plateau. Here *pahn* is the only official who holds service land, and he gets half a *patti*, or not quite two standard *bighas*. He performs the village *pūjas*, and often does the work of a *mahato*, when the owner of the village is an absentee. But even then the landlord sometimes employs a bailiff, called *barhill*, to collect the rents.

In the tract known as the Five Parganās including Tāmār, Bundu, Silli, Rāhe, and Barandā, as well as in the Mānipatti, or that part of Sonpur *pargana* which borders on Singbhum district, we meet with *mankis* and *mūndas*, who are undoubtedly the descendants of the original chiefs, and still hold the villages which their ancestors founded. Here the *parha* divisions exist in their entirety, as groups of from twelve to twenty-four villages each of which has its own *mūnda* or village head; while the whole commune is subject to a divisional headman called *manki*, who collects the fixed rents payable by the *mūndas*. The chief village officer is the *pahn*, who holds from one to five *kats* of land rent-free as *dalikatari*. A *kat* in this sense is a measure of land analogous to, if not identical with, the *khandi* of the Kolhān in Singbhum, and denotes the quantity of land which can be sown with one *kat* of seed. In this part of the country the *mūnda* sometimes has a deputy called *diwan*, who assists him to collect his rents, and *bhandāris* are occasionally met with.

INDEX

B

C

D

E

N

Q

R

T

U

V

W

X

Y

Z

PRINTED BY WILLIAM CLOWES AND SONS, LIMITED, LONDON AND BECCLES.

PLATE I.

FROM A PHOTOGRAPH BY DR. SIMPSON.

KHAMTI FEMALE.

The chief seat of the Khamtis, who are a branch of the Shan or Tai race, is in Bor Khamti, a Province of Burma, on the Upper Irrawady. Several colonies from thence have settled in Upper Assam on both banks of the Brahmaputra River, east of Sadiya. They are Buddhists in religion, and by far the most intelligent of the tribes of the North-Eastern Frontier.

This is a very typical representation of a young Khamti woman. The elevation of the hair on the crown of the head indicates that she is married, and the style is recommended as dignified and becoming. Unmarried girls wear it in a roll low down on the occiput. They are exceedingly industrious, spin, weave, dye, and embroider, and can themselves make up all that they wear. The jacket is ordinarily of cotton, dyed blue; the petticoat of the same material, and round the waist a coloured silk scarf as a sash. But the dress of the lady in the illustration is of richer material—black velvet bodice and silk skirt. The ear ornaments are of amber.

PLATE I.

PLATE II.

FROM A PHOTOGRAPH BY DR. SIMPSON.

CHULIKATA WOMAN.

A typical, but not a favourable specimen of a Chulikata, or crop-haired, Mishmi woman. This tribe occupies the hills north of Sadiya, but their country is so difficult of access, that very little is known about it. They trade between Tibet and Assam, when at peace; but they are considered the most treacherous and aggressive of all the North-Eastern tribes, though more skilled in arts and manufactures than their neighbours, the Abors to the East, and the Mishmis to the West. They are called Chulikata, or crop-haired, from their having originated the modern fashion of cutting the hair straight across the forehead. The men cut theirs to the level of the rims of their wicker helmets as far as the back of the ear; both sexes wear it long behind.

PLATE II.

PLATES III & IV.

FROM PHOTOGRAPHS BY DR. SIMPSON.

MALE AND FEMALE OF THE TAIN OR DIGARU MISHMI TRIBE.

These are both good average specimens of the tribe. They are, as a rule, fairer and with softer features than the Abors, acquiring from their journeys across the snow a becoming ruddiness of complexion. The young women have generally pretty figures, which their costume shows to advantage. The frontlet, a thin plate of bright silver, is a picturesque and becoming ornament, worn on the forehead by all women who can afford it. They are a quiet, inoffensive people, occupying the hills and skirts of the hills between the Digaru and Dilli Rivers, two of the north hill-affluents of the Brahmaputra, and devoting themselves chiefly to trade.

PLATE III.

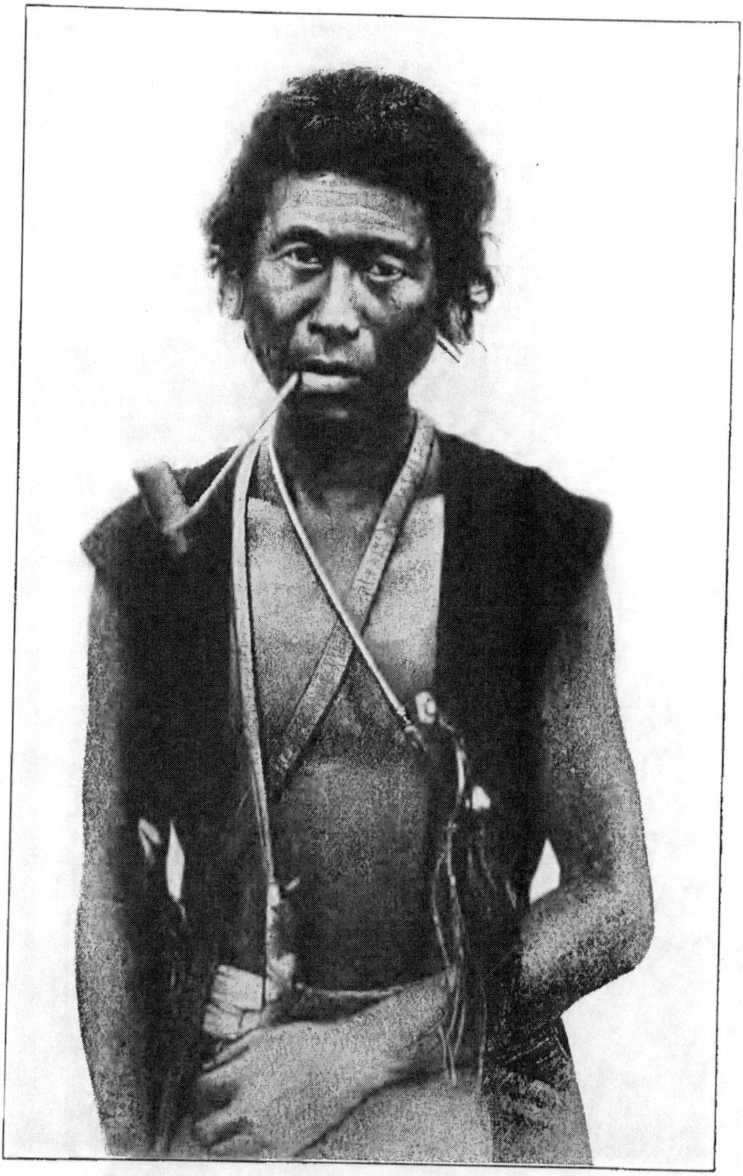

PLATE IV.

PLATE V.

FROM A PHOTOGRAPH BY DR. SIMPSON.

BOR ABOR GIRL.

A Bor Abor girl, belonging probably to some village near the great Dihong River in the Sub-Himalayan range. These ladies crop their hair all round as the least troublesome method of disposing of it. The illustration gives a capital representation of their strongly marked Mongolian features, and their coarse, good-tempered faces. This young girl's costume and the ornaments are all apparently from the North; the blue vitreous turquoise-like beads, which our glass manufacturers cannot imitate, and cornelian and agate pebbles.

PLATE V.

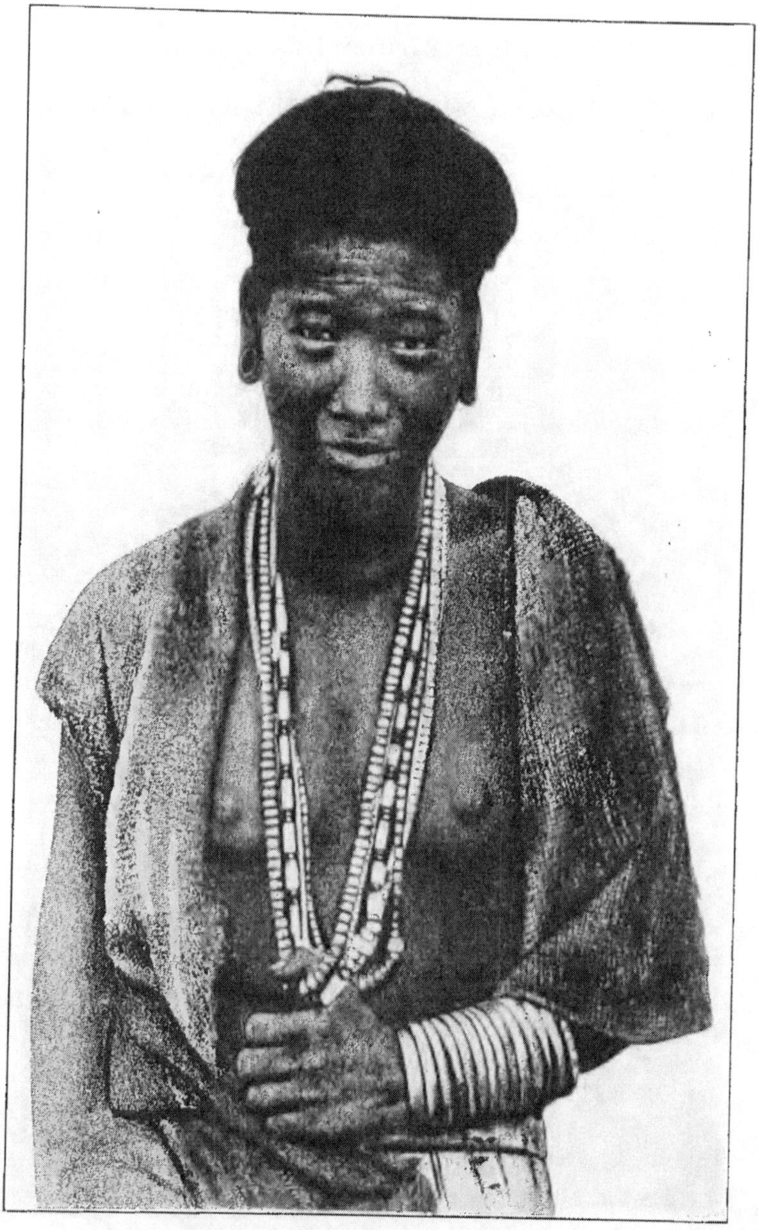

PLATE VI.

FROM A PHOTOGRAPH BY DR. SIMPSON.

A CHULIKATA MISHMI CHIEF IN FULL DRESS.

PLATE VI.

PLATES VII & VIII.

MALE AND FEMALE OF THE LOWER NAGA GROUP.

These are admirable illustrations of one of the Naga tribes, who are found in the hills south of the Nowgong district, between the Doyang and Kopili Rivers, in the Assam Province. There is nothing that I know of except the name to connect these clans with the tribes east of the Doyang. Their features are harsher, more decidedly Mongolian ; and their language, which is quite different, associates them with the Manipuri and Kuki tribes and their cognates.

PLATE VII.

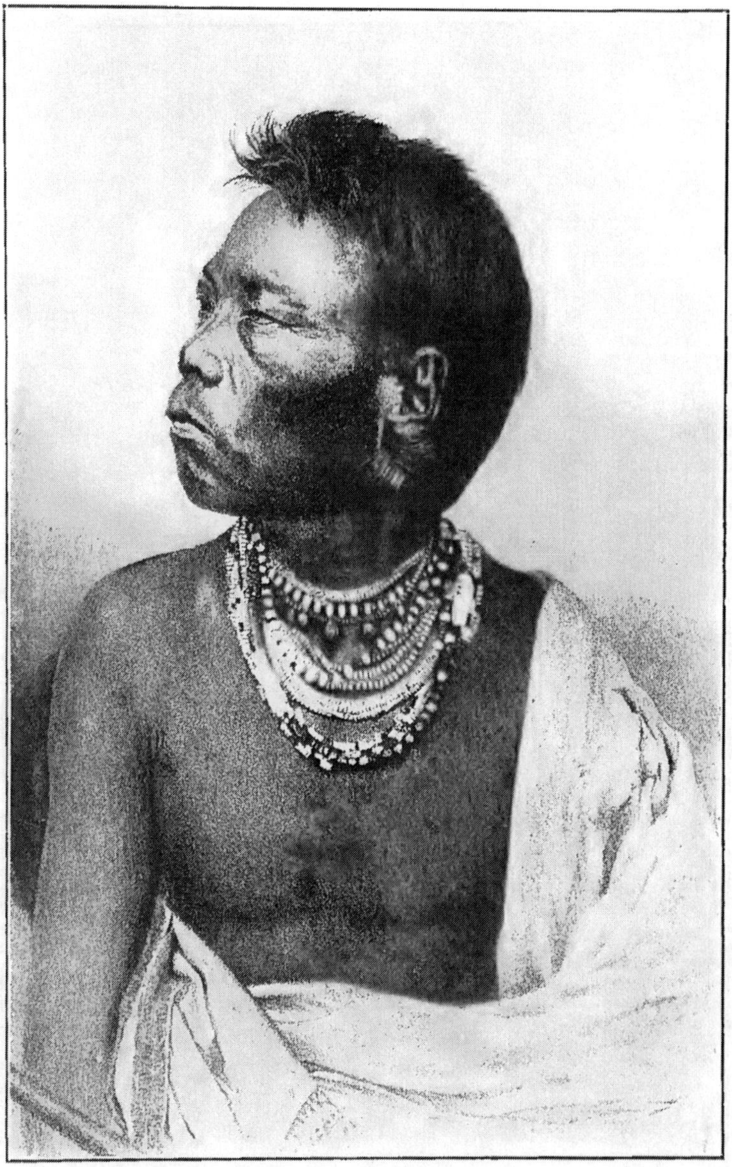

PLATE VIII.

PLATES IX & X.

FROM PHOTOGRAPHS BY DR. SIMPSON.

LEPCHAS (SIKKIM).

The Lepchas are found in Western Bhutan, Eastern Nepal, and in the small State between both, called Sikkim. They are well known at Darjeeling.

PLATE IX.

PLATE X.

PLATES XI & XII.

PHOTOGRAPHED BY DR. SIMPSON.

LIMBU, MALE AND FEMALE.

The very respectable-looking gentleman here represented and the richly bedizened old lady belong, I presume, to the upper class of Limbu society. The Limbus or Kirantis are represented by Mr. Hodgson and others as approximating in appearance to the darker Turanian race in colour and feature, but the old lady is apparently of light complexion, and has a very Mongolian type of face.

NOTE.—The use of Kiranti as a synonym for Limbu is not strictly correct. The Limbu tribe is only one member of the Kiranti group, which includes also the Khambu (Rai or Rai Jimdār) and the Yākhā. The term Turanian is now obsolete as a race designation.

H. H. R.

PLATE XI.

PLATE XII.

PLATE XIII.

FROM A PHOTOGRAPH BY DR. SIMPSON.

A 'HO' OR KOL OF SINGHBHUM.

This is a good typical representation of a young Singhbhum Ho or Kol of the clan, or Kili, *Koadadah.* In his right hand he grasps the national weapon called 'tangi.' This division of the Kols, called also the Larka, or warlike Kols, are found only in Singhbhum.

PLATE XIII.

PLATES XIV & XV.

FROM PHOTOGRAPHS BY DR. SIMPSON.

MUNDAS OF CHUTIA NAGPUR, MALE AND FEMALE.

The above are Mundas of villages close to Ranchi, the capital of the Province of Chutia Nagpur, who living with Oraons have adopted their style of decoration. They are good typical representatives of the race, though not handsome specimens. They show the breadth of face and obliquity of eye, which affirm the north-eastern origin ascribed to them.

NOTE.—The Mundas are now generally classed as Dravidians and the theory of their 'north-eastern origin' has been abandoned.

H. H. R.

PLATE XIV.

PLATE XV.

PLATE XVI.

FROM A PHOTOGRAPH BY DR. SIMPSON.

A GROUP OF KORWAS.

This is one of the wildest of the Kolarian tribes. They are found in the hills of the Sarguja and Jashpur States in the Province of Chutia Nagpur.

PLATE XVI.

PLATES XVII & XVIII.

FROM PHOTOGRAPHS BY DR. SIMPSON.

ORAONS, MALE AND FEMALE.

These are very fair specimens of the great Oraon tribe who have been sometimes called the 'navvies' of India. The nucleus of the tribe is in Chutia Nagpur proper, from whence they have spread as settlers to all the surrounding districts, and as labourers to Assam, Kachar, Mauritius, the West Indies, and other British and French Colonies.

PLATE XVII.

PLATE XVIII.

PLATES XIX & XX.

FROM PHOTOGRAPHS BY THE LATE MR. TOSCO PEPPÉ.

JUANG MAN AND GIRLS.

The photographs of the young Juang man and girls were taken by the late Mr. Tosco Peppé at Gonasika in Keonjhar, one of the Cuttack Tributary States, the legendary cradle of the race. The young man keeps his spare arrows hanging by the barbs from his matted black hair, as is also the custom of the Korwas. The beads or bugles forming the girdles worn by the girls are of fine earthenware made by themselves. The bracelets are of brass and the necklaces of glass beads or flowers. The rest of the attire is of leaves. Mr. Peppé had immense difficulty in inducing these wild timid creatures to pose before him, and it was not without many a tear that they resigned themselves to the ordeal. It is right to mention that they were brought in from the forest, where they had been searching for their daily bread, which chiefly consists of forest produce, and their leaves were not as neatly arranged as they would have been if the girls had had time to make a fresh toilette.

NOTE.—The origin of Juang millinery is obscure. According to one legend the goddess of the Baitarni river caught a party of Juangs dancing naked, and ordained for the women, on pain of divine displeasure, the costume shown in the illustration. This consists of the young shoots of any tree with long soft leaves, stuck through the girdle in front and behind, and suitably draped. As long as the leaves are fresh they are comfortable enough; when they get dry they are unpleasantly prickly. For the men the goddess prescribed a shred of bark from the Tumba tree, which has now given place to an exiguous strip of cloth. The Juang ladies, according to Colonel Dalton, repudiated this scandalous tale, and alleged that their attire expressed their genuine conviction that women's dress should be cheap and simple, and that fashions should never change. How much this was worth was seen a year or so later when a sympathetic Political Agent took the prevailing fashion in hand. An open air durbar, fitted out with a tent and a bonfire, was held in the Juang hills. One by one the women of the tribe filed into the tent and were robed by a female attendant in Manchester *sāris* provided at the Agent's expense. As they came out they cast their discarded *Swadeshi* attire into the bonfire. Thus ended a picturesque survival.

PLATE XIX.

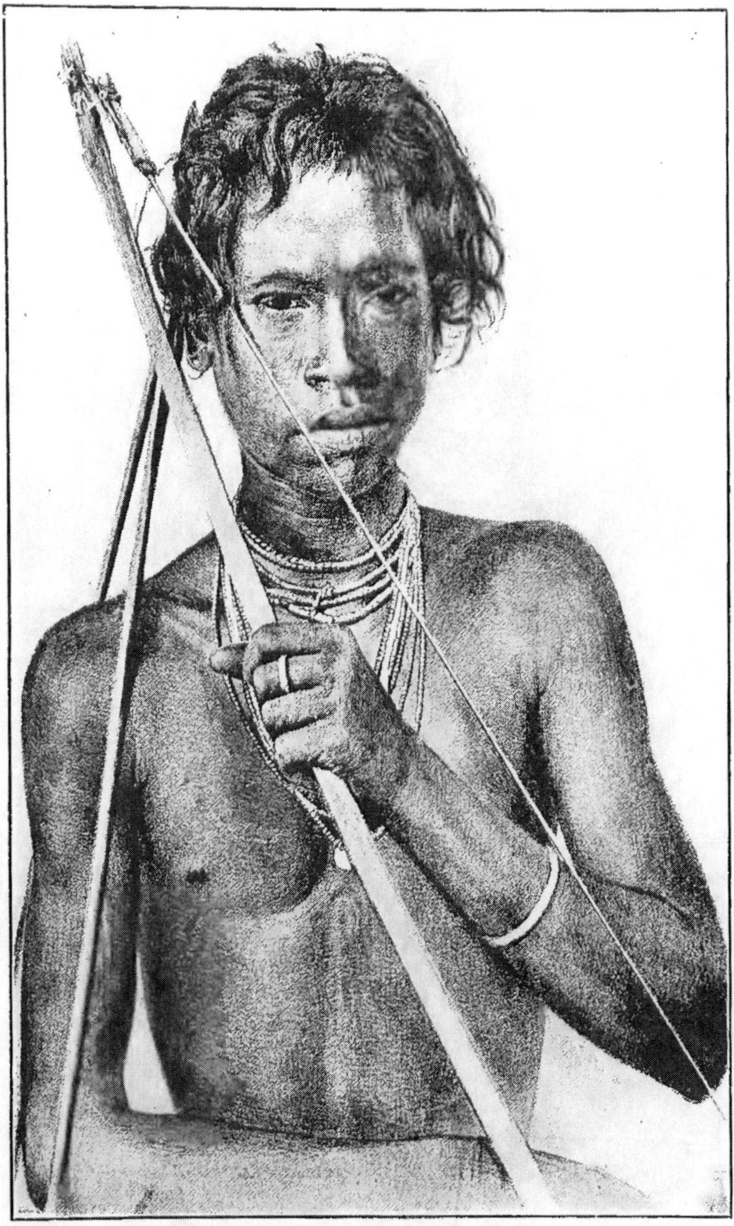

PLATE XX.

PLATES XXI & XXII.

FROM PHOTOGRAPHS BY THE LATE MR. TOSCO PEPPÉ.

MALE AND FEMALE OF THE BENDKAR TRIBE.

I have assigned to the Bendkars of Keonjhar a relationship with the Sauras or Savaras. They have only been met with in Keonjhar, and they are found there in small communities widely separated. The man holds the only implement that they use in tillage. It is the origin of the plough! The handle with the crook is all one piece of wood; in the illustration the crook is made to appear as if it was fitted on to the handle, but this is incorrect, there is no joint, and there should have been no shade at the junction. The only use they ever make of cattle is to offer them as sacrifice to the gods. Thus we have in the Bendkars a people who in their agriculture use neither iron nor cattle.

NOTE.—The typical form of the Bendkar plough is a straight piece of a branch of a tree with a shorter piece of another branch growing out of it. The long piece forms the handle, the short one the share.

H. H. R.

PLATE XXI.

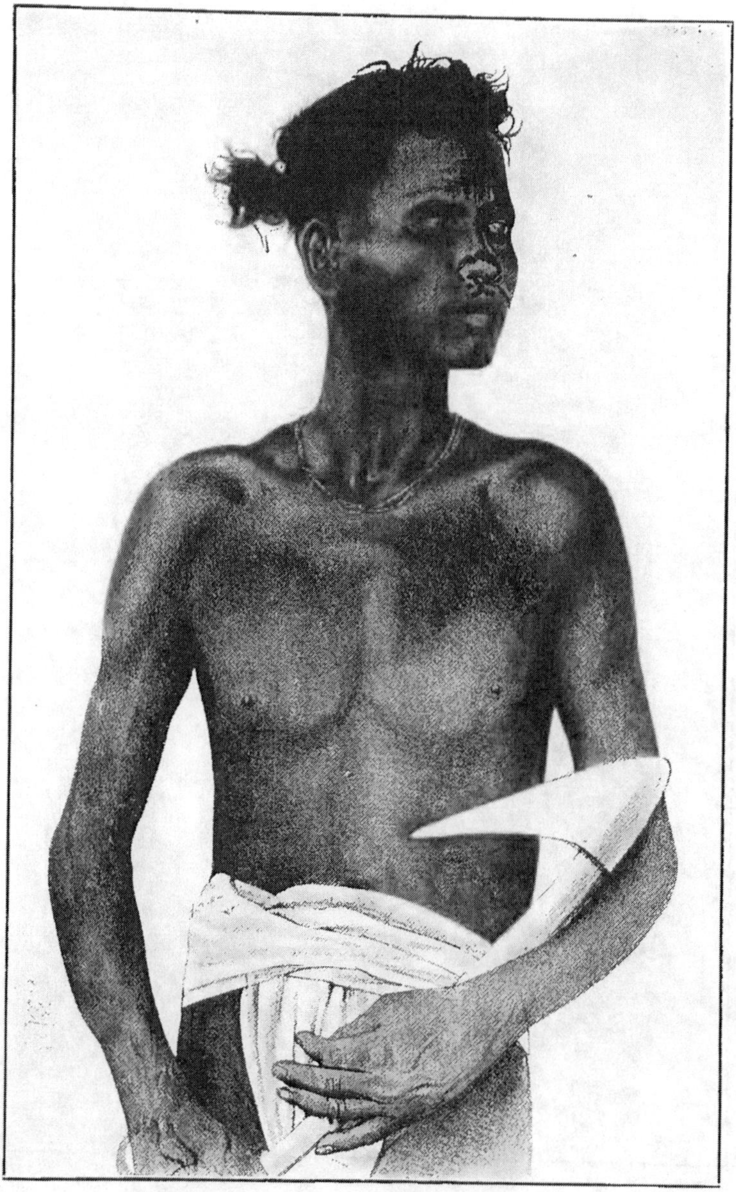

PLATE XXII.

PLATE XXIII.

FROM A PHOTOGRAPH RECEIVED FROM MR. E. H. MANN.

A GROUP OF ANDAMANESE AT GOVERNMENT HOUSE, PORT BLAIR, ANDAMAN ISLANDS: NEGRITO TYPE.

The Andamanese represent a type found only in these islands, and have affinity with no other race on the Indian continent. They are probably a remnant of a Negrito people at one time inhabiting Burma or the Malay Peninsula. In ancient times the Andaman Islands seem to have been connected with the Malay Peninsula, and thus migration became possible. As regards physical characteristics, the Andamanese are short in stature, the skin when clean is black, and the hair so excessively woolly, that when separated from the head, it is almost unrecognisable as human hair. They are nomadic, having, generally speaking, no fixed dwelling-places. Their numbers have considerably decreased owing to infertility, high infant mortality, an increase in the death-rate among adults, the last due to change of environment under the influence of civilisation, and to imported diseases.

PLATE XXIII.

PLATE XXIV.

FROM A PHOTOGRAPH BY MAJOR NICOLAS, DERA GHAZI KHAN.

SŪBAHDĀR-MAJOR SHER BAHĀDUR KHĀN, KAISRĀNI BALOCH: TURKO-IRANIAN TYPE.

The Baloch are believed to have entered their present territory from the west in the 14th and 15th centuries A.D. They are a fine, manly race, expert horsemen, and fight well under officers whom they know and trust. The ordinary tribesman usually carries a sword, knife, and shield, and rides to combat, but fights on foot. In physical characteristics they present a contrast to their Afghan neighbours, being shorter in build, more spare and wiry. The hair is usually worn long, in oily curls, and cleanliness is considered a mark of effeminacy. They have a bold bearing, frank manner, and are fairly truthful. Courage is the highest virtue, and hospitality a sacred duty. Owing to their custom of admitting outsiders into their septs, they are heterogeneous in origin. Their adherence to Islam is little more than a veneer over their primitive Animism, but, unlike the Afghan, they are seldom fanatical.

PLATE XXIV.

PLATE XXV.

PHOTOGRAPH BY PANDIT GIRAJ KISHOR DUTT, RAI BAHADUR.

PANDIT DULI CHAND, VIDYAPATI BRĀHMAN OF AGRA: INDO-ARYAN TYPE.

This is a fine picture of the old-fashioned, learned Brāhman of Northern India, whose life is devoted to the study of Sanskrit literature and the observance of an intricate form of ritual. He has been little influenced by Western culture. He wears wooden clogs, held between his toes by a brass peg, because the touch of leather is a source of ceremonial pollution. He carries a rosary, by the help of which he mutters prayers or holy texts, and recites the names of the Deity whom he worships. He is in many ways like the Nambutiri Brāhman of Malabar, the most primitive type of Brāhman. But the latter have preserved their isolation more successfully than their Northern brethren, who have lived for centuries under foreign Governments. His title Vidyāpati implies that he is a master of learning.

PLATE XXV.

PLATE XXVI.

From a Photograph received from Rai Bahadur B. A. Gupte.

A GROUP OF SUTĀRS, CARPENTERS, BENGAL: MONGOLO-DRAVIDIAN TYPE.

The carpenters of Bengal, like other craftsmen, hold a low rank, and Brāhmans will not take water from their hands. Besides ordinary work in wood, they carve conch-shells into bracelets, make images of the gods, and paint religious pictures. They are probably recruited from the non-Aryan or indigenous races. Their chief object of worship is Visvakarma, the divine architect of the Universe, sometimes represented as a white man with three eyes and bearing a club; but more usually he is symbolised by the tools used by the householder, which are set up and decorated with flowers; offerings are presented to them, and the god is besought to favour his votaries in their profession during the coming year.

PLATE XXVI.

PLATE XXVII.

FROM A PHOTOGRAPH RECEIVED FROM RAI BAHADUR B. A. GUPTE.

A GROUP OF MOCHIS, SHOEMAKERS, BENGAL: MONGOLO-DRAVIDIAN TYPE.

The Mochis or Muchis are a branch of the Chamār caste, whose business is tanning leather. Their association with this material renders them impure in the estimation of high-caste Hindus. The Mochis' chief business is the making of the slipper-like shoes worn by their customers. They also, as in the illustration, manufacture drums. The covering is made of goat skins, while strips of cowhide are used for tightening the parchment. In all native drums, at one or both ends, black circles are inscribed with a paste of iron filings and rice in order to improve the pitch. Muchi women never act as midwives, like those of the Chamār caste.

PLATE XXVII.

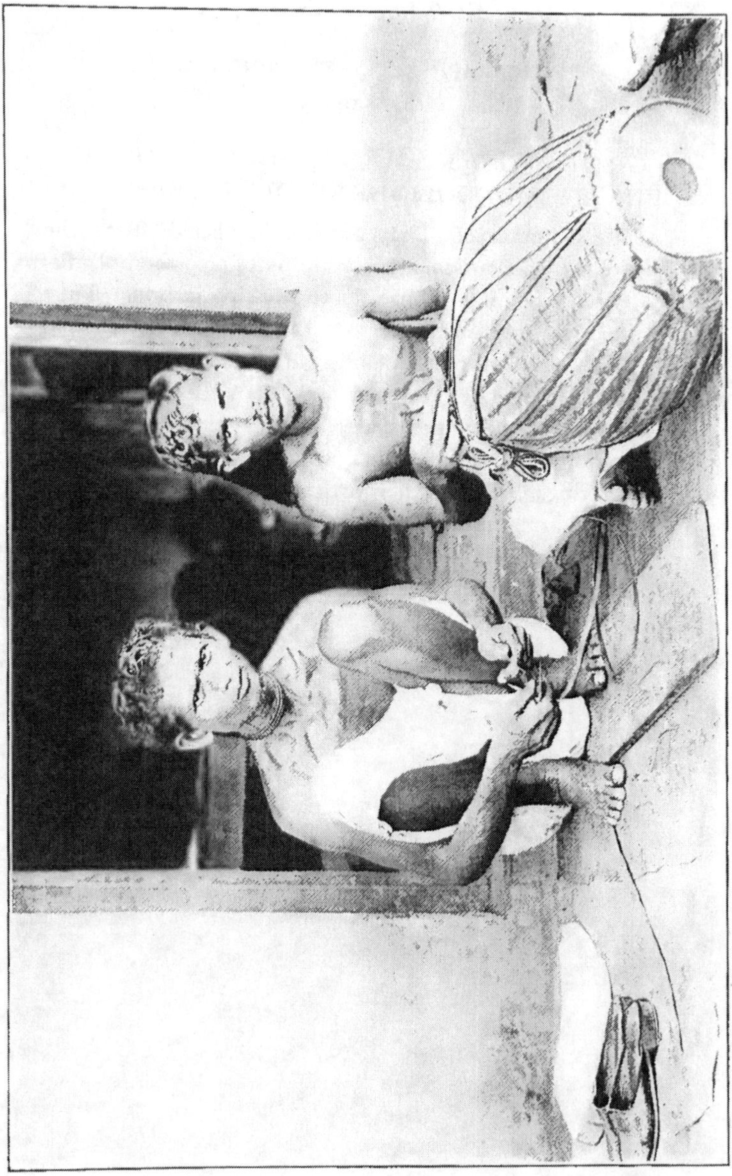

PLATE XXVIII.

From a Photograph received from Rai Bahadur B. A. Gupte.

A GROUP OF KĀMĀRS, BLACKSMITHS, BIHĀR: MONGOLO-DRAVIDIAN TYPE.

The Kāmārs of Bihār are distinguished from the Lohārs, the ordinary blacksmiths of Northern India, by not confining themselves to working in iron. They work in gold and silver also, and in Eastern Bengal make cooking vessels of brass and other similar alloys. Hence they hold a higher rank than the Lohārs, and Brāhmans will take water from their hand. They pride themselves on not allowing their women to wear noserings. Like other artizan castes, they worship Visvakarma, the divine architect of the Universe, who is often represented by the hammer, anvil, and other tools used in their handicraft.

PLATE XXVIII.

PLATE XXIX.

FROM A PHOTOGRAPH BY MESSRS. JOHNSTON AND HOFFMANN, CALCUTTA.

A KUMBU FROM NEPAL: MONGOLOID TYPE.

The Kumbus are one of the Nepal tribes which supply recruits to our Gurkha regiments. Their religion is nominally Buddhism, but their real faith is a form of primitive Animism. Some of them bury their dead; others cremate the corpse on a hill top, and throw the ashes in the air. At a funeral a man of the tribe recites texts, supposed to lay at rest the spirit of the deceased, and to prevent it from annoying the survivors.

PLATE XXIX.

PLATE XXX.

FROM A PHOTOGRAPH BY MESSRS. JOHNSTON AND HOFFMANN, CALCUTTA.

A LAMA WOMAN FROM THE TIBETAN FRONTIER: MONGOLOID TYPE.

Lāma or Lā-ma is a Tibetan word meaning "Superior One," and was formerly restricted to the head of a monastery. It is now strictly applicable only to abbots and to the higher class of Buddhist monks, though out of courtesy it is given to almost all monks and priests, and on the British frontier it is extended to a sept of the Gurung tribe. In many families the first-born son is often dedicated to the profession of religion. As in the case of the lady in the illustration, to use the words of Lt.-Col. Waddell: "Their inveterate craving for material protection against malignant gods and demons has caused them to pin their faith on charms and amulets, which are to be seen everywhere dangling from the dress of every man, woman, and child."

PLATE XXX.

PLATE XXXI.

FROM A PHOTOGRAPH BY MESSRS. JOHNSTON AND HOFFMANN, CALCUTTA.

A LEPCHA FROM SIKKIM: MONGOLOID TYPE.

The Lepchas are a Mongolian tribe, found in Sikkim, western Bhutan, eastern Nepal, and Darjiling. They are short in stature, of fair complexion, and their features are markedly Mongolian. The total absence of beard and the fashion of parting the hair along the crown of the head add to a somewhat feminine expression of countenance in the men, and the use of a jacket like a loose bed-gown, with wide sleeves, contributes still more to the difficulty of distinguishing the sexes, especially in middle age. Their dirty habits render them unpleasant inmates of a close dwelling, but in the rainy season, when they move about and are frequently wet, they become partially clean. They are remarkably honest, and seldom quarrel among themselves. When they are ill-treated, they escape to the jungle and live on yams and other innutritious vegetables. They are nominally Buddhists. They have no caste prejudices about food, but in Nepal they are obliged to conform to the law prohibiting the slaughter of cattle. Pork is their favourite dish, but they will eat carrion, the flesh of a dead elephant being specially prized.

PLATE XXXI.

PLATE XXXII.

FROM A PHOTOGRAPH BY MESSRS. JOHNSTON AND HOFFMANN, CALCUTTA.

THE MAHĀRĀNI OF NEPAL, WITH ATTENDANTS: MIXED INDO-ARYAN AND MONGOLOID TYPES.

The Gurkhas, the ruling race of Nepal, who defeated the indigenous Newārs and occupied the country in 1769 A.D., are the result of a mixture of fugitives of Rājputs and other high-caste people of the Plains, who escaped to the hills during the Muhammadan invasion of the 12th century, and on their arrival in Nepal formed alliances with the Newārs. The remarkable skirt worn by the Mahārāni in the illustration has been described in a lively fashion by Lady Dufferin: "The first view of her was that of a mass of light gauze above and a pair of legs clothed in white trousers below. The thin pink and yellow striped material was not a petticoat, and I am quite at a loss to imagine how it was put on, or how many hundred yards were in it. It looked just as if a great piece had been unrolled, and unrolled, and then picked up and half wound round and half carried by the wearer. When she sat down it was in a great fluff, and when

PLATE XXXII.

PLATE XXXIII.

PHOTOGRAPH RECEIVED FROM MR. E. THURSTON, C.I.E.

A SHOLAGA FROM THE NĪLGIRI HILLS, MADRAS: PURE DRAVIDIAN TYPE.

The Sholagas are a jungle tribe inhabiting the British District of Coimbatore and the adjoining parts of the Mysore State. They live on millet paste and yams, supplemented by sundry jungle animals and birds, but they will not eat parroquets, which they say are their children. Their main occupation is the collection of various jungle fruits, roots, bark, and honey from cavities in the rocks. They bury their dead, and after the funeral erect in the burial-ground of the sept to which the dead man belonged a memorial stone to serve as an abode for the spirit. They are excellent trackers of game, and some of them have recently begun to do a little rude cultivation. Those of the better class have a simple form of marriage ceremony; but the poorer members merely elope with their brides to a distant jungle, and return home only after a child has been born.

PLATE XXXIII.

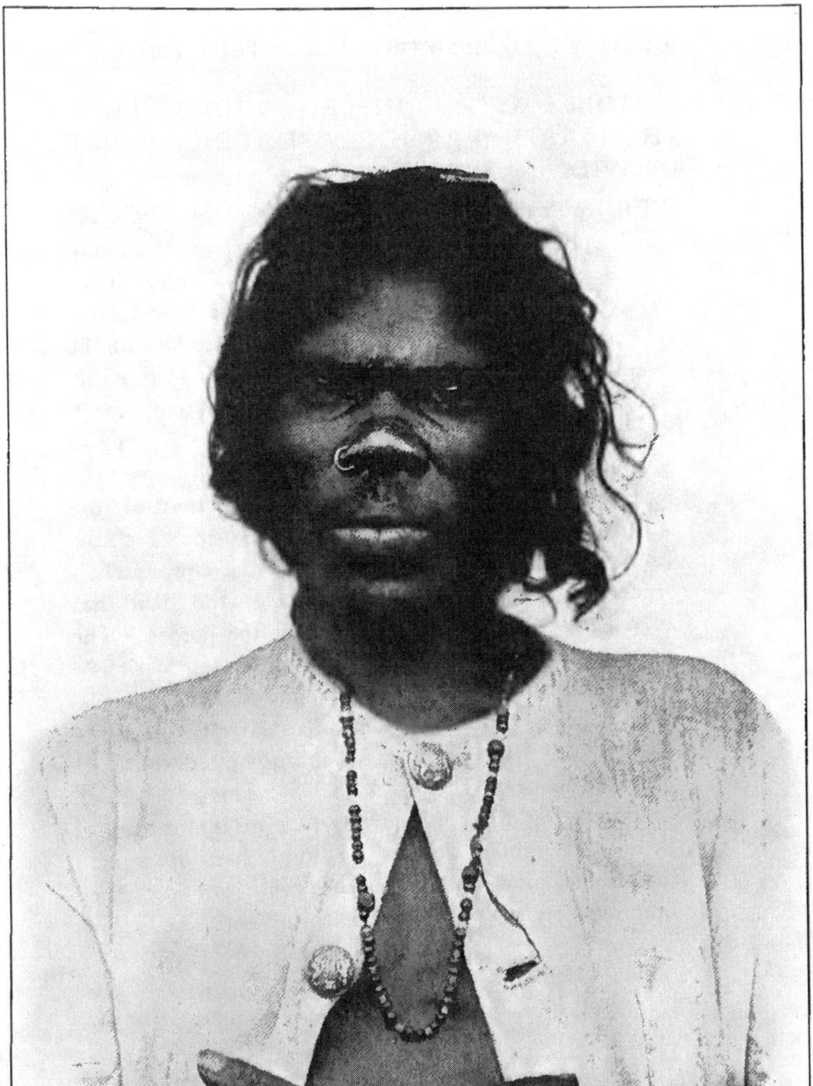

PLATE XXXIV.

PHOTOGRAPH RECEIVED FROM MR. E. THURSTON, C.I.E.

A KĀDIR, WITH CHIPPED TEETH, FROM THE ĀNAIMALAI HILLS, MADRAS: PURE DRAVIDIAN TYPE.

The Kādirs are a jungle tribe found in the Ānaimalai or Elephant Hills of Madras and other ranges extending southwards into the State of Travancore. They are of short stature, with a dark skin and broad nose. They are a happy people, living on the produce of the forests where they reside. They are nomad in habit, building neat huts at places which they temporarily occupy; good trackers and expert in the pursuit of game; wonderfully clever in climbing high trees, their method of ascent closely resembling that of the Dayaks of Borneo. They have a horror of cattle, and will not touch the products of the cow. Their reticence in regard to the disposal of the dead has given rise to a legend that they eat the corpse. The remarkable custom of chipping the teeth curiously resembles that of the Jakuns of the Malay Peninsula. The Kādirs chip all or some of the upper and lower incisors into the form of a sharp-pointed, but not serrated, cone. This is done by means of a chisel, bill-hook, and file. Both sexes undergo the operation; it is said that it makes an ugly man or woman handsome, and that a person who has not been improved in this way has teeth and eats like a cow.

PLATE XXXIV.

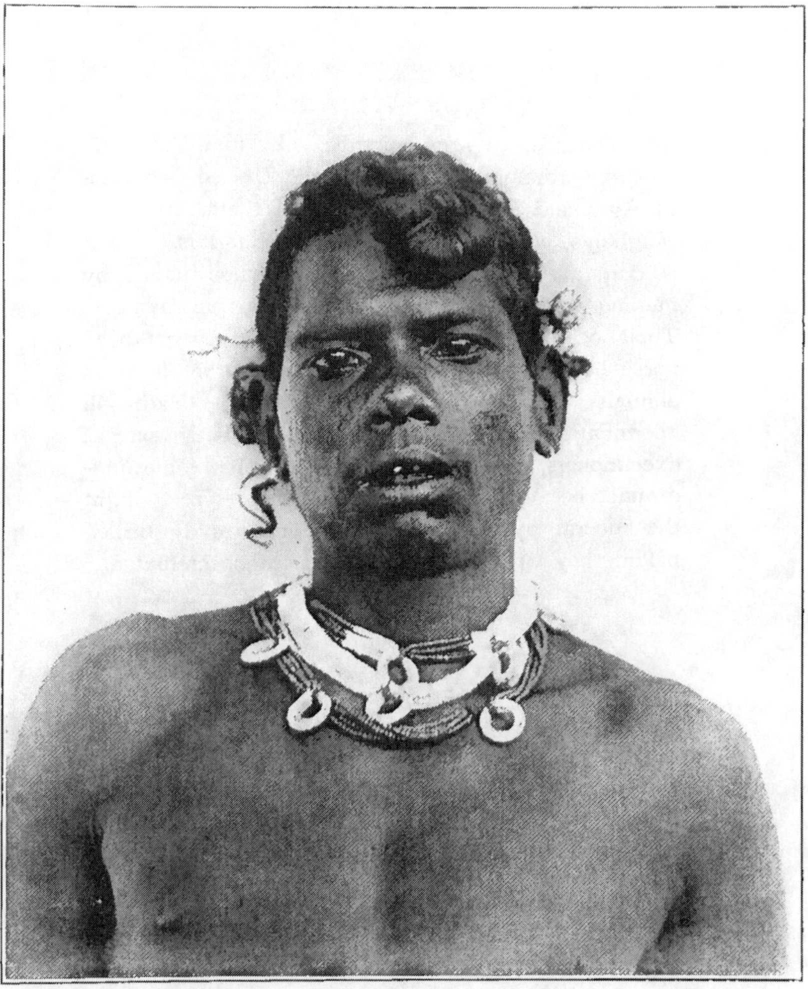

PLATE XXXV.

FROM A PHOTOGRAPH RECEIVED FROM RAI BAHADUR B. A. GUPTE.

A GROUP OF DOM BASKET-MAKERS FROM BIHĀR: MIXED DRAVIDIAN TYPE.

The Doms are a semi-nomadic tribe found in Bihār and the adjoining districts of the United Provinces of Agra and Oudh. One group of them, known as Maghaiya, are habitual thieves and burglars. Other sections are more or less settled, and live mainly by making mats and baskets out of slips of bamboo. Their social status is very low, because they eat beef, pork, horse-flesh, field-rats, and even the flesh of animals which have died a natural death—all abominations to orthodox Hindus. They act as executioners, and at holy places lord it at the burning-ground, because they alone can supply fire to light the funeral pyre, and they must be heavily bribed before they will permit the corpse to be cremated.

PLATE XXXV.

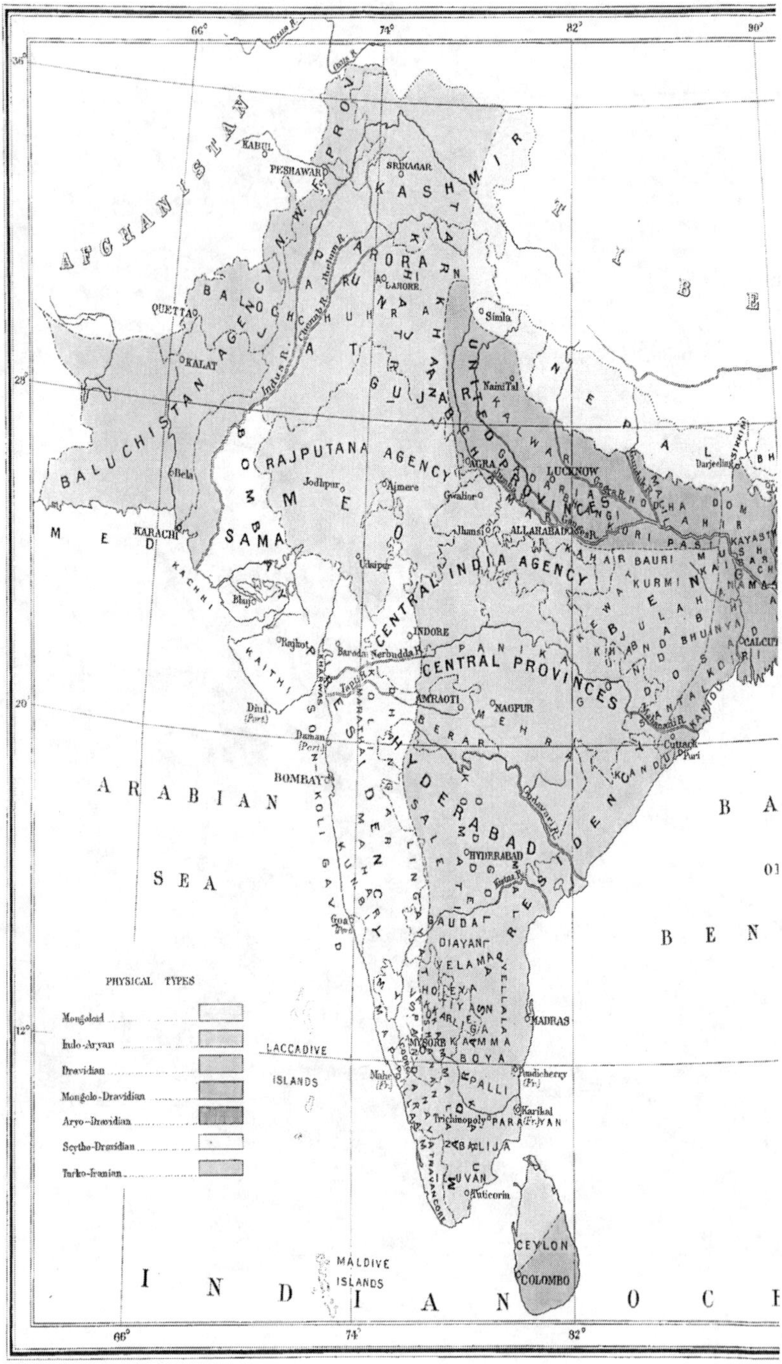

AFGHANISTAN
KABUL
PESHAWAR
QUETTA
KALAT
BALUCHISTAN AGENCY
BALUCHISTAN
Bela
KARACHI
KASHMIR
SRINAGAR
LAHORE
Simla
Naini Tal
TIBET
NEPAL
Darjeeling
SIKKIM
RAJPUTANA AGENCY
Jodhpur
Ajmere
Udaipur
UNITED PROVINCES
AGRA
LUCKNOW
Gwalior
Jhansi
ALLAHABAD
CENTRAL INDIA AGENCY
INDORE
CENTRAL PROVINCES
NAGPUR
AMRAOTI
BERAR
Rajkot
Baroda
Nerbudda R.
Diu
(Port)
Daman
(Port)
BOMBAY
Cuttack
Puri
HYDERABAD
Godavari R.
Kistna R.
Goa
(Port)
MADRAS
MYSORE
Mahe
(Fr.)
Pondicherry
(Fr.)
Karikal
(Fr.)
Trichinopoly
Tuticorin
TRAVANCORE
CEYLON
COLOMBO
ARABIAN SEA
LACCADIVE ISLANDS
MALDIVE ISLANDS
INDIAN OCEAN
PHYSICAL TYPES
Mongoloid
Indo-Aryan
Dravidian
Mongolo-Dravidian
Aryo-Dravidian
Scytho-Dravidian
Turko-Iranian
66°
74°
82°
90°
36°
28°
20°
12°

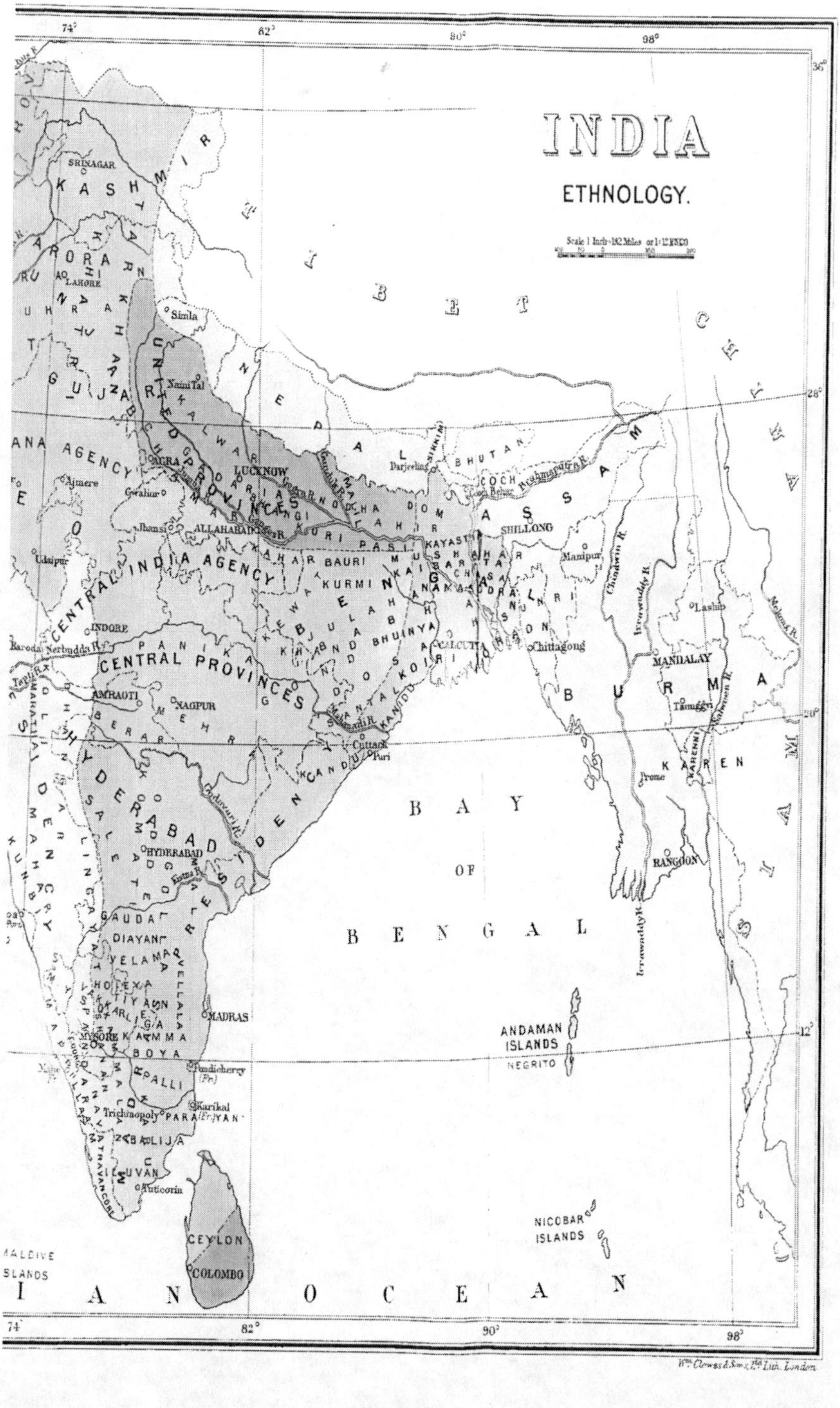

Wm. Clowes & Sons, Ltd. Lith. London